D0076162

This list is continued inside the back cover.

Bonus!

Prepaid access to LearnE-Commerce.net

As a reader of *E-commerce: Business. Technology. Society.* by Kenneth Laudon and Carol Traver, you are entitled to prepaid access to LearnE-Commerce.net, the world's first site designed exclusively to help you learn E-commerce and keep you in-the-know! This Web site will be a key resource in helping you succeed in your study of electronic commerce.

This prepaid subscription gives you full access to all student support areas of this Web site, including:

- Editorials relevant to your course, written by the book's authors.
- Timely reviews of E-commerce research literature.
- Regular e-mail notification of cutting-edge developments in E-commerce.
- Testing and diagnostic tools to help you assess your basic understanding of the material.
- Interactive exercises and Web-based projects to enhance your understanding of the topics.

To activate your prepaid access:
1. Point your web browser to www.LearnE-Commerce.net
2. Scratch off the area below to reveal your pre-assigned Registration Code
3. Enter your Registration Code exactly as it appears below

REGISTRATION CODE:

4. Select "Submit"
5. Complete the online registration form to establish your personal User ID and Password
6. Once your personal User ID and Password are confirmed, you can begin using LearnE-Commerce.net!

This Activation ID and Password can only be used once to establish a subscription. This subscription to LearnE-Commerce.net is not transferable.

WARNING
If the activation code above is showing, it may not be valid.
To obtain access to LearnE-Commerce.net, please purchase a new copy of this textbook or visit www.LearnE-Commerce.net.

E-commerce

business. technology. society.

Kenneth C. Laudon
New York University

Carol Guercio Traver
Azimuth Interactive, Inc.

Addison
Wesley

Boston San Francisco New York
London Toronto Sydney Tokyo Singapore Madrid
Mexico City Munich Paris Cape Town Hong Kong Montreal

Executive Editor:	Susan Hartman Sullivan
Development Editor:	Rebecca Ferris
Senior Production Supervisor:	Juliet Silveri
Production Services:	Kathy Smith
Composition and Text illustration:	Publishers' Design and Production Services, Inc.
Design Supervisor:	Regina Hagen Kolenda
Cover Designer:	Diana Coe
Text Designer and Art Editor:	The Davis Group, Inc.
Marketing Manager:	Michael Hirsch
Print Buyer:	Hugh Crawford
Rights and Permissions Advisor:	Dana Weightman
Cover image:	© 2001 by EyeWire.

Credit lines appear on page 739 at the back of the book.

Library of Congress Cataloging-in-Publication Data

Laudon, Kenneth C., 1944–

    E-commerce : business, technology, society / Kenneth C. Laudon, Carol Guercio Traver.

      p.   cm.

    Includes index.

    ISBN 0-201-74815-0

      1. Electronic commerce. 2. Internet marketing. 3. Information technology.

I. Traver, Carol Guercio. II. Title.

HF5548.32.L38 2001

658.8′4—dc21   2001045881

For information on obtaining permission for the use of material from this work, please submit a written request to Pearson Education, Inc., Rights and Contracts Department, 75 Arlington St., Suite 300, Boston, MA 02116 or fax your request to 617-848-7047.

1 2 3 4 5 6 7 8 9 10—DOC—0504030201

PREFACE

WELCOME TO THE NEW E-COMMERCE

In the few years since 1995, electronic commerce has grown in the United States from a standing start to a $60 billion retail business and a $700 billion business-to-business juggernaut, bringing about enormous change in business firms, markets, and consumer behavior. Economies and business firms around the globe, in Europe, Asia, and Latin America, are being similarly affected. In the next five years, e-commerce in all of its forms is projected to continue growing at double-digit rates, becoming the fastest growing form of commerce in the world. Just as automobiles, airplanes, and electronics defined the twentieth century, so will e-commerce of all kinds define business and society in the twenty-first century. The rapid movement towards an e-commerce economy and society is being led by both established business firms such as Wal-Mart, JCPenney, and General Electric, and new entrepreneurial firms such as E*Trade, Expedia, and eBay. Students of business and information technology need a thorough grounding in electronic commerce in order to be effective and successful managers in the next decade. This book is written for tomorrow's managers.

The focus of our book is on the new breed of e-commerce — what we call E-commerce II — that is emerging from the explosive entrepreneurial growth period of e-commerce that occurred from 1995 to Spring 2000 (E-commerce I). The defining characteristic of E-commerce II firms is that they are profitable, sustainable, efficient, and innovative firms with powerful brand names. Students must understand how to build these kinds of e-commerce businesses in order to prepare for entry into the E-commerce II period.

Since Spring 2000, many of the once high-flying dot.coms have failed, and what seemed like a never-ending supply of venture capital to support them turns out to be quite finite. It would be foolish to ignore the lessons learned in the E-commerce I period. Like so many technology revolutions in the past — automobiles, electricity, telephones, television, and biotechnology — there is an explosion of entrepreneurial efforts, followed by consolidation, and yet continued rapid deployment. We do not shy away from making critical, yet sympathetic, assessments of this early, exciting period in e-commerce.

In 2001, e-commerce is alive, well, and growing very fast; bringing about extraordinary changes to markets, industries, individual businesses and society as a whole. Today, e-commerce has moved into the mainstream life of established businesses that have the market brands and financial muscle required for the long-term deployment of e-commerce technologies and methods. If you are working in an established business, chances are the firm's e-commerce capabilities and Web presence are important factors for its success.

BUSINESS. TECHNOLOGY. SOCIETY.

We believe that in order for business and technology students to really understand e-commerce, they must understand the relationships among e-commerce business concerns, Internet technology, and the social and legal context of e-commerce. These three themes permeate all aspects of e-commerce, and therefore in each chapter we present material that explores the business, technological, and social aspects of that chapter's main topic.

Given the continued growth and diffusion of e-commerce, all students — regardless of discipline or function — must also understand the basic economic and business forces driving e-commerce. E-commerce is creating new electronic markets where prices are transparent, global, and highly efficient, though not perfect. E-commerce is having a direct impact on the firm's relationship with suppliers, customers, competitors, and partners, as well as how we market products, advertise, and use brands. Whether you are interested in marketing and sales, design, production, finance, information systems, or logistics, you will need to know how e-commerce technologies can be used to reduce supply chain costs, increase production efficiency, and tighten the relationship with customers. This text is written to help you understand the fundamental business issues in e-commerce.

We spend a considerable amount of effort analyzing the business models and strategies of "pure-play" online companies and established businesses now forging "bricks-and-clicks" business models. We explore why many early e-commerce firms failed and the strategic, financial, marketing, and organizational challenges they faced. We also describe how contemporary e-commerce firms learned from the mistakes of early firms, and how established firms are using e-commerce to succeed. Above all, we attempt to bring a strong sense of business realism and sensitivity to the often exaggerated descriptions of e-commerce. As founders of a dot.com company and participants in the E-commerce I period, we have learned that the "E" in e-commerce does not stand for easy.

E-commerce is driven by Internet technology. Internet technology, and information technology in general, is perhaps the star of the show. Without the Internet, e-commerce would be virtually nonexistent. Accordingly, we provide four specific chapters on the Internet and e-commerce technology, and in every chapter we provide continuing coverage by illustrating how the topic of the chapter is being shaped by new information technologies. For instance, Internet technology drives developments in payment systems, security, marketing strategies and techniques, financial applications, business-to-business trade, and retail e-commerce. We describe new wireless and mobile commerce technology, new telecommunications technologies that lower business costs, new software languages such as XML for expediting the flow of documents among business firms, new Internet technologies for making payments over the Internet, and new types of Internet-based information systems that support electronic business-to-business markets.

E-commerce is not only about business and technology, however. The third part of the equation for understanding e-commerce is society. E-commerce and Internet technologies have important social consequences that business leaders can ignore only at their peril. E-commerce has challenged our concepts of privacy, intellectual property, and even our ideas about national sovereignty and governance. Advertising networks maintain profiles on millions of U.S. and foreign online shoppers. Entire e-commerce industries — such as digital music — are based on challenging the intellectual property rights of record labels and artists. And many countries — including the United States — are demanding to control the content of Web sites displayed within their borders. As a result of these challenges to existing institutions, e-commerce and the Internet are the subject of increasing investigation, litigation, and legislation. Business leaders need to understand these societal developments, and they cannot afford to assume any longer that the Internet is borderless, beyond social control and regulation, or a place where market efficiency is the only consideration. In addition to an entire chapter devoted to the social and legal implications of e-commerce, each chapter contains material highlighting the social implications of e-commerce.

FEATURES AND COVERAGE

Real-World Business Firm Focus From Akamai Technologies to Zoomerang.com, *E-commerce: Business. Technology. Society.* contains well over one hundred real-company examples that place coverage in the context of actual dot.com businesses. You'll find these examples in each chapter, as well as in special features such as chapter-opening and chapter-closing cases, and "Insight on" boxes.

E-Commerce in Action Cases Part IV of the book analyzes the business strategies and financial operating results of seventeen e-commerce companies in retail, services, B2B, auctions, portals, communities, and digital media content. Among the companies we analyze are Yahoo, Buy.com, JCPenney, Lands'End, FashionMall, E*Trade.com, Hotjobs.com, Expedia.com, eBay.com, FreeMarkets, and Ariba. For each company, we perform a brief strategic and financial analysis of the firm and assess the near-term future prospects for the firm. These cases are ideal real-world instructional guides for students interested in understanding the financial foundation of e-commerce firms, their strategic visions and customer value propositions, and their changing strategic objectives.

In-depth Coverage of B2B Commerce We devote an entire chapter to an examination of B2B commerce. In writing this chapter, we developed a unique and easily understood classification schema to help students understand this complex arena of e-commerce. This chapter covers Net marketplaces, including e-distributors, e-procurement companies, exchanges and industry consortia, as well as the development of private industrial networks and collaborative commerce.

Current and Future Technology Coverage Internet and related information technologies continue to change rapidly. What was once a shortage of telecommunications capacity has now turned into a surplus, PC prices have continued to fall, new client-side devices have emerged, and Internet high-speed connections are continuing to show double-digit growth. While we thoroughly discuss the current Internet environment, we devote considerable attention to describing Internet II technologies and applications such as the advanced network infrastructure, fiber optics, wireless Web and 3G technologies, WiFi, IP Multicasting, and future guaranteed service levels.

Up-to-date Coverage of the Research Literature We have sought to include where appropriate references and analysis of the latest e-commerce research findings, as well as many classic articles, in all of our chapters. We have drawn especially on the disciplines of economics, marketing, and information systems and technologies, as well as law journals and broader social science research journals and sources.

Special Attention to the Social and Legal Aspects of E-commerce We have paid special attention throughout the book to the social and legal context of e-commerce. Chapter 9 is devoted to a thorough exploration of four ethical dimensions of e-commerce: information privacy, intellectual property, governance, and protecting public welfare on the Internet. We have included an analysis of the latest Federal Trade Commission and other regulatory and nonprofit research reports, and their likely impact on the e-commerce environment.

OVERVIEW OF THE BOOK

The book is organized into four parts.

Part 1, "Introduction to E-commerce," provides an introduction to the major themes of the book. Chapter 1 defines e-commerce, distinguishes between e-commerce and e-business, defines the different types of e-commerce, and introduces the two periods of E-commerce I and E-commerce II. Chapter 2 introduces and defines the concepts of business model and revenue model, describes the major e-commerce business and revenue models for both B2C and B2B firms, and introduces the basic business concepts required throughout the text for understanding e-commerce firms including industry structure, value chains, and firm strategy.

Part 2, "Technology Infrastructure for E-commerce," focuses on the technology infrastructure that forms the foundation for all e-commerce. Chapter 3 traces the historical development of Internet I — the first Internet — and thoroughly describes how today's Internet works. A major focus of this chapter is the new Internet II that is now under development and will shape the near-term future of e-commerce. Chapter 4 builds on the Internet chapter by focusing on the steps managers need to follow in order to build a commercial Web site. This e-commerce infrastructure chapter covers the systems and analysis and design process that should be followed in building an e-commerce Web site; the major decisions surrounding the decision to outsource site development and/or hosting; and how to choose software, hardware, and other tools that can improve Web site performance.

Chapter 5 focuses on Internet security and encryption, building on the e-commerce infrastructure discussion of the previous chapter by describing the ways security can be provided over the Internet. This chapter defines security, describes the major threats to security, and then discusses both the technology and policy solutions available to business managers seeking to secure their firm's sites. Chapter 6 focuses on payment systems. This chapter identifies the stakeholders in payment systems, the dimensions to consider in creating payment systems, and the various types of systems, and then describes in some detail digital wallets, digital cash, digital credit cards, digital checking, smart cards, B2B payment systems, and electronic billing and presentment systems.

Part 3, "Business Concepts and Social Issues," focuses directly on the business and social–legal issues that surround the development of e-commerce. Chapter 7 focuses on e-commerce consumer behavior, the Internet audience, and introduces the student to the basics of online marketing and branding, including online marketing technologies and marketing strategies. Chapter 8 is devoted to online marketing communications, such as online advertising and e-mail marketing,.

Chapter 9 provides a thorough introduction to the social and legal environment of e-commerce. Here, the student will find a description of the ethical and legal dimensions of e-commerce, including a thorough discussion of the latest developments in personal information privacy, intellectual property, Internet governance, jurisdiction, and public health and welfare.

Part 4, "E-commerce in Action," focuses on real-world e-commerce experiences in retail, services, business-to-business, auctions, portals, communities, and digital media. Chapter 10 takes a close look at the experience of firms in the retail marketplace, including both "pure-play" online firms such as Amazon, and mixed strategy "clicks and bricks" firms such as Wal-Mart and JCPenney. Chapter 11 examines the online services industries, with an in-depth look at online financial (banking, brokerage, real estate and insurance), travel, and career services. Chapter 12 explores the world of B2B commerce, describing both electronic Net marketplaces and the less heralded, but very large arena of private industrial networks and the movement toward collaborative commerce. Chapter 13 explores the online world of auctions, portals, and communities. We describe a number of successful ventures here, including eBay.com and Yahoo, and communities such as iVillage and Alloy Online. Chapter 14 explores the world of online content and digital media, and examines the online publishing, entertainment, and learning industries.

CHAPTER OUTLINE

Each chapter contains a number of elements designed to make learning easy as well as interesting.

Learning Objectives A list of learning objectives that highlights the key concepts in the chapter guides student study.

Loudcloud
What Is 100% Uptime Worth?

The day that Chris Wong's company, SkillsVillage.com, which helps businesses find, hire, and manage skilled contract workers, went live, he got an early morning call from the FBI. It seems within hours of launching the site, hackers had taken over SkillsVillage and used it as a front to attack a Canadian corporation.

Wong had launched the site without installing a firewall, security software that could have prevented such a hacker assault, thinking that he'd do it later. There were more important issues to deal with, or so he thought. The call from the FBI prompted Wong to change his thinking and consider outsourcing.

To handle the problem, SkillsVillage turned to another start-up, Loudcloud, a company started by Netscape co-founder Marc Andreeson. Loudcloud provides businesses with outsourced Web site infrastructure services, including all the equipment, software, Internet access, and technical support a site requires. According to Andreeson, Loudcloud has developed software it calls opsware, using off-the-shelf applications that it has customized, that supposedly systematizes all the hard work around Web operations, such as provisioning (determining what components to use), scaling (having enough capacity), and site management and monitoring.

By handing off the work to Loudcloud, clients such as SkillsVillage experience improved site performance and the ability to almost instantaneously add capacity as the site grows. Loudcloud guarantees 100% uptime — absolutely no downtime. If users ever are denied access to a site, Loudcloud provides substantial discounts off its monthly service fees, which typically run in the tens of thousands of dollars. Fortunately for Loudcloud, so far that has not happened.

177

Chapter-Opening Cases
Each chapter opens with a story about a leading e-commerce company that relates the key objectives of the chapter to a real-life e-commerce business venture.

"Insight on" Boxes Each chapter contains real-world vignettes, drawn from the popular press, illustrating the themes of technology, business, and society. These vignettes create an integrated framework and coverage throughout the book for describing and analyzing the full breadth of the field of e-commerce. The boxes probe such issues as Web accessibility for the physically challenged, wireless privacy, hiring "tiger teams" of hackers to locate security threats, and online marketing's targeting of children.

Marginal Glossary

Throughout the text, key terms and their definitions appear in the text margin where they are first introduced.

Real-Company Examples

Drawn from actual e-commerce ventures, well over 100 pertinent examples are used throughout the text to illustrate concepts. Full-color screenshots further enliven the presentation.

Chapter-Closing Cases Each chapter concludes with a robust case study based on a real-world organization. These cases help students synthesize chapter concepts and apply this knowledge to concrete problems and scenarios such as evaluating the legality of Napster and assessing the business model behind Priceline.com.

Chapter-Ending Pedagogy Each chapter contains end-of-chapter materials designed to reinforce the learning objectives of the chapter.

Key Concepts Keyed to the learning objectives, Key Concepts present the key points of the chapter to aid student study.

Review Questions Thought-provoking questions prompt students to demonstrate their comprehension and apply chapter concepts to management problem solving.

Projects At the end of each chapter are a number of projects that encourage students to apply chapter concepts. Many make use of the Internet and require students to present their findings in an oral presentation or written report. For instance, students are asked to evaluate publicly available information about a company's financials at the SEC Web site, assess payment system options for companies across international boundaries, or search for the top ten cookies on their own computer and the sites they are from.

Web Resources A Web section at the end of the chapter directs students to resources that can extend their knowledge of each chapter with projects and exercises and additional content at **www.LearnE-commerce.net.**

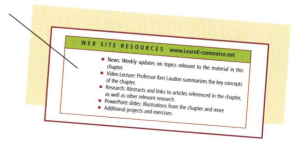

Companion Web Site Integrating Technology and Learning Available at **www.LearnE-commerce.net**, the Web site provides online access to innovative teaching and learning tools. This best-of-breed Web site in the e-commerce educational marketspace offers significant additional content, including:

- Weekly updates on the topics relevant to the materials in each chapter
- Timely reviews of the research literature
- Streaming video lectures for each chapter
- Editorials by the authors
- Additional exercises and Web-based projects

The Companion Web site system includes an online syllabus builder that allows instructors to create a calendar of assignments for each class and to track student activity and quiz grades with an electronic gradebook.

In addition to the Companion Web site, the Web content is available in Course Compass™, WebCT, and BlackBoard versions. CourseCompass™ is a nationally hosted, dynamic, interactive online course management system powered by BlackBoard, leaders in the development of Internet-based learning tools. This easy-to-use and customizable program enables professors to tailor content and functionality to meet individual course needs. To see a demo, visit www.coursecompass.com. Please contact your local sales representative for more information on obtaining Web content in these various formats.

SUPPORT PACKAGE

The following supplementary materials are available to qualified instructors at the text's Web site, www.LearnE-commerce.net. Contact your Addison-Wesley sales representative for information about obtaining a password. (You can also request an Instructor's Resource CD-ROM with these materials from your sales representative.)

Instructor's Manual This comprehensive manual pulls together a wide variety of teaching tools so that instructors can use the text easily and effectively. Each chapter contains an overview of key topics, a recap of the key learning objectives, lecture tips, discussion of the chapter-ending case, and detailed answers to the Case Study Questions, Review Questions, and Student Projects. To aid instructors, the manual also includes a variety of suggested course syllabi and a detailed description of the resources available at the text's Web site.

Test Bank For quick test preparation, the Test Bank contains 50 questions per chapter in multiple-choice, true/false, and short-essay format emphasizing critical/creative thinking about the issues evoked by the chapter. The Test Bank is available in Microsoft Word and in Addison-Wesley's easy-to-use testing software (Test-Gen EQ with QuizMaster-EQ for Windows and Macintosh), which allows instructors to view, edit, and add questions.

PowerPoint Lecture Presentation Slides illustrate key points, tables, and figures as well as Web site information from the text in lecture note format. The slides can be easily converted to transparencies or viewed electronically in the classroom.

ACKNOWLEDGMENTS

Addison-Wesley sought the advice of many excellent reviewers, all of whom strongly influenced the organization and substance of this book. The following individuals provided extremely useful evaluations:

Prasad Bingi, Indiana-Purdue University, Fort Wayne

Tom Critzer, Miami University

Abhijit Deshmukh, University of Massachusetts

Brian L. Dos Santos, University of Louisville

John H. Gerdes, University of California, Riverside

Philip Gordon, University of California at Berkeley

Marios Koufaris, CUNY Baruch

Zoonky Lee, University of Nebraska, Lincoln

Haim Levkowitz, University of Massachusetts, Lowell

John Mendonca, Purdue University

Kent Palmer, MacMurray College

Jay Rhee, San Jose State University

Amber Settle, DePaul CTI

Sumit Sircar, University of Texas at Arlington

Pamela Specht, University of Nebraska at Omaha

David Zolzer, Northwestern State University

We also want to thank Bruce Buchanan, Professor of Marketing, New York University Stern School of Business, and Edward T. Stohr, Professor of Information Systems, Stevens Institute of Technology for generously sharing with us materials they created for their e-commerce classes. Special thanks to Jane Laudon for contributing ideas and suggestions, and discussing topics in the book.

We would also like to thank Jupiter Media Metrix for their permission to include data and figures from their research reports in our text. Jupiter Media Metrix is a global leader in Internet and new technology analysis and measurement, combining data and analysis to provide businesses with unmatched resources for understanding and profiting from the Internet.

In addition, we would like to thank all those at Addison-Wesley who have worked so hard to make sure that this book is the very best that it can be. Susan Hartman Sullivan, Executive Editor, led the team, set the targets and goals, and pushed the project through to completion; her warm encouragement spurred us forward. Rebecca Ferris, Development Editor, coordinated, read, and commented on our drafts and provided invaluable moral support. Roberta Lewis, Development Editor, developmentally edited our manuscript and provided excellent suggestions for improvement. A special thanks is also owed to Kathy Smith, our Project Manager, who, along with Juliet Silveri, Senior Production Supervisor, did a superb job. Dana C. Weightman, Rights and Permissions Advisor, helped us secure permission for the figures and screenshots that are so integral to the text. Regina Hagen Kolenda, Senior Designer, Diana Coe, Cover Designer, and Geri Davis, Text Designer and Art Editor, have collaborated to provide us with a wonderful cover, interior design, and artwork. Michael Hirsch, Executive Marketing Manager, helped to make us aware of the needs and desires of the professors and students who will be using the text. A special thanks also to Frank Ruggirello, Publisher at Addison-Wesley when we began this project, and now Publisher at Benjamin-Cummings. Once again, his belief in our abilities gave us the courage to tackle yet another mountain.

We would also like to thank Marcia Layton Turner and Robin Pickering for their assistance in providing background research and drafts of cases and other materials, and to Russell Polo, Technical Director at Azimuth Interactive, Inc. for his review of the technical material in the text.

Finally, last but not least, we would like to thank our family and friends, without whose support this book would not have been possible.

Kenneth C. Laudon

Carol Guercio Traver

Brief Contents

Contents

PART 2 Technology Infrastructure for E-commerce

---

4 **BUILDING AN E-COMMERCE WEB SITE**   **176**

5	SECURITY AND ENCRYPTION	228

6   **E-COMMERCE PAYMENT SYSTEMS**   **280**

PART 3 Business Concepts and Social Issues

7 E-COMMERCE MARKETING CONCEPTS 332

PART 4   E-commerce in Action

10   RETAILING ON THE WEB   524

Chapters 13 and 14 are available on the Web at www.LearnE-commerce.net

---

13   **AUCTIONS, PORTALS, AND COMMUNITIES**

PART **1**

Introduction to E-commerce

CHAPTER 1

The Revolution Is Just Beginning

After reading this chapter, you will be able to:

- Define e-commerce and describe how it differs from e-business.
- Identify the unique features of e-commerce technology and their business significance.
- Describe the major types of e-commerce.
- Understand the visions and forces behind the E-commerce I era.
- Understand the successes and failures of E-commerce I.
- Identify several factors that will define the E-commerce II era.
- Describe the major themes underlying the study of e-commerce.
- Identify the major academic disciplines contributing to e-commerce research.

Amazon.com:
Before and After

Amazon.com's first Web site

December 1999: Jeff Bezos, the founder and Chief Executive Officer of Amazon .com, the online retailer, graces the cover of *Time* magazine as its Person of the Year. In the same month, Amazon's stock reaches a peak of $113.00 per share.

January 2001: Amazon reports a net loss of $545 million for the fourth quarter of 2000, and a whopping $1.411 billion as its overall loss for the year. Its stock is trading in the low teens. On January 31, 2001, it lays off 1,300 employees, constituting about 15% of its workforce. Questions about its long-term viability abound. Yet at the same time, there are many who continue to believe in its future.

The story of Amazon.com, the most well-known e-commerce company in the United States, in many ways mirrors the story of e-commerce itself. So, let's take a closer look at Amazon's path to preview many of the issues we'll be discussing throughout this book.

The ideas behind Amazon had their genesis in 1994, when Jeff Bezos, then a 29-year old senior vice president at D.E. Shaw, a Wall Street investment bank, read that Internet usage was growing at 2,300% per year. To Bezos, that number represented an extraordinary opportunity. He quit his job and investigated what products he might be able to sell successfully online.

He quickly hit upon books—with over three million in print at any one time, no physical bookstore could stock more than a small percentage. A "virtual bookstore" could offer a much greater selection. He also felt consumers would feel less need to actually "touch and feel" a book before buying it. The comparative dynamics of the book publishing, distributing, and retailing industry were also favorable. With over 2,500 publishers in the United States, and the two largest retailers, Barnes and Noble and Borders, accounting for only 12% of total sales, there were no "800-pound gorillas" in the market. The existence of two large distributors, Ingram Books and Baker and Taylor, meant that Amazon would have to stock only minimal inventory.

Bezos easily raised several million dollars from private investors and in July 1995, Amazon.com opened for business on the Web. Amazon offered consumers four compelling reasons to shop there: selection (a database of 1.1 million titles, convenience (shop anytime, anywhere, with ordering simplified by Amazon's patented "1-Click" express shopping technology), price (high discounts on bestsellers), and service (e-mail and telephone customer support, automated order confirmation, tracking and shipping information, and more).

In January 1996, Amazon moved from a small 400-square foot office into a 17,000-square foot warehouse. By the end of 1996, Amazon had almost 200,000 customers. Its revenues had climbed to $15.6 million, but the company posted an overall loss of $6.24 million.

In May 1997, Amazon went public, raising $50 million. Its initial public offering documents identified several ways in which Amazon expected to have a lower cost structure than traditional book stores—it would not need to invest in expensive retail real estate, it would have reduced personnel requirements, and it would not have to carry extensive inventory, since it was relying in large part on book distributors.

During 1997, Amazon continued to grow. It served its one-millionth unique customer, expanded its Seattle warehouse, and built a second 200,000-square foot distribution center in Delaware. By the end of 1997, revenues had expanded to $148 million for the year, but at the same time, losses also grew, to $31 million.

In 1998, Amazon expanded its product line, first adding music CDs and then videos and DVDs. Amazon was no longer satisfied with merely selling books: Its business strategy was now "to become the best place to buy, find, and discover *any product or services* available online." Revenues for the year increased significantly, to $610 million, but the losses also continued to mount, quadrupling to $125 million.

The year 1999 was a watershed year for Amazon. Bezos's announced goal was for Amazon to become the "Earth's Biggest Store." In February, Amazon borrowed over $1 billion dollars, using the funds to finance expansion and cover operating losses. During the year, it added electronics, toys, home improvement products, software, and video games to its product lines. It also introduced several marketplaces, including Amazon.com Auctions (similar to that offered by eBay), zShops (online storefronts for small retailers), and sothebys.amazon.com, a joint venture with the auction house Sotheby's. To service these new product lines, Amazon significantly expanded its warehouse and distribution capabilities, adding eight new distribution centers comprising approximately

SOURCES: "Amazon Says on Target for Profit," *New York Times*, June 5, 2001; Amazon.com, Inc. Form 10-Q for the Quarter ended March 31, 2001, filed with the Securities and Exchange Commission on April 24, 2001; "The Trials of Jeff Bezos," by Miguel Helft, *The Industry Standard*, April 23, 2001; "Amazon's True Believer," by Eric J. Savitz, *The Industry Standard*, April 23, 2001; Amazon.com, Inc. Form 10-K for the Fiscal Year Ended December 31, 2000, filed with the Securities and Exchange Commission on March 23, 2001 "Amazon Profits Coming—Now What?," by Jen Muehlbauer, *The Industry Standard*, January 31, 2001; "Amazon's Conundrum," by John Frederick Moore, *Business2.0*, December 12, 2000; "The Amazon Question," by Miguel Helft, *The Industry Standard*, July 10, 2000; "Who's Writing the Book on Web Business?" by William C. Taylor, *Fast Company*, October 1996.

four million square feet. By the end of 1999, Amazon had more than doubled its 1998 revenues, recording sales of $1.6 billion. But at the same time, Amazon's losses showed no signs of abating, reaching $720 million for the year.

Although Bezos and Amazon were still riding high at the end of December 1999, in hindsight, it's possible to say that the handwriting was on the wall. Wall Street analysts, previously willing to overlook continuing and mounting losses as long as the company was expanding into new markets and attracting customers, began to wonder if Amazon would ever show a profit. They pointed out that as Amazon built more and more warehouses brimming with goods, and hired more and more employees (it had 9,000 by the end of 2000), it strayed farther and farther from its original vision of being a "virtual" retailer with lean inventories, low headcount, and significant cost savings over traditional bookstores. Lehman Brothers bond analyst Ravi Suria was one of Amazon's fiercest critics, issuing a report in June 2000 contending that Amazon.com showed "the financial characteristics that have driven innumerable retailers to disaster throughout history" — losing money on every sale and living on borrowed cash.

The year 2000 ended on a much different note than 1999 for Amazon. No longer the darling of Wall Street, its stock price had fallen significantly from its December 1999 high. In January 2001, it struggled to put a positive spin on its financial results for 2000, noting that while it had recorded a staggering $1.4 billion loss on revenues of $2.7 billion, its fourth-quarter loss was slightly less than analysts' projections. For the first time, it also announced a target for profitability, promising a "pro-forma operating profit" by the fourth quarter of 2001. Few analysts were impressed, pointing out that the method by which Amazon was suggesting its profit be calculated was not in accordance with generally accepted accounting principles and excluded, among other items, interest expense on its over $1 billion in debt. They further noted that growth had slowed in Amazon's core books, music, and video business, and that profit margins were slim in the faster growing categories, such as consumer electronics.

At the same time, though, Amazon continues to have its supporters. Lisa Rapuano, research director for Legg Mason, a large mutual fund, believes Amazon can make money. Its assets include an incredibly powerful, trusted brand, and a large lead on the competition. As other e-commerce sites fall by the wayside, it may be one of the few left standing. It has served over 30 million customers since 1995, and as Rapuano notes, "the customers love it; the customers aren't leaving." In her view, Amazon has extraordinary growth potential and many alternatives for future expansion.

In April 2001, Amazon reported a net loss of $234 million for the first quarter of 2001, compared to $308 million for the comparable quarter in 2000, and in June 2001, announced that it was still on target for the pro-forma operating profit it had promised by the fourth quarter of 2001. But at this point, whether Amazon will be recorded in the history books as a success or failure still remains unknown.

1.1 E-COMMERCE: THE REVOLUTION IS JUST BEGINNING

In 1994, e-commerce as we now know it did not exist. Today, just a few years later, more than thirty million American consumers are expected to spend about $65 billion purchasing products and services on the Internet's World Wide Web (Dykema, 2000). (Although the terms *Internet* and *World Wide Web* are often used interchangeably, they are actually two very different things: The Internet is a worldwide network of computer networks and the World Wide Web is one of the Internet's most popular services, providing access to over two billion Web pages. We describe both more fully later in this section and in Chapter 3.) Businesses in 2001 are expected to spend about $470 billion purchasing goods and services on the Web from other businesses (Jupiter Media Metrix, 2001). From a standing start in 1995, this type of commerce, called *electronic commerce* or *e-commerce*, has experienced growth rates of well over 100% a year and become the foundation for the first digital electronic marketplace. And even more impressive than its spectacular growth is its future predicted growth. By 2006, analysts estimate that consumers will be spending around $250 billion and businesses about $5.4 trillion in online transactions (Dykema, 2000; Jupiter Media Metrix, 2001).

It is important to realize that the rapid growth and change that has occurred in the first five to six years of e-commerce represents just the beginning — what could be called the first thirty seconds of the e-commerce revolution. The twenty-first century will be the age of a digitally enabled social and commercial life, the outlines of which we can barely perceive at this time. It appears likely that e-commerce will eventually impact nearly all commerce, or that all commerce will be e-commerce by the year 2050.

Business fortunes are made — and lost — in periods of extraordinary change such as this. The next five years hold out extraordinary opportunities — as well as risks — for new and traditional businesses to exploit digital technology for market advantage. For society as a whole, indeed for the world's societies, the next few decades offer the possibility of extraordinary gains in social wealth as the digital revolution works its way through larger and larger segments of the world's economy, offering the possibility of high rates of productivity and income growth in an inflation-free environment.

e-commerce
the use of the Internet and the Web to transact business. More formally, digitally enabled commercial transactions between and among organizations and individuals

This book will help you perceive and understand the opportunities and risks that lay ahead. By the time you finish, you will be able to identify the technological, business, and social forces that have shaped the first era of e-commerce and extend that understanding into the years ahead.

WHAT IS E-COMMERCE?

Our focus in this book is **e-commerce** — the use of the Internet and the Web to transact business. More formally, we focus on digitally enabled commercial transactions between and among organizations and individuals. Each of these components of our working definition of e-commerce is important. *Digitally enabled transactions* include all transactions mediated by digital technology. For the most part, this means transactions that occur over the Internet and the Web. *Commercial transactions* involve the exchange of value (e.g., money) across organizational or individual boundaries in return for products and services. Exchange of value is important for understanding the limits of e-commerce: Without an exchange of value, no commerce occurs.

THE DIFFERENCE BETWEEN E-COMMERCE AND E-BUSINESS

There is a debate among consultants and academics about the meaning and limitations of both e-commerce and e-business. Some argue that e-commerce encompasses the entire world of electronically based organizational activities that support a firm's market exchanges — including a firm's entire information system's infrastructure (Rayport and Jaworksi, 2001). Others argue, on the other hand, that e-business encompasses the entire world of internal and external electronically based activities, including e-commerce (Kalakota and Robinson, 2001).

We think that it is important to make a distinction between e-commerce and e-business because we believe they refer to different phenomena. For purposes of this text, we will use the term **e-business** to refer primarily to the digital enablement of transactions and processes *within* a firm, involving information systems under the control of the firm. For the most part, in our view, e-business does not include commercial transactions involving an exchange of value across organizational boundaries. For example, a company's online inventory control mechanisms are a component of e-business, but such internal processes do not directly generate revenue for the firm from outside businesses or consumers, as e-commerce, by definition, does. It is true, however, that a firm's e-business infrastructure can also support e-commerce exchanges. And e-commerce and e-business systems can and do blur together at the business firm boundary, at the point where internal business systems link up with suppliers, for instance. E-business applications turn into e-commerce precisely when an exchange of value occurs. We will examine this intersection further in Chapter 14, *Business-to-Business E-commerce, Supply Chain Management and Collaborative Commerce*.

Figure 1.1 illustrates the differences and complex relationship between e-commerce and e-business.

e-business

the digital enablement of transactions and processes within a firm, involving information systems under the control of the firm

WHY STUDY E-COMMERCE?

Why are there college courses and textbooks on e-commerce when there are no courses or textbooks on "TV Commerce," "Radio Commerce," "Direct Mail Commerce," "Rail-

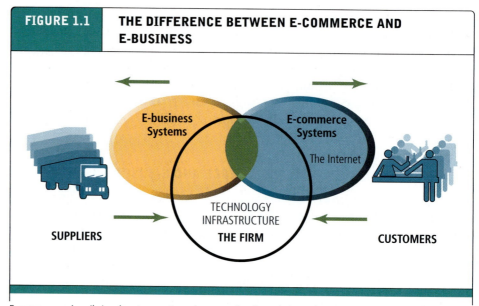

FIGURE 1.1	THE DIFFERENCE BETWEEN E-COMMERCE AND E-BUSINESS

E-commerce primarily involves transactions that cross firm boundaries. E-business primarily concerns the application of digital technologies to business processes within the firm.

road Commerce," or "Highway Commerce," even though these technologies have had profound impacts on commerce in the twentieth century and account for far more commerce than e-commerce? The reason, as you shall see, is that e-commerce technology (discussed in detail in Chapters 3 and 4) is different and more powerful than any of the other technologies we have seen in the past century.

Prior to the development of e-commerce, the process of marketing and selling goods was a mass-marketing and salesforce-driven process. Consumers were viewed as passive targets of advertising "campaigns" and branding blitzes intended to influence consumers' long-term product perceptions and immediate purchasing behavior. Selling was conducted in well-insulated "channels." Consumers were considered to be trapped by geographical and social boundaries, unable to search widely for the best price and quality. Information about prices, costs, and fees could be hidden from the consumer, creating profitable "information asymmetries" for the selling firm. **Information asymmetry** refers to any disparity in relevant market information among parties in a transaction.

E-commerce has challenged much of this traditional business thinking. Table 1.1 lists seven unique features of e-commerce technology that both challenge traditional business thinking and explain why we have a high interest in e-commerce.

information asymmetry
any disparity in relevant market information among parties in a transaction

TABLE 1.1	SEVEN UNIQUE FEATURES OF E-COMMERCE TECHNOLOGY
E-COMMERCE TECHNOLOGY DIMENSION	**BUSINESS SIGNIFICANCE**
Ubiquity—Internet/Web technology is available everywhere: at work, at home, and elsewhere via mobile devices, anytime.	The marketplace is extended beyond traditional boundaries and is removed from a temporal and geographic location. "Marketspace" is created; shopping can take place anywhere. Customer convenience is enhanced, and shopping costs are reduced.
Global Reach—The technology reaches across national boundaries, around the earth.	Commerce is enabled across cultural and national boundaries seamlessly and without modification. "Marketspace" includes potentially billions of consumers and millions of businesses worldwide.
Universal Standards—There is one set of technology standards, namely Internet standards.	There is one set of technical media standards across the globe.
Richness—Video, audio, and text messages are possible.	Video, audio, and text marketing messages are integrated into a single marketing message and consuming experience.
Interactivity—The technology works through interaction with the user.	Consumers are engaged in a dialog that dynamically adjusts the experience to the individual, and makes the consumer a co-participant in the process of delivering goods to the market.
Information Density—The technology reduces information costs and raises quality.	Information processing, storage, and communication costs drop dramatically, while currency, accuracy, and timeliness improve greatly. Information becomes plentiful, cheap, and accurate.
Personalization/Customization—The technology allows personalized messages to be delivered to individuals as well as groups.	Personalization of marketing messages and customization of products and services are based on individual characteristics.

SEVEN UNIQUE FEATURES OF E-COMMERCE TECHNOLOGY

Each of the dimensions of e-commerce technology and their business significance listed in Table 1.1 deserves a brief exploration, and comparison to both traditional commerce and other forms of technology-enabled commerce.

Ubiquity

In traditional commerce, a marketplace is a physical place you visit in order to transact. For example, television and radio are typically directed to motivating the consumer to go someplace to make a purchase. E-commerce is **ubiquitous**, meaning that is it available just about everywhere, at all times. It liberates the market from being restricted to a physical space and makes it possible to shop from your desktop, at home, at work, or even from your car, using mobile commerce. The result is called a **marketspace** — a marketplace extended beyond traditional boundaries and removed

ubiquity
available just about everywhere, at all times. A unique feature of e-commerce technology

marketspace
marketplace extended beyond traditional boundaries and removed from a temporal and geographic location

from a temporal and geographic location. From a consumer point of view, ubiquity reduces *transaction costs* — the costs of participating in a market. To transact, it is no longer necessary that you spend time and money traveling to a market. At a broader level, the ubiquity of e-commerce lowers the cognitive energy required to transact in a marketspace. *Cognitive energy* refers to the mental effort required to complete a task. Humans generally seek to reduce cognitive energy outlays. When given a choice, humans will choose the path requiring the least effort — the most convenient path (Shapiro and Varian, 1999; Tversky and Kahneman, 1981).

Global Reach

E-commerce technology permits commercial transactions to cross cultural and national boundaries far more conveniently and cost effectively than is true in traditional commerce. As a result, the potential market size for e-commerce merchants is roughly equal to the size of the world's online population (over 400 million in 2001, and growing rapidly, according to the Computer Industry Almanac). The total number of users or customers an e-commerce business can obtain is a measure of its **reach** (Evans and Wurster, 1997).

reach
the total number of users or customers an e-commerce business can obtain

In contrast, most traditional commerce is local or regional — it involves local merchants or national merchants with local outlets. Television and radio stations, and newspapers, for instance, are primarily local and regional institutions with limited but powerful national networks that can attract a national audience. In contrast to e-commerce technology, these older commerce technologies do not easily cross national boundaries to a global audience.

Universal Standards

One strikingly unusual feature of e-commerce technologies is that the technical standards of the Internet, and therefore the technical standards for conducting e-commerce, are **universal standards** — they are shared by all nations around the world. In contrast, most traditional commerce technologies differ from one nation to the next. For instance, television and radio standards differ around the world, as does cell telephone technology. The universal technical standards of e-commerce greatly lower *market entry costs* — the cost merchants must pay just to bring their goods to market. At the same time, for consumers, universal standards reduce *search costs* — the effort required to find suitable products. And by creating a single, one-world marketspace, where prices and product descriptions can be inexpensively displayed for all to see, *price discovery* becomes simpler, faster, and more accurate (Bakos, 1997; Kambil, 1997). With e-commerce technologies, it is possible for the first time in history to easily find all the suppliers, prices, and delivery terms of a specific product anywhere in the world. Although this is not necessarily realistic today for all or many products, it is a potential that will be exploited in the future.

universal standards
standards that are shared by all nations around the world

Richness

Information **richness** refers to the complexity and content of a message (Evans and Wurster, 1997; 1999). Traditional markets, national salesforces, and small retail stores have great richness: They are able to provide personal, face-to-face service using aural and visual cues when making a sale. The richness of traditional markets makes them a powerful selling or commercial environment. Prior to the development of the Web, there was a trade-off between richness and reach: the larger the audience reached, the less rich the message (see Figure 1.2).

richness
the complexity and content of a message

Interactivity

Unlike any of the commercial technologies of the twentieth century, with the possible exception of the telephone, e-commerce technologies are **interactive**, meaning they allow for two-way communication between merchant and consumer. Television, for instance, cannot ask the viewer any questions, enter into a conversation with a viewer, or request customer information be entered into a form. In contrast, all of these activities are possible on an e-commerce Web site. Interactivity allows an online

interactive
technology that allows for two-way communication between merchant and consumer

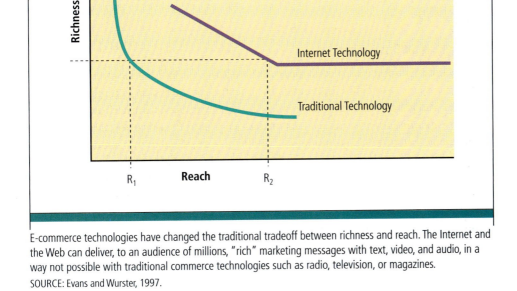

| FIGURE 1.2 | THE CHANGING TRADE-OFF BETWEEN RICHNESS AND REACH |

E-commerce technologies have changed the traditional tradeoff between richness and reach. The Internet and the Web can deliver, to an audience of millions, "rich" marketing messages with text, video, and audio, in a way not possible with traditional commerce technologies such as radio, television, or magazines.
SOURCE: Evans and Wurster, 1997.

merchant to engage a consumer in ways similar to a face-to-face experience, but on a much more massive, global scale.

Information Density

information density

the total amount and quality of information available to all market participants

The Internet and the Web vastly increase **information density** — the total amount and quality of information available to all market participants, consumers, and merchants alike. E-commerce technologies reduce information collection, storage, processing, and communication costs. At the same time, these technologies increase greatly the currency, accuracy, and timeliness of information — making information more useful and important than ever. As a result, information becomes more plentiful, cheaper, and of higher quality.

A number of business consequences result from the growth in information density. In e-commerce markets, prices and costs become more *transparent*. *Price transparency* refers to the ease with which consumers can find out the variety of prices in a market; *cost transparency* refers to the ability of consumers to discover the actual costs merchants pay for products (Sinha, 2000). But there are advantages for merchants as well. Online merchants can discover much more about consumers; this allows merchants to segment the market into groups willing to pay different prices, and permits them to engage in *price discrimination* — selling the same goods, or nearly the same goods, to different targeted groups at different prices. For instance, an online merchant can discover a consumer's avid interest in expensive exotic vacations, and then pitch expensive exotic vacation plans to that consumer at a premium price — knowing this person is willing to pay extra for an exotic vacation, while pitching the same vacation plan at a lower price to more price-sensitive consumers (Shapiro and Varian, 1999).

Personalization/Customization

personalization

the targeting of marketing messages to specific individuals by adjusting the message to a person's name, interests, and past purchases

customization

changing the delivered product or service based on a user's preferences or prior behavior

E-commerce technologies permit **personalization**: Merchants can target their marketing messages to specific individuals by adjusting the message to a person's name, interests, and past purchases. The technology also permits **customization** — changing the delivered product or service based on a user's preferences or prior behavior. Given the interactive nature of e-commerce technology, a great deal of information about the consumer can be gathered in the marketplace at the moment of purchase. With the increase in information density, a great deal of information about the consumer's past purchases and behavior can be stored and used by online merchants. The result is a level of personalization and customization unthinkable with existing commerce technologies. For instance, you may be able to shape what you see on television by selecting a channel, but you cannot change the contents of the channel you have chosen. In contrast, the *Wall Street Journal Online* allows you to select the type of news stories you want to see first, and to be alerted when certain events happen.

Now, let's return to the question that motivated this section: Why study e-commerce? To reiterate, the answer is simply that e-commerce technologies — and the digital markets that result — promise to bring about some very fundamental, unprecedented shifts in commerce. One of these shifts, for instance, appears to be a very large reduction in information asymmetry among all market participants (consumers and merchants). In the past, merchants and manufacturers were able to prevent consumers from learning about their costs, their price discrimination strategies, and their profits from sales. This becomes more difficult with e-commerce, and the entire marketplace potentially becomes very price competitive.

On the other hand, the unique dimensions of e-commerce technologies listed in Table 1.1 also suggest many new possibilities for marketing and selling — a powerful set of interactive, personalized, and rich messages are available for delivery to segmented, targeted audiences. E-commerce technologies make it possible for merchants to know much more about consumers and use this information more effectively than was ever true in the past. Potentially, online merchants could use this new information to develop new information asymmetries, enhance their ability to brand products, charge premium prices for high-quality service, and segment the market into an endless number of subgroups, each receiving a different price. To complicate matters further, these same technologies make it possible for merchants to know more about other merchants than was ever true in the past. This presents the possibility that merchants might collude on prices rather than compete and drive overall average prices up. This strategy works especially well when there are just a few suppliers (Varian, 2000b). We examine these different visions of e-commerce — friction-free commerce versus a brand-driven imperfect marketplace — further in Section 1.2 and throughout the book.

TYPES OF E-COMMERCE

There are a variety of different types of e-commerce and many different ways to characterize these types. Table 1.2 lists the five major types of e-commerce discussed in this book.[1]

For the most part, we distinguish different types of e-commerce by the nature of the market relationship — who is selling to whom. The exceptions are P2P and m-commerce, which are technology-based distinctions.

B2C. The most commonly discussed type of e-commerce is **Business-to-Consumer (B2C) e-commerce**, in which online businesses attempt to reach individual consumers. Even though B2C is comparatively small (about $65 billion in 2001), it has

Business-to-Consumer (B2C) e-commerce
online businesses selling to individual consumers

---

[1]B2G — Business to Government e-commerce can be considered yet another type of e-commerce. For the purposes of this text, we subsume B2G e-commerce within B2B e-commerce, viewing the government as simply a form of business when it acts as a procurer of goods and/or services.

TABLE 1.2	MAJOR TYPES OF E-COMMERCE
TYPE OF E-COMMERCE	EXAMPLE
B2C—Business to Consumer	Amazon.com is a general merchandiser that sells consumer products to retail consumers.
B2B—Business to Business	eSteel.com is a steel industry exchange that creates an electronic market for steel producers and users.
C2C—Consumer to Consumer	eBay.com creates a marketspace where consumers can auction or sell goods directly to other consumers.
P2P—Peer to Peer	Gnutella is a software application that permits consumers to share music with one another directly, without the intervention of a market maker as in C2C e-commerce.
M-commerce—Mobile commerce	Wireless mobile devices such as PDAs (personal digital assistants) or cell phones can be used to conduct commercial transactions.

grown exponentially since 1995, and is the type of e-commerce that most consumers are likely to encounter. Within the B2C category there are many different types of business models. Chapter 2 has a detailed discussion of seven different B2C business models: portals, online retailers, content providers, transaction brokers, market creators, service providers, and community providers.

Business-to-Business (B2B) e-commerce
online businesses selling to other businesses

B2B. **Business-to-Business (B2B) e-commerce**, in which businesses focus on selling to other businesses, is the largest form of e-commerce with about $700 billion in transactions in 2001. In 2001, there was an estimated $12 trillion in business-to-business exchanges of all kinds, online and offline, suggesting that B2B e-commerce has significant growth potential. The ultimate size of B2B e-commerce could be huge. At first, B2B e-commerce primarily involved inter-business exchanges, but a number of other B2B business models have developed, including e-distributors, B2B service providers, matchmakers, and infomediaries that are widening the use of B2B e-commerce.

Consumer-to-Consumer (C2C) e-commerce
consumers selling to other consumers

C2C. **Consumer-to-Consumer (C2C) e-commerce** provides a way for consumers to sell to each other, with the help of an online market maker such as the auction site eBay. The size of this market is estimated to be over $5 billion and growing rapidly (eBay.com, 2001). In C2C e-commerce, the consumer prepares the product for market, places the product for auction or sale, and relies on the market maker to provide catalog, search engine, and transaction-clearing capabilities so that products can be easily displayed, discovered, and paid for.

P2P. Peer-to-peer technology enables Internet users to share files and computer resources directly without having to go through a central Web server. In peer-to-peer's purest form, no intermediary is required. For instance, Gnutella is a peer-to-peer freeware software application that permits users to directly exchange musical tracks, typically without any charge. Since 1999, entrepreneurs and venture capitalists have attempted to adapt various aspects of peer-to-peer technology into **Peer-to-Peer (P2P) e-commerce.** Napster.com, which was established to aid Internet users in finding and sharing online music files known as *MP3 files*, is perhaps the most well-known example of peer-to-peer e-commerce, although purists note that Napster is only partially peer-to-peer because it relies on a central database to show which users are sharing music files. In 2000, the Recording Industry of America, a trade organization of the largest recording companies, successfully sued Napster for violating copyright law by allowing Napster members to exchange copyrighted music tracks without compensation to the copyright holders. Read the case study at the end of the chapter for a further look at how Napster worked and the issues it raises.

> **Peer-to-Peer (P2P) e-commerce**
> use of peer-to-peer technology, which enables Internet users to share files and computer resources directly without having to go through a central Web server, in e-commerce

M-commerce. **Mobile commerce**, or **m-commerce**, refers to the use of wireless digital devices to enable transactions on the Web. These devices are described more fully in Chapter 3, but essentially, they utilize wireless networks to connect cell phones and handheld devices such as the PalmVIIx to the Web. Once connected, mobile consumers can conduct many types of transactions, including stock trades, in-store price comparisons, banking, travel reservations, and more. Thus far, m-commerce is used most widely in Japan and Europe (especially Finland), where cell phones are more prevalent than in the United States, but, as discussed in the next section, it is expected to grow rapidly in the United States over the next five years.

> **mobile commerce (m-commerce)**
> use of wireless digital devices to enable transactions on the Web

GROWTH OF THE INTERNET AND THE WEB

The technology juggernaut behind e-commerce is the Internet and the World Wide Web.

Without both of these technologies, e-commerce as we know it would be impossible. We describe the Internet and the Web in some detail in Chapter 3. The Internet is a worldwide network of computer networks built on common standards. Created in the late 1960s to connect a small number of mainframe computers and their users, the Internet has since grown into the world's largest network, connecting about 350 million computers worldwide. The Internet links businesses, educational institutions, government agencies, and individuals together, and provides users with services such as e-mail, document transfer, newsgroups, shopping, research, instant messaging, music, videos, and news.

Figure 1.3 illustrates one way to measure the growth of the Internet, by looking at the number of Internet host computers (Web server computers with an Internet

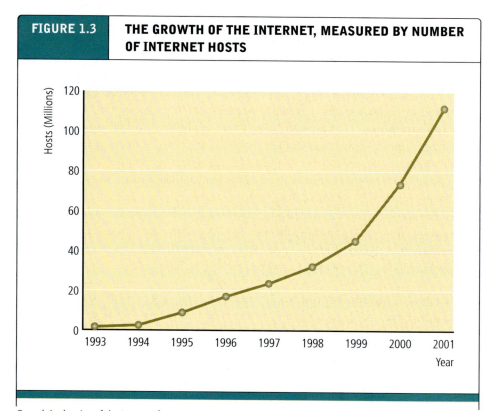

FIGURE 1.3 | THE GROWTH OF THE INTERNET, MEASURED BY NUMBER OF INTERNET HOSTS

Growth in the size of the Internet from 1993–2000, as measured by the number of Internet hosts (servers) with domain names.

SOURCE: Internet Domain Survey, Internet Software Consortium, 2001.

address). In 2000, there were over 70 million Internet host computers in over 245 countries, with the number growing at about a rate of 45% a year (Tehan, 2000)

The Internet has shown extraordinary growth patterns when compared to other electronic technologies of the past. It took radio 38 years to achieve a 30% share of United States households. It took television 17 years to achieve a 30% share. Since the invention of a graphical user interface for the World Wide Web in 1993, it has taken only seven years for the Internet/Web to achieve a 30% share of United States households.

The World Wide Web is the most popular service that runs on the Internet infrastructure. The Web is the "killer application" that made the Internet commercially interesting and extraordinarily popular. The Web was developed in the early 1990s and hence is of much more recent vintage than the Internet. We describe the Web in some detail in Chapter 3. The Web provides access to over one billion pages or documents created in a language called *HTML (HyperText Markup Language)*. These HTML pages contain information — including text, graphics, animations, and other objects —

made available for public use. You can find an exceptionally wide range of information on Web pages, ranging from the entire catalog of Sears Roebuck, to the entire collection of public records from the Securities and Exchange Commission, to the card catalog of your local library, millions of music tracks (some of them legal), and video clips. Even entire videos are available. The Internet prior to the Web was primarily used for text communications, file transfers, and remote computing. The Web introduced far more powerful and commercially interesting, colorful multimedia capabilities of direct relevance to commerce. In essence, the Web added color, voice, and video to the Internet, creating a communications infrastructure and information storage system that rivals television, radio, magazines, and even libraries.

Web content has grown exponentially since 1993. A variety of groups have estimated there are between one billion and two billion Web pages in 2000. Each day about seven million new Web pages are added. By the end of 2001, at this rate of growth there will be about four billion Web pages (Cyveillance, Inc. 2000; Inktomi 2000). Figure 1.4 describes the growth of Web content in the form of Web pages.

Read *Insight on Technology: Spider Webs and Bow Ties*, for the latest view of researchers on the structure of the Web.

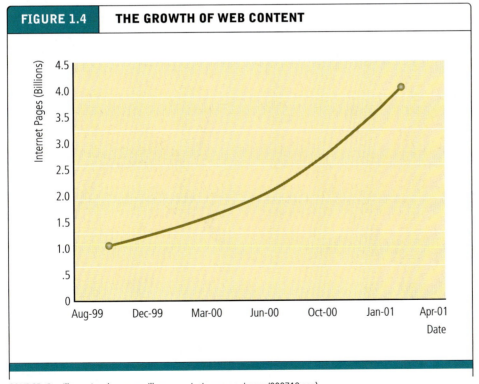

| FIGURE 1.4 | THE GROWTH OF WEB CONTENT |

SOURCE: Cyveillance, Inc. (www.cyveillance.com/us/newsroom/pressr/000710.asp)

INSIGHT ON TECHNOLOGY

SPIDER WEBS AND BOW TIES

The World Wide Web conjures up images of a giant spider web where everything is connected to everything else, and you can go from one edge of the web to another by just following the right links. Theoretically, that's what makes the Web different from a typical index system: You can follow hyperlinks from one page to another. In the "small world" theory of the Web, every Web page is thought to be separated from any other Web page by an average of about 19 clicks. The small world theory was supported by early research on a small sampling of Web sites. But recent research conducted jointly by scientists at IBM, Compaq, and AltaVista found something entirely different. These scientists used AltaVista's Web crawler "Scooter" to identify 200 million Web pages and follow 1.5 billion links on these pages.

The research discovered that the Web was not like a spider web at all, but rather like a bow tie (see figure below). The bow-tie Web has a "strongly connected component" (SCC) composed of about 56 million Web pages. On the right side of the bow tie is a set of 44 million OUT pages that you can get to from the center, but cannot return to the center from. OUT pages tend to be corporate intranet and other Web site pages that are designed to trap you at the site when you land. On the left side of the bow tie is a set of 44

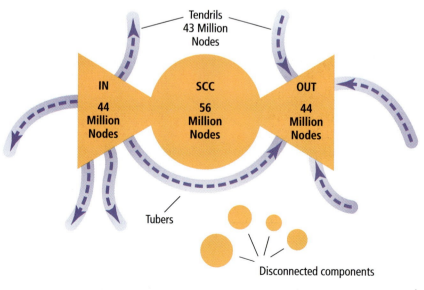

Tendrils
43 Million
Nodes

IN

44
Million
Nodes

SCC

56
Million
Nodes

OUT

44
Million
Nodes

Tubers

Disconnected components

(continued)

million IN pages from which you can get to the center, but that you cannot travel to from the center. These are recently created "newbie" pages that have not yet been linked to by many center pages. 43 million pages were classified as "tendrils," which are pages that do not link to the center, and cannot be linked to from the center. However, the tendril pages may be linked to IN and OUT pages. Occasionally, tendrils link to one another without passing through the center (these are called "tubes"). Finally, there were 16 million pages totally disconnected from everything.

The picture of the Web that emerges from this research is quite different from earlier reports and claims. The notion that most pairs of Web pages are separated by a handful of links, almost always under 20, and that the number of connections would grow exponentially with the size of the Web, is not supported. In fact, there is a 75% chance that there is no path from one randomly chosen page to another. With this knowledge it now becomes clear why the most advanced Web search engines only index about six million Web sites, when the overall population of Web sites is over 70 million. Most Web sites cannot be found by search engines because their pages are not well-connected or linked to the central core of the Web. Because e-commerce revenues in part depend on customers being able to find a Web site using search engines, Web site managers need to take steps to ensure their Web pages are part of the connected central core of the Web. One way to do this is to make sure the site has as many links as possible to and from other relevant sites, especially to other sites within the SCC.

SOURCES: "Graph Structure in the Web" by A. Broder; R. Kumar; F. Maghoul; P. Raghaven; S. Rajagopalan; R. Stata; A. Tomkins; and J. Wiener, Proceedings of the 9th International World Wide Web Conference, Amsterdam, The Netherlands, pages 309-320. Elsevier Science, May 2000; "Study Reveals Web As Loosely Woven," by Ian Austen, *New York Times*, May 18, 2000; "The Bowtie Theory Explains Link Popularity," by John Heard, www.searchengineposition.com/Articles/bowtie.html

ORIGINS AND GROWTH OF E-COMMERCE

It is difficult to pinpoint just when e-commerce begins. There are many precursors to e-commerce. In the late 1970s, a pharmaceutical firm named Baxter Healthcare initiated a primitive form of B2B e-commerce by using a telephone-based modem that permitted hospitals to reorder supplies from Baxter. This system was later expanded during the 1980s into a PC-based remote order entry system and was widely copied throughout the United States long before the Internet became a commercial environment. Electronic Data Interchange (EDI) standards were developed in the 1980s that permitted firms to exchange commercial documents and conduct digital commercial transactions across private networks.

In the B2C arena, the first truly large-scale digitally enabled transaction system was deployed in France in 1981. The French Minitel was a videotext system that combined a telephone with an 8-inch screen. By the mid-1980s more than 3 million Mini-

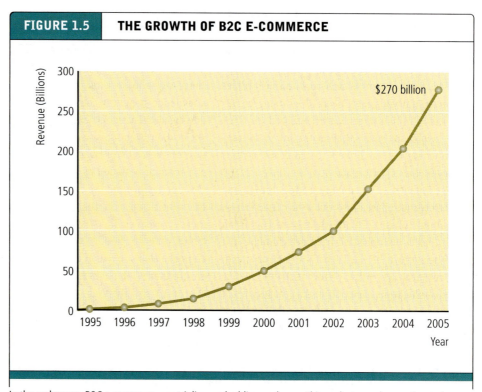

FIGURE 1.5 **THE GROWTH OF B2C E-COMMERCE**

In the early years, B2C e-commerce was tripling or doubling each year. This explosive early growth rate has since slowed. In future years, B2C e-commerce is expected to grow at about 45% to 55% per year, with seasonal spikes showing stronger year-to-year gains.
SOURCE: Dykema, 2000.

tels were deployed, and today there are about 15 million in use throughout France. Over 25,000 different services can be found on Minitel, including ticket agencies, travel services, retail products, and online banking. Purchases are paid for by means of the monthly telephone bill. No credit cards are needed (Tagliabue, 2001).

Yet none of these precursor systems had the functionality of the Internet. Generally, when we think of e-commerce today, it is inextricably linked to the Internet. For our purposes we will say e-commerce begins in 1995, following the appearance of the first banner advertisements placed by ATT, Volvo, Sprint and others on Hotwired.com in late October 1994, and the first sales of banner ad space by Netscape and Infoseek in early 1995. Since then, e-commerce has been the fastest growing form of commerce in the United States. Figures 1.5 and 1.6 chart the development of B2C e-commerce and B2B e-commerce, respectively, with projections through 2005.

FIGURE 1.6	THE GROWTH OF B2B E-COMMERCE

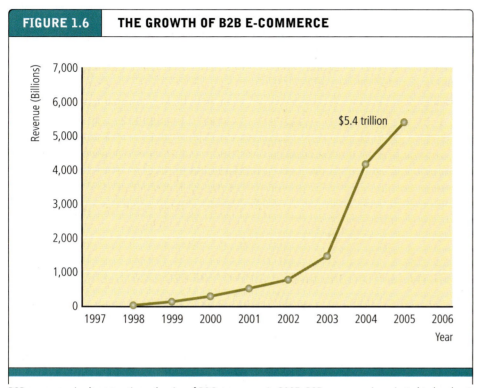

B2B commerce is about ten times the size of B2C commerce. In 2005, B2B commerce is projected to be about $5.4 trillion. About a third of all B2B purchases will take place online.

Source: Jupiter Media Metrix, 2001.

Both graphs show a strong projected growth rate, but the dollar amounts of B2B e-commerce dwarf those of B2C.

TECHNOLOGY AND E-COMMERCE IN PERSPECTIVE

Although in many respects, e-commerce is new and different, it is also important to keep e-commerce in perspective. First, the Internet and the Web are just two of a long list of technologies that have greatly changed commerce in the United States and around the world. Each of these other technologies spawned business models and strategies designed to leverage the technology into commercial advantage and profit and were also accompanied by explosive early growth, characterized by thousands of entrepreneurial start-up companies, followed by painful retrenchment, and then a long-term successful exploitation of the technology by larger established firms. In the case of automobiles, for instance, in 1915, there were over 250 automobile manufacturers in the United States. By 1940, there were five. In the case of radio, in 1925, there were over two thousand radio stations across the United States, most broadcasting to local neighborhoods and run by amateurs. By 1990, there were fewer than 500 independent stations. There is every reason to believe e-commerce will follow the same pattern — with notable differences discussed throughout the text.

Second, although e-commerce has grown explosively, there is no guarantee it will continue to grow forever at these rates, and much reason to believe e-commerce growth will cap as it confronts its own fundamental limitations. For instance, B2C e-commerce is still a small part (about 1%) of the overall retail market. With current growth rates, in 2005, all of B2C e-commerce will roughly equal the annual revenue of Wal-Mart — the world's largest and most successful retailer.

POTENTIAL LIMITATIONS ON THE GROWTH OF B2C E-COMMERCE

There are several limitations on B2C e-commerce that have the potential to cap its growth rate and ultimate size. Table 1.3 describes some of these limitations.

Some of these limitations may be eradicated in the next decade. For instance, it is likely that the price of entry-level PCs will fall to $200 by the year 2005. This, coupled with enhancements in capabilities such as integration with television, access to entertainment film libraries on a pay-per-view basis, and other software enhancements, will likely raise U.S. household penetration rates to the level of cable television penetration (about 80%) by 2005. The PC operating system will also likely evolve from the current Windows platform to far simpler choice panels similar to the interface found on Palm handheld devices.

The most significant technology that can reduce barriers to Internet access is wireless Web technology (described in more detail in Chapter 3). Currently about 3.2 million wireless Web appliances are in use in the United States (about 21.5 million worldwide with penetration in Europe and Asia far ahead of the United States). By 2005, these devices are expected to be used by an estimated 115 million persons in the United States and almost 600 million worldwide, accounting for 55.4% of total Internet access in the United States and 71% worldwide (eTForecasts, 2000). Figure 1.7 illustrates the extremely rapid growth projected for wireless Web devices.

On the other hand, some of the limitations noted in Table 1.3 are likely to continue to persist. For instance, it is very unlikely that the digital shopping experience can ever equal the social and cultural experience that many seek from the traditional shopping environment. Furthermore, most of the world's population will not be able to access the Internet in 2005 because of limited access to the technology and language barriers.

TABLE 1.3	LIMITATIONS ON THE GROWTH OF B2C E-COMMERCE
LIMITING FACTOR	**COMMENT**
Home penetration of PCs	Currently only 48% of households have PCs and the penetration rate is not growing rapidly.
Expensive technology	Using the Internet requires a $500 PC (minimal) and a $20/month connect charge.
Complex software interface	Using the Web requires installation of a complex operating system and application suite that is far more difficult to operate than a television or telephone.
Sophisticated skill set	The skills required to make effective use of the Internet and e-commerce capabilities are far more sophisticated than, say, for television or newspapers.
Persistent cultural attraction of physical markets and traditional shopping experiences	For many, shopping is a cultural and social event where people meet directly with merchants and other consumers. This experience cannot yet be duplicated in digital form.
Persistent global inequality limiting access to telephones and personal computers	Most of the world's population does not have telephone service, PCs, or cell phones.

On balance, the current technological limits on e-commerce growth, while real, are likely to recede in importance over the next decade. The social and cultural limitations of e-commerce are less likely to change.

1.2 E-COMMERCE I AND II

Although e-commerce is a very recent phenomenon of the 1990s, it already has a history. The history of e-commerce can be divided into two periods we call E-commerce I and E-commerce II. The **E-commerce I** era was a period of explosive growth, beginning in 1995 with the first widespread use of the Web to advertise products, and ending in 2000 when stock market valuations for dot.com companies began to collapse.

The **E-commerce II** era began in January 2001, by which time a sobering reassessment of e-commerce companies and the value of their stock had occurred.

E-commerce I
a period of explosive growth in e-commerce, beginning in 1995 and ending in 2000

E-commerce II
the current era of e-commerce, beginning in 2001

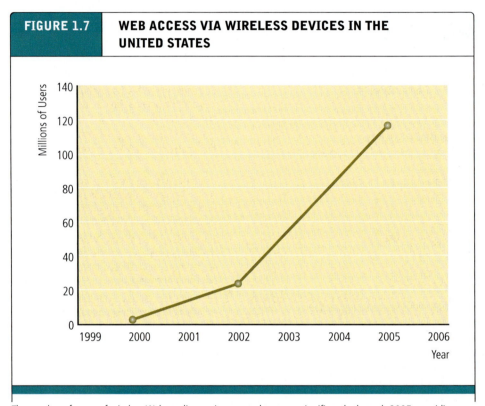

FIGURE 1.7 **WEB ACCESS VIA WIRELESS DEVICES IN THE UNITED STATES**

The number of users of wireless Web appliances is expected to grow significantly through 2005, providing a significant stimulus to e-commerce.

SOURCE: eTForecasts, 2000

Each of these periods of e-commerce is characterized by a set of visions and driving forces.

THE VISIONS AND FORCES BEHIND E-COMMERCE I: 1995–2000

E-commerce I was one of the most euphoric of times in American commercial history. Thousands of dot.com companies were formed, backed by over $125 billion in financial capital — one of the largest outpourings of venture capital in United States history (PriceWaterhouseCoopers, 2001). Table 1.4 details the amounts invested in various e-commerce sectors in the period 1996–2000.

For computer scientists and information technologists, E-commerce I was a powerful vindication of a set of information technologies that had developed over a period of forty years — extending from the development of the early Internet to the PC, to local area networks. The vision was of a universal communications and computing

TABLE 1.4	AMOUNTS RAISED BY VENTURE-BACKED INTERNET COMPANIES IN 1996–2000 (IN MILLIONS)				
	1996 TOTAL	1997 TOTAL	1998 TOTAL	1999 TOTAL	2000 TOTAL
TYPE OF E-COMMERCE					
Business Services	$780.42	$1,270.03	$3,409.02	$14,749.50	$29,536.22
Content	$233.72	$276.05	$455.02	$1,977.78	$2,301.25
B2C/Retail	$108.25	$159.51	$540.66	$4,209.14	$1,941.79
Infrastructure	$466.67	$879.88	$1,388.81	$4,589.29	$13,860.46
ISPs	$369.41	$561.27	$1,030.25	$3,499.10	$7,577.11
Software/Database	$1,132.67	$1,634.05	$2,459.00	$7,132.39	$15,124.71
Estimated Amount	$11.40	$14.15	$79.12	$540.14	$2,069.48
Total Internet Financings for Yr	**$3,102.54**	**$4,794.95**	**$9,361.86**	**$36,697.33**	**$72,411.02**

SOURCE: PriceWaterhouse Coopers MoneyTree Survey, 2001

environment that everyone on earth could access with cheap, inexpensive computers; a worldwide universe of knowledge stored on HTML pages created by hundreds of millions of individuals and thousands of libraries, governments, and scientific institutes. They celebrated the fact that the Internet was not controlled by anyone, by any nation, but was free to all. They believed the Internet — and the e-commerce that rose on this infrastructure — should remain a self-governed, self-regulated environment.

For economists, e-commerce raised the realistic prospect of a perfect *Bertrand market* — a market where price, cost, and quality information is equally distributed, where a nearly infinite set of suppliers compete against one another, and where customers have access to all relevant market information worldwide. Merchants in turn would have equal direct access to hundreds of millions of customers. In this near-perfect information marketspace, transaction costs would plummet because the cost of searching for prices, product descriptions, payment settlement, and order fulfillment would all fall drastically (Bakos, 1997). New "shopping bot" programs would automatically search the entire Web for the best prices and delivery times. For merchants, the cost of searching for customers would also fall — reducing the need for wasteful advertising. Prices and even costs would be increasingly transparent to the consumer, who could now know exactly and instantly the worldwide best cost, quality, and availability of most products. Information asymmetry would be greatly reduced. Given the instant nature of Internet communications, the availability of powerful sales infor-

disintermediation

displacement of market middlemen who traditionally are intermediaries between producers and consumers by a new direct relationship between manufacturers and content originators with their customers

friction-free commerce

a vision of commerce in which information is equally distributed, transaction costs are low, prices can be dynamically adjusted to reflect actual demand, intermediaries decline, and unfair competitive advantages are eliminated

first mover

a firm that is first to market in a particular area and that moves quickly to gather market share

network effect

occurs where users receive value from the fact that everyone else uses the same tool or product

mation systems, and the low cost involved in changing prices on a Web site (low *menu costs*), producers could *dynamically price* their products to reflect actual demand, ending the idea of one national price, or one suggested manufacturer's list price. In turn, market middlemen would disappear (**disintermediation**) — the distributors, wholesalers, and other factors in the marketplace who are intermediates between producers and consumers, each demanding a payment and raising costs while adding little value. Manufacturers and content originators would develop a direct market relationship with their customers. The resulting intense competition, the decline of intermediaries, and the lower transaction costs would eliminate product brands, and along with it, the possibility of *monopoly profits* based on brands, geography, or special access to factors of production. Prices for products and services would fall to the point where prices covered costs of production plus a fair, "market rate" of return on capital, plus additional small payments for entrepreneurial effort (that would not last long). Unfair competitive advantages (which occur when one competitor has an advantage others cannot purchase) would be eliminated, as would extraordinary returns on invested capital. This vision was called **friction-free commerce** (Smith et al.,2000).

For real-world entrepreneurs, their financial backers, and marketing professionals in the E-commerce I period, the idea of friction-free commerce was far from their own visions. For these players, e-commerce represented an extraordinary opportunity to earn far above normal returns on investment, far above the cost of borrowing capital. The e-commerce marketspace represented access to millions of consumers worldwide who used the Internet and a set of marketing communications technologies (e-mail and Web pages) that was universal, inexpensive, and powerful. These new technologies would permit marketers to practice what they always had done — segmenting the market into groups with different needs and price sensitivity, targeting the segments with branding and promotional messages, and positioning the product and pricing for each group — but with even more precision. In this new marketspace, extraordinary profits would go to **first movers** — those firms who were first to market in a particular area and who moved quickly to gather market share. First movers could establish a large customer base quickly, build brand name recognition early, build an entirely new distribution channel, and then inhibit competitors (new entrants) by building in *switching costs* for their customers through proprietary interface designs and features available only at one site. Online businesses using the new technology could create informative, community-like features unavailable to traditional merchants. These "communities of consumption" also would add value and be difficult for traditional merchants to imitate. The thinking was that once customers became accustomed to using a company's unique Web interface and feature set, they could not easily be switched to competitors. In the best case, the entrepreneurial firm would invent proprietary technologies and techniques that most everyone adopted, creating a network effect. A **network effect** occurs where all participants receive value from the fact that everyone else uses the same tool or product, such as a common operating system, telephone system, or software application such as instant messaging, all of which increase in value as more people adopt them[2]. Successful first movers would become the *new intermediaries* of e-commerce, displacing traditional retail merchants and suppliers of content, and becoming profitable by charging fees of one sort or another for the value customers perceived in their services and products.

To initiate this process, entrepreneurs argued that prices would have to be very low to attract customers and fend off potential competitors. E-commerce was, after all, a totally new way of shopping that would have to offer some immediate cost benefits to consumers. However, because doing business on the Web was supposedly so much more efficient when compared to traditional "bricks and mortar" businesses, and even when compared to direct mail catalog business, and because the costs of customer acquisition and retention would supposedly be so much lower, profits would inevitably materialize out of these efficiencies. Given these dynamics, market share, the number of visitors to a site ("eyeballs"), and revenue became far more important in the earlier stages than earnings or profits. Entrepreneurs and their financial backers in the E-commerce I era expected that extraordinary profitability would come, but only after several years of losses.

Thus, the E-commerce I period was driven largely by visions of profiting from new technology, with the emphasis on quickly achieving very high market visibility. The source of financing was venture capital funds. The ideology of the period emphasized the ungoverned "Wild West" character of the Web, and the feeling that governments and courts could not possibly limit or regulate the Internet, that traditional corporations were too slow and bureaucratic, too stuck in the old ways of doing business, to "get it" — to be competitive in e-commerce. Young entrepreneurs were therefore the driving force behind E-commerce I ventures, backed by huge amounts of money invested by venture capitalists. The emphasis was on *deconstructing* (destroying) traditional distribution channels and disintermediating existing channels, using new pure online companies who aimed to achieve impregnable first mover advantages. Overall, E-commerce I was characterized by experimentation, capitalization, and hypercompetition (Varian, 2000a). Read *Insight on Business: A Short History of Dot.com IPOs* for a further look at the E-commerce I era.

E-COMMERCE II 2001–2006

The crash in stock market values for E-commerce I companies throughout 2000 is a convenient marker for ending that period. There were a number of reasons for that crash. A part of the run-up in technology stocks, especially those traded on the

---

[2]The network effect is quantified by Metcalfe's Law, which postulates that the value of a network grows by the square of the number of participants.

A SHORT HISTORY OF DOT.COM IPOS

E-commerce I was built using Internet technology, but what made it run was money, big money. Between 1998 and 2000, venture capitalists poured an estimated $120 billion into approximately 12,450 dot.com start-up ventures. Investment bankers then took 1,262 of these companies public in what is called an *initial public offering (IPO)* of stock. To prepare for an IPO, investment bankers analyze a company's finances and business plans and attempt to arrive at an estimate of how much the company is worth—how much the investing public might be willing to pay for the shares and how many shares might be purchased by the public and other institutions. The bankers then underwrite the stock offering and sell the stock on a public stock exchange, making enormous fees for underwriting in the process.

In the E-commerce I heyday, 1998–2000, dot.com IPOs shares often skyrocketed within minutes of hitting the trading floor. Some shares tripled and quadrupled in the first day, and a 50% "pump" (or increase in value) was considered just a reasonable showing. IPO shares for dot.com companies were often targeted to open at around $15 per share, and it was not uncommon for them to be trading at $45 a share or even much more later the same day. Therefore, getting in on the ground floor of an IPO—which meant arranging to purchase a fixed number of shares prior to actual trading on the first day—was a privilege reserved for other large institutions, friends of the investment bankers, or other investment bankers.

In what was called "stock spinning," the underwriter would sell IPO shares to entrepreneurs it hoped to obtain business from in the future. The Securities and Exchange Commission made this practice illegal in 1999.

What has happened to the dot.com IPOs of this period? According to a financial services research firm, Thomson Financial, 12% of the companies that went public between 1998 and 2000 were trading at $1 or less a share in April 2001, a fairly shocking development when one considers that just a relatively short time previously, those companies' shares were trading at upwards of 10 to 100 times that price. In comparison, during the period 1986–1995, only 1% of IPOs on average traded below $1 dollar a year after going public. Here are just a few of the dot.com IPOs that were trading below $1 in April 2001, listed together with their stock highs:

Ask Jeeves.com: $190.50

Autoweb.com: $50:00

Buy.com: $35.44

Coolsavings.com: $7.13

Theglobe.com: $48.50

Webvan.com: $34.00

MyPoints.com: $97.69

Drkoop.com: $45.75

DSL.net: $32.56

iBeam Broadcasting: $29.44

IVillage.com: $130.00

24/7 Media: $69.63

Salon.com: $15.13

Drugstore.com: $70.00

Launchmedia.com: $36.69

NetZero: $40.00

Razorfish.com: $56.94

Varsitybooks.com: $13.13

Quokka Sports: $18.75

HealthCentral.com: $14.38

Barnesandnoble.com: $26.50

Clearly there were many dot.com start-up firms that had poor business plans and should never have been allowed to go public. But as one investment banker noted, there was an insatiable market for IPO shares at the time. For the moment, given the recent poor track record of many dot.com IPOs, the ability of dot.coms to sell shares to the public via IPOs has evaporated.

SOURCES: Thomson Financial Services, Venture Economics News, April 2000 (http://www.ventureeconomics.com/news_ve/1999VEpress/PerfQ400final .htm); "Just Who Brought Those Duds to Market?" by Andrew Ross Sorkin, *New York Times*, April 15, 2001; Venture Capital Journal, April 2001 (www. venturecapitaljournal.net).

NASDAQ market, was due to an enormous information technology capital expenditure of large American firms who were rebuilding their internal business systems to withstand the challenges of Y2K. The simple change from year 1999 to 2000 was believed to be a major threat to corporate systems. Once these systems were rebuilt, this information technology capital expenditure declined, sending the earnings forecasts of technology companies down.

Second, in early 2000, it became clear that the telecommunications industry had built excess capacity in high-speed fiber optic networks. Prices wars were breaking out in telecommunications markets, and it was clear that earnings in this sector would fall dramatically, with many smaller firms going bankrupt, unable to pay their debts incurred to build high-speed networks. An estimated $250 billion in telecommunications sector debt will not be repaid.

Third, the 1999 e-commerce Christmas season provided less sales growth than anticipated, and more important, demonstrated that e-commerce was not easy. Many dot.com retailers — such as eToys.com — could not deliver in a timely fashion. This hurt the credibility of B2C e-commerce in general.

Fourth, and perhaps most important, the valuations of dot.com and technology companies had risen so high that even supporters were questioning whether earnings of these companies could ever grow fast enough to justify the prices of the shares. Some high tech companies had stock values 400 times their earnings, while the shares of traditional companies were selling for 10 to 15 times their earnings. And as it turned out, most dot.com companies — those specifically devoted to e-commerce — in fact did not have any earnings! Most, in fact, were losing money while showing revenue growth. Even supporters of the e-commerce phenomenon began to wonder if the dot.com companies would ever become profitable.

The stock market crash of dot.com companies led to a sobering reassessment of the prospects for e-commerce and the methods of achieving business success. E-commerce II — the second period in the evolution of e-commerce — begins in January 2001. We will end this period in 2006, five years from now: This is about as far out as technology and business projections can reasonably be made.

E-commerce Today: Successes and Failures

Looking back at E-commerce I, it is apparent that e-commerce has been, for the most part, a stunning *technological* success as the Internet and the Web ramped up from a few thousand to billions of e-commerce transactions per year, generating over $60 billion in B2C revenues, and 100 million online customers in the United States, and another 100 million worldwide by 2000. With enhancements and strengthening, described in later chapters, it is clear the e-commerce's digital infrastructure is solid enough to sustain significant growth in e-commerce during the next decade. The "e" in e-commerce has been an overwhelming success.

From a business perspective, though, E-commerce I was a mixed success. Only about 10% of dot.coms formed since 1995 survive as independent companies in 2001. Only a very tiny percentage of these survivors are profitable. Yet online B2C sales of goods and services in 2001 are still growing at 45% to 55% per year (depending on the source of the projection). B2C revenues are expected to grow from $65 billion in 2001 (about 1.5% of all retail revenue) to $269 billion by 2005 (about 8% of total retail sales). In addition, consumers have learned to use the Web as a powerful source of information about products they actually purchase though other channels, such as at a traditional "bricks and mortar" store. This is especially true of expensive consumer durables such as appliances, automobiles, and electronics. This "Internet-influenced" commerce was estimated at $13 billion in 2000 and projected to grow to $378 billion by 2005. Altogether then, B2C e-commerce could amount to $647 billion in 2005, about 18.5% of total retail sales (Dykema, 2000; Bakos, 2001). The "commerce" in e-commerce therefore is basically very sound, at least in the sense of attracting customers and generating revenues.

While the E-commerce II period continues an extremely rapid pace of growth in customers and revenues, it is clear that many of the visions for e-commerce developed during E-commerce I have not been fulfilled. For instance, economists' visions of "friction-free" commerce have not been entirely realized. Prices are sometimes lower on the Web, but the low prices are primarily a function of entrepreneurs selling products below their costs. Consumers are less price sensitive than expected; surprisingly, the Web sites with the highest revenue also have the highest prices. There remains considerable persistent price dispersion on the Web, and the concept of one world, one market, one price has weakened as entrepreneurs discover new ways to differentiate their products and services. For instance, prices on books and CDs vary by as much as 50%, prices for airline tickets as much as 20% (Bailey, 1998a, b; Brynjolfsson and Smith, 1999; Clemons, Hann and Hitt, 2000). Brands remain very important in e-commerce — consumers trust some firms more than others to deliver a high-quality product on time (Shankar, et. al., 1998). The Bertrand model of extreme market efficiency has not entirely come to pass. Information asymmetries are continually being introduced by merchants and marketers. Search costs may have fallen overall, but the overall transaction cost of actually completing a transaction in e-commerce remains very high because users have a bewildering number of new decisions to make (Will the merchant actually deliver? What is the time frame of delivery? Does the merchant really have stock on this item?) About 65% of e-commerce purchases are terminated in the shopping cart stage because of these consumer uncertainties. In many product areas, it is easier to call a trusted catalog merchant than order on a Web site. Finally, intermediaries have not disappeared as predicted, and few manufacturers or producers have actually developed a one-to-one sales relationship with their ultimate consumers. If anything, e-commerce has created many new opportunities for middlemen to aggregate content, products, and services into portals and thereby introduce themselves as the "new" intermediaries. Yahoo.com and Amazon.com are two examples of this kind of new intermediary.

Nor have the visions of many entrepreneurs and venture capitalists for e-commerce during the E-commerce I era materialized exactly as predicted. First-mover advantage appears to have succeeded only for a very small group of sites. Historically, first movers have been long-term losers, with the early-to-market innovators usually being displaced by established "fast follower" firms with the financial, marketing, legal, and production assets needed to develop mature markets, and this has proved true for e-commerce as well. A number of e-commerce first movers, such as eToys.com, FogDog.com (sporting goods), Furniture.com, and Eve.com (beauty products) are out of business. Customer acquisition and retention costs have turned out to be extraordinarily high, with some firms, such as E-Trade.com and other financial service firms paying up to $400 to acquire a new customer. The overall costs of doing business on the Web — including the costs of technology, site design and maintenance, and warehouses for fulfillment — are no lower than the costs faced by the most efficient brick and mortar stores. The start-up costs can be staggering. Attempting to achieve profitability by raising prices has often led to large customer defections. From the e-commerce merchant's perspective, the "e" in e-commerce does not stand for "easy."

Table 1.5 summarizes some of the most important differences between E-commerce I and E-commerce II.

PREDICTIONS FOR THE FUTURE

The future of E-commerce II is now more clear, although not certain. There are five main factors that will help define the future of e-commerce. First, there is little doubt

TABLE 1.5	E-COMMERCE I AND E-COMMERCE II COMPARED
E-COMMERCE I	**E-COMMERCE II**
Technology-driven	Business-driven
Revenue growth emphasis	Earnings and profits emphasis
Venture capital financing	Traditional financing
Ungoverned	Stronger regulation and governance
Entrepreneurial	Large traditional firms
Disintermediation	Strengthening intermediaries
Perfect markets	Imperfect markets, brands, and network effects
Pure online strategies	Mixed "clicks and bricks" strategies
First mover advantages	Strategic follower strength

that the technology of e-commerce — the Internet, the Web, and the growing number of wireless Internet appliances — will continue to propagate through all commercial activity. The overall revenues from e-commerce will continue to rise on a very steep growth path, most likely in the range of 40% to 50% per year until 2006. The number of products and services sold on the Web and the number of unique visitors (Web e-commerce traffic) are both growing. Big-ticket items such as computer hardware and travel services of all kinds are particularly strong (see Table 1.6). Overall traffic at e-commerce sites is expanding at nearly 60% per year.

Second, e-commerce prices will rise to cover the real costs of doing business on the Web, and to pay investors a reasonable rate of return on their capital. Third, e-commerce margins (the difference between the revenues from sales and the cost of goods) and profits will rise to levels more typical of all retailers. Fourth, the cast of players will change radically. In the B2C and B2B marketspaces, traditional well-endowed, experienced Fortune 500 companies will play a growing and dominant role in e-commerce. There will also be a continuation of audience consolidation on the Internet in general, with the top few sites garnering over 90% of the audience share. Table 1.7 shows the top 25 Web properties visited by consumers in March 2001.

Table 1.8 shows the top e-commerce sites in 2001 and an unmistakable trend toward the appearance in the top twenty sites of some very well known, traditional brands from strong traditional businesses — such as Wal-Mart, Sears, JC Penney, Spiegel, JCrew, Staples, Victoria's Secret, the Gap, and Old Navy.

Fifth, the number of successful pure online companies will decline further, and most successful e-commerce firms will adopt mixed "clicks and bricks" strategies, combining traditional sales channels such as physical stores and printed catalogs with

TABLE 1.6	APRIL 2001 NRF/FORRESTER ONLINE RETAIL INDEX		
CATEGORY	TOTAL SPENT IN APRIL (IN THOUSANDS)	TOTAL SPENT IN MARCH (IN THOUSANDS)	FEBRUARY INDEX RESULTS (APRIL/MARCH)
Small-Ticket Items			
Software	$106,360	$135,830	0.78
Books	$155,070	$147,888	1.04
Music	$103,399	$102,385	1.00
Videos	$66,466	$81,315	0.81
Office supplies	$122,584	$104,919	1.16
Apparel	$290,944	$177,543	1.63
Footwear	$72,623	$53,731	1.35
Jewelry	$104,328	$85,118	1.22
Flowers	$63,532	$41,416	1.53
Linens/Home Decor	$87,728	$55,719	1.57
Health and Beauty	$172,141	$110,994	1.55
Small appliances	$89,010	$37,038	2.40
Toys/Video Games	$82,964	$102,702	0.80
Sporting Goods	$45,342	$64,028	0.70
Tools and Hardware	$36,465	$42,719	0.85
Garden Supplies	$51,887	$24,547	2.11
Big-Ticket Items			
Computer hardware	$368,328	$400,543	0.91
Consumer Electronics	$154,285	$207,211	0.74
Appliances	$3,943	$23,778	0.16
Furniture	$88,790	$36,559	2.42
Food/Beverages	$126,716	$96,897	1.30
Airline Tickets	$776,259	$572,417	1.35
Car Rental	$246,969	$133,531	1.84
Hotel Reservations	$511,651	$310,685	1.64
Other	$358,600	$362,260	0.98
Total Spending	**$4,286,384**	**$3,511,685**	**1.22**
Number of Buyers	**15,691**	**13,349**	**1.17**
Average Spent per Consumer	**$273.18**	**$263.07**	**1.04**

SOURCE: Forrester Online Retail Index. www.cyberatlas.com/markets/retailing. May 15, 2001.

TABLE 1.7	TOP 25 PROPERTIES OF MARCH 2001 (Combined Home & Work)		
RANK	PROPERTY	UNIQUE AUDIENCE	TIME PER PERSON (hr:min:sec)
1.	AOL Time Warner	79,168,000	1:08:51
2.	Yahoo!	69,139,000	1:54:34
3.	MSN	61,260,000	1:28:43
4.	Microsoft	39,976,000	0:13:29
5.	Terra Lycos	35,472,000	0:18:44
6.	Excite@Home	30,900,000	0:40:04
7.	About.com	26,033,000	0:11:16
8.	Walt Disney Internet Group	26,020,000	0:37:11
9.	Amazon.com	22,751,000	0:17:23
10.	eBay.com	21,265,000	2:08:26
11.	NBC Internet	18,967,000	0:15:20
12.	CNET Networks	18,834,000	0:17:56
13.	eUniverse Network	18,421,000	0:18:21
14.	Ask Jeeves.com	15,531,000	0:10:18
15.	Napster Inc.	14,674,000	0:21:17
16.	GoTo.com	13,621,000	0:04:19
17.	Weather Channel.com	13,475,000	0:13:58
18.	AltaVista.com	13,458,000	0:11:31
19.	Google.com	13,125,000	0:23:35
20.	American Greetings	13,037,000	0:13:32
21.	Bonzi.com	12,914,000	0:04:02
22.	LookSmart.com	12,858,000	0:06:11
23.	The Go2Net Network	12,675,000	0:11:09
24.	Viacom International	12,482,000	0:20:01
25.	Real Networks	11,793,000	0:08:11

SOURCE: Nielsen/ Net Ratings Inc. http://cyberatlas.internet.com/big_picture/traffic_patterns/article/0,,5931_741721,00.html

online efforts. Amazon.com will increasingly use printed catalogs; Proctor and Gamble will continue to develop informative Web sites such as Tide.com; and the major automotive companies will continue to improve the content and value of their Web sites even if they do not enter into direct sales relationships with consumers but instead use the Web to assist sales through dealers (thereby strengthening traditional intermediaries and channels).

TABLE 1.8		**TOP 20 WEB RETAILERS AMONG U.S. HOME USERS** (January, 2001)				
JAN. RANK	DEC. RANK	WEB SITE	PROJECTED BUYERS (000)	OVERALL REACH (%)	UNIQUE USERS (000)	BUY RATE (%)
1	1	amazon.com	2,330	23.6	22,934	10.2
2	2	barnesandnoble.com	638	7.2	6,998	9.1
3	9	ticketmaster.com	636	5.6	5,473	11.6
4	7	half.com	567	8.7	8,396	6.8
5	4	jcpenney.com	545	4.1	3,967	13.7
6	10	drugstore.com	322	2.5	2,473	13.0
7	5	walmart	286	5.7	5,491	5.2
8	3	cdnow.com	263	7.2	6,959	3.8
9	—	shopintuit.com	245	1.4	1,358	18.1
10	6	sears.com	215	3.2	3,070	7.0
11	8	etoys.com	188	2.4	2,306	8.2
12	30	staples.com	186	2.3	2,226	8.4
13	24	cyberrebate.com	185	8.3	8,089	2.3
14	19	spiegel.com	159	141	1,391	11.4
15	11	buy.com	153	3.2	3,120	4.9
16	20	jcrew.com	136	1.1	1,066	12.8
17	34	victoriassecret.com	133	3.3	3,154	4.2
18	13	gap.com	122	2.3	2,275	5.3
19	15	oldnavy.com	122	2.1	2,072	5.9
20	16	1800flowers.com	115	1.6	1,525	7.5

SOURCE: PC Data Online, Top E-Tailers of January 2001. http://www.cyberatlas.internet.com/markets/retailing/article/0,,6061_589061,00.html

Another feature of the E-commerce II period will be the growth of regulatory activity both in the United States and worldwide. Governments all around the world are challenging the early vision of computer scientists and information technologists that the Internet remain a self-regulating and self-governing phenomenon. The Internet and e-commerce have been so successful and powerful, so all-pervasive, that they directly involve the social, cultural, and political life of entire nations and cultures. Throughout history, whenever technologies have risen to this level of social importance, power, and visibility, they become the target of efforts to regulate and control the technology to ensure that positive social benefits result from its use and to ensure the public's health and welfare. Radio, television, automobiles, electricity, and railroads are all the subject of regulation and legislation. Likewise, with E-commerce II.

In the U.S. Congress, there have already been more than one hundred pieces of legislation proposed to control various facets of the Internet and e-commerce, from consumer privacy to pornography, child abuse, gambling, and encryption. We can expect these efforts at regulation in the United States and around the world to increase as e-commerce extends it reach and importance.

In summary, E-commerce II will become primarily business-driven, with a view to producing profits, dominated by large traditional business firms and increasingly subject to national and global regulations.

1.3 UNDERSTANDING E-COMMERCE: ORGANIZING THEMES

Understanding e-commerce in its totality is a difficult task for students and instructors because there are so many facets to the phenomenon. No single academic discipline is prepared to encompass all of e-commerce. After teaching the e-commerce course for several years and preparing this book, we have come to realize just how difficult it is to "understand" e-commerce. We have found it useful to think about e-commerce as involving three broad interrelated themes: technology, business, and society. We do not mean to imply any ordering of importance here because this book and our thinking freely ranges over these themes as appropriate to the problem we are trying to understand and describe. Nevertheless, as in previous technologically driven commercial revolutions, there is an historic progression. Technologies develop first, and then those developments are exploited commercially. Once commercial exploitation of the technology becomes widespread, a host of social, cultural, and political issues arise.

TECHNOLOGY: INFRASTRUCTURE

The development and mastery of digital computing and communications technology is at the heart of the newly emerging global digital economy we call e-commerce. To understand the likely future of e-commerce, you need a basic understanding of the information technologies upon which it is built. E-commerce is above all else a technologically driven phenomenon that relies on a host of information technologies as well as fundamental concepts from computer science developed over a 50-year period. At the core of e-commerce are the Internet and the World Wide Web, which we describe in detail in Chapter 3. Behind these technologies are a host of complementary technologies — personal computers, local area networks, relational databases, client/server computing, and fiber optic switches, to name just a few. These technologies lie at the heart of sophisticated business computing applications such as enterprise-wide computing systems, supply chain management systems, manufacturing resource planning systems, and customer relationship management systems. E-commerce relies on all these basic technologies — not just the Internet. The Internet — while representing a sharp break from prior corporate computing and communications technologies — is nevertheless just the latest development in the evolution of corporate computing and part of the continuing chain of computer-based innovations in business.

Figure 1.8 illustrates the major stages in the development of corporate computing and indicates how the Internet and the Web fit into this development trajectory.

FIGURE 1.8   THE INTERNET AND THE EVOLUTION OF CORPORATE COMPUTING

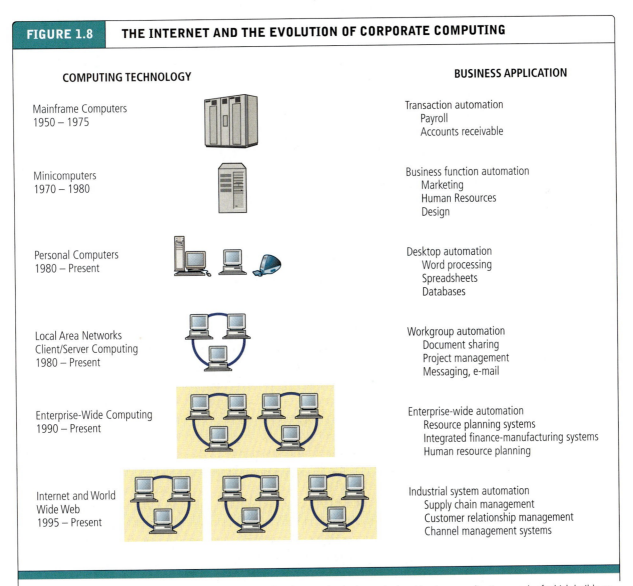

COMPUTING TECHNOLOGY

Mainframe Computers
1950 – 1975

Minicomputers
1970 – 1980

Personal Computers
1980 – Present

Local Area Networks
Client/Server Computing
1980 – Present

Enterprise-Wide Computing
1990 – Present

Internet and World
Wide Web
1995 – Present

BUSINESS APPLICATION

Transaction automation
    Payroll
    Accounts receivable

Business function automation
    Marketing
    Human Resources
    Design

Desktop automation
    Word processing
    Spreadsheets
    Databases

Workgroup automation
    Document sharing
    Project management
    Messaging, e-mail

Enterprise-wide automation
    Resource planning systems
    Integrated finance-manufacturing systems
    Human resource planning

Industrial system automation
    Supply chain management
    Customer relationship management
    Channel management systems

The Internet and World Wide Web are the latest in a chain of evolving technologies and related business applications, each of which builds on its predecessors.

To truly understand e-commerce, then, you will need to know something about client/server computing, packet-switched communications, protocols such as TCP/IP, Web servers, and HTML. All of these topics are described fully in Section II of the book (Chapters 3–6).

BUSINESS: BASIC CONCEPTS

While the technology provides the infrastructure, it is the business applications — the potential for extraordinary returns on investment — that create the interest and excitement in e-commerce. New technologies present businesses and entrepreneurs with new ways of organizing production and transacting business. New technologies change the strategies or plans of existing firms: Old strategies are made obsolete and new ones need to be invented. New technologies are the birthing grounds where thousands of new companies spring up with new products and services. To truly understand e-commerce you will need to be familiar with some key business concepts, such as the nature of electronic markets, information goods, business models, firm and industry value chains, industry structure, and consumer behavior in electronic markets. We'll examine each of these concepts further in Chapter 2 and throughout the book.

SOCIETY: TAMING THE JUGGERNAUGHT

With 170 million Americans now using the Internet, many for e-commerce purposes, and 400 million users worldwide, the impact of the Internet and e-commerce are significant and global. Increasingly, e-commerce is subject to the laws of nations and global entities. You will need to understand the pressures that global e-commerce places on contemporary society in order to conduct a successful e-commerce business or understand the e-commerce phenomenon. The primary societal issues we discuss in this book are intellectual property, individual privacy, and public policy. Because the cost of distributing digital copies of copyrighted *intellectual property* — tangible works of the mind such as music, books and videos — are nearly zero on the Internet, e-commerce poses special challenges to the various methods societies have used in the past to protect intellectual property rights.

Since the Internet and the Web are exceptionally adept at tracking the identity and behavior of individuals online, e-commerce raises difficulties for preserving *privacy* — the ability of individuals to place limits on the type and amount of information collected about them, and to control the uses of their personal information. Read *Insight on Society: Keeping Your Clickstream Private* to get a view of some of the ways e-commerce sites use personal information.

The global nature of e-commerce also poses public policy issues of equity, equal access, content regulation, and taxation. For instance, in the United States, public telephone utilities are required under public utility and public accommodation laws to make basic service available at affordable rates so everyone can have telephone service. Should these laws be extended to the Internet and the Web? If goods are purchased by a New York state resident from a Web site in California, shipped from a center in Illinois, and delivered to New York, what state has the right to collect a sales tax? If some societies choose to ban selected images, selected commercial activity (such as gambling) or political messages from their public media, then how can that society exercise content and activity control over a global e-commerce site? What rights do nation-states and their citizens have with respect to the Internet, the Web, and e-commerce?

ACADEMIC DISCIPLINES CONCERNED WITH E-COMMERCE

The phenomenon of e-commerce is so broad that a multi-disciplinary perspective is required. See Figure 1.9. There are two primary approaches to e-commerce: technical and behavioral.

Technical Approaches

Computer scientists are interested in e-commerce as an exemplary application of Internet technology. They are concerned with the development of computer hardware, software, and telecommunications systems, as well as standards, encryption, and database design and operation. Management scientists are primarily interested in building mathematical models of business processes and optimizing these processes. They are interested in e-commerce as an opportunity to study how business firms can exploit the Internet to achieve more efficient business operations.

FIGURE 1.9	DISCIPLINES CONCERNED WITH E-COMMERCE

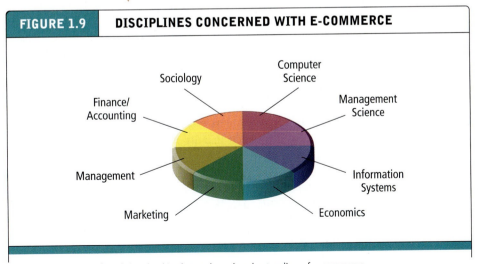

Many disciplines are directly involved in the study and understanding of e-commerce.

KEEPING YOUR CLICKSTREAM PRIVATE

One of the virtues, or vices (depending on your perspective), of e-commerce technology is that it permits online merchants to send you advertising that reflects personal information the merchant has gathered about you. This personal information might include what products you have previously purchased from the merchant, what kind of content you have viewed at its site, how you arrived at the site (where you were previously), as well as all of your clicking behavior at the site. This "*clickstream*" becomes the basis for constructing a digital profile of you. Your clicksteam and resulting profile is a marketer's and merchant's goldmine: If you know what people like and what they have recently purchased, you stand a good chance of being able to sell them something else. To exploit this data, new e-commerce-oriented advertising companies such as DoubleClick, 24/7 Media, and Engage Technology have created networks of thousands of e-commerce Web sites that pool your clickstream data and then serve you banner ads and other marketing material based on your behavior when visiting the network member sites.

Many people feel that such one-to-one marketing techniques constitute an invasion of privacy. They believe that while it may increase sales in the short term, violating personal privacy on the Web is bad business. For instance, a survey of 3,000 Web shoppers com-

missioned by IBM found that 48% decided not to purchase at a site because of privacy concerns. Yet a recent survey commissioned by the Personalization Consortium, an industry trade group, of 4,500 Web shoppers found that 73% of consumers found it helpful and convenient when a Web site remembers basic information about them. Only 15% would be unwilling to provide personal information that improved online service.

How is it possible for e-merchants and advertising networks to monitor your clickstream? As you will learn in later chapters, Web server computers keep a complete contact log of every click you make, and every object you choose to see on the Web. This data is stored and can be mined to create a profile of your behavior. Web sites also use cookies and Web bugs. A *cookie* is small text file downloaded onto your hard drive by a Web site. The cookie file contains whatever identifying information the merchant chooses to put in it. They can be read by other Web sites you visit and used to track your movement among sites. A *Web bug* is a tiny graphic, typically one pixel wide and one pixel deep, embedded within a Web page or e-mail. It usually is transparent or blends into the background color. A Web bug in a Web page can report information such as a visitor's IP address, cookie information, and referring URL back to the sending server or to the server of a third party, such as a Web advertising company. In e-mail messages, a Web

(continued)

bug can tell the merchant whether you opened the e-mail, and even more alarming to privacy advocates, can match the e-mail address with a previously set cookie, thereby allowing the merchant to coordinate a specific individual with their actions on the Web.

Can you protect your privacy in the Internet age (and still use the Web for convenient shopping)? There are some merchant privacy policy solutions. New laws will need to be written. And there are some new technologies that can help. Indeed, there is a whole new privacy protection industry arising on the Web. One group of companies, called *anonymizers*, were born out of the "cyberpunk" community of cryptographers and programmers. Companies such as Zero-Knowledge Systems, PrivacyX.com, and Anonymizer.com have developed software packages and their own Web servers that you can use to hide your identity online. With Anonymizer.com, for instance, you connect to the Web through an Anonymizer computer that hides your identity from merchants, government agencies, and others interested in invading your privacy. Or using Zero-Knowl-

edge's Freedom software package (available for free at its site, www.zero-knowledge.com), you are assigned a pseudonym and temporary Internet address. Your personal information is encrypted so that not even Zero-Knowledge can know who you are, let alone outsiders. This means that even if Zero-Knowledge's records are subpoenaed, the firm cannot supply a customer's personal information.

Most Web merchants are learning that it pays to be sensitive to customers' concerns about privacy. Trust is critical to successful e-commerce. According to a Pew Foundation survey, 87% of online customers fear online credit card theft, and 43% say they fear online crime. Almost all sites have "opt out" check boxes that allow visitors the option to not receive e-mail and other marketing information from the site. Many sites have "opt in" policies that require the customer to check a box if they want to receive additional marketing messages. All of the Web's top twenty e-merchants, as well as many others, have privacy policies posted on their sites.

SOURCES: "Fear of Online Crime" by Susannah Fox and Oliver Lewis, Pew Internet & American Life Project, April 2, 2001 (www.pewinternet.org); "Privacy Policies Critical to Online Consumer Trust." Columbus Group and Psos-Reid, March 1, 2001; "Congressional Group to Study Web Bugs," by Christopher Saunders, *Internet News*, February 9, 2001; "Click and Cover," by Edward Robinson, *Business2.0*, September 12, 2000; "Personalization and Privacy Survey," Personalization Consortium, April 5, 2000, www.personalization.org; "IBM Multi-National Consumer Privacy Survey," IBM Global Services, October 1999. (See www.privacyexchange.org for a complete listing of recent surveys.)

Behavioral Approaches

In the behavioral sector, information systems researchers are primarily interested in e-commerce because of its implications for firm and industry value chains, industry structure, and corporate strategy. The information systems discipline spans the technical and behavioral approaches. For instance, technical groups within the information systems specialty also focus on data mining, search engine design, and artificial intelligence. Economists have focused on consumer behavior at Web sites, and on the features of digital electronic markets. In both of these areas, economists share an interest with marketing scholars who have focused on e-commerce consumer response to marketing and advertising campaigns, and the ability of firms to brand, segment markets, target audiences, and position products to achieve above-normal returns on investment. Management scholars have focused on entrepreneurial behavior and the challenges faced by young firms who are required to develop organizational structures in short time spans. Finance and accounting scholars have focused on e-commerce firm valuation and accounting practices. Sociologists — and to a lesser extent psychologists — have focused on general population studies of Internet usage, the role of social inequality in skewing Internet benefits, and the use of the Web as a personal and group communications tool. Legal scholars have become interested in issues such as preserving intellectual property, privacy, and content regulation.

No one perspective dominates research about e-commerce. The challenge is to learn enough about a variety of academic disciplines so that you can grasp the significance of e-commerce in its entirety.

CASE STUDY

Napster Rocked
But Was It Legal?

In early 1999, two college students, Shawn Fanning and Sean Parker, convinced some leading Silicon Valley venture capital firms to invest $2 million in seed money in a Web-based music distribution system Fanning and Parker called Napster. Fanning, a computer science student at Northeastern University in Boston, created Napster in response to his roommates' complaints about the difficulties of finding MP3 files (a form of digital music files) on the Web. The name Napster was Fanning's high school nickname. The system used a unique technology called *peer-to-peer computing* with a central pointer index that permitted users to share music files stored on their own PCs.

In the heady days of E-commerce I, few questioned the legality of permitting millions of music fans to share copyrighted musical tracks. Napster supporters felt that the Internet had ushered in a new era of "free information" in which old ideas such as copyrights would be destroyed by an all-powerful technology. The slogan of the time was "information wants to be free."

Here's how Napster worked in its early days. To use Napster, first you downloaded and installed the Napster software onto your computer and signed up for a free account at Napster.com. Clicking the Napster icon on your desktop would then take you to the Napster.com Web site, where you could enter the name of the music track you were looking for in a search window. The Napster software tracks all users who are connected at a particular time and provides access to tracks stored on users' hard drives. When Napster found the song you wanted, it would set up a connection between your computer and the other Napster member's computer. The transfer of the track could take hours using a home modem operating at 56 Kpbs, but on a college campus network with a 100 Mbps communications link, it would take only a few minutes to transfer a title. In essence, Napster functioned as a giant, constantly updated index of all tracks currently available from connected users. Although it was not required, good citizenship for Napster users meant making and storing some music titles on your computer as a contribution to the network, as well as allowing other users to scan your hard drive for titles. To contribute a title, a user "ripped" or converted the title from a musical CD (where the files are stored as digital .wav files) and copied it to their hard drive as an MP3 file.

Napster.com launched in May 1999 with backing from some of Silicon Valley's most prestigious venture capital firms, such as Kleiner Perkins Caufield & Byers and

Hummer Winblad Partners, along with several Silicon Valley entrepreneurs, such as Andy Bechtolshein, co-founder of Sun Microsystems and Saheer Bhatia, founder of Hotmail, among others. These sophisticated investors apparently were not restrained by the possibility that Napster's business model was based on copyright infringement, nor the fact that the business model itself was somewhat murky. Napster provided its services for free. Its business plan called for future revenue from advertising and selling information on the music-listening habits and e-mail addresses of its users. It believed that a database containing the music selections of 48 million music fans worldwide ultimately would be invaluable to existing record label firms.

The year 1999 was a period of extraordinary innovation in Web-based music services. A number of other free downloaded music sites opened in the same period, such as MP3.com, Myplay.com, Riffage.com, Launch.com, EMusic.com and Epitonic.com. Internet radio sites such as Spinner.com, Sonicnet.com, and WiredPlanet.com launched. Many offered personalized music services such as shared personal play lists. Music guides such as Listen.com and InSound.com offered guides and expert reviews. Recommendation engines such as MongoMusic and Gigabeat offered users access to databases to help them find music they liked. New versions of Web music player software from RealNetworks, Liquid Audio, and MusicMatch improved the quality of streaming music over the Web.

Napster proved an immediate success, and it quickly became one of the most popular destinations on the Web (see the chart below). On college campuses such as Indiana University, Napster accounted for 60% of all traffic between the campus and

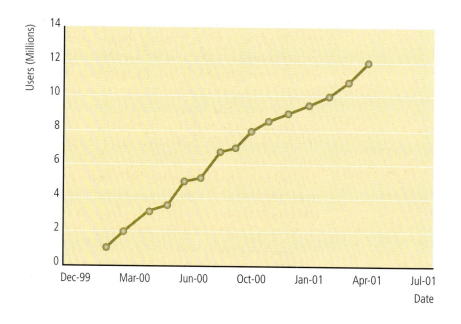

the Internet. As a result, IU and many other colleges attempted to ban Napster, both for technological as well as legal reasons.

Napster's success did not go unnoticed by the music industry. In December 1999, the Recording Industry Association of America (RIAA), which represents the interests of the five major music labels in the world — Universal, Sony, BMG (Bertelsmann AG), Warner, and EMI — sued Napster for copyright infringement. In April 2000, music groups Metallica and Dr. Dre also sued Napster for copyright infringement and racketeering (engaging in an organized conspiracy).

Napster defended itself by arguing that there was nothing illegal with users sharing copies of musical tracks they had purchased. Under the "fair use" doctrine of copyright law, individuals are permitted to make copies of musical records, tapes, or CDs, and share those copies with friends, or use them in portable devices. Napster argued that it just assisted the ability of users to share music, and that it was performing a valuable legal service for music fans around the world. Napster pointed out that more than 48 million music fans had registered at the site, and that nearly a million users might be connected during peak times. Supporters argued that nothing could stop the sharing of music on the Web because the technology Napster used could not be regulated and certainly not stopped by courts.

On July 26, 2000, the United States federal district court in San Francisco ruled that Napster indeed was systematically infringing the copyrights of music companies and artists by assisting millions of music fans in the sharing of music without compensation to the copyright owners. Judge Marilyn Hall Patel did not accept the idea that these activities constituted "fair use" of copyrighted works, and agreed with the record labels that Napster harmed the market for music owned by the labels. After an unsuccessful appeal, and faced with a complete shut down, Napster agreed to do what before it had claimed was technically impossible — remove individual titles for which it did not have a permission from the music companies from its central index. The music companies have since supplied Napster with lists containing over 100,000 copyrighted titles that Napster must remove from its site.

In October 2000, Bertelsmann, which had been one of Napster's key foes, provided Napster with a loan of more than $50 million to create a legal version of its service, in exchange for Napster agreeing to give Bertelsmann the option to purchase a controlling interest in Napster in the future. Napster is currently developing a subscription-based music distribution system in which fans would pay a monthly fee — around $10 — to download copyrighted music. In June 2001, Napster announced it had also struck a distribution deal with MusicNet, another music subscription service jointly created by Real Networks, Warner Music Group, Bertelsman, and EMI, which would provide Napster users with legal access to mainstream music offered by three of the five major record labels for an additional fee.

However, Napster's future, like so many others in e-commerce, still remains unclear. In the past, when faced with fees, millions of subscribers to free Web services

SOURCES: "Napster Strikes Deal With Labels," *Associated Press*, June 6, 200; "Vivendi Deal for MP3.com Highlights Trend," by Matt Richtel, *New York Times*, May 22, 2001; "Record Labels Sending Napster List of 135,000 Songs to Block," by Matt Richtel, *New York Times*, March 10, 2001; "Can Napster Change Its Tune," by Dan Godin, *The Industry Standard*, February 18, 2001; "Napster Suffers a Rout in Appeals Court," by Lee Gomes and Anna Wilde Matthews, *Wall Street Journal*, February 13, 2001; "Which Direction Now for Digital Music?" by Laura M. Holson, *New York Times*, November 20, 2000; "Napster Users Mourn End of Free Music," by Amy Harmon, *New York Times*, November 1, 2000; "Music Companies Fight Back, Hoping Downloads for Fees Can Prove as Popular as Free," by Don Clark and Martin Peers, *Wall Street Journal*, June 20, 2000; "Starting to Feel Left Out of the Fun?" by Thomas E. Weber, *Wall Street Journal*, June 20, 2000; "Napster Alters Its Software in a Bid to Appease Colleges," by Lee Gomes, *Wall Street Journal*, March 23, 2000.

have dropped out and refused to pay. In a recent survey by the research firm Webnoise, 87% of the 3,000 users polled said they would go to other unauthorized file-trading services after Napster started charging a fee. Yet Napster and many others in the recording industry believe that millions of users will probably be willing to pay some subscription fee in return for access to huge libraries of music, music reviews, and recommendations.

In the meantime, the competitive landscape in which Napster operates has changed significantly. In 1999, many believed that Napster and the other upstarts like it would challenge the major record labels as the predominant distributors of music. Today, many of those upstarts are gone, either closed (such as Riffage.com) or absorbed (MP3.com, WiredPlanet, MongoMusic, EMusic.com, and others) by the very companies they set out to challenge. The result, industry analysts say, is that the five major record companies may end up actually consolidating their power and influence.

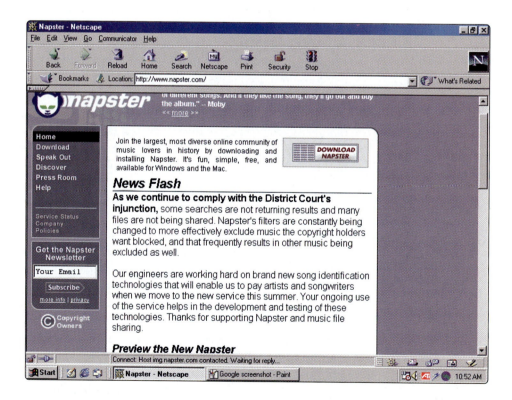

Case Study Questions

1. Identify the elements of the Napster case study that are indicative of the E-commerce I and E-commerce II eras, respectively.

2. Into which category or categories of e-commerce does Napster fall?

3. What social issues did Napster's operations raise? Were colleges right to ban Napster from the campus?

4. Follow up on events at Napster subsequent to June 2001. Is Napster still in business? How many users have signed up and are paying a subscription fee? Is Napster making money? Has Napster been acquired by Bertelsmann?

1.5 REVIEW

KEY CONCEPTS

■ **Define e-commerce and describe how it differs from e-business.**

E-commerce involves:
- digitally enabled commercial transactions between and among organizations and individuals. Digitally enabled transactions include all those transactions mediated by digital technology, meaning, for the most part, transactions that occur over the Internet and the Web. Commercial transactions involve the exchange of value (e.g. money) across organizational or individual boundaries in return for products or services.

E-business refers primarily to the:
- digital enablement of transactions and processes *within* a firm, involving information systems under the control of the firm. For the most part, e-business does not involve commercial transactions across organizational boundaries where value is exchanged.

■ **Identify the unique features of e-commerce technology and their business significance.**

There are seven features of e-commerce technology that are unique to this medium. E-commerce technology:
- is ubiquitous, meaning that is it available just about everywhere, at all times, making it possible to shop from your desktop, at home, at work, or even from your car.
- has global reach, permitting commercial transactions to cross cultural and national boundaries far more conveniently and cost effectively than is true in traditional commerce.

- operates according to universal standards shared by all nations around the world. In contrast, most traditional commerce technologies differ from one nation to the next.
- provides information richness, which refers to the complexity and content of a message. It enables an online merchant to deliver to an audience of millions marketing messages with text, video, and audio, in a way not possible with traditional commerce technologies such as radio, television, or magazines.
- is interactive, meaning it allows for two-way communication between merchant and consumer and enables the merchant to engage a consumer in ways similar to a face-to-face experience, but on a much more massive, global scale.
- increases information density (the total amount and quality of information available to all market participants). The Internet reduces information collection, storage, processing, and communication costs while increasing the currency, accuracy, and timeliness of information.
- permits personalization and customization: merchants can target their marketing messages to specific individuals by adjusting the message to a person's name, interests, and past purchases. Because of the increase in information density, a great deal of information about the consumer's past purchases and behavior can be stored and used by online merchants. The result is a level of personalization and customization unthinkable with existing commerce technologies.

■ **Describe the major types of e-commerce.**

There are five major types of e-commerce:
- B2C involves businesses selling to consumers and is the type of e-commerce that most consumers are likely to encounter. In 2001, consumers will spend about $65 billion in B2C transactions.
- B2B e-commerce involves businesses selling to other businesses and is the largest form of e-commerce, with an estimated $700 billion in transactions occurring in 2001.
- C2C is a means for consumers to sell to each other. In C2C e-commerce, the consumer prepares the product for market, places the product for auction or sale, and relies on the market maker to provide catalog, search engine, and transaction clearing capabilities so that products can be easily displayed, discovered, and paid for.
- P2P technology enables Internet users to share files and computer resources directly without having to go through a central Web server. Music and file sharing services, such as Gnutella, are a prime example of this type of e-commerce, because consumers can transfer files directly to other consumers without a central server involved.
- M-commerce involves the use of wireless digital devices to enable transactions on the Web.

■ Understand the visions and forces behind the E-commerce I era.

The E-commerce I era was a period of explosive growth in e-commerce, beginning in 1995 with the first widespread use of the Web to advertise products and ending in 2000 with the collapse in stock market valuations for dot.com ventures. Among the visions for e-commerce expressed during the period were the following:

* For computer scientists, e-commerce was part of their vision of a universal communications and computing environment that everyone on earth could access with cheap, inexpensive computers.
* For economists, e-commerce raised the realistic prospect of a perfect Bertrand market — a market where price, cost, and quality information is equally distributed — and friction-free commerce.
* For entrepreneurs and their financial backers, e-commerce represented an extraordinary opportunity to earn far above normal returns on investment.

Overall, the E-commerce I period was driven largely by visions of profiting from new technology, with the emphasis on quickly achieving very high market visibility. The source of financing was venture capital funds. The ideology of the period emphasized the ungoverned "Wild West" character of the Web, and the feeling that governments and courts could not possibly limit or regulate the Internet, that traditional corporations were too slow and bureaucratic, too stuck in the old ways of doing business to "get it," that is, to be competitive in e-commerce.

■ Understand the successes and failures of E-commerce I.

E-commerce during the E-commerce I era has been :

* a technological success, with the digital infrastructure created during the period solid enough to sustain significant growth in e-commerce during the next decade.
* a mixed business success, with significant revenue growth and customer usage, but low profit margins.

E-commerce during the E-commerce I era has not:

* fulfilled economists' visions of the perfect Betrand market and friction-free commerce
* fulfilled the visions of entrepreneurs and venture capitalists for first mover advantages, low customer acquisition and retention costs, and low costs of doing business.

■ Identify several factors that will define the E-commerce II era.

Factors that will define e-commerce over the next five years include the following:

* E-commerce technology will continue to propagate through all commercial activity, with overall revenues from e-commerce, the number of products and services sold over the Web, and the amount of Web traffic all rising.
* E-commerce prices will rise to cover the real costs of doing business on the Web.
* E-commerce margins and profits will rise to levels more typical of all retailers.

- Traditional well-endowed and experienced Fortune 500 companies will play a growing and more dominant role.
- The number of successful pure online companies will continue to decline and most successful e-commerce firms will adopt a mixed "clicks and bricks" strategy.
- Regulation of e-commerce and the Web by government will grow both in the United States and worldwide.

■ **Describe the major themes underlying the study of e-commerce.**

E-commerce involves three broad interrelated themes:

- *Technology*: To understand e-commerce, you need a basic understanding of the information technologies upon which it is built, including the Internet and the World Wide Web, and a host of complimentary technologies — personal computers, local area networks, client/server computing, packet-switched communications, protocols such as TCP/IP, Web servers, HTML, and relational databases, among others.
- *Business*: While technology provides the infrastructure, it is the business applications — the potential for extraordinary returns on investment — that create the interest and excitement in e-commerce. New technologies present businesses and entrepreneurs with new ways of organizing production and transacting business. Therefore, you also need to understand some key business concepts such as electronic markets, information goods, business models, firm and industry value chains, industry structure, and consumer behavior in electronic markets
- *Society*: Understanding the pressures that global e-commerce places on contemporary society is critical to being successful in the e-commerce marketplace. The primary societal issues are intellectual property, individual privacy, and public policy.

■ **Identify the major academic disciplines contributing to e-commerce research.**

There are two primary approaches to e-commerce: technical and behavioral. Each of these approaches is represented by several academic disciplines. On the technical side:

- Computer scientists are interested in e-commerce as an application of Internet technology.
- Management scientists are primarily interested in building mathematical models of business processes and optimizing them to learn how businesses can exploit the Internet to improve their business operations.
- Information systems professionals are interested in e-commerce because of its implications for firm and industry value chains, industry structure, and corporate strategy.
- Economists have focused on consumer behavior at Web sites, and on the features of digital electronic markets.

On the behavioral side:

- Sociologists have focused on studies of Internet usage, the role of social inequality in skewing Internet benefits, and the use of the Web as a personal and group communications tool.
- Finance and accounting scholars have focused on e-commerce firm valuation and accounting practices.
- Management scholars have focused on entrepreneurial behavior and the challenges faced by young firms who are required to develop organizational structures in short time spans.
- Marketing scholars have focused on consumer response to online marketing and advertising campaigns, and the ability of firms to brand, segment markets, target audiences, and position products to achieve higher returns on investment.

QUESTIONS

1. What is e-commerce? How does it differ from e-business? Where does it intersect with e-business?
2. What is information asymmetry?
3. What are some of the unique features of e-commerce technology?
4. What is a marketspace?
5. What are three benefits of universal standards?
6. Compare online and traditional transactions in terms of richness.
7. Name three of the business consequences that can result from growth in information density.
8. Give examples of B2C, B2B, C2C, and P2P Web sites besides those listed in the chapter materials.
9. How are the Internet and the Web similar to or different from other technologies that have changed commerce in the past?
10. What are the major limitations on the growth of e-commerce? Which is potentially the toughest to overcome?
11. What are three of the factors that will contribute to greater Internet penetration in U.S. households?
12. Define disintermediation and explain the benefits to Internet users of such a phenomenon. How does disintermediation impact friction-free commerce?
13. What are some of the major advantages and disadvantages of being first mover?
14. What are the four main reasons cited for the stock market crash in the technology sector in late 2000?
15. Discuss the ways in which the E-commerce I era can be considered both a success and a failure.
16. What are five of the major differences between E-commerce I and II?
17. What factors will help define the future of e-commerce over the next five years?

18. Why is a multi-disciplinary approach necessary if one hopes to understand e-commerce?

PROJECTS

1. Search the Web for an example of each of the five major types of e-commerce described in Section 1.1 Create a PowerPoint presentation or written report describing each Web site (take a screenshot of each, if possible), and explain why it fits into one of the five types of e-commerce.

2. Choose an e-commerce Web site and assess it in terms of the seven unique features of e-commerce technology described in Table 1.1. Which of the features does the site implement well, and which features poorly, in your opinion? Prepare a short memo to the president of the company you have chosen detailing your findings and any suggestions for improvement you may have.

3. Given the development and history of E-commerce I from 1995–2000, what do you predict we will see during the next five years of E-commerce II? Describe some of the technological, business, and societal shifts that may occur as the Internet continues to grow and expand. Prepare a brief PowerPoint presentation or written report to explain your vision of what E-commerce II looks like.

4. Follow up on events at Amazon subsequent to June 2001 (when the opening case was prepared). Has Amazon moved any closer to profitability? What are its current prospects for success or failure? Prepare a short report on your findings.

CHAPTER 2

E-commerce Business Models and Concepts

LEARNING OBJECTIVES

After reading this chapter you will be able to:

- Identify the key components of e-commerce business models.
- Describe the major B2C business models.
- Describe the major B2B business models.
- Recognize business models in other emerging areas of e-commerce.
- Understand key business concepts and strategies applicable to e-commerce.

Kozmo Finally Crashes

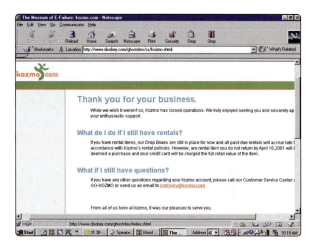

What do you do when you're a New Yorker or Bostonian with a late night craving for Ben & Jerry's ice cream? Last year, instead of traipsing to the local convenience store, you could have logged onto Kozmo.com and placed an order for food, videos, or personal care items, and had it at your door within an hour. But no more. In April 2001, after three years of struggling to find a business model that worked, Kozmo.com finally called it quits.

Targeting the "delivery culture" of Manhattan, Joseph Park and Yong Kang began developing the ideas behind Kozmo in 1997. Their business model: Use the Internet to combine the convenience of a catalog with the immediate gratification of in-store shopping by offering entertainment, food, and convenience products delivered within one hour, with no minimum order required and no delivery charges.

To implement their plan, they created a Web site that featured localized offerings based on customer zip codes, product listings accessible by browsing or key word search, and customizable delivery. An order placed on the Web site would be transmitted directly to Kozmo's distribution center, packed, then handed off to a "Kozmonaut"—an employee in a van, or on a bike or motor scooter—whose mission was to complete the delivery within one hour.

Launched during the heyday of the E-commerce I era, Kozmo attracted an impressive list of backers, including Chase Venture Capital, Flatiron Partners, Dreamworks SKG, Starbucks, and Warner Brothers, who together invested more than $250 million. Venture capital in hand, Kozmo embarked on a program of rapid expansion and intensive spending in an effort to gain market share and brand recognition, without concern for short-term profitability.

Now fast forward to Fall 2000. The ability to show that a business model can be profitable had become paramount. Kozmo had expanded into ten cities in addition to its hometown of New York, and had a reported loyal customer base of over 300,000, but had yet to show a profit. It also had learned some painful lessons about its business model in the process.

The first lesson: It's hard to make money delivering low-priced convenience store items. The second lesson: Its business model didn't work everywhere. The third lesson: A company's founders are not necessarily its best managers.

To survive, Kozmo tried to adjust its business model. Its founders relinquished day-to-day control to a more experienced management team. It shuttered poorly performing operations in San Diego and Houston and laid off employees. And it began to focus on how to make a profit. Since many Kozmo orders did not even cover the cost of processing and delivery, increasing the average order size was key. To do so, Kozmo began adding more items to its order menu — especially more expensive ones such as DVD players, Palm Pilots, and phone headsets. It also imposed a $5 minimum order requirement and added a new delivery fee on small orders. Kozmo also began to shift its marketing emphasis from Gen-Y'ers to older, more prosperous consumers. By January 2001, the changes in its business model had helped Kozmo show a profit in New York and San Francisco, and moved it close to breaking even in Boston, Seattle, and Washington, D.C. Average order size had grown from $10 to $25. That in turn was enough to attract some further venture capital from its existing investors.

In February 2001, Kozmo announced plans to publish a print catalog of high-end products available for delivery, and decided to drop the ".com" from its name. It continued cost-cutting and in March, it cancelled a five-year $150 million marketing alliance with Starbucks that put Kozmo video drop-off bins in hundreds of Starbucks around the country. But in April, one of the companies that had committed to fund it in January backed out, leaving the company short of cash. On April 11, 2001, Kozmo announced it had shut down, effective immediately, laying off 1,100 workers.

Gerry Burdo, Kozmo's president, said, "Given more time and more hospitable market conditions, Kozmo would have succeeded in rounding the corner." After reading this chapter, see whether you agree.

SOURCES: "Behind Kozmo's Demise: Thin Profit Margins," by Jayson Blair, *New York Times*, April 13, 2001; "Kozmo Calls It Quits," by Keith Regan, *E-Commerce Times*, April 12, 2001; "Silicon Alley 100," *Silicon Alley Reporter*, February 2001; "Kozmo Closes 2 Markets, Cuts 120 More Jobs," by Kenneth Li, *Industry Standard*, January 8, 2001; "Glimpse at Profit Earns $30 Million for Kozmo," by Jayson Blair, *New York Times*, December 30, 2000; "Online Delivery Sites Finding that Manhattan Can Be a Hard Place to Make It," by Jayson Blair, *New York Times*, October 1, 2000; Kozmo.com S-1, filed with the Securities and Exchange Commission on March 21, 2000.

The story of Kozmo.com illustrates just how difficult it can be for a new firm to establish a profitable e-commerce business in an entirely new market niche.

Thousands of firms in the E-commerce I era discovered they could spend other people's invested capital much faster than they could get customers to pay for their products or services. In most instances of failure, the business model of the firm was faulty from the very beginning. In contrast, successful e-commerce firms have business models that are able to leverage the unique qualities of the Web, avoid legal and social entanglements that can harm the firm, and produce profitable business results. But what is a business model and how can you tell if a firm's business model is going to produce a profit?

In this chapter we will focus on business models and basic business concepts that you must be familiar with in order to understand e-commerce.

2.1 E-COMMERCE BUSINESS MODELS

INTRODUCTION

A **business model** is a set of planned activities (sometimes referred to as *business processes*) designed to result in a profit in a marketplace. The business model is at the center of the business plan. A **business plan** is a document that describes a firm's business model. An **e-commerce business model** aims to use and leverage the unique qualities of the Internet and the World Wide Web (Timmers, 1998).

business model
a set of planned activities designed to result in a profit in a marketplace

business plan
a document that describes a firm's business model

e-commerce business model
a business model that aims to use and leverage the unique qualities of the Internet and the World Wide Web

EIGHT KEY INGREDIENTS OF A BUSINESS MODEL

If you hope to develop a successful business model in any arena, not just e-commerce, you must make sure that the model effectively addresses the eight elements listed in Table 2.1. These eight elements are value proposition, revenue model, market opportunity, competitive environment, competitive advantage, market strategy, organizational development, and management team (Ghosh, 1998). Many writers focus on a firm's value proposition and revenue model. While these may be the most important and easily identifiable aspects of a company's business model, the other elements are equally important when evaluating business models and plans, or when attempting to understand why a particular company has succeeded or failed (Kim and Mauborgne, 2000). In the following section, we describe each of the key business model elements more fully.

Value Proposition

A company's value proposition is at the very heart of its business model. A **value proposition** defines how a company's product or service fulfills the needs of customers (Kambil, Ginsberg, and Bloch, 1998). To develop and/or analyze a value proposition,

value proposition
defines how a company's product or service fulfills the needs of customers

TABLE 2.1	KEY INGREDIENTS OF A BUSINESS MODEL
BUSINESS MODEL COMPONENTS	**KEY QUESTIONS**
Value proposition	Why should the customer buy from you?
Revenue model	How will you earn money?
Market opportunity	What marketspace do you intend to serve, and what is its size?
Competitive environment	Who else occupies your intended marketspace?
Competitive advantage	What special advantages does your firm bring to the marketspace?
Market strategy	How do you plan to promote your products or services to attract your target audience?
Organizational development	What types of organizational structures within the firm are necessary to carry out the business plan?
Management team	What kinds of experiences and background are important for the company's leaders to have?

you need to answer the following key questions: Why will customers choose to do business with your firm instead of another company? What will your firm provide that other firms do not and cannot? From the consumer point of view, successful e-commerce value propositions include: personalization and customization of product offerings, reduction of product search costs, reduction of price discovery costs, and facilitation of transactions by managing product delivery (Kambil, 1997; Bakos, 1998).

Kozmo.com, for instance, sold the same snacks, entertainment, and toiletries that other businesses did, but Kozmo made speedy home deliveries. Although convenience stores, restaurants, and pharmacies could also offer home delivery to their customers, another Kozmo advantage was that they could bundle items from several types of businesses and drop them off within an hour. Convenience and speed were Kozmo's two main value propositions.

Before Amazon.com existed, most customers personally traveled to book retailers to place an order. In some cases, the desired book might not be available and the customer would have to wait several days or weeks, and then return to the bookstore to pick it up. Amazon made it possible for book lovers to shop for virtually any book in print from the comfort of their home or office, 24 hours a day, and to know immediately whether a book is in stock. Amazon's primary value propositions are unparalleled selection and convenience.

In many cases, companies develop their value proposition based on current market conditions or trends. Consumers' increasing reliance on delivery services was surely a trend Kozmo.com's founders took note of, just as Starbucks' founders saw the growing interest in and demand for coffee bars nationwide. Both companies watched the market and then developed their value proposition to meet what they perceived to be consumers' demand for certain products and services.

Revenue Model

A firm's **revenue model** describes how the firm will earn revenue, generate profits, and produce a superior return on invested capital. We use the terms *revenue model* and *financial model* interchangeably. The function of business organizations is both to generate profits and to produce returns on invested capital that exceed alternative investments. Profits alone are not sufficient to make a company "successful" (Porter, 1985). In order to be considered successful, a firm must produce returns greater than alternative investments. Firms that fail this test go out of existence.

Retailers, for example, sell a product, such as a personal computer, to a customer who pays for the computer using cash or a credit card. This produces revenue. The merchant typically charges more for the computer than it pays out in operating expenses, producing a profit. But in order to go into business, the computer merchant had to invest capital — either by borrowing or by dipping into personal savings. The profits from the business constitute the return on invested capital, and these returns must be greater than the merchant could obtain elsewhere, say, by investing in real estate or just putting the money into a savings account.

Although there are many different e-commerce revenue models that have been developed, most companies rely on one, or some combination, of the following major revenue models: the advertising model, the subscription model, the transaction fee model, the sales model, and the affiliate model.

In the **advertising revenue model**, a Web site that offers its users content, services, and/or products also provides a forum for advertisements and receives fees from advertisers. Those Web sites that are able to attract the greatest viewership or that have a highly specialized, differentiated viewership and are able to retain user attention ("stickiness") are able to charge higher advertising rates. Yahoo.com, for instance, derives its primary revenue from selling advertising such as banner ads. This model, originally one of the primary revenue models for the Web, has fallen somewhat into disfavor, although it remains a primary source for Web-based revenue.

revenue model
describes how the firm will earn revenue, produce profits, and produce a superior return on invested capital

advertising revenue model
a company provides a forum for advertisements and receives fees from advertisers

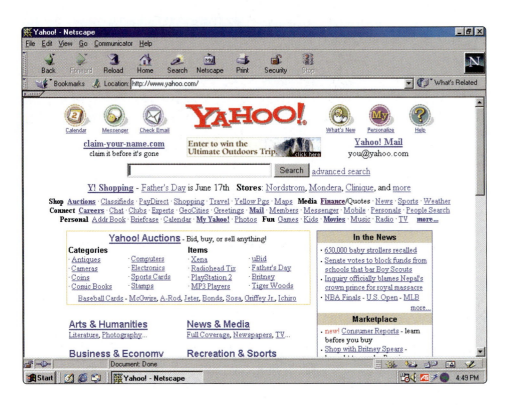

subscription revenue model

a company offers its users content or services and charges a subscription fee for access to some or all of its offerings

In the **subscription revenue model**, a Web site that offers its users content or services charges a subscription fee for access to some or all of its offerings. For instance, Consumer Reports Online provides access to its content only to subscribers, who have a choice of paying a $3.95 monthly subscription fee or a $24.00 annual fee. Experience with the subscription revenue model indicates that to successfully overcome the disinclination of users to pay for content on the Web, the content offered must be perceived as a high-value-added, premium offering that is not readily available elsewhere nor easily replicated.

transaction fee revenue model

a company receives a fee for enabling or executing a transaction

In the **transaction fee revenue model**, a company receives a fee for enabling or executing a transaction. For example, eBay.com created an online auction marketplace and receives a small transaction fee from a seller if the seller is successful in selling the item. E-Trade.com, an online stockbroker, receives transaction fees each time it executes a stock transaction on behalf of a customer.

sales revenue model

a company derives revenue by selling goods, information, or services

In the **sales revenue model**, companies derive revenue by selling goods, information, or services to customers. Companies such as Amazon.com, which sells books, music, and other products, DoubleClick.net, which gathers information about online users and then sells it to other companies, and Salesforce.com, which sells sales force management services over the Web, all have sales revenue models.

In the **affiliate revenue model**, sites that steer business to an "affiliate" receive a referral fee or percentage of the revenue from any resulting sales. For example, MyPoints.com makes money by connecting companies with potential customers by offering special deals to its members. When they take advantage of an offer and make a purchase, members earn "points" they can redeem for freebies, and MyPoints.com receives a fee.

Table 2.2 summarizes these major revenue models.

affiliate revenue model
a company steers business to an affiliate and receives a referral fee or percentage of the revenue from any resulting sales

TABLE 2.2	FIVE PRIMARY REVENUE MODELS	
REVENUE MODEL	**EXAMPLE**	**REVENUE SOURCE**
Advertising	Yahoo.com	Fees from advertisers in exchange for advertisements
Subscription	WSJ.com, Consumerreports.org, Sportsline.com	Fees from subscribers in exchange for access to content or services
Transaction Fee	eBay.com, E-Trade.com	Fees (commissions) for enabling or executing a transaction
Sales	Amazon.com, DoubleClick.net, Salesforce.com	Sales of goods, information, or services
Affiliate	MyPoints.com	Fees for business referrals

Market Opportunity

The term **market opportunity** refers to the company's intended **marketspace** (i.e., an area of actual or potential commercial value) and the overall potential financial opportunities available to the firm in that marketspace. The market opportunity is usually divided into smaller market niches. The realistic market opportunity is defined by the revenue potential in each of the market niches where you hope to compete.

For instance, let's assume you are analyzing a software training company that creates software-learning systems for sale to corporations over the Internet. The overall size of the software training market for all market segments is approximately $70 billion. The overall market can be broken down, however, into two major market segments: instructor-led training products, which comprise about 70% of the market ($49 billion in revenue), and computer-based training, which accounts for 30% ($21 billion). Within each of those major market segments there are further market niches,

market opportunity
refers to the company's intended marketspace and the overall potential financial opportunities available to the firm in that marketspace

marketspace
the area of actual or potential commercial value in which a company intends to operate

such as the Fortune 1000 computer-based training market, and the small business computer-based training market. Because the firm is a start-up firm, it cannot compete effectively in the large business, computer-based training market (about $15 billion). Large brand-name training firms dominate this niche. Its real market opportunity is to sell to the thousands of small business firms who spend about $6 billion on computer-based software training and who desperately need a cost-effective training solution. This then is the size of the firm's *realistic* market opportunity (see Figure 2.1).

Competitive Environment

A firm's **competitive environment** refers to the other companies operating in the same marketspace selling similar products. The competitive environment for a company is influenced by several factors: how many competitors are active, how large their operations are, what the market share of each competitor is, how profitable these firms are, and how they price their products.

Firms typically have both direct and indirect competitors. *Direct competitors* are those companies that sell products and services that are very similar and into the same market segment. For example, Priceline.com and Hotwired.com, both of whom sell discount airline tickets online, are direct competitors because both companies sell products that can be considered close substitutes for one another. *Indirect competitors* are companies that may be in different industries but still compete indirectly. Priceline.com and Amazon.com, for instance, can be considered indirect competitors: While Amazon.com currently does not offer airline tickets, its expertise in developing online commerce and in facilitating Internet traffic, either alone or in conjunction

competitive environment
refers to the other companies operating in the same marketspace selling similar products

FIGURE 2.1 **MARKETSPACE AND MARKET OPPORTUNITY IN THE $70 BILLION SOFTWARE TRAINING MARKET**

Market spaces are composed of many market segments. Your realistic market opportunity will typically focus on one or a few market segments.

with other e-commerce or offline companies, gives it the ability to quickly do so. Automobile manufacturers and airline companies operate in different industries but they still compete indirectly because they offer consumers alternative means of transportation. The online music service provided by MyMP3.com competes indirectly with Amazon.com's book sales because both Web sites offer consumers alternative modes of entertainment.

The existence of a large number of competitors in any one segment may be a sign that the market is saturated and that it may be difficult to become profitable. On the other hand, a lack of competitors could either signal an untapped market niche ripe for the picking or a market that has already been tried without success because there is no money to be made. Analysis of the competitive environment can help you decide which it is.

Competitive Advantage

Firms achieve a **competitive advantage** when they can produce a superior product and/or bring the product to market at a lower price than most, or all, of their competitors (Porter, 1985). Firms also compete on scope. Some firms can develop global markets while other firms can only develop a national or regional market. Firms that can provide superior products at lowest cost on a global basis are truly advantaged. Firms achieve competitive advantages because they have somehow been able to obtain differential access to the factors of production that are denied to their competitors — at least in the short term (Barney, 1991). Perhaps the firm has been able to obtain very favorable terms from suppliers, shippers, or sources of labor. Or perhaps the firm has more experienced, knowledgeable, loyal employees than any competitors. Perhaps the firm has a patent on a product that others cannot imitate, or access to investment capital through a network of former business colleagues or a brand name and popular image that other firms cannot duplicate. An **asymmetry** exists whenever one participant in a market has more resources — financial backing, knowledge, information, and/or power — than other participants. Asymmetries lead to some firms having an edge over others, permitting them to come to market with better products, faster than competitors, and sometimes at lower cost.

For instance, when Papa John's Pizza began advertising that its founder was the former founder of Pizza Hut, the company earned instant credibility. Similarly, when Geraldine Laybourne left her senior position at Disney to start the online women's network, Oxygen.com, her company was given better-than-average odds of success simply because of her background and her connections, which included several larger investors who were willing to invest significant capital to start the company.

One rather unique competitive advantage derives from being first mover. A **first mover advantage** is a competitive market advantage for a firm that results from being the first into a marketplace with a serviceable product or service. If first movers develop a loyal following or a unique interface that is difficult to imitate, they can sus-

competitive advantage
achieved by a firm when it can produce a superior product and/or bring the product to market at a lower price than most, or all, of its competitors

asymmetry
exists whenever one participant in a market has more resources than other participants

first mover advantage
a competitive market advantage for a firm that results from being the first into a marketplace with a serviceable product or service

tain their first mover advantage for long periods (Arthur, 1996). Amazon.com provides a good example. However, in the history of technology-driven business innovation, most first movers lack the resources to sustain their advantages, and often follower firms reap the largest rewards (Rigdon, 2000; Teece, 1986).

Some competitive advantages are called "unfair." An **unfair competitive advantage** occurs when one firm develops an advantage based on a factor that other firms cannot purchase (Barney, 1991). For instance, a brand name cannot be purchased and is in that sense an "unfair" advantage. As we will discuss in Chapter 8, brands are built upon loyalty, trust, reliability, and quality. Once obtained, they are difficult to copy or imitate, and they permit firms to charge premium prices for their products.

In **perfect markets**, there are no competitive advantages or asymmetries because all firms have access to all the factors of production (including information and knowledge) equally. However, real markets are imperfect, and asymmetries leading to competitive advantages do exist at least in the short term. Most competitive advantages are short term, although some — such as the competitive advantage enjoyed by Coca-Cola because of the Coke brand name — can be sustained for very long periods. But not forever: Coke's sweet soft drink is increasingly challenged by fruit, health, and unique flavor drinks.

Companies are said to **leverage** their competitive assets when they use their competitive advantages to achieve more advantage in surrounding markets. For instance, Amazon.com's move into the online auction arena leveraged the company's huge customer database, offering customers one more way to buy from Amazon and giving them new access to just about any item someone else had to sell. Amazon's competitive advantages included the years of e-commerce experience the company had already amassed by the time it ventured into online auctions, plus its database of millions of customers.

Market Strategy

No matter how tremendous a firm's qualities, its marketing strategy and execution are often just as important. The best business concept, or idea, will fail if it is not properly marketed to potential customers.

Everything you do to promote your company's products and services to potential customers is known as marketing. **Market strategy** is the plan you put together that details exactly how you intend to enter a new market and attract new customers.

Part of Kozmo.com's marketing strategy, for instance, was to use partners such as Starbucks Coffee to help attract new customers. By partnering with other companies that could benefit from fast customer deliveries, Kozmo attempted to extend its reach.

Other companies, such as Yahoo.com, have used a different marketing strategy. They invest heavily in advertising to get the word out about their site. Simply introducing someone to a new site can be all that is needed to encourage them to use it. AOL, in contrast, used sampling to attract new users. AOL enclosed CDs with a free

---

unfair competitive advantage

occurs when one firm develops an advantage based on a factor that other firms cannot purchase

perfect market

a market in which there are no competitive advantages or asymmetries because all firms have equal access to all the factors of production

leverage

when a company uses its competitive advantages to achieve more advantage in surrounding markets

market strategy

the plan you put together that details exactly how you intend to enter a new market and attract new customers trial offer in magazines and newspapers across the country. By distributing a huge volume of samples, AOL hoped that at least a small percentage would opt to try the software and decide to become a new subscriber. This strategy has proven to be very successful for AOL, and today they have almost 30 million subscribers.

Organizational Development

Although many entrepreneurial ventures are started by one visionary individual, it is rare that one person alone can grow an idea into a multi-million dollar company. In most cases, fast-growth companies — especially e-commerce businesses — need employees and a set of business procedures. In short, all firms — new ones in particular — need an organization to efficiently implement their business plans and strategies. Many e-commerce firms and many traditional firms who attempt an e-commerce strategy have failed because they lacked organizational structures and supportive cultural values required to support new forms of commerce (Kanter, 2001).

Companies that hope to grow and thrive need to have a plan for **organizational development** that describes how the company will organize the work that needs to be accomplished. Typically, work is divided into functional departments, such as production, shipping, marketing, customer support, and finance. Jobs within these functional areas are defined, and then recruitment begins for specific job titles and responsibilities. Typically, in the beginning, generalists who can perform multiple tasks are hired. As the company grows, recruiting becomes more specialized. For instance, at the outset, a business may have one marketing manager. But after two or three years of steady growth, that one marketing position may be broken down into seven separate jobs done by seven individuals.

For instance, eBay.com founder Pierre Omidyar started an online auction site to help his girlfriend trade Pez dispensers with other collectors, but within a few months the volume of business had far exceeded what he alone could handle. So he began hiring people with more business experience to help out. Soon the company had many employees, departments, and managers who were responsible for overseeing the various aspects of the company.

Management Team

Arguably, the single most important element of a business model is the **management team** responsible for making the model work. A strong management team gives a model instant credibility to outside investors, immediate market-specific knowledge, and experience in implementing business plans. A strong management team may not be able to salvage a weak business model, but they should be able to change the model and redefine the business as it becomes necessary.

Eventually, most companies get to the point of having several senior executives or managers. How skilled managers are, however, can be a source of competitive

organizational development plan
describes how the company will organize the work that needs to be accomplished

management team
employees of the company responsible for making the business model work

advantage or disadvantage. The challenge is to find people who have both the experience and the ability to apply that experience to new situations.

To be able to identify good managers for a business start-up, first consider the kinds of experiences that would be helpful to a manager joining your company. What kind of technical background is desirable? What kind of supervisory experience is necessary? How many years in a particular function should be required? What job functions should be fulfilled first: marketing, production, finance, or operations? Especially in situations where financing will be needed to get a company off the ground, do prospective senior managers have experience and contacts for raising financing from outside investors?

CATEGORIZING E-COMMERCE BUSINESS MODELS: SOME DIFFICULTIES

There are many e-commerce business models, and more are being invented every day. The number of such models is limited only by the human imagination, and our list of different business models is certainly not exhaustive. However, despite the abundance of potential models, it is possible to identify the major generic types (and subtle variations) of business models that have been developed for the e-commerce arena and describe their key features. It is important to realize, however, that there is no one correct way to categorize these business models.

Our approach is to categorize business models according to the different e-commerce sectors — B2C, B2B, C2C, etc. — in which they are utilized. You will note, however, that fundamentally similar business models may appear in more than one sector. For example, the business models of online retailers (often called *e-tailers*) and e-distributors are quite similar. However, they are distinguished somewhat by the market focus of the sector in which they are used. In the case of e-tailers in the B2C sector, the business model focuses on sales to the individual consumer, while in the case of the e-distributor, the business model focuses on sales to another business.

The type of e-commerce technology involved can also affect the classification of a business model. *M-commerce*, for instance, refers to e-commerce conducted over wireless networks. The e-tail business model, for instance, can also be used in m-commerce, and while the basic business model may remain fundamentally the same as that used in the B2C sector, it will nonetheless have to be adapted to the special challenges posed by the m-commerce environment.

Finally, you will also note that some companies use multiple business models. For instance, eBay.com can be considered as a B2C market maker. At the same time, eBay can also be considered as having a C2C business model. If eBay adopts wireless mobile computing, allowing customers to bid on auctions from their telephones or wireless web machines, then eBay may also be described as having a B2C m-commerce business model. We can expect many companies will have closely related B2C, B2B, and m-commerce variations on their basic business model. Such is the expanding nature of e-commerce on the Web.

2.2 MAJOR BUSINESS-TO-CONSUMER (B2C) BUSINESS MODELS

Business-to-consumer (B2C) e-commerce, in which online businesses seek to reach individual consumers, is the most well-known and familiar type of e-commerce.

Table 2.3 illustrates the major business models utilized in the B2C arena.

TABLE 2.3	B2C BUSINESS MODELS			
BUSINESS MODEL	VARIATIONS	EXAMPLES	DESCRIPTION	REVENUE MODEL
Portal	Horizontal/General	Yahoo.com, AOL.com, MSN.com, Excite@home.com	Offers an integrated package of services and content such as search, news, e-mail, chat, music downloads, video streaming, and calendars. Seeks to be a user's home base.	Advertising, subscription fees, transaction fees
	Vertical/Specialized (Vortal)	iBoats.com	Offers services and products to specialized marketspace.	Advertising, subscription fees, transaction fees
E-tailer	Virtual Merchant	Amazon.com	Online version of retail store, where customers can shop at any hour of the day or night without leaving home or office.	Sales of goods
	Clicks and Mortar	Walmart.com	Online distribution channel for company that also has physical stores.	Sales of goods
	Catalog Merchant	LandsEnd.com	Online version of direct mail catalog.	Sales of goods
	Online Mall	Fashionmall.com	Online version of mall.	Sales of goods, transaction fees
	Manufacturer-direct	Dell.com	Online sales made directly by manufacturer.	Sales of goods
Content Provider		WSJ.com, Sportsline.com, CNN.com	Information and entertainment providers such as newspapers, sports sites, and other online sources that offer customers up-to-date news and special interest, how-to guidance, and tips and/or information sales.	Advertising, subscription fees, affiliate referral fees

(continued)

TABLE 2.3	B2C BUSINESS MODELS (*CONTINUED*)			
BUSINESS MODEL	VARIATIONS	EXAMPLES	DESCRIPTION	REVENUE MODEL
Transaction Broker		E-Trade.com, Expedia.com, Monster.com	Processors of online sales transactions, such as stock brokers and travel agents, that increase customers' productivity by helping them get things done faster and more cheaply.	Transaction fees
Market Creator	Auctions and other forms of dynamic pricing	eBay.com, Priceline.com	Web-based businesses that use Internet technology to create markets that bring buyers and sellers together.	Transaction fees
Service Provider		xDrive.com, whatsitworthtoyou.com, myCFO.com	Companies that make money by selling users a service, rather than a product.	Sales of services
Community Provider		About.com, iVillage.com, BlackPlanet.com	Sites where individuals with particular interests, hobbies, and common experiences can come together and compare notes.	Advertising, subscription, affiliate referral fees

PORTAL

portal

offers users powerful Web search tools as well as an integrated package of content and services all in one place

Portals such as Yahoo.com, AOL.com, and MSN.com offer users powerful Web search tools (see *Insight on Technology: Google.com* at the end of Section 2.2) as well as an integrated package of content and services — such as news, e-mail, instant messaging, calendars, shopping, music downloads, video streaming, and more, all in one place. While five years ago, portals sought to be viewed as "gateways" to the Internet, today, the portal business model is to be a destination site. Portals do not sell anything directly — or so it seems — and in that sense they can present themselves as unbiased. The market opportunity is very large — in 2001, about 170 million people in the United States had access to the Internet (Neilsen/Net Ratings, 2001). Portals generate revenue primarily by charging advertisers for ad placement, collecting referral fees for steering customers to other sites, and charging for premium services. AOL and MSN — which in addition to being portals are also *Internet Service Providers (ISPs)* that provide access to the Internet and the Web — add an additional revenue stream: monthly subscription fees of around $22–$24 per month.

Although there are numerous portal/search engine sites, the top ten sites gather more than 90% of the search engine traffic because of their superior brand recognition (www.searchenginewatch.com, 2001). Many of the top sites were among the first to appear on the Web and therefore had first mover advantages. Being first confers advantage because customers come to trust a reliable provider and experience switching costs if they change to late arrivals in the market. By garnering a large chunk of the marketplace, first movers — just like a single telephone network — can offer customers access to commonly shared ideas, standards, and experiences (something called *network externalities* that we describe in later chapters).

Yahoo, AOL, MSN, and others like them are considered to be *horizontal portals* because they define their marketspace to include all users of the Internet. *Vertical portals* (sometimes called *vortals*) attempt to provide similar services as horizontal portals, but are focused around a particular subject matter or market segment. For instance, iBoats.com specializes in the consumer boating market that contains about 16 million Americans who own or rent boats. Although the total number of vortal users may be much lower than the number of portal users, if the market segment is attractive enough, advertisers are willing to pay a premium in order to reach a targeted audience.

E-TAILER

Online retail stores, often called **e-tailers**, come in all sizes and shapes, from giant Amazon.com to tiny local stores who have a Web site. E-tailers are much like the typical brick-and-mortar storefront, except that customers only have to dial into the Internet to check their inventory and place an order. Some e-tailers, sometimes referred to as "clicks and mortar" or "clicks and bricks" are subsidiaries of existing physical stores and carry the same products. JCPenney, Barnes & Noble, Wal-Mart, and Staples are four examples of companies with complementary online stores. Others, however, operate only in the virtual world, without any ties to physical locations. Amazon.com, iBaby.com, and MarthaStewart.com are examples of these. Several other variations of e-tailers — such as online versions of direct mail catalogs, online malls, and manufacturer-direct online sales — also exist (Gulati and Garino, 2000).

Given that the overall retail market in the United States in 2000 was estimated to be about $3.2 trillion dollars, the market opportunity for e-tailers is very large (ICSC Econstats USA, 2001). With the growing population of Internet users approaching about 60% of U.S. households in 2001, representing about 170 million potential consumers, there has literally been an explosion in B2C e-tailers (Neilsen/Net Ratings, 2001). Every Internet user is a potential customer. Customers who feel time-starved are even hotter prospects, since they want shopping solutions that will eliminate the need to drive to the mall or store (Bellman, Lohse, and Johnson, 1999). The e-tail revenue model is product-based, with customers paying for the purchase of a particular item.

This sector is extremely competitive, however. Since **barriers to entry** (the total cost of entering a new marketplace) into the Web e-tail market are low, tens of thou-

e-tailer
online retail store

barriers to entry
the total cost of entering a new marketplace

sands of small e-tail shops have sprung up on the Web. Becoming profitable and surviving is very difficult for e-tailers with no prior brand name or experience. Since 1999, hundreds, if not thousands, of e-tailers have failed and closed shop. The e-tailer's challenge is differentiating its business from existing stores. How is a new toy e-tailer going to perform better than or differently from eToys.com, an online toy e-tailer, for example, which was well-funded and still couldn't survive?

Companies that try to reach every online consumer are likely to deplete their resources quickly. Those that develop a niche strategy, clearly identifying their target market and its needs, are best prepared to make a profit. Keeping expenses low, selection broad, and inventory controlled are keys to success in e-tailing, with inventory being the most difficult to gauge. The holiday season of 1999 proved to be a fiasco for e-tailers that were caught without adequate inventory, for instance. eToys.com was one of the hardest hit, causing a public relations nightmare and thousands of disgruntled customers who were unlikely to trust the business again when holiday gifts were not delivered on time, as promised. That slip-up is one of the reasons for eToys' big sell-off of inventory little more than a year later — they lost their customers' trust (Glasner, 2001).

CONTENT PROVIDER

intellectual property
refers to all forms of human expression that can be put into a tangible medium such as text, CDs, or the Web

content provider
distributes information content, such as digital news, music, photos, video, and artwork over the Web

Although there are many different ways the Internet can be useful, "information content," which can be defined broadly to include all forms of intellectual property, is one of the largest types of Internet usage. **Intellectual property** refers to all forms of human expression that can be put into a tangible medium such as text, CDs, or the Web (Fisher, 1992). **Content providers** distribute information content, such as digital news, music, photos, video, and artwork over the Web. Retrieving and paying for content is the second largest revenue source for B2C e-commerce, accounting for 14.9% of online sales in 2000 (Dykema, 2000). More Internet users go on the Web to retrieve information than to purchase products (70% versus 53%) (Rainie and Packel, 2000).

Content providers make money by charging subscribers a subscription fee. For instance, in the case of MP3.com, a monthly subscription fee provides users with access to thousands of song tracks. Other content providers, such as WSJ.com (the *Wall Street Journal*'s online newspaper), *Harvard Business Review*, and many others, charge customers for content downloads in addition to or in place of a subscription fee. Micropayment systems technology, such as the Qpass system, provides content providers with a cost effective method for processing high volumes of very small monetary transactions (anywhere from $.25 to $5.00 per transaction). Micropayment systems have greatly enhanced the revenue model prospects of content providers who wish to charge by the download. Content providers such as MP3.com also make money by selling advertising space on their sites.

Of course, not all online content providers charge for their information — just look at Sportsline.com, CIO.com, Thestandard.com, and the online versions of many other newspapers and magazines. Users can access news and information at these sites without paying a cent. These popular sites make money in other ways, such as through advertising and partner promotions on the site.

The key to becoming a successful content provider is owning the content. Traditional owners of copyrighted content — publishers of books and newspapers, broadcasters of radio and television content, music publishers, and movie studios — have powerful advantages over newcomers to the Web. Some content providers, however, do not own content, but syndicate (aggregate) and then distribute content produced by others. *Syndication* is a major variation of the standard content provider model. IntoNetworks.com, and intertainment.com, for instance, license content such as games, videos, and software training programs from owners and then distribute the content on high-speed Internet connections to small businesses and homes (Werbach, 2000).

Any e-commerce start-up that intends to make money by providing content is likely to face difficulties unless it has a unique information source that others cannot access. For the most part, this business category is dominated by traditional content providers.

One example of a successful content provider start-up is drudgereport.com, a political and entertainment site started by a would-be journalist with no training or experience. Through word-of-mouth, its founder, Matt Drudge, garnered support and a long list of information tipsters. Ultimately a tipster leaked word of the Monica Lewinsky scandal and *The Drudge Report* was the first media source anywhere to report it. Since then, the site has grown tremendously, and has inked licensing deals with AOL and TV and radio shows. Despite Matt Drudge's lack of experience and business savvy, *The Drudge Report* has attracted thousands of regular readers through smart promotional moves — and luck.

TRANSACTION BROKER

Sites that process transactions for consumers normally handled in person, by phone, or mail are **transaction brokers**. The largest industries using this model are financial services, travel services, and job placement services. Online stockbrokers such as E-Trade.com, Ameritrade.com, and Schwab.com, for instance, have captured about 20% of retail stock transactions. The online transaction broker's primary value propositions are savings of money and time. In addition, most transaction brokers provide timely information and opinion. Sites such as Monster.com offer job searchers a national marketplace for their talents, and offer employers a national resource for talent. Both employers and job seekers are attracted by the convenience and currency of information. Online stock brokers charge commissions that are considerably less than traditional brokers, with many offering substantial deals, such as cash and a certain number of free trades, to lure new customers (Bakos, Lucas, et al., 2000).

Given rising consumer interest in financial planning and the stock market, the market opportunity for online transaction brokers appears to be large. However, while

transaction broker
site that processes transactions for consumers that are normally handled in person, by phone, or mail

millions of customers have shifted to online brokers, many have been wary to switch from their traditional broker who provides personal advice and a brand name. Fears of privacy invasion and the loss of control over personal financial information also contribute to market resistance. Consequently, the challenge for online brokers is to overcome consumer fears, by emphasizing the security and privacy measures in place.

Transaction brokers make money each time a transaction occurs. Each stock trade, for example, nets the company a fee, based either on a flat rate or a sliding scale related to the size of the transaction. Attracting new customers and encouraging them to trade frequently are the keys to generating more revenue for these companies. Job sites generate listing fees from employers up front, rather than a fee when a position is filled.

Competition among brokers has become more fierce in the past few years, due to new entrants offering ever more appealing offers to consumers to sign on. Those who prospered initially were the first movers such as E-Trade.com, Ameritrade.com, Datek.com, and Schwab.com. During the E-commerce I era, many of these firms engaged in expensive marketing campaigns and were willing to pay up to $400 to acquire a single customer. However, online brokerages are now in direct competition with traditional brokerage firms who have now joined the online marketspace. Significant consolidation is occurring in this industry. The number of job sites has also multiplied, but the largest sites — those with the largest number of job listings — are pulling ahead of smaller niche companies. In both industries, only a few, very large firms are likely to survive in the long term.

MARKET CREATOR

market creator
builds a digital environment where buyers and sellers can meet, display products, search for products, and establish a price for products

Market creators build a digital environment where buyers and sellers can meet, display products, search for products, and establish a price for products. Prior to the Internet and the Web, market creators relied on physical places to establish a market. Beginning with the medieval marketplace, extending to today's New York Stock Exchange, a market has meant a physical space for transacting. There were few private digital network marketplaces prior to the Web. The Web changed this by making it possible to separate markets from physical space. A prime example is Priceline.com, which allows consumers to set the price they are willing to pay for various travel accommodations and other products (sometimes referred to as a *reverse auction*) and eBay.com, the online auction site utilized by both businesses and consumers.

For example, eBay's auction business model is to create a digital electronic environment for buyers and sellers to meet, agree on a price, and transact. This is different from transaction brokers who actually carry out the transaction for their customers, acting as agents in larger markets. At eBay, the buyers and sellers are their own agents. Each sale on eBay nets the company a fee, in addition to a listing fee upfront. eBay is one of the few Web sites that has been profitable virtually from the beginning. Why? One answer is that eBay has no inventory or production costs. It is a simply a middleman.

The market opportunity for market creators is potentially vast, but only if the firm has the financial resources and marketing plan to attract sufficient sellers and buyers to the marketplace. About seven million people use eBay each month and this makes for an efficient market: There are many sellers and buyers for each type of product, sometimes for the same product, for example, laptop computer models. New firms wishing to create a market require an aggressive branding and awareness program to attract a sufficient critical mass of customers. Some very large Web-based firms such as Amazon.com have leveraged their large customer base and started auctions. Many other digital auctions have sprung up in smaller, more specialized vertical market segments such as jewelry and automobiles.

In addition to marketing and branding, a company's management team and organization can make a difference in creating new markets, especially if some managers have had experience in similar businesses. Speed is often the key in such situations. The ability to become operational quickly can make the difference between success and failure.

SERVICE PROVIDER

While e-tailers sell products online, **service providers** offer services online. Some charge a fee, while others generate revenue from other sources, such as advertising and by collecting personal information that is useful in direct marketing. Obviously, some services cannot be provided online; plumbing and car repair, for example, cannot be completed via the Internet. Arrangements can be made, however, for car repair and for plumbing via the Internet. Many service providers are computer-related, such as information storage at xDrive.com, or provide consulting services, such as at whatsitworthtoyou.com, where consumers can have antiques and collectibles appraised online or myCFO.com, which provides advice and services to high net-worth individuals. Grocery shopping services such as Netgrocer.com can also be considered service providers.[1] To complicate matters a bit, most financial transaction brokers (described above) provide services such as college tuition and pension planning. Travel brokers also provide vacation-planning services, not just transactions with airlines and hotels.

The basic value proposition of service providers is that they offer consumers a valuable, convenient, time-saving, and low-cost alternative to traditional service providers. Research has found, for instance, that a major factor in predicting online

service provider
offers services online

---

[1]Netgrocer and other similar e-commerce businesses can also be classified as online retailers insofar as they warehouse commonly purchased items and make a profit based on the spread between their buy and sell prices. Often they charge a premium or have minimum order sizes.

buying behavior is *time starvation*. Time-starved people tend to be busy professionals who work long hours and simply do not have the time to pick up packages or buy groceries (Bellman, Lohse, and Johnson, 1999). Service providers make money through subscription fees (if there is a recurring need for the service), through one-time payments for single use of the service, or through commissions on items purchased or delivered. When a new subscriber signs on for monthly information storage, xDrive.com makes money. Much like retailers, who trade products for cash, service providers trade knowledge, expertise, and effort for revenue.

The market opportunity for service providers is as large as the variety of services that can be provided and potentially is equal to the market opportunity for physical goods. We live in a service-based economy and society; witness the growth of fast food restaurants, package delivery services, and wireless cellular phone services. Consumers' increasing demand for convenience products and services bodes well for current and future service providers.

Marketing of service providers must allay consumer fears about hiring a vendor online, as well as build confidence and familiarity among current and potential customers. Name recognition is the first challenge, in order to build comfort, with the second challenge being enticing consumers to try the service.

COMMUNITY PROVIDER

community provider

sites that create a digital online environment where people with similar interests can transact (buy and sell goods), communicate with like-minded people, and receive interest-related information

Although community providers are not a new entity, the Internet made such sites for like-minded individuals to meet and converse much easier, without the limitations of geography to hinder participation. **Community providers** are sites that create a digital online environment where people with similar interests can transact (buy and sell goods), communicate with like-minded people, receive interest-related information, and even play out fantasies by adopting online personalities (Armstrong and Hagel, 1996). The basic value proposition of community providers is to create a fast, convenient, one-stop site where users can focus on their most important concerns and interests. Community providers typically rely on a hybrid revenue model that includes subscription fees, sales revenues, transaction fees, affiliate fees, and advertising fees from other firms who are attracted by a tightly focused audience.

Community sites such as ParentSoup.com, Oxygen.com, and About.com make money through affiliate relationships with retailers and from advertising. For instance, a parent might visit ParentSoup.com for tips on diapering a baby and be presented with a link to Huggies.com; if the parent clicks the link and then makes a purchase from Huggies.com, ParentSoup gets a commission. Likewise, banner ads also generate revenue. At About.com, visitors can share tips and buy recommended books from Amazon.com, giving About.com a commission on every purchase. Some of the oldest communities on the Web are Well.com, which provides a forum for technology and Internet-related discussions, and The MotleyFool (Fool.com), which provides financial advice, news, and opinions.

INSIGHT ON TECHNOLOGY

GOOGLE.COM — SEARCHING FOR PROFITS

The Web's hottest search engine isn't Yahoo or AltaVista, it's Google. Although the name sounds a bit juvenile, it's actually based on complex mathematics — google is the common pronunciation of *googol*, or 10^{100}. Google was started in 1998 by two enterprising Stanford grad students, Sergey Brin and Larry Page, who were studying data mining and the process of analyzing data for patterns. That research later became the basis of their business, Google, which has indexed over a billion Web pages.

What makes Google so notable is its proprietary technology. Some search engines merely count how many times a search term appears on a given Web page to determine where to rank a particular page. Clever marketers can exploit the system and jury-rig a page so that it will receive a higher ranking, leaving users with lists of pages that may not be truly relevant to their searches. Google's engine, on the other hand, uses outside criteria to validate that a search result is likely to be relevant — the more outside links there are to a particular page, the higher it jumps in Google's ranking structure. Google also factors in other information, such as link structure, fonts, heading, and text of nearby pages. The company uses extremely sophisticated

software algorithms to carry out each search, drawing on the power of up to 6,000 computers. In addition to a higher probability of returning relevant results, other Google technology hallmarks include quick search times, and ease of use.

However, if there's one thing that's become clear in the E-commerce II era, it's that a "cool" technology does not a successful business model make. Brin and Page have decided to focus Google purely on the search engine business, in contrast to AltaVista, Excite, Lycos, and other competitors that began as search engines but then tried to broaden their business model into the portal arena. Right now, Google makes money primarily through advertising and licensing its search technology to over 120 other Web sites. Yahoo, for instance, recently dropped its relationship with search engine Inktomi, replacing it with Google.

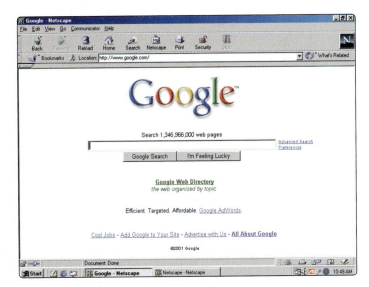

(continued)

While such a relationship is undoubtedly good for Google's image in the financial community, Yahoo still may not be the gravy train the company needs. Co-founder Page expects the company to be making an average of a penny per search from advertising in the near future, which equates to about $14 million a quarter. But they're not there yet. Page claims Google could be profitable right away. But, "We are in this for the long term, and we want to do the right thing for our business. Being profitable immediately isn't the right thing." For instance, unlike many other search engines, Google currently refuses to accept payments from companies in exchange for a higher ranking.

How long Page and Brin can maintain that position is open to question. Google has some strong backers, including venture capital firms Kleiner Perkins and Sequoia Capital, and hopes to go public at some point. The company's traffic figures are also on the rise, growing at about 20% per month, due mainly to word of mouth. With the amount of information available online increasing exponentially and the need for users to find what they are searching for becoming more difficult, Google may just be in the right place at the right time—if it can find a way to become profitable.

SOURCES: "The Virtuous Search Engine," by Mindy Charski, *Interactive Week*, June 4, 2001; "Google Buys Deja Unit," by Michael Liedtke, *Washington Post*, February 12, 2001; "Search Us, Says Google," by Robert McGarvey, *Technology Review*, November 2000; "A Great Product isn't Everything," by Anne Schukat, *Fortune*, August 14, 2000; "Anatomy of a Large-Scale Hypertextual Web Search Engine," by Sergey Brin and Larry Page, *WWW7/Computer Networks*, 1998.

Consumers' interest in communities seems to be increasing, with the market opportunity expanding as well. The key in developing a new community is to carve out a well-defined niche that is currently not being served. Targeting large market segments will only pit a company against bigger, better established competitors. Small pockets — subsegments of larger markets — have the potential for future growth without as much competitive pressure. The greatest challenge faced by community sites is balancing the cost of high-quality content with the revenue derived from advertising. Currently, community sites are finding it difficult to make a profit, and considerable consolidation in community sites will occur.

Firm qualities that are important among community providers are breadth and depth of knowledge. Since the purpose of communities is to link consumers with similar interests and personal situations, having managers who can relate to such experiences is crucial. Community members frequently request guidance and advice. Lack of experienced personnel can severely hamper the growth of a community, which needs facilitators and managers to keep discussions on course and relevant.

Enticing new participants to join a community is the focus of most marketing strategies, with larger communities generating powerful word-of-mouth advertising and rising commissions. The more community members, the higher the advertising rates that can be charged and the better the chances for sales at partner sites.

2.3 MAJOR BUSINESS–TO-BUSINESS (B2B) BUSINESS MODELS

In Chapter 1, we noted that business-to-business (B2B) e-commerce, in which businesses focus on selling to other businesses, is about three times the size of B2C e-commerce, even though most of the public attention has focused on B2C. For instance, total revenues for all types of B2C e-commerce in 2001 were estimated to be about $65 billion (Dykema, 2000; Bakos, 2001), compared to an estimated $470 billion for all types of B2B commerce in 2001 (Jupiter Media Metrix, 2001). Experts predict that B2B purchasing will grow to $5.4 trillion by 2006, or about one-third of total inter-firm purchasing at that time (Jupiter Media Metrix, 2001).

Table 2.4 lists the major business models utilized in the B2B arena.

MARKETPLACE/EXCHANGE (B2B HUB)

Marketplace/exchanges, or **B2B hubs,** have garnered most of the B2B attention and funding because of their potential market size. A marketplace/exchange is a digital electronic marketplace where suppliers and commercial purchasers can conduct transactions (Kaplan and Sawhney, 2000). GartnerGroup's Dataquest reports approximately $100 billion in business was handled by these all-encompassing industry portals in 2000, with that figure expected to grow to $2.7 trillion by the year 2004 (Knight, 2001).

For buyers, B2B hubs make it possible to gather information, check out suppliers, collect prices, and keep up-to-date on the latest happenings all in one place. Sellers, on the other hand, benefit from expanded access to buyers. The greater the number of potential buyers, the lower the sales cost and the higher the chances of making a sale. Some sites also have experienced higher average revenue per buyer, according to a Grainger Consulting Services study (Grainger Consulting Services, 1999).

Marketplaces make it significantly less expensive and time consuming to identify potential suppliers, customers, and partners, and to do business with each other. As a result, they can lower *transaction costs* — the cost of making a sale or purchase. For instance, the cost for a corporate purchasing agent to place an order typically starts at $100. B2B hubs can also lower product costs and *inventory-carrying costs* — the cost of keeping a product on hand, in a warehouse.

Vertical marketplaces serve specific industries, such as the steel, automobile, chemical, floral, or logging industry, while *horizontal marketplaces* sell specific products and services to a wide range of companies. Vertical marketplaces supply a smaller number of companies with products and services of specific interest to their industry, while horizontal marketplaces supply companies in different industries with a particular type of product and service, such as marketing-related, financial, or computing. One of the largest vertical B2B marketplaces is Covisint, the auto parts

marketplace/exchange (B2B hub)

a digital electronic marketplace where suppliers and commercial purchasers can conduct transactions

TABLE 2.4	**B2B BUSINESS MODELS**			
BUSINESS MODEL	VARIATIONS	EXAMPLES	DESCRIPTION	REVENUE MODEL
Marketplace/ Exchange (B2B Hub)	Vertical	DirectAg.com, e-Steel.com	Helps bring buyers and sellers together to reduce procurement costs for a specific industry.	Transaction fees
	Horizontal	TradeOut.com	Same as vertical except focused on specific types of products and services.	Transaction fees
E-Distributor		Grainger.com	Connecting businesses directly with other businesses, reducing sales cycles and mark-up.	Sales of goods
B2B Service Provider	Traditional	Employeematters.com	Supports companies through online business services.	Sales of services
	Application Service Provider (ASP)	Salesforce.com, Corio.com	Rents Internet-based software applications to businesses.	Rental fees
Matchmaker		iShip.com	Helps businesses find what they want and need on the Web.	Transaction fees
Infomediary	Audience Broker	DoubleClick.net	Gathers information about consumers and uses it to help advertisers find the most appropriate audience.	Sales of information
	Lead Generator	AutoByTel.com	Gathers customer data, and uses it to direct vendors to customers.	Referral fee

exchange backed by DaimlerChrysler, Ford, General Motors, Renault, CommerceOne, and Oracle. Formed in October 2000, by December 2000, Covisint had logged over $350 million in transactions, conducted 100 auctions, and placed over 100 catalogs online (Morneau, 2001).

Likewise, DirectAg.com serves the agricultural market, providing farmers and suppliers with news, commodities pricing, and forecasts, as well as volume purchasing opportunities that help users save time and money on purchases. Read *Insight on Business: e-Steel.com Breaks Its Mold* for a more in-depth look at B2B exchange business models.

TradeOut.com, in comparison, auctions surplus equipment off to the highest bidder in any industry, which is why it is an example of a horizontal marketplace. It specializes in helping companies with excess inventory and idle assets sell their products and services to other companies that have a need for them. Businesses can buy from and sell to each other, freeing up cash and unloading inventory that is no longer of any use to them.

The key to success with marketplaces is size — the size of the industry and the number of registered users. If the industry that the marketplace seeks to serve is not large enough, it is not likely that the site will be profitable. Similarly, if the site cannot reach critical mass by attracting a large number of buyers and sellers, users will go elsewhere. In the next few years, experts predict a sharp consolidation within e-marketplaces, with the number of such sites diminishing dramatically, leaving just a few major B2B hubs (Wise and Morrison, 2000). In addition, the concept of a centralized hub may slowly be replaced by direct peer-to-peer exchanges similar to those enabled by Napster in the music marketspace described below (McAfee, 2000).

E-DISTRIBUTOR

Companies that supply products and services directly to individual businesses are **e-distributors**. W.W. Grainger, for example, is the largest distributor of maintenance, repair, and operations (MRO) supplies. In the past it relied on catalog sales and physical distribution centers in metropolitan areas. Its catalog of equipment went online in 1995 at grainger.com, giving businesses access to more than 220,000 items. Company purchasing agents can search by type of product, such as motors, HVAC, or fluids, or by specific brand name.

> **e-distributor**
> a company that supplies products and services directly to individual businesses

Whereas B2B hubs pull together many businesses, making it possible for them to do business with other companies, e-distributors are set up by one company seeking to serve many customers. However, as with B2B hubs, critical mass is a factor. With e-distributors, the more products and services a company makes available on its site, the more attractive that site is to potential customers. One-stop shopping is always preferable to having to visit numerous sites to locate a particular part or product.

Although W.W. Grainger established its Web site in order to conduct business with its customers, General Electric Aircraft Engines backed into its role as an e-distributor. GE Aircraft Engines is such a large purchaser of aircraft engine parts that other purchasers in the aircraft industry almost always need the same parts GE is ordering from vendors. GE decided to make its internal procurement system public, allowing fellow buyers of industrial products and equipment to visit its site, geae.com, in search of needed parts and machinery. GE and other purchasers can buy together and receive larger discounts for larger orders. In setting itself up as a focal point for such purchasing inquiries, GE improved its own purchasing power and relationships. This decision has created a new profit center for GE and reduced its own cost of acquisition.

B2B SERVICE PROVIDER

Just as e-distributors provide products to other companies, **B2B service providers** sell business services to other firms. "Traditional" B2B service providers offer online equivalents to common business services, such as accounting, financial services, human resource management, printing, and so on. Application service providers are another type of B2B service provider. An **application service provider (ASP)** is a

> **B2B service provider**
> sells business services to other firms

> **application service provider (ASP)**
> a company that sells access to Internet-based software applications to other companies

company that sells access to Internet-based software applications to other companies. Salesforce.com, for instance, enables companies to manage their sales forces. Businesses license Salesforce.com's software based on the number of salespeople who will be accessing the system. This eliminates the need for firms to buy or install a complex sales force automation system.

B2B service providers make money through transaction fees, fees based on the number of workstations using the service, or annual licensing fees (the method used by Salesforce.com). They offer purchasing firms significant advantages. Services tend to be knowledge-intensive, based on expensive professional employees. Computer-based software management systems are difficult to build or customize to one's business. A B2B service provider such as Salesforce.com can build an expensive sales force management system and then spread the cost of the system over many users — achieving what economists call *scale economies*. Scale economies arise when large fixed-cost production systems (such as factories or software systems) can be operated at full capacity with no idle time. In the case of software, the marginal cost of a digital copy of a software program is nearly zero, and finding additional buyers for an expensive software program is exceptionally profitable. This is much more efficient than having every firm build its own sales force management system, and it permits Salesforce.com to specialize in a single type of system and offer the marketplace a "best of breed" system.

MATCHMAKER

matchmaker
a company that makes money by linking other businesses and taking a cut of any business that occurs via a transaction or usage fee

Companies that make money by linking other businesses and taking a cut of any business that occurs via a transaction or usage fee are called **matchmakers**. They are a form of the transaction brokers familiar in the B2C area.

For example, iShip.com, acquired in May 2001 by United Parcel Service from Stamps.com, helps businesses find the cheapest shipper for their packages. Although other companies sell expensive multicarrier shipping software, iShip lets companies access its Web site free of charge to compare the rates from several major carriers, including Federal Express, Airborne, and the U.S. Postal Service. Once a company has located the cheapest shipper for its particular package, it pays iShip a fee in order to proceed with the shipment.

INFOMEDIARY

infomediary
a company whose business model is premised upon gathering information about consumers and selling it to other businesses

The term **infomediary** was originally coined by Hagel and Rayport to describe a new breed of company that would act as custodians, agents, and brokers of customer information, marketing it to businesses on consumers' behalf while protecting their privacy at the same time. Today, although the privacy-protection aspects of their proposed definition have not necessarily come to fruition, there are a number of companies whose business model is premised upon gathering information about consumers and selling it to other businesses.

INSIGHT ON BUSINESS

E-STEEL.COM BREAKS ITS MOLD

e-Steel.com is one of the estimated 1,000 or so B2B online marketplaces launched between 1998 and 2001. With more than 3,500 member companies trading globally, e-Steel is considered a leading exchange. And when U.S. Steel, the largest steel manufacturer in the United States, decided not only to join but also invest in e-Steel, the exchange's prestige and notoriety went up another notch.

That's not to suggest that e-Steel is anywhere near profitable yet — it's not. But it has managed to bring together an impressive number of metals industry manufacturers and buyers for the purpose of doing business online. Members can buy and sell prime and non-prime steel products, such as hot rolled, cold rolled, coated, and plate steel.

e-Steel uses a private negotiation model rather than the auction model that many other exchanges have adopted, and enables users to make inquiries or offers, search for products, and negotiate the full details of a transaction online. It developed proprietary e-commerce software, called SteelDirect, based on the BroadVision One-to-One Enterprise Relationship Management system, that allows users to both target and block specific companies from receiving its sensitive information; pricing information may be shared with potential customers, for example, but not with direct competitors.

The exchange raised more than $65 million to get started, some from Paul Allen's Vulcan Ventures, as well as from Goldman Sachs and GE Capital. When it first launched in September 1998, e-Steel presented itself to the steel industry as an independent intermediary — a neutral marketplace where buyers and sellers could meet online. Within six months, it had registered 1,800 companies and posted $80 million of materials, and appeared well on its way to success.

However, by February 2000, the environment around e-Steel had changed. Other competitors had joined the fray, including MetalSite, a steel industry consortium formed by Bethlehem Steel, LTV Steel, and others. e-Steel needed more capital. So, when U.S. Steel expressed an interest in purchasing a stake in e-Steel, e-Steel was in no position to turn it down.

While the move improved e-Steel's financial position, it has also raised questions about whether the exchange will continue to be viewed as a purely neutral player or whether it will now be perceived as somehow favoring U.S. Steel. e-Steel claims that it will continue to operate on a strictly neutral basis and that the existence of industry investors will have a positive rather than negative impact on other members, indicating acceptance of the marketplace by industry leaders. In e-Steel's view, there will ultimately be only one or perhaps two successful B2B exchanges in each vertical industry, and it is doing everything it can to assure that it is one of those left standing at the end of the day.

SOURCES: "Traditional Industries Stole the E-Marketplace Initiative from Dot-Coms. Now What?," by Rob Spiegal, *E-Commerce Business*, December 18, 2000; "e-Steel Moves Industry Value Chain Online," by Rob Spiegal, *E-Commerce Business*, November 6, 2000; "B2B In a State of Flux," by Gordon McConnell, *B2B Magazine*, September 2000; "B2B Marketplaces Struggle," by Edward Iwata, *USA Today*, May 16, 2000; "U.S. Steel Finds B2B E-commerce Riveting," by Mary Hillebrand, *E-Commerce Times*, February 25, 2000.

A vendor-oriented infomediary sells the information it gathers to vendors who use it to target products, services, and promotions to particular consumers. Vendor-oriented infomediaries can be classified into two basic subcategories: audience brokers and lead generators.

Audience brokers capture information about customers and use it to help advertisers reach the most appropriate audiences for their advertising. A leading example is DoubleClick.

Lead generators gather customer data, from which they then create customer profiles and preferences. They then direct vendors of products and services that fit these customer profiles to the customers. One example of a lead generator is AutoByTel, which operates a national network of auto dealers to whom Web users are referred in return for a fee per lead (Hagel and Rayport, 1997a, b).

2.4   BUSINESS MODELS IN EMERGING E-COMMERCE AREAS

When we think about a business, we typically think of a business firm that produces a product or good, and then sells it to a customer. But the Web has forced us to recognize new forms of business, such as consumer-to-consumer e-commerce, peer-to-peer e-commerce, and m-commerce. Table 2.5 lists some of the business models that can be found in these emerging markets.

CONSUMER-TO-CONSUMER (C2C) BUSINESS MODELS

Consumer-to-consumer (C2C) ventures provide a way for consumers to sell to each other, with the help of an online business. The first and best example of this type of business is eBay.com, utilizing a market creator business model.

TABLE 2.5	BUSINESS MODELS IN EMERGING E-COMMERCE AREAS			
TYPE	MODEL	EXAMPLE	DESCRIPTION	REVENUE MODEL
Consumer-to-consumer	Market Creator	eBay.com, Half.com	Helps consumers connect with other consumers who have items to sell.	Transaction fees
Peer-to-peer	Content Provider	Napster.com, My.MP3.com	Technology enabling consumers to share files and services via the Web.	Subscription fees, advertising, transaction fees
M-commerce	Various	Amazon.com	Extending business applications using wireless technology.	Sales of goods

Before eBay, individual consumers used garage sales, flea markets, and thrift shops to both dispose of and acquire used merchandise. With the introduction of online auctions, consumers no longer had to venture out of their home or office in order to bid on items of interest, and sellers could relinquish expensive retail space that was no longer needed in order to reach buyers. In return for linking like-minded buyers and sellers, eBay takes a small commission. The more auctions, the more eBay makes money. In fact, it is the one Web site that has been profitable from day one — and has stayed so for several years.

Consumers that don't like auctions but still want to find used merchandise can visit Half.com, which enables consumers to sell off unwanted books, movies, music, and games to other consumers. Unlike eBay, it allows sellers to set a fixed-price for each item, rather than putting it up for bid. In return for facilitating a transaction, Half.com takes a 15% commission on the sale, plus a fraction of the shipping fee it charges. It, too, is doing well.

PEER-TO-PEER (P2P) BUSINESS MODELS

Like the C2C models, P2P ventures link users, enabling them to share files and computer resources without a common server. The focus in P2P companies is on helping individuals make information available for anyone's use by connecting users on the Web. C2C companies, on the other hand, link consumers so that they can buy and sell goods and services on the Web. Because historically, peer-to-peer technology has been used to allow file sharing among users for free, the challenge for P2P ventures is to develop a viable business model that will enable them to make money. In Chapter 1, we discussed the difficulties faced by Napster.com, one of the most prominent examples of a P2P business model. Another music site, MP3.com, took a slightly different tack than Napster with its My.MP3.com service. Like Napster, MP3.com makes it possible for music lovers to share files and to download free MP3 songs at My.MP3.com. (See Figure 2.2.) MP3.com also stores songs made available for free by lesser known artists and bands, who have given permission for the music to be stored at the MP3 site. MP3 has become a haven for bands waiting to be discovered. MP3.com makes money through advertising and charging for some downloads and has recently been acquired by Vivendi Universal, a major music industry player.

M-COMMERCE BUSINESS MODELS

M-commerce, short for *mobile-commerce*, takes traditional e-commerce models and leverages emerging new wireless technologies — described more fully in Chapter 3 — to permit mobile access to the Web. Traditional e-commerce provides access to anyone, anytime via the Internet. The major advantage of m-commerce is that it provides access to anyone, anytime, and *anywhere*, using wireless devices.

In essence, wireless networks utilize newly available bandwidth and communication protocols to connect mobile users to the Internet. While existing wireless net-

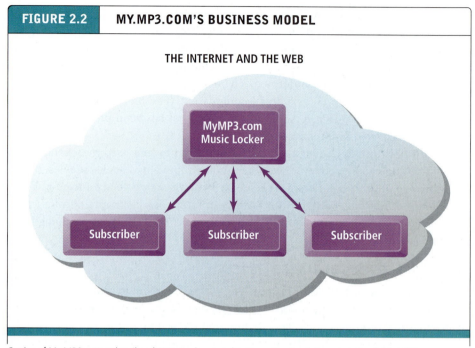

FIGURE 2.2	MY.MP3.COM'S BUSINESS MODEL

THE INTERNET AND THE WEB

Copies of My.MP3.com subscribers' CDs can be stored in the subscriber's "music locker." My.MP3.com software then permits the subscriber to download and play the music from any computer on the Web, or to make a CD copy on their PC. Also, a user who has purchased a music CD online with a credit card at the site can immediately listen to the MP3 version of the CD online.

works have limited bandwidth capacity, soon their capacity will increase significantly. These technologies have already taken off in Japan and Europe, and will expand greatly in the United States in a few years.

In general, wireless Web technology will enable the extension of existing Web business models to service the mobile work force and consumer of the future. For instance, Amazon.com recently made its site accessible by wireless mobile devices. Currently, there are many more cell phone subscribers than there are Internet users, with an estimated 800 million cell phone users worldwide in 2001, versus roughly 400 million Internet users. Forecasters predict that the number of mobile users will rise to more than one billion by 2002 (Micrologic Research, 2001). When cell phones finally become truly Web-ready, a development expected within the next several years, analysts predict an explosion of interest in m-commerce.

However, as with all areas of e-commerce, the challenge for businesses will be finding ways to use m-commerce to make money. With cell phone service providers in the United States currently charging relatively high per-minute fees, users have little incentive to use mobile devices to access the Internet for any lengthy period of time. However, a shift to flat-fee charges — which consumers are demanding — is

WHO'S CALLING — WIRELESS PRIVACY

You're walking past the local Pizza Hut and your cell phone rings. Who's calling? No, it's not your significant other or a parent or friend. It's Pizza Hut. They just wanted to let you know that pizzas are on sale — two for one, until 6 p.m. today.

This scenario might seem far-fetched, but it's just around the corner. By October 2001, all wireless companies will be required to have global-positioning-system (GPS) or other technologies in place to identify the location of people who dial 911 on their cell phones.

While the primary goal is enhanced public safety, companies are already developing business models centered around applications that will allow them to exploit the technology. And with over 100 million cell phone users in the United States today and the number continuing to grow rapidly, it's not surprising that many of these business models revolve around advertising and pushing unsolicited information to a customer's mobile device.

The specter of more unsolicited, unwanted phone calls coupled with Big Brother-like location tracking has privacy advocates raising an alarm. "Developing wireless technology shows many indications of repeating two privacy disasters of the wired Internet — spam and nonconsensual tracking," said one privacy expert.

The wireless industry, mindful of the privacy issues raised in the online e-commerce context, has issued calls for stringent self-regulation in an attempt to avoid government-imposed regulation. For instance, a wireless industry trade group whose members include AT&T Wireless, Sprint, and Microsoft has recommended that consumers be given the choice as to whether they want to participate in such services.

How to implement giving consumers that choice is also controversial, however. For instance, most privacy advocates recommend a "double opt-in" system, where customers are not subjected to receiving services or information unless they specifically request them and then confirm that request. Many companies, on the other hand, would rather implement choice through an "opt-out" system, which allows them to send a customer information or services until the customer informs the company that he or she does not want to receive them.

For now, wireless location-based services remain unregulated. Will consumers be so enthralled with the idea of services tailored to their specific location that they won't mind being tracked? Privacy watchdogs don't think so and predict that any company whose business model is predicated on that assumption is underestimating the increasing sensitivity of the American public to privacy concerns in the E-commerce II era.

SOURCES: "CDT Urges FCC to Adopt Privacy Rules for Wireless Location Information," Center for Democracy and Technology, April 10, 2001; "Talking about Wireless Privacy," by Keith Perine, *Industry Standard*, December 15, 2000; "Wireless Services Hit Snags," by Carmen Nobel and Dennis Callaghan, *eWeek*, December 18, 2000; "Location Information Could Invade Wireless Privacy," by Matt Hamblen, *Computerworld*, October 5, 2000.

expected to significantly increase usage. M-commerce business models that hope to rely on push advertising, as described in *Insight on Society: Who's Calling — Wireless Privacy*, also may face an uphill battle.

E-COMMERCE ENABLERS: THE GOLD RUSH MODEL

Of the nearly 500,000 miners who descended on California in the Gold Rush of 1849, fewer than 1% ever achieved significant wealth. However, the banking firms, shipping companies, hardware companies, real estate speculators, and clothing companies such as Levi Strauss built long-lasting fortunes. Likewise in e-commerce. No discussion of e-commerce business models would be complete without mention of a group of companies whose business model is focused on providing the infrastructure necessary for e-commerce companies to exist, grow, and prosper. These are the *e-commerce enablers*: the Internet infrastructure companies. They provide the hardware, operating system software, networks and communications technology, applications software, Web designs, consulting services and other tools that make e-commerce over the Web possible. (See Table 2.6.) While these firms may not be conducting e-commerce per se (although in many instances, e-commerce in its traditional sense is in fact one of their sales channels), they as a group have perhaps profited the most from the development of e-commerce. We will discuss many of these players in the following chapters.

TABLE 2.6	E-COMMERCE ENABLERS
INFRASTRUCTURE	**PLAYERS**
Hardware: Web Servers	IBM, Sun, Compaq, Dell
Software: Operating Systems and Server Software	Microsoft, Sun, Apache Software Foundation
Networking: Routers	Cisco
Security: Encryption Software	CheckPoint, VeriSign
E-commerce Software Systems (B2C, B2B)	IBM, Microsoft, iPlanet, CommerceNet, Ariba
Streaming Media Solutions	Real Networks, Microsoft
Customer Relationship Management Software	PeopleSoft
Payment Systems	PayPal, CyberCash
Performance Enhancement	Akamai, Cache Flow, Inktomi, Cidera, Digital Island
Databases	Oracle, Sybase
Hosting Services	Exodus, Equinex, Global Crossing

2.5 HOW THE INTERNET AND THE WEB CHANGE BUSINESS: BASIC BUSINESS CONCEPTS

Now that you have a clear grasp of the variety of business models used by e-commerce firms, you also need to understand how the Internet and the Web have changed the business environment in the last decade, including industry structures, industry and firm operations (value chains), and business strategy. We will return to these concepts throughout the book as we explore the e-commerce phenomenon.

Recall Table 1.1 in Chapter 1 that describes the truly unique features of e-commerce technology. Table 2.7 suggests some of the implications of each unique feature for the overall business environment — industry structure, business operations, and strategies.

TABLE 2.7	SEVEN UNIQUE FEATURES OF E-COMMERCE TECHNOLOGY
FEATURE	SELECTED IMPACTS ON BUSINESS ENVIRONMENT
Ubiquity	Alters industry structure by creating new marketing channels and expanding size of overall market. Creates new efficiencies in industry operations and lowers costs of firms' sales operations. Enables new differentiation strategies.
Global reach	Changes industry structure by lowering barriers to entry, but greatly expands market at the same time. Lowers cost of industry and firm operations through production and sales efficiencies. Enables competition on global scope.
Universal standards	Changes industry structure by lowering barriers to entry and intensifying competition within an industry. Lowers costs of industry and firm operations by lowering computing and communications costs. Enables broad-scope strategies.
Richness	Alters industry structure by reducing strength of powerful distribution channels. Changes industry and firm operations cost by lessening reliance on sales forces. Enhances post-sales support strategies.
Interactivity	Alters industry structure by reducing threat of substitutes through enhanced customization. Reduces industry and firm costs by lessening reliance on sales forces. Enables differentiation strategies.
Personalization/ Customization	Alters industry structure by reducing threats of substitutes, raising barriers to entry. Reduces value chain costs in industry and firm by lessening reliance on sales forces.
Information density	Changes industry structure by weakening powerful sales channels, shifting bargaining power to consumer. Reduces industry and firm operations costs by lowering costs of obtaining, processing, and distributing information about suppliers and consumers.

INDUSTRY STRUCTURE

industry structure
refers to the nature of the players in an industry and their relative bargaining power

E-commerce changes industry structure, in some industries more than others. **Industry structure** refers to the nature of the players in an industry and their relative bargaining power. An industry's structure is characterized by five forces: *rivalry* among existing competitors, the *threat of substitute products*, *barriers to entry* into the industry, the *bargaining power of suppliers*, and the *bargaining power of buyers*. When you describe an industry's structure, you are describing the general business environment in an industry, and the overall profitability of doing business in that environment. E-commerce has the potential to change the relative strength of these competitive forces. (See Figure 2.3.)

industry structural analysis
an effort to understand and describe the nature of competition in an industry, the nature of substitute products, the barriers to entry, and the relative strength of consumers and suppliers

When you consider a business model and its potential long-term profitability, you should always perform an industry structural analysis. An **industry structural analysis** is an effort to understand and describe the nature of competition in an industry, the nature of substitute products, the barriers to entry, and the relative strength of consumers and suppliers.

E-commerce can affect the structure of industries in very different ways. Some industries — such as the popular music industry — have been deeply affected as new technology-based competitors such as Napster entered the industry and consumers

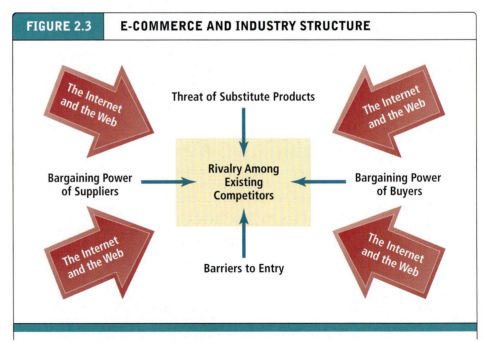

| FIGURE 2.3 | E-COMMERCE AND INDUSTRY STRUCTURE |

E-commerce technologies impact an industry's structure.
SOURCE: Adapted from Porter, March 2001.

began to use the Internet to bypass traditional music distributors and producers entirely. Other industries, such as the chemical or automobile industry, have not been affected as much by e-commerce because e-commerce technology has not fundamentally altered the competitive forces — the bargaining power of suppliers, barriers to entry, bargaining power of buyers, the threat of substitutes, or the rivalry among competitors — within the industry.

New forms of distribution created by new market entrants can completely change the competitive forces in an industry. For instance, if a software firm such as Microsoft discovers that consumers will gladly substitute a $50 or even free encyclopedia on a CD-ROM (a digital information product) for a $2,500 set of Britannica encyclopedias (a physical information product), then the competitive forces in the encyclopedia industry are radically changed. Even if the substitute is an inferior product, consumers are able to satisfy their anxieties about their children's education at a much lower cost (Gerace, 1999).

Inter-firm rivalry (competition) is one area of the business environment where e-commerce technologies have had an impact on most industries. It has been relatively easy for existing firms to adopt e-commerce technology and attempt to use it to achieve competitive advantage vis-à-vis rivals. For instance, the Internet inherently changes the scope of competition from local and regional to national and global. Because consumers have access to global price information, the Internet produces pressures on firms to compete by lowering prices (and lowering profits). On the other hand, the Internet has made it possible for some firms to differentiate their product or services from others. Amazon.com has patented one-click purchasing for instance, while eBay has created a unique, easy-to-use interface and a differentiating brand name. REI, Inc. — a specialty mountain climbing-oriented sporting goods company — has been able to use its Web site to maintain its strong niche focus on outdoor gear.

It is impossible to determine if e-commerce technologies have had an overall positive or negative impact on firm profitability. Each industry is unique, so it is necessary to perform a separate analysis for each one. Clearly, in some industries, in particular information product industries, such as the music, newspaper, book, and software industries, as well as other information-intense industries such as financial services, e-commerce has shaken the foundations of the industry. In these industries, the power of consumers has grown relative to providers, prices have fallen, and overall profitability has been challenged. Nevertheless, despite firms such as Napster and other online content distributors, thus far, profits of music and book publishers have remained relatively stable. In other industries, especially manufacturing, the Internet has not greatly changed relationships with buyers, but has changed relationships with suppliers. Increasingly, manufacturing firms in entire industries have banded together to aggregate purchases, create industry digital exchanges or marketplaces, and outsource industrial processes in order to obtain better prices from suppliers. Throughout this book we will document these changes.

INDUSTRY VALUE CHAINS

While an industry structural analysis helps us understand the impact of e-commerce technology on the overall business environment in an industry, a more detailed industry value chain analysis can help identify more precisely just how e-commerce may change business operations at the industry level (Benjamin and Wigand, 1995). One of the basic tools for understanding the impact of information technology on industry and firm operations is the value chain. The concept of a value chain is quite simple: A **value chain** is the set of activities performed in an industry or in a firm that transforms raw inputs into final products and services. Each of these activities adds economic value to the final product; hence, the term *value chain* as an interconnected set of value-adding activities. Figure 2.4 illustrates the six generic players in an industry value chain: suppliers, manufacturers, transporters, distributors, retailers, and customers.

value chain

the set of activities performed in an industry or in a firm that transforms raw inputs into final products and services

By reducing the cost of information, the Internet offers each of the key players in an industry value chain new opportunities to maximize their positions by lowering costs and/or raising prices. For instance, manufacturers can reduce costs they pay for goods by developing Web-based B2B exchanges with their suppliers. Manufacturers can develop direct relationships with their customers through their own Web sites, bypassing the costs of distributors and retailers. Distributors can develop highly efficient inventory management systems to reduce their costs; retailers can develop

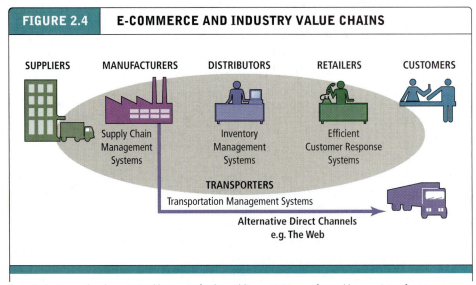

| FIGURE 2.4 | E-COMMERCE AND INDUSTRY VALUE CHAINS |

Every industry can be characterized by a set of value-adding activities performed by a variety of actors. E-commerce potentially affects the capabilities of each player as well as the overall operational efficiency of the industry.

highly efficient customer relationship management systems to strengthen their service to customers. Customers in turn can use the Web to search for best quality, delivery, and prices, thereby lowering their transaction costs and reducing prices they pay for final goods. Finally, the operational efficiency of the entire industry can increase, lowering prices and adding value to consumers, and helping the industry to compete with alternative industries. Dell Computer Corporation, for instance, employs a number of these stratagems, most notably a sales model for personal computers that bypasses traditional retail distribution channels by selling directly to consumers over the Web. Dell also has developed a highly efficient supply chain management system to reduce its costs, and an equally efficient customer relationship management system to support customers and add to the value of its products.

FIRM VALUE CHAINS

The concept of value chain can be used to analyze a single firm's operational efficiency as well. The question here is: How does e-commerce technology potentially affect the value chains of firms within an industry? A **firm value chain** is the set of activities a firm engages in to create final products from raw inputs. Each step in the process of production adds value to the final product. In addition, firms develop support activities that coordinate the production process and contribute to overall operational efficiency. Figure 2.5 illustrates the key steps and support activities in a firm's value chain.

firm value chain
the set of activities a firm engages in to create final products from raw inputs

The Internet offers firms many opportunities to increase their operational efficiency and differentiate their products. For instance, firms can use the Internet's communications efficiency to outsource some primary and secondary activities to specialized, more efficient providers without such outsourcing being visible to the consumer. In addition, firms can use the Internet to more precisely coordinate the steps in the value chains and reduce their costs. Finally, firms can use the Internet to provide users with more differentiated and high-value products. For instance, Amazon.com uses the Internet to provide consumers with a much larger inventory of books to choose from, at a lower cost, than traditional book stores. It also provides many services — such as instantly available professional and consumer reviews, and information on buying patterns of other consumers — that traditional bookstores cannot.

BUSINESS STRATEGY

A **business strategy** is a set of plans for achieving superior long-term returns on the capital invested in a business firm. A business strategy is therefore a plan for making profits in a competitive environment over the long term. **Profit** is simply the difference between the price a firm is able to charge for its products and the cost of producing and distributing goods. Profit represents economic value. Economic value is created anytime customers are willing to pay more for a product than it costs to pro-

business strategy
a set of plans for achieving superior long-term returns on the capital invested in a business firm

profit
the difference between the price a firm is able to charge for its products and the cost of producing and distributing goods

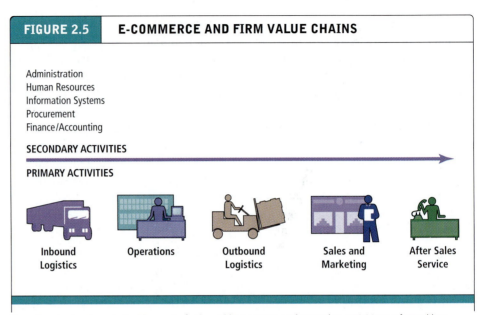

FIGURE 2.5	E-COMMERCE AND FIRM VALUE CHAINS

Administration
Human Resources
Information Systems
Procurement
Finance/Accounting

SECONDARY ACTIVITIES

PRIMARY ACTIVITIES

| **Inbound Logistics** | **Operations** | **Outbound Logistics** | **Sales and Marketing** | **After Sales Service** |

Every firm can be characterized by a set of value-adding primary and secondary activities performed by a variety of actors in the firm. A simple firm value chain performs five primary value-adding steps: inbound logistics, operations, outbound logistics, sales and marketing, and after-sales support.
SOURCE: Porter, 1980; Porter and Millar, 1985.

duce. Why would anyone pay more for a product than it costs to produce? There are multiple answers. The product may be unique (there are no other suppliers), it may be the least costly product of its type available, you may be able to purchase the product anywhere in the world, or it may satisfy some unique needs that other products do not. Each of these sources of economic value define a firm's strategy for positioning its products in the marketplace. There are four generic strategies for achieving a profitable business: *differentiation, cost, scope,* and *focus.* We describe each of these below. The specific strategies that a firm follows will depend on the product, the industry, and the marketplace where competition is encountered. The Internet is a unique marketplace, and we can expect that successful firms will devise Internet-specific strategies that leverage its capabilities (Porter, 2001).

Differentiation refers to all the ways producers can make their products unique and distinguish them from those of competitors. The opposite of differentiation is **commoditization**—a situation where there are no differences among products or services, and the only basis of choosing a product is price. As economists tell us, when price alone becomes the basis of competition and there are many suppliers and many customers, eventually the price of the good falls to the cost to produce it (marginal revenues from the nth unit equal marginal costs). And then profits are zero! This

differentiation

refers to all the ways producers can make their products unique and different to distinguish them from those of competitors

commoditization

a situation where there are no differences among products or services, and the only basis of choosing products is price is an unacceptable situation for any business person. The solution is to differentiate your product and to create a monopoly-like situation where you are the only supplier.

There are many ways businesses differentiate their products. A business may start with a core generic product, but then create expectations among users about the "experience" of consuming the product — "Nothing refreshes like a Coke!" or "Nothing equals the experience of driving a BMW." Businesses may also augment products by adding features to make them different from those of competitors. And businesses can differentiate their products further by enhancing the products' abilities to solve related consumer problems. For instance, tax programs such as Turbo Tax can import data from spreadsheet programs, as well as be used to electronically file tax returns. These capabilities are enhancements to the product that solve a customer's problems. The purpose of marketing is to create these differentiation features and to make the consumer aware of the unique qualities of products, creating in the process a "brand" that stands for these features. We discuss marketing and branding in Chapter 8.

In their totality, the differentiation features of a product constitute the customer value proposition we described in earlier sections of this chapter. The Internet and the Web offer some truly unique ways to differentiate products. The ability of the Web to personalize the shopping experience and to customize the product or service to the particular demands of each consumer are perhaps the most significant ways in which the Web can be used to differentiate products. E-commerce businesses can also differentiate products by leveraging the ubiquitous nature of the Web (by making it possible to purchase the product from home, work, or on the road); the global reach of the Web (by making it possible to purchase the product anywhere in the world); richness and interactivity (by creating Web-based experiences for people who use the product, such as unique interactive content, videos, stories about users, and reviews of users); and information density (by storing and processing information for consumers of the product, such as warranty information on all products purchased through a site or income tax information online).

Adopting a strategy of cost competition means a business has discovered some unique set of business processes or resources that other firms cannot obtain in the marketplace. Business processes are the atomic units of the value chain. For instance, the set of value-creating activities called Inbound Logistics in Figure 2.5 is in reality composed of many different collections of activities performed by people on the loading docks and in the warehouses. These different collections of activities are called *business processes* — the set of steps or procedures required to perform the various elements of the value chain.

When a firm discovers a new, more efficient set of business processes, it can obtain a cost advantage over competitors. Then it can attract customers by charging a lower price, while still making a handsome profit. Eventually, its competitors go out of business as the market decisively tilts toward the lowest cost provider. Or, when a business discovers a unique resource, or lower cost supplier, it can also compete effectively on cost. For instance, switching production to low wage cost areas of the world is one way to lower costs.

Competing on cost can be a short-lived affair and very tricky. Competitors can also discover the same or different efficiencies in production. And competitors can also move production to low-cost areas of the world. Also, competitors may decide to lose money for a period as they compete on cost.

The Internet offers some new ways to compete on cost — at least in the short term. Firms can leverage the Internet's ubiquity by lowering the costs of order entry (the customer fills out all the forms, so there is no order entry department); leverage global reach and universal standards by having a single order entry system world-wide; leverage richness, interactivity, and personalization by creating customer profiles online and treating each individual consumer differently — without the use of an expensive sales force that performed these functions in the past; finally, firms can leverage the information intensity of the Web by providing consumers with detailed information on products, without maintaining either expensive catalogs or a sales force.

While the Internet offers powerful capabilities for intensifying cost competition, making cost competition appear to be a viable strategy, the danger is that competitors have access to the same technology. The *factor markets* — the markets where producers buy their supplies — are open to all. Assuming they have the skills and organizational will to use the technology, competitors can buy many of the same cost-reducing techniques in the marketplace. Even a skilled labor force can be purchased, ultimately. However, self-knowledge, proprietary tacit knowledge (knowledge that is not published or codified), and a loyal, skilled workforce are in the short term difficult to purchase in factor markets. Therefore, cost competition remains a viable strategy.

Two other generic business strategies are scope and focus. A *scope strategy* is a strategy to compete in all markets around the globe, rather than merely in local, regional, or national markets. The Internet's global reach, universal standards, and ubiquity can certainly be leveraged to assist businesses in becoming global competitors. Yahoo, for instance, along with all of the other top twenty e-commerce sites, has readily attained a global presence using the Internet. A *focus strategy* is a strategy to compete within a narrow market segment or product segment. This is a specialization strategy with the goal of becoming the premier provider in a narrow market. For instance, Amazon.com started out focusing on books, and later CDs (rather than attempt to become a general retail department store); L.L. Bean uses the Web to continue its historic focus on outdoor sports apparel; and W.W. Grainger — the Web's most frequently visited B2B site — focuses on a narrow market segment called MRO: maintenance, repair, and operations of commercial buildings. The Internet offers some obvious capabilities that enable a focus strategy. Firms can leverage the Web's rich interactive features to create highly focused messages to different market segments; the information intensity of the Web makes it possible to focus e-mail and other marketing campaigns on small market segments; personalization — and related customization — means the same product can be customized and personalized to fulfill the very focused needs of specific market segments and consumers.

Industry structure, industry and firm value chains, and business strategy are central business concepts used throughout this book to analyze the viability of and prospects for e-commerce sites. In particular, the signature case studies found at the end of each chapter are followed with questions that may ask you to identify and analyze the competitive forces in the case, or how the case illustrates changes in industry structure, industry and firm value chains, and business strategy.

Priceline.com
Can This Business Model Be Saved?

Priceline.com is one of the Web's most well-known companies. Its "name your price" reverse-auction pricing system (what the company refers to as a *demand collection* system) is a unique business model that uses the information sharing and communications power of the Internet to create a new way of pricing products and services. It offers a compelling value proposition to customers, allowing them to save money by trading off flexibility about brands, product features, and/or sellers in return for lower prices; vendors also can gain additional revenue by selling products they might not otherwise be able to sell by accepting below-retail price offers, without disrupting their existing distribution channels or retail pricing structure. Since beginning operations in April 1998, Priceline has registered over nine million users and sold six million airline tickets. Sounds like a promising e-commerce story.

However, Priceline has yet to achieve profitability, losing millions in the process. Its stock price has fallen from a high in the mid-$100s to a low in the single digits. Key executives have resigned. Headlines such as "Priceline on the Ropes" and "Curtain Call for Priceline.com" predominate.

The question is: Can Priceline survive? What went wrong with a business model that seemed so promising?

Priceline commenced operations on April 6, 1998, with the sale of airline tickets. To purchase a ticket, a customer logs onto Priceline.com's Web site, specifies the origin and destination of the trip, the dates he or she wishes to depart, the price the customer is willing to pay, and a valid credit card to guarantee the offer. The customer must agree to fly on any major airline, leave at any time of day between 6 A.M. and 10 P.M., accept at least one stop or connection, receive no frequent flier miles or upgrades, and accept tickets that cannot be refunded or changed. Upon receiving the offer, Priceline checks the available fares, rules, and inventory provided by its participating airlines and determines whether it will fulfill the order at the requested price. If so, it notifies the customer within an hour that his or her offer has been accepted.

On the consumer side, a central premise of Priceline's business model is that in many product and service categories, there are a significant number of consumers for whom brands, product features, and sellers are interchangeable, particularly if agreeing to a substitution among brands or sellers will result in saving money. On the vendor side, the Priceline business model is predicated on the assumption that sellers almost invariably have excess inventory or capacity that they would sell at lower prices, if they could do so without either lowering their prices to retail customers or advertising that lower prices are available. Priceline believed that its business model was ideally suited to industries characterized by expiring or rapidly aging inventory (for example, airline seats not sold by the time a flight takes off or hotel rooms not rented), although it did not think that it would be limited to such industries.

Priceline extended its system to hotel reservations in October 1998, and in January 1999 introduced home financing services. It went public in March 1999, and later that year, it added rental cars and even new cars to the mix. To promote its products and the Priceline brand, Priceline embarked on an extensive (and expensive) advertising campaign, hiring William Shatner to become the voice of Priceline, and it quickly became one of the most recognizable brands on the Web.

At the beginning of 2000, Priceline licensed its patented "Name Your Own Price" business model to several affiliates, including Priceline Webhouse Club, which attempted to extend the model to groceries and gasoline, and Perfect Yardsale, which used the model to sell used goods online, and added long distance calling and travel insurance. Priceline also had ambitious plans to expand internationally, and in 2000

licensed its business model to companies planning to set up similar operations in Asia and Australia.

However, by fall 2000, the picture no longer looked so rosy. In October 2000, after only 10 months of operation, Priceline's affiliate Priceline Webhouse Club, unable to raise additional financing, shut down its business, after running through $363 million. The financial climate at the time, with its renewed emphasis on profitability, made it impossible for Jay Walker, Priceline's founder, to raise the additional hundreds of millions that would be required before Webhouse might become profitable. Walker did not see the closure as a failure of the Priceline business model, however. Instead, he characterized it as the result of the "fickle sentiments" of investors: "It's like having your baseball game rained out when you're ahead," he said, "It doesn't say anything about your ball team. It's just about the weather."

Many analysts did not accept Walker's characterization. Instead, they pointed to other factors. First, many of the major manufacturers of food and dried goods chose not to participate in Priceline Webhouse. So, to generate consumer interest, Priceline Webhouse subsidized discounts on most products itself. Although some major manufacturers, such as Kellogg's and Hershey's, did eventually sign up, many, such as Kraft, Procter & Gamble, and Lever Brothers, did not. The second miscalculation was that bidding on groceries and gasoline did not exactly provide a "hassle-free" way to shop. Customers were required to bid on and pay for groceries online, then use a special identification card to pick them up at a participating supermarket. If the particular items purchased were not available at the store, the customer would either have to go to another store, or return at another time. To many, the demise of Priceline Webhouse highlighted potential cracks in the Priceline business model and raised strong concerns about its ultimate extensibility.

Even Priceline's core business was facing problems. It missed earnings estimates for both the 3rd and 4th quarters in 2000. It received major adverse publicity when the Connecticut Better Business Bureau expelled it for three months that Fall after receiving more than 300 complaints, ranging from misrepresentation of services to failure to make promised refunds. Its Chief Financial Officer, Heidi Miller, quit in November and its Chairman and founder, Jay Walker stepped down in December. An airline-backed Web site, Hotwired.com, which also offered discount tickets and hotel reservations, formally opened for business, offering new competition to Priceline on both its supply side and its sell side.

Opinions differ on how Priceline might pull out of its tailspin. Some feel that Priceline should focus solely on its core airline-ticket business, where it presumably has the greatest chance of making its model a success. Analysts noted that the ticket business has strong profit potential, but that Priceline's failed efforts to expand had drained those profits. Others note that investors had been initially attracted to Priceline based on the assumption that the business model could in fact be extended to other industries. If it cannot, then the company would become nothing more than a glorified online travel agency.

SOURCES: "Is Priceline Back? Travel Site Beats Street, Predicts Q2 Profit," by Michael Mahoney, *E-Commerce Times* , May 2, 2001; "Priceline.com Narrows Net Losses, But Still Fails to Meet Forecasts," by Julia Angwin, *Wall Street Journal*, February 16, 2001; "Priceline Reports Losses and Slow Sales," by Alex Berenson, *New York Times*, February 16, 2001; "Curtain Call For Priceline.com," by Dan Selicaro, *Upside*, February 2001; "Priceline Wonders if System Can Be Expanded Profitably," by Julia Angwin, *Wall Street Journal*, January 25, 2001; "Priceline Founder Exits Board," by Clare Saliba and Nora Macaluso, *E-Commerce Times*, December 29, 2000; "Priceline on the Ropes," by Ronna Abramson and Ben Hammer, *Industry Standard*, October 16, 2000; Priceline.com Incorporated 10-Q, filed with the Securities and Exchange Commission (SEC) on October 30, 2000; Priceline.com Incorporated 10-K, filed with the SEC on March 30, 2000; Priceline.com Incorporated S-1/A filed with the SEC on August 10, 1999.

Priceline's announced plan is to curtail plans for expansion into nontravel areas — but only for the time being. Once it is profitable, they intend to try to grow again, but in a "careful, low expense" way, says its Chairman, Richard Braddock. "Priceline will entertain selective expansion … with stringent financial controls. We're going to make money on this and move forward."

Early indications are that Priceline's plans may be working. In May 2001, it announced a loss for the first quarter of 2001 that was lower than expected by Wall Street analysts, and that it expected to show a profit for the first time for the second quarter of 2001. But although right now, it looks as if Priceline will survive, the question still remains: Will it ever really succeed?

Case Study Questions

1. What are the core components of Priceline.com's business model?

2. Do you think Priceline will ultimately succeed or fail? Why?

3. How has Priceline impacted the travel services industry?

4. Follow up on developments at Priceline since June 2001, when this case study was prepared. Has its business model and/or strategy changed at all, and if so, how? Who are its strongest competitors? Has it achieved profitability or is it still operating at a loss?

2.7 REVIEW

KEY CONCEPTS

■ Identify the key components of e-commerce business models.

A successful business model effectively addresses eight key elements:

- *Value proposition* — how a company's product or service fulfills the needs of customers. Typical e-commerce value propositions include personalization, customization, convenience, and reduction of product search and price delivery costs.
- *Revenue model* — how the company plans to make money from its operations. Major e-commerce revenue models include the advertising model, subscription model, transaction fee model, sales model, and affiliate model.
- *Market opportunity* — the revenue potential within a company's intended marketspace.

- *Competitive environment* — the direct and indirect competitors doing business in the same marketspace, including how many there are and how profitable they are.
- *Competitive advantage* — the factors that differentiate the business from its competition, enabling it to provide a superior product at a lower cost.
- *Market strategy* — the plan a company develops that outlines how it will enter a market and attract customers.
- *Organizational development* — the process of defining all the functions within a business and the skills necessary to perform each job, as well as the process of recruiting and hiring strong employees.
- *Management team* — the group of individuals retained to guide the company's growth and expansion.

■ **Describe the major B2C business models.**

There are a number of different business models being used in the B2C e-commerce arena. The major models include the following:

- *Portal* — offers powerful search tools plus an integrated package of content and services; typically utilizes a combined subscription/advertising revenue/transaction fee model; may be general or specialized (vortal).
- *E-tailer* — online version of traditional retailer; includes virtual merchants (online retail store only), clicks and mortar e-tailers (online distribution channel for a company that also has physical stores); catalog merchants (online version of direct mail catalog); online malls (online version of mall); manufacturers selling directly over the Web.
- *Content provider* — information and entertainment companies that provide digital content over the Web; typically utilizes an advertising, subscription, or affiliate referral fee revenue model.
- *Transaction broker* — processes online sales transactions; typically utilizes a transaction fee revenue model.
- *Market creator* — uses Internet technology to create markets that bring buyers and sellers together; typically utilizes a transaction fee revenue model.
- *Service provider* — offers services online.
- *Community provider* — provides an online community of like-minded individuals for networking and information sharing; revenue is generated by referral fees, advertising, and subscriptions.

■ **Describe the major B2B business models.**

The major business models used to date in the B2B arena include:

- *Hub*, also known as *marketplace/exchange* — electronic marketplace where suppliers and commercial purchasers can conduct transactions; may be general (a horizontal marketplace) or specialized (a vertical marketplace).
- *E-distributor* — supplies products directly to individual businesses.
- *B2B service provider* — sells business services to other firms.

- *Matchmaker* — links businesses together, charges transaction or usage fees.
- *Infomediary* — gathers information and sells it to businesses.

■ **Recognize business models in other emerging areas of e-commerce.**

A variety of business models can be found in the consumer-to-consumer
e-commerce, peer-to-peer e-commerce, and m-commerce areas:

- *C2C business models* connect consumers with other consumers. The most successful has been the market creator business model used by eBay.com and
  Half.com.
- *P2P business models* enable consumers to share files and services via the Web
  without common servers. A challenge has been finding a revenue model that
  works.
- *M-commerce business models* take traditional e-commerce models and leverage
  emerging wireless technologies to permit mobile access to the Web.
- *E-commerce enablers' business models* focus on providing the infrastructure necessary for e-commerce companies to exist, grow, and prosper.

■ **Understand key business concepts and strategies applicable to e-commerce.**

The Internet and the Web have had a major impact on the business environment in
the last decade, and has affected:

- *Industry structure* — the nature of players in an industry and their relative bargaining power — by changing the basis of competition among rivals, the barriers
  to entry, the threat of new substitute products, the strength of suppliers, and the
  bargaining power of buyers.
- *Industry value chains* — the set of activities performed in an industry by suppliers, manufacturers, transporters, distributors and retailers that transforms raw
  inputs into final products and services — by reducing the cost of information and
  other transaction costs
- *Firm value chains* — the set of activities performed within an individual firm to
  create final products from raw inputs — by increasing operational efficiency.
- *Business strategy* — a set of plans for achieving superior long-term returns on the
  capital invested in a firm — by offering unique ways to differentiate products,
  obtain cost advantages, compete globally, or compete in a narrow market or
  product segment.

QUESTIONS

1. What is a business model? How does it differ from a business plan?
2. What are the eight key components of an effective business model?
3. What are Amazon.com's primary customer value propositions?
4. Describe the five primary revenue models used by e-commerce firms.
5. Why is targeting a market niche generally smarter for a community provider
   than targeting a large market segment?

6. Besides music, what other forms of information could be shared through peer-to-peer sites such as Napster and MP3, using shareware such as Gnutella?
7. Would you say that Amazon.com and Half.com are direct or indirect competitors? (You may have to visit the Web sites to answer.)
8. What are some of the specific ways that a company can obtain a competitive advantage?
9. Besides advertising and product sampling, which Yahoo and AOL have used almost exclusively as their marketing strategy, what are some other market strategies?
10. What elements of Kozmo's business model may have been faulty?
11. Why is it difficult to categorize e-commerce business models?
12. Besides the examples given in the chapter, what are some other examples of vertical and horizontal portals in existence today?
13. What are the major differences between virtual storefronts, such as marthastewart.com, and clicks and bricks operations, such as walmart.com? What are the advantages and disadvantages of each?
14. Besides news and articles, what other forms of information or content do content providers offer?
15. What is a reverse auction? What company is an example of this type of business?
16. What are the key success factors for B2B hubs? How are they different from portals?
17. What is an application service provider?
18. What are some business models seen in the consumer-to-consumer and peer-to-peer e-commerce areas?
19. How have the unique features of e-commerce technology changed industry structure?
20. Who are the major players in an industry value chain and how are they impacted by e-commerce technology?
21. What are four generic business strategies for achieving a profitable business?

PROJECTS

1. Select an e-commerce company. Visit its Web site and describe its business model based on the information you find there. Identify its customer value proposition, its revenue model, the marketspace it operates in, who its main competitors are, any comparative advantages you believe the company possesses, and what its market strategy appears to be. Also try to locate information about the company's management team and organizational structure (check for a page labeled "the Company," "About Us," or something similar).

2. Examine the experience of shopping on the Web versus shopping in a traditional environment. Imagine that you have decided to purchase a digital camera (or any other item of your choosing). First, shop for the camera in a

traditional manner. Describe how you would do so (for example, how you would gather the necessary information you would need to choose a particular item, what stores you would visit, how long it would take, prices, etc.). Next, shop for the item on the Web. Compare and contrast your experiences. What were the advantages and disadvantages of each? Which did you prefer and why?

3. Visit the eBay.com Web site and look at the many types of auctions available. If you were considering establishing a rival specialized online auction business, what are the top three market opportunities you would pursue, based on the goods and auction community in evidence at eBay? Prepare a slide presentation to support your analysis and approach.

4. During the E-commerce I era, first mover advantage was touted as one way to success. On the other hand, some suggest that being a market follower can yield rewards as well. Which approach has proven to be more successful — first mover or follower? Choose two e-commerce companies that prove your point, and prepare a brief presentation to explain your analysis and position.

5. Prepare a 3- to 5 page research report on the current and potential future impacts of e-commerce technology on the publishing industry.

WEB SITE RESOURCES www.LearnE-commerce.net

- News: Weekly updates on topics relevant to the material in this chapter.
- Video Lecture: Professor Ken Laudon summarizes the key concepts of the chapter.
- Research: Abstracts and links to articles referenced in the chapter, as well as other relevant research.
- PowerPoint slides: Illustrations from the chapter and more
- Additional projects and exercises

PART **2**

Technology
Infrastructure
for E-commerce

CHAPTER 3

The Internet and World Wide Web: E-commerce Infrastructure

Akamai Technologies:
Speeding Internet Performance with Math

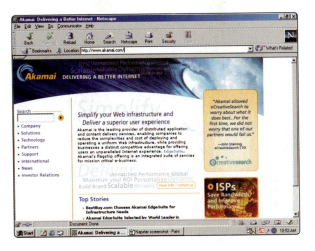

Most people love the Web, but hate the wait. Studies have shown that most people won't stay on a site if the page and its contents take more than eight seconds to load. That's bad news for anyone seeking to use the Web for e-commerce.

Slow-loading Web pages sometimes result from poor design, but more often than not, the problem stems from the underlying infrastructure of the Internet. As you'll learn in this chapter, the Internet was originally developed to carry text-based e-mail messages among a relatively small group of researchers, not bandwidth-hogging graphics, sound, and video files to millions of people.

Akamai Technologies is seeking to provide a solution by improving the "World Wide Wait" with existing Internet infrastructure technologies. Akamai (which means intelligent, clever, or "cool" in Hawaiian) was founded by Tom Leighton, an MIT professor of applied mathematics, and Daniel Lewin, an MIT grad student. Leighton and Lewin wondered: What if Web traffic could be monitored all over the world, just like traffic reporters monitor road traffic, and users seeking access to congested sites diverted on the fly to less busy Web servers (computers that "serve up" Web pages)? A simple idea in concept, but difficult to implement. It took three years to perfect mathematical algorithms that could perform such complex routing in real time.

Officially launched in August 1998, Akamai's software constantly monitors the entire Internet, locating potential sluggish areas and devising faster routes for information to travel. Frequently used portions of a client's Web site, or large files that would be difficult to send to users quickly, are stored on Akamai's 8000 servers in over 50 countries around the world. Akamai's software

SOURCES: Akamai Technologies Inc. Report 10-K, filed with the Securities and Exchange Commission on February 12, 2001; "Tom Leighton Unclogging the Web's Plumbing," by Dori Jones Yang, *U.S. News & World Report*, December 25, 2000; "Content Bridge over Troubled Waters," by Elinor Abreu and Jason Krause *The Industry Standard*, February 19, 2001; "On the Edge: An Interview with Akamai's George Conrades," by Nicholas G. Carr, *Harvard Business Review*, May-June 2000; "Product or Service? Internet Infrastructure's Battling Business Model," by Lawrence M. Fisher, Business+Strategy /Booz Allen Hamilton, Fourth Quarter 2000.

determines which server is optimum for the user and then transmits the "Akamaized" content locally.

Akamai passed its most visible public test in October 1999, when it supported the Webcast of NetAid's Concert against Hunger, which attracted millions of hits within a very short period of time. It also helped client Barnes & Noble cut the average wait time on its home page from four seconds at Christmas 1999 to 1.5 seconds by Christmas 2000, and assisted CNN.com in dealing with the sudden surge when millions of voters went looking for election day updates virtually simultaneously in November 2000.

Akamai makes money by selling its service to a wide range of clients, from Yahoo to Nasdaq to Martha Stewart Living. In 2000, it had revenues of approximately $90 million. However, Akamai is not alone in providing enhanced Web site performance. Its closest competitor is Inktomi, which uses a similar technology. The field is also likely to continue to attract further entrants. As one analyst notes, the Web has yet to approach performance standards that were once commonplace in the days of mainframe computers, and "until typical performance gets down to the subsecond range, anyone who can improve performance would have a good business."

The Akamai story illustrates how much the Internet as it currently exists (what we call *Internet I*) and the World Wide Web are strained by the extraordinary growth in Web traffic over the last few years, as millions of people sign on to a small number of high-traffic sites such as Barnesandnoble.com, Amazon.com, and others. But equally important, the Akamai case also illustrates how important it is for a business to understand how the Internet and related technologies work. Implementing key Web business strategies such as personalization, customization, market segmentation, and price discrimination all require that business people understand Web technology. Looking forward five years to the emerging Internet II of 2006, the business strategies of the future will require a firm understanding of these new technologies.

This chapter examines the Internet and World Wide Web of today and tomorrow, how it evolved, how it works, and how the present and future infrastructure of the Internet and the Web enables e-commerce.

3.1 THE INTERNET: TECHNOLOGY BACKGROUND

What is the Internet? Where did it come from, and how did it support the growth of the World Wide Web? What are the Internet's most important operating principles?

As noted in Chapter 1, the **Internet** is an interconnected network of thousands of networks and millions of computers (sometimes called *host computers* or just *hosts*) linking businesses, educational institutions, government agencies, and individuals together. The Internet provides around 400 million people around the world (and over 170 million people in the United States) with services such as e-mail, newsgroups, shopping, research, instant messaging, music, videos, and news. No one organization controls the Internet or how it functions, nor is it owned by anybody, yet it has provided the infrastructure for a transformation in commerce, scientific research, and culture. The word *Internet* is derived from the word *internetwork* or the connecting together of two or more computer networks. The **World Wide Web**, or **Web** for short, is one of the Internet's most popular services, providing access to over one billion Web pages, which are documents created in a programming language called HTML and which can contain text, graphics, audio, video, and other objects, as well as "hyperlinks" that permit a user to jump easily from one page to another.

Internet
an interconnected network of thousands of networks and millions of computers linking businesses, educational institutions, government agencies, and individuals together

World Wide Web (Web)
one of the Internet's most popular services, providing access to over one billion Web pages

THE EVOLUTION OF THE INTERNET 1961–2000

Internet I — today's Internet — has evolved over the last forty years. In this sense, the Internet is not "new"; it did not happen yesterday. Although journalists and pundits talk glibly about "Internet" time — suggesting a fast-paced, nearly instant, worldwide global change mechanism, in fact, it has taken forty years of hard work to arrive at today's Internet.

The history of the Internet can be segmented into three phases (see Figure 3.1). In the first phase, the *Innovation Phase*, from 1961 to 1974, the fundamental building blocks of the Internet were conceptualized and then realized in actual hardware and software. The basic building blocks are: packet-switching hardware, client/server computing, and a communications protocol called TCP/IP (all described more fully below). The original purpose of the Internet, when it was conceived in the late 1960s, was to link together large mainframe computers on college campuses. This kind of one-to-one communication between campuses was previously only possible through the telephone system or postal mail.

In the second phase, the *Institutional Phase*, from 1975 to 1995, large institutions such as the Department of Defense and the National Science Foundation provided funding and legitimization for the fledging invention called the *Internet*. Once the concept of the Internet had been proven in several government-supported demonstration projects, the Department of Defense contributed a million dollars to develop the concepts and demonstration projects into a robust military communications system that could withstand nuclear war. This effort created what was then called ARPANET (Advanced Research Projects Agency Network). In 1986, the National Science Foundation assumed responsibility for the development of a civilian Internet (then called NSFNet) and began a ten-year-long $200 million expansion program.

In the third phase, the *Commercialization Phase*, from 1995–2001, government

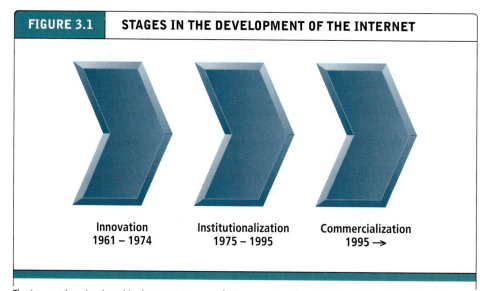

| FIGURE 3.1 | STAGES IN THE DEVELOPMENT OF THE INTERNET |

Innovation
1961 – 1974

Institutionalization
1975 – 1995

Commercialization
1995 →

The Internet has developed in three stages over a forty-year period from 1961 to 2000. In the Innovation stage, basic ideas and technologies were developed; in the Institutional stage, these ideas were brought to life; in the Commercialization stage, once the ideas and technologies had been proven, private companies brought the Internet to millions of people worldwide.

agencies encouraged private corporations to take over and expand both the Internet backbone and local service to ordinary citizens — families and individuals across America and the world who were not students on campuses. By 2000, the Internet's use had expanded well beyond military installations and research universities. The E-commerce I period begins — arguably — in 1994 with the first effort to advertise and market on the Web.

See Figure 3.2 for a closer look at the development of the Internet from 1961 on.

FIGURE 3.2	DEVELOPMENT OF THE INTERNET: TIMELINE	
YEAR	EVENT	SIGNIFICANCE
INNOVATION PHASE 1961–1974		
1961	Leonard Kleinrock (MIT) publishes a paper on "packet switching" networks.	The concept of packet switching is born.
1961	Lawrence Roberts (MIT) connects a computer in Cambridge to a computer in California using a low-speed data line.	This is the first demonstration of a wide area network[a] using telephone circuits. It demonstrated that computers could retrieve data and run programs remotely (and that the phone system was too noisy and slow for this purpose).
1962	J.C.R. Licklider (MIT) writes memos calling for a "Galactic Network" of computers.	**The vision of a global computer network is born.**
1963	Licklider heads up Department of Defense (DOD) ARPA[b] network development.	This is the beginning of military interest and funding. ARPA becomes the largest funder of early Internet efforts.
1966	Lawrence Roberts convinces ARPA to fund development of ARPANET using packet switching.	The first effort begins to build a global packet switched wide-area network.
1968	ARPA requests quotes from various companies to build packet switches.	The concept of packet switching moves toward physical reality.
1969	The first packet switches are installed at UCLA and Stanford by Bolt, Beranek and Newman (BBN), a defense contractor.	**The concept of packet switching is realized in hardware.**
1969	The first packet-switched message is sent from UCLA to Stanford.	The communications technology hardware of the Internet is born — the first "Inter Network." The questions now are: How could this new technology be used? And for what purpose?

[a] A "wide area network" is a network that connects computers and other devices over distances longer than 1,000 meters. Early "local" networks connected dumb terminals in the same building (less than 1,000 meters) to centralized mainframe computers. These early networks essentially sent keyboard and display commands back and forth from the terminals to the mainframe computers. The new wide area networks proposed in the 1960s were much more powerful: These new networks promised to permit remote computers to transfer entire files, send e-mail messages, and execute programs on a local computer.

[b] ARPA refers to the Advanced Research Projects Agency of the United States Department of Defense. ARPA is essentially the research and development unit within the Department of Defense; it invests in promising new technologies that could have military significance.

FIGURE 3.2	DEVELOPMENT OF THE INTERNET: TIMELINE (*CONTINUED*)

YEAR	EVENT	SIGNIFICANCE
1972	E-mail is invented by Ray Tomlinson of BBN. The first ARPANET application is demonstrated at ICCC[c] conference. Roberts writes the first e-mail utility program permitting listing, forwarding, and responding to e-mails.	The first "killer app" of the Internet is born.
1973	Bob Metcalfe (XeroxPARC Lab) invents Ethernet and local area networks.	**Client/server computing is invented.** Ethernet permitted the development of local area networks and client/server computing in which thousands of fully functional desktop computers could be connected into a short distance (<1,000 meters) network to share files, run applications, and send messages. Although the Apple and IBM personal computers had not yet been invented, at XeroxPARC the first powerful desktop computers were created in the late 1960s. Xerox's Ethernet StarNetwork connected these early desktop machines into a functioning office network that could share files, programs, and send messages.
1974	"Open architecture" networking and TCP/IP concepts are presented in a paper by Vint Cerf (Stanford) and Bob Kahn (BBN).	**TCP/IP invented.** The conceptual foundation for a single common communications protocol that could potentially connect any of thousands of disparate local area networks and computers, and a common addressing scheme for all computers connected to the network, is born. These developments made possible **"peer-to peer" "open" networking.** Prior to this, computers could only communicate if they shared a common proprietary network architecture, e.g., IBM's System Network Architecture. With TCP/IP, computers and networks could work together regardless of their local operating systems or network protocols.

INSTITUTIONAL PHASE 1980–1993		
1980	TCP/IP is officially adopted as the DOD standard communications protocol	The single largest computing organization in the world adopts TCP/IP and packet-switched network technology.
1980	Personal computers are invented.	Altair, Apple, and IBM personal desktop computers are invented. These computers become the foundation for today's Internet, affording millions of people access to the Internet and the Web.
1983	ARPA creates a separate military network (MILNET) and ARPANET contains only civilian university traffic.	The idea of a "civilian" Internet is born.
1983	Telnet and File Transfer Protocol (FTP) services are deployed.	Telnet permits remote computers to link into a local computer and operate programs. FTP permits easy file transfers on the Internet. These services join e-mail as new "killer apps."

[c] ICCC stands for International Computer Communication Conference, one of the first technical engineering groups devoted to communications among computers.

(continued)

FIGURE 3.2	DEVELOPMENT OF THE INTERNET: TIMELINE (*CONTINUED*)

YEAR	EVENT	SIGNIFICANCE
1984	Apple Computer releases the HyperCard program as part of its graphical user interface operating system called Macintosh.	The concept of "hyperlinked" documents and records that permit the user to jump from one page or record to another is commercially introduced.
1986	The National Science Foundation (NSF) adopts the Internet as its interuniversity network.	NSF begins $200 million program to develop a university network. It requires all universities receiving NSF funds to make access available campus-wide.
1988	NSF encourages development of private long-haul backbone communication carriers to privatize the Internet.	Private firms such as PSI and UUNet form to handle commercial Internet traffic.
1989	Tim Berners-Lee at the CERN physics lab in Switzerland proposes a worldwide network of hyperlinked documents based on a common markup language called HTML — HyperText Markup Language.	**The concept of an Internet-supported service called the World Wide Web is born.** The Web would be constructed from "pages" created in a common markup language, with "hyperlinks" that permitted easy access among the pages. The idea does not catch on rapidly and most Internet users rely on cumbersome FTP and Gopher protocols to find documents.
1990	NSF plans and assumes responsibility for civilian Internet backbone and creates NSFNET.[d] ARPANET is decommissioned.	The concept of a "civilian" Internet open to all is realized through non-military funding by NSF.
1990	The Internet backbone grows.	By 1990, the backbone had grown from six nodes connected at 56 Kbps to 21 nodes connected at 45 Mbps. 50,000 networks were now connected on all continents, with 29,000 in the United States alone.
1993	The first graphical Web browser called *Mosaic* is invented by Mark Andreesen and others at the National Center for Supercomputing at the University of Illinois.	Mosaic makes it very easy for ordinary users to connect to HTML documents anywhere on the Web. The browser-enabled Web takes off.
1994	NSF report plans the development of a "information superhighway supporting universities, business and civilians."	Congress and the President's Office propose the creation of a national information superhighway to support research, education, commercial, and private interests.
1994	Andreesen and Jim Clark form Netscape Corporation.	First commercial Web browser — Netscape — becomes available.
1994	The first banner advertisements appear on Hotwired.com.	**The E-commerce I era begins.**

[d] "Backbone" refers to the U.S. domestic trunk lines that carry the heavy data traffic across the nation, from one metropolitan area to another. Universities are given responsibility for developing their own campus networks that must be connected to the national backbone.

(continued)

FIGURE 3.2	DEVELOPMENT OF THE INTERNET: TIMELINE (*CONTINUED*)	
YEAR	EVENT	SIGNIFICANCE
COMMERCIALIZATION PHASE 1995–PRESENT		
1995	NSF privatizes the backbone, and commercial carriers take over backbone operation.	The fully commercial civilian Internet is born. Major long-haul networks such as ATT, Sprint, GTE, UUNet, and MCI take over operation of the backbone. Network Solutions (a private firm) is given a monopoly to assign Internet addresses.
1996	Internet2 Consortium formed	Thirty-four government agencies, universities, and business firms plan the development of an Internet 100 to 1,000 times faster than the existing Internet I.
1998	The U.S. federal government encourages the founding of Internet Corporation for Assigning Numbers and Names (ICANN).	Governance over domain names and addresses passes to a private nonprofit international organization.

Source: Based on Leiner, et. al., 2000.

THE INTERNET: KEY TECHNOLOGY CONCEPTS

In 1995, the Federal Networking Council (FNC) took the step of passing a resolution formally defining the term *Internet*. (See Figure 3.3)

Based on that definition, the Internet means a network that uses the IP addressing scheme, supports the Transmission Control Protocol (TCP), and makes services available to users much like a telephone system makes voice and data services available to the public.

FIGURE 3.3	RESOLUTION OF THE FEDERAL NETWORKING COUNCIL

"The Federal Networking Council (FNC) agrees that the following language reflects our definition of the term "Internet."

"Internet" refers to the global information system that—

(i) is logically linked together by a globally unique address space based on the Internet Protocol (IP) or its subsequent extensions/follow-ons;

(ii) is able to support communications using the Transmission Control Protocol/Internet Protocol (TCP/IP) suite or its subsequent extensions/follow-ons, and/or other IP-compatible protocols; and

(iii) provides, uses or makes accessible, either publicly or privately, high level services layered on the communications and related infrastructure described herein."

Last modified on October 30, 1995.

Behind this formal definition are three extremely important concepts that are the basis for understanding the Internet: packet switching, the TCP/IP communications protocol, and client/server computing. Although the Internet has evolved and changed dramatically in the last 30 years, these three concepts are at the core of how the Internet functions today and are the foundation for Internet II.

Packet Switching.   **Packet switching** is a method of slicing digital messages into parcels called "**packets**," sending the packets along different communication paths as they become available, and then reassembling the packets once they arrive at their destination (see Figure 3.4). Prior to the development of packet switching, early computer networks used leased, dedicated telephone circuits to communicate with terminals and other computers. In circuit-switched networks such as the telephone system, a complete point-to-point circuit is put together, and then communication can proceed. However, these "dedicated" circuit-switching techniques were expensive and wasted available communications capacity — the circuit would be maintained regardless of whether any data was being sent. For nearly 70% of the time, a dedicated voice circuit is not being fully used because of pauses between words and delays in assembling the circuit segments, both of which increased the length of time required to find and connect circuits. A better technology was needed.

The first book on packet switching was written by Leonard Kleinrock in 1964 (Kleinrock, 1964), and the technique was further developed by others in the defense research labs of both the United States and England. With packet switching, the communications capacity of a network can be increased by a factor of 100 or more. The communications capacity of a digital network is measured in terms of bits per second.[1] Imagine if the gas mileage of your car went from 15 miles per gallon to 1,500 miles per gallon — all without changing too much of the car!

In packet-switched networks, messages are first broken down into packets. Appended to each packet are digital codes that indicate a source address (the origination point) and a destination address, as well as sequencing information and error-control information for the packet. Rather than being sent directly to the destination address, in a packet network, the packets travel from computer to computer until they reach their destination. These computers are called routers. **Routers** are special-purpose computers that interconnect the thousands of different computer networks that make up the Internet and route packets along to their ultimate destination as they travel. To ensure that packets take the best available path toward their destination, the routers use computer programs called **routing algorithms.**

Packet switching does not require a dedicated circuit but can make use of any spare capacity that is available on any of several hundred circuits. Packet switching

packet switching
a method of slicing digital messages into packets, sending the packets along different communication paths as they become available, and then reassembling the packets once they arrive at their destination

packet
the parcels into which digital messages are sliced for transmission over the Internet

routers
special-purpose computers that interconnect the computer networks that make up the Internet and route packets to their ultimate destination as they travel the Internet

routing algorithm
computer program that ensures that packets take the best available path toward their destination

[1]A bit is a binary digit, 0 or 1. A string of eight bits constitutes a byte. A home telephone modem connects to the Internet usually at 56 Kbps (56,000 bits per second). Mbps refers to millions of bits per second.

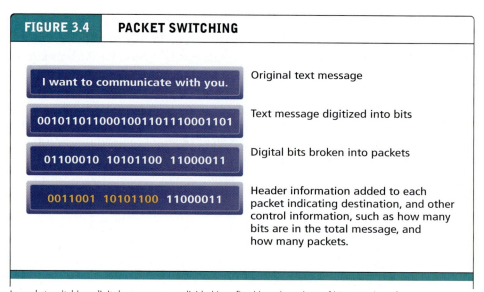

FIGURE 3.4 | **PACKET SWITCHING**

I want to communicate with you. — Original text message

00101101100010011011110001101 — Text message digitized into bits

01100010 10101100 11000011 — Digital bits broken into packets

0011001 10101100 11000011 — Header information added to each packet indicating destination, and other control information, such as how many bits are in the total message, and how many packets.

In packet switching, digital messages are divided into fixed length packets of bits. Header information indicates both the origin and the ultimate destination address of the packet, the size of the message, and the number of packets the receiving node should expect. Because the packets are sent individually on any available line, some packets may arrive before others, producing a delay called *latency*.

TCP (Transmission Control Protocol)
protocol that establishes the connections among sending and receiving Web computers, handles the assembly of packets at the point of transmission, and their reassembly at the receiving end

IP (Internet Protocol)
protocol that provides the Internet's addressing scheme

protocol
a set of rules for formatting, ordering, compressing, and error checking messages

makes nearly full use of almost all available communication lines and capacity. Moreover, if some lines are disabled or too busy, the packets can be sent on any available line that eventually leads to the destination point.

TCP/IP.   While packet switching was an enormous advance in communications capacity, there was no universally agreed upon method for breaking up digital messages into packets, routing them to the proper address, and then reassembling them into a coherent message. This was like having a system for producing stamps, but no postal system (a series of post offices and a set of addresses).

TCP/IP answered the problem of what to do with packets on the Internet and how to handle them. **TCP** refers to the Transmission Control Protocol (TCP). **IP** refers to the Internet Protocol (IP). A **protocol** is a set of rules for formatting, ordering, compressing, and error-checking messages. It may also specify the speed of transmission and means by which devices on the network will indicate they have stopped sending and/or receiving messages. Protocols can be implemented in either hardware or software. TCP/IP is implemented in Web software called *server software* (described below). TCP is the agreed upon protocol for transmitting data packets over the Web. TCP establishes the connections among sending and receiving Web computers, handles the assembly of packets at the point of transmission, and their reassembly at the receiving end.

TCP/IP is divided into four separate layers, with each layer handling a different aspect of the communication problem (see Figure 3.5). The Network Interface Layer is responsible for placing packets on and receiving them from the network medium, which could be a Local Area Network (Ethernet) or Token Ring Network, or other network technology. TCP/IP is independent from any local network technology and can adapt to changes in the local level. The Internet Layer is responsible for addressing, packaging, and routing messages on the Internet. The Transport Layer is responsible for providing communication with the application by acknowledging and sequencing the packets to and from the application. The Application Layer provides a wide

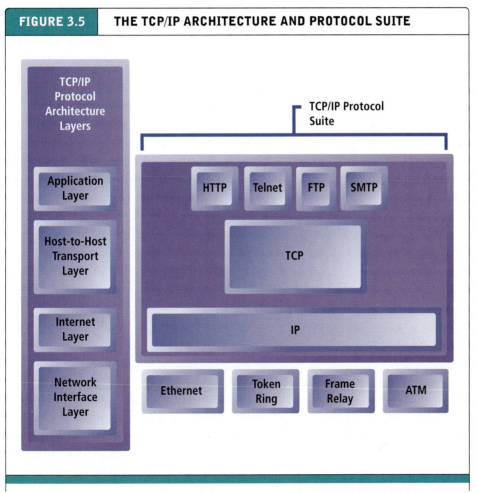

FIGURE 3.5   **THE TCP/IP ARCHITECTURE AND PROTOCOL SUITE**

TCP/IP is an industry standard suite of protocols for large internetworks developed in 1969 by the U.S. Department of Defense Advanced Research Projects Agency (DARPA). The purpose of TCP/IP is to provide high-speed communication network links.

variety of applications with the ability to access the services of the lower layers. Some of the best known applications are HyperText Transfer Protocol (HTTP), File Transfer Protocol (FTP), and Simple Mail Transfer Protocol (SMTP), all of which we will discuss later in this chapter.

IP Addresses.   TCP handles the packetizing and routing of Internet messages. IP provides the Internet's addressing scheme. Every computer connected to the Internet must be assigned an address — otherwise it cannot send or receive TCP packets. For instance, when you sign onto the Internet using a dial-up telephone modem, your computer is assigned a temporary address by your Internet Service Provider.

> **IP addresses**
> Internet addresses expressed as 32-bit numbers that appear as a series of four separate numbers marked off by periods, such as 201.61.186.227

Internet addresses, known as **IP addresses**, are 32-bit numbers that appear as a series of four separate numbers marked off by periods, such as 201.61.186.227. Each of the four numbers can range from 0–255. This "dotted quad" addressing scheme contains up to 4 billion addresses (2 to the 32nd power). The leftmost number typically indicates the network address of the computer, while remaining numbers help to identify the specific computer within the group that is sending (or receiving) a message.

The current version of IP is called Version 4, or IPv4. Because many large corporate and government domains have been given millions of IP addresses each (to accommodate their current and future work forces), and with all the new networks and new Internet-enabled devices requiring unique IP addresses being attached to the Internet, a new version of the IP protocol, called IPv6 is being adopted. This scheme contains 128-bit addresses, or about one quadrillion (10 to the 15th power) (National Research Council, 2000).

Figure 3.6 illustrates how TCP/IP and packet switching work together to send data over the Internet.

> **domain name**
> IP address expressed in natural language
>
> **domain name system (DNS)**
> system for expressing numeric IP addresses in natural language
>
> **uniform resource locator (URL)**
> the address used by a Web browser to identify the location of content on the Web

Domain Names and URLs.   Most people cannot remember 32-bit numbers. IP addresses can be represented by a natural language convention called **domain names. The domain name system (DNS)** allows expressions such as cnet.com to stand for numeric IP addresses (cnet.com's numeric IP is 216.200.247.134).[2] **Uniform resource locators (URLs)**, which are the addresses used by Web browsers to identify the location of content on the Web, also use domain names as part of the URL. A typical URL contains the protocol to be used when accessing the address, followed by its location. For instance, the URL httttp://www.azimuth-interactive.com/flash_test refers to the IP address 208.148.84.1 with the domain name "azimuth-interactive.com" and the protocol being used to access the address, Hypertext Transfer Protocol (HTTP). A resource called "flash_test" is located on the server directory path /flash_test. A URL can have from two to four parts, for example name1.name2.

[2]You can check the IP address of any domain name on the Internet. In Windows, bring up the DOS program or use Start/Run/command to start the DOS prompt. Type "Ping < Domain Name". You will receive the IP address in return.

FIGURE 3.6	ROUTING INTERNET MESSAGES: TCP/IP AND PACKET SWITCHING

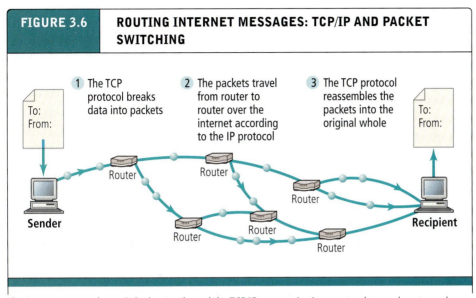

The Internet uses packet-switched networks and the TCP/IP communications protocol to send, route, and assemble messages. Messages are broken into packets, and packets from the same message can travel along different routes.

name3.org. We discuss domain names and URLs further in Section 3.4. Table 3.1 summarizes the important components of the Internet addressing scheme.

TABLE 3.1	PIECES OF THE INTERNET PUZZLE: NAMES AND ADDRESSES
IP addresses	Every computer connected to the Internet must have a unique address number called an *Internet Protocol address*. Even computers using a modem are assigned a temporary IP address.
Domain names	The DNS (domain name system) allows expressions such as aw.com (Addison Wesley's Web site) to stand for numeric IP locations.
DNS servers	DNS servers are databases that keep track of IP addresses and domain names on the Internet.
Root servers	Root servers are central directories that list all domain names currently in use. DNS servers consult root servers to look up unfamiliar domain names when routing traffic.
ICANN	The Internet Corporation for Assigned Numbers and Names (ICANN) was established in 1998 to set the rules for domain names and IP addresses and also to coordinate the operation of root servers. It took over from private firms such as NetSolutions.com.

Client/Server Computing.   While packet switching exploded the available communications capacity and TCP/IP provided the communications rules and regulations, it took a revolution in computing to bring about today's Internet and the Web. That revolution is called *client/server computing* and without it, the Web — in all its richness — would not exist. In fact, the Internet is a giant example of client/server computing in which over 70 million host server computers store Web pages and other content that can be easily accessed by nearly a million local area networks and hundreds of millions of client machines worldwide (Computer Industry Almanac Inc., 2001.)

client/server computing
a model of computing in which very powerful personal computers are connected together in a network with one or more servers.

Client/server computing is a model of computing in which very powerful personal computers called **clients** are connected together in a network together with one or more server computers. These clients are sufficiently powerful to accomplish complex tasks such as displaying rich graphics, storing large files, and processing graphics and sound files, all on a local desktop or handheld device. **Servers** are networked computers dedicated to common functions that the client machines on the network need, such as storing files, software applications, utility programs such as Web connections, and printers. (See Figure 3.7.)

client
a very powerful personal computer that is part of a network. They are capable of displaying rich graphics, storing large files, and processing graphics and sound files

To appreciate what client/server computing makes possible, you must understand what preceded it. In the mainframe computing environment of the 1960s and 1970s, computing power was very expensive and limited. For instance, the largest commercial mainframes of the late 1960s had 128k of RAM and 10 megabyte disk drives, and occupied hundreds of square feet. There was insufficient computing capacity to support graphics or color in text documents, let alone sound files or hyperlinked documents and databases.

server
networked computer dedicated to common functions that the client machines on the network need, such as storing files, software applications, utility programs such as Web connections, and printers

With the development of personal computers and local area networks during the late 1970s and early 1980s, client/server computing became possible. Client/server

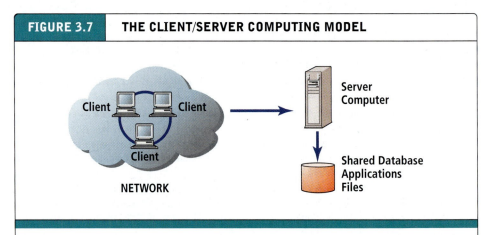

| FIGURE 3.7 | THE CLIENT/SERVER COMPUTING MODEL |

In the client/server model of computing, client computers are connected in a network together with one or more servers.

computing has many advantages over centralized mainframe computing. For instance, it is easy to expand capacity by adding servers and clients. Also, client/server networks are less vulnerable than centralized computing architectures. If one server goes down, backup or mirror servers can pick up the slack; if a client machine is inoperable, the rest of the network continues operating. Moreover, processing load is balanced over many powerful smaller machines rather than being concentrated in a single huge machine that performs processing for everyone. Both software and hardware in client/server environments can be built more simply and economically.

Today there are about 450 million PCs in existence worldwide (Computer Industry Almanac Inc., 2001). Most of these PCs can display and process graphics, sound files, and colored text. They have memories up to 512MB, 20 gigabyte hard drives, and occupy about two square feet. These personal "supercomputers," when tied together in local area networks or into large wide area networks such as the Web, make it possible for millions of people to enjoy "rich" Web documents and experiences. Soon these capabilities will move to handheld devices such as the Palms and HP Jornada, and wireless cell phones (much "thinner clients"). In the process, more computer processing will be performed by central servers (reminiscent of mainframe computers of the past).

OTHER INTERNET PROTOCOLS AND UTILITY PROGRAMS

There are many other Internet protocols that provide services to users in the form of Internet applications that run on Internet clients and servers. These Internet services are based on universally accepted protocols — or standards — that are available to everyone who uses the Internet. They are not owned by any one organization but are services that were developed over many years and given to all Internet users.

HTTP: Hypertext Documents.   **HTTP** (short for **HyperText Transfer Protocol**) is the Internet protocol used for transferring Web pages (described in the following section). The HTTP protocol runs in the Application Layer of the TCP/IP model shown in Figure 3.5. An HTTP session begins when a client's browser requests a Web page from a remote Internet server. When the server responds by sending the page requested, the HTTP session for that object ends. Because Web pages may have many objects on them — graphics, sound or video files, frames, and so forth — each object must be requested by a separate HTTP message.

SMTP, POP, and IMAP: Sending E-mail.   E-mail is one of the oldest, most important, and frequently used Internet services. **STMP (Simple Mail Transfer Protocol)** is the Internet protocol used to send mail to a server. **POP (Post Office Protocol)** is used by the client to retrieve mail from an Internet server. You can see how your browser handles SMTP and POP by looking in your browser's Preferences or Tools section, where the mail settings are defined. You can set POP to retrieve e-mail mes-

HTTP (HyperText Transfer Protocol)
the Internet protocol used for transferring Web pages

STMP (Simple Mail Transfer Protocol)
the Internet protocol used to send mail to a server

POP (Post Office Protocol)
a protocol used by the client to retrieve mail from an Internet server

sages from the server and then delete the messages on the server, or retain them on the server. **IMAP (Internet Message Access Protocol)** is a more current e-mail protocol supported by many servers and all browsers. IMAP allows users to search, organize, and filter their mail prior to downloading it from the server.

IMAP (Internet Message Access Protocol)

a more current e-mail protocol that allows users to search, organize, and filter their mail prior to downloading it from the server

FTP: Transferring Files.

FTP (File Transfer Protocol) is one of the original Internet services. It is a part of the TCP/IP protocol and permits users to transfer files from the server to their client machine, and vice versa. The files can be documents, programs, or large database files. FTP is the fastest and most convenient way to transfer files larger than 1 megabyte, which many mail servers will not accept. (See Figure 3.8.)

FTP (File Transfer Protocol)

one of the original Internet services. Part of the TCP/IP protocol that permits users to transfer files from the server to their client machine, and vice versa

SSL: Security.

SSL (Secure Sockets Layer) is a protocol that operates between the Transport and Application Layers of TCP/IP and secures communications between the client and the server. SSL helps secure e-commerce communications and payments through a variety of techniques such as message encryption and digital signatures that we will discuss further in Chapter 5.

SSL

a protocol that secures communications between the client and the server

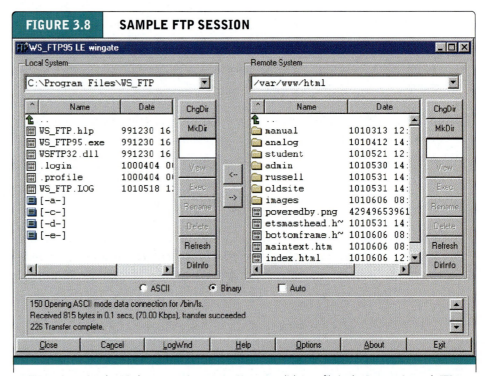

FIGURE 3.8 **SAMPLE FTP SESSION**

An FTP session using the Windows operating system. Users can click on a file in the Remote System's FTP directory and transfer the file to a directory in the local system. FTP is especially good for moving large files or programs.

Telnet: Running Remote.   **Telnet** is a terminal emulation program that runs in TCP/IP. You can run Telnet from your client machine. When you do so, your client emulates a mainframe computer terminal. (The industry standard terminals defined in the days of mainframe computing are VT-52, VT-100, and IBM 3250.) You can then attach yourself to a computer on the Internet that supports Telnet and run programs or download files from that computer. Telnet was the first "remote work" program that permitted users to work on a computer from a remote location.

Finger: Finding People.   You can find out who is logged onto a remote network by using Telnet to connect to a server, and then typing "finger" at the prompt. **Finger** is a utility program supported by UNIX computers. When supported by remote computers, finger can you tell you who is logged in, how long they have been attached, and their user name. Obviously there are security issues involved with supporting finger, and most Internet host computers do not support finger today.

Ping: Testing the Address.   You can "**ping**" a host computer to check the connection between your client and the server (see Figure 3.9). The ping (Packet InterNet Groper) program will also tell you the time it takes for the server to respond, giving you some idea about the speed of the server and the Internet at that moment. You can run ping from the DOS prompt on a personal computer with a Windows operating system by typing: Ping <domain name>. We will discuss ping further in Chapter 5, because one way to slow down or even crash a domain computer is to send it millions of ping requests.

Tracert: Checking Routes.   **Tracert** is one of a several route-tracing utilities that allow you to follow the path of a message you send from your client to a remote computer on the Internet. Figure 3.10 shows the result of route tracking a message sent to a

FIGURE 3.9	THE RESULT OF A PING

```
Command Prompt
C:\>
C:\>
C:\>ping www.yahoo.com

Pinging www.yahoo.com [204.71.200.72] with 32 bytes of data:

Reply from 204.71.200.72: bytes=32 time=100ms TTL=240
Reply from 204.71.200.72: bytes=32 time=100ms TTL=240
Reply from 204.71.200.72: bytes=32 time=130ms TTL=240
Reply from 204.71.200.72: bytes=32 time=100ms TTL=240

C:\>
```

A ping is used to verify an address and test the speed of the round trip from your client to a host and back.

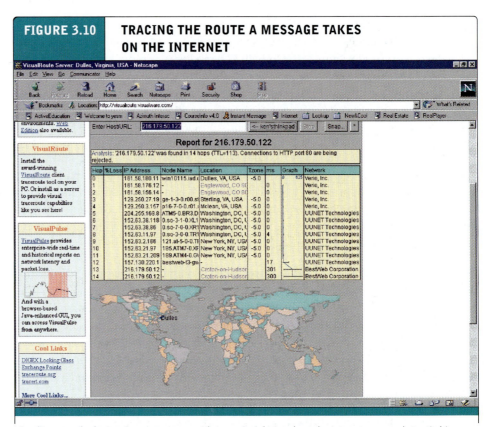

FIGURE 3.10 **TRACING THE ROUTE A MESSAGE TAKES ON THE INTERNET**

VisualRoute and other tracing programs provide some insight into how the Internet uses packet switching. This particular message traveled from a computer in Dulles, Virginia to Croton-on-Hudson, New York.

remote host using a visual route-tracing program called VisualRoute (available from Visualware).

3.2 THE INTERNET TODAY

By 2001, there were approximately 400 million Internet users worldwide, up from 100 million users at year-end 1997. That figure is projected to continue to grow to close to 800 million by 2003 (Computer Industry Almanac Inc., 2001; Global Reach, 2001). One would think that with such incredible growth, the Internet would be overloaded. However, this has not been true for several reasons. First, client/server computing is highly extensible: By simply adding servers and clients, the population of Internet users can grow indefinitely. Second, the Internet architecture is built in layers so that each layer can change without disturbing developments in other layers. For instance, the technology used to move messages through the Internet can go through radical changes to make service faster without being disruptive to your desktop applications running on the Internet.

Figure 3.11 illustrates the "hourglass" architecture of the Internet. The Internet can be viewed conceptually as having four layers: the network technology substrate, trans-

---

FIGURE 3.11 | **THE HOURGLASS MODEL OF THE INTERNET**

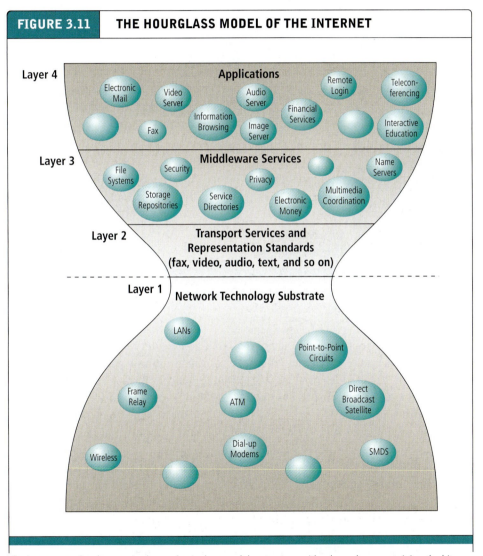

The Internet can be characterized as an hour-glass modular structure with a lower layer containing the bit-carrying infrastructure (including cables and switches) and an upper layer containing user applications such as e-mail and the Web. In the narrow waist are transportation protocols such as TCP/IP.

Source: Adapted from Computer Science and Telecommunications Board (CSTB), 2000.

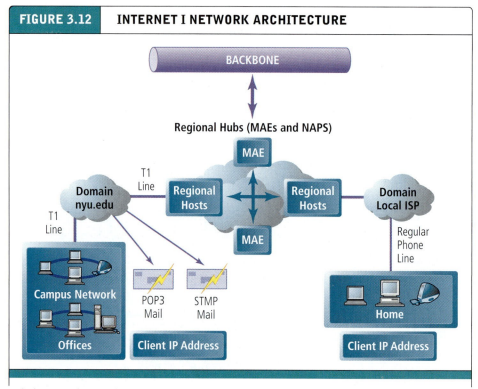

FIGURE 3.12   INTERNET I NETWORK ARCHITECTURE

Today's Internet has a multi-tiered open network architecture featuring a national backbone, regional hubs, "campus" networks, and local client machines.

middleware

the "glue" that ties the applications to the communications networks, and includes such services as security, authentication, addresses, and storage repositories

backbone

high-bandwidth fiber optic cable that transports data across the Internet

Network Service Provider (NSP)

owns and controls one of the major networks comprising the Internet's backbone

port services and representation standards, middleware services, and applications.[3] The network technology substrate is composed of telecommunications networks and protocols. The transport layer houses the TCP/IP protocol. The applications layer contains client applications such as the World Wide Web, e-mail, and audio or video playback. **Middleware** is the glue that ties the applications to the communications networks, and includes such services as security, authentication, addresses, and storage repositories. Users work with applications (such as e-mail) and rarely become aware of middleware that operates in the background. Because all layers use TCP/IP and other common standards linking all four layers, it is possible for there to be significant changes in the network layer without forcing changes in the applications layer. The network layer is described below.

THE INTERNET BACKBONE

Figure 3.12 illustrates the main physical elements of today's Internet. The Internet's **backbone** is formed by **Network Service Providers (NSPs)**, which own and control

---

[3]Recall that the TCP/IP communications protocol also has layers, not to be confused with the Internet architecture layers.

TABLE 3.2	MAJOR U.S INTERNET BACKBONE OWNERS
AT&T	Qwest
Cable & Wireless	Level 3
Genuity	Williams
MCI Worldcom	Global Crossing
Sprint	Broadwing
PSI Net	

the major networks (see Table 3.2). The backbone has been likened to a giant pipeline that transports data around the world in milliseconds. In the United States, the backbone is composed entirely of fiber-optic cable (described more fully below), with bandwidths ranging from 155 Mbps to 2.5 Gbps. **Bandwidth** measures how much data can be transferred over a communications medium within a fixed period of time, and is usually expressed in bits per second (bps), kilobits (thousands of bits) per second (Kbps), megabits (millions of bits) per second (Mbps), or gigabits (billions of bits) per second (Gbps).

Connections to other continents are made via a combination of undersea fiber optic cable and satellite links. The backbones in foreign countries typically are operated by a mixture of private and public owners. The U.S. backbone is one of the most developed because the Internet's infrastructure was developed here. The backbone has built-in redundancy so that if one part breaks down, data can be rerouted to another part of the backbone. **Redundancy** refers to multiple duplicate devices and paths in a network.

NETWORK ACCESS POINTS AND METROPOLITAN AREA EXCHANGES

In the United States there are a number of hubs where the backbone intersects with regional and local networks, and where the backbone owners connect with one another (see Figure 3.13). These hubs are called **Network Access Points (NAPs)** or **Metropolitan Area Exchanges (MAEs),** and use high-speed switching computers to connect the backbone to regional and local networks, and exchange messages with one another. The regional and local networks are owned by local Bell operating companies (RBOCs — pronounced "ree-bocks"), and private telecommunications firms such as MFS Corporation; they generally are fiber optic networks operating at over 100 Mbps. The regional networks lease access to Internet Service Providers, private companies, and government institutions.

bandwidth
measures how much data can be transferred over a communications medium within a fixed period of time; is usually expressed in bits per second (bps), kilobits per second (Kbps), or megabits (or millions of bits) per second (Mbps)

redundancy
multiple duplicate devices and paths in a network

Network Access Point (NAP)
one of the hubs where the backbone intersects with regional and local networks, and where the backbone owners connect with one another

Metropolitan Area Exchanges (MAEs)
another name for one of the hubs where the backbone intersects with regional and local networks, and where the backbone owners connect with one another

FIGURE 3.13	INTERNET NAPS AND MAES

MAJOR U.S. INTERCONNECT POINTS

Location	Owner/Operator
Chicago NAP	Ameritech Advanced Data Services and Bellcorp
Santa Clara, CA	CIX Commercial Internet Exchange
Palo Alto, CA	Digital IX/PAIX
Mountain View, CA (FIX-West)	Federal Internet Exchange (FIX)
College Park, MD (FIX-East)	
San Jose (MAE-West)	MCI WorldCom
San Francisco	
Los Angeles	
Chicago	
Dallas	
Houston	
Washington D.C. (MAE-East)	
New York NAP (Pennsauken, NJ)	SprintLink
San Francisco NAP	Pacific Bell

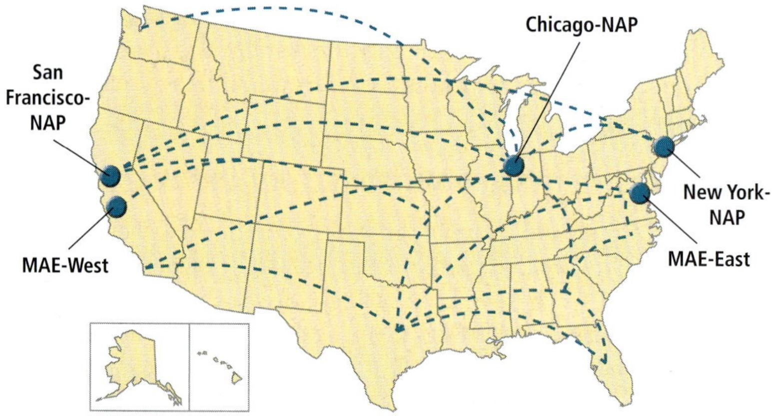

The Internet backbone connects regional networks, which in turn provide access to the Internet to Internet Service Providers, large firms, and government agencies.

CAMPUS NETWORKS

There are an estimated one million campus networks attached to the Internet worldwide (Computer Industry Almanac Inc., 2001). **Campus networks** are generally local area networks operating with a single organization — such as New York University or Microsoft Corporation. In fact, most large organizations have hundreds of such local area networks. These organizations (representing about 60 million workers) are sufficiently large that they lease access to the Web directly from regional and national carriers. These local area networks generally are running Ethernet (a local area network protocol) and have operating systems such as Windows 2000 (NT), Novell, or others that permit desktop clients to connect to the Internet through a local Internet server attached to their campus networks. Connection speeds in campus networks are in the range of 10–100 Mbps to the desktop.

campus networks
generally local area networks operating with a single organization that leases access to the Web directly from regional and national carriers

INTERNET SERVICE PROVIDERS

The firms that provide the lowest level of service in the multi-tiered Internet architecture by leasing Internet access to home owners, small businesses, and some large institutions are called **Internet Service Providers (ISPs)**. ISPs are retail providers — they deal with "the last mile of service" to the curb, the home, the business office. About 45 million American households connect to the Internet through either national or local ISPs. ISPs typically connect to the Internet and MAEs or NAPs with high-speed telephone or cable lines (up to 45 Mbps).

There are major ISPs such as America Online, MSN Network, and AT&T WorldNet and about 5,000 local ISPs in the United States, ranging from local telephone companies offering dial-up and DSL telephone access, to cable companies offering cable modem service, to small "mom and pop" Internet shops that service a small town, city, or even county with mostly dial-up phone access (Boardwatch, 2001). If you have home or small business Internet access, an ISP will be providing you the service.

Table 3.3 summarizes the variety of services, speeds, and costs of ISP Internet connections. There are two types of ISP service: narrowband and broadband. **Narrowband** service is the traditional telephone modem connection now operating at 56.6 Kbps (although the actual throughput hovers around 30 Kbps due to line noise that causes extensive resending of packets). This is the most common form of connection worldwide. **Broadband** service is based on DSL, cable modem, telephone (T1 and T3 lines), and satellite technologies. Broadband — in the context of Internet service — refers to any communication technology that permits clients to play streaming audio and video files at acceptable speeds — generally anything above 100 Kbps.

Internet Service Provider (ISP)
firm that provides the lowest level of service in the multi-tiered Internet architecture by leasing Internet access to home owners, small businesses, and some large institutions

narrowband
the traditional telephone modem connection, now operating at 56.6 Kbps

broadband
refers to any communication technology that permits clients to play streaming audio and video files at acceptable speeds — generally anything above 100 Kbps

TABLE 3.3	ISP SERVICE LEVELS CHOICES	
BANDWIDTH CHOICES		
Service	Cost/Month	Speed to Desktop (Kbps)
Telephone Modem	$21–25	30–56 Kbps
DSL Lite	$50–75	150–384 Kbps
DSL Regular	$100–150	385Kbps–1 Mbps
Cable Modem	$50–75	350Kbps–1Mbps
Satellite Dish	$35–50	250Kbps–1Mbps
T1	$1000–2000	1.554 Mbps

The actual throughput of data will depend on a variety of factors including noise in the line and the number of subscribers requesting service

DSL (digital subscriber line)
a telephone technology for delivering high-speed access through ordinary telephone lines found in homes or businesses

cable modem
a cable television technology that piggybacks digital access to the Internet on top of the analog video cable providing television signals to a home

T1
an international telephone standard for digital communication that offers guaranteed delivery at 1.54 Mbps

T3
an international telephone standard for digital communication that offers guaranteed delivery at 43 Mbps

The term **DSL** refers to **digital subscriber line** service, which is a telephone technology for delivering high-speed access through ordinary telephone lines found in your home or business. Service levels range from about 150 Kbps all the way up to 1 Mbps. DSL service requires that customers live within two miles (about 4,000 meters) of a neighborhood telephone switching center.

Cable modem refers to a cable television technology that piggybacks digital access to the Internet on top of the analog video cable providing television signals to a home. Cable modem services ranges from 350 Kbps up to 1 Mbps. Cable service may degrade if many people in a neighborhood log on and demand high-speed service all at once.

T1 and **T3** are international telephone standards for digital communication. T1 lines offer guaranteed delivery at 1.54 Mbps, while T3 lines offer delivery at 43 Mbps. T1 lines cost about $1,000–$2,000 per month, and T3 lines between $10,000 and $30,000 per month. These are leased, dedicated, guaranteed lines suitable for corporations, government agencies, and businesses such as ISPs requiring high-speed guaranteed service levels.

Some satellite companies are offering broadband high-speed digital downloading of Internet content to homes and offices that deploy 18″ satellite antennas. Service is available beginning at 256 Kbps up to 1 Mbps. In general, satellite connections are not viable for homes and small businesses because they are only one-way — you can download from the Internet at high speed, but cannot upload to the Internet at all. Instead, users require a phone or cable connection for their uploading.

Broadband service — DSL and cable modem — will be available to approximately 8–10 million homes and small businesses in 2001. Most professional organizations and nearly all large business firms and government agencies have broadband connections to the Internet. About 60 million other homes — the vast majority of Internet users — still use the much slower 56.6 Kbps modem and ordinary telephone connections. Demand for broadband service is growing because customers are frustrated by the lengthy delays experienced using telephone modems when downloading large files (see Table 3.4). As the quality of Internet service offerings expands to include Hollywood movies, music, games, and other rich media steaming content, the demand for broadband access will swell rapidly. Currently, Internet I cannot deliver these types of services to millions of users simultaneously.

INTRANETS AND EXTRANETS

The very same Internet technologies that make it possible to operate a worldwide public network can also be used by private and government organizations as internal networks. An **intranet** is a TCP/IP network located within a single organization for purposes of communications and information processing. Many corporations are moving away from proprietary local area networks such as Windows 2000 and Novell, and toward a single internal intranet to handle the firm's information processing and communication needs. Internet technologies are generally far less expensive than proprietary networks, and there is a global source of new applications that can run on intranets. In fact, all the applications available on the public Internet can be used in private intranets.

intranet
a TCP/IP network located within a single organization for purposes of communications and information processing

TABLE 3.4	TIME TO DOWNLOAD A 10 MEGABYTE FILE BY TYPE OF INTERNET SERVICE	
TYPE OF INTERNET SERVICE	TIME TO DOWNLOAD	
Narrowband Services		
Telephone modem	25 minutes	
Broadband Services		
DSL lite	9 minutes	
DSL regular	3.5 minutes	
Cable modem	3.5 minutes	
T-1	51 seconds	
T-3	2 seconds	

Extranets are formed when firms permit outsiders to access their internal TCP/IP networks. For instance, General Motors permits parts suppliers to gain access to GM's intranet that contains GM's production schedules. In this way, parts suppliers know exactly when GM needs parts, and where and when to deliver the parts.

Intranets and extranets generally do not involve commercial transactions in a marketplace, and they are mostly beyond the scope of this text. Extranets will receive some attention as a type of B2B exchange.

WHO GOVERNS THE INTERNET?

Aficionados and promoters of the Internet often claim that the Internet is governed by no one, and indeed cannot be governed, and that it is inherently above and beyond the law. In fact, the Internet is tied into a complex web of governing bodies, national legislatures, and international professional societies. There is no one governing body that controls activity on the Internet. Instead, there are several organizations that influence the system and monitor its operations. Among the governing bodies of the Internet are:

- The *Internet Architecture Board (IAB)*, which helps define the overall structure of the Internet.
- The *Internet Corporation for Assigned Names and Numbers (ICANN)*, which assigns IP addresses, and the *Internet Network Information Center (InterNIC)*, which assigns domain names.
- The *Internet Engineering Steering Group (IESG)*, which oversees standard setting with respect to the Internet.
- The *Internet Engineering Task Force (IETF)*, which forecasts the next step in the growth of the Internet, keeping watch over its evolution and operation.
- The *Internet Society (ISOC)*, which is a consortium of corporations, government agencies, and nonprofit organizations that monitors Internet policies and practices.
- The *World Wide Web Consortium (W3C)*, which sets HTML and other programming standards for the Web.

While none of these organizations has actual control over the Internet and how it functions, they can and do influence government agencies, major network owners, ISPs, corporations, and software developers with the goal of keeping the Internet operating as efficiently as possible.

In addition to these professional bodies, the Internet must also conform to the laws of the sovereign nation-states in which it operates, as well as the technical infrastructures that exist within the nation-state. Although in the early years of the Internet and the Web there was very little legislative or executive interference, this situation will change in the near future as the Internet plays a growing role in the distribution of information and knowledge, including content that some find objectionable. Read

Insight on Society: Yahoo France for a further look at the issue of government regulation of the Internet.

3.3	**INTERNET II: THE FUTURE INFRASTRUCTURE**

To appreciate the benefits of Internet II, you must first understand the limitations of the Internet's current infrastructure.

LIMITATIONS OF INTERNET I

Much of the Internet's current infrastructure is several decades old (equivalent to a century in Internet time). It suffers from a number of limitations, including:

- *Bandwidth limitations.* There is insufficient capacity throughout the backbone, the metropolitan switching centers, and most importantly, to the "last mile" to the house and small business. The result is slow service (congestion) and a very limited ability to handle video and voice traffic.

- *Quality of service limitations.* Today's information packets take a circuitous route to get to their final destinations. This creates the phenomenon of **latency** — delays in messages caused by the uneven flow of information packets through the network. In the case of e-mail, latency is not noticeable. However, with streaming video and synchronous communication, such as a telephone call, latency is noticeable to the user and perceived as "jerkiness" in movies or delays in voice communication. Today's Internet uses "best efforts" quality of service, (QOS), which makes no guarantees about when or whether data will be delivered, and provides each packet with the same level of service, no matter who the user is or what type of data is contained in the packet. A higher level of service quality is required if the Internet is to keep expanding into new services (such as video on demand or telephony). (CSTB, 2000).

latency

delays in messages caused by the uneven flow of information packets through the network

- *Network architecture limitations.* Today, a thousand requests for a single music track from a central server will result in a thousand efforts by the server to download the music to each requesting client. This slows down network performance as the same music track is sent out a thousand times to clients that might be located in the same metropolitan area. This is very different from television, where the program is broadcast once to millions of homes.

- *Language development limitations.* HTML, the language of Web pages, is fine for text and simple graphics, but poor at defining and communicating "rich documents" such as databases, business documents, or graphics. The tags used to define an HTML page are fixed and generic.

Now imagine an Internet at least 100 times as powerful as today's Internet, an Internet not subjected to the limitations of bandwidth, protocols, architecture, and

YAHOO! FRANCE — GOVERNMENT REGULATION OF THE INTERNET

Who controls the Internet? It seems France wants some control, at least over what its citizens can access on the World Wide Web.

In November 2000, French judge Jean-Jacques Gomez ruled that U.S.-based Yahoo! must block French users from access to Nazi-related memorabilia available on the site. In France, Nazi paraphernalia is illegal.

But should France have the authority to determine what all other Internet users can and can't see and buy? Yahoo! thinks not and, although it has contested the ruling both on the grounds that it's impossible to block access and that the French court does not have jurisdiction, the company did remove all Nazi items in January, 2001. Web portal sites often claim they are "common carriers" and cannot technically control the content their users post, and in any event, are not responsible for what their users say or post to the site.

Such growing restrictions on the Internet are making many people nervous. Just the fact that Yahoo! took action to appease the two groups that sued the company — the League Against Racism and Anti-Semitism (LICRA) and the Union of French Jewish Students — has raised some eyebrows. Yahoo! denies that it acted because of the lawsuit, stating that it decided on its own that the Nazi items were unacceptable.

However, if other countries gain authority to police Web sites according to the laws of their own countries, we're going to see some major inequities with respect to who sees what. South Korea, for example, has outlawed access to gambling Web sites, some Muslim countries forbid religious discussions, and China holds Web sites responsible for any illegal content found on the site. But illegal according to whose laws? That's the question. And can and should companies be forced to police content on their Web sites at all?

Attempting to enforce the various and often contradictory laws of every country is what some are calling "legal harmonization." However, instead of creating harmony, such efforts are likely to do anything but. In the end, we may end up with a "lowest common denominator standard for protected speech on the Net," cautions *New York Times* writer Carl Kaplan, where what is acceptable is what is legal absolutely everywhere. This means that there won't be much information available.

The irony here is that the Internet was developed as a means of fostering global communication. Yet it is now very clear that many countries will put stricter limits on freedom of expression than the United States. The practicalities of a global perspective are proving more difficult socially and politically than the Internet's founders had hoped.

SOURCES: "Yahoo Defies Court Ruling over Nazi Memorabilia," by Kristi Essick, *The Standard*, February 21, 2001; "Will Cyberspace Look Like France or America?," by James K. Glassman *Reason Online*, January 22, 2001; "Experts See Online Speech Case as Bellwether," by Carl S. Kaplan, *New York Times*, January 5, 2001; "Yahoo Bans Hate Propaganda," by Jean Eaglesham, *Financial Times*, January 3, 2001; "From France, Yahoo Case Resonates Around Globe," by Victoria Shannon, *International Herald Tribune*, November 22, 2000.

language detailed above. Welcome to the world of Internet II, and the next generation of e-commerce services and products.

THE INTERNET2® PROJECT

Internet2® is a consortium of more than 180 universities, government agencies, and private businesses that are collaborating to find ways to make the Internet more efficient.[4] Their work together is a continuation of the kind of cooperation among government, private, and educational organizations that created the original Internet.

The idea behind Internet2 is to create a "giant test bed" where new technologies can be tested without impacting the existing Internet.

The three primary goals of Internet2 are to:

- Create a leading edge network capability for the national research community;
- Enable revolutionary Internet applications; and
- Ensure the rapid transfer of new network services and applications to the broader Internet community.

Some of the areas Internet2 participants are focusing on in this pursuit are advanced network infrastructure, new networking capabilities, middleware, and advanced applications. We discuss each of these in the following sections.

Advanced Network Infrastructure.   The advanced networks created and in use by Internet2 members provide the environment in which new technologies can be tested and enhanced. Several new networks have been established, including Abilene and vBNS (a Worldcom/NSF partnership). Abilene and vBNS (short for very high performance Backbone Network Service) are high performance backbone networks with bandwidths ranging from 2.5 Gbps to 9.6 Gbps that interconnect the gigaPoPs used by Internet2 members to access the network. A **gigaPoP** is a regional Gigabit Point of Presence, or point of access to the Internet2 network that supports data transfers at the rate of 1 Gbps or higher (see Figure 3.14).

New Networking Capabilities.   Internet2 is identifying, developing, and testing new networking services and technologies to provide the reliable performance advanced applications require. Internet2 networking projects include:

- deploying the IPV6 addressing protocol;
- developing and implementing new quality of service technologies that will enable the Internet to provide differing levels of service depending on the type and importance of the data being transmitted;
- developing more effective routing practices;

[4]The Internet2® project is just one aspect of the larger second generation Internet we call Internet II.

Internet2®
a consortium of more than 180 universities, government agencies, and private businesses that are collaborating to find ways to make the Internet more efficient

GigaPop
a regional Gigabit Point of Presence, or point of access to the Internet2 network that supports at least one gigabit (1 billion bits) per second information transfer

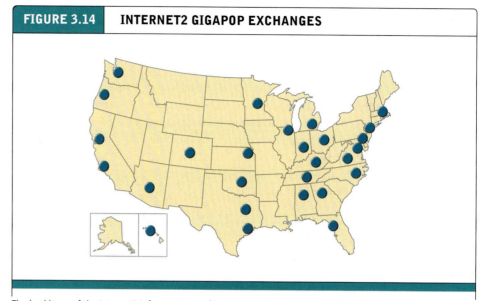

FIGURE 3.14 | **INTERNET2 GIGAPOP EXCHANGES**

The backbone of the Internet2 infrastructure is fiber-optic cable connecting regional "GigaPoP" servers (represented by the blue circles) that operate at billions of bits per second.
Source: www.Internet2.edu

- coordinating the interconnection of the different components of the Internet2 infrastructure — backbones, GigaPoPs, campus LANs, and exchange points; and
- creating an infrastructure to efficiently handle one-to-many communications over the Internet (multicasting, described further in the next section).

Middleware.   Internet2 is developing new middleware capabilities. Researchers are developing standardized middleware that incorporates identification, authentication, authorization, directory, and security services that today are often handled as a part of applications running on the Internet. Internet2 researchers believe advanced middleware will aid application development, increase robustness, assist data management, and provide overall operating efficiencies.

Advanced Applications.   Internet2 work teams are collaborating on a number of advanced applications, including distributed computation, virtual laboratories, digital libraries, distributed learning, tele-immersion, and a synthesis of all of these working in combination. We will discuss these applications in greater depth in Section 3.5.

In the end, the basic goal of Internet2 is to radically enhance the transmission of video and audio and rich documents to enable wider and more extensive use of the Internet for communications and knowledge sharing.

THE LARGER INTERNET II TECHNOLOGY ENVIRONMENT

The Internet2 project is just the tip of the iceberg when it comes to near-term future enhancements to the Internet. In fact, we believe that a whole new era is about to begin that we call *Internet II*. For instance, **NGI (Next Generation Internet)** is another project initiated and sponsored by the federal government that is focused on developing advanced applications and networking capabilities needed by U.S. government agencies such as NASA and the Department of Energy. In addition, other groups — mostly private corporations and industries — are making extraordinary efforts to expand Internet capacity in order to support new services and products that they believe the public will demand in the near future.

Fiber Optics and the Bandwidth Explosion.   Total Internet bandwidth supply has been growing at nearly 150% each year for the past several years in response to increasing demand from more than 400 million worldwide users of the Internet. Improvements are being driven primarily by fiber optic technology companies and large telecommunications companies, many of whom currently operate the backbone of the Internet. **Fiber-optic cable** consists of up to hundreds of strands of glass or plastic that use light to transmit data. It is frequently replacing existing coaxial and twisted pair cabling because it can transmit much more data at faster speeds, with less interference and better data security. Fiber-optic cable is also thinner and lighter, taking up less space during installation. The hope is to use fiber optics to expand network bandwidth capacity in order to prepare for the expected increases in Web traffic once Internet2 services are widely adopted. Figure 3.15 shows actual and projected growth rates for the fiber-optic market. By 2003, there is expected to be 120 million kilometers (74.5 million miles) of fiber-optic cable installed globally.

Network providers are currently using fiber optics to enhance bandwidth by:

- replacing older transmission lines with fiber-optic cable;
- improving fiber-optic-based communications technology; and
- improving fiber-optic switching speeds.

Some of the major **photonics** (the study of communicating with light waves) technologies that will make the dream of Internet II a reality in the future include Dense Wave Division Multiplexing (DWDM), optical and fiber switches, optical switching components, optical integrated circuits, and optical networks (see Table 3.5).

- **Dense Wavelength Division Multiplexing (DWDM)** is an optical technology used to increase bandwidth over existing fiber-optic backbones. DWDM works by combining and transmitting multiple signals simultaneously at different wavelengths on the same fiber. In effect, a single strand of fiber is transformed into multiple virtual fibers.

NGI (Next Generation Internet)
another project initiated and sponsored by the federal government focused on developing advanced applications and networking capabilities need by U.S. government agencies

fiber-optic cable
consists of up to hundreds of strands of glass or plastic that use light to transmit data

photonics
the study of communicating with light waves

Dense Wavelength Division Multiplexing (DWDM)
an optical technology used to increase bandwidth over existing fiber optic backbones

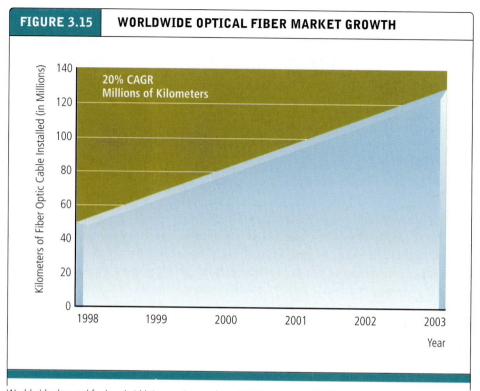

| FIGURE 3.15 | **WORLDWIDE OPTICAL FIBER MARKET GROWTH** |

Worldwide demand for bandwidth is growing at about 150% per year, with fiber-optic cable sales growing at a 20% compounded annual growth rate, according to Corning, a leading supplier of fiber-optic cable.

- Optical switches and transmission equipment will enable capacity expansion and transmission speed increases, along with reduced service costs.
- Gigabit Ethernet using fiber switches is another technological jump that will permit access to larger Metropolitan Regional Networks, with greater bandwidth and a shorter connection to the Internet backbone.
- Optical service accounting platforms will impact how data transmission fees are charged, by fostering packet-sized metering and billing.
- Optical switching components will form the building blocks for all optical systems, such as switches and transmission equipment, as well as circuits and networks.
- Optical integrated circuits are powerful optical chips with mirrors and lasers that can be built into new hardware.
- Passive Optical Networks (PON) are high bandwidth fiber-optic networks that have lower cost and high performance.

TABLE 3.5	MAJOR PHOTONICS OPPORTUNITIES AND PLAYERS	
TECHNOLOGY	OPPORTUNITY	PLAYERS
Dense Wavelength Division Multiplexing	Transform single strand of fiber-optic cable into multiple virtual fibers	Cisco, Cogent Communications
Optical switches and transmission equipment	Expand capacity, drop costs, speed service	BrightLink, Corvis
Gigabit Ethernet over fiber switches	Increased access to metro regional networks	Worldwide Packets; Zuma
Optical service accounting platforms	Packet size metering and billing; bytes to bucks	Ellacoya Networks
Optical switching components	Building blocks for all optical systems	Altitun; Cronos; Coretek
Optical integrated circuits	Powerful optical chips with mirrors and lasers	Bookham; Kymata; Nonovation
Passive Optical Networks (PON)	Low cost, high performance networks	LuxN, Quantum, Teraware
Fiber-optic cable	The highway material	Corning; ATT

Together these improvements will allow the Internet to move from narrowband to broadband digital services, and from stationary Web access to mobile Web access. The next step, "**Big Band**," can accommodate upwards of 10 Gbps, enabling applications such as interactive TV, HDTV, medical imaging, remote labs, multi-user video conferencing, and tele-immersion. The work of collaborators on Internet2 will likely determine what comes after Big Band, as the teams develop new very high bandwidth applications. Figure 3.16 gives a comparative look at bandwidth demand for various applications.

Insight on Business: Enkido — A View of the Future of Networks, examines how one company, Enkido, is using fiber optics and new technologies to create a "Big Band" network on a limited scale.

Wireless Web and 3G Technologies.

While Internet I is mostly a land-based technology that requires the user's client machine to be attached to a cable, Internet II will increasingly rely on wireless technology to connect users' handheld telephones and personal organizers to the Web. The primary technology for wireless connections to the Internet is cellular telephone technology using a variety of cellular standards such as **GSM (Global System for Mobile Communications),** widely used in Europe and Asia, and **CDMA (Code Division Multiple Access),** widely used in the United States. GSM uses narrowband Time Division Multiple Access (TDMA), which allows up to eight calls on a single radio frequency. CDMA is different in that it does

Big Band
can accommodate upwards of 1 Gbps, enabling high bandwidth applications

GSM (Global System for Mobile Communications)
mobile communications system widely used in Europe and Asia that uses narrowband Time Division Multiple Access (TDMA)

CDMA (Code Division Multiple Access)
mobile communications system widely used in the United States that uses the full spectrum of radio frequencies and digitally encrypts each call

---

FIGURE 3.16	BANDWIDTH DEMAND OF VARIOUS WEB APPLICATIONS

Narrowband
Peripheral sharing

Telemetry
Radio e-mail

Wireless alarms,
pagers, text,
e-mail

Broadband
Video conferencing
Multimedia distance learning
File transfer
WWW voice

CD transfer rates
Simulations
High-definition graphics
ASPs/LSPs possible

BigBand
TV, HDTV
Interactive TV
Hollywood on the Web
Internet 2:
    Extensive ASP/LSP possible
    Medical images
    Remote labs
    Multi-person video conferencing
    Ubiquitous netpliance computing

1 Kbps	1 Mbps	1 Gbps	1 Tbps

Protocol: modem vbis90 56.6Kbps Ethernet 10Mbps FDDI/Sonet 100Mbps ATM

Media: Cellular/WAP   Twisted pair   DSL   COAX Cable   Fiber Cable   OC-68

Future e-commerce applications involving streaming video and audio will require much higher levels of bandwidth to the home than Internet I.

GPRS (General Packet Radio Switching)
next generation technology carries data in packets, just like the Internet, but over radio frequencies that make wireless communication possible

WAP (Wireless Application Protocol)
a relatively new protocol that can support virtually any wireless network and is supported by every operating system

Wireless Markup Language (WML)
programming language for devices using WAP

not assign a specific frequency to each caller. Rather, it uses the full spectrum of radio frequencies and digitally encrypts each call.

A secondary wireless technology that is rapidly growing is radio packet switching that uses radio frequencies for the connection. Called **GPRS** for **General Packet Radio Switching**, this next generation technology carries data in packets, just like the Internet, but over radio frequencies that make wireless communication possible. Europe is in the process of establishing a GPRS network, and VoiceStream Wireless has stated its intention to develop one in the United States by year-end 2001.

Currently, most cellular phones can access the Web at only 9.6 Kbps and display only four lines of text, while most PDAs are limited to transmission speeds of up to 19.2 Kbps. Two protocols are used to deliver Web pages to wireless users: WAP and iMode. **WAP (Wireless Application Protocol)** is a relatively new protocol that enables PDA users to access the Web. WAP can support virtually any wireless network and is supported by every operating system. Information that is sent via WAP must be written in **Wireless Markup Language (WML).** This means an existing Web site must rewrite its HTML pages as WML pages. On the other hand, WAP was designed specifically for small PDAs with small screens and no keyboard. Although WAP is a new technology, it is supported by some major players in the wireless arena: Nokia, Ericsson, Motorola, and wireless software developer Unwired Planet.

INSIGHT ON BUSINESS

ENKIDO
A View of the Future of Networks

You'd think that by now the biggest telecommunications providers would have broken through the 10 Gbps barrier that is limiting Internet traffic flow. With all their money and resources, most analysts expected that companies such as AT&T or MCI WorldCom would be the first to offer faster connection speeds. But they were wrong. Enkido was first.

Start-up private carrier Enkido, Inc., based in Hackensack, New Jersey, is leading the way with OC-768 service—telecommunications jargon for 40 Gbps connections on an optical network, the fastest anywhere (OC stands for Optical Carrier). Granted, OC-768 is currently only available in New York City, but Enkido has already bought 20,000 miles of fiber optic cable and has 20-year leases on facilities in New York, Los Angeles, and San Francisco. And some big name customers have signed on, showing support for this technology leader: Deutsche Telecom, NBC, Disney, NASA, and the Department of Defense Advanced Research Projects Agency (DARPA).

Enkido's founder and majority shareholder, Nayel Shafei, is a former Qwest executive who has a knack for development of new technologies. Perhaps his boldest pronouncement is his vision for the future of communications networks.

Most existing communications networks are composed of layers. Enkido aims to get rid of some of the layers. Today the most widely used technology is *Sonet*, for *synchronous optical network*, which is commonly layered with another technology called *ATM*, for *asynchronous transfer mode*, which packages voice, audio, or video data into a cell. Within each ATM cell are the services that we rely on—Internet connections, telephone calls, and data transfer activities. Essentially, the ATM cell is found within the Sonet layer, which runs on the fiber optic cable.

Enkido wants to do away with the Sonet and ATM layers, leaving a modified Internet protocol to travel directly over the fiber optic cable. The end result is faster speeds, even faster than the 40 Gbps that Enkido already offers. A radical idea that has merit, say many analysts. Others are skeptical. So far, however, Enkido is the only company to have achieved OC-768 on a commercial basis.

Part of the reason Enkido has achieved such a feat is that the company has the support and resources of major networking vendors, such as Cisco and Lucent, which have provided free prototypes of new technologies for Enkido to use and test. The company gets paid by customers and vendors who need help developing technological solutions. Last year, in addition to completing its work on its high-speed network, work for its customers netted Enkido more than $50 million in revenue.

SOURCES: "Simplicity and Power Are Driving Data Delivery; A Little-Known Company May Mirror the Future," by Seth Schiesel, *New York Times*, July 27, 2000; Enkido Web site, www.enkido.com ; "Big Apple, Big Pipes," by Mary Jander, *Light Reading*, August 11, 2000; "From the Ether…," by Bob Metcalfe, *InfoWorld*, May 1, 2000.

iMode
wireless standard that is a proprietary service of the Japanese company NTT DoCoMo

The other current wireless standard, **iMode**, is a proprietary service of the Japanese company NTT DoCoMo and is widely available in Japan where it has several million subscribers. Although U.S. companies have been resistant to using iMode, analysts report that iMode is more consumer-friendly and easier to program than WAP. It is text-based and always connected, another difference between it and WAP. iMode applications are written in cHTML which is based on HTML. Conversion of existing Web pages is quite easy. However, iMode is text-based currently and is not as capable as WML at handling graphics. DoCoMo recently announced a partnership with AOL as a means of entering the U.S. market, potentially giving iMode the footing it needs in the United States.

3G
new generation of cellular phone standards that can connect users to the Web at 2.4 Mbps

Whatever standard is adopted, the critical constraint will be bandwidth. A new generation of cellular phone standards, called **3G** for "third generation," is emerging. Already being installed in Japan, 3G cellular can connect users to the Web at 2.4 Mbps. Another technology called W-CDMA or Wideband CDMA can connect users at 2 Mbps.

These new communications technologies, coupled with far more powerful and somewhat larger handheld phones and personal organizers, will permit users nearly complete access to Web services including e-mail, video, audio, and voice-driven browsers. (See Table 3.6.)

Wireless LANs.   The wireless revolution extends far beyond cellular phones and PDAs. It also includes connecting laptops and other computers to one another and to other digital devices such as home appliances, vending machines, and remote sensors of all kinds (such as home heating systems). **Bluetooth** is a new technology standard for short-range wireless communication under 100 meters. It constantly scans its environment looking for compatible devices to connect with that are located within about 30 feet of it.

Bluetooth
new technology standard for short-range wireless communication under 100 meters

TABLE 3.6	WIRELESS WEB PRODUCTS AND PLAYERS
COMPANY	PRODUCT
Innovative Global Solution	Neopoint 1000
Mitsubishi	Mobile Access 120 Series
Motorola	i1000Plus
Nokia	9000il Communicator
Palm Computing	Palm VII
Qualcomm	PDQ Smart Phone, Thin Phone
Samsung	Duette

Today, these communications are typically handled by local area networks based on coaxial cables strung throughout buildings. Another standard is 802.11B or **Wi-Fi**, also known as **Wireless Fidelity**, which is the standard for Ethernet with greater speed and range than Bluetooth. Both of these new technologies rely on short range radio frequencies — similar to garage door openers.

As the standard is sorted out, applications of the technology will broaden from computing and office equipment to the home and public domain, such as shopping malls, doctors' offices, and libraries.

Potential wireless LAN applications include:

- Handheld devices can become multi-functional units, serving as a credit card, identification badge, and key all in one.
- Laptops can synchronize with phones to exchange data and download needed information.
- Vending machine purchases can be processed via a handheld device.
- Highway tolls can be paid via PDA.
- Documents can be printed by any printer within range, or faxed via a local machine.

Internet Appliances: The Changing Client Computer.
Internet II infrastructure will make it possible to connect nearly all the electronic devices in our lives to the Internet and private intranets. The personal computer will still be with us as a lightweight, portable, but full-function client. But nearly half of all Internet data traffic and uses will originate with newer, much smaller clients.

With the PC or handheld device as the driver, or controller, users will be able to activate and deactivate virtually any device that can be connected to the Internet. By interlinking appliances, the user can control multiple devices from one source. These products include home appliances, such as TV and stereo, telephones, games, security systems, cars. and Net PCs.

Some of these examples fit the definition of **"thin client" computing**, where the receiving device — the client — relies totally on the Internet server to handle all information processing; the device itself has no processing ability. Thin client computing has become a popular buzzword because of the market trend toward smaller, thinner client devices that require most data processing to be done by the server. But thin client also refers to PCs without hard drives, and therefore no processing power; fat clients, on the other hand, are PCs with drives.

These innovations affect the hardware side of the equation, but on the software side, keep an eye out for software subscription rentals. Major software development companies, including Microsoft, are planning to introduce software by subscription. By purchasing a subscription, a client can be assured of always having the latest version and only need pay for the software while it's needed. This service is expected to

Wi-Fi (Wireless Fidelity)
also referred to as 802.11B. Wireless standard for Ethernet networks with greater speed and range than Bluetooth

thin client computing
where the receiving device — the client — relies totally on the Internet server to handle all information processing; the device itself has no processing ability

make larger, more expensive software packages affordable for small businesses and individuals.

BENEFITS OF INTERNET II TECHNOLOGIES

The increased bandwidth and expanded network connections of the Internet II era will result in benefits beyond faster access and richer communications. Enhanced reliability and quality of Internet transmissions will create new business models and opportunities. Some of the major benefits of these technological advancements include IP multicasting, latency solutions, guaranteed service levels, lower error rates, and declining costs.

IP Multicasting.   **IP multicasting** is a set of technologies that enables efficient delivery of data to many locations on a network. Rather than making multiple copies of a message intended to be distributed to multiple recipients at the point of origin of a message, multicasting initially sends just one message and does not copy it to the individual recipients until it reaches the closest common point on the network, thereby minimizing the bandwidth consumed. (See Figure 3.17.) Network performance is significantly improved because it isn't bogged down with the processing and transmission of several large data files; each receiving computer doesn't have to query the transmitting server for the file. Multicasting technologies are already making their way into today's Internet through the use of Mbone (a special-purpose backbone for delivering video data).

Latency Solutions.   One of the challenges of packet switching, where data is divided into chunks and then sent separately to meet again at the destination, is that the Internet does not differentiate between high-priority packets, such as video clips, and those of lower priority, such as self-contained e-mail messages. Because the packets cannot yet be simultaneously reassembled, the result is distorted audio and video streams.

Internet II, however, holds the promise of **diffserve**, or differentiated quality of service — a new technology that assigns levels of priority to packets based on the type of data being transmitted. Videoconference packets, for example, which need to reach their destination almost instantaneously, would receive much higher priority than e-mail messages. In the end, the quality of video and audio will skyrocket without undue stress on the network. Live and on-demand TV and video will be possible once Internet II is completed.

Guaranteed Service Levels.   In today's Internet, there is no service-level guarantee and no way to purchase the right to move data through the Internet at a fixed pace. The Internet is democratic — it speeds or slows everyone's traffic alike. With Internet II, it will be possible to purchase the right to move data through the network at a guaranteed speed in return for higher fees.

IP multicasting
a set of technologies that enables efficient delivery of data to many locations on a network

diffserve (differentiated quality of service)
a new technology that assigns levels of priority to packets based on the type of data being transmitted

FIGURE 3.17 | IP MULTICASTING

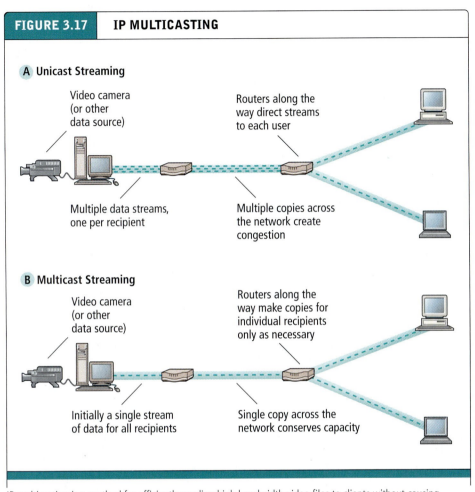

A Unicast Streaming

Video camera (or other data source)

Routers along the way direct streams to each user

Multiple data streams, one per recipient

Multiple copies across the network create congestion

B Multicast Streaming

Video camera (or other data source)

Routers along the way make copies for individual recipients only as necessary

Initially a single stream of data for all recipients

Single copy across the network conserves capacity

IP multicasting is a method for efficiently sending high bandwidth video files to clients without causing Internet congestion and delay for other traffic.

Source: www.Internet2.edu

Lower Error Rates. Improved capacity and packet switching will inevitably impact quality of data transmissions, reducing error rates and boosting customer satisfaction.

Declining Costs. As the Internet pipeline is upgraded, the availability of broadband service will expand beyond major metropolitan areas, significantly reducing the costs of access. More users means lower cost, as products and technology catch on in the mass market. Higher volume usage enables providers to lower the cost of both access devices, or clients, and the service required to use such products. Both broadband and wireless service fees are expected to decline as geographic service areas increase, in part due to competition for that business.

3.4 THE WORLD WIDE WEB

Without the World Wide Web, there would be no e-commerce. The invention of the Web brought an extraordinary expansion of digital services to millions of amateur computer users, including color text and pages, formatted text, pictures, animations, video, and sound. In short, the Web makes nearly all the rich elements of human expression needed to establish a commercial marketplace available to nontechnical computer users worldwide.

DEVELOPMENT OF THE WEB

While the Internet began to evolve starting in the 1960s, the Web was not invented until 1989–1991 by Dr. Tim Berners-Lee of the European Particle Physics Laboratory, better known as CERN (Berners-Lee et al., 1994). Several earlier authors — such as Vannevar Bush (in 1945) and Ted Nelson (in the 1960s) — had suggested the possibility of organizing knowledge as a set of interconnected pages that users could freely browse (Bush, 1945; Ziff Davis Publishing, 1998). Berners-Lee and his associates at CERN built on these ideas and developed the initial versions of HTML, HTTP, a Web server, and a browser, the four essential components of the Web.

First, Berners-Lee wrote a computer program that allowed formatted pages within his own computer to be linked using keywords (hyperlinks). Clicking on a keyword in a document would immediately move him to another document. Berners-Lee created the pages using a modified version of a powerful text markup language called SGML (Standard Generalized Markup Language).

He called this language HyperText Markup Language, or HTML. Berners-Lee then came up with the idea of storing his HTML pages on the Internet. Remote client machines could access these pages by using HTTP (introduced earlier in Section 3.2 and described more fully below). But these early Web pages still appeared as black and white text pages with hyperlinks expressed inside brackets. The early Web was still based on text only: The original Web browser only provided a line interface.

Information being shared on the Web remained text-based until 1993, when Marc Andreesen and others at the NCSA (National Center for Supercomputing Applications at the University of Illinois) created a Web browser with a graphical user interface (GUI) called **Mosaic** that made it possible to view documents on the Web graphically — using colored backgrounds, images, and even primitive animations. Mosaic was a software program that could run on any graphically based interface such as Macintosh, Windows, or UNIX. The Mosaic browser software read the HTML

Mosaic
Web browser with a graphical user interface (GUI) that made it possible to view documents on the Web graphically

text on a Web page and displayed it as a graphical interface document within a graphical user interface operating system such as Windows or Macintosh. Liberated from simple black and white text pages, HTML pages could now be viewed by anyone in the world who could operate a mouse and use a Macintosh or PC.

Aside from making the content of Web pages colorful and available to the world's population, the graphical Web browser created the possibility of **universal computing**, the sharing of files, information, graphics, sound, video, and other objects across all computer platforms in the world, regardless of operating system. A browser could be made for each of the major operating systems, and the Web pages created for one system, say, Windows, would also be displayed exactly the same, or nearly the same, on computers running the Macintosh or UNIX operating systems. As long as each operating system had a Mosaic browser, the same Web pages could be used on all the different types of machines and operating systems. This meant no matter what kind of computer you used, anywhere in the world, you would see the same Web pages. The browser and the Web have introduced us to a whole new world of computing and information management that was unthinkable prior to 1993.

In 1994 Andreesen and Jim Clark founded Netscape, which created the first commercial browser, **Netscape Navigator**. Although Mosaic had been distributed free of charge, Netscape initially charged for its software. In August 1995, Microsoft Corporation released its own version of a browser, called **Internet Explorer (IE)**. In the ensuing years, Netscape would falter, falling from a 100% market share to less than 20% in 2001. The fate of Netscape illustrates an important e-commerce business lesson: Innovators usually are not long-term winners, whereas smart followers often have the assets needed for long-term survival.

HYPERTEXT

Web pages can be accessed through the Internet because the Web browser software operating your PC can request Web pages stored on an Internet host server using the HTTP protocol. **Hypertext** is a way of formatting pages with embedded links that connect documents to one another, and that also link pages to other objects such as sound, video, or animation files. When you click on a graphic and a video clip plays, you have clicked on a hyperlink. For example, when you type a Web address in your browser such as http://www.sec.gov, your browser sends an HTTP request to the sec.gov server requesting the home page of sec.gov.

HTTP is the first set of letters at the start of every Web address, followed by the domain name. The domain name specifies the organization's server computer that is housing the document. Most companies have a domain name that is the same as or closely related to their official corporate name. The directory path and document name are two more pieces of information within the Web address that help the browser track down the requested page. Together, the address is called a Uniform Resource Locator, or URL. When typed into a browser, a URL tells it exactly where to

universal computing
the sharing of files, information, graphics, sound, video, and other objects across all computer platforms in the world, regardless of operating system

Netscape Navigator
the first commercial Web browser

Internet Explorer (IE)
Microsoft's Web browser

Hypertext
a way of formatting pages with embedded links that connect documents to one another, and that also link pages to other objects such as sound, video, or animation files

look for the information. For example, in the following URL: http://www.megacorp. com/content/features/082602.html

http = the protocol used to display Web pages

www.megacorp.com = domain name

content/features = the directory path that identifies where on the domain Web server the page is stored

082602.html = document name and its format (an html page)

The most common domain extensions currently available and officially sanctioned by ICANN are shown in the list below. Countries also have domain names such as .uk, .au, and .fr (United Kingdom, Australia, and France). Also shown in the list below are recently approved top-level domains .biz and .info, as well as new domains under consideration. In the near future, this list will expand to include many more types of organizations and industries.

.com   Commercial organizations/businesses

.edu   Educational institutions

.gov   U.S. government agencies

.mil   U.S. military

.net   Network computers

.org   Nonprofit organizations and foundations

New Top-Level Domains approved May 15, 2001:

.biz   business firms

.info   information providers

New Top-Level Domains proposed:

.aero   Air transport industry   .

.coop   Cooperatives

.museum   Museums

.name   Individuals

.pro   Professionals

MARKUP LANGUAGES

Standard Generalized Markup Language (SGML)
a early version of Generalized Markup Language (GML)

Although the most common Web page formatting language is HTML, the concept behind document formatting actually had its roots in the 1960s with the development of Generalized Markup Language (GML).

SGML.   In 1986, the International Standards Organization adopted a variation of GML called **Standard Generalized Markup Language**, or **SGML**. The purpose of

| FIGURE 3.18 | EXAMPLE HTML CODE (A) AND WEB PAGE (B) |

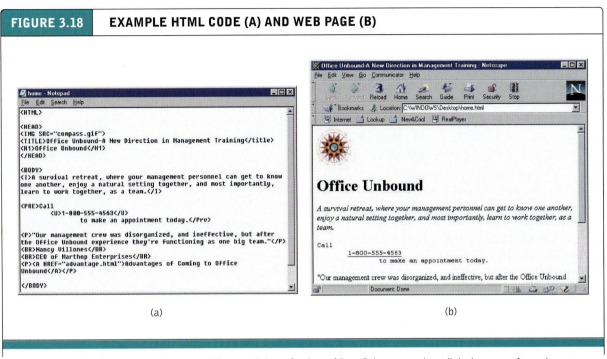

(a)　　　　　　　　　　　　　　　　　　(b)

HTML is a text markup language used to create Web pages. It has a fixed set of "tags" that are used to tell the browser software how to present the content on screen. The HTML shown in Figure 3.18 (a) creates the Web page seen in Figure 3.18 (b).

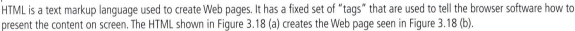

SGML was to help very large organizations format and categorize large collections of documents. The advantage of SGML is that it can run independent of any software program but, unfortunately, it is extremely complicated and difficult to learn. Probably for this reason, it has not been widely adopted.

HTML　　HTML (HyperText Markup Language) is a GML that is relatively easy to use. HTML provides Web page designers with a fixed set of markup "tags" that are used to format a Web page (see Figure 3.18). When these tags are inserted into a Web page, they are read by the browser and interpreted into a page display. You can see the source HTML code for any Web page by simply clicking on the "Page Source" command found in all browsers. In Figure 3.18, the HTML code in the first screen produces the display in the second screen.

HTML functions to define the structure and style of a document, including the headings, graphic positioning, tables, and text formatting.[5] Since its introduction, the

HTML (HyperText Markup Language)
one of the next generation of GMLs that is relatively easy to use in Web page design. HTML provides Web page designers with a fixed set of markup "tags" that are used to format a Web page

---

[5]A detailed discussion of how to use HTML is beyond the scope of this text. The reader is referred to *The Web Wizard's Guide to HTML* by Wendy Lehnert (Addison-Wesley, 2002).

two major browsers — Netscape's Navigator and Microsoft's Internet Explorer — have continuously added features to HTML to enable programmers to further refine their page layouts. Unfortunately, many of the enhancements only work in one company's browser, and this development threatens the attainment of a universal computing platform. Worse, building browsers with proprietary functionality adds to the costs of building e-commerce sites. Whenever you build an e-commerce site, special care must be taken to ensure the pages can be viewed by major browsers, even outdated versions of browsers.

HTML Web pages can be created with any text editor, such as Notepad or Wordpad, using Microsoft Word (simply save the Word document as a Web page) or any one of several Web page editors (See Table 3.7).

Extensible Markup Language (XML)

a new markup language specification developed by the W3C (the World Wide Web Consortium) that is designed to describe data and information

XML. **Extensible Markup Language (XML)** takes Web document formatting a giant leap forward. **XML** is a new markup language specification developed by the W3C (the World Wide Web Consortium). XML is a markup language like HTML, but it has very different purposes. Whereas the purpose of HTML is to control the "look and feel" and display of data on the Web page, XML is designed to describe data and information. For example, consider the sample XML document in Figure 3.19. The first line in the sample document is the XML declaration, which is always included. It defines the XML version of the document. In this case, the document conforms to the 1.0 specification of XML. The next line defines the first element of the document (the root element): < note >. The next four lines define four child elements of the root (to, from, heading, and body). The last line defines the end of the root element. Notice that XML says nothing about how to display the data, or how the text should look on the screen. HTML is used for information display in combination with XML, which is used for data description.

TABLE 3.7	HTML TOOLS
SOFTWARE TOOL	COMMENTS
Text editor, e.g. Notepad or Wordpad	Suitable for creating simple Web pages, text.
PageMill	Solid basic page editor.
FrontPage	Strong candidate for Web page creation, design, and site management tools. Good at creating and integrating graphics and other objects.
DreamWeaver	Professional Web page and site development tool. Good at creating graphics, animations, and other special effects.

FIGURE 3.19   **SAMPLE XML CODE**

Sample XML Code

```
<?xml version="1.0"?>
<note>
<to>George</to>
<from>Carol</from>
<heading>Just a Reminder</heading>
<body>Don't forget to order the groceries from WebVan!</body>
</note>
```

Source: www.xml101.com/xml

For instance, if you want to send a patient's medical record — including diagnosis, personal identity, medical history information, and any doctor's notes — from a database in Boston to a hospital in New York over the Web, it would be impossible using HTML. However, with XML, these rich documents (database records) for patients could be easily sent over the Web and displayed. For example, Figure 3.20 shows how XML can be used to define database records. Tags such as < doctor name > can be changed to be appropriate for a single firm or an entire industry. This flexibility will enable organizations to put most of their information processing functions into an Internet processing environment.

As can be seen in Figure 3.20, XML is "extensible," which means the tags used to describe and display data are defined by the user, whereas in HTML the tags are limited and predefined. XML can also transform information into new formats, such as

FIGURE 3.20   **SAMPLE XML CODE FOR A MEDICAL RECORD**

```
<?xml version="1.0"?>
<list>
<medical record patient id=456 45 3498>
<name>John Q. Williams<name>
<address>52 Oregon Road<address>
<city>Ann Arbor<city>
<state>Michigan<state>
<zip code>45678<zip code>
<doctor name>Frank Lucretis<doctor name>
<list>
```

by importing information from a database and displaying it as a table. With XML, information can be analyzed and displayed selectively, making it a more powerful alternative to HTML. This means that business firms, or entire industries, can describe all of their invoices, accounts payable, payroll records, and financial information using a Web-compatible markup language. Once described, these business documents can be stored on intranet Web servers and shared throughout the corporation.

XML is not yet a replacement for HTML. Currently, XML is fully supported only by Microsoft's Internet Explorer 5, and is not supported by Netscape (although this may change). Whether XML eventually supplants HTML as the standard Web formatting specification depends a lot on whether it is supported by future Web browsers. Currently, XML and HTML work side by side on the same Web pages. HTML is used to define how information should be formatted, and XML is being used to describe the data itself.

WEB SERVERS AND CLIENTS

We have already described client/server computing and the revolution in computing architecture brought about by client/server computing. You already know that a server is a computer attached to a network that stores files, controls peripheral devices, interfaces with the outside world — including the Internet — and does some processing for other computers on the network.

Web server software
software that enables a computer to deliver Web pages written in HTML to client machines on a network that request this service by sending an HTTP request

But what is a Web server? **Web server software** refers to the software that enables a computer to deliver Web pages written in HTML to client machines on a network that request this service by sending an HTTP request. The two leading brands of Web server software are Apache, which is free Web server shareware that accounts for about 60% of the market, and Microsoft's NT Server software, which accounts for about 20% of the market.

Aside from responding to requests for Web pages, all Web servers provide some additional basic capabilities such as the following:

- *Security services* — These consist mainly of authentication services that verify that the person trying to access the site is authorized to do so. For Web sites that process payment transactions, the Web server also supports Secure Sockets Layer (SSL), the Internet protocol for transmitting and receiving information securely over the Internet. When private information such as names, phone numbers, addresses, and credit card data need to be provided to a Web site, the Web server uses SSL to ensure that the data passing back and forth from the browser to the server is not compromised.

- *File Transfer Protocol (FTP)* — This protocol allows users to transfer files to and from the server. Some sites limit file uploads to the Web server, while others restrict downloads, depending on the user's identity.

- *Search engine* — Just as search engine sites enable users to search the entire Web for particular documents, search engine modules within the basic Web server software package enable indexing of the site's Web pages and content, and permit easy keyword searching of the site's content. When conducting a search, a search engine makes use of an *index*, which is a list of all the documents on the server.. The search term is compared to the index to identify likely matches.

- *Data capture* — Web servers are also helpful at monitoring site traffic, capturing information on who has visited a site, how long the user stayed there, the date and time of each visit, and which specific pages on the server were accessed. This information is compiled and saved in a log file, which can then be analyzed by a user log file. By analyzing a log file, a site manager can find out the total number of visitors, average length of each visit, and the most popular destinations, or Web pages.

The term *Web server* is sometimes also used to refer to the physical computer that runs Web server software. Leading manufacturers of Web server computers are IBM, Compaq, Dell, and Hewlett Packard. Although any personal computer can run Web server software, it is best to use a computer that has been optimized for this purpose. To be a Web server, a computer must have the Web server software described above installed and be connected to the Internet. Every Web server machine has an IP address. For example, if you type *http://www.aw.com/laudon*, in your browser, the browser software sends a request for HTTP service to the Web server whose domain name is *aw.com*. The server then locates the page named "laudon" on its hard drive, sends the page back to your browser, and displays it on your screen.

Aside from the generic Web server software packages, there are actually many types of specialized servers on the Web, from **database servers** that access specific information with a database, to **ad servers** that deliver targeted banner ads, to **mail servers** that provide mail messages, and **video servers** that provide video clips. At a small e-commerce site, all of these software packages might be running on a single machine, with a single processor. At a large corporate site, there may be hundreds of discrete machines, many with multiple processors, running specialized Web server functions described above. We discuss the architecture of e-commerce sites in greater detail in Chapter 4.

A **Web client**, on the other hand, is any computing device attached to the Internet that is capable of making HTTP requests and displaying HTML pages. The most common client is a Windows PC or Macintosh, with various flavors of UNIX machines a distant third. However, the fastest growing category of Web clients are not computers at all, but personal digital assistants (PDAs) such as the Palm and HP Jornada, and cellular phones outfitted with wireless Web access software. In general, Web clients can be any device — including a refrigerator, stove, home lighting system, or automobile instrument panel — capable of sending and receiving information from Web servers.

database server
server designed to access specific information with a database

ad server
server designed to deliver targeted banner ads

mail server
server that provides mail messages

video server
server that serves video clips

Web client
any computing device attached to the Internet that is capable of making HTTP requests and displaying HTML pages, most commonly a Windows PC or Macintosh

WEB BROWSERS

The primary purpose of Web browsers is to display Web pages, but browsers also have added features, such as e-mail and newsgroups (an online discussion group or forum).

Currently 94% of Web users use either Internet Explorer or Netscape Navigator, but recently some new browsers have been developed that are beginning to attract attention. The browser Opera is becoming very popular because of its speed — it is currently the world's fastest browser — and because it is much smaller than existing browsers (it can almost fit on a single diskette). It can also remember the last Web page you visited, so the next time you surf, you can start where you left off. And like the big two, you can get it for free; the catch is that you have to watch blinking ads in one corner, or pay $40 for the ad-free version of Opera.

The browser NeoPlanet is also gaining new fans, primarily because of the 500+ *skins*, or design schemes, that come with it. Using skins, you can design the browser to look and sound just the way you'd like it to, rather than being limited to the standard look provided by Navigator and Internet Explorer. However, NeoPlanet requires Internet Explorer's technology in order to operate, so you must also have IE installed on your computer.

3.5   THE INTERNET AND THE WEB: FEATURES

The Internet and the Web have spawned a number of powerful new software applications upon which the foundations of e-commerce are built.

E-MAIL

electronic mail (e-mail)
the most-used application of the Internet. Uses a series of protocols to enable messages containing text, images, sound, and video clips to be transferred from one Internet user to another

Since its earliest days, **electronic mail**, or e-mail, has been the most-used application of the Internet. An estimated 3.5 billion business e-mails and 2.7 billion personal e-mails are sent every day in the United States (McGrane, 2001). Worldwide, more than 8 billion e-mails are sent each day. E-mail uses a series of protocols to enable messages containing text, images, sound, and video clips to be transferred from one Internet user to another. Because of its flexibility and speed, it is now the most popular form of business communication — more popular than the phone, fax, or snail mail (the U.S. Postal Service).

In addition to text typed within the message, e-mail also allows **attachments**, which are files inserted within the e-mail message. The files can be documents, images, or sound or video clips.

attachment
a file inserted within the e-mail message

Although e-mail was designed to be used for interpersonal messages, it can also be a very effective marketing tool. E-commerce sites purchase e-mail lists from list providers and send mail to prospective customers, as well as existing customers. The response rate from targeted e-mail campaigns can be as high as 20%, extraordinary when compared to banner ad response rates of less than 1%. Most e-commerce sites also have a "Contact Us" section that includes an e-mail contact, to make requests and comments easier for customers.

However, in addition to this acceptable practice of communicating with people who have requested such contact, some companies also use e-mail as a mass mailing technique, also known as **spam,** or unsolicited e-mail. There are a number of state laws against spamming, but it is still the bane of the Web.

SEARCH ENGINES

Search engines can be Web sites themselves, such as Google and AltaVista, or a service within a site that allows users to ask for information about various topics. A **search engine** identifies Web pages that appear to match keywords, also called *queries,* typed by the user and provides a list of the best matches. A query can be a question, a series of words, or a single word for the search engine to look for.

How exactly individual search engines work is a proprietary secret, and at times defies explanation. Some search engines — among them Alta Vista — seek to visit every Web page in existence, read the contents of the home page, identify the most common words or keywords, and create a huge database of domain names with keywords. Sometimes the search engines will just read the meta tags and other keyword sections of the home page. This is faster, but Web designers often stuff an extraordinary number of keywords into their meta tags. The program that search engines unleash on the Web to perform this indexing function is called a *spider* or *crawler*. Unfortunately, as the number of Web pages climbs to over two billion, more and more pages are missed by the search engines. Google, perhaps the most complete search engine, contains references to only about half (one billion) of all Web pages. And the engines do not always overlap, which means you may miss a page on one engine, but pick it up on another. It's best therefore to use multiple search engines.

Other search engines use different strategies. As you learned in Chapter 2, Google uses a collaborative filtering technique: It indexes and ranks sites based on the number of users who request and land at a site. This method is biased by volume: You see the Web pages others have asked to see. Yahoo, on the other hand, uses a staff of human indexers to organize as many pages as they can. It is very difficult to get your site registered on Yahoo because of the limitations of their method, which is biased toward sites that somehow come to the attention of Yahoo staff. Once again, the best advice is to use several different search engines.

Figure 3.21 lists the top search engines, based on the percentage of users estimated to have visited them during February 2001.

One of the newest trends in search engines is focus; instead of trying to cover every possible information need that users have, some search engines are electing to specialize in one particular area. By limiting their coverage to such topics as sports,

spam
unsolicited e-mail

search engine
identifies Web pages that appear to match keywords, also called queries, typed by the user and provides a list of the best matches

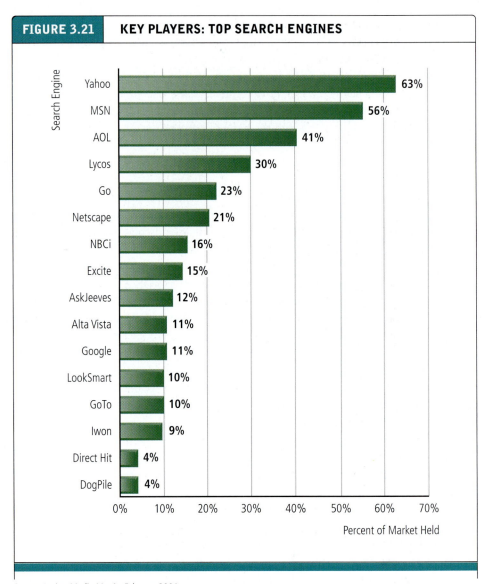

FIGURE 3.21 | **KEY PLAYERS: TOP SEARCH ENGINES**

Source: Jupiter Media Metrix, Feburary 2001

news, medicine, or finance, niche search engines are hoping to differentiate themselves from the crowd and provide better quality results for users. FindLaw.com, a search engine and directory of legal information, has seen its searches rising steadily. The same is true of Moreover.com, a search engine that specializes in collecting and reporting news headlines from more than 1,800 news sites.

Although the major search engines are used for tracking down general information of interest to users, such as a site for buying beer-making supplies, or statistics on Internet usage in Barbados, they have also become a crucial tool within e-commerce sites. Customers can more easily search for the exact item they want with the help of a search program; the difference is that within Web sites, the search engine is limited to finding matches from that one site. Sites without search engines are asking visitors to spend lots of time exploring the site — something few people are willing to do — when most sites offer a quick-and-easy way to find what they're looking for.

INTELLIGENT AGENTS (BOTS)

Intelligent agents, or **software robots** (**bots** for short) are software programs that gather and/or filter information on a specific topic, and then provide a list of results for the user. Intelligent agents were originally invented by computer scientists interested in the development of artificial intelligence (a family of related technologies that attempt to imbue computers with human-like intelligence). However, with the advent of e-commerce on the Web, interest quickly turned to exploiting intelligent agent technology for commercial purposes. Today, there are a number of different types of bots used in e-commerce on the Web, and more are being developed every day. See Table 3.8.

For instance, as previously noted, many search engines employ *web crawlers* or *spiders* that crawl from server to server, compiling lists of URLs that form the database for the search engine. These web crawlers and spiders are actually bots.

The *shopping bot* is another common type of bot. Shopping bots search online retail sites all over the Web and then report back on the availability and pricing of a range of products. For instance, you can use MySimon.com's shopping bot to search for a Sony digital camera. The bot provides a list of online retailers that carry a particular camera model, as well as report about whether it is in inventory and what the price and shipping charges are.

Another type of bot, called an *update bot*, allows you to monitor for updated materials on the Web, and will e-mail you when a selected site has new or changed information. *News bots* will create custom newspapers or clip articles for you in newspapers around the world.

Read *Insight on Technology: Chatterbots at Work*, to see how a bot with academic roots has morphed into an e-commerce tool.

INSTANT MESSAGING

E-mail messages have a time lag of several seconds to minutes between when messages are sent and received, but **instant messaging (IM)** displays words typed on a computer almost instantaneously. Recipients can then respond immediately to the sender the same way, making the communication more like a live conversation than is possible through e-mail.

intelligent agents (software robots or bots)
software programs that gather and/or filter information on a specific topic and then provide a list of results for the user

instant messaging (IM)
displays words typed on a computer almost instantaneously. Recipients can then respond immediately to the sender the same way, making the communication more like a live conversation than is possible through e-mail

TABLE 3.8	TYPES OF WEB BOTS
TYPE	**EXAMPLE**
Search Bot	Altavista.com Webcrawler.com
Shopping Bot	MySimon.com Jango.com DealTime.com
Update Bot	UrlyWarning.com
News Bot	WebClipping.com Sportspider.net
Chatter Bot	Lucy (ArtificialLife.com) Eve (eGain.com) Nicole (NativeMinds.com)

America Online (AOL) was the first to introduce a widely accepted Instant Messaging system several years ago, which is credited with the company's sudden surge in users. AOL's system is proprietary. One of the key components of an IM service is a *buddy list*, as AOL called it. The buddy list is a private list of people with whom you might want to communicate. If a person is on your buddy list, AOL will alert you when that individual signs on, enabling an IM to be sent.

The downside is that IM systems are proprietary — no standard has been set yet — so that competing sites have created their own IM services. Yahoo has IM, as does MSN, but neither works in conjunction with the others.

Interestingly, despite the wild popularity of such services, no one seems to know yet how to make money from it. AOL, Yahoo, and MSN have all offered IM free to their users and have no immediate plans to start charging a fee. True, it is a marketing draw that brings in new users, but that doesn't necessarily translate into profits.

Nevertheless, some companies have added IM to their Web sites as a means of offering instant access to customer service. For example, Sotheby's, an auction house, encourages visitors to chat live with a Sotheby's representative online. The hope is that by encouraging consumers' need for immediate gratification — whether in the form of a question answered or product ordered — IM will boost revenues and customer satisfaction.

chat
enables users to communicate via computer in real time, that is, simultaneously. Unlike IM, chat can occur among several users.

CHAT

Like IM, **chat** enables users to communicate via computer in real time, that is, simultaneously. However, unlike IM, which can only work between two people, chat can occur between several users.

For many Web sites, developing a community of like-minded users has been critical for their growth and success. Just look at eBay.com, which would probably have been unsuccessful without its corps of auction fans, or About.com, which exists to serve communities of consumers with similar interests. Once those community members come together on a site, chat can be a service that enables them to further bond and network, endearing them further to the Web site.

Chat is also used frequently in distance learning, for class discussions and online discussions sponsored by a company. When a celebrity appears on an entertainment Web site, for example, they use chat software in order to see and respond to questions from audience members out in cyberspace.

MUSIC, VIDEO, AND OTHER STANDARD FILES

Although the low bandwidth of Internet I era connections has made audio and video files more difficult to share, with Internet II, these files will become more commonplace. Today it is possible to send and receive files containing music or other audio information, video clips, animation, photographs, and other images, although the download times can be very long, especially for those using a 56 Kbps modem.

Video clips, Flash animations, and photo images are now routinely displayed either as part of Web sites, or sent as attached files. Companies that want to demonstrate use of their product have found video clips to be extremely effective. And audio reports and discussions have also become commonplace, either as marketing materials or customer reports. Photos, of course, have become an important element of most Web sites, helping to make site designs more interesting and eye catching, not to mention helping to sell products, just as catalogs do.

STREAMING MEDIA

Streaming media enables music, video, and other large files to be sent to users in chunks so that when received and played, the file comes through uninterrupted. Streamed files must be viewed "live": They cannot be stored on client hard drives. RealAudio and RealVideo are the most widely used streaming tools. Streaming audio and video segments used in Web ads or CNN news stories are perhaps the most frequently used streaming services.

Macromedia's Shockwave is commonly used to stream audio and video for instructional purposes. Macromedia's Flash vector graphics program is the fastest growing streaming audio and video tool. Flash has the advantage of being built into most client browsers; no plug-in is required to play Flash files.

COOKIES

Cookies are a tool used by Web sites to store information about a user. When a visitor enters a Web site, the site sends a small text file (the cookie) to the user's computer

streaming media
enables music, video, and other large files to be sent to users in chunks so that when received and played, the file comes through uninterrupted

cookie
a tool used by Web sites to store information about a user. When a visitor enters a Web site, the site sends a small text file (the cookie) to the user's computer so that information from the site can be loaded more quickly on future visits. The cookie can contain any information desired by the site designers

CHATTERBOTS AT WORK

In the early 1960s, Joseph Weizenbaum, a professor of computer science at the Massachusetts Institute of Technology, created a software program known as Eliza. Eliza was one of the first software programs to allow a computer to "converse" with a human in natural language. Weizenbaum programmed Eliza so that it was able to recognize certain key words in a statement or question. Eliza would then respond based on a set of pre-programmed rules. Sometimes Eliza was able to carry on a passable conversation — for a short period of time. More often than not, though, the conversation quickly degenerated into something no person would mistake for a human interaction.

From this rudimentary beginning sprang chatterbots: intelligent agents that can converse with a user over the Web. Since the early days of Eliza, tremendous advances have been made in artificial intelligence and natural language processing. Chatterbots today have become surprisingly articulate and responsive, and in many cases are represented graphically as animated characters that respond with facial expressions and gestures that are linked to a huge database of words. For instance, bots created by Artificial Life, one of the leaders in intelligent agent technologies, can smile, laugh, wink, blink, and scowl, all in context-specific situations. The most sophisticated bots also learn as they interact and remember the actions users took and the preferences they expressed.

Chatterbots are being viewed as one possible answer to the customer service difficulties plagu-ing many e-commerce sites, problems that cost e-tailers billions of dollars in 2000. For instance, one study found that the response times of Fortune 100 companies to simple e-mail queries left much to be desired, with only 13% responding within 24 hours. Another study found that over 65% of those who start to fill up a shopping cart abandon it before going through the check-out process, for a variety of reasons, including poor Web site design, a confusing check-out process, or questions that were unanswered.

Chatterbots can handle a number of functions that real-world sales assistants might normally handle — greeting you when you visit a site, engaging you in chat, remembering your preferences. They can serve as a virtual tour guide to the site, whisking you to the page you need without drill-down menus, click-throughs, or site maps. In addition, the cost of a chatterbot is much less than that of a representative working via the telephone — less than $1 per incident for a chatterbot compared to $20–$35 per incident for a telephone representative.

Chatterbots are already starting to make their presence known on a variety of e-tail sites. For instance, Artificial Life's animated sales representative, Kim, sells cellular phones online for the German telecom company MobilCom. A chatterbot created by Extempo represents Proctor & Gamble's Mr. Clean character at the www.mrclean.com Web site. And Ford Motor Company has recently announced plans to deploy Virtual Representatives created by NativeMinds to provide online technical and support assistance to

(continued)

over 5,000 Ford and Lincoln Mercury dealerships in the United States and Canada.

The use of chatterbots does present some issues. According to Extempo, 90% of the customers who click on one of its bots will chat for over 10 minutes, and more than 90% of customers asked a personal question by a bot will respond with an answer. According to Robert Pantaro, chief financial officer of Artificial Life, "Small talk capability gets people comfortable. People start talking about themselves, volunteering a lot of important stuff that's beneficial to companies— name, age, occupation. No offense to people mining click data or cookie data, like DoubleClick, but we're taking online marketing to the next level. People find cookies intrusive and are more apt to turn them off. Not so for our agents." What a site does with the information extracted by a chatterbot is obviously a privacy concern that has to be addressed as chatterbots become more prevalent.

▬▬▬ Sources: "To Bot or Not to Bot," by Kristin Zhivago, *Business 2.0*, March 6, 2001; "Recruiting the Chatterbots," by Michael Leaverton, *C/Net Tech Trends*, October 2, 2000; "Invasion of the Virbots," by Dolly Setton, *Forbes*, September 11, 2000; "Talk to the Bot," by Jenny Oh, *Industry Standard*, June 12, 2000.

so that information from the site can be loaded more quickly on future visits. The cookie can contain any information desired by the site designers, including customer number, pages visited, products examined, and other detailed information on the behavior of the consumer at the site. Cookies are useful to consumers because the site will recognize returning patrons and not ask them to register again. Cookies can also help personalize a site by allowing the site to recognize returning customers and make special offers to them based on their past behavior at the site. Cookies can also permit customization and market segmentation — the ability to change the product or the price based on prior consumer information (described more fully in later chapters). As we will discuss throughout the book, cookies also can pose a threat to consumer privacy, and at times they are bothersome. Many people clear their cookies at the end of every day. Some disable them entirely.

INTERNET II AND E-COMMERCE: EMERGING FEATURES AND SERVICES

The Internet II infrastructure will permit the rapid deployment of new services and greatly expand e-commerce opportunities. New technologies, increased bandwidth, and greater reliance on the Internet for communications will create new e-commerce product and service opportunities and potentially replace existing modes of communication. Telephone communication is one area destined for change.

Internet Telephony.   Internet telephony is not entirely new. **IP telephony** is a general term for the technologies that use the **Voice Over Internet Protocol (VOIP)** and the Internet's packet-switched network to transmit voice, fax, and other forms of

IP telephony
a general term for the technologies that use VOIP and the Internet's packet-switched network to transmit voice and other forms of audio communication over the Internet

Voice Over Internet Protocol (VOIP)
protocol that allows for transmission of voice and other forms of audio communication over the Internet

audio communication over the Internet. The major advantage, of course, is the cost: It's free. VOIP avoids the long distance charges imposed by phone companies.

The problem with VOIP has been that breaking calls into packets in order to transmit them via the Internet often results in poor voice quality. However, with new high bandwidth connections, quality problems will diminish; use of VOIP is expected to rise dramatically. New communications services will also be introduced that combine voice and computer functioning, such as call forwarding on Internet lines that can send callers to voice mail or e-mail, or the ability to click on a buddy list member and initiate voice chat, rather than text-based Instant Messaging. Because of these new capabilities, analysts are expecting major increases in the amount and type of VOIP usage in the very near future.

Although VOIP accounted for just 1.4% of all phone calls in the year 2000, by 2004 that percentage will hit close to 14%, according to analysts. In revenue terms, Internet voice traffic yielded $1.6 billion in 2000, versus a projected $18.7 billion in 2004. (See Figure 3.22.)

In the past, voice and fax were the exclusive provenance of the regulated telephone networks. With the convergence of the Internet and telephony, however, this dominance is already starting to change, with local and long distance telephone providers and cable companies becoming ISPs, and ISPs getting into the phone market (see Table 3.9). Part of the attraction to this market may be that, unlike traditional phone services, IP telephony is currently free of governmental oversight, with the FCC (Federal Communications Commission) stating that it has no immediate intention of stepping in.

Digital Libraries.   As bandwidth capabilities of the Internet increase, distribution of software applications by Application Service Providers (ASPs) over the Internet is also expected to increase. Digital libraries of software applications will emerge as companies and individuals elect to rent software rather than buy it. Accessing a Web server will enable a user to download the desired software, paying a subscription fee instead of a purchase price. This service will be especially useful for expensive software packages, such as graphic design or software development tools, that few individuals could afford. Multimedia digital libraries, with automated video and audio indexing, navigation, and search and retrieval, will also be available.

Distributed Storage.   ASPs can assist both in processing data and in storing it, dispersing it to multiple servers rather than having it reside on one. Although compiling information from multiple sources used to be a challenge for computers, it has become commonplace today. Sophisticated software, such as XML, can now extract pieces of data from various sources, analyze it, and report the results in a predetermined fashion.

FIGURE 3.22	THE GROWTH OF INTERNET TELEPHONY

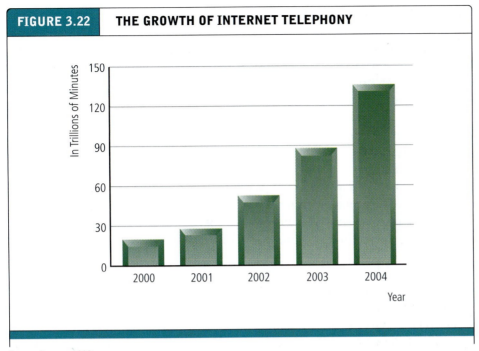

Source: Sweeny, 2000

TABLE 3.9	KEY TELEPHONY PLAYERS

COMPANY	SPECIALTY
Cisco	Equipment
VocalTec	Equipment
3Com	Equipment
Netspeak	Equipment
Nortel	Equipment
Lucent	Equipment, service provider
ITXC	Service provider
Comcast	Service provider
AT&T	Service provider (in trial period)
IBasis	Service provider

Distance Learning.   Perhaps one of the biggest educational initiatives in recent years, the distance learning opportunity has pushed schools, colleges, and universities worldwide to make courses and whole degree programs available online. The sticking point has been the lack of interactivity available through the Internet. Some schools have tried to get around this by providing videos of actual lectures and encouraging regular chat sessions as class supplements, but two-way communication between student and teacher had a significant time lag. Now, through videoconferencing, students can watch in real time as professors give lectures. Student interactions and questions can also incorporate a visual image of the student in action, rather than a text-only message.

Development of the application software required to merge video, audio, and voice at once is a prime opportunity for an ASP, rather than for the schools themselves. Distributing the software from the company's server will also reduce the data load on school computing systems and place the burden for reliability on the ASP (Center for Media Education, 2000).

Digital Video.   Ted Hanss, Internet2 Director for Applications Development, considers digital video to be the "killer app" for Internet II. Future digital video networks will be able to deliver better-than-broadcast quality video over the Internet to computers and other devices. High quality interactive video and audio will make sales presentations and demonstrations more effective and lifelike and enable companies to develop new forms of customer support. New video, audio, and presentation approaches could also dramatically change the nature of the media and news business.

Video Teleconferencing.   Although video teleconferencing has been available for years, few companies and individuals have made use of it simply because both the cost of equipment and rental fees have been high. Internet II will significantly reduce that cost, making it affordable for most workers to use video conferencing to share information that involves either an image or audio component. Meetings of geographically dispersed workers or colleagues will be easy to arrange, using VOIP technology, and the quality of image and audio transmission will be much higher.

Tele-immersion.   One of the newest services to come onto the market will be tele-immersion, a merger of virtual reality and video conferencing, where participants can see each other and collaborate on visual projects. For instance, at the University of Illinois at Chicago, researchers are working on CALVIN, a testbed for using virtual reality in architectural design. Researchers believe high-speed connectivity, collaborative design systems that allow customers and vendors to interactively design and develop new products, coupled with virtual reality modeling and simulation such as this could dramatically reduce the time required for new product development.

M-commerce Applications.   Combining voice, data, images, audio, and video on one wireless device will become possible during Internet II. As one commentator noted, "when high-bandwidth wireless and the fiber-optic based Internet2 converge, that's when we go from e-business to e-life" (McGarr, 2000). We will describe many m-commerce applications in later chapters.

Into Networks

Into Networks was founded in 1996 by Ric Fulop, then a 21-year-old Internet wunderkind who had already founded and sold two companies; Derek Atkins, an MIT Media Lab computer scientist; and Rouzeh Yassini, the inventor of the cable modem. Originally named Arepa, Inc., Into Networks' goal was to create a way to deliver high-bandwidth CD-ROM content over the Internet, while eliminating the need to actually download and install the software on a user's PC. Their vision was real-time delivery of "software-on-demand" — users would be able to "click and play" any one of thousands of software titles with no wait for access.

But how could they hope to achieve this goal when it can take up to 18 hours to download a 450 MB CD using a 56k modem connection?

The answer rests in part in the broadband distribution networks that were beginning to be developed in the mid-1990s: Cable, DSL, and satellite networks all offered "fatter pipes" that promised to increase throughput on the Internet. Although a necessary ingredient, the existence of fat broadband pipes was not sufficient in and of itself. Even with a broadband connection and a cable modem, it still takes over an hour to download a 450 MB CD-ROM. Delays in transmission (latency) that result from the packet-switching nature of the Internet also can interfere with the seamless delivery of software over the Net. There were a number of other problems that also needed to addressed, such as developing a payment mechanism for software-on-demand as well as the security concerns of the software creators.

With early funding from Yassini's YAS Corporation, Fidelity Ventures, Venrock Associates, and Intel, a team of MIT-trained engineers at Into Networks began by developing a patent-pending system, which it calls *briqing,* to encode CD-ROM content. The briqing process essentially breaks existing software into small pieces that can be delivered efficiently over a broadband network without affecting the underlying source code. In addition to being broken apart and then compressed, briqing also encrypts each CD-ROM file so that it can be delivered in a secure manner.

The second part of Into Network's solution addressed the latency issue. Once briqued, a copy of the encoded content is stored on each of Into Network's last-mile, RAFT (Random Access File Transfer) content servers located throughout the country at broadband network head ends. This allows Into Networks to more efficiently stream software in real time. When an end user requests a particular CD-ROM title, the request goes to the local RAFT. Only executable and any other necessary files are delivered at that time. Then, when the user has additional requirements, such as advancing to the next level of a game or utilizing a particular feature of a piece of software, that file is delivered. If a user repeats a request, the file is delivered either from the cache on the user's machine or from the cache at the broadband head end. To the user, the software appears to be running seamlessly.

Into Networks coupled its distributed content network with a centrally hosted system located on a secure server at its headquarters in Massachusetts. The centrally hosted system provides a storefront that serves as the point of initial interaction with an end user, provides access to software titles, handles the authorization of end-user access to requested titles, and provides the e-commerce billing solution.

Even though it now has its technology in place, Into Networks faces many challenges before its vision becomes a viable reality. It has inked alliances with most of the major distributors of cable and DSL broadband services. However, broadband service, though growing, is still only a very small piece of the overall Internet pie. For instance, as of 2001, there were only about 6 million homes in the United States with broadband access, compared to 40 million with 56.6k or less dial-up service. Commentators point to a chicken and egg problem: It is hard to attract new broadband subscribers unless they can be offered content that is compelling and different, but until broadband achieves a higher penetration rate, it does not make economic sense to cre-

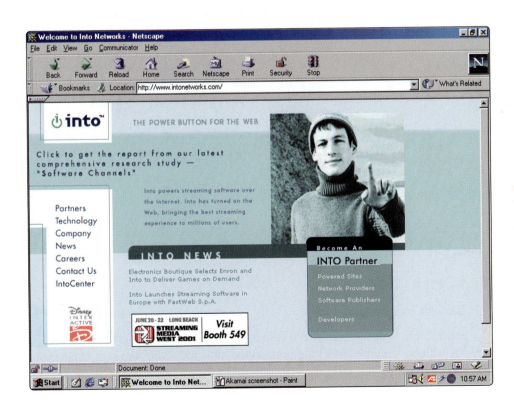

SOURCES: "Monetizing the Bits," by Vincent Grosso, *Internet Industry Magazine,* Fall/Winter 2000/2001; "Games and Software: Flowing Streams," by Greg Frame, *Streaming Media,* October 12, 2000; "ASP Makes Play for Consumer Market," by Eric Ladley, *ISP Business News,* October 16, 2000; "A Software Tryout Service for Broadband Customers," *Internet World,* August 1, 2000; "Subscription Software Services Could Reshape the Industry," *Wall Street Journal,* June 19, 2000.

ate broadband content. Into Networks hopes to be a partial solution to that problem by allowing content providers to utilize existing content.

Convincing content providers to sign up is another challenge. The software rental and subscription revenue models are new to the software industry. Software subscription prices are very low in order to attract subscribers, and about 20% of the monthly software subscription revenue goes to the local broadband service owner. This does not leave much left over for the content providers. Software providers also must be assured that they will not cannibalize existing distribution channels by offering their software on a pay-per-play, rental, or subscription basis via Into Networks. So far, only around 30 software publishers have signed up with Into Networks and have made approximately 700 software titles available to subscribers, a mere drop in the bucket.

Attracting customers and getting them to pay is another issue. Overcoming the "I want it free" mentality is perhaps the greatest challenge Into Networks faces.

Case Study Questions

1. Why does Intro Networks need RAFT servers for interactive software content?

2. If you were a software content owner, would you sign up for the Into Network solution? Why or why not?

3. Would you be willing to use Into Networks for software services such as word processing or spreadsheet programs? How much would you be willing to pay monthly for access to a word processing or spreadsheet program?

4. If you were a venture capital investor, what factors would encourage you to invest in Into Networks? What factors would discourage your investment?

3.7 REVIEW

KEY CONCEPTS

■ Discuss the origins of the Internet.

The Internet has evolved from a collection of mainframe computers located on a few U.S. college campuses to an interconnected network of thousands of networks and millions of computers worldwide.

The history of the Internet can be divided into three phases:
- During the Innovation Phase (1961–1974), its purpose was to link researchers nationwide via computer.
- During the Institutional Phase (1975–1995), the Department of Defense and National Science Foundation provided funding to expand the fundamental building blocks of the Internet into a complex military communications system and then into a civilian system.
- During the Commercialization Phase (1995 to the present), government agencies encouraged corporations to assume responsibility for further expansion of the network and private business began to exploit the Internet for commercial purposes.

■ **Relate the key technology concepts behind the Internet.**

The Internet's three key technology components are:
- *Packet switching*, which slices digital messages into packets, routes the packets along different communication paths as they become available, and then reassembles the packets once they arrive at their destination.
- *TCP/IP*. TCP establishes the connections among sending and receiving Web computers and handles the assembly of packets at the point of transmission, as well as their reassembly at the receiving end. IP provides the addressing scheme, enabling messages to arrive at the proper destination computer.
- *Client/server technology*, which makes it possible for large amounts of information to be stored on Web servers and shared with individual users on their client computers.

■ **Describe the role of Internet protocols and utility programs.**

Internet protocols and utility programs make the following Internet services possible:
- *HTTP* delivers requested Web pages, allowing users to view them.
- *STMP* and *POP* enable mail to be routed to a mail server and then picked up by the recipient's server, while *IMAP* enables mail to be sorted before being downloaded by the recipient.
- *FTP* is used to transfer files from servers to clients and vice versa.
- *SSL* ensures that information transmissions are encrypted.
- *Telnet* is a utility program that enables work to be done remotely.
- *Finger* is a utility program that allows you to find out who is logged onto a remote network.
- *Ping* is a utility program that allows users to verify a connection between client and server.
- *Tracert* lets you track the route a message takes from a client to a remote computer.

■ **Explain the structure of the Internet today.**

The main structural elements of the Internet are:
- The *backbone*, which is composed primarily of high-bandwidth fiber optic cable operated by a variety of providers.
- *NAPs* and *MAEs*, which are hubs that use high-speed switching computers to connect the backbone with regional and local networks.
- *Campus networks*, which are local area networks operating within a single organization that connect directly to regional networks.
- *Internet Service Providers*, which deal with the "last mile" of service to homes and offices. ISPs offer a variety of types of service, ranging from dial-up service to broadband DSL, cable modem, T1 and T3 lines, and satellite link service.

■ **Understand the limitations of today's Internet.**

To envision what the Internet of tomorrow — Internet II — will look like, we must first look at the limitations of today's Internet.
- *Bandwidth limitations*: Today's Internet is slow and incapable of effectively sharing and displaying large files, such as video and voice files.
- *Quality of service limitations*: Data packets don't all arrive in the correct order, at the same moment, causing latency; latency creates jerkiness in video files and voice messages.
- *Network architecture limitations*: Servers can't keep up with demand. Future improvements to Internet infrastructure will improve the way servers process requests for information, thus improving overall speed.
- *Language development limitations*: The nature of HTML restricts the quality of "rich" information that can be shared online. Future languages will enable improved display and viewing of video and graphics.

■ **Describe the potential capabilities of Internet II.**

Internet2 is a consortium working together to develop and test new technologies for potential use on the Internet. Internet2 participants are working in a number of areas, including
- advanced network infrastructure;
- new networking capabilities;
- middleware; and
- advanced applications that incorporate audio and video to create new services.

In addition to the Internet2 project, other groups are working to expand Internet bandwidth via improvements to fiber optic technologies and through photonics technologies such as Dense Wavelength Division Multiplexing, optical and fiber switches, optical switching components, optical integrated circuits, and optical networks. Wireless Web and 3G technologies will provide users of cellular phones and PDAs with increased access to the Internet and its various services. The increased bandwidth and expanded connections of the Internet II era will result in a number of benefits, including

- IP multicasting, which will enable more efficient delivery of data;
- latency solutions such as diffserve (differentiated quality of service), which assigns levels of priority to packets based on the type of data being transmitted;
- guaranteed service levels;
- lower error rates; and
- declining costs.

■ **Understand how the World Wide Web works.**

The Web was developed during 1989–1991 by Dr. Tim Berners-Lee, who created a computer program that allowed formatted pages stored on the Internet to be linked using keywords (hyperlinks). In 1993, Marc Andreesen created the first graphical Web browser, which made it possible to view documents on the Web graphically and created the possibility of universal computing. The key concepts you need to be familiar with in order to understand how the Web works are the following:

- *Hypertext*, which is a way of formatting pages with embedded links that connect documents to one another and that also link pages to other objects.
- *HTTP (HyperText Transfer Protocol)*, which is the protocol used to transmit Web pages over the Internet.
- *URLs (uniform resource locators)*, which are the addresses at which Web pages can be found.
- *HTML*, which is the programming language used to create most Web pages and which provides designers with a fixed set of tags that are used to format a Web page
- *XML*, which is a newer markup language that allows designers to describe data and information.
- *Web server software*, which is software that enables a computer to deliver Web pages written in HTML to client machines that request this service by sending an HTTP request. Web server software also provides security services, FTP, search engine, and data capture services. The term *Web server* also is used to refer to the physical computer that runs the Web server software.
- *Web clients*, which are computing devices attached to the Internet that are capable of making HTTP requests and displaying HTML pages.
- *Web browsers*, which display Web pages and also have added features such as e-mail and newsgroups.

■ **Describe how Internet and Web features and services support e-commerce.**

Together, the Internet and the Web make e-commerce possible by allowing computer users to access product and service information and to complete purchases online. Some of the specific features that support e-commerce include:

- *Electronic mail (e-mail)*, which uses a series of protocols to enable messages containing text, images, sound, and video clips to be transferred from one Internet user to another. E-mail is used in e-commerce as a marketing and customer support tool.
- *Search engines*, which identify Web pages that match a query submitted by a user. Search engines assist users in locating Web pages related to items they may want to buy.
- *Intelligent agents or software robots*, which are software programs that gather and/or filter information on a specific topic and then provide a list of results for the users.
- *Instant messaging*, which allows messages to be sent between two users almost instantly, allowing parties to engage in a two-way conversation. In e-commerce, companies are using instant messaging as a customer support tool.
- *Chat*, which allows two or more users to communicate via computer in real time (simultaneously) and is being used in e-commerce as a community-building tool.
- *Music, video, and other standard files* (such as photos, etc.), which are used in e-commerce as digital content that may be sold and as marketing tools.
- *Streaming media*, which enables music, video, and other large files to be sent to users in chunks so that when received and played, the file comes through uninterrupted. Like standard digital files, streaming media may be sold as digital content and used as a marketing tool.
- *Cookies*, which are small text files that allow a Web site to store information about a user, and are used by e-commerce as a marketing tool. Cookies allow Web sites to personalize the site to the user and also permit customization and market segmentation.

The Internet II infrastructure will permit the rapid deployment of new services and greatly expand e-commerce opportunities. Emerging services include

- *Internet telephony*, which uses VOIP to transmit audio communication over the Internet;
- *digital libraries*, which will allow distribution of software applications by ASPs to increase;
- *distributed storage*, which will allow ASPs to store data on multiple servers;
- *distance learning through videoconferencing* that will permit real-time two-way communication;
- *digital video networks* that will be able to deliver better-than-broadcast quality video over the Internet;
- *high-quality video teleconferencing*;
- *tele-immersion* (the merger of virtual reality and video conferencing); and
- *m-commerce applications*.

QUESTIONS

1. What are the three basic building blocks of the Internet?

2. What is latency and how does it interfere with Internet functioning?
3. Explain how packet switching works.
4. How is the TCP/IP protocol related to information transfer on the Internet?
5. What technological innovation made client/server computing possible? What impact has client/server computing had on the Internet?
6. Despite the number of PCs connected to the Internet, rich information sharing is still limited. Why?
7. Why isn't the Internet overloaded? Will it ever be at capacity?
8. What types of companies form the Internet backbone today?
9. What function do the NAPs/MAEs serve?
10. What is a campus network and who uses them?
11. Compare and contrast intranets, extranets, and the Internet as a whole.
12. What are the four major limitations of today's Internet?
13. What are some of the challenges of policing the Internet? Who has the final say when it comes to content, such as with Yahoo! France?
14. What does photonics have to do with improving how the Internet functions?
15. Compare and contrast WAP and iMode.
16. What is the difference between NGI and Internet2, if any?
17. What are some of the new wireless standards, and are how are they relevant to Internet II?
18. What are the major technological advancements that are anticipated will accompany Internet II? Define and discuss the importance of each.
19. Why was the development of the browser so significant for the growth of the Web?
20. Name the different Web markup languages and explain the differences between them.
21. Name and describe five services currently available through the Web.
22. What are at least three new services that will be available through the next generation of the Internet?

PROJECTS

1. Visit the MySimon.com Web site and investigate the following types of purchases: an MP3 player, a copy of the book *Seabiscuit: An American Legend*, and a dozen red roses. What did you find as you searched for these items? Describe the process, the search results, and any limitations you encountered. What are the major advantages and disadvantages of such intelligent agents?

2. Locate where cookies are stored on your computer. (They are probably in a folder entitled "cookies" within your browser program.) List the top 10 cookies you find and write a brief report describing what kinds of sites these are. What purpose do you think the cookies serve? Also, what do you believe are the major advantages and disadvantages of cookies? In your opinion, do the advantages outweigh the disadvantages, or vice versa?

3. Call a local ISP, cable provider, and DSL provider to request information on their services. Prepare a brief report summarizing the features, benefits, and costs of each. Which is the fastest? What, if any, are the downsides of selecting any of the three for Internet service (such as additional equipment purchases)?

4. Select two countries (excluding the United States) and prepare a short report describing their basic Internet infrastructure. Are they public or commercial? How and where do they connect to backbones within the United States?

5. We have mentioned several high-speed gigabit networks throughout this chapter. Investigate the topic of high-speed networks on the Web and try to find the fastest recorded network (usually used for research purposes). Then try to find the fastest commercial network handling routine Internet traffic.

CHAPTER 4

Building an E-commerce Web Site

After reading this chapter you will be able to:

- Explain the process that should be followed in building an e-commerce Web site.
- Describe the major issues surrounding the decision to outsource site development and/or hosting.
- Identify and understand the major considerations involved in choosing Web server and e-commerce merchant server software.
- Understand the issues involved in choosing the most appropriate hardware for an e-commerce site.
- Identify additional tools that can improve Web site performance.

Loudcloud

What Is 100% Uptime Worth?

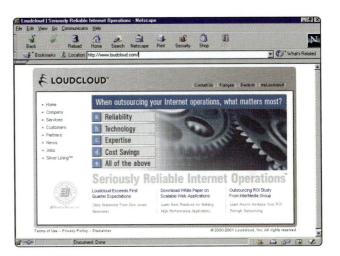

The day that Chris Wong's company, SkillsVillage.com, which helps businesses find, hire, and manage skilled contract workers, went live, he got an early morning call from the FBI. It seems within hours of launching the site, hackers had taken over SkillsVillage and used it as a front to attack a Canadian corporation.

Wong had launched the site without installing a firewall, security software that could have prevented such a hacker assault, thinking that he'd do it later. There were more important issues to deal with, or so he thought. The call from the FBI prompted Wong to change his thinking and consider outsourcing.

To handle the problem, SkillsVillage turned to another start-up, Loudcloud, a company started by Netscape co-founder Marc Andreeson. Loudcloud provides businesses with outsourced Web site infrastructure services, including all the equipment, software, Internet access, and technical support a site requires. According to Andreeson, Loudcloud has developed software it calls *opsware*, using off-the-shelf applications that it has customized, that supposedly systematizes all the hard work around Web operations, such as provisioning (determining what components to use), scaling (having enough capacity), and site management and monitoring.

By handing off the work to Loudcloud, clients such as SkillsVillage experience improved site performance and the ability to almost instantaneously add capacity as the site grows. Loudcloud guarantees 100% uptime—absolutely no downtime. If users ever are denied access to a site, Loudcloud provides substantial discounts off its monthly service fees, which typically run in the tens of thousands of dollars. Fortunately for Loudcloud, so far that has not happened.

SOURCES: Loudcloud Inc. Report on 10-K for the year ended January 31, 2001, filed with the Securities and Exchange Commission on April 25, 2001; "Loudcloud's Early ASP Clients Give their Verdict," by Lisa Phifer, *ASPnews.com*, November 6, 2000; "Cradle-to-Grave Site Management," by Jade Boyd, *Internet Week*, August 28, 2000; "Crank It Up," by David Sheff, *Wired*, August 8, 2000; "Ahead in the Clouds," by Carol Pickering, *Business 2.0*, March 1, 2000; "Loudcloud Puts Mouth Where Money Is," by Alexei Oreskovic, *Industry Standard*, February 7, 2000.

Loudcloud's message is "Focus on your own core competency and let us build a customized infrastructure." With $68 million in backing from venture capital firms such as Benchmark Capital and Morgan Stanley Dean Witter, as well as $150 million from an IPO in February 2001, Loudcloud is poised to be market leader in the infrastructure outsourcing category.

If Loudcloud's deal with SkillsVillage is any indication, Loudcloud has a promising future. SkillsVillage pays Loudcloud more than $1 million per year for its services. But according to CEO Wong, it's a win-win for both company. Wong estimates that Loudcloud's fee in fact represents a 25% savings over what it would cost to hire technical workers, buy all the needed hardware and software, and manage the site internally.

I n Chapter 3 we examined the Internet and Web's infrastructure, e-commerce's technological foundation. Now its time to take the next step: building an e-commerce site.

In this chapter we will describe the important factors that a manager needs to consider when building an e-commerce site. Our focus will be on the managerial business decisions you must make, such as those faced by SkillsVillage in the opening case. As you will see, building a sophisticated e-commerce site isn't easy; in fact, it can be so complicated that companies such as Loudcloud are basing their entire business model on building and running e-commerce sites for others.

4.1 BUILDING AN E-COMMERCE WEB SITE: A SYSTEMATIC APPROACH

Building a successful e-commerce site is a complex endeavor that requires a keen understanding of business, technology, and social issues, as well as a systematic approach. In many firms today, e-commerce is just too important to be left totally to technologists and programmers.

The two most important management challenges in building a successful e-commerce site are (a) developing a clear understanding of your business objectives and (b) knowing how to choose the right technology to achieve those objectives. The first challenge requires you to build a plan for developing your firm's site. The second challenge requires you to understand some of the basic elements of e-commerce infrastructure.

Even if you decide to outsource the entire e-commerce site development and operation to a service provider such as Loudcloud, you will still need to have a site development plan and some understanding of the basic e-commerce infrastructure issues such as cost, capability, and constraints. Without a plan and a knowledge base, you will not be able to make sound management decisions about e-commerce within your firm (Laudon and Laudon, 2001).

PIECES OF THE SITE-BUILDING PUZZLE

Let's assume you are a manager for a medium-sized, industrial parts firm of around 10,000 employees worldwide, operating in ten countries in Europe, Asia, and North America. Senior management has given you a budget of $1 million to build an e-commerce site within one year. The purpose of this site will be to sell and service the firm's 20,000 customers, who are mostly small machine and metal fabricating shops around the world. Where do you start?

First, you must be aware of the main areas where you will need to make decisions (see Figure 4.1). On the organizational and human resources front, you will have to bring together a team of individuals who possess the skill sets needed to build and

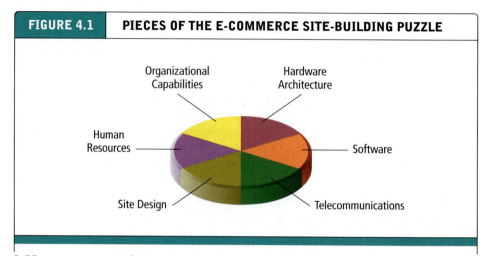

FIGURE 4.1	PIECES OF THE E-COMMERCE SITE-BUILDING PUZZLE

Building an e-commerce Web site requires that you systematically consider the many factors that go into the process.

manage a successful e-commerce site. This team will make the key decisions about technology, site design, and the social and information policies that will be applied at your site. The entire site development effort must be closely managed if you hope to avoid the disasters that have occurred at some firms.

You will also need to make decisions about your site's hardware, software, and telecommunications infrastructure. While you will have technical advisors help you make these decisions, ultimately the operation of the site is your responsibility. The demands of your customers should drive your choices of technology. Your customers will want technology that enables them to find what they want easily, view the product, purchase the product, and then receive the product from your warehouses quickly. You will also have to carefully consider your site's design. Once you have identified the key decision areas, you will need to think about a plan for the project.

PLANNING: THE SYSTEMS DEVELOPMENT LIFE CYCLE

Your second step in building an e-commerce site will be creating a plan document. In order to tackle a complex problem such as building an e-commerce site, you will have to proceed systematically through a series of steps. One methodology for developing an e-commerce site plan is the systems development life cycle. The **systems development life cycle (SDLC)** is a methodology for understanding the business objectives of any system and designing an appropriate solution. Adopting a life cycle methodology does not guarantee success, but it is far better than having no plan at all. The SDLC method also helps in creating documents that communicate to senior management the objectives of the site, important milestones, and the uses of resources. The five major steps involved in the systems development life cycle for an e-commerce site are:

systems development life cycle (SDLC)

a methodology for understanding the business objectives of any system and designing an appropriate solution

- Systems Analysis
- Systems Design
- Building the System
- Testing
- Implementation

SYSTEMS ANALYSIS: IDENTIFY BUSINESS OBJECTIVES, SYSTEM FUNCTIONALITY, AND INFORMATION REQUIREMENTS

The systems analysis step of the SDLC tries to answer the question, "What do we want the e-commerce site to do?" We will assume here that you have identified a business strategy and chosen a business model to achieve your strategic objectives (see Chapter 2). But how do you translate your strategies, business models, and ideas into a working e-commerce site?

One way to start is to identify the specific business objectives for your site, and then develop a list of system functionalities and information requirements. **Business objectives** are simply a list of capabilities you want your site to have. **System functionalities** are a list of the types of information systems capabilities you will need to achieve your business objectives. The **information requirements** for a system are the information elements that the system must produce in order to achieve the business objectives. You will need to provide these lists to system developers and programmers so they know what you as the manager expect them to do.

Table 4.1 describes some basic business objectives, system functionalities, and information requirements for a typical e-commerce site. As shown in the table, there are nine basic business objectives that an e-commerce site must deliver. These objectives must be translated into a description of system functionalities and ultimately into a set of precise information requirements. The specific information requirements for a system typically are defined in much greater detail than Table 4.1 indicates. To a large extent, the business objectives of an e-commerce site are not that different from those of an ordinary retail store. The real difference lies in the system functionalities and information requirements: In an e-commerce site, the business objectives must be provided entirely in digital form without buildings or salespeople, twenty-four hours a day, seven days a week.

SYSTEM DESIGN: HARDWARE AND SOFTWARE PLATFORMS

Once you have identified the business objectives and system functionalities, and have developed a list of precise information requirements (see Table 4.1), you can begin to consider just how all this functionality will be delivered. You must come up with a **system design specification** — a description of the main components in a system and their relationship to one another. The system design itself can be broken down into two components: a logical design and a physical design. A **logical design** includes a data flow diagram that describes the flow of information at your

business objectives
a list of capabilities you want your site to have

system functionalities
a list of the types of information systems capabilities you will need to achieve your business objectives

information requirements
the information elements that the system must produce in order to achieve the business objectives

system design specification
description of the main components in a system and their relationship to one another

logical design
describes the flow of information at your e-commerce site, the processing functions that must be performed, the databases that will be used, the security and emergency backup procedures that will be instituted, and the controls that will be used in the system

TABLE 4.1	SYSTEM ANALYSIS: BUSINESS OBJECTIVES, SYSTEM FUNCTIONALITY, AND INFORMATION REQUIREMENTS FOR A TYPICAL E-COMMERCE SITE	
BUSINESS OBJECTIVE	**SYSTEM FUNCTIONALITY**	**INFORMATION REQUIREMENTS**
Display goods.	Digital catalog	Dynamic text and graphics catalog.
Provide product information.	Product database	Product description, stock numbers, inventory levels.
Personalize/customize product.	Customer on-site tracking	Site log for every customer visit. Data mining capability to identify common customer paths and appropriate responses.
Execute a transaction.	Shopping cart/payment system	Secure credit card clearing; multiple payment options.
Accumulate customer information.	Customer database	Name, address, phone, and e-mail for all customers. Online customer registration.
Provide after-sale customer support.	Sales database	Customer ID, product, order date, payment, shipment date.
Coordinate marketing/advertising program.	Ad server, e-mail server, e-mail campaign manager, ad banner manager	Site behavior log of prospects and customers linked to e-mail and banner ad campaigns.
Understand marketing effectiveness.	Site tracking and reporting system	Number of unique visitors, pages visited, products purchased, identified by marketing campaign.
Provide production and supplier links.	Inventory management system	Product and inventory levels, supplier ID and contact, order quantity data by product.

e-commerce site, the processing functions that must be performed, and the databases that will be used. The logical design also includes a description of the security and emergency backup procedures that will be instituted, and the controls that will be used in the system.

physical design
translates the logical design into physical components

A **physical design** translates the logical design into physical components. For instance, the physical design details the specific model of server to be purchased, the software to be used, the size of the telecommunications link that will be required, the way the system will be backed up and protected from outsiders, and so on.

Figure 4.2(a) presents a data flow diagram for a simple high-level logical design for a very basic Web site that delivers catalog pages in HTML in response to HTTP requests from the client's browser, while Figure 4.2(b) shows the corresponding physical design. Each of the main processes can be broken down into lower level designs that are much more precise in identifying exactly how the information flows and what equipment is involved.

FIGURE 4.2 | **A LOGICAL AND PHYSICAL DESIGN FOR A SIMPLE WEB SITE**

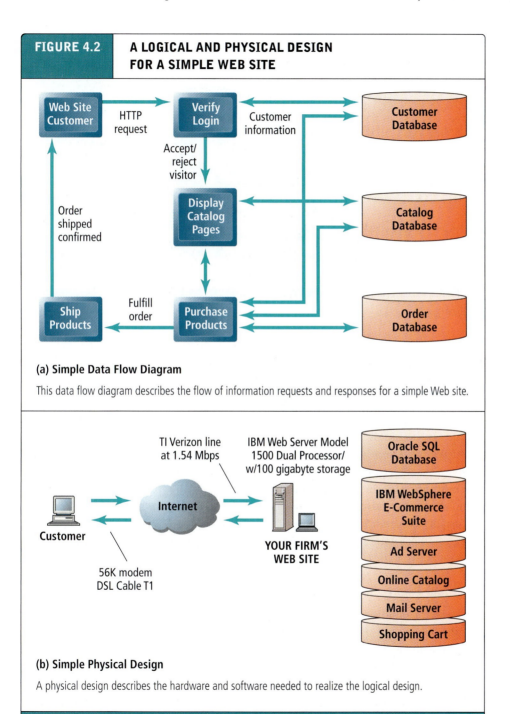

(a) Simple Data Flow Diagram

This data flow diagram describes the flow of information requests and responses for a simple Web site.

(b) Simple Physical Design

A physical design describes the hardware and software needed to realize the logical design.

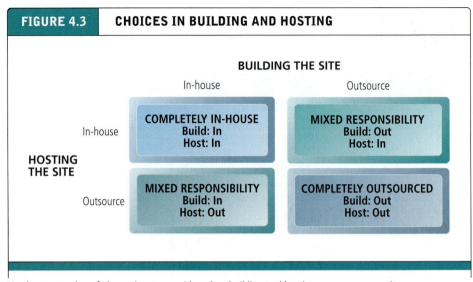

FIGURE 4.3 — **CHOICES IN BUILDING AND HOSTING**

You have a number of alternatives to consider when building and hosting an e-commerce site.

BUILDING THE SYSTEM: IN-HOUSE VS. OUTSOURCING

outsourcing

hiring an outside vendor to provide the services you cannot perform with in-house personnel

Now that you have a clear idea of both the logical and physical design for your site, you can begin considering how to actually build the site. There are many choices here. They range from outsourcing everything (including the actual systems analysis and design) to building everything in-house. **Outsourcing** means that you will hire an outside vendor to provide the services involved in building the site that you cannot perform with in-house personnel. You also have a second decision to make: Will you host (operate) the site on your firm's own servers or will you outsource the hosting to a Web host provider? These decisions are independent of each other, but they are usually considered at the same time. There are some vendors who will design, build, and host your site (such as Loudcloud), while others will either build or host (but not both). Figure 4.3 illustrates the alternatives.

Build Your Own versus Outsourcing

Let's take the building decision first. If you elect to build your own site, you will need a multi-skilled staff of programmers, graphic artists, Web designers, and managers. You will also have to select and purchase hardware and software tools. There are a broad variety of tools available for building your own e-commerce site, ranging from those that help you build everything yourself from scratch, such as Dreamweaver and Front Page, to top-of-the-line prepackaged site-building tools that can create sophisticated sites customized to your needs, to prebuilt templates that merely require you to input text, graphics, and other data. (See Figure 4.4.) We will look more closely at the variety of e-commerce software available in Section 4.2.

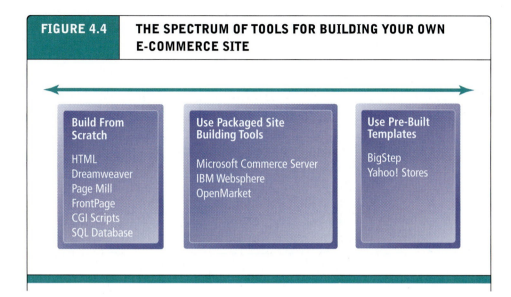

FIGURE 4.4 THE SPECTRUM OF TOOLS FOR BUILDING YOUR OWN E-COMMERCE SITE

The decision to build your own site entirely has a number of risks. Given the complexity of features such as shopping carts, credit card authentication and processing, inventory management, and order processing, the costs involved are high, as are the risks of doing a poor job. You will be reinventing what other specialized firms have already built, and your staff may face a long, difficult learning curve, delaying your entry to market. Your efforts could fail (Albrecht and Gaffney, 1983). On the positive side, you may be better able to build a site that does exactly what you want, and more important, develop the in-house knowledge to allow you to change the site rapidly if necessary due to a changing business environment.

If you choose more expensive site-building packages, you will be purchasing state-of-the art software that is well tested. You could get to market sooner. However, in order to make a sound decision, you will have to evaluate many different packages and this can take a long time. You may have to modify the packages to fit your business needs and perhaps hire additional outside vendors to modify the package. Costs rise rapidly as modifications mount (see Figure 4.5). If you choose the template route, you will be limited to the functionality already built into the templates, and you will not be able to add to the functionality or change it.

Brick-and-mortar retailers in need of an e-commerce site generally design the site themselves (because they already have the skilled staff in place and have extensive investments in IT capital such as databases and telecommunications), but they use outside vendors and consultants to build the sophisticated e-commerce applications. Small start-ups may build their own sites from scratch using in-house technical people in an effort to keep costs low. Medium-size start-ups will often purchase a sophisti-

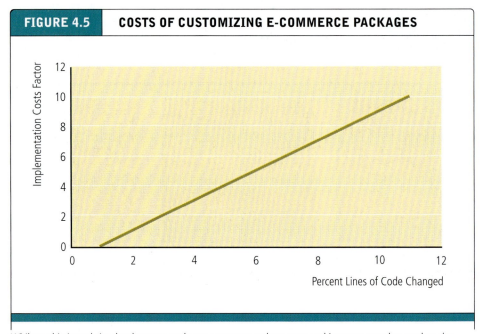

| FIGURE 4.5 | COSTS OF CUSTOMIZING E-COMMERCE PACKAGES |

While sophisticated site development packages appear to reduce costs and increase speed to market, the modifications required to fit the package to your business needs rise exponentially. A $4,000 package can easily become a $40,000 to $60,000 development project.
SOURCE: Laudon and Laudon, 2001.

cated package and then modify it to suit their needs. Very small mom-and-pop firms seeking simple storefronts will use templates.

Host Your Own versus Outsourcing

Now let's look at the hosting decision. Most businesses chose to outsource hosting and to pay a company to host their Web site, which means that the hosting company is responsible for ensuring the site is "live," or accessible, twenty-four hours a day. By agreeing to a monthly fee, the business need not concern itself with many of the technical aspects of setting up a Web server and maintaining it, nor with staffing needs.

You can also choose to *co-locate*. With a **co-location** agreement, your firm purchases or leases a Web server (and has total control over its operation), but locates the server in a vendor's physical facility. The vendor maintains the facility, communications lines, and the machinery. See Table 4.2 for a list of some of the major hosting/co-location providers.

Hosting and co-location have become a commodity and a utility: Costs are driven by very large providers (such as Exodus, IBM, and Qwest) who can achieve large

co-location

when a firm purchases or leases a Web server (and has total control over its operation) but locates the server in a vendor's physical facility. The vendor maintains the facility, communications lines, and the machinery.

TABLE 4.2	KEY PLAYERS: HOSTING/CO-LOCATION SERVICES	
Exodus	Qwest	
Equinex	Verio	
IBM	Rackspace	

economies of scale by establishing huge "server farms" located strategically around the country and the globe. The capital expenditures for building these server farms, associated telecommunications links, and emergency power supplies are very large. Small ISPs also can be used as hosts, but service reliability is an issue. Will the small ISP be able to provided uninterrupted service, 24x7x365? Will they have service staff available when you need it?

The disadvantage of outsourcing hosting is that as the online business grows, the company may need more power and services than the hosting company can provide. That is why some corporations elect to do their own hosting. When you host your own site, you are in total control of the operation. Keep in mind that your costs may be higher than if you had used a large outsourcing firm. You will have to purchase hardware and software, have a physical facility, lease communications lines, hire a staff, and build security and backup capabilities.

TESTING THE SYSTEM

Once the system has been built and programmed, you will have to engage in a testing process. Depending on the size of the system, this could be fairly difficult and lengthy. Testing is required whether the system is outsourced or built in-house. A complex e-commerce site can have thousands of pathways through the site, each of which must be documented and then tested. **Unit testing** involves testing the site's program modules one at a time. **System testing** involves testing the site as a whole, in a way the typical user will in using the site. Because there is no truly "typical" user, system testing requires that every conceivable path be tested. Final **acceptance testing** requires that the firm's key personnel and managers in marketing, production, sales, and general management actually use the system as installed on a test Internet or intranet server. This acceptance test verifies that the business objectives of the system as originally conceived are in fact working. It is important to note that testing is generally underbudgeted. As much as 50% of the software effort can be consumed by testing and rebuilding (usually depending on the quality of initial design).

IMPLEMENTATION AND MAINTENANCE

Most people unfamiliar with systems erroneously think that once an information system is installed, the process is over. In fact, while the beginning of the process is over,

unit testing
involves testing the site's program modules one at a time

system testing
involves testing the site as a whole, in a way the typical user will in use the site

acceptance testing
verifies that the business objectives of the system as originally conceived are in fact working

the operational life of a system is just beginning. Systems break down for a variety of reasons — most of them unpredictable. Therefore, they need continual checking, testing, and repair. Systems maintenance is vital, but sometimes not budgeted for. In general, the annual system maintenance cost will roughly parallel the development cost. A $40,000 e-commerce site will likely require a $40,000 annual expenditure to maintain. Very large e-commerce sites experience some economies of scale, so that, for example, a million dollar site will likely require a maintenance budget of $500,000 to $700,000.

Why does it cost so much to maintain an e-commerce site? Unlike payroll systems, for example, e-commerce sites are always in a process of change, improvement, and correction. Studies of traditional systems maintenance have found 20% of the time is devoted to debugging code and responding to emergency situations (a new server was installed by your ISP, and all your hypertext links were lost and CGI scripts disabled — the site is down!) (Lientz and Swanson, 1980; Banker and Kemerer, 1989). Another 20% of the time is concerned with changes in reports, data files, and links to backend databases. The remaining 60% of maintenance time is devoted to general administration (making product and price changes in the catalog) and making changes and enhancements to the system. E-commerce sites are never finished: They are always in the process of being built and rebuilt. They are dynamic — much more so than payroll systems.

The long-term success of an e-commerce site will depend on a dedicated team of employees (the Web team) whose sole job is to monitor and adapt the site to changing market conditions. The Web team must be multi-skilled; it will typically include programmers, designers, and business managers drawn from marketing, production, and sales support. One of the first tasks of the Web team is to listen to customers' feedback on the site, and respond to that feedback as necessary. A second task is to develop a systematic monitoring and testing plan to be followed weekly to ensure all the links are operating, prices are correct, and pages are updated. A large business may have thousands of Web pages, many of them interlinked, that require systematic monitoring. Other important tasks of the Web team include **benchmarking** (a process in which the site is compared with those of competitors in terms of response speed, quality of layout, and design) and keeping the site current on pricing and promotions. The Web is a competitive environment where you can very rapidly frustrate and lose customers with a dysfunctional site (see *Insight on Technology: What Boo Did Wrong*).

benchmarking
a process in which the site is compared with those of competitors in terms of response speed, quality of layout, and design

4.2   CHOOSING SERVER SOFTWARE

What you are able to do at an e-commerce site is largely a function of the software. As a business manager in charge of building the site, you will need to know some basic

INSIGHT ON TECHNOLOGY

WHAT BOO DID WRONG

It all started out with so much promise. Boo.com was the darling of the Internet media, a high-flying start-up backed with $185 million from such heavy hitters as JP Morgan, Goldman Sachs, Bain Capital, Bernard Arnault (chairman of LVMH-Moet Hennessy Louis Vuitton), the Benetton family, and others. Its founders were on the cover of *Fortune* magazine's Cool Companies of 1999. It had hired staff with stunning pedigrees from companies such as Barney's, Virgin, and Boston Consulting Group. It claimed that it would have a "killer Web site" on top of a "global business model," which would give it a significant first-mover advantage. And on the surface, it offered a compelling business plan: a global fashion e-tailer, selling urban chic, with service in seven different languages and 18 different currencies.

But a mere 18 months later, the world came crashing down. The company's doors were shuttered and its assets put up for liquidation. How did things go so terribly wrong for Boo?

Although the story is a complicated one, with many intertwining factors, the mistakes Boo made in building its e-commerce Web site clearly played a major role in bringing about Boo's downfall.

Mistake #1: For many months, Boo had no development plan. When one former employee, who joined Boo in August 1999, with the launch already behind schedule by three months, asked to see the project plan, he was told one didn't exist. "People were working on bits and pieces of the project without communicating with other people they were affecting."

Mistake #2: The concept for the Web site was extraordinarily ambitious — ultimately, too ambitious. Planned to launch from the ground up in multiple countries, Boo's system needed to handle multiple languages, multiple currencies, on-the-fly tax calculation and integration with multiple fulfillment parties. Each of these issues presented its own challenges; for example, to implement multiple languages, Boo found that it could not rely on translation software and instead had to have the copy translated by hand. Implementing multiple currencies also turned out to be extremely complex, as was on-the-fly tax calculation. Taken all together, the challenges were insurmountable.

Mistake # 3: Boo's Web site design failed to take into account something very important. Boo founders had envisioned the ultimate catalog, where clothes rotate so you can see what they would look like from the back, with virtual mannequins that allow you to try clothes on, and with a 3-D shopping bot, "Miss Boo," to assist shoppers with everything from product questions to sizing. But, in going for the "cool," Boo forgot the customer.

When the site finally launched in November 1999, six months late, "it wasn't great" said one of the founders, in perhaps the understatement of the year. In fact, one critic chided, "the site seemed actively designed to stop people from just buying stuff," with an interface that was "memo-

(continued)

rably bad." For starters, Boo demanded users have the Flash plug-in. It hid navigation under cute graphics, launched new windows at every opportunity, forced users to navigate pages of animations to get to where they could actually order something, and frequently crashed browsers. Customers with Macintoshes could not log on at all. Boo also demanded a high-speed connection, which 99% of European homes and 98% of U.S. homes lacked at the time. All in all, it was a wildly overdesigned site, and completely out of touch with most Web retailers' visions of quick shopping and ease of use. Within one week of the launch, Federated Department Stores had backed away from a commitment to invest $10 million, signaling the beginning of the end of the fairy tale.

SOURCES: "Boo.com Tries Again, Humbled and Retooled," by Michelle Slatella, *New York Times*, January 11, 2001; "From Big Idea to Big Bust: The Wild Ride of Boo.com," by Andrew Ross Sorkin, *New York Times*, December 13, 2000; "Boo.com Buys High, Sells Low," by Jen Muehlbauer, *Industry Standard*, May 30, 2000; "It All Ends in Tears at Boo," by John Cassy and Mary O'Hara, *The Guardian*, May 19, 2000; "Boo.com Burns Out," by Keith Regan and Paul A. Greenberg, *E-commerce Times*, May 18, 2000; "Boo.com's Bold Fashion Statement," by James Ledbetter, *Industry Standard*, May 10, 1999.

information about e-commerce software. The more sophisticated the software and the more ways you can sell goods and services, the more effective your business will be. In this section we will describe the software needed to operate a contemporary e-commerce site. Then, in Section 4.3, we discuss the hardware you will need to handle the demands of the software.

SIMPLE VERSUS MULTI-TIERED WEB SITE ARCHITECTURE

Prior to the development of e-commerce, Web sites simply delivered Web pages to users who were making requests through their browsers for HTML pages. Web site software was appropriately quite simple — it consisted of a server machine running basic Web server software. We might call this arrangement a single-tier system architecture. **System architecture** refers to the arrangement of software, machinery, and tasks in an information system needed to achieve a specific functionality (much like a home's architecture refers to the arrangement of building materials to achieve a particular functionality) .

system architecture
refers to the arrangement of software, machinery, and tasks in an information system needed to achieve a specific functionality

However, the development of e-commerce required a great deal more functionality, such as the ability to respond to user input (name and address forms), take customer orders for goods and services, clear credit card transactions on the fly, consult price and product databases, and even adjust advertising on the screen based on user characteristics. This kind of extended functionality required the development of *Web application servers* and a multi-tiered system architecture to handle the processing loads. Web application servers, described more fully later in this section, are specialized software programs that perform a wide variety of transaction processing required by e-commerce.

In addition to having specialized application servers, e-commerce sites must be able to pull information from and add information to pre-existing corporate databases. These older databases that predate the e-commerce era are called *backend* or *legacy* databases. Corporations have made massive investments in these systems to store their information on customers, products, employees, and vendors. These backend systems constitute an additional layer in a multi-tiered site.

Figure 4.6 illustrates a simple two-tier and more complex multi-tier e-commerce system architecture. In **two-tier architecture**, a Web server responds to requests for Web pages and a database server provides backend data storage. In a **multi-tier architecture**, in contrast, the Web server is linked to a middle-tier layer that typically

FIGURE 4.6	TWO-TIER AND MULTI-TIER E-COMMERCE ARCHITECTURES

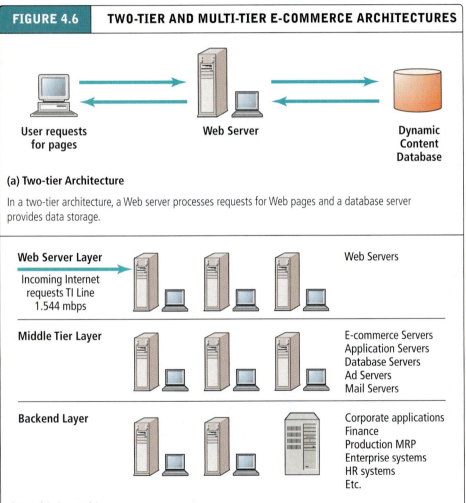

User requests for pages   **Web Server**   **Dynamic Content Database**

(a) Two-tier Architecture

In a two-tier architecture, a Web server processes requests for Web pages and a database server provides data storage.

Web Server Layer   Web Servers

Incoming Internet requests TI Line 1.544 mbps

Middle Tier Layer   E-commerce Servers
Application Servers
Database Servers
Ad Servers
Mail Servers

Backend Layer   Corporate applications
Finance
Production MRP
Enterprise systems
HR systems
Etc.

(b) Multi-tier Architecture

In a multi-tier architecture, the Web server is linked to a middle-tier layer of servers and a backend layer of existing corporate systems.

includes a series of application servers that perform specific tasks, as well as to a back-end layer of existing corporate systems containing product, customer, and pricing information. A multi-tiered site typically employs several or more physical computers, each running some of the software applications and sharing the work load across many physical computers.

In the remainder of this section we will describe basic Web server software functionality and the various types of Web application servers.

WEB SERVER SOFTWARE

All e-commerce sites require basic Web server software to answer requests from customers for HTML and XML pages. The leading Web server software choices are shown in Figure 4.7.

When you choose Web server software, you will also be choosing an operating system for your site's computers. The leading Web server software, with over 60% of the market, is Apache HTTP, which works only with the Unix operating system. Unix is the original programming language of the Internet and Web. Apache was developed by a worldwide community of Internet innovators. Apache is free and can be downloaded from many sites on the Web, and comes installed on most IBM Web servers. Literally thousands of programmers have worked on Apache over the years; thus, it is extremely stable. There are thousands of utility software programs written for Apache that can provide all the functionality required for a contemporary e-commerce site. In order to use Apache, you will require staff knowledgeable in the operation of the Unix operating system (or its PC variant, Linux).

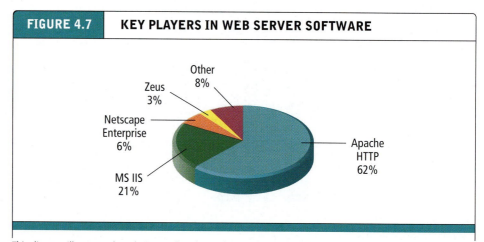

| FIGURE 4.7 | **KEY PLAYERS IN WEB SERVER SOFTWARE** |

This diagram illustrates the relative market share of the most popular Web server software. As you can see, Apache HTTP dominates the market.

SOURCE: Netcraft Web Server Survey, May 2001.

Microsoft Internet Information Server (IIS) is the second major Web server software available, albeit a distant second to Apache, with only about 20% of the market. IIS is based on the Windows 2000 (Windows NT) operating system and is compatible with a wide selection of Microsoft utility and support programs.

There are also at least one hundred other smaller providers of Web server software, most of them based on Unix. Note that the choice of Web server has little effect on users of your system. The pages they see will look the same regardless of the development environment. There are many advantages to the Microsoft suite of development tools — they are integrated, powerful, and easy to use. The Unix operating system, on the other hand, is exceptionally reliable and stable, and there is a worldwide open software community that develops and tests Unix-based Web server software.

Table 4.3 shows the basic functionality provided by all Web servers.

Site Management Tools

We have described most of the basic functionality of Web servers listed in Table 4.3 in Chapter 3. One functionality not described previously is **site management tools**. Site management tools are essential if you want to keep your site working, and if you want to understand how well it is working. Site management tools verify that links on pages are still valid and also identify *orphan files*, or files on the site that are not linked to any pages. By surveying the links on a Web site, a site management tool can

site management tools
verify that links on pages are still valid and also identify orphan files

TABLE 4.3	BASIC FUNCTIONALITY PROVIDED BY WEB SERVERS
FUNCTIONALITY	DESCRIPTION
Processing of HTTP requests	Receive and respond to client requests for HTML pages.
Security services (Secure Sockets Layer)	Verify username and password; process certificates and private/public key information required for credit card processing and other secure information.
File Transfer Protocol	Permits transfer of very large files from server to server.
Search engine	Indexing of site content; keyword search capability.
Data capture	Log file of all visits, time, duration, and referral source.
E-mail	Ability to send, receive, and store e-mail messages.
Site management tools	Calculate and display key site statistics, such as unique visitors, page requests, and origin of requests. Check links on pages.

quickly report on potential problems and errors that users may encounter. Links to URLs that have moved or been deleted are called *dead links*; these can cause error messages for users trying to access that link. Regularly checking that all links on a site are operational helps prevent irritated users who may take their business elsewhere.

Additional site management software and services, such as those provided by Webtrends.com, can be purchased in order to more effectively monitor customer purchases and marketing campaign effectiveness, as well as keep track of standard hit counts and page visit information.

Dynamic Page Generation Tools

One of the most important innovations in Web site operation has been the development of dynamic page generation tools. Prior to the development of e-commerce, Web sites primarily delivered unchanging static content in the form of HTML pages. While this capability might be sufficient to display pictures of products, consider all the elements of a typical e-commerce site today by reviewing Table 4.1, or visit what you believe is an excellent e-commerce site. The content of successful e-commerce sites is always changing, often day by day. There are new products and promotions, changing prices, news events, and stories of successful users. E-commerce sites must intensively interact with users, who not only request pages, but also request product, price, availability, and inventory information. One of the most dynamic sites is eBay.com — the auction site. There, the content is changing minute by minute. E-commerce sites are just like real markets — they are dynamic.

The dynamic and complex nature of e-commerce sites requires a number of specialized software applications in addition to static HTML pages. Perhaps one of the most important is dynamic page generation software. With **dynamic page generation**, the contents of a Web page are stored as objects in a database, rather than being hard-coded in HTML. When the user requests a Web page, the contents for that page are then fetched from the database. The objects are retrieved from the database using CGI (Common Gateway Interface), ASP (Active Server Pages), JSP (Java Server Pages) or other server-side programs. CGI, ASP, and JSP are described in the last section of this chapter. This technique is much more efficient than working directly in HTML code. It is much easier to change the contents of a database than it is to change the coding of an HTML page. A standard data access method called *Open DataBase Connectivity (ODBC)* makes it possible to access any data from any application regardless of what database is used. ODBC is supported by most of the large database suppliers such as Oracle, Sybase, and IBM. ODBC makes it possible for HTML pages to be linked to backend corporate databases regardless of who manufactured the database. Web sites must be able to pull information from, and add information to, these databases. For example, when a customer clicks on a picture of a pair of boots, the site can access the product catalog database stored in a DB2 database, and access the inventory

dynamic page generation

the contents of a Web page are stored as objects in a database, rather than being hard-coded in HTML. When the user requests a Web page, the contents for that page are then fetched from the database.

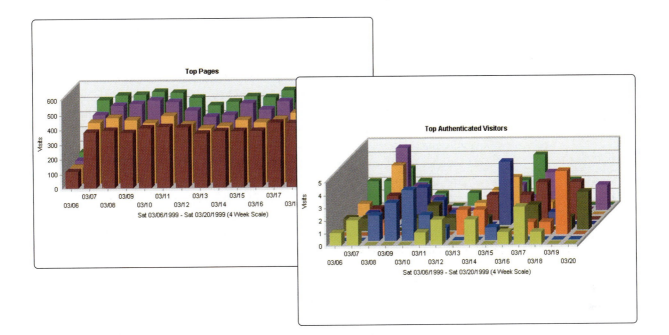

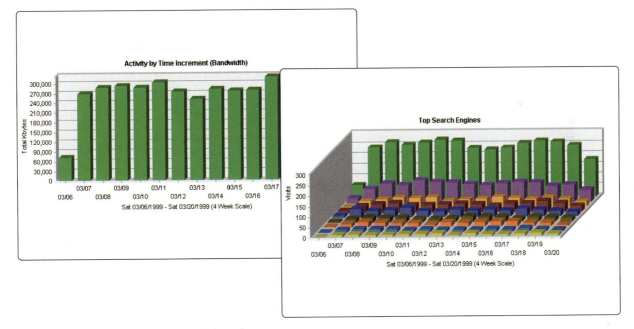

Using a site management program such as WebTrends,
you can easily and quickly learn who is visiting your site, where they come from, when they visit, and what pages they visit.

database stored in an Oracle database to confirm that the boots are still in stock and report the current price (Hughes and Birznieks, 2001).

Dynamic page generation gives e-commerce several significant capabilities that generate cost and profitability advantages over traditional commerce. Dynamic page generation lowers *menu costs* (the costs incurred by merchants for changing product descriptions and prices). Dynamic page generation also permits easy online *market segmentation* — the ability to sell the same product to different markets. The same capability makes possible nearly cost-free *price discrimination* — the ability to sell the same product to different customers at different prices. For instance, you might want to sell the same product to corporations and government agencies — but use different marketing themes. Based on a cookie you placed on client files, or in response to a question on your site that asks visitors if they are from a government agency or a corporation, you would be able to use different marketing and promotional materials for corporate clients and government clients. You might want to reward loyal customers with lower prices, say on CDs or musical tracks, when compared to first-time buyers. In summary, dynamic page generation allows you to approach different customers with different messages, and prices.

APPLICATION SERVERS

web application server
software programs that provide the specific business functionality required of a Web site

Web application servers are software programs that provide the specific business functionality required of a Web site. The basic idea of application servers is to isolate the business applications from the details of displaying Web pages to users on the front end and the details of connecting to databases on the back end. Application servers are a kind of *middleware software* that provides the glue connecting traditional corporate systems to the customer as well as providing all the functionality needed to conduct e-commerce. In the early years, a number of software firms developed specific separate programs for each function, but increasingly these specific programs are being replaced by integrated software tools that combine all the needed functionality for an e-commerce site into a single development environment, a packaged software approach.

Table 4.4 illustrates the wide variety of application servers available in the marketplace. The table focuses on "sell side" servers that are designed to enable selling products on the Web. So-called "buy side" and "link" servers focus on the needs of businesses to connect with partners in their supply chains or find suppliers for specific parts and assemblies. These buy side and link servers are described more fully in Chapter 12, *B2B E-commerce, Supply-Chain Management, and Collaborative Commerce*.

There are several thousand software vendors that provide application server software. For UNIX environments, many of these capabilities are available free on the Internet from various sites. Most businesses — faced with this bewildering array of choices — choose to use integrated software tools called *merchant server software*.

TABLE 4.4	APPLICATION SERVERS AND THEIR FUNCTION
APPLICATION SERVER	**FUNCTIONALITY**
Catalog display	Provides a database for product descriptions and prices.
Transaction processing (shopping cart)	Accepts orders and clears payments.
List server	Creates and serves mailing lists and manages e-mail marketing campaigns.
Proxy server	Monitors and controls access to main Web server; implements firewall protection.
Mail server	Manages Internet e-mail.
Audio/video server	Stores and delivers streaming media content.
Chat server	Creates an environment for online real-time text and audio interactions with customers.
News server	Provides connectivity and displays Internet news feeds.
Fax server	Provides fax reception and sending using a Web server.
Groupware server	Creates work group environments for online collaboration.
Database server	Stores customer, product, and price information.
Ad server	Maintains Web-enabled database of advertising banners that permits customized and personalized display of advertisements based on consumer behavior and characteristics.
Auction server	Transaction environment for conducting online auctions.
B2B Server	Implements buy, sell, and link marketplaces for commercial transactions.

E-COMMERCE MERCHANT SERVER SOFTWARE FUNCTIONALITY

E-commerce merchant server software provides the basic functionality needed for online sales, including an online catalog, order taking via an online shopping cart, and online credit card processing.

Online Catalog

A company that wants to sell products on the Web must have a list, or **online catalog**, of its products, available on its Web site. Merchant server software typically includes a database capability that will allow for construction of a customized online catalog. The complexity and sophistication of the catalog will vary depending on the size of the company and its product lines. Small companies, or companies with small product lines, may post a simple list with text descriptions and perhaps color photos.

e-commerce merchant server software

software that provides the basic functionality needed for online sales, including an online catalog, order taking via an online shopping cart, and online credit card processing

online catalog

list of products available on a Web site

A larger site might decide to add sound, animations, or videos (useful for product demonstrations) to the catalog, or interactivity, such as customer service representatives available via Instant Messaging to answer questions.

Shopping Carts

shopping cart

allows shoppers to set aside desired purchases in preparation for checkout, review what they have selected, edit their selections as necessary, and then actually make the purchase by clicking a button

Online **shopping carts** are much like their real-world equivalent; both allow shoppers to set aside desired purchases in preparation for checkout. The difference is that the online variety is part of a merchant server software program residing on the Web server, and allows consumers to select merchandise, review what they have selected, edit their selections as necessary, and then actually make the purchase by clicking a button. Shopping cart data is automatically stored by the merchant server software.

Credit Card Processing

A site's shopping cart typically works in conjunction with credit card processing software, which verifies the shopper's credit card and then puts through the debit to the card and the credit to the company's account at checkout. Integrated e-commerce software suites typically supply the software for this function. Otherwise, you will have to make arrangements with a variety of credit card processing banks and intermediaries.

MERCHANT SERVER SOFTWARE PACKAGES (E-COMMERCE SUITES)

merchant server software package (e-commerce server suite)

offers an integrated environment that provides most or all of the functionality and capabilities needed to develop a sophisticated, customer-centric site

Rather than build your site from a collection of disparate software applications, it is easier, faster, and generally more cost effective to purchase a **merchant server software package** (also called an **e-commerce server suite**). Merchant server software/e-commerce suites offer an integrated environment that promises to provide most or all of the functionality and capabilities you will need to develop a sophisticated, customer-centric site. E-commerce suites come in three general ranges of price and functionality.

Basic packages for elementary e-commerce business applications are provided by B-City, Bizland, Hypermart, Yahoo! Stores, GeoShops, ShopBuilder, and Virtual Spin.

Midrange suites include IBM's WebSphere Commerce Start Edition and Microsoft's Commerce Server 2000. High-end enterprise solutions for large global firms are provided by OpenMarket, Interworld, Broadvision, and others. There are over a hundred software firms that provide e-commerce suites. Table 4.5 lists some of the most widely adopted midrange and high-end e-commerce suites.

Choosing an E-commerce Suite

With all of these vendors, how do you choose the right one? Evaluating these tools and making a decision is one of the most important and uncertain decisions you will make in building an e-commerce site. The real costs are hidden — they involve training your staff to use the tools and integrating the tools into your business processes

TABLE 4.5	WIDELY USED MIDRANGE AND HIGH-END E-COMMERCE SUITES	
PRODUCT	**APPROXIMATE PRICE**	
Microsoft Commerce Server 2000	$8,500 per processor	
IBM WebSphere Commerce Suite	$9,000 single workstation for Start edition; $45,000 for Professional edition (per processor)	
InterWorld Commerce Exchange	$65,000	
Open Market Transact	$125,000	
Intershop Enfinity Suite	$125,000–$250,000	
Broadvision One-to-One Enterprise	$250,000–$500,000	
Blue Martini Customer Interaction System	$1,000,000+	

and organizational culture (Glass, 1999; Valdes, 2000). The following are some of the key factors to consider:

- Functionality
- Support for different business models
- Business process modeling tools
- Visual site management tools and reporting
- Performance and scalability
- Connectivity to existing business systems
- Compliance with standards
- Global and multicultural capability
- Local sales tax and shipping rules

For instance, although e-commerce suites promise to do everything, your business may require special *functionality* — such as streaming audio and video. You will need a list of business functionality requirements. Your business may involve several different business models — such as a retail side and a business-to-business side; you may run auctions for stock excess as well as fixed price selling. Be sure the package can *support all of your business models*. You may wish to change your business processes — such as order taking and order fulfillment. Does the suite contain *tools for modeling business process and work flows*? Understanding how your site works will require *visual reporting tools* that make its operation transparent to many different people in your business. A poorly designed software package will drop off significantly in performance as visitors and transactions expand into the thousands per hour, or minute. Check for *performance and scalability* by stress testing a pilot edition or obtaining data from the vendor about performance under load. You will have to connect the e-commerce suite to your traditional business systems. How will this *connection to existing systems* be made, and is your staff skilled in making the connection? Because of the changing technical environment — in particular, changes in mobile commerce platforms — it is important to document exactly *what standards are supported* by the suite now, and what is the migration path toward the future. Finally, your e-commerce site may have to work both globally and locally. You may need a foreign language edition using foreign currency denominations. And you will have to collect sales taxes across many local, regional, and national tax systems. Does the e-commerce suite support this level of *globalization* and *localization*?

BUILDING YOUR OWN E-COMMERCE SOFTWARE

If you decide to attempt to build your own e-commerce capabilities, there are a number of increasingly powerful tools available to help you. For very simple e-commerce sites, services such as Freemerchant.com offer a free turnkey (complete) solution for building a simple online store. BigStep.com takes users step by step through the process of building an online store. eCongo.com, Tripod.com, and Yahoo! Store all provide easy-to-use site-building tools and e-commerce templates for simple e-commerce sites. An e-commerce template is a predesigned Web site that allows users to customize the look and feel of the site to fit their business needs and provides a standard set of functionality. Most templates today contain ready-to-go site designs with built-in commerce features. WebSite Professional, a popular program by O'Reilly, for example, bundles Web development and e-commerce capabilities together, making it unnecessary to purchase separate packages for that purpose.

There are many providers of sophisticated (and much more expensive) e-commerce site development tools such as those licensed by BEA Systems, for instance. BEA Systems bundles basic e-commerce page and site creation tools with a number of powerful e-commerce applications such as customer and product databases, onsite customer tracking, and customer relationship management tools; it also provides interfaces with backend databases containing product and price information

You can of course build everything for your site from scratch yourself, but this requires that you have the necessary personal knowledge or support staff. You can use Microsoft FrontPage, PageMill, or Dreamweaver (Macromedia) to build your basic pages for the catalog. Then, in order to take orders and interact with the client, you will need to know how to write CGI scripts, and you will have to understand how to work with a database package such as SQL. Often the challenges of building an e-commerce site are so great that businesses decide to use e-commerce suites instead.

Once you have selected the software tools needed for your e-commerce site, you will have to select the computer hardware and telecommunications links needed to realize your vision of the site.

SMALL TOWN DOESN'T MEAN SMALL BUSINESS ANYMORE

Despite the fact that few rural areas have access to the high-speed Internet connections supposedly required for successful e-commerce ventures, more and more examples of thriving small-town Internet businesses are cropping up. Approximately 60 million people live in small communities, many of which are growing smaller as residents leave for better opportunities in urban areas. But not all small towns are dying; in fact, many are seeing a rebirth, primarily due to entrepreneurs looking for new customers online.

Take The Geiger Cos., based in Harleysville, PA, population 7,405. By starting two new e-commerce sites in mid-2000, the company reached out beyond its East Coast territory to build its wholesale and consumer horticulture business. The day the wholesale site, Hortnet.com, went live, the company received an inquiry from New Zealand. Instead of limiting its sales territory from Connecticut to North Carolina, Geiger is now a global venture, thanks to the Internet.

In addition to increasing revenue by significantly expanding its territory, more business has meant more jobs at Geiger—five have been added to the existing 100 jobs in the last year alone.

In another town even smaller than Harleysville, Wendy and Shep Moyle started a party-supply Web site called ShindigZ, an online division of a 75-year-old catalog retailer, Stumps. Since launching the Web site, business has grown so much that the company has added 100 jobs

and expects to add that many more this year. For South Whitley, Indiana, with just 1,700 residents, 200 more jobs is a tremendous boost to the local economy—one that can be attributed solely to Internet sales.

Some companies, however, have no interest in expanding their work force. Apple computer reseller Small Dog Electronics, based in Waitsfield, Vermont, population 1,600, has been profitable since day one and aims to stay that way. But as revenues have grown, thanks to a customer base spread from Vermont to Guam and beyond, the company has worked to keep its employee size small. At $15 million in sales, Small Dog still has just 14 workers and has no plans to increase that figure significantly.

Perhaps one of the smallest success stories is TractorBoy, an e-commerce venture started part time by partners Steve Waters and Wade Griffin. Selling only two products—men's underwear in three styles and baseball caps emblazoned with the TractorBoy logo—the company has reached out to the gay community from its base in Blackshear, Georgia. With a Web site built by Griffin, who taught himself Web site design, the company is now looking for about $200,000 in financing to take it to the next level, increasing its inventory and enabling one of the founders to commit full time to the venture.

These small town success stories have caught the eye of some venture capital firms, which are now turning their attention to Internet-based companies outside of major metropolitan areas.

(continued)

Instead of Silicon Valley and Manhattan, some VCs are watching small town America to see which companies are demonstrating consistent growth. The one holdup seems to be access to high-speed Internet lines. Only 5% of towns with fewer than 10,000 residents have high-speed service, hampering the efforts of new e-commerce ventures.

▬ **SOURCES:** "No Longer Limited by Location, Rural Entrepreneurs Unfold on the Internet," by Jim Hopkins, *USA Today*, February 20, 2001; "Profits Take Root at Geiger," by Mia Geiger, *Philadelphia Business Journal*, August 25, 2000; "The Village Vanguard," by Andy Serwer, *Fortune*, July 10, 2000; "Hot Dogs," by Larissa K. Vigue, *Business People*, January 2000.

4.3 CHOOSING THE HARDWARE FOR AN E-COMMERCE SITE

As the manager in charge of building an e-commerce site, you will be held account-able for its performance. Whether you host your own site or outsource the hosting and operation of your site, you will need to understand certain aspects of the com-puting hardware platform. The **hardware platform** refers to all the underlying com-puting equipment that the system uses to achieve its e-commerce functionality. Your objective is to have enough platform capacity to meet peak demand (avoiding an overload condition), but not so much platform that you are wasting money. Failing to meet peak demand can mean your site is slow, or actually crashes. Remember, the Web site may be your only or principal source of cash flow. How much computing and telecommunications capacity is enough to meet peak demand? How many hits per day can your site sustain?

To answer these questions, you will need to understand the various factors that affect the speed, capacity, and scalability of an e-commerce site.

RIGHT-SIZING YOUR HARDWARE PLATFORM: THE DEMAND SIDE

The most important factor affecting the speed of your site is the demand that cus-tomers put on the site. Table 4.6 lists the most important factors to consider when esti-mating the demand on a site.

The first factor to consider is the number of simultaneous users who will likely visit your site. In general, the load created by an individual customer on a server is typically quite limited and short-lived. A Web session initiated by the typical user is **stateless**, meaning that the server does not have to maintain an ongoing, dedicated interaction with the client. A Web session typically begins with a page request, then a server replies, and the session is ended. The sessions may last from tenths of a sec-ond per user, to a minute. Nevertheless, system performance does degrade as more

hardware platform

refers to all the underlying computing equipment that the system uses to achieve its e-commerce functionality

stateless

refers to fact that the server does not have to maintain an ongoing, dedicated interaction with the client

TABLE 4.6	FACTORS IN RIGHT-SIZING AN E-COMMERCE PLATFORM
LOAD FACTORS	SIGNIFICANCE
Number of simultaneous users and their frequency, e.g., hits per day	The more visitors you have, the greater the demand on your system.
Nature of customer requests	Viewing dynamic pages requires far more capacity than viewing static Web pages.
Type of content	The more dynamic pages and the more large multimedia files you have, the greater will be the load on the system.
Bandwidth to site	The greater the bandwidth connection, the higher the maximum number of requests will be.

and more simultaneous users request service. Fortunately, degradation (measured as "transactions per second" and "latency" or delay in response) is fairly graceful over a wide range, up until a peak load is reached and service quality becomes unacceptable. (See Figure 4.8.)

FIGURE 4.8	DEGRADATION IN PERFORMANCE AS NUMBER OF USERS INCREASE

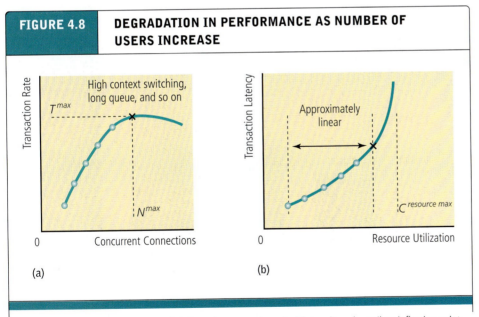

(a) As the number of concurrent users (N) rises, the transaction rate (T) rises linearly until an inflection point (X) is reached, after which performance falls at a nonlinear rate until a crash is experienced. (b) Likewise, latency increases to a point where it becomes exponential and service quality is unacceptable.

SOURCE: Microsoft, "Capacity Model for Internet Transactions," 1999.

I/O intensive

requires input/output operations rather than heavy-duty processing power

In general, a robust single-processor Web server (with, for example, a Pentium III or Xeon processor at 500 Mhz), serving only static Web pages, can handle about 8,000 concurrent users. Serving up static Web pages is **I/O intensive**, which means it requires input/output operations rather than heavy-duty processing power. As a result, Web site performance is constrained primarily by the server's input/output (I/O) limitations and the telecommunications connection, rather than speed of the processor.

Below we discuss some of the steps you can take to ensure you stay within an acceptable service quality. One step is to simply purchase a server with faster CPU processors or more CPU processors, or larger hard disk drives. However, the improvement that results is not linear and at some point becomes cost ineffective. Figure 4.9 shows the performance of a Windows 2000 Server as processors are added from a single processor up to eight processors. By increasing processors by a factor of eight, you get only three times more load capacity.

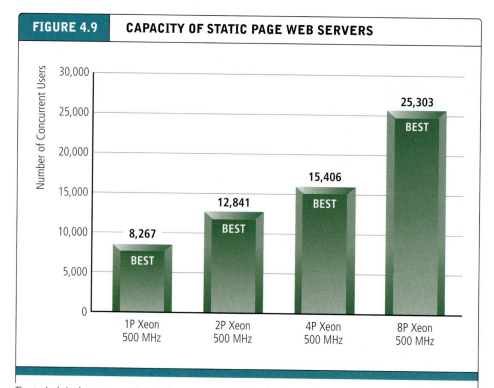

| FIGURE 4.9 | CAPACITY OF STATIC PAGE WEB SERVERS |

The typical single-processor Web static page server can handle about 8,000 concurrent users. With eight processors, the same machine could handle about 25,000 concurrent users.
SOURCE: Microsoft, 2000.

TABLE 4.7	VISITOR PROFILE AT TYPICAL E-COMMERCE SITES
VISITOR ACTIVITY	**PERCENTAGE OF VISITORS**
Browse	80%
Search for content	9%
Add items to shopping carts	5%
Purchase goods	4%
Register at site	2%

SOURCE: Intel, 1999.

A second factor to consider on the demand side is the **user profile**, which refers to the nature of customer requests and customer behavior on your site (how many pages customers request and the kind of service they want). An Intel study found 80% of visitors to the typical e-commerce site simply browse — requesting static Web pages. (See Table 4.7.)

Web servers can be very efficient at serving static Web pages (80% of the load as noted in Table 4.7). However, as customers request more advanced services, such as searches of site, registration, order taking via shopping carts, or downloads of large multimedia audio and video files, all of which require more processing power, performance can deteriorate rapidly.

The nature of the content your site offers is a third factor to consider. If your site uses dynamic page generation, then the load on the processor rises rapidly and performance will degrade. Dynamic page generation and business logic (such as a shopping cart) are **CPU-intensive** operations — they require a great deal of processing power. For instance, a site with only dynamic page content can expect performance of a single processor server to fall to one-tenth the levels described in Figure 4.9. Instead of effectively serving 8,000 users, you can only service 1,000 concurrent users. Microsoft has estimated that its Web server software operating on a 200 mhz Pentium II can handle only about 400 concurrent users of dynamic ASP pages (Microsoft, 1999). Any interaction with the user requiring access to a database — filling out forms, adding to carts, purchasing, and questionnaires — puts a heavy processing load on the server.

CPU-intensive
operations that require a great deal of processing power

Figure 4.10 shows the impact of increasing dynamic page content from 25% to 50% on a variety of processor configurations.

A final factor to consider is the telecommunications link that your site has to the Web, and also the changing nature of the client connection to the Web. Figure 4.11 shows that the number of hits per second your site can handle depends on the band-

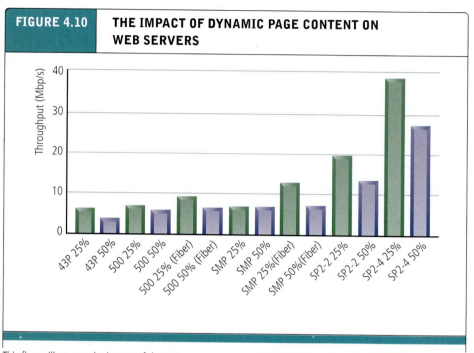

FIGURE 4.10	THE IMPACT OF DYNAMIC PAGE CONTENT ON WEB SERVERS

This figure illustrates the impact of dynamic page content on IBM RS6000 servers with different processors, ranging from a single processor, to dual processor, quad processor, and finally to a parallel processor machine. In each instance, doubling dynamic content from 25% to 50% reduces throughput by up to one third.
SOURCE: Robinson, Merenda, and Curtis, 1999.

width connection between your server and the Web. The larger the bandwidth available, the more customers can simultaneously hit your site. For example, if your connection to the Web is a 150 Kbps lite DSL line, the maximum number of visitors per second for 1 kilobyte files is probably about ten. Most businesses host their sites at an ISP or other provider that contractually is (or should be) obligated to provide enough bandwidth for your site to meet peak demands. However, there are no guarantees and ISPs can blame Web congestion for their own bandwidth limitations. Check your ISP's bandwidth and your site performance daily.

While server bandwidth connections are less a constraint today with the widespread deployment of fiber optic cable, the connection to the client is improving. By 2002, it is expected that about 13 million Americans will have broadband connections from their homes and small businesses to the Web (Jupiter Media Metrix, 2000). This means they will be able to make far more frequent requests and demand far richer content and experiences from your site. This demand will translate quickly into dynamic content and the need for additional capacity.

FIGURE 4.11 | **THE RELATIONSHIP OF BANDWIDTH TO HITS**

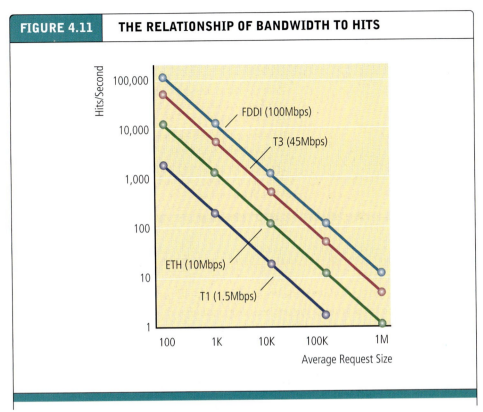

SOURCE: Robinson, Merenda, and Curtis, 1999.

RIGHT-SIZING YOUR HARDWARE PLATFORM: THE SUPPLY SIDE

Once you estimate the likely demand on your site, you will need to consider how to scale up your site to meet demand. **Scalability** refers to the ability of a site to increase in size as demand warrants. There are three steps you can take to meet the demands for service at your site: you can scale hardware vertically, scale hardware horizontally, and/or improve the processing architecture of the site. (See Table 4.8.)

You can scale your site vertically by upgrading the servers from a single processor to multiple processors. (See Figure 4.12.) For instance, you can change your hardware from a single-processor Pentium III, to a dual processor with two Pentium IIIs or Xeon processor. You can keep adding up to 20 processors to a machine and changing chip speeds as well.

There are two drawbacks to vertical scaling. First, it can become expensive to purchase new machines with every growth cycle, and second, your entire site becomes dependent on a small number of very powerful machines. If you have two such

scalability
refers to the ability of a site to increase in size as demand warrants

TABLE 4.8	SCALING YOUR SITE TO MEET DEMAND
SCALING METHOD	**DESCRIPTION**
Vertical scaling	Increase your processing supply by improving your hardware but maintaining the physical footprint and the number of servers.
Horizontal scaling	Increase your processing supply by adding servers and increasing your physical facility.
Improve processing architecture	Improve your processing supply by identifying operations with similar workloads, and using dedicated tuned servers for each type of load.

machines and one goes down, half of your site, or perhaps your entire site may become unavailable.

Horizontal scaling involves adding multiple single-processor servers to your site and balancing the load among the servers. You can also then partition the load so that some servers handle only requests for HTML or ASP pages, while others are dedicated

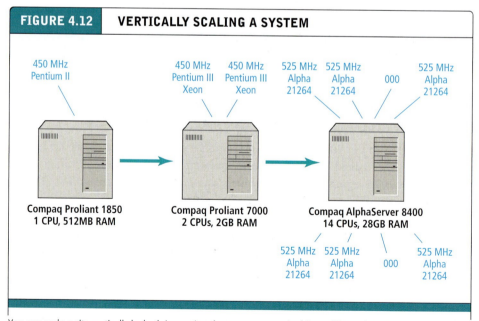

FIGURE 4.12   **VERTICALLY SCALING A SYSTEM**

You can scale a site vertically by both improving the processors and adding additional CPUs into a single physical server.

SOURCE: Microsoft, 1999.

to handling database applications. You will need special load-balancing software (provided by a variety of vendors such as Cisco, Microsoft, and IBM) to direct incoming requests to various servers. (See Figure 4.13.)

There are many advantages to horizontal scaling. It is inexpensive and often can be accomplished using older PCs that otherwise would be disposed of. Horizontal scaling also introduces redundancy — if one machine fails, chances are that another

FIGURE 4.13	HORIZONTALLY SCALING A SYSTEM

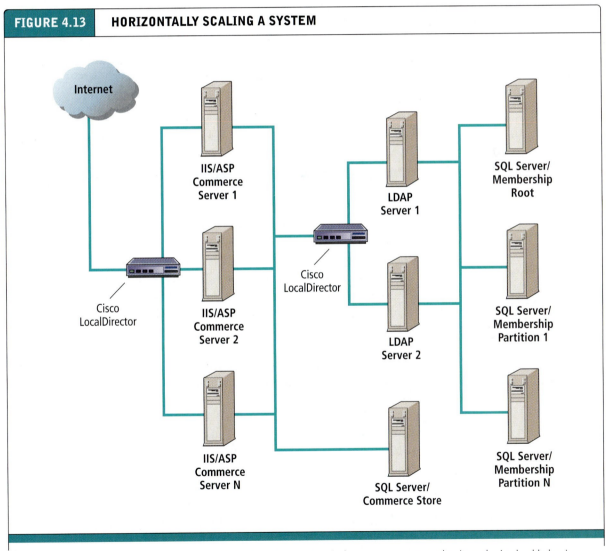

You can horizontally scale a system to meet demands by adding inexpensive single-processor servers to the site and using load-balancing software to allocate incoming customer requests to the correct server, shown in the diagram as a Cisco LocalDirector.

TABLE 4.9	IMPROVING THE PROCESSING ARCHITECTURE OF YOUR SITE
ARCHITECTURE IMPROVEMENT	DESCRIPTION
Separate static content from dynamic content.	Use specialized servers for each type of workload.
Cache static content.	Increase RAM to the gigabyte range and store static content in RAM.
Cache database lookup tables.	Cache tables used to look up database records.
Consolidate business logic on dedicated servers.	Put shopping cart, credit card processing, and other CPU-intensive activity on dedicated servers.
Optimize ASP code.	Examine your code to ensure it is operating efficiently.
Optimize the database schema.	Examine your database search times and take steps to reduce access times.

machine can pick up the load dynamically. However, when your site grows from a single machine to perhaps ten to twenty machines, the size of the physical facility required (the "footprint") increases and there is added management complexity.

A third alternative — improving the processing architecture — is a combination of vertical and horizontal scaling, combined with artful design decisions. Table 4.9 lists some of the more common steps you can take to greatly improve performance of your site.

Most of these steps involve splitting the workload into I/O-intensive activities (such as serving Web pages), and CPU-intensive activities (such as taking orders). Once you have this work separated, you can fine-tune the servers for each type of load. One of the least expensive fine-tuning steps is to simply add RAM to a few servers and store all your HTML pages in RAM. This reduces load on your hard drives and increases speed dramatically. RAM is thousands of times faster than hard disks, and RAM is inexpensive. The next most important step is to move your CPU-intensive activities, such as order taking, onto a high-end, multiple processor server that is totally dedicated to handling orders and accessing the necessary databases.

Taking these steps can permit you to reduce the number of servers required to service 10,000 concurrent users from 100 down to 20, according to one estimate.

4.4   OTHER E-COMMERCE SITE TOOLS

Now that you understand the key factors that affect the speed, capacity, and scalability of your site, we can consider some other important requirements for your Web site. You will need a coherent Web site design effort that makes business sense — not necessarily a site to wow visitors or excite them, but to sell them something. You will also need to know how to build active content and interactivity into your site — not just display static HTML pages. You will definitely want to be able to track customers who come, leave, and return to your site in order to be able to greet return visitors ("Hi Sarah, Glad to Have You Return!"). You will also want to track customers throughout your site so you can personalize and customize their experience. Finally, you will need to establish a set of information policies for your site — privacy, accessibility, and access to information policies.

In order to achieve these business capabilities, you will need to be aware of some design guidelines and additional software tools that can cost-effectively achieve the required business functionality.

WEB SITE DESIGN: BASIC BUSINESS CONSIDERATIONS

This is not a text about how to design Web sites. (In Chapter 8, we discuss Web site design issues from a marketing perspective.) Nevertheless, from a business manager's perspective, there are certain design objectives you must communicate to your Web site designers to let them know how you will evaluate their work. At a minimum, your customers will need to find what they need at your site, make a purchase, and leave.

We have all experienced poorly designed e-commerce sites. Some critics believe poor design is more common than good design. It appears easier to describe what irritates people about Web sites than to describe how to design a good Web site. The worst e-commerce sites make it difficult to find information about their products and complicated to make a purchase; they have missing pages and broken links, a confusing navigation structure, and annoying graphics or sounds that you cannot turn off. Table 4.10 restates these negative experiences as positive goals for Web site design.

Tools for Interactivity and Active Content

As a manager responsible for building a Web site, you will want to ensure users can interact with your Web site quickly and easily. As we describe in later chapters, the more interactive a Web site is, the more effective it will be in generating sales and encouraging return visitors.

Although functionality and ease of use are the supreme objectives in site design, you will also want to interact with the user and present the user with a lively "active" experience. You will want to personalize the experience for customers by addressing

TABLE 4.10	THE EIGHT MOST IMPORTANT FACTORS IN SUCCESSFUL E-COMMERCE SITE DESIGN
FACTOR	DESCRIPTION
Functionality	Pages that work, load quickly, and point the customer toward your product offerings.
Informational	Links that customers can easily find to discover more about you and your products.
Ease of use	Simple fool-proof navigation.
Redundant navigation	Alternative navigation to the same content.
Ease of purchase	One or two clicks to purchase.
Multi-browser functionality	Site works with the most popular browsers.
Simple graphics	Avoids distracting, obnoxious graphics and sounds that the user cannot control.
Legible text	Avoids backgrounds that distort text or make it illegible.

their individual needs, and customize the content of your offerings based on their behavior or expressed desires. For example, you may want to offer customers free mortgage calculations or free pension advice, based on their interaction with programs available at your site. In order to achieve these business objectives, you will need to consider carefully the tools needed to build these capabilities. Simple interactions such as a customer submitting a name, along with more complex interactions involving credit cards, user preferences, and user responses to prompts, all require special programs. Here is a brief description of some commonly used software tools for achieving high levels of site interactivity.

CGI (Common Gateway Interface)
a set of standards for communication between a browser and a program running on a server that allows for interaction between the user and the server

CGI (Common Gateway Interface) is a set of standards for communication between a browser and a program running on a server that allows for interaction between the user and the server. CGI permits an executable program to access all the information within incoming requests from clients. The program can then generate all the output required to make up the return page (the HTML, script code, text, etc.), and send it back to the client via the Web server. CGI programs can be written in nearly any programming language as long as they conform to CGI standards. Generally, CGI programs are used with UNIX servers.

For instance, if a user clicks the button "Display the Contents of My Shopping Cart," the server receives this request and executes a CGI program. The CGI program retrieves the contents of the shopping cart from the database and returns it to the server. The server sends an HTML page that displays the contents of the shopping cart on the user's screen. Notice all the computing takes place on the server side (this is why CGI programs and others like it are referred to as "server-side" programs).

Active Server Pages (ASP) is Microsoft's version of server-side programming for Windows. Invented by Microsoft in late 1996, ASP has grown rapidly to become the major technique for server-side Web programming in the Windows environment. ASP enables developers to easily create and open records from a database and execute programs within an HTML page, as well as handle all the various forms of interactivity found on e-commerce sites. Like CGI, ASP permits an interaction to take place between the browser and the server. ASP uses the same standards as CGI for communication with the browser. ASP programs are restricted to use on Windows 2000 and Windows NT Web servers running Microsoft's IIS Web server software.

Java, Java Server Pages (JSP) and JavaScript

Java is a programming language that allows programmers to create interactivity and active content on the client machine — thereby saving considerable load on the server. Java was invented by Sun Microsystems in 1990 as a platform-independent programming language for consumer electronics. The idea was to create a language whose programs could operate on any machine regardless of operating system, so-called Write Once Run Anywhere (WORA) programs. This would be possible if every operating system (Macintosh, Windows, DOS, UNIX, and mainframe MVS systems) had a Java Virtual Machine (VM) installed that would interpret the Java programs for that environment.

By 1995, it had become clear, however, that Java was more applicable to the Web than to consumer electronics. Java programs (known as *Java applets*) could be downloaded to the client over the Web and executed entirely on the client's computer. Applet tags could be included in an HTML page. To enable this, each browser would have to include a Java VM. Today, the leading browsers do include a VM to play Java programs. When the browser accesses a page with an applet, a request is sent to the server to download and execute the program and allocate page space to display the results of the program. Java can be used to display interesting graphics, create interactive environments (such as a mortgage calculator), and directly access the Web server.

Different vendors, including Microsoft, IBM, HP, and others, have produced several versions of the Java language, and even different VMs. Java applets built using Microsoft Java can play well only on Microsoft's Internet Explorer browser. Therefore, the objective of having Java applets play the same on all Web clients has not succeeded. Many corporations will not allow Java applets through their firewalls for security reasons. Despite the fact that Java applets do not have access to local client system resources (they operate in a "sandbox" for security reasons), IS managers are extremely suspicious of allowing applets served from remote servers to come through the firewall. Many Java applets crash or do not perform well, wasting system resources, and when they do perform, the functions are often trivial (such as flashing logos).

Active Server Pages (ASP)
a proprietary software development tool that enables programmers using Microsoft's IIS package to build dynamic pages

Java
a programming language that allows programmers to create interactivity and active content on the client machine—thereby saving considerable load on the server

Java Server Pages (JSP)

like CGI and ASP, a Web page coding standard that allows developers to dynamically generate Web pages in response to user requests

Java Server Pages (JSP), like CGI and ASP, is a Web page coding standard that allows developers to use a combination of HTML, JSP scripts, and Java to dynamically generate Web pages in response to user requests. JSP uses Java "servlets," small Java programs that are specified in the Web page and run on the Web server to modify the Web page before it is sent to the user who requested it. Java Server Pages are supported by most of the popular application servers on the market today.

JavaScript

a programming language invented by Netscape that is used to control the objects on an HTML page and handle interactions with the browser

JavaScript is a programming language invented by Netscape that is used to control the objects on an HTML page and handle interactions with the browser. It is most commonly used to handle verification and validation of user input, as well as to implement business logic. For instance, JavaScript can be used on customer registration forms to confirm that a valid phone number, zip code, or even e-mail address has been given. Before a user finishes completing a form, the e-mail address given can be tested for validity. JavaScript appears to be much more acceptable to corporations and other environments in large part because it is more stable and it is restricted to the operation of requested HTML pages.

Active X and VBScript

ActiveX

a programming language created by Microsoft to compete with Java

VBScript

a programming language invented by Microsoft to compete with JavaScript

Microsoft — not to be outdone by Sun Microsystems and Netscape — invented the **ActiveX** programming language to compete with Java and **VBScript** to compete with JavaScript. When the browser receives an HTML page with an ActiveX control (comparable to a Java applet), the browser simply executes the program. Unlike Java, however, ActiveX has full access to all the client's resources — printers, networks, hard drives. VBScript performs in the same way as JavaScript. Of course, ActiveX and VBScript work only if you are using Internet Explorer. Otherwise, that part of the screen is blank.

In general, given the conflicting standards for Java, ActiveX, and VBScript and the diversity of user client machines, most e-commerce sites steer clear of these tools. CGI scripts, JSP, and JavaScript are the leading tools for providing active, dynamic content.

ColdFusion

ColdFusion

an integrated server-side environment for developing interactive Web applications

ColdFusion is an integrated server-side environment for developing interactive Web applications. Developed by Macromedia, ColdFusion combines an intuitive tag-based scripting language and a tag-based server scripting language (CFML) that lowers the cost of creating interactive features. ColdFusion offers a powerful set of visual design, programming, debugging, and deployment tools.

PERSONALIZATION TOOLS

You will definitely want to know how to treat each customer on an individual basis and emulate a traditional face-to-face marketplace. *Personalization* (the ability to treat people based on their personal qualities and prior history with your site) and *cus-*

tomization (the ability to change the product to better fit the needs of the customer) are two key elements of e-commerce that potentially can make it nearly as powerful as a traditional marketplace, and perhaps even more powerful than direct mail or shopping at an anonymous suburban shopping mall. Speaking directly to the customer on a one-to-one basis, and even adjusting the product to the customer is quite difficult in the usual type of mass marketing, one-size-fits-all commercial transaction that characterizes much of contemporary commerce.

There are a number of methods for achieving personalization and customization. For instance, you could personalize Web content if you knew the personal background of the visitor. You could also analyze the pattern of clicks and sites visited for every customer who visits your site. We discuss these methods in later chapters on marketing. The primary method for achieving personalization and customization is through the placement of cookie files on the user's client machine. As we discussed in Chapter 3, a cookie is a small text file placed on the user's client machine that can contain any kind of information about the customer, such as customer ID, campaign ID, or purchases at the site. And then, when the user returns to the site, or indeed goes further into your site, the customer's prior history can be accessed from a database. Information gathered on prior visits can then be used to personalize the visit and customize the product.

For instance, when a user returns to a site, you can read the cookie to find a customer ID, look the ID up in a database of names, and greet the customer ("Hello Mary! Glad to have you return!"). You could also have stored a record of prior purchases, and then recommend a related product ("How about the wrench tool box now that you have purchased the wrenches?"). And you could think about customizing the product ("You've shown an interest in the elementary training programs for Word. We have a special "How to Study" program for beginners in Office software. Would you like to see a sample copy online?")

We will describe the use of cookies and their effectiveness in achieving a one-to-one relationship with the customer in Chapter 8, *E-commerce Marketing*.

THE INFORMATION POLICY SET

In developing an e-commerce site, you will also need to focus on the set of information policies that will govern the site. You will need to develop a **privacy policy** — a set of public statements declaring to your customers how you treat their personal information that you gather on the site. You will need to establish **accessibility rules** — a set of design objectives that ensure disabled users can effectively access your site. There are more than forty million Americans who are disabled and require special access routes to buildings as well as computer systems (see *Insight on Society: Web Accessibility for the Physically Challenged*). Finally, you will need to establish a set of **financial reporting policies** — statements declaring how you will account for revenues and costs at your site. E-commerce information policies are described in greater depth in Chapter 9.

---

privacy policy
a set of public statements declaring to your customers how you treat their personal information that you gather on the site

accessibility rules
a set of design objectives that ensure disabled users can effectively access your site

financial reporting policies
statements declaring how you will account for revenues and costs at your site

INSIGHT ON SOCIETY

WEB ACCESSIBILITY FOR THE PHYSICALLY CHALLENGED

If designing a Web site to be accessible to the physically challenged is easy to do, as advocates for the disabled argue, why aren't more Web sites built with accessibility in mind? Part of the problem is that retrofitting an existing site is very difficult, according to online merchants. Building an accessible site from scratch is far easier than trying to improve on an old site, which may require that tens of thousands of pages be rewritten.

Today's graphically rich, multimedia-enabled sites make it more difficult for the approximately 54 million disabled Americans to access Web sites. Blind users, for example, rely on a screen reader that uses software and a speech synthesizer to describe what is on a Web page. But sites that fail to use descriptive tags to explain links or images make it impossible for the screen reader to provide complete information. In the end, only 10% to 20% of all Web sites are accessible to the close to 10 million blind Americans.

Other site design elements make it difficult for the disabled to even navigate through a site. For instance, sites with small or crowded links make it more difficult for people with impaired motor skills to click on a particular link. Sites without closed-captioning cause the hearing impaired to miss built-in audio messages altogether.

In 1998, the U.S. government stepped in to force Web sites of federally funded organizations to be accessible to users who are blind, deaf, blind and deaf, or unable to use a mouse, but so far it has stayed away from enforcing the Americans with Disabilities Act in the e-commerce environment. Unless they do business with the federal government, companies with physical storefronts must be accessible to the physically challenged, but associated Web sites currently do not.

That may change, however. The National Federation of the Blind, for example, filed suit against America Online (AOL) in 2000 to try and force the site to become more accessible. The suit was later dropped after AOL agreed to design its next software package to be compatible with programs for the visually impaired. Other major sites may be targeted next.

Fortunately for these sites, some of the strategies Web designers can use to improve accessibility are fairly simple. Embedding text descriptions behind images is one example that allows screen readers to announce those descriptions. So instead of saying "Image," when a screen reader passes over an image, the visually impaired user can hear "Photo of a cruise ship sitting in a harbor." Allowing users to set the color and font schemes can also make a difference for the visually impaired. Adding screen magnification tools and sound labels where hyperlinks appear are two additional ways to increase accessibility.

These are examples of "equivalent alternatives" to visual content that disability advocates suggest should be required, both for visual and auditory content, to ensure that the disabled have equal access to information that appears on-screen. Other guidelines for creating accessible Web sites include ensuring that text and graphics are understandable when viewed without color, using features that enable activation of page elements via a variety of input devices (such as keyboard, head wand, or Braille reader), and providing clear navigation mechanisms (such as navigation bars or a site map) to aid users.

Making page design simpler and easier to follow sounds like good advice for sites trying to appeal to the disabled and well-bodied alike. But should Web sites be required by law to meet everyone's needs?

SOURCES: "Enlighten Launches Accessibility Initiative," *PR Newswire*, March 12, 2001; "Progress Made in Making Web Sites Accessible to the Blind," by Evan Koblentz, *eWeek*, January 31, 2001; "Advocates of People with Disabilities Take Online Stores to Task," by Bob Tedeschi, *New York Times*, January 1, 2001; "Law, Taxes, Money: Group Drops Lawsuit against AOL over Internet Access for the Blind," *Philanthropy News Network Online*, July 28, 2000; "Net to Get More Accessible to Disabled," by Doug Brown, *Interactive Week*, June 5, 2000; "Designing Accessible Web Pages for the Internet," National Arts and Disability Center, nadc.ucla.edu/dawpi.htm; "Web Content Accessibility Guidelines 1.0, W3C Recommendation," www.w3.org/TR/WAI-WEBCONTENT, May 5, 1999.

REI

A Homegrown Success Story

Washington-based Recreational Equipment, Inc. (REI) is the world's largest online retailer of outdoor gear. Here's how they succeeded while so many others have failed.

REI is a somewhat unusual company. It was founded in 1938 by Lloyd and Mary Anderson, mountain climbers from Seattle, Washington. The Andersons imported a special ice axe from Austria for themselves and decided to set up a cooperative to help their friends and other fellow outdoor enthusiasts acquire high-quality climbing and camping gear at reasonable prices. Today REI is the largest consumer cooperative in the United States, with 1.8 million members paying a one-time membership fee of $15 that entitles them to an annual dividend equal to about 10% of their annual purchases. An estimated 85% of the company's earnings are paid out as that member dividend. And the business has grown: Today REI operates 60 retail stores in 24 states, three online stores, an international mail order operation, and REI Adventures, a travel agency.

REI first started exploring the Internet in the summer of 1995. Netscape had just gone public, and the E-commerce I era was just beginning. As with many business success stories, REI's online venture began with senior executives who recognized the potentially transformative power of the Web, and the mixture of opportunity and possible threat that it represented.

Many traditional "bricks and mortar" retailers at that time feared cannibalization of their retail and/or catalog sales if they introduced an online sales outlet. Their nightmare was that starting an online store would merely "steal" their own customers from their regular sales channels. But REI wasn't deterred. As Dennis Madsen, REI's president and chief executive officer, said, "We knew that if we could not serve our customers who were looking to shop with us online, they would turn to someone else online. It was never a question for us. Being online meant better serving the customer. Our experience has proven that cannibalization is largely a myth and that our multi-channel customers are our best customers.

REI charged Matt Hyde, who had previously helped start REI Adventures, the company's travel service, with the mission of launching REI's first Web site on a budget of approximately $500,000. At the time, Netscape was the only company offering a complete e-commerce suite, so REI chose Netscape's Merchant Server software installed on an IBM RS/6000 server. And although Hyde recognized that REI was a retailer by trade, not a programming shop, he chose to keep design of the site in-house, using off-the-shelf Web authoring tools, rather than outsource creation of the Web site. The rationale: "When [we] took the leap of faith that we could launch this compelling value proposition, and that it could be big, [we] realized we needed to make this a core competency. It couldn't be outsourced." The decision was not without its costs, however: Managing rei.com's growth internally, with no outsourcing, strained REI's human resources. REI soon discovered that finding people with the requisite skills could be difficult, and even if they did find them, they were a lot more expensive than salespeople. For instance, REI's Seattle store employs around 400 people, while the company's online stores have just 90, but the payrolls for the two organizations are about the same.

In September 1996, at a time when few traditional retailers were even looking at online sales, rei.com launched, promoted primarily through direct mail and in-store notices. The first order arrived 20 minutes later. By February 1997, Hyde and his team knew they were on the right track. Traffic was up by 50% in the two months following Christmas. But that in itself posed a problem. As Hyde remembers, "We chose Netscape early on, and they were clearly the leader [at that time]. But not long after getting the system up, we realized that it was too limited. When you go from a few

thousand people checking out your site, to a million every month, you need a lot of infrastructure."

He also noted "On the surface, e-commerce sounds relatively easy. It's not until you have experience trying to integrate a high-volume, high-functionality Web site into existing business processes and applications that you realize that it's a lot harder than it seems. It's like an iceberg — the view from the browser is only 10% of what it takes to build a successful and profitable Web site."

REI had originally hoped to upgrade with Netscape, but, as Hyde said, "that wasn't working out." This time they had more of a choice, and looked at offerings from all the major vendors, including Microsoft, IBM, Broadvision, and OpenMarket. "When you change commerce packages, there's a huge learning curve. I was going to make this change once, but I wasn't going to do it again, so I wanted to pick the right package . . . for the next several years." In early 1998, REI decided on IBM's Net.Commerce server software. An important factor in the decision was IBM's ability to preserve all the custom coding REI had done over the past two years to connect its online store to its legacy system. "I had hundreds of thousands, if not millions of dollars tied up in this [system], and we didn't want to throw it away. And since Net.Commerce [would also lessen] the need to do custom coding in the future, it's a two-fold benefit."

In August 1998, REI launched a second Web site, rei-outlet.com, using Net.Commerce server software. Once rei-outlet.com was successfully launched, REI then turned to migrating rei.com to the new system, completing the move in October 1998.

Today, rei.com offers more than 78,000 individual items — more than any of its physical stores — at prices that are the same as in the retail stores; 45,000 pages of in-depth product information; an interactive community system; and a complete adventure travel service. The outlet store, rei-outlet.com, sells merchandise that the company buys specifically for the outlet.

To run its two Web sites, REI has multiple IBM RS/6000 web application servers and an IBM AS/400 back-end server. To handle transactions for the Web site, the rei.com and rei-outlet.com sites run separate web, application, and database servers that connect to an order-processing application database server shared by both sites. The order-processing server interfaces with the REI back-end AS/400 system that provides fulfillment, inventory, and product SKU information.

The system appears to be working well. Keynote Systems' 2000 e-Shopping Holiday Report ranked rei.com among the best sites for performance and availability, while the Holistix Performance Index placed REI.com in the top one percent of 300,000 sites tested for page download and server response time during November 1999, one of the busiest months of the year for e-commerce sales.

With its Internet stores functional, REI came back to an idea management had had several years earlier — developing proprietary information systems within its stores to allow employees to access product information more easily. That idea hadn't

SOURCES: "REI's Online Business Reports $92 Million in 2000 Sales, *REI.com Press Release*, February 15, 2001; "See You at the Top," by Alicia Neuman, *The Standard*, November 10, 2000; "REI Treks to Profits on Web," by Ken Yamada, *Red Herring*, May 9, 2000; "REI Climbs Online," by Lawrence M. Fisher, *Strategy +Business*, First Quarter, 2000; "Recreational Equipment, Inc.: An Internet Retailing Innovator," *IBM e-business case study*, 1999.

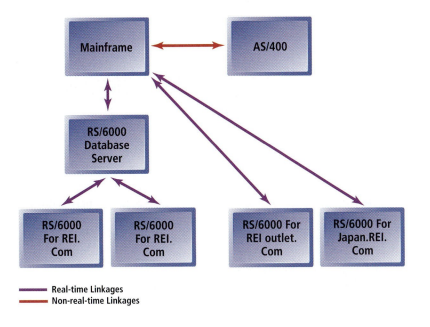

— Real-time Linkages
— Non-real-time Linkages

been developed because of the costs involved. But now, the idea became simpler to implement: Web-enabled kiosks and cash registers allow customers and employees alike to access REI's sites on the Web. Before the Internet, the kiosk concept was viewed purely as an expense, but after the Internet, the kiosk is now a profit center. For instance, they allow customers to find whatever product they need, determine whether that particular retail location has it in stock or not, and gather any background information or instruction.

REI's clicks-and-bricks strategy has paid off handsomely. In addition to improving relationships with existing customers, the online stores have helped create new customers. About 36% of the online customers are not members of the REI cooperative, meaning they are likely new customers, compared to 15% of REI's retail customers. And despite management's early fears, the online stores haven't cannibalized traditional store stales. In fact, the opposite has occurred: Online customers who also shopped in traditional REI stores spent over 20% more in those stores than in the previous year. The online stores have also increased REI's revenue and strengthened the company's position as industry leader. In February 2001, for instance, REI reported sales of $125 million for its online stores, a 125% increase over 1999 and topping sales figures for its largest store. Furthermore, REI's online venture was profitable within its second full year of operations, something not many e-commerce sites can claim.

Case Study Questions

1. Create a simple logical design and physical design for the REI.com Web site using information provided in the case study, supplemented as necessary by your own research.

2. After reading the case study, identify the key reasons for REI.com's success thus far.

3. Visit the REI.com Web site and rate its performance on the eight factors listed in Table 4.10 on a scale of 1 to 10 (with 1 being the lowest, and 10 the highest). Provide reasons for your ratings.

4. Prepare a short industry analysis of the online outdoor sporting goods and apparel industry. Who are REI's primary competitors?

4.6 REVIEW

KEY CONCEPTS

■ **Explain the process that should be followed in building an e-commerce Web site.**

Factors you must consider when building an e-commerce site include:
- hardware architecture
- software
- telecommunications capacity
- site design
- human resources
- organizational capabilities

The systems development life cycle (a methodology for understanding the business objectives of a system and designing an appropriate solution) for building an e-commerce Web site involves five major steps:
- Identify the specific business objectives for the site and then develop a list of system functionalities and information requirements.
- Develop a system design specification (both logical design and physical design).
- Build the site, either by in-house personnel or by outsourcing all or part of the responsibility to outside contractors.
- Test the system (unit testing, system testing, and acceptance testing).
- Implement and maintain the site.

The nine basic business and system functionalities an e-commerce site should contain include:

- A *digital catalog* — allows a site to display goods using text and graphics.
- *Product database* — provides product information, such as a description, stocking number, and inventory level.
- *Customer on-site tracking* — enables a site to create a site log for each customer visit, aiding in personalizing the shopping experience and identifying common customer paths and destinations.
- *Shopping cart/payment system* — provides an ordering system, secure credit-card clearing, and other payment options.
- *Customer database* — includes customer information such as the name, address, phone number, and e-mail address.
- *Sales database* — contains information regarding the customer ID, product purchased, date, payment, and shipment to be able to provide after-sale customer support.
- *Ad server* — tracks the site behavior of prospects and customers that come through e-mail or banner ad campaigns.
- *Site tracking and reporting system* — monitors the number of unique visitors, pages visited, and products purchased.
- *Inventory management system* — provides a link to production and suppliers in order to facilitate order replenishment.

■ **Describe the major issues surrounding the decision to outsource site development and/or hosting.**

Advantages of building a site in-house include:
- the ability to change and adapt the site quickly as the market demands, and
- the ability to build a site that does exactly what the company needs.

Disadvantages of building a site in-house include:
- the costs may be higher;
- the risks of failure may be greater, given the complexity of issues such as security, privacy, and inventory management;
- the process may be more time-consuming than if you had hired an outside specialist firm to manage the effort; and
- staff may experience a longer learning curve that delays your entry into the market.

Using design templates cuts development time, but pre-set templates can also limit functionality.

A similar decision is also necessary regarding outsourcing the hosting of the site versus keeping it in-house. Relying on an outside vendor to ensure that the site is live twenty-four hours a day places the burden of reliability on someone else, in return for a monthly hosting fee. The downside is that if the site requires fast upgrades due to heavy traffic, the chosen hosting company may or may not be capable of keeping up. Reliability versus scalability are the issues in this instance.

■   Identify and understand the major considerations involved in choosing Web server and e-commerce merchant server software.

Early Web sites used single-tier system architecture and consisted of a single-server computer that delivered static Web pages to users making requests through their browsers. The extended functionality of today's Web sites required the development of a multi-tiered systems architecture, which utilizes a variety of specialized Web servers, as well as links to pre-existing "back-end" or "legacy" corporate databases..

All e-commerce sites require basic Web server software to answer requests from customers for HTML and XML pages. When choosing Web server software, companies are also choosing what operating system the site will run on; Apache, which runs on the Unix system, is the market leader.

Web servers provide a host of services, including
- processing user HTML requests,
- security services,
- file transfer protocol,
- search engine,
- data capture,
- e-mail, and
- site management tools.

Dynamic server software allows sites to deliver dynamic content, rather than static, unchanging information. Web application server programs enable a wide range of e-commerce functionality, including creating a customer database, creating an e-mail promotional program, accepting and processing orders, as well as many other services.

E-commerce merchant server software is another important software package that provides catalog displays, information storage and customer tracking, order taking (shopping cart), and credit card purchase processing. E-commerce suites can save time and money, but customization can significantly drive up costs. Factors to consider when choosing an e-commerce suite include its functionality, support for different business models, visual site management tools and reporting systems, performance and scalability, connectivity to existing business systems, compliance with standards, and global and multicultural capability.

■   Understand the issues involved in choosing the most appropriate hardware for an e-commerce site.

Speed, capacity, and scalability are three of the most important considerations when selecting an operating system, and therefore the hardware that it runs on.

To evaluate how fast the site needs to be, companies need to assess the number of simultaneous users the site expects to see, the nature of their requests, the type of information requested, and the bandwidth available to the site. The answers to these questions will provide guidance regarding the processors necessary to meet customer demand. In some cases, adding additional processing power can add capacity, thereby improving system speed.

Scalability is also an important issue. Increasing processing supply, by scaling up to meet demand, can be done through:

- *Vertical scaling* — improving the processing power of the hardware, but maintaining the same number of servers;
- *Horizontal scaling* — adding more of the same processing hardware; and
- *Improving processing architecture* — identifying operations with similar workloads and using dedicated tuned servers for each type of load.

■ **Identify additional tools that can improve Web site performance.**

In addition to providing a speedy Web site, companies must also strive to have a well-designed site that encourages visitors to buy. Building in interactivity improves site effectiveness, as does personalization techniques that provide the ability to track customers while they are visiting the site. Commonly used software tools for achieving high levels of Web site interactivity and customer personalization include:

- *Common gateway interface (CGI) scripts* — a set of standards for communication between a browser and a program on a server that allows for interaction between the user and the server.
- *Active Server Pages (ASP)* — a Microsoft tool that also permits interaction between the browser and the server.
- *Java Applets* — programs written in the Java programming language that also provide interactivity.
- *JavaScript* — used to validate user input, such as an e-mail address.
- *ActiveX* and *VBScript* — Microsoft version of Java and JavaScript, respectively
- *Cookies* — text files stored on the user's hard drive that provide information regarding the user and his or her past experience at a Web site.

QUESTIONS

1. Name the six main pieces of the e-commerce site puzzle.
2. Define the systems development life cycle and discuss the various steps involved in creating an e-commerce site.
3. Discuss the differences between a simple logical and simple physical Web site design.
4. Why is system testing important? Name the three types of testing and their relation to each other.
5. Compare the costs for system development and system maintenance. Which is more expensive, and why?
6. Why is a Web site so costly to maintain? Discuss the main factors that impact cost.
7. What are the main differences between single-tier and multi-tier site architecture?

8. Name five basic functionalities a Web server should provide.
9. What are the three main factors to consider when choosing the best platform for your Web site?
10. Why is Web server bandwidth an important issue for e-commerce sites?
11. Compare and contrast the various scaling methods. Explain why scalability is a key business issue for Web sites.
12. What are the eight most important factors impacting Web site design, and how do they affect a site's operation?
13. What are Java and JavaScript? What role do they play in Web site design?
14. Name and describe three tools used to treat customers individually. Why are they significant to e-commerce?
15. What are some of the policies e-commerce businesses must develop before launching a site and why?

PROJECTS

1. Go to www.bigstep.com or Yahoo! Store (store.yahoo.com). Both sites allow you to create a simple e-tailer Web site for a free trial period. The site should feature at least four pages, including a home page, product page, shopping cart, and contact page. Extra credit will be given for additional complexity and creativity. Come to class prepared to present your e-tailer concept and Web site.

2. Visit several e-commerce sites, not including those mentioned in this chapter, and evaluate the effectiveness of the sites according to the nine basic criteria/functionalities listed in Table 4.1. Choose one site you feel does an excellent job on all the aspects of an effective site and create a presentation, including screen shots, to support your choice.

3. Imagine that you are the head of IT for a fast-growth e-commerce start-up. You are in charge of development of the company's Web site. Consider your options for building the site in-house with existing staff, or outsourcing the entire operation. Decide which strategy you believe is in your company's best interest and create a brief presentation outlining your position. Why choose that approach? And what are the estimated associated costs, compared with the alternative? (You'll need to make some educated guesses here — don't worry about being exact.)

4. Choose two of the e-commerce suite software packages listed in Table 4.5 and prepare an evaluation chart that rates the packages on the key factors discussed in the section "Choosing an E-commerce Suite." Which package would you choose if you were developing a Web site of the type described in this chapter, and why?

WEB SITE RESOURCES   www.LearnE-commerce.net

- News: Weekly updates on topics relevant to the material in this chapter.
- Video Lecture: Professor Ken Laudon summarizes the key concepts of the chapter.
- Research: Abstracts and links to articles referenced in the chapter, as well as other relevant research.
- PowerPoint slides: Illustrations from the chapter and more.
- Additional projects and exercises
- Tutorials: Learn more about CGI, Active Server Pages and Java Server Pages, Java and ActiveX, JavaScript and VBScript, and Web site design.

Security and Encryption

After reading this chapter, you will be able to:

- Understand the scope of e-commerce crime and security problems.
- Describe the key dimensions of e-commerce security.
- Understand the tension between security and other values.
- Identify the key security threats in the e-commerce environment.
- Describe how various forms of encryption technology help protect the security of messages sent over the Internet.
- Identify the tools used to establish secure Internet communications channels.
- Identify the tools used to protect networks, servers, and clients.
- Appreciate the importance of policies, procedures, and laws in creating security.

The Merchant Pays

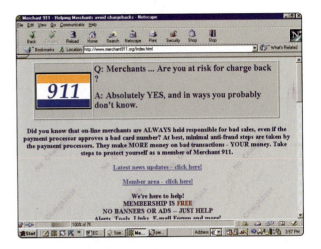

Cracker Hits Western Union Site." "Vast Online Credit Card Threat Revealed." "FBI Warns of Credit Card Rings That Prowl Web." It's no wonder many consumers are still leery of using credit cards to order merchandise online. But what's ironic is that while all the attention is being paid to the risks consumers face from online credit card fraud—a risk that is actually relatively minimal for the customer—it is usually the merchant who ends up being the victim.

Victor Stein is a case in point. Stein, a New York sugar broker who runs an e-commerce site about billiards on the side, was happy to process an order from a customer calling herself Amina Hadir for a $700 billiard encyclopedia in early 2000; the fact that the shipment was to be made to Morocco was no problem. Visa authorized the purchase and Stein mailed the book off, just as with all his other online customers. Except that Ms. Hadir denied that she had purchased the book, or that she had received it. As a result, Stein's bank did what is known as a "chargeback": It deducted the $700 that had originally been deposited into his Visa merchant account and returned it to Ms. Hadir. Not only did he lose the sale, but he lost the merchandise as well.

Travel site Expedia.com had a similar experience, losing more than $4 million when airline tickets were purchased through the site using stolen credit cards. Once the tickets were received, the thieves sold them, pocketing the cash. Expedia was liable for the retail cost of all the tickets purchased on the site through chargebacks from the credit card companies.

In the "off-line" world, when a credit card is stolen and then used to purchase merchandise, if the merchant has followed proper procedures (such as obtaining a signature and checking it against the signature on the back of the card), the credit card issuer absorbs the cost.

However, many of the security procedures that the credit card companies rely on are not applicable in an online environment. Internet credit card charges fall under the heading of CNP (cardholder not present) transactions. As a result, typically there is no tangible signature to check and hold as proof that a customer actually placed an order. Internet speed means that a high volume of purchases can be processed before the credit card company or consumer becomes aware that a card has been stolen. The global nature of the Internet is another consideration: Credit card companies can verify addresses of U.S. residents, but not those of international buyers, such as Victor Stein's customer. And in some instances, as in the case of digitally delivered products such as downloads of software, there is no address—the product is "shipped" directly and immediately to the purchaser's computer.

As a result, credit card companies have shifted most of the risks associated with e-commerce credit card transactions to the merchant, even though the credit card company supposedly authorizes the transaction. So, although a card owner is only liable for the first $50 of unauthorized purchases, online merchants that are victims of credit card fraud are generally liable for everything they ship.

The percentage of Internet transactions that are charged back to the online merchant is much higher than for traditional retailers—from 3% to 5% for online retailers compared to ½ of 1% for traditional retailers, according to industry estimates. However, the full extent of the problem is difficult to peg, as the major credit card companies and most major online retailers refuse to divulge actual figures. There's no doubt, however, that international fraud is a major problem, and as the Internet encourages global trading, more fraud is bound to occur. In fact, MSNBC estimates that overseas criminals account for up to one-third of all online fraud within the United States today.

So how can an online merchant protect itself? Some refuse to process purchases from overseas customers; others no longer take orders from free account e-mail holders. Many insist that the billing address on the credit card and the shipping address match. Larger companies often use screening software that looks for anomalies and flags potential purchases that may be problematic for further investigation. There are also other steps merchants could take to make the process more secure, such as requiring a digital certificate that more reliably authenticates the customer, but to do so, the merchant must be willing to forgo the sale in the event the customer doesn't have a certificate. At this point, that's a step many merchants are not willing to take as they consider the risks and rewards of e-commerce.

SOURCES: "Credit-Card Scams Bedevil E-Stores," by Julia Angwin, *Wall Street Journal*, September 19, 2000; "Expedia Stung by Major Credit Card Fraud," by Paul Greenberg, *E-Commerce Times*, March 2, 2000; "E-business versus the Perfect Cybercrime," by Mike Brunker, MSNBC, March 3, 2000.

As "The Merchant Pays" illustrates, doing business on the Web is more risky than doing business with local customers. Stolen credit cards, disputed charges, off-shore shipping destinations, the power of credit card companies to force merchants to pay for fraud, and the lack of international laws governing global e-commerce problems are just some of the security problems with which e-commerce merchants must grapple. For consumers, on the other hand, the risk in e-commerce is really no greater than in ordinary commerce. Although there have been some spectacular losses of credit card information involving a tiny percentage of companies, because of a variety of laws, consumers are largely insolated from the impact of stolen credit cards and credit card information. Nevertheless, as the transaction volumes and monetary value of e-commerce continue to expand, so do the risks for both merchants and consumers. In this chapter we will examine e-commerce security issues, identify the major risks, and describe the variety of solutions currently available.

5.1 THE E-COMMERCE SECURITY ENVIRONMENT

For most law-abiding citizens, the Internet holds the promise of a global marketplace, providing access to people and businesses worldwide. For criminals, the Internet has created entirely new — and lucrative — ways to steal. From products and services to cash to information, it's all there for the taking on the Internet.

It's also less risky to steal online. The potential for anonymity on the Internet cloaks many criminals in legitimate-looking identities, allowing them to place fraudulent orders with online merchants, steal information by intercepting e-mail, or simply to shut down e-commerce sites by using software viruses. In the end, however, the actions of such cybercriminals are costly for both businesses and consumers, who are then subjected to higher prices and additional security measures.

THE SCOPE OF THE PROBLEM

It is difficult to estimate the actual amount of e-commerce crime for a variety of reasons. In many instances, e-commerce crimes are not reported because companies fear losing the trust of legitimate customers (Thibodeau, 2001). And even when crimes are reported, it may be hard to quantify the losses incurred. For instance, a recent survey of 538 security practitioners in U.S. corporations and government agencies conducted by the Computer Security Institute reported that 85% of the respondents had detected breaches of computer security within the last 12 months and that 64% acknowledged financial loss as a result. Only 35%, however, were willing and/or able to quantify their financial loss, which totaled $377 million in the aggregate. The most serious losses involved theft of proprietary information and financial fraud.

Forty percent reported attacks from outside the organization, 38% experienced denial of service attacks (attempts from outside the organization to disable a site, described later), and 94% detected virus attacks (Computer Security Institute, 2001).

The FBI's Internet Fraud Complaint Center (IFFC) is another source of data on computer crime, and one that is focused more particularly on consumers and e-commerce. The IFCC has received over 15,000 consumer complaints since May 2000, of which approximately 4,000 have been referred to law enforcement agencies. Figure 5.1 presents data on e-commerce crime from the IFFC.

The FBI data is useful for gauging the types of e-commerce crime most likely to be reported by consumers and the typical amount of loss experienced. Most complaints to the IFFC regarding online fraud during 2000 resulted from online auctions, where either the buyer or the seller felt cheated. Although the average loss of "referred cases" — those actually brought to a prosecutor — was only about $1,000, the largest loss referred was $366,248. The total dollar loss for all referred cases was $4.6 million during a six-month period in 2000.

As noted in the opening case, online credit card fraud is perhaps the most high profile form of e-commerce crime. Private research firms estimate that total credit card fraud in the United States exceeded $1.5 billion in 2000 and could reach $15 billion by 2003 (Finfacts, 2001). While it is hard to determine exactly how much online credit card fraud comprises of this overall figure, industry estimates place the amount somewhere in the $500 million range. In Europe, the European Commission esti-

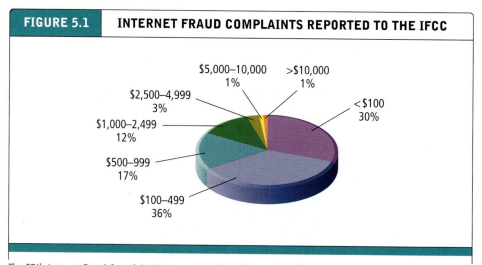

| FIGURE 5.1 | INTERNET FRAUD COMPLAINTS REPORTED TO THE IFCC |

The FBI's Internet Fraud Complaint Center reports that the most common Internet crime involves auction fraud, and the average dollar loss is $1,259.

SOURCE: National White Collar Crime Center and the Federal Bureau of Investigation, 2000.

mated that online credit card fraud in the European Union during 2000 was also in the $500 million range (Reuters, 2001).

Not every cybercriminal is after money. In some cases, such criminals aim to just deface, vandalize and/or disrupt a Web site, rather than actually steal goods or services. The cost of such an attack includes not only the time and effort to make repairs to the site but also damage done to the site's reputation and image as well as revenues lost as a result of the attack. Estimates of the overall cost of the various forms of cybervandalism range into the billions (Yankee Group, 2000).

From this and other reports we can conclude that while the overall size of cybercrime may be unclear, cybercrime against e-commerce sites is significant, the amount of losses is growing rapidly, and the managers of e-commerce sites must prepare for a variety of criminal assaults.

WHAT IS GOOD E-COMMERCE SECURITY?

What is a secure commercial transaction? Any time you go into a marketplace, you take risks, including the loss of privacy (information about what you purchased). The prime risk as a consumer is that you do not get what you paid for. In fact, you might pay and get nothing! Worse, someone steals your money while you are at the market! As a merchant in the market, your risk is that you don't get paid for what you sell. Thieves take merchandise and then either walk off without paying anything, or pay you with a fraudulent instrument, stolen credit card, or forged currency.

E-commerce merchants and consumers face many of the same risks as participants in traditional commerce, albeit in a new digital environment. Theft is theft, regardless of whether it is digital theft or traditional theft. Burglary, breaking and entering, embezzlement, trespass, malicious destruction, vandalism — all crimes in a traditional commercial environment — are present also in e-commerce. However, reducing risks in e-commerce is a complex process that involves new technologies, organizational policies and procedures, and new laws and industry standards that empower law enforcement officials to investigate and prosecute offenders. Figure 5.2 illustrates the multi-layered nature of e-commerce security.

To achieve the highest degree of security possible, new technologies are available and should be used. But these technologies by themselves do not solve the problem. Organizational policies and procedures are required to ensure the technologies are not subverted. Finally, industry standards and government laws are required to enforce payment mechanisms, as well as investigate and prosecute violators of laws designed to protect the transfer of property in commercial transactions.

What the history of security in commercial transactions teaches is that any security system can be broken if enough resources are put against it. Security is not absolute. In addition, perfect security forever is not needed, especially in the information age. There is a time value to information — just as there is to money. Sometimes it is sufficient to protect a message for a few hours, days, or years. Also, because

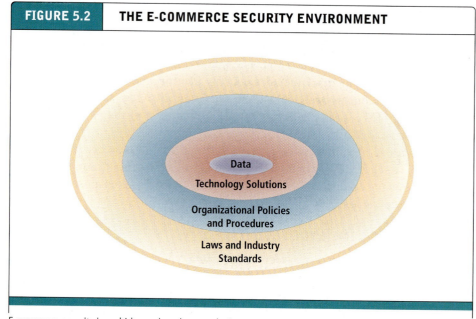

FIGURE 5.2	THE E-COMMERCE SECURITY ENVIRONMENT

E-commerce security is multi-layered, and must take into account new technology, policies and procedures, and laws and industry standards.

security is costly, we always have to weigh the cost against the need. Finally, we have also learned that security is a chain, a chain that breaks most often at the weakest link. Our locks are often much stronger than our management of the keys.

We can conclude then that good e-commerce security requires a set of laws, procedures, policies, and technologies, that, to the extent feasible, protect individuals and organizations from unexpected behavior in the e-commerce marketplace (Garfinkel and Spafford, 1997).

DIMENSIONS OF E-COMMERCE SECURITY

There are six key dimensions to e-commerce security: integrity, nonrepudiation, authenticity, confidentiality, privacy, and availability (See Table 5.1).

integrity

the ability to ensure that information being displayed on a Web site or transmitted or received over the Internet, has not been altered in any way by an unauthorized party

Integrity refers to the ability to ensure that information being displayed on a Web site, or transmitted or received over the Internet, has not been altered in any way by an unauthorized party. For example, if an unauthorized person intercepts and changes the contents of an online communication, such as by redirecting a bank wire transfer into a different account, the integrity of the message has been compromised because the communication no longer represents what the original sender intended.

An e-commerce customer may question a message's integrity if the contents seem suspicious and out of character for the person who supposedly sent it. And a

TABLE 5.1	CUSTOMER AND MERCHANT PERSPECTIVES ON THE DIFFERENT DIMENSIONS OF E-COMMERCE SECURITY	
DIMENSIONS	**CUSTOMER'S PERSPECTIVE**	**MERCHANT'S PERSPECTIVE**
Integrity	Has information I transmit or receive been altered?	Has data on the site been altered without authorization? Is the data being received from customers valid?
Nonrepudiation	Can a party to an action with me later deny taking the action?	Can a customer deny ordering products?
Authenticity	Who am I dealing with? How can I be assured that the person or entity is who they claim to be?	What is the real identity of the customer?
Confidentiality	Can someone other than the intended recipient read my messages?	Are messages or confidential data accessible to anyone other than those authorized to view them?
Privacy	Can I control the use of information about myself transmitted to an e-commerce merchant?	What use, if any, can be made of personal data collected as part of an e-commerce transaction? Is the personal information of customers being used in an unauthorized manner?
Availability	Can I get access to the site?	Is the site operational?

system administrator must deal with the issue of integrity when determining who should have authorization to change data on the Web site; the more people with authority to change data, the greater the threat of integrity violations from both inside and out.

Nonrepudiation refers to the ability to ensure that e-commerce participants do not deny (i.e., repudiate) their online actions. For instance, free e-mail accounts make it easy for a person to post comments or send a message and perhaps later deny doing so. As discussed in the opening vignette, even when a customer uses a real name and e-mail address, it is easy for that customer to order merchandise online and then later deny doing so. In most cases, because merchants typically do not obtain a physical copy of a signature, the credit card issuer will side with the customer because the merchant has no legally valid proof that the customer ordered the merchandise.

Authenticity refers to the ability to identify the identity of a person or entity with whom you are dealing on the Internet. How does the customer know that the Web site operator is who it claims to be? How can the merchant be assured that the customer is really who she says she is? Someone who claims to be someone they are not is "spoofing" or misrepresenting themselves.

Confidentiality refers to the ability to ensure that messages and data are available only to those who are authorized to view them. Confidentiality is sometimes con-

nonrepudiation
the ability to ensure that e-commerce participants do not deny (i.e., repudiate) their online actions

authenticity
the ability to identify the identity of a person or entity with whom you are dealing on the Internet

confidentiality
the ability to ensure that messages and data are available only to those who are authorized to view them

privacy

the ability to control the use of information about oneself

availability

the ability to ensure that an e-commerce site continues to function as intended

fused with **privacy**, which refers to the ability to control the use of information a customer provides about himself or herself to an e-commerce merchant.

E-commerce merchants have two concerns related to privacy: They must establish internal policies that govern their own use of customer information, and they must protect that information from illegitimate or unauthorized use. For example, if hackers break into an e-commerce site and gain access to credit card or other information, this not only violates the confidentiality of the data, but also the privacy of the individuals who supplied the information.

Availability refers to the ability to ensure that an e-commerce site continues to function as intended.

E-commerce security is designed to protect these six dimensions. When any one of them is compromised, it is a security issue.

THE TENSION BETWEEN SECURITY AND OTHER VALUES

Can there be too much security? Contrary to what some may believe, security is not an unmitigated good. Computer security adds overhead and expense to business operations, and also gives criminals new opportunities to hide their intentions and their crimes.

Ease of Use

There are inevitable tensions between security and ease of use. When traditional merchants are so fearful of robbers that they do business in locked shops, ordinary customers are discouraged from walking in. The same can be true on the Web. In general, the more security measures added to an e-commerce site, the more difficult it is to use and the slower the site becomes. As you will discover reading this chapter, digital security is purchased at the price of slowing down processors and adding significantly to data storage demands on storage devices. Security is a technological and business overhead that can detract from doing business. Too much security can harm profitability, while not enough security can potentially put you out of business.

Public Safety and the Criminal Uses of Security

There is also an inevitable tension between the desires of individuals to act anonymously (to hide their identity) and the needs of public officials to maintain public safety that can be threatened by criminals or terrorists. This is not a new problem, or even new to the electronic era. The U.S. government began informal tapping of telegraph wires during the Civil War in the mid-1860s, and the first police wiretaps of local telephone systems were in place by the 1890s — twenty years after the invention of the phone (Schwartz, 2001). No nation-state has ever permitted a technological haven to exist where criminals can plan crimes without fear of official surveillance or investigation. In this sense, the Internet is no different from any other communication system. Drug cartels make extensive use of voice, fax, and data encryption devices; one individual — Carlos Felipe Salgado, Jr. — stole 100,000 credit card numbers from the University of California at San Francisco and then used encrypted e-mail and CD-ROMs to sell the numbers; encrypted files were used by Ramsey Yousef — a member of a terrorist group responsible for bombing the World Trade Center in 1993 — to hide plans for bombing eleven U.S. airliners; and the Aum Shinrikyo religious cult in Japan that spread poison gas in the Tokyo subway in March 1995 (killing twelve and hospitalizing 6,000 people) stored their records detailing plans for attacks on other countries on computers using a powerful form of encryption called RSA, described later. Fortunately, authorities were lucky to find the encryption key stored on a floppy disk (Deming and Bauugh, 1999).

The criminal uses of computer security have sparked a lively debate and even a clash of international proportions. On one side, governments — especially the U.S. federal government — have taken strong positions in policy and law seeking to restrict the development and export of "strong encryption" systems that cannot be easily penetrated by law enforcement agencies. Most foreign countries have rejected these U.S. pressures. On the other side, computer security manufacturing firms, civil libertarians, and others have sought unrestricted development of powerful encryption systems, arguing that the primary enemy of privacy and confidentiality is the government.

We will review this debate and legislation at the end of the chapter. As we will see, modern technologies provide criminals with a host of new opportunities for mischief. The balance between security, privacy, anonymity, and public safety changes as societies act to resolve perceived threats and exploit new opportunities for economic growth.

5.2 SECURITY THREATS IN THE E-COMMERCE ENVIRONMENT

From a technology perspective, there are three key points of vulnerability when dealing with e-commerce: the client, the server, and the communications pipeline. Figure 5.3 illustrates a typical e-commerce transaction involving the use of a credit card by a consumer to purchase a product. Figure 5.4 illustrates some of the things that can go wrong at each major vulnerability point in the transaction — over Internet communications channels, at the server level, and at the client level.

In this section we will be describing the seven most common and most damaging forms of security threats to e-commerce sites: malicious code, hacking and cybervandalism, credit card fraud/theft, spoofing, denial of service attacks, sniffing, and insider jobs.

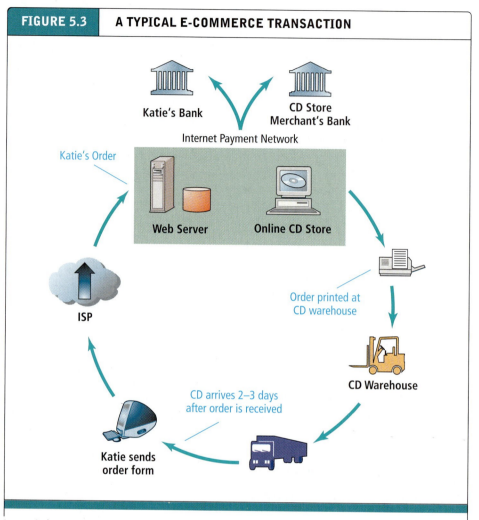

| FIGURE 5.3 | A TYPICAL E-COMMERCE TRANSACTION |

In a typical e-commerce transaction, the customer uses a credit card and the existing credit payment system. The transaction has many vulnerable points.
SOURCE: Boncella, 2000.

malicious code (malware)
includes a variety of threats such as viruses, worms, Trojan horses, and "bad applets"

virus
a computer program that has the ability to replicate or make copies of itself, and spread to other files

MALICIOUS CODE

Malicious code (sometimes referred to as "malware") includes a variety of threats such as viruses, worms, Trojan horses, and "bad applets." A **virus** is a computer program that has the ability to replicate or make copies of itself, and spread to other files. In addition to the ability to replicate, most computer viruses deliver a "payload." The payload may be relatively benign, such as the display of a message or image, or it may

FIGURE 5.4 — VULNERABLE POINTS IN AN E-COMMERCE ENVIRONMENT

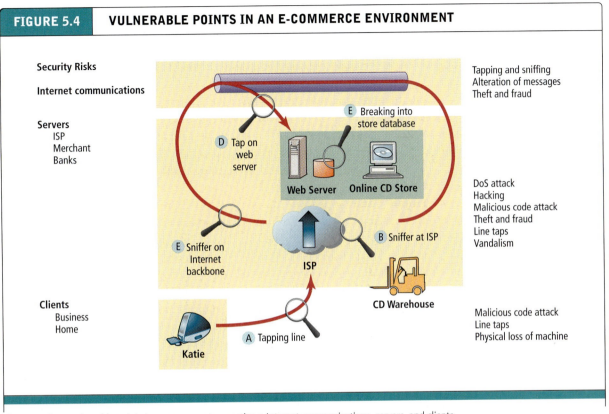

There are three vulnerable points in e-commerce transactions: Internet communications, servers, and clients.
SOURCE: Boncella, 2000.

be highly destructive — destroying files, reformatting the computer's hard drive, or causing programs to run improperly.

The most common type of virus is a *macro virus*; close to 75% to 80% of all viruses are believed to fall into this category (International Computer Security Association, 2000). Macro viruses are application-specific, meaning that the virus affects only the application for which it was written, such as Microsoft Word, Excel, and PowerPoint. When a user opens an infected document in the appropriate application, the virus copies itself to the templates in the application, so that when new documents are created, they are infected with the macro virus as well. Macro viruses can easily be spread when sent in an e-mail attachment.

File-infecting viruses usually infect executable files, such as *.com, *.exe, *.drv, and *.dll files. They may activate every time the infected file is executed by copying themselves into other executable files. File-infecting viruses are also easily spread through e-mails and any file transfer system.

Script viruses are written in script programming languages such as VBScript (Visual Basic Script) and JavaScript. The viruses are activated simply by double-clicking an infected *.vbs or *.js file. The ILOVEYOU virus (also know as the Love Bug), which overwrites *.jpg and *.mp3 files, is the most famous example of a script virus.

Macro, file-infecting, and script viruses are often combined with a worm. Instead of just spreading from file to file, a **worm** is designed to spread from computer to computer. A worm does not necessarily need to be activated by a user or program in order for it to replicate itself. For instance, the ILOVEYOU virus was both a script virus and a worm that rapidly spread by sending itself to the first 50 addresses in a user's Microsoft Outlook address book

A **Trojan horse** appears to be benign, but then does something other than expected. The Trojan horse is not itself a virus because it does not replicate, but is often a way for viruses or other malicious code to be introduced into a computer system. The term *Trojan horse* is based on the huge wooden horse in Homer's *Iliad* that the Greeks gave their opponents, the Trojans — a gift that actually contained hundreds of Greek soldiers. Once the people of Troy let the massive horse within their gates, the soldiers revealed themselves and captured the city. In today's world, a Trojan horse may masquerade as a game, but actually hide a program to steal your passwords and e-mail them to another person.

Java applets and ActiveX controls are programs that run from within browsers. They add functionality to Web sites and make them interactive. Although these technologies enhance the usefulness of Web sites, they represent an increased security risk because they may be activated merely by surfing to a Web site and downloading the applet or control to the user's PC. *Bad applets*, also referred to as *malicious mobile code*, are expected to become an increasing problem as Java and ActiveX controls become more commonplace.

Malicious code such as that described above is a threat at both the client and the server level, although servers generally engage in much more thorough anti-virus activities than do consumers. At the server level, malicious code can bring down an entire Web site, preventing millions of people from using the site. Such incidents are infrequent. Much more frequent malicious code attacks occur at the client level, but the amount of damage is limited to a single machine.

Malicious code is a threat to a system's integrity and continued operation, often changing how a system functions or altering documents created on the system. In some cases, the affected user is unaware of the attack until it is underway, such as with the macros that use e-mail address books to send out copies of the virus to everyone in the user's address book. Not only does this slow down the computer, but it can create hundreds or thousands of bogus messages that appear to be coming from the user, thereby spreading the virus further each time it is opened and activated. Ford Motor Company experienced such an attack in the spring of 2000 on its global e-mail

---

worm

malware that is designed to spread from computer to computer

Trojan horse

appears to be benign, but then does something other than expected. Often a way for viruses or other malicious code to be introduced into a computer system.

network. The ILOVEYOU virus had infected 1,000 of its corporate computers and forced a shutdown of all network activities for more than a day while programmers eradicated the virus and cleared out the more than 140,000 contaminated e-mail messages that had been sent (Bradsher, 2000). Table 5.2 lists some of the more well-known examples of malicious code on the Internet.

HACKING AND CYBERVANDALISM

A **hacker** is an individual who intends to gain unauthorized access to a computer system. Within the hacking community, the term **cracker** is typically used to denote a

hacker
an individual who intends to gain unauthorized access to a computer system

cracker
within the hacking community, term typically used to denote a hacker with criminal intent

TABLE 5.2	EXAMPLES OF MALICIOUS CODE	
NAME	**TYPE**	**DESCRIPTION**
Melissa	Macro virus/worm	First spotted in March 1999. At the time, Melissa was the fastest spreading infectious program ever discovered. It attacked Microsoft Word's normal.dot global template, ensuring infection of all newly created documents and mailed an infected Word file to the first 50 entries in each user's Microsoft Outlook address book.
ILOVEYOU (Love Bug)	Script virus/worm	ILOVEYOU struck in May 2000, unseating Melissa as the fastest spreading virus. It used Microsoft Outlook to send a message with an attachment file "Love-Letter-For-You.TXT.vbs". When opened, the virus erased .mp3 and .jpg files. The virus used Microsoft Outlook and mIRC (Internet Relay Chat) to propagate itself to other systems.
ExploreZip	Trojan horse/worm	ExploreZip was first discovered in June 1999 and used Microsoft Outlook to propagate itself. When opened, it sought certain files and reduced their file size to zero, rendering them useless and unrecoverable.
Chernobyl	File infecting virus	This virus first appeared in 1998 and is very destructive. It wipes out the first megabyte of data on a hard disk (making the rest useless) every April 26, the anniversary of the nuclear disaster at Chernobyl.
BackOrifice 2000	Trojan horse	Once installed on a victim's machine, BackOrifice can gather information, perform system commands, redirect network traffic, and reconfigure the victim's computer.

hacker with criminal intent, although in the public press, the terms *hacker* and *cracker* are used interchangeably (Sinrod and Reilly, 2000). Hackers and crackers gain unauthorized access by finding weaknesses in the security procedures of Web sites and computer systems, often taking advantage of various features of the Internet that make it an open system that is easy to use. Hackers and crackers are computer aficionados excited by the challenge of breaking into corporate and government Web sites. Sometimes they are satisfied merely by breaking into the files of an e-commerce site. Others have more malicious intentions and commit **cybervandalism**, intentionally disrupting, defacing, or even destroying the site. For instance, on April Fools Day 2001, hackers targeted sites running Microsoft's Internet Information Server for defacement, hitting such high-profile and diverse victims as Walt Disney Company, the *Wall Street Journal*'s WebWatch, Ringling Brothers and Barnum & Bailey Circus, and the ASPCA (Greene, 2001). Some hackers, motivated by "hacktivism," launch politically motivated attacks with the same effect. For instance, also in April 2001, South Korean hackers crashed a Japanese education ministry Web site as part of a protest against a controversial history textbook, which protesters claimed distorted history and justified Japan's past wartime aggression against Asian countries.

The hacker phenomenon has diversified over time. And hacker activities have broadened beyond mere system intrusion to include theft of goods and information, as well as vandalism and system damage. Groups of hackers called *tiger teams* are used by corporate security departments to test their own security measures. By hiring hackers to break into the system from outside, the company can identify weaknesses in the computer system's armor. These "good hackers" became known as **white hats** because of their role in helping organizations locate and fix security flaws. White hats do their work under contract, with agreement from clients that they will not be prosecuted for their efforts to break in.

In contrast, **black hats** are hackers who engage in the same kinds of activities but without pay or any buy-in from the targeted organization, and with the intention of causing harm. They break into Web sites and reveal the confidential or proprietary information they find. These hackers believe strongly that information should be free, so sharing previously secret information is part of their mission.

Somewhere in the middle are the **grey hats**, hackers who believe they are pursuing some greater good by breaking in and revealing system flaws. Grey hats discover weaknesses in a system's security and then publish the weakness without disrupting the site or attempting to profit from their finds. Their only reward is the prestige of discovering the weakness. Grey hat actions, however, are suspect, especially when the hackers reveal security flaws that make it easier for other criminals to gain access to a system.

cybervandalism
intentionally disrupting, defacing, or even destroying a site

white hats
"good" hackers that help organizations locate and fix security flaws

black hats
hackers who act with the intention of causing harm

grey hats
hackers who believe they are pursuing some greater good by breaking in and revealing system flaws

CREDIT CARD FRAUD

What is one of the most-feared occurrences on the Internet? Theft of credit card data. Fear that their credit card information will be stolen frequently prevents users from making online purchases. Interestingly, this fear appears to be largely unfounded. Incidences of stolen credit card information are much lower than users think. For instance, a study by ActivMedia Research reports that 58% of consumers reported a fear of online credit card theft, when only a 2% occurrence was reported. It is unclear at this time if the realistic threat to consumers for credit card fraud is greater in e-commerce than in traditional commerce.

In traditional commerce, there is substantial credit card fraud, but the consumer is largely insured against the losses by federal law. Credit card fraud amounts to approximately $1 to $1.5 billion a year. The most common cause of credit card fraud is a lost or stolen card that is used by someone else, followed by employee theft of customer numbers, and stolen identities (criminals applying for credit cards using false identities). Federal law limits the liabilities of individuals to $50 for a stolen credit card. For amounts over $50, the credit card company generally pays the amount, although in some cases the merchant may be held liable if it failed to verify the account or consult published lists of invalid cards. The costs of credit card fraud are recouped by banks by charging higher interest rates on unpaid balances, and by merchants who raise prices to cover the losses.

E-commerce adds some nuances to traditional credit card fraud. While in traditional commerce the greatest threat to a consumer is physically losing the card and suffering a $50 liability, in e-commerce the greatest threat to the consumer is that the merchant's server with which the consumer is transacting will "lose" the credit information or permit it to be diverted for a criminal purpose. Credit card files are a major target of Web site hackers. Moreover, e-commerce sites are wonderful sources of customer personal information — name, address, and phone number. Armed with this information, criminals can assume a new identity and establish new credit for their own purposes. As discussed in the opening vignette, "The Merchant Pays," for e-commerce merchants, one of the greatest credit card threats is repudiation.

International orders have been particularly prone to repudiation. If an international customer places an order and then later disputes it, online merchants often have no way to verify that the package was actually delivered and that the credit card holder is the person who placed the order.

The solution for many Web sites is to institute new identity verification mechanisms that are currently in development; these will be discussed in the next section. Until a customer's identity can be guaranteed, online companies are at a much higher risk of loss than traditional offline companies. *Insight on Society: E-Signatures — Bane or Boon to E-commerce?* looks at the federal government's attempt to address this issue.

INSIGHT ON SOCIETY

E-SIGNATURES—BANE OR BOON TO E-COMMERCE?

The goal of the Electronic Signature in Global and National Commerce Act (the "E-Sign Law"), which went into effect on October 1, 2000, is to make it faster, easier, and less expensive to do business on the Internet. For a document—such as a purchase agreement or sales receipt—to be legally binding, a company or individual needs to be able to prove that it was actually signed by the person entering into the agreement. Online transactions have been hampered by the fact that it has been difficult to either obtain or verify the signature of someone who has placed an online order.

By effectively giving as much legal weight to an electronic signature as to a pen-and-ink version, lawmakers are attempting to encourage consumers to conduct more business online. Enhancing the status of online signatures—giving them legitimacy—will hopefully reduce or even eliminate incidents of repudiation, where consumers can easily deny having made a purchase or having entered into a contract.

With that loophole gone, the whole e-commerce industry will change. Or will it? Although e-signatures have gained stature in the United States and some European countries, many other countries so far have not instituted such legislation.

Some estimates suggest that as many as 35% to 40% of online users who express interest in setting up an online financial, insurance, or retail account fail to follow through because of the additional paperwork required. Printing out and mailing in original signatures has proved to be too much to ask of potential customers, who want a fast and instantaneous process. With e-signatures, however, that additional paperwork is eliminated.

But do consumers really want to go through the trouble of making it easier for online companies to process transactions? In order to validate an e-signature, new measures will need to be introduced that serve to verify an individual's identity — measures such as digital certificates, additional passwords, thumb prints, or a photo image of the signer's face. Some sites may even require additional financial information as a backup. All of these measures provide online companies with additional personal information about users, something that many users are hesitant to share.

As Internet usage grows, so do the number of stories regarding stolen identities, fraudulent purchases, and personal information becoming public. All of these reports serve to make users more nervous and less willing to reveal personal information. So will e-signatures really make users more willing to engage in online transactions?

Thus far (one year after its passage), the law does not appear to be having much impact, and some analysts suggest that the law may require significant revision (for instance, limiting liability for "stolen" e-signatures in a manner similar to what is done for credit cards) if e-signatures are to be widely accepted by the American consumer.

SOURCES: "E-Signatures: Unsigned, Unsealed, Undelivered," by Paul Greenwood, *E-commerce Times*, June 5, 2001; E-Signing Law Seen as a Boon to E-Business," by Barnaby Feder, *New York Times*, June 29, 2000; "E-Signatures: Ties that Bind" and "E-Signatures Spread to E-Commerce," by George Hulme, *InformationWeek*, July 3, 2000, "Electronic-Signature Bill is Passed by U.S. House," by Jeri Clausing, *New York Times*, June 15, 2000."

SPOOFING

Hackers attempting to hide their true identity often **spoof**, or misrepresent themselves by using fake e-mail addresses or masquerading as someone else. Spoofing also can involve redirecting a Web link to an address different from the intended one, with the site masquerading as the intended destination. Links that are designed to lead to one site can be reset to send users to a totally unrelated site, one that benefits the hacker.

Although spoofing does not directly damage files or network servers, it threatens the integrity of a site. For example, if hackers redirect customers to a fake Web site that looks almost exactly like the true site, they can then collect and process orders, effectively stealing business from the true site. Or, if the intent is to disrupt rather than steal, hackers can alter orders — inflating them or changing products ordered — and then send them on to the true site for processing and delivery. Customers become dissatisfied with the improper order shipment and the company may have huge inventory fluctuations that impact its operations.

In addition to threatening integrity, spoofing also threatens authenticity by making it difficult to discern the true sender of a message. Clever hackers can make it almost impossible to distinguish between a true and fake identity or Web address.

DENIAL OF SERVICE (DoS) ATTACKS

In a **Denial of Service (DoS)** attack, hackers flood a Web site with useless traffic to inundate and overwhelm the network. A **distributed Denial of Service (dDoS)** attack uses numerous computers to attack the target network from numerous launch points.

DoS attacks may cause a network to shut down, making it impossible for users to access the site. For busy e-commerce sites such as eBay and Buy.com, these attacks are costly; while the site is shut down, customers cannot make purchases. And the longer a site is shut down, the more damage is done to a site's reputation.

Although such attacks do not destroy information or access restricted areas of the server, they are nuisances that interfere with a company's operations. In February 2000, for instance, a series of hacker attacks caused many Web sites to shut down for several hours. EBay was down for 5 long hours, Amazon for just under 4 hours, CNN for 3.5, and E-Trade for under 3. Yahoo, Buy.com, and ZDNet were also affected for 3 to 4 hours (McConnell, 2000).

One type of DoS attack, called a *smurf*, brings a network down by sending out a request to many broadcast addresses — an address that can communicate with up to 255 host computers — to verify that the address is working. (This is called a PING request, for Packet Internet Groper, discussed in Chapter 3.) When the 255 hosts on each broadcast address reply to the verification request, the hacker spoofs the IP address, listing a particular company's server as the supposed reply address. Soon the

spoof
to misrepresent oneself by using fake e-mail addresses or masquerading as someone else

Denial of Service (DoS) attack
flooding a Web site with useless traffic to inundate and overwhelm the network

distributed Denial of Service (dDoS) attack
uses numerous computers to attack the target network from numerous launch points

victim company's server is quickly inundated with thousands of PING responses that tie it up.

DoS attacks are threats to a system's operation because they can shut it down indefinitely. Major Web sites such as Yahoo and even Microsoft have recently experienced such attacks, making the companies aware of their vulnerability and the need to introduce new measures to prevent future attacks (Gaither, 2001; Bridis, 2001).

SNIFFING

sniffer

a type of eavesdropping program that monitors information traveling over a network

A **sniffer** is a type of eavesdropping program that monitors information traveling over a network. When used legitimately, sniffers can help identify potential network trouble-spots, but when used for criminal purposes, they can be damaging and very difficult to detect. Sniffers enable hackers to steal proprietary information from anywhere on a network, including e-mail messages, company files, and confidential reports.

E-mail wiretaps are a new variation on the sniffing threat. An e-mail wiretap is hidden code in an e-mail message that allows someone to monitor all succeeding messages forwarded with the original message. For example, suppose an employee reports a manufacturing flaw that she has discovered to her supervisor, who then cascades that message throughout an organization. Someone using an e-mail wiretap will be privy to all of the subsequent e-mails that are shared on the topic. When sensitive internal communication occurs, this type of eavesdropping can be damaging and dangerous (Smith, 2001; McCormick, 2001).

The threat of sniffing is that confidential or personal information will be made public. For both companies and individuals, such an occurrence can be disruptive.

INSIDER JOBS

We tend to think of security threats to a business as originating outside the organization. In fact, the largest financial threat to business institutions come not from robberies, but from embezzlement by insiders. The same is true for e-commerce sites: Some of the largest disruptions to service, destruction to sites, and diversion of customer credit data and personal information have come from insiders — once trusted employees. Employees have access to privileged information, and in the presence of sloppy internal security procedures, they are often able to roam throughout an organization's systems without leaving a trace.

Here's one example. Jose Oquendo worked as a computer security specialist for Collegeboardwalk.com, which shared office space and a computer network with Five Partners Asset Management, one of its investors. Oquendo altered the start-up commands on the Five Partners network to automatically send the password file from the system to an e-mail account he controlled each time the Five Partners system was rebooted. After Collegeboardwalk.com failed, Oquendo secretly installed a sniffer program that intercepted and recorded electronic traffic on the Five Partners network, including unencrypted passwords. Oquendo was later caught when he used the sniffer to snare a password into the network of another company, and then erased that company's database (NIPC press release, 2001).

5.3 TECHNOLOGY SOLUTIONS

The first line of defense against the wide variety of security threats to an e-commerce site is a set of tools that can make it difficult for outsiders to invade or destroy a site. Figure 5.5 illustrates the major tools available to achieve site security. Below we describe these tools in greater detail.

PROTECTING INTERNET COMMUNICATIONS

Because e-commerce transactions must flow over the public Internet, and therefore involve thousands of routers and servers through which the transaction packets flow, security experts believe the greatest security threats occur at the level of Internet communications. This is very different from a private network where a dedicated communication line is established between two parties. A number of tools are avail-

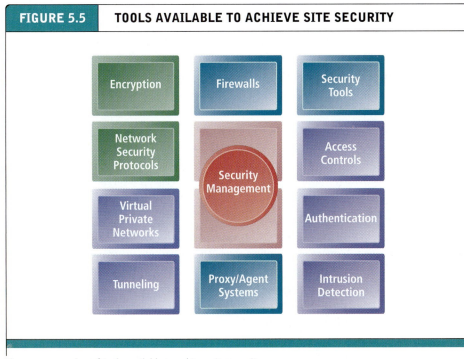

FIGURE 5.5   TOOLS AVAILABLE TO ACHIEVE SITE SECURITY

There are a number of tools available to achieve site security.

able to protect the security of Internet communications, the most basic of which is message encryption.

ENCRYPTION

Encryption is the process of transforming plain text or data into **cipher text** that cannot be read by anyone outside of the sender and the receiver. The purpose of encryption is (a) to secure stored information and (b) to secure information transmission. Encryption can provide four of the six key dimensions of e-commerce security referred to in Table 5.1:

- *Message integrity* — provides assurance that the message has not been altered.
- *Nonrepudiation* — prevents the user from denying he or she sent the message.
- *Authentication* — provides verification of the identity of the person (or machine) sending the message.
- *Confidentiality* — gives assurance that the message was not read by others.

This transformation of plain text to cipher text is accomplished by using a key or cipher. A **key** (or **cipher**) is any method for transforming plain text to cipher text. Encryption has been practiced since the earliest forms of writing and commercial transactions. Ancient Egyptian and Phoenician commercial records were encrypted using substitution and transposition ciphers. In a **substitution cipher**, every occurrence of a given letter is replaced systematically by another letter. For instance, if we used the cipher "letter plus two" — meaning replace every letter in a word with a new letter two places forward — then the word "Hello" in plain text would be transformed into the following cipher text: "JGNNQ." In a **transposition cipher**, the ordering of the letters in each word is changed in some systematic way. Leonardo Da Vinci recorded his shop notes in reverse order, making them readable only with a mirror. The word "Hello" can be written backwards as "OLLEH." A more complicated cipher would (a) break all words into two words and (b) spell the first word with every other letter beginning with the first letter, and then spell the second word with all the remaining letters. In this cipher, "HELLO" would be written as "HLO EL."

Symmetric Key Encryption

In order to decipher these messages, the receiver would have to know the secret cipher that was used to encrypt the plain text. This is called **symmetric key encryption** or **secret key encryption**. In symmetric key encryption, both the sender and the receiver use the same key to encrypt and decrypt the message. How do the sender and the receiver have the same key? They have to send it over some communication media or exchange the key in person.

Symmetric key encryption was used extensively throughout World War II and is still a part of Internet encryption. The Germans added a new wrinkle in the 1940s

encryption
the process of transforming plain text or data into cipher text that cannot be read by anyone outside of the sender and the receiver. The purpose of encryption is (a) to secure stored information and (b) to secure information transmission.

cipher text
text that has been encrypted and thus cannot be read by anyone besides the sender and the receiver

key (cipher)
any method for transforming plain text to cipher text

substitution cipher
every occurrence of a given letter is replaced systematically by another letter

transposition cipher
the ordering of the letters in each word is changed in some systematic way

symmetric key encryption (secret key encryption)
both the sender and the receiver use the same key to encrypt and decrypt the message

with the invention of the *Enigma machine*. Every day, the Enigma machine would generate a new secret cipher that used both substitution and transposition based on the settings made by a mechanical device. As long as all Enigma machines around the world were set to the same settings, they could communicate securely, and every day the codes would change, hindering code breakers from breaking the code in a timely fashion. The Allies captured several Enigma machines, examined their operation, understood the role of time in changing the codes, and eventually were able to routinely decipher German military and diplomatic messages.

The possibilities for simple substitution and transposition ciphers are endless, but they all suffer from common flaws. First, in the digital age, computers are so powerful and fast that these ancient means of encryption can be broken quickly. Second, symmetric key encryption requires that both parties share the same key. In order to share the same key, they must send the key over a presumably insecure medium where it could be stolen and used to decipher messages. If the secret key is lost or stolen, the entire encryption system fails. Third, in commercial use where we are not all part of the same team or army, you would need a secret key for each of the parties with whom you transacted, that is, one key for the bank, another for the department store, and another for the government. In a large population of users, this could result in as many as n(n − 1) keys. In a population of millions of Internet users, thousands of millions of keys would be needed to accommodate all e-commerce customers (estimated at about 35 million purchasers in the United States). Potentially, (35 million) ^{2} different keys would be needed. Clearly this situation would be too unwieldy to work in practice.

Modern encryption systems are digital. The ciphers or keys used to transform plain text into cipher text are digital strings. Computers store text or other data as binary strings composed of 0s and 1s. For instance, the binary representation of the capital letter "A" in ASCII computer code is accomplished with eight binary digits (bits): 01000001. One way in which digital strings can be transformed into cipher text is by multiplying each letter by another binary number, say, an eight-bit key number 0101 0101. If we multiplied every digital character in our text messages by this eight-bit key, sent the encrypted message to a friend along with the secret eight-bit key, the friend could decode the message easily.

The strength of modern security protection is measured in terms of the length of the binary key used to encrypt the data. In the above example, the eight-bit key is easily deciphered because there are only 2^8 or 256 possibilities. If the intruder knows you are using an eight-bit key, then he or she could decode the message in a few seconds using a modern desktop PC just by using the brute force method of checking each of the 256 possible keys. For this reason, modern digital encryption systems use keys with 56, 128, 256, or 512 binary digits. With encryption keys of 512 digits, there are 2^{512} possibilities to check out. It is estimated that all the computers in the world would need to work for ten years before stumbling upon the answer.

Data Encryption Standard (DES)

the most widely used symmetric key encryption, developed by the National Security Agency (NSA) and IBM. Uses a 56-bit encryption key.

public key cryptography

two mathematically related digital keys are used: a public key and a private key. The private key is kept secret by the owner, and the public key is widely disseminated. Both keys can be used to encrypt and decrypt a message. However, once the keys are used to encrypt a message, that same key cannot be used to unencrypt the message.

The most widely used symmetric key encryption on the Internet today is the **Data Encryption Standard (DES)** developed by the National Security Agency (NSA) and IBM in the 1950s. DES uses a 56-bit encryption key. To cope with much faster computers, it has been improved recently by *Triple DES* — essentially encrypting the message three times each with a separate key. There are many other symmetric key systems with keys up to 2048 bits.[1] Like all symmetric key systems, DES requires the sender and the receiver to exchange and share the same key, and requires a different set of keys for each set of transactions.

Public Key Encryption

In 1976, an entirely new way of encrypting messages called **public key cryptography** was invented by Whitfield Diffie and Martin Hellman. Public key cryptography solves the problem of exchanging keys. In this method, two mathematically related digital keys are used: a public key and a private key. The private key is kept secret by the owner, and the public key is widely disseminated. Both keys can be used to encrypt and decrypt a message. However, once the keys are used to encrypt a message, that same key cannot be used to unencrypt the message. The mathematical algorithms used to produce the keys are *one-way functions*. A one-way irreversible mathematical function is one in which, once the algorithm is applied, the input cannot be subsequently derived from the output. Most food recipes are like this. For instance, it is easy to make scrambled eggs, but impossible to retrieve whole eggs from the scrambled eggs. Public key cryptography is based on the idea of irreversible mathematical functions. The keys are sufficiently long (128-, 256-, and 512-bit keys) that it would take enormous computing power to derive one key from the other using the largest and fastest computers available. Figure 5.6 illustrates a simple use of public key cryptography and takes you through the important steps in using public and private keys.

Public Key Encryption Using Digital Signatures and Hash Digests

In public key encryption, some elements of security are missing. Although we can be quite sure the message was not understood or read by a third party (message confidentiality), there is no guarantee the sender really is the sender — that is, there is no authentication of the sender. This means the sender could deny ever sending the message (repudiation). And there is no assurance the message was not altered somehow in transit. For example, the message "Buy Cisco @ $25" could have been accidentally or intentionally altered to read "Sell Cisco @ $25." This suggests a potential lack of integrity in the system.

A more sophisticated use of public key cryptography can achieve authentication, nonrepudiation, and integrity. Figure 5.7 illustrates this more powerful approach.

[1]For instance: DESX and RDES with 168-bit keys; the RC Series: RC2, RC4, and RC5 with keys up to 2048 bits; the IDEA algorithm, the basis of PGP, e-mail public key encryption software described later in this chapter, using 128-bit keys.

FIGURE 5.6	PUBLIC KEY CRYPTOGRAPHY — A SIMPLE CASE

STEP	DESCRIPTION
1. The sender creates a digital message.	The message could be a document, spreadsheet, or any digital object.
2. The sender obtains the recipient's public key from a public directory and applies it to the message.	Public keys are distributed widely and can be obtained from recipients directly.
3. Application of the recipient's key produces an encrypted cipher text message.	Once encrypted using the public key, the message cannot be reverse-engineered or unencrypted using the same public key. The process is irreversible.
4. The encrypted message is sent over the Internet.	The encrypted message is broken into packets and sent through several different pathways, making interception of the entire message difficult (but not impossible).
5. The recipient uses his/her private key to decrypt the message.	The only person who can decrypt the message is someone who has possession of the recipient's private key. Hopefully, this is the legitimate recipient.

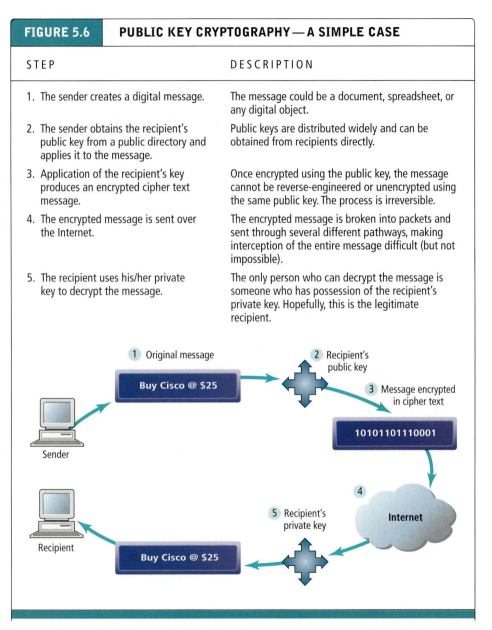

In the simplest use of public key cryptography, the sender encrypts a message using the recipient's public key, and then sends it over the Internet. The only person who can decrypt this message is the recipient, using his or her private key. However, this simple case does not ensure confidentiality or an authentic message.

FIGURE 5.7	PUBLIC KEY CRYPTOGRAPHY WITH DIGITAL SIGNATURES

STEP	DESCRIPTION
1. The sender creates an original message.	The message could be any digital file.
2. The sender applies the hash function, producing a 128-bit hash result.	Hash functions create a unique digest of the message based on the message's contents
3. The sender encrypts the message and hash result using recipient's public key.	This irreversible process creates a cipher text that can be read only by the recipient using his/her private key
4. The sender encrypts the result, again using his or her private key.	The sender's private key is a digital signature. There is only one person who could create this digital mark.
5. The result of this double encryption is sent over the Internet.	The message traverses the Internet as a series of independent packets.
6. The receiver uses the sender's public key to authenticate the message.	Only one person could send this message, namely, the sender.
7. The receiver uses his or her private key to decrypt the hash function and the original message. The receiver checks to ensure that the original message and the hash function results conform to one another.	The hash function is used here to check the original message. This ensures the message was not changed in transit.

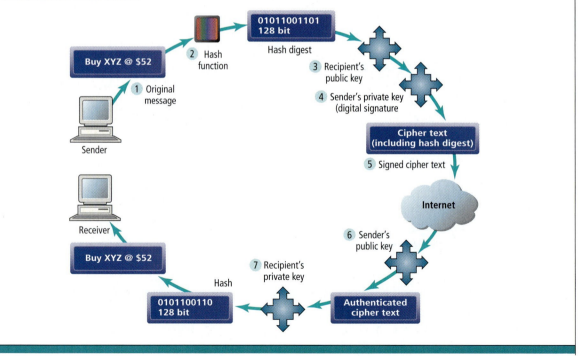

A more realistic use of public key cryptography uses hash functions and digital signatures to both ensure the confidentiality of the message and authenticate the sender. The only person who could have sent the above message is the owner or the sender using his/her private key. This authenticates the message. The hash function ensures the message was not altered in transit. As before, the only person who can decipher the message is the recipient, using his/her private key.

To check the confidentiality of a message and ensure it has not been altered in transit, a hash function is used first to create a digest of the message. A **hash function** is an algorithm that produces a fixed-length number called a *hash* or *message digest*. A hash function can be simple, and count the number of digital "1s" in a message, or it can be more complex, and produce a 128-bit number that reflects the number of 0s and 1s, the number of 00s, 11s, and so on. Standard hash functions are available (MD4 and MD5 produce 128- and 160-bit hashes) (Stein, 1998). These more complex hash functions produce hashes or hash results that are unique to every message. The results of applying the hash function are sent by the sender to the recipient. Upon receipt, the recipient applies the hash function to the received message and checks to verify the same result is produced. If so, the message has not been altered. The sender then encrypts both the hash result and the original message using the recipient's public key (as in Figure 5.6), producing a single block of cipher text.

One more step is required. To ensure the authenticity of the message, and to ensure nonrepudiation, the sender encrypts the entire block of cipher text one more time using the sender's private key. This produces a **digital signature** (also called an *e-signature*) or "signed" cipher text that can be sent over the Internet.

A digital signature is a close parallel to a handwritten signature. Like a handwritten signature, a digital signature is unique — only one person presumably possesses the private key. When used with a hash function, the digital signature is even more unique than a handwritten signature. In addition to being unique to a particular individual, when used to sign a hashed document, the digital signature is also unique to the document, and changes for every document.

The recipient of this signed cipher text first uses the sender's public key to authenticate the message. Once authenticated, the recipient uses his or her private key to obtain the hash result and original message. As a final step, the recipient applies the same hash function to the original text, and compares the result with the result sent by the sender. If the results are the same, the recipient now knows the message has not been changed during transmission. The message has integrity.

Digital Envelopes

Public key encryption is computationally slow. If one used 128- or 256-bit keys to encode large documents — such as this chapter or the entire book — significant declines in transmission speeds and increases in processing time would occur. Symmetric key encryption is computationally faster — but as we pointed out above — has a weakness, namely, the symmetric key must be sent to the recipient over insecure transmission lines. One solution is to use the more efficient symmetric encryption and decryption for large documents, but public key encryption to encrypt and send the symmetric key. This technique is called using a **digital envelope**. Figure 5.8 shows how a digital envelope works.

---

hash function
an algorithm that produces a fixed-length number called a hash or message digest

digital signature (e-signature)
"signed" cipher text that can be sent over the Internet

digital envelope
a technique that uses symmetric encryption for large documents, but public key encryption to encrypt and send the symmetric key

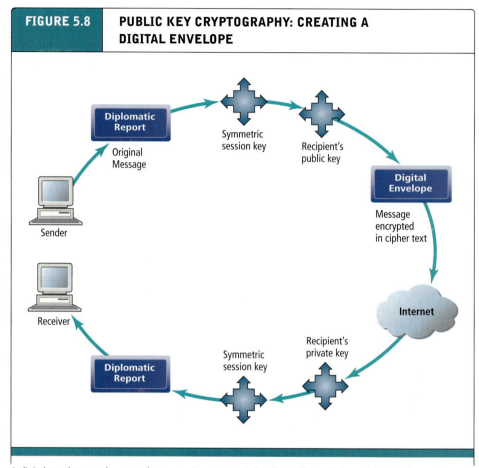

FIGURE 5.8 PUBLIC KEY CRYPTOGRAPHY: CREATING A DIGITAL ENVELOPE

A digital envelope can be created to transmit a symmetric key that will permit the recipient to decrypt the message and be assured the message was not intercepted in transit.

In Figure 5.8, a diplomatic document is encrypted using a symmetric key. The symmetric key — which the recipient will require to decrypt the document — is itself encrypted, using the recipient's public key. So we have a "key within a key" or what is called a *digital envelope*. The encrypted report and the digital envelope are sent across the Web. The recipient first uses his/her private key to decrypt the symmetric key. And then the recipient uses the symmetric key to decrypt the report. This method saves time because both encryption and decryption are faster with symmetric keys.

Digital Certificates and Public Key Infrastructure (PKI)

There are still some deficiencies in the message security regime described above. How do we know that people and institutions are who they claim to be? Anyone can

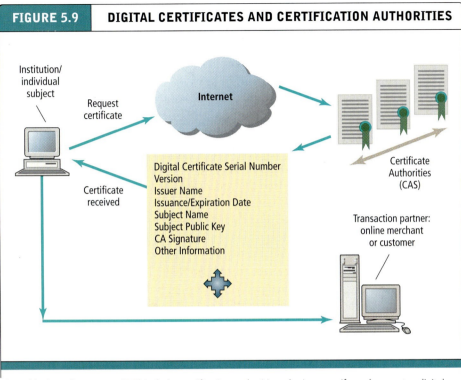

FIGURE 5.9   DIGITAL CERTIFICATES AND CERTIFICATION AUTHORITIES

Institution/individual subject

Request certificate

Internet

Certificate received

Certificate Authorities (CAS)

Digital Certificate Serial Number
Version
Issuer Name
Issuance/Expiration Date
Subject Name
Subject Public Key
CA Signature
Other Information

Transaction partner:
online merchant
or customer

The public key infrastructure (PKI) includes certification authorities who issue, verify, and guarantee digital certificates that are used in e-commerce to assure the identity of transaction partners.

make up a private and public key combination and claim to be the Defense Department or Santa Claus. Before you place an order with an online merchant such as Amazon.com, you want to be sure it really is Amazon.com you have on the screen and not a spoofer masquerading as Amazon. In the physical world, if someone asks who you are and you show a social security number, they may well ask to see a picture ID or a second form of certifiable or acceptable identification. If they really doubt who you are, they may ask for references to other authorities and actually interview these other authorities. Similarly in the digital world, we need a way to know who people and institutions really are.

Digital certificates, and the supporting public key infrastructure, are an attempt to solve this problem of digital identity. A **digital certificate** is a digital document issued by a trusted **certification authority (CA)** that contains the name of the subject or company, the subject's public key, a digital certificate serial number, an expiration date, an issuance date, the digital signature of the certification authority (the name of the CA encrypted using the CA's private key), and other identifying information. (See Figure 5.9.)

digital certificate
a digital document issued by a certification authority that contains the name of the subject or company, the subject's public key, a digital certificate serial number, an expiration date, an issuance date, the digital signature of the certification authority, and other identifying information

certification authority (CA)
a trusted third party that issues digital certificates

A CA is an institution — a so-called "trusted third party." In the United States, private corporations such as VeriSign and government agencies such as the U.S. Postal Service, act as CAs. In fact, a hierarchy of CAs is emerging with less well known CAs being certified by larger and better known CAs, creating a community of mutually verifying institutions. **Public key infrastructure (PKI)** refers to the certification authorities and digital certificate procedures that are accepted by all parties.

To create a digital certificate, the user generates a public/private key pair and sends a request for certification to a CA along with the user's public key. The CA verifies the information (how this is accomplished differs from CA to CA). The CA issues a certificate containing the user's public key and other related information. Finally, the CA creates a message digest from the certificate itself (just like a hash digest) and signs it with the CA's private key. This signed digest is called the *signed certificate*. We end up with a totally unique cipher text document — there can be only one signed certificate like this in the world.

There are several ways the certificates are used in commerce. Before initiating a transaction, the customer can request the signed digital certificate of the merchant and decrypt it using the merchant's public key to obtain both the message digest and the certificate as issued. If the message digest matches the certificate, then the merchant and the public key are authenticated. The merchant may in return request certification of the user, in which case the user would send the merchant his or her individual certificate. There are many types of certificates: personal, institutional, Web server, software publisher, and CAs themselves.

You can easily obtain a public and private key at the Pretty Good Privacy site, www.pgpi.org. **Pretty Good Privacy (PGP)** was invented in 1991 by Phil Zimmerman, and has become one of the most widely used e-mail public key encryption software tools in the world. Using PGP software installed on your computer, you can compress and encrypt your messages as well as authenticate both yourself and the recipient.

Limitations to Encryption Solutions

Public key infrastructure is a powerful technological solution to security issues, but it has many limitations. PKI applies mainly to protecting messages in transit on the Internet and is not effective against insiders — employees — who have legitimate access to corporate systems including customer information. Most e-commerce sites do not store customer information in encrypted form. Other limitations are apparent. For one, how is your private key to be protected? Most private keys will be stored on insecure desktop or laptop machines. There is no guarantee the person using your computer — and your private key — is really you. Under many digital signature laws (such as those in Utah and Washington), you are responsible for whatever your private key does even if you were not the person using the key. This is very different from mail-order or telephone order credit card rules, where you have a right to dis-

---

public key infrastructure (PKI)

certification authorities and digital certificate procedures that are accepted by all parties

---

Pretty Good Privacy (PGP)

a widely used e-mail public key encryption software program

pute the credit card charge. Second, there is no guarantee the verifying computer of the merchant is secure. Third, CAs are self-selected organizations seeking to gain access to the business of authorization. They may not be authorities on the corporations or individuals they certify. For instance, how can a CA know about all the industries and corporations within an industry to determine who is or is not legitimate? A related question concerns the method used by the CA to identify the certificate holder. Was this an e-mail transaction verified only by claims of applicants who filled out an online form? For instance, in March 2001, Verisign acknowledged that in January 2001, it had mistakenly issued two digital certificates to someone fraudulently claiming to represent Microsoft. Last, what are the policies for revoking or renewing certificates? The expected life of a digital certificate or private key is a function of the frequency of use and the vulnerability of systems that use the certificate. Yet most CAs have no policy or just an annual policy for re-issuing certificates (Ellison, and Schneier, 2000). Read *Insight on Technology: Everlasting Security?* for a look at the search for ever more secure encryption technologies.

SECURING CHANNELS OF COMMUNICATION

The concepts of public key encryption are used routinely for securing channels of communication.

Secure Sockets Layer (SSL)

The most common form of securing channels is through the *secure sockets layer (SSL)* of TCP/IP (described briefly in Chapter 3). When you receive a message from a server on the Web that you will be communicating through a secure channel, this means you will be using SSL to establish a secure negotiated session (notice that the URL changes from HTTP to HTTPS). A **secure negotiated session** is a client-server session in which the URL of the requested document, along with the contents, contents of forms, and the cookies exchanged, are encrypted (see Figure 5.10). For instance, your credit card number that you entered into a form would be encrypted. Through a series of handshakes and communications, the browser and the server establish one another's identity by exchanging digital certificates, decide on the strongest shared form of encryption, and then proceed to communicate using an agreed-upon session key. A **session key** is a unique symmetric encryption key chosen just for this single secure session. Once used, it is gone forever. Figure 5.10 shows how it works.

In practice, most private individuals do not have a digital certificate. In this case, the merchant server will not request a certificate, but the client browser will request the merchant certificate once a secure session is called for by the server.

The SSL protocol provides data encryption, server authentication, optional client authentication, and message integrity for TCP/IP connections. SSL is available in 40-bit and 128-bit levels, depending on what version of browser you are using. The strongest shared encryption is always chosen.

secure negotiated session
a client-server session in which the URL of the requested document, along with the contents, contents of forms, and the cookies exchanged, are encrypted

session key
a unique symmetric encryption key chosen for a single secure session

INSIGHT ON TECHNOLOGY

EVERLASTING SECURITY?

Michael O. Rabin, computer science professor at Harvard and recipient of the A.C.M. Turing Award in computer science, claims to have invented, together with his graduate student Yan Zong Bing, a method for achieving everlasting security based on a disappearing encryption key. According to Rabin, it is the first mathematically provable unbreakable code. Others have attempted this feat and failed. Rabin says his method works.

Recall that one of the big weaknesses of Public Key Infrastructure (PKI) occurs when you lose your private key, someone steals your machine (or borrows it) and uses your private key, or a government investigator or private lawyer forces you to reveal your private key as part of an investigation. How nice it would be if the key just vanished!

Here is Rabin's idea. Imagine a machine that produces billions of random numbers per second. Then imagine this machine broadcasting from a satellite. When two parties want to send an encrypted message, they start recording from the random string of numbers at precisely the same time. They keep recording until they have sampled enough numbers to produce a level of security they desire — say, 1024 bits. The sender immediately uses this 1024-bit key to encode the message and send it, while simultaneously the receiver uses this 1024-bit key to decrypt the message. The same key is used to encrypt and decrypt — so this is a symmetric key encryption method. When the message is finished being transmitted, the sender destroys the key. The receiver destroys the key upon reception and decoding. The key vanishes. Now there is no key for investigators to discover, no key that can be stolen, and virtually no way the message, even if intercepted, could be decrypted.

Why does this idea work? Rabin's idea rests on storage limitations. The string of random numbers being generated is so large that no computer system in the world could possibly store the numbers without filling up quickly. Rabin's idea rests also on computational limitations — the symmetric key is so long that after the message is sent, no network of existing computers would be able to use brute force tactics to find the key.

Professional security consultants and Internet cyberpunks immediately started working on ways to crack Rabin's ideas. They pointed out that given the large size of the key, it would be impractical for large messages, and perhaps impractical to guarantee a reliable satellite transmission that could not be overridden locally. Another weakness: An intruder could intercept the start message (the point where the random number sequence is recorded) and start recording precisely at the same moment as the sender and receiver. Rabin's system works only if the sender and receiver share a truly secure channel of communication. Some hackers noted that the system's security seemed to rest entirely on the fact that the data volume was too enormous for current computers to store, but that might not always be the case. Also, the system appeared to rely on a true random number-generator machine that

(continued)

Rabin apparently assumed could not be hacked and replaced by a psuedo-random number generator.

Others noted that existing encryption is so strong that an even better system was pointless. Some felt that cryptography is not the answer to the security problem anyway, because there are weaker links in the chain. As one hacker noted "if you're in this business of stealing information, you need something reliable and cheap — like the three Bs: burglary, bribery or blackmail. There are other ways to get the message, just maybe not by cryptanalysis [the process of converting an encrypted message to plain text]."

Rabin's response: Just because there are other weaknesses in communication systems does not mean that secure encryption is unimportant. To Rabin, the pursuit of everlasting perfect security is a worthwhile goal, even if his theories are never actually implemented.

SOURCES: "The Key Vanishes: Scientist Outlines Unbreakable Code," by Gina Kolata, *New York Times*, February 20, 2001; "Disappearing Keys," http://www.edsworld.com/about_eds/hompage/home_page_encrypt.shtml; "Information Theoretically Secure Communication in the Limited Storage Space Model," by Yonatan Aumann and Michael O. Rabin, *Springer LINK: Lecture Notes in Computer Science 1966*, December 16, 1999.

FIGURE 5.10   SECURE NEGOTIATED SESSIONS USING SSL

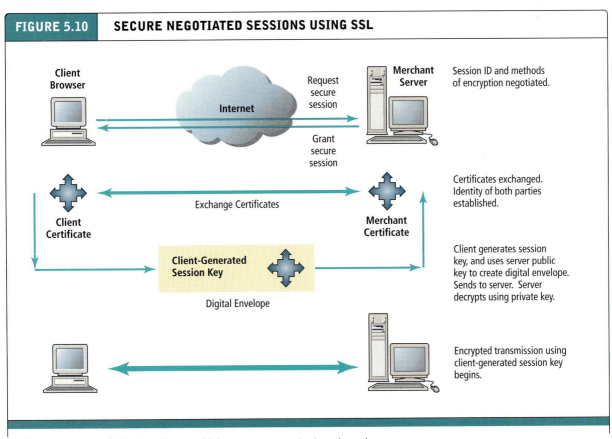

Certificates play a key role in using SSL to establish a secure communications channel.

SSL was designed to address the threat of authenticity by allowing users to verify another user's identity, or the identity of a server. It also protects the integrity of the messages exchanged. However, once the merchant receives the encrypted credit and order information, that information is typically stored in unencrypted format on the merchant's servers.

While the SSL protocol provides secure transactions between merchant and consumer, it only guarantees server side authentication. Client authentication is optional. In addition, SSL cannot provide irrefutability — consumers can order goods or download information products, and then claim the transaction never occurred. Other protocols for protecting financial transactions such as *SET (Secure Electronic Transaction Protocol)* have emerged that require all parties to a transaction to use digital certificates. SET is discussed further in Chapter 6.

S-HTTP

S-HTTP (Secure Hypertext Transfer Protocol)

a secure message-oriented communications protocol designed for use in conjunction with HTTP. Cannot be used to secure non-HTTP messages.

A competing method is called **S-HTTP (Secure Hypertext Transfer Protocol)**. S-HTTP is a secure message-oriented communications protocol designed for use in conjunction with HTTP. It is designed to coexist with HTTP and to be easily integrated with HTTP applications. Whereas SSL is designed to establish a secure connection between two computers, S-HTTP is designed to send individual messages securely. Not all browsers and not all Web sites support S-HTTP. You know you are dealing with a supporting site when the URL starts with "SHTTP". The use of this as part of an anchor tag indicates that the target server is S-HTTP capable. Using S-HTTP, any message may be signed, authenticated, encrypted, or any combination of these. Basically S-HTTP attempts to make HTTP more secure.

Virtual Private Networks (VPN)

virtual private networks (VPN)

allow remote users to securely access internal networks via the Internet, using the Point-to-Point Tunneling Protocol (PPTP)

Point-to-Point Tunneling Protocol (PPTP)

an encoding mechanism that allows one local network to connect to another using the Internet as the conduit

Virtual private networks (VPN) allow remote users to securely access internal networks via the Internet, using the **Point-to-Point Tunneling Protocol (PPTP)**. PPTP is an encoding mechanism that allows one local network to connect to another using the Internet as the conduit. A remote user can dial into a local ISP, and PPTP makes the connection from the ISP to the corporate network as if the user had dialed into the corporate network directly. The process of connecting one protocol (PPTP) through another (IP) is called *tunneling* because PPTP creates a private connection by adding an invisible wrapper around a message to hide its content. As the message travels through the Internet between ISP and corporate network, it is shielded from prying eyes by PPTP's encrypted wrapper.

A virtual private network is "virtual" in the sense that it appears to users as a dedicated secure line when in fact it is a temporary secure line. The primary use of VPNs is to establish secure communications among business partners — larger suppliers or customers. A dedicated connection to a business partner can be very expensive. Using the Internet and PPTP as the connection method significantly reduces the cost of secure communications.

PROTECTING NETWORKS

Once you have protected communications as well as possible, the next set of tools to consider are those that can protect your networks, and the servers and clients on those networks.

Firewalls

Firewalls and proxy servers are intended to build a wall around your network, and the attached servers and clients, just like physical-world firewalls protect you from fires for a limited period of time. Firewalls and proxy servers share some similar functions, but they are quite different. **Firewalls** are software applications that act as filters between a company's private network and the Internet. They prevent remote client machines from attaching to your internal network. Firewalls monitor and validate all incoming and outgoing communications. Every message that is to be sent or received from the network is processed by the firewall software, which determines if the message meets security guidelines established by the business. If it does, it is permitted to be distributed, and if it doesn't, the message is blocked.

firewall
a software application that acts as a filter between a company's private network and the Internet itself

There are two major methods firewalls use to validate traffic: packet filters and application gateways. *Packet filters* examine data packets to determine whether they are destined for a prohibited port, or originate from a prohibited IP address (as specified by the security administrator). The filter specifically looks at the source and destination information, as well as the port and packet type, when determining whether the information may be transmitted. One downside of the packet filtering method is that it is susceptible to spoofing, since authentication is not one of its roles.

Application gateways are a type of firewall that filters communications based on the application being requested, rather than the source or destination of the message. Such firewalls also process requests at the application level, farther away from the client computer than packet filters. By providing a central filtering point, application gateways provide greater security than packet filters, but can compromise system performance.

Proxy servers (proxies) are software servers (usually located on a dedicated machine) that handle all communications originating from or being sent to the Internet, acting as a spokesperson or bodyguard for the organization. Proxies act primarily to limit access of internal clients to external Internet servers, although some proxy servers act as firewalls as well. Proxy servers are sometimes called *dual home systems* because they have two network interfaces. To internal machines, a proxy server is

proxy server (proxy)
software server that handles all communications originating from or being sent to the Internet, acting as a spokesperson or bodyguard for the organization

262

CHAPTER 5   Security and Encryption

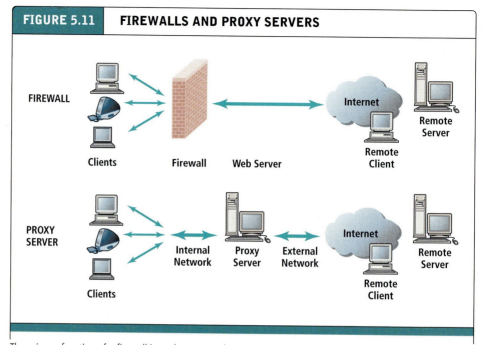

FIGURE 5.11   FIREWALLS AND PROXY SERVERS

The primary function of a firewall is to deny access by remote client machines to local machines. The primary purpose of a proxy server is to provide controlled access from local machines to remote machines.

known as the *gateway*, while to external machines it is known as a *mail server* or *numeric address*.

When a user on an internal network requests Web pages, the request is routed first to the proxy server. The proxy server validates the user and the nature of the request, and then sends the request onto the Internet. Pages sent by external Internet servers first pass to the proxy server. If acceptable, the pages pass onto the internal network Web server and then to the client desktop. By prohibiting users from communicating directly with the Internet, companies can restrict access to certain types of sites, such as pornographic, auction, or stock-trading sites. Proxy servers also improve Web performance by storing frequently requested Web pages locally, reducing upload times, and hiding the internal network's address, thus making it more difficult for hackers to monitor. Figure 5.11 illustrates how firewalls and proxy servers protect a local area network from Internet intruders and prevent internal clients from reaching prohibited Web servers.

PROTECTING SERVERS AND CLIENTS

Operating system features and anti-viral software can help further protect servers and clients from certain types of attacks.

Operating System Controls

Computer operating systems typically have a built-in username and password requirement that provides a level of authentication. Some operating systems also have an access control function that automates user access (or more commonly denies access by clients) to various areas of the network. For instance, operating systems security can manage access to selected network paths so that only authorized personnel can obtain access to payroll information. Application software — including Microsoft Office and all server-side database packages — contain extensive security management features that can be used on networks and intranets to manage access to data files.

Anti-Virus Software

The easiest and least expensive way to prevent threats to system integrity is to install anti-virus software. Programs by McAfee and Symantec provide inexpensive tools to identify and eradicate the most common types of viruses as they enter a computer, as well as destroy those already lurking on a hard drive. It is not enough, however, to simply install the software once. Since new viruses are being developed daily, routine updates are needed in order to prevent new threats from being loaded.

Another similar type of software, which is more complex and expensive, is an intrusion detection system. Such programs work much like anti-virus software in that they look for recognized hacker tools or signature actions. Designed to trigger an alarm when such an action is noted, these systems must be monitored by staff members or intrusion-detection services in order to work properly. Sensors set up on a computer network will trigger hundreds of alarms, with only a very small percentage being a potential security threat. Regular monitoring and analysis help weed out the insignificant from the potentially harmful. Despite the extra work involved in eliminating false alarms, intrusion detection systems also serve as a first line of defense against hacker attacks.

5.4 POLICIES, PROCEDURES, AND LAWS

Most CEOs and CIOs of existing e-commerce operations believe that technology is not the key issue in managing the risk of e-commerce. The technology provides a foundation, but in the absence of intelligent management policies even the best technology can be easily defeated. Public laws and active enforcement of cybercrime statutes

| FIGURE 5.12 | DEVELOPING AN E-COMMERCE SECURITY PLAN |

There are five steps involved in building an e-commerce security plan.

are also required to both raise the costs of illegal behavior on the Internet and guard against corporate abuse of information. Let's consider briefly the development of management policy.

A SECURITY PLAN: MANAGEMENT POLICIES

In order to minimize security threats, e-commerce firms must develop a coherent corporate policy that takes into account the nature of the risks, the information assets that need protecting, and the procedures and technologies required to address the risk, as well as implementation and auditing mechanisms. Figure 5.12 illustrates the key steps in developing a solid security plan.

A security plan begins with **risk assessment** — an assessment of the risks and points of vulnerability. The first step is to inventory the information and knowledge assets of the e-commerce site and company. What information is at risk? Is it customer information, proprietary designs, business activities, secret processes, or other internal information, such as price schedules, executive compensation, or payroll? For each type of information asset, try to estimate the dollar value to the firm if this information were compromised and then multiply that amount by the probability of

risk assessment

an assessment of the risks and points of vulnerability

the loss occurring. Once you have done so, rank order the results. You now have a list of information assets prioritized by their value to the firm.

Based on your quantified list of risks, you can start to develop a **security policy** — a set of statements prioritizing the information risks, identifying acceptable risk targets, and identifying the mechanisms for achieving these targets. You will obviously want to start with the information assets that you determined to be the highest priority in your risk assessment. Who generates and controls this information in the firm? What existing security policies are in place to protect the information? What enhancements can you recommend to improve security of these most valuable assets? What level of risk are you willing to accept for each of these assets? Are you willing, for instance, to lose customer credit data once every ten years? Or will you pursue a hundred-year hurricane strategy by building a security edifice for credit card data that can withstand the once in a hundred year disaster? You will need to estimate how much it will cost to achieve this level of acceptable risk. Remember, total and complete security may require extraordinary financial resources. By answering these questions, you will have the beginnings of a security policy.

Next consider an **implementation plan** — the action steps you will take to achieve the security plan goals. Specifically, you must determine how you will translate the levels of acceptable risk into a set of tools, technologies, policies, and procedures. What new technologies will you deploy to achieve the goals, and what new employee procedures will be needed?

To implement your plan, you will need an organizational unit in charge of security, and a security officer — someone who is in charge of security on a daily basis. For a small e-commerce site, the security officer will likely be the person in charge of Internet services or the site manager; whereas for larger firms, there typically is a dedicated team with a supporting budget. The **security organization** educates and trains users, keeps management aware of security threats and breakdowns, and maintains the tools chosen to implement security.

The security organization typically administers access controls, authentication procedures, and authorization policies. **Access controls** determine which outsiders and insiders can gain legitimate access to your networks. Outsider access controls include firewalls and proxy servers, while insider access controls typically consist of login procedures (usernames, passwords, and access codes).

Authentication procedures include the use of digital signatures, certificates of authority, and public key infrastructure. Now that e-signatures have been given the same legal weight as an original pen-and-ink version, companies are in the process of devising ways to test and confirm a signer's identity. Attaching a digital thumbprint and showing a live video image of the signer are two methods under consideration. Companies frequently have signers type their full name and click on a button indicating their understanding that they have just signed a contract or document.

Biometric devices are used along with digital signatures to verify physical attributes associated with an individual, such as a fingerprint or retina (eye) scan or

security policy
a set of statements prioritizing the information risks, identifying acceptable risk targets, and identifying the mechanisms for achieving these targets

implementation plan
the action steps you will take to achieve the security plan goals

security organization
educates and trains users, keeps management aware of security threats and breakdowns, and maintains the tools chosen to implement security

access controls
determine who can gain legitimate access to a network

authentication procedures
include the use of digital signatures, certificates of authority, and public key infrastructure

biometrics

the study of measurable biological or physical characteristics

speech recognition system. (**Biometrics** is the study of measurable biological, or physical, characteristics.) A company could require, for example, that an individual undergo a fingerprint scan before being allowed access to a Web site, or before being allowed to pay for merchandise with a credit card. Biometric devices make it even more difficult for hackers to break into sites or facilities, significantly reducing the opportunity for spoofing.

authorization policies

determine differing levels of access to information assets for differing levels of users

Authorization policies determine differing levels of access to information assets for differing levels of users. **Authorization management systems** establish where and when a user is permitted to access certain parts of a Web site. Their primary function is to restrict access to private information within a company's Internet infrastructure. Although there are several authorization management products currently available, most operate in the same way: The system encrypts a user session to function like a passkey that follows the user from page to page, allowing access only to those areas that the user is permitted to enter, based on information set at the system database. By establishing entry rules up front for each user, the authorization management system knows who is permitted to go where at all times.

authorization management system

establishes where and when a user is permitted to access certain parts of a Web site

The last step in developing an e-commerce security plan is performing a security audit. A **security audit** involves the routine review of access logs (identifying how outsiders are using the site as well as how insiders are accessing the site's assets). A monthly report should be produced that establishes the routine and non-routine accesses to the systems and identifies unusual patterns of activities. Tiger teams are often used by large corporate sites to evaluate the strength of existing security procedures. A **tiger team** is a group whose sole job activity is attempting to break into a site (stopping just short of actually making any unauthorized changes to the site). Many small firms have sprung up in the last five years to provide these services to large corporate sites. See *Insight on Business: Tiger Teams — Hiring Hackers to Locate Threats* for a further look at tiger teams.

security audit

involves the routine review of access logs (identifying how outsiders are using the site as well as how insiders are accessing the site's assets)

tiger team

a group whose sole job activity is attempting to break into a site

Given the dynamic nature of attacks on sites, the growing number of worldwide users and hackers, and the changes in technology, the process of developing security for e-commerce sites is never finished. Instead, it is an ongoing effort requiring commitment and vigilance.

CERT

CERT Coordination Center

monitors and tracks online criminal activity reported to it by private corporations and government agencies that seek out its help

The good news is that e-commerce sites are not alone in their battle to achieve security on the Internet. Several organizations — some public and some private — are devoted to tracking down criminal organizations and individuals engaged in attacks against Internet and e-commerce sites. Once of the better known private organizations is the **CERT Coordination Center** (formerly known as the Computer Emergency Response Team) at Carnegie Mellon University. CERT monitors and tracks online criminal activity reported to it by private corporations and government agencies that seek out its help. CERT is composed of full-time and part-time computer

INSIGHT ON BUSINESS

TIGER TEAMS—HIRING HACKERS TO LOCATE THREATS

The concept of "tiger teams" of computer experts originated in the 1970s with the U.S. Air Force, which used special teams of experts to test security vulnerability at bases. The idea spread throughout the government and, in 1973, the Department of Defense documented the use of tiger teams to assess computer security. By the 1980s and into the 1990s, the use of tiger teams had spread into the corporate arena, with companies hiring elite squads of consultants to break into their computer networks by any means necessary.

Big consulting firms such as Ernst & Young and PricewaterhouseCoopers pull together tiger teams on behalf of their clients. And companies such as IBM Research coordinate their own investigative teams, using white hat hackers as contractors. In some cases, corporations considering partnering with smaller firms require that they consent to a tiger team assessment, with a failing grade meaning the alliance goes no further.

Some clients have been surprised at the lengths to which these teams will go to break into secure networks, including dumpster diving for scraps of computer paper, stealing ID badges, and crawling through ceiling tiles to access computer rooms. But since hackers will seemingly go to any extent to break in, tiger teams must mimic their actions. In the end, clients gain a true assessment of both their weaknesses and the likelihood of a break-in.

One thing most companies will not do is hire known grey or black hats for tiger team assignments. Although some claim to have "gone straight" and work only under contract, security consulting firms are wary of them, afraid that in breaking into a client facility, these grey or black hats may try to profit from the assignment.

Some grey hats are so dedicated to improving the operations of computer networks everywhere that they run their own drills, testing major sites and then publicly reporting on weaknesses they discover. Most also provide fixes so that the site can rectify any problems the grey hats discover. Some industry observers decry the fact that the hackers give criminals the needed ammunition to break into sites, while other analysts see value in the pressure such groups place on companies to improve their operations. Either way, organizations are being pushed to consistently improve and upgrade their security measures—whether by paid tiger teams or self-appointed evaluators.

SOURCES: "In a World of Hackers, Good Guys and Bad Guys are Often a Blur," by Katie Hafner, *New York Times*, February 12, 2000; "The Hack Attack," by Elinor Abreu, *The Industry Standard*, February 21, 2000; "The Internet Under Siege: Stalking the Hackers," by David Hamilton and David Cloud, *Wall Street Journal*, February 10, 2000.

experts who can trace the origins of attacks against sites despite the complexity of the Internet. Its staff members also assist organizations in identifying security problems, developing solutions, and communicating with the public about widespread hacker threats. The CERT Coordination Center also provides product assessments, reports, and training in order to improve the public's knowledge and understanding of security threats and solutions.

THE ROLE OF LAWS AND PUBLIC POLICY

The public policy environment for the E-commerce II era is very different than that for E-commerce I. The net result is that the Internet is no longer an ungoverned, unsupervised, self-controlled technology juggernaut. Just as with financial markets in the last 70 years, there is a growing awareness that e-commerce markets work only when a powerful institutional set of laws and enforcement mechanisms are in place These laws help ensure orderly, rational, and fair markets. This growing public policy environment is becoming just as global as e-commerce itself. Despite some spectacular internationally based attacks on U.S. e-commerce sites, the sources and persons involved in major harmful attacks have almost always been uncovered and, where possible, prosecuted.

Voluntary and private efforts have both played a very large role in identifying criminal hackers, and assisting law enforcement. As e-commerce has grown in significance, national and local law enforcement activity has expanded greatly since 1995. New laws have been passed that grant local and national authorities new tools and mechanisms for identifying, tracing, and prosecuting cyber criminals. Table 5.3 lists the most significant federal e-commerce security legislation.

Following passage of the National Information Infrastructure Protection Act of 1996, which makes DoS attacks and virus distribution federal crimes, the FBI and the

TABLE 5.3	E-COMMERCE SECURITY LEGISLATION
LEGISLATION	SIGNIFICANCE
Computer Fraud and Abuse Act (1986)	Primary federal statute used to combat computer crime.
Electronic Communications Privacy Act (1986)	Imposes fines and imprisonment for individuals who access, intercept, or disclose private e-mail communications of others.
National Information Infrastructure Protection Act (1996)	Makes DoS attacks illegal. Creates NIPC in the FBI.
Cyberspace Electronic Security Act (CESA; 2000)	Reduces export restrictions.

Department of Justice established the **National Infrastructure Protection Center** (NIPC). Acting as a unit within the FBI, this organization's sole mission is to identify and combat threats against the United States' technology and telecommunications infrastructure.

By increasing the punishment for cybercrimes, the U.S. government is attempting to create a deterrent to further hacker actions. And by making such actions federal crimes, the government is able to extradite international hackers and prosecute them within the United States.

Government Policies and Controls on Encryption Software

As noted in the beginning of this chapter, governments have sought to restrict availability and export of encryption systems as a means of detecting and preventing crime and terrorism. In the United States, both Congress and the executive branch have sought to regulate the uses of encryption. At the international level, four organizations have influenced the international traffic in encryption software: OECD (Organization for Economic Cooperation and Development), G-7/G-8 (the heads of state of the top eight industrialized countries in the world), the Council of Europe, and the Wassnaar Arrangement (law enforcement personnel from the top 33 industrial-

National Infrastructure Protection Center (NIPC)
a unit within the FBI whose sole mission is to identify and combat threats against the United States' technology and telecommunications infrastructure

TABLE 5.4 GOVERNMENT EFFORTS TO REGULATE AND CONTROL ENCRYPTION

REGULATORY EFFORT	IMPACT
Restrict export of strong security systems	Export restrictions on strong security supported primarily by the United States. Widespread distribution of encryption schemes weakens this policy. The policy is changing to permit exports except to pariah countries.
Key escrow/key recovery schemes	France, the United Kingdom, and the United States supported this effort in the late 1990s, but now it has largely been abandoned. There are few trusted third parties.
Lawful access and forced disclosure	There is growing support in recent U.S. legislation and in OECD countries.
Official hacking	All countries are rapidly expanding budgets and training for law enforcement "technical centers" aimed at monitoring and cracking computer-based, encryption activities of suspected criminals. The FBI's DCS100 system is currently in use.

ized counties in the world) (EPIC, 2000). Various governments have proposed schemes for controlling encryption software, or at least preventing criminals from obtaining strong encryption tools. See Table 5.4.

Because the U.S. government has strongly opposed exporting powerful commercial encryption software since the 1990s, many encryption firms have moved operations off shore, and foreign companies have provided access to strong encryption schemes over the Internet. Today, export controls have largely been eliminated. Several key escrow/recovery schemes have been proposed in which strong encryption schemes would be universally allowed, but copies of the decryption keys (private keys) would be held by a trusted third party (such as a court of law) and made available to law enforcement agencies upon showing a reasonable basis for suspecting criminal activity. In general, these schemes have not been successful anywhere in the world.

Following rejection of key escrow schemes, a number of countries — including the United States — are considering legislation permitting lawful access and forced disclosure. In this legislation, individuals would be required to disclose encryption keys to law enforcement officials or face criminal penalties for failure to assist in a lawful investigation. Additionally, nearly all industrialized countries are expanding the ability of law enforcement agencies to monitor computer-based communications and storage equipment of suspected criminals. Perhaps the most extensive national effort is **DCS100**, an e-mail sniffing software program formerly known as **Carnivore**, developed by the Federal Bureau of Investigation (FBI). DCS100 can copy and filter all data sent from a user's computer to a local ISP.

DCS100 (Carnivore)

an e-mail sniffing software program developed by the FBI that can copy and filter all data sent from a user's computer to a local ISP

CASE STUDY

VeriSign
The Web's Security Blanket

When the University of Pittsburgh decided to open e-Store, an e-commerce Web site to replace its on-campus computer store, it faced a number of challenges. One challenge was security. Pitt had to make sure that e-Store customers were actually part of the university community entitled to educational discounts and so needed to limit access to the site to registered students, faculty, and staff (about 50,000 people). Pitt also wanted to assure students, faculty, and staff that their use of credit cards or university debit cards was relatively risk-free. Rather than rely on a simple password access system that could easily be circumvented or attempt to develop its own security system, Pitt turned to VeriSign, Inc. — the Web's largest provider of Internet trust services.

Pitt signed up for VeriSign OnSite — a public key infrastructure system that uses digital certificates to authenticate user identity and authorize access to university services, including the e-Store. To obtain a digital certificate, a user first accesses the e-Store at e-store.pitt.edu and provides his or her University Computer Account name, password, and Social Security number. The name and password are automatically checked against the University's internal authentication system. Then the certificate request goes to VeriSign, which issues a digital certificate with a public and private key to each valid user. So far, VeriSign has issued about 2,000 digital certificates to University of Pittsburgh users. The system was implemented in three weeks, from time of signing to operation.

When a user wants to access the e-Store, the user's digital certificate is used to authenticate the requesting computer as one that is entitled to access. The e-Store's servers are also equipped with digital certificates to encrypt credit card transactions and assure users that they have reached a server belonging to the organization they expect, making the buying process more secure.

This is just one example of the kind of services offered by the Web's largest provider of managed security services. VeriSign was formed in 1995 as a spinoff of RSA Inc., an early pioneer in public key encryption technology. Stratton Sclavos, VeriSign's CEO, joined the company shortly after it was formed, because "clearly, you were going to need security, identification and authentication services if commerce on the Internet was going to take off. VeriSign was going to be in a unique position to take advantage of that."

Building on public key encryption technology that it licensed from RSA Inc., VeriSign was one of the first companies to develop digital certificate technology. Its position in the nascent e-commerce security industry was given a significant boost when Netscape decided to integrate VeriSign's digital certificates into the SSL protocol that Netscape was developing to help facilitate secure commerce. This alliance gave VeriSign a major lead on the competition.

Today, VeriSign dominates the Web site encryption services market with an overwhelming 75% market share. As of June 2001, it had issued over 305,000 Web site digital certificates, with over 90,000 of those certificates issued in the first quarter of 2001 alone. It had also sold OnSite solutions similar to the one developed for the University of Pittsburgh to over 2000 customers. VeriSign currently employs about 2,300 employees and had revenues of almost $500 million in 2000.

VeriSign's corporate mission is to "Enable everyone, everywhere to use the Internet with confidence." Its CEO, Stratton Sclavos, likes to refer to VeriSign as a "trust utility."

To fulfill that mission, VeriSign has been on an acquisition binge, purchasing companies such as Signio, a major player in the Internet payment processing market, and Network Solutions, the Web site domain registration company. In the process, VeriSign picked up Network Solutions' exclusive contract to maintain the Registry for the .com, .net., and .org top-level domains — the definitive database of over 30.6 million .com, .net, and .org names. VeriSign operates 12 global top-level domain name servers that answer domain name look-ups in the .com, .net, and .org zones, and provides the associated IP addresses for every .com, .net, and .org domain name on the Internet. Says Sclavos: "At some point, every company on the Internet will be touching one of our systems."

Right now, VeriSign been most successful in the business-to-business arena. The rush by companies to buy and sell over the Internet is driving an unprecedented demand for sophisticated encryption products to encode e-mail, purchase orders, and other sensitive information flowing over the Internet. While consumers are at risk of losing a few hundred dollars on an e-commerce transaction gone awry, large firms purchasing over the Internet could be facing losses in the millions of dollars on a single purchase. Authenticating parties and encoding messages, therefore, is very important to large firms engaging in B2B exchanges. Rather than build their own security, many large firms are outsourcing their entire encryption operation to service providers such as VeriSign.

Sclavos believes the success of VeriSign will ultimately revolutionize Internet security and make the Web safe for all kinds of transactions that today are mostly still accomplished by paper and pen. With the recent passage of a federal law giving digital signatures legal validity, people can conceivably use the Internet to sign up for bank accounts, sign legal documents, even obtain prescriptions from doctors. But that's only if they have a digital certificate.

Business analysts wonder just how fast consumers will start using digital certificates. Although VeriSign's certificates are integrated into Netscape's implementation

SOURCES: VeriSign Inc. Report on Form 10-K for the year ended December 31, 2000, filed with the Securities and Exchange Commission on March 28, 2001; "VeriSign Issues False Microsoft Digital Certificates," by Brian Fonseca, *InfoWorld*, March 22, 2001; "The Web's Virtual Vault: VeriSign," by Jim Kerstetter, *BusinessWeek Online*, October 23, 2000; "VeriSign: Witness to the Future?", by Farhad Manjoo, *WiredNews*, October 18, 2000; "Special Report: B2B e-commerce The Internet's Trust Utility," by Mike Wiebner, *www.larsten.net*, July/August 2000; "At the U. of Pittsburgh, Digital Certificates Begin Replacing Passwords," by Florence Olson, *The Chronicle of Higher Education*, March 23, 2000; "VeriSign is Clicking With Its Encryption Outsourcing," by William M. Bulkeley, *Wall Street Journal*, March 7, 2000; VeriSign Inc. S-1 filed with the Securities and Exchange Commission on November 21, 1997.

of SSL, right now, very few consumers use digital certificates to authenticate themselves or others, or to encrypt their e-mail. Frank Prince, a Forrester Research analyst, says "Just because somebody can sign a mortgage online, doesn't mean they will." Prince thinks the public will eventually use certificates, but it will be a long learning curve — perhaps five years or more.

There's another, mostly unspoken, issue surrounding VeriSign and its security services — just how much security do they really provide? As discussed in the chapter, public key infrastructure, like any security solution, is only as good as the weakest link in the chain. In the case of PKI, the weak links include the initial security procedures set up to obtain the certificates (witness VeriSign's issuance of two digital certificates to someone masquerading as a representative of Microsoft), and the subsequent storage of private keys on a personal computer (which are usually unsecured in most homes and businesses). PKI does not guarantee, for instance, that the person using the client computer is in fact a legitimate user.

Case Study Questions

1. Make a list of five documents that you have been asked to sign or receive as part of a transaction. Which of these documents would you feel secure about executing online with a digital certificate system in place?

2. What are the social implications of a single firm such as VeriSign dominating the market for digital certificates? Who oversees VeriSign? Is there a need for legislation to regulate the digital certificate industry, and if so, what kind of regulations do you think might be appropriate?

3. What additional security technologies would be useful to ensure the authenticity of the actual operator of a client computer?

5.6 REVIEW

KEY CONCEPTS

■ **Understand the scope of e-commerce crime and security problems.**

While the overall size of cybercrime is unclear at this time, cybercrime against e-commerce sites is growing rapidly, the amount of losses is growing, and the management of e-commerce sites must prepare for a variety of criminal assaults.

■ **Describe the key dimensions of e-commerce security.**

There are six key dimensions to e-commerce security:
- *Integrity* — the ability to ensure that information displayed on a Web site, or sent or received via the Internet has not been altered in any way by an unauthorized party.
- *Nonrepudiation* — the ability to ensure that e-commerce participants do not deny (repudiate) their online actions.
- *Authenticity* — refers to the ability to verify an individual or business's identity.
- *Confidentiality* — determines whether information shared online, such as through e-mail communication or an order process, can be viewed by anyone other than the intended recipient.
- *Privacy* — deals with the use of information shared during an online transaction. Consumers want to limit the extent to which their personal information can be divulged to other organizations, while merchants want to protect such information from falling into the wrong hands.

- *Availability* — determines whether a Web site is accessible and operational at any given moment.

E-commerce security is designed to protect these six dimensions; when any one of them is compromised, it is a security issue.

■ **Understand the tension between security and other values.**

Although computer security is considered necessary to protect e-commerce activities, it is not without a downside. Two major areas where there are tensions between security and Web site operations include:

- *Ease of use*: The more security measures that are added to an e-commerce site, the more difficult it is to use and the slower the site becomes, hampering ease of use. Security is purchased at the price of slowing down processors and adding significantly to data storage demands. Too much security can harm profitability, while not enough can potentially put a business out of business.
- *Public safety*: There is a tension between the claims of individuals to act anonymously and the needs of public officials to maintain public safety that can be threatened by criminals or terrorists.

■ **Identify the key security threats in the e-commerce environment.**

The seven most common and most damaging forms of security threats to e-commerce sites include:

- *Malicious code* — viruses, worms, Trojan horses, and "bad applets" are a threat to a system's integrity and continued operation, often changing how a system functions or altering documents created on the system.
- *Hacking and cybervandalism* — intentionally disrupting, defacing, or even destroying a site.
- *Credit card fraud/theft* — one of the most-feared occurrences and one of the main reasons more consumers do not participate in e-commerce. The most common cause of credit card fraud is a lost or stolen card that is used by someone else, followed by employee theft of customer numbers, and stolen identities (criminals applying for credit cards using false identities).
- *Spoofing* — occurs when hackers attempt to hide their true identities or misrepresent themselves by using fake e-mail addresses or masquerading as someone else. Spoofing also can involve redirecting a Web link to an address different from the intended one, with the site masquerading as the intended destination.
- *Denial of service attacks* — hackers flood a Web site with useless traffic to inundate and overwhelm the network, frequently causing it to shut down and damaging a site's reputation and customer relationships.
- *Sniffing* — a type of eavesdropping program that monitors information traveling over a network, enabling hackers to steal proprietary information from anywhere on a network, including e-mail messages, company files, and confidential reports. The threat of sniffing is that confidential or personal information will be made public.

- *Insider jobs* — although the bulk of Internet security efforts are focused on keeping outsiders out, the biggest threat is from employees who have access to sensitive information and procedures.

■ **Describe how various forms of encryption technology help protect the security of messages sent over the Internet.**

Encryption is the process of transforming plain text or data into cipher text that cannot be read by anyone other than the sender and the receiver. Encryption can provide four of the six key dimensions of e-commerce security:

- *Message integrity* — provides assurance that the sent message has not been altered.
- *Nonrepudiation* — prevents the user from denying that he or she sent a message.
- *Authentication* — provides verification of the identity of the person (or machine) sending the message.
- *Confidentiality* — gives assurance that the message was not read by others.

There are a variety of different forms of encryption technology currently in use. They include:

- *Symmetric key encryption* — Both the sender and the receiver use the same key to encrypt and decrypt a message. DES (Data Encryption Standard), a 56-bit encryption key developed by NSA and IBM in the 1950s, is the most widely used symmetric key encryption system on the Internet today.
- *Public key cryptography* — Two mathematically related digital keys are used: a public key and a private key. The private key is kept secret by the owner, and the public key is widely disseminated. Both keys can be used to encrypt and decrypt a message. Once the keys are used to encrypt a message, the same keys cannot be used to unencrypt the message.
- *Public key encryption using digital signatures and hash digests* — This method uses a mathematical algorithm called a hash function to produce a fixed-length number called a hash digest. The results of applying the hash function are sent by the sender to the recipient. Upon receipt, the recipient applies the hash function to the received message and checks to verify that the same result is produced. The sender then encrypts both the hash result and the original message using the recipient's public key, producing a single block of cipher text. To ensure the authenticity of the message and to ensure nonrepudiation, the sender encrypts the entire block of cipher text one more time using the sender's private key. This produces a digital signature or "signed" cipher text that can be sent over the Internet to ensure the confidentiality of the message and authenticate the sender.
- *Digital envelope* — This method uses symmetric encryption to encrypt and decrypt the document, but public key encryption to encrypt and send the symmetric key.
- *Digital certificates and public key infrastructure* — This method relies on certification authorities who issue, verify, and guarantee digital certificates (a digital

document that contains the name of the subject or company, the subject's public key, a digital certificate serial number, an expiration date, an issuance date, the digital signature of the certification authority and other identifying information).

■ **Identify the tools used to establish secure Internet communications channels.**

In addition to encryption, there are several other tools that are used to secure Internet channels of communication, including:

* *Secure Sockets Layer (SSL)* — This is the most common form of securing channels. The SSL protocol provides data encryption, server authentication, client authentication, and message integrity for TCP/IP connections.
* *S-HTTP (Secure Hypertext Transfer Protocol)* — S-HTTP secures only Web protocols and cannot be used to secure non-HTTP messages.
* *Virtual private networks (VPN)* — These allow remote users to securely access internal networks via the Internet, using the Point-to-Point Tunneling Protocol (PPTP), an encoding mechanism that allows one local network to connect to another using the Internet as the conduit.

■ **Identify the tools used to protect networks, servers, and clients.**

After communications channels are secured, tools to protect networks, the servers, and clients should be implemented. These include:

* *Firewalls* — software applications that act as filters between a company's private network and the Internet itself, denying unauthorized remote client machines from attaching to your internal network .
* *Proxies* — software servers that act primarily to limit access of internal clients to external Internet servers and are frequently referred to as the gateway.
* *Operating system controls* — built-in username and password requirements that provide a level of authentication. Some operating systems also have an access control function that controls user access to various areas of a network.
* *Anti-virus software* — a cheap and easy way to identify and eradicate the most common types of viruses as they enter a computer, as well as to destroy those already lurking on a hard drive.

■ **Appreciate the importance of policies, procedures, and laws in creating security.**

In order to minimize security threats:

* e-commerce firms must develop a coherent corporate policy that takes into account the nature of the risks, the information assets that need protecting, and the procedures and technologies required to address the risk, as well as implementation and auditing mechanisms.
* Public laws and active enforcement of cybercrime statutes are also required to both raise the costs of illegal behavior on the Internet and guard against corporate abuse of information.

The key steps in developing a security plan are:
- *Perform a risk assessment* — an assessment of the risks and points of vulnerability.
- *Develop a security policy* — a set of statements prioritizing the information risks, identifying acceptable risk targets, and identifying the mechanisms for achieving these targets.
- *Create an implementation plan* — a plan that determines how you will translate the levels of acceptable risk into a set of tools, technologies, policies and procedures.
- *Create a security team* — the individuals who will be responsible for ongoing maintenance, audits, and improvements.
- *Perform periodic security audits.*

QUESTIONS

1. Why are some online merchants hesitant to ship to international addresses? What are some of the risks of doing so?
2. Explain how Internet security measures can actually create opportunities for criminals to steal, rather than preventing them.
3. Why is it less risky to steal online? Explain some of the ways criminals deceive consumers and merchants.
4. Explain why an e-commerce site might not want to report being the target of cybercriminals.
5. Discuss why new and improved security measures are not enough to stop online crime. What is the missing ingredient?
6. Give an example of security breaches as they relate to each of the seven dimensions of e-commerce security. For instance, what would be a privacy incident?
7. Explain why the U.S. government wants to restrict the export of strong encryption systems. And why would other countries be against it?
8. Name the major points of vulnerability in a typical online transaction.
9. Describe the differences between three major types of malicious code: script, file-infecting, and macro viruses.
10. How does spoofing threaten a Web site's operations?
11. What are some of the steps a company can take to curtail cybercriminal activity from within a business?
12. Explain some of the modern-day flaws associated with encryption. Why is encryption not as secure today as it was earlier in the century?
13. Briefly explain how public key cryptography works. How does the addition of a digital signature change the process?
14. Compare and contrast firewalls and proxy servers and their security functions.
15. Is a computer with anti-virus software protected from viruses? Why or why not?
16. Identify and discuss the five steps in developing an e-commerce security plan.

17. How do biometric devices help improve security? What particular type of security breach do they particularly reduce?
18. What are tiger teams, who uses them, and what are some of the tactics they use in their work?
19. Name an organization involved in tracking and studying cybercriminal activity.

PROJECTS

1. Imagine you are the owner of an e-commerce Web site. What are some of the signs that your site has been hacked? Discuss the major types of attacks you could expect to experience and the resulting damage to your site. Prepare a brief summary presentation.

2. Given the shift toward m-commerce, identify and discuss the new security threats to this type of technology. Prepare a presentation outlining your vision of the new opportunities for cybercrime.

3. Find three certification authorities and compare the features of each company's digital certificates. Provide a brief description of each company as well, including number of clients. Prepare a brief presentation of your findings.

4. Visit Netcraft's Web page, "What is this SSL site running," http://www.netcraft.com/sslwhats, and run SSL queries for five sites of your choosing. For each site, identify the digital certificate owner, the Web server software being used, the encryption algorithms supported by the server, the administrative details of the certificate (the period during which it was valid and the serial number) and the certification authority that issued the certificate.

WEB SITE RESOURCES www.LearnE-commerce.net

- News: Weekly updates on topics relevant to the material in this chapter.
- Video Lecture: Professor Ken Laudon summarizes the key concepts of the chapter.
- Research: Abstracts and links to articles referenced in the chapter, as well as other relevant research.
- PowerPoint slides: Illustrations from the chapter and more.
- Additional projects and exercises

CHAPTER 6

E-commerce Payment Systems

After reading this chapter you will be able to:

- Describe the features of traditional payment systems.
- Discuss the current limitations of online credit card payment systems.
- Understand the features and functionality of digital wallets.
- Describe the features and functionality of the major types of digital payment systems in the B2C arena.
- Describe the features and functionality of the major types of digital payment systems in the B2B arena.
- Describe the features and functionality of electronic billing presentment and payment systems.

PayPal
The Money's in the E-mail

On November 16, 1999, Peter Theil sat with friends at a restaurant. When the bill arrived, Theil used his Palm Pilot to "beam" his share to a friend sitting across the table. Theil and fellow co-founder Max Levchin had built a system that would allow them to send money to one another via a Palm Pilot's infrared links. From this idea sprang one of the first "peer-to-peer" payment systems: PayPal.com, which allows individuals to send money to one another via e-mail.

PayPal emphasizes ease of use for both senders and receivers of cash. Here's a brief synopsis of how it works. First, you create a PayPal account at the PayPal Web site by filling out a one-page application form and providing credit card or bank account information. Only PayPal is privy to this information, not the receiving party. Then, when you use PayPal to pay for a purchase, money is drawn from the credit card or bank account and transmitted to the Automated ClearingHouse (ACH) Network, a privately operated financial intermediary that tracks and transfers funds between financial institutions. The party who is to receive the payment is notified via e-mail that money is waiting. If the receiving party has a PayPal account, the funds are automatically deposited into the account; if the person does not have a PayPal account, he or she must set one up, and then the money is credited to his or her account. Once the funds are in the PayPal account, the recipient can then transfer them electronically to a checking account, request a paper check, or use PayPal to send the funds to someone else.

Levchin and Theil originally conceived of PayPal as a method for payments between individuals who knew one another. However, they quickly realized that it would also work for a company such as eBay, providing purchasers and sellers with a way to short-cut the time-consuming and cumbersome process of mailing checks and money orders and waiting for checks to clear before shipping items. Theil and Levchin were right. Today, PayPal is the largest and most popular online payment service, growing from a handful of users when it launched in late 1999 to over 9 million in August 2001. About 20,000 new users and around 3,000 business accounts sign up each day.

PayPal filled a niche that credit card companies avoided. Before PayPal, it was very difficult, if not impossible, for individuals to accept credit card payments. To date, PayPal is one of e-commerce's major success stories. PayPal earns money in two ways. First, online sellers (who may be individuals or small businesses that do not want the difficulties or high fees associated with obtaining a merchant credit card account) pay a small transaction fee for the service (1.9% of the transaction, plus 25 cents, which is half the cost a merchant typically pays for a credit card transaction). Consumers are not charged for use of the account. Second, PayPal earns revenue by collecting the interest earned on consumer funds not yet transferred out of the PayPal system.

The strength of PayPal is in part its simplicity: It piggybacks on existing credit card and checking payment systems. This is also one of its weaknesses, however. PayPal reportedly suffers relatively high levels of fraud related to the credit card system on which it relies. To protect against fraud, PayPal requires special authorization for payments over $200.

Although PayPal is the largest peer-to-peer payment service, there are several others in existence, all of which enhance and facilitate the operation of existing payment mechanisms such as bank checking accounts, credit cards in the United States, and debit cards in Europe. The major credit card companies have long ignored the demands of ordinary consumers for convenient online peer-to-peer payment systems. Yet the major credit card associations — under the pressure of an antitrust suit in which they are accused of stifling competition in the $1.7 trillion-a-year U.S. credit card market — are searching for competitive alternatives to PayPal. Western Union, with MoneyZap, AOL with its AOLQuickCash, and Citibank with C2it, are just three of the major players entering the market with payment alternatives. So far, though, PayPal remains ahead of the pack.

SOURCES: "Credit Card Firms Still Need a Strong Hand in Web Game," by Jathon Sapsford and Paul Beckett, *Wall Street Journal*, April 2, 2001; "Online: Auction Web Sites: Are You Buying or Selling?" by David Rowley, *The Guardian*, February 22, 2001; "New Economy: For Many Online Companies, Customer Service is Hardly a Priority. Just Try to Find a Phone Number," by Susan Stellin, *New York Times*, February 19, 2001; "Basics: With Debts Paid Online, Check Is in the E-mail," by Jessica Seigal, *New York Times*, July 27, 2000; "When Cash Will No Longer Count," by Tim Jackson, *Financial Times*, May 8, 2000.

C ollecting revenue from sales is at the heart of running a business. E-commerce poses some unique issues for merchants who want to reliably and efficiently collect revenue from customers, and for customers who would like a reliable, trustworthy way to pay for goods and services online. E-commerce has also created the potential for new forms of payment systems. Companies such as PayPal illustrate some of the market opportunities entrepreneurial firms have to improve on existing payment systems while at the same time extending the functionality of these systems. And although entrepreneurial firms such as PayPal face severe competition from traditional banking and credit card companies that dominate the payments industry, there appears to be plenty of room for competition: Electronic payments on and off the Web are growing by $75 billion a year (Sapsford and Beckett, 2001).

In this chapter we will review existing payments systems, identify the universal features of these systems, describe current and future e-commerce payment systems in both the B2C and B2B arenas, and describe the use of the Internet as an electronic bill paying and presentment system.

6.1 PAYMENT SYSTEMS

In order to understand e-commerce payment systems, you first need to be familiar with the various types of generic payment systems. Then you will be able to clarify the different requirements that e-commerce payments systems must meet and identify the opportunities provided by e-commerce technology for developing new types of payment systems.

TYPES OF PAYMENT SYSTEMS

There are five main types of payment systems: cash, checking transfer, credit cards, stored value, and accumulating balance.

Cash

Cash, which is legal tender defined by a national authority to represent value, is the most common form of payment in terms of number of transactions (see Figure 6.1).

The key feature of cash is that it is instantly convertible into other forms of value without the intermediation of any other institution. For instance, free airline miles are not cash because they are not instantly convertible into other forms of value—they require intermediation by a third party (the airline) in order to be exchanged for value (an airline ticket). Private organizations sometimes create a form of private cash called *scrip* that can be instantly redeemed by participating organizations for goods or cash. Examples include Green Stamps and other forms of consumer loyalty currency.

cash
legal tender defined by a national authority to represent value

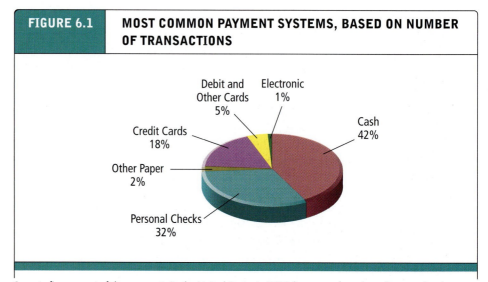

FIGURE 6.1

MOST COMMON PAYMENT SYSTEMS, BASED ON NUMBER OF TRANSACTIONS

Seventy-five percent of the payments in the United States in 2000 (in terms of number of transactions) were made by cash or personal check.

SOURCE: Statistical Abstract of the United States, 2001.

Why is cash still so popular today? Cash is portable, requires no authentication, and provides instant purchasing power for those who possess it. Cash allows for *micropayments* (payments of small amounts). The use of cash is "free" in that neither merchants nor consumers pay a transaction fee for using it. Using cash does not require any complementary assets, such as special hardware or the existence of an account, and it puts very low cognitive demands on the user. Cash is anonymous and difficult to trace, and in that sense it is "private." Other forms of payment require significant use of third parties and leave an extensive digital or paper trail.

On the other hand, cash is limited to smaller transactions (you can't easily buy a car or house with cash), it is easily stolen, and it does not provide any "**float**" (the period of time between a purchase and actual payment for the purchase); when it is spent, it is gone. With cash, purchases tend to be final and irreversible (i.e., they are irrefutable) unless otherwise agreed by the seller.

float
the period of time between a purchase and actual payment for the purchase

checking transfers
funds transferred directly via a signed draft or check from a consumer's checking account to a merchant or other individual

Checking Transfer

Checking transfers, which are funds transferred directly via a signed draft or check from a consumer's checking account to a merchant or other individual, are the second most common form of payment in terms of number of transactions (see Figure 6.1), and the most common in terms of total amount spent (see Figure 6.2).

Checks can be used for both small and large transactions, although typically they are not used for micropayments. Checks have some float (it can take up to ten days

FIGURE 6.2 MOST COMMON PAYMENT SYSTEMS, BASED ON DOLLAR AMOUNT

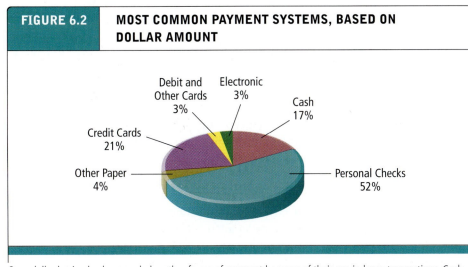

On a dollar basis, checks overwhelm other forms of payment because of their use in large transactions. Cash remains the leading form of payment for small transactions.

SOURCE: Statistical Abstract of the United States, 2001.

for out-of-state checks to clear), and the unspent balances can earn interest. Checks are not anonymous and require third-party institutions to work. Checks also introduce security risks for merchants: They can be forged more easily than cash; hence authentication is required. For merchants, checks also present some additional risk compared to cash because they can be canceled before they clear the account or they may bounce if there is not enough money in the account.

Money orders, cashiers checks, and travelers checks are *ensured checks* that address some of the limitations of personal checks described above. Ensured checks reduce the security risk of a personal check by requiring an up-front payment to a *trusted third party* — a bank or money transfer company such as American Express, Wells Fargo, or Western Union. These trusted third parties then issue a guaranteed payment draft called a *money order* that is as good as cash, although less anonymous. Merchants are guaranteed the funds in any transaction with an ensured check. Trusted third parties make money by charging consumers a fee and receiving interest on the money consumers deposited with them. Ensured checks provide merchants with lower risk, but they add costs for the consumer. In return, consumers have a payment instrument that is accepted nearly everywhere and in some cases is ensured against loss.

Credit Card

credit card

represents an account that extends credit to consumers, permits consumers to purchase items while deferring payment, and allows consumers to make payments to multiple vendors at one time

A **credit card** represents an account that extends credit to consumers, permits consumers to purchase items while deferring payment, and allows consumers to make payments to multiple vendors at one time. **Credit card associations** such as Visa and MasterCard are nonprofit associations that set standards for the **issuing banks**—such as CitiBank—that actually issue the credit cards and process transactions. Other third parties (called **processing centers** or **clearinghouses**) usually handle verification of accounts and balances. Credit card issuing banks act as financial intermediaries, minimizing the risk to transacting parties.

credit card associations

nonprofit associations that set standards for issuing banks

Credit cards offer consumers a line of credit and the ability to make small and large purchases instantly. They are widely accepted as a form of payment, reduce the risk of theft associated with carrying cash, and increase consumer convenience. Credit cards also offer consumers considerable float. With a credit card, for instance, a consumer typically need not actually pay for goods purchased until receiving a credit card bill thirty days later. Merchants benefit from increased consumer spending resulting from credit card use, but they pay a hefty transaction fee of 3% to 5% of the purchase price to the issuing banks. In addition, federal Regulation Z places the risks of the transaction (such as credit card fraud, repudiation of the transaction, or nonpayment) largely on the merchant and credit card issuing bank. Regulation Z limits cardholder liability to $50 for unauthorized transactions that occur before the card issuer is notified. Once a card is reported stolen, consumers are not liable for any subsequent charges.

issuing banks

the banks that actually issue credit cards and process transactions

processing centers (clearinghouses)

institutions that handle verification of accounts and balances

Credit cards have less finality than other payment systems because consumers can refute or repudiate purchases under certain circumstances, and they limit risk for consumers while raising it for merchants and bankers.

Stored Value

stored-value payments systems

accounts created by depositing funds into an account and from which funds are paid out or withdrawn as needed

Accounts created by depositing funds into an account and from which funds are paid out or withdrawn as needed are **stored-value payments systems**. Stored-value payment systems are similar in some respects to checking transfers—which also store funds—but do not involve writing a check. Examples include debit cards, gift certificates, prepaid cards, and smart cards (described in greater detail later in the chapter). **Debit cards** look like credit cards, but rather than providing access to a line of credit, they instead immediately debit a checking or other demand-deposit account. For many consumers, the use of a debit card eliminates the need to write a paper check. Because debit cards are dependent on funds being available in a consumer's bank account, however, larger purchases are still generally paid for by credit card. Also, consumers in the United States have not embraced debit cards to a great extent because they do not have the protections provided by Regulation Z and do not provide any float.

debit cards

immediately debit a checking or other demand-deposit account

Peer-to-peer (P2P) payment systems such as PayPal are variations on the stored value concept. P2P payment systems do not insist on prepayment, but do require an account with stored value, either a checking account with funds available or a credit card with an untapped credit balance.

Accumulating Balance

Accounts that accumulate expenditures and to which consumers make periodic payments are **accumulating balance payment systems**. Traditional examples include utility, phone, and American Express accounts, all of which accumulate balances, usually over a specified period (typically a month), and then are paid in full at the end of the period.

Table 6.1 summarizes how payment systems differ on a variety of dimensions noted above and highlights a number of points about payment systems. First, evaluating payment systems is a complex process; there are many dimensions that must be considered. Table 6.1 suggests how difficult it is for entrepreneurs to devise new payment mechanisms to displace current payment systems (cash, checks, and credit cards). As we will discuss below, consumers in the United States have not, as a general matter, accepted most online payment systems.

Table 6.1 also suggests that the various parties that have an interest in payment systems (stakeholders) may have different preferences with respect to the different dimensions. The main stakeholders in payment systems are consumers, merchants, financial intermediaries, and government regulators.

Consumers are interested primarily in low-risk, low-cost, refutable (able to be repudiated or denied), convenient, and reliable payment mechanisms. Consumers have demonstrated they will not use new payment mechanisms unless they are equally or more beneficial to them than existing systems (Winn, 1999). In general, most consumers use cash, checks, and/or credit cards. The specific payment system chosen will change depending on the transaction situation. For instance, cash may be preferred to keep certain transactions private and anonymous, but the same consumer may want a record of transaction for the purchase of a car.

Merchants are interested primarily in low-risk, low-cost, irrefutable (i.e., final), secure, and reliable payment mechanisms. Merchants currently carry much of the risk of checking and credit card fraud, refutability of charges, and much of the hardware cost of verifying payments. Merchants typically prefer payments made by cash, check, and to a lesser extent credit cards, which usually carry high fees and allow transactions to be repudiated after the fact by consumers.

Financial intermediaries, such as banks and credit card networks, are primarily interested in secure payment systems that transfer risks and costs to consumers and merchants, while maximizing transaction fees payable to themselves. The preferred

accumulating balance payment systems
accounts that accumulate expenditures and to which consumers make periodic payments

TABLE 6.1	DIMENSIONS OF PAYMENT SYSTEMS				
DIMENSION	CASH	PERSONAL CHECK	CREDIT CARD	STORED VALUE (DEBIT CARD)	ACCUMULATING BALANCE
Instantly convertible without intermediation	yes	no	no	no	no
Low transaction cost for small transactions	yes	no	no	no	yes
Low transaction cost for large transactions	no	yes	yes	yes	yes
Low fixed costs for merchant	yes	yes	no	no	no
Refutable (able to be repudiated)	no	yes	yes	no (usually)	yes
Financial risk for consumer	yes	no	up to $50	limited	no
Financial risk for merchant	no	yes	yes	no	yes
Anonymous for consumer	yes	no	no	no	no
Anonymous for merchant	yes	no	no	no	no
Immediately respendable	yes	no	no	no	no
Security against unauthorized use	no	some	some	some	some
Tamper-resistant	yes	no	yes	yes	yes
Requires authentication	no	yes	yes	yes	yes
Special hardware required	no	no	yes — by merchant	yes — by merchant	yes — by merchant
Buyer keeps float	no	yes	yes	no	yes
Account required	no	yes	yes	yes	yes
Has immediate monetary value	yes	no	no	yes	no

SOURCE: Adapted from MacKie-Mason and White, 1996.

payment mechanisms for financial intermediaries are checking transfers, debit cards, and credit cards.

Government regulators are interested in maintaining trust in the financial system. Regulators seek to protect against fraud and abuse in the use of payment systems, ensure that the interests of consumers and merchants are balanced against the interests of the financial intermediaries whom they regulate, and enforce information reporting laws. The most important regulations of payment systems are Regulation Z, Regulation E, and the Electronic Funds Transfer Act (EFTA) of 1978, regulating ATM machines. Regulation Z limits the risk to consumers when using credit cards. In contrast, EFTA and Regulation E place more risk on consumers when using debit or ATM cards. For instance, if you lose an ATM card or debit card, you are potentially liable for any losses to the account. However, Visa and MasterCard have issued policies that limit consumer risk for loss of debit cards to the same $50 that applies to credit cards.

OVERVIEW OF CURRENT E-COMMERCE PAYMENT SYSTEMS

The emergence of e-commerce has created new financial needs that in many cases cannot be effectively fulfilled by traditional payment systems. For instance, new types of purchasing relationships—such as auctions between individuals online—have resulted in the need for peer-to-peer payment methods that allow individuals to e-mail payments to other individuals. New types of online information products require micropayments. Merchants would like to sell online products such as individual music tracks, columns from newspapers, and chapters of textbooks. In turn, e-commerce technology offers a number of possibilities for creating new payment systems that substitute for existing systems, as well as for creating enhancements to existing systems. In this section we provide an overview of e-commerce payment systems in use today. Sections 6.2 and 6.3 provide a more detailed description of how online payments work.

Current Online Payment Systems

In 2000, credit cards accounted for 95% of online payments and about $47 billion of online transactions in the United States. (See Figure 6.3.)

While credit cards are the dominant form of online payment in the United States, this is not true in other parts of the world. Only 50% of consumers outside the United States use credit cards for online purchases. Consumers in Europe rely much more on checks or cash on delivery (COD) for payments. Consumers in Japan rely on bank transfers, CODs (using local convenience stores as the drop-off point), and accumulated balance accounts with the telephone company. Online payment outside the United States is heavily influenced by the host country's financial infrastructure (Lawrence, 2000).

In the United States, the dominance of online credit card payments is being challenged by a number of new forms of electronic payment. The fastest growth in pay-

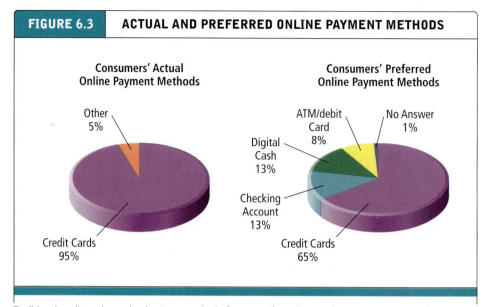

FIGURE 6.3 | ACTUAL AND PREFERRED ONLINE PAYMENT METHODS

Consumers' Actual Online Payment Methods

Other 5%

Credit Cards 95%

Consumers' Preferred Online Payment Methods

ATM/debit Card 8%

No Answer 1%

Digital Cash 13%

Checking Account 13%

Credit Cards 65%

Traditional credit cards are the dominant method of payment for online purchases. However, according to a Jupiter Research survey, some consumers would prefer to use other payment methods, such as e-cash, checking accounts, or debit cards, although they do not currently do so.

SOURCE: Jupiter Media Metrix, 2000.

ment systems is the "Other" category noted in Figure 6.3. Experts predict that these "other" forms of payments will account for nearly one-quarter of online purchases by 2003.

These new forms of payment include:

- **Digital cash**: Systems that generate a private form of currency that can be spent at e-commerce sites.
- **Online stored value systems**: Systems that rely on prepayments, debit cards, or checking accounts to create value in an account that can be used for e-commerce shopping.
- **Digital accumulating balance payment systems**: Systems that accumulate small charges and bill the consumer periodically. These systems are especially suited for processing micropayments for digital content.
- **Digital credit accounts**: Systems that extend the online functionality of existing credit card payment systems.
- **Digital checking**: Systems that create digital checks for e-commerce remittances and extend the functionality of existing bank checking systems.

In Section 6.3 we describe these new digital payment systems in detail and in Section 6.4 we discuss digital payment systems used in business-to-business transactions.

6.2   CREDIT CARD E-COMMERCE TRANSACTIONS

Because credit cards are the dominant form of online payment, it is important to understand how online credit card transactions work and to recognize the strengths and weaknesses of this payment system.

HOW AN ONLINE CREDIT CARD TRANSACTION WORKS

Online credit card transactions are processed much the same way that in-store purchases are, with the major differences being that online merchants never see the actual card being used, no card impression is taken, and no signature is available. Online credit card transactions most closely resemble *MOTO transactions* (mail order-telephone order) transactions. As you learned in Chapter 5, these types of purchases are also called *CNP* (Card Not Present) transactions and are the major reason that charges can be disputed later by consumers. Since the merchant never sees the credit card, nor receives a hand-signed agreement to pay from the customer, when disputes arise, the merchant faces the risk that the transaction may be disallowed and reversed, even though he has already shipped the goods or the user has downloaded a digital product.

Figure 6.4 illustrates the online credit card purchasing cycle. There are five parties involved in an online credit card purchase: consumer, merchant, clearinghouse, merchant bank (sometimes called the "acquiring bank"), and the consumer's card issuing bank. In order to accept payments by credit card, online merchants must have a merchant account established with a bank or financial institution. A **merchant account** is simply a bank account that allows companies to process credit card payments and receive funds from those transactions.

As shown in Figure 6.4, an online credit card transaction begins with a purchase (#1). When a consumer wants to make a purchase, he or she adds the item to the merchant's shopping cart. When the consumer wants to pay for the items in the shopping cart, a secure tunnel through the Internet is created using SSL (Secure Sockets Layer), described in Chapter 5. Using encryption, SSL secures the session during which credit card information will be sent to the merchant and protects the information from interlopers on the Internet (#2). SSL does not authenticate either the merchant or the consumer. The transacting parties have to trust one another.

Once the consumer credit card information is received by the merchant, the merchant software contacts a clearinghouse (#3). As previously noted, a clearinghouse is a financial intermediary that authenticates credit cards and verifies account balances. The clearinghouse contacts the issuing bank to verify the account information (#4).

merchant account
a bank account that allows companies to process credit card payments and receive funds from those transactions

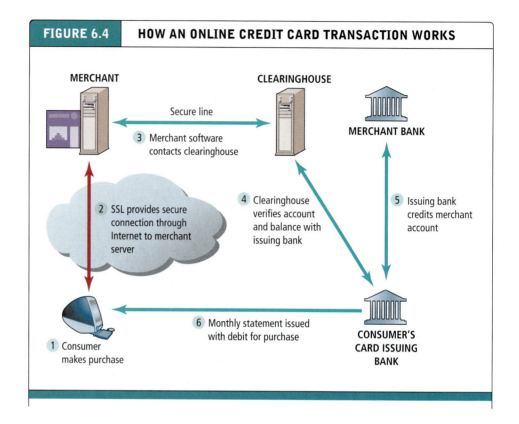

FIGURE 6.4   **HOW AN ONLINE CREDIT CARD TRANSACTION WORKS**

MERCHANT

CLEARINGHOUSE

MERCHANT BANK

Secure line

3 Merchant software contacts clearinghouse

2 SSL provides secure connection through Internet to merchant server

4 Clearinghouse verifies account and balance with issuing bank

5 Issuing bank credits merchant account

6 Monthly statement issued with debit for purchase

1 Consumer makes purchase

CONSUMER'S CARD ISSUING BANK

Once verified, the issuing bank credits the account of the merchant at the merchant's bank (usually this occurs at night in a batch process) (#5). The debit to the consumer account is transmitted to the consumer in a monthly statement (#6).

CREDIT CARD E-COMMERCE ENABLERS

Companies that have a merchant account still need to buy or build a means of handling the online transaction; securing the merchant account is only step one in a two-part process. Today, Internet payment service providers can provide both a merchant account and the software tools needed to process credit card purchases online.

For instance, VeriSign, a leader in Internet security services, is also an Internet payment service provider. VeriSign will help a merchant secure a merchant account with one of its merchant account provider partners and provides payment processing software that a merchant installs on its server. The software collects the transaction information from the merchant's site and then routes it via the VeriSign "payment gateway" to the appropriate bank, ensuring that customers are authorized to make their purchases. The funds for the transaction are then transferred to the merchant's merchant account.

LIMITATIONS OF ONLINE CREDIT CARD PAYMENT SYSTEMS

There are a number of limitations to the existing credit card payment system. The most important limitations involve security, merchant risk, cost, and social equity. The existing system offers very poor security. Neither the merchant nor the consumer can be fully authenticated. The merchant could be a criminal organization designed to collect credit card numbers, and the consumer could be using stolen or fraudulent cards. The risk facing merchants is high: Consumers can repudiate charges even though the goods have been shipped or the product downloaded. Costs for merchants are also significant—roughly 3.5% of the purchase plus a transaction fee of 20–30 cents per transaction, plus other set-up fees. The high costs make it undesirable to sell goods on the Web for less than $10. The sale of individual articles, music tracks, or other small items is not feasible with credit cards.

Credit cards are not very democratic, even though they seem ubiquitous. As discussed in *Insight on Society: The Right to Shop*, millions of young adults do not have credit cards, along with almost 100 million other adult Americans who cannot afford cards or who are considered poor risks because of low incomes. Alternative payment systems described in Section 6.3 overcome many of these limitations. The credit card industry itself has attempted to solve the security issue through the development of a new standard Internet protocol called SET.

SET: SECURE ELECTRONIC TRANSACTION PROTOCOL

Central issues for merchants and credit issuing banks involve authentication and refutability of charges. Although the SSL protocol provides secure transactions between merchant and consumer, it does not and cannot provide authentication. In addition, SSL cannot provide irrefutability: Consumers can order goods or download information products and then claim the transaction never occurred.

SET, for **Secure Electronic Transaction Protocol**, is intended to address the weaknesses of ordinary online credit card transactions by authenticating cardholder and merchant identity and making it impossible to refute charges through the use of digital signatures. SET is an open standard for the e-commerce industry developed and offered by MasterCard and Visa, the two major credit card issuers in the United States, as a way to facilitate and encourage improved security for credit card transactions.

SET uses a *digital certificate*, discussed in Chapter 5, which is an attachment to a message that verifies a sender's identity, as one way of improving payment security. Credit card companies issue digital certificates to their cardholders just as they issue plastic cards; the digital certificate is stored in a digital wallet (described more fully in the next section) for use during online transactions. Merchants are issued similar certificates by the bank providing merchant account status. By using SET, merchants can

Secure Electronic Transaction Protocol (SET)

an open standard for the e-commerce industry developed and offered by MasterCard and Visa as a way to facilitate and encourage improved security for credit card transactions

INSIGHT ON SOCIETY

THE RIGHT TO SHOP

How would you feel if the only way you could take advantage of a great bargain was to purchase the item online—but you didn't have access to a computer or the Internet, or even if you did, the merchant could only process payments by credit card, and you didn't have one. If you think that would be unfair, you're not alone. Although the right to purchase merchandise online may not yet have risen to the level of an inalienable right, over the past several years increasing attention has been focused on the equity (or social fairness) issues raised by the fact that some groups don't have the same access to computers and the Internet as do others. This gap between the "haves" and "have nots" is often called the "digital divide."

A U.S. Department of Commerce study done in 1998 entitled "Falling Through the Net II: New Data on the Digital Divide," forecast growing challenges for the digital "have nots" in America, primarily households with incomes below $35,000, those without college educations, people living in rural areas, African Americans, Hispanics, seniors over 65, and the disabled. The report predicted that members of these groups would have an even more difficult time functioning in an economy that was Internet-dependent. Without access to a computer and the Internet, the report suggested, these Americans would have limited access to career improvement, be shut off from communications with family and friends, and lose out on purchasing opportunities.

Thankfully, the picture looks somewhat more promising today. According to the most recent U.S. Department of Commerce study, "Falling Though the Net: Toward Digital Inclusion," since 1998, Americans in all of the above groups have gained access to computers and the Internet in record numbers. The so-called digital divide has narrowed significantly just in the space of a few years. Two of the main reasons have been falling computer prices and free Internet service providers.

Still, there remain groups that are behind national averages in terms of computer ownership and Internet usage. Overall, according to the study, as of August 2000, 41.5% of Americans had Internet access in their homes, leaving 58.5% without. Noticeable divides still exist between those with different levels of income and education, different racial and ethnic groups, the old and the young, single and dual-parent families, and individuals with and without disabilities. For instance, only 12.7 % of households with incomes below $15,000 and 21.3% of households with incomes between $15,000 and $24,999 have Internet access compared to 60% of all households earning between $50,000 and $75,000. African American and Hispanic households have the lowest household Internet penetration of major ethnic groups—23.5% and 23.6%, respectively.

Now consider that credit card payments account for more than 95% of all online payments in the United States. Consider further that somewhere between 70 and 100 million adults in the United States do not have a credit card. Although there are a number of alternative online payment

(continued)

systems, many continue to rely on the underlying possession of a credit card. When you couple the digital divide numbers with those of Americans without credit cards, you end up with an even greater divide — the digital payments divide.

▬ **SOURCES:** "New Economy? You Ain't Seen Nothin' Yet," by Alvin and Heidi Toffler, *Wall Street Journal*, March 29, 2001; "Cheap PCs Helping to Narrow Digital Divide," by Gwendolyn Mariano, CNET News.com, March 13, 2001; "Falling Through the Net: Toward Digital Inclusion," National Telecommunications and Information Administration, U.S. Department of Commerce, October 2000; "Falling Through the Net: New Data on the Digital Divide," National Telecommunications and Information Administration, U.S. Department of Commerce, July 1998.

be assured that received orders have not been altered somewhere in the process. SET also authenticates both the consumer and the merchant. Figure 6.5 illustrates how SET transactions work.

The SET transaction process itself is similar to a standard online credit card transaction, except that there is more identity verification involved. As shown in Figure 6.5, after completing an online order form, the consumer selects the "Payment with SET" option at the site and then indicates which credit card he or she wants to use (#1). On receiving the order form, the merchant's computer accesses the consumer's

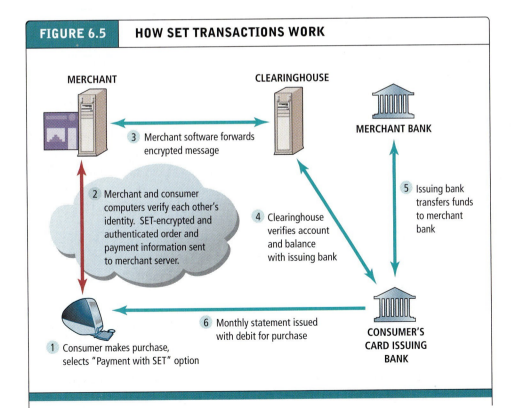

FIGURE 6.5 | **HOW SET TRANSACTIONS WORK**

MERCHANT

CLEARINGHOUSE

MERCHANT BANK

3 Merchant software forwards encrypted message

2 Merchant and consumer computers verify each other's identity. SET-encrypted and authenticated order and payment information sent to merchant server.

4 Clearinghouse verifies account and balance with issuing bank

5 Issuing bank transfers funds to merchant bank

6 Monthly statement issued with debit for purchase

CONSUMER'S CARD ISSUING BANK

1 Consumer makes purchase, selects "Payment with SET" option

digital wallet to learn the details of the credit card payment. The merchant's server verifies the consumer's identity using the digital certificate in the digital wallet, just as the consumer's computer verifies the merchant's identity the same way. Once verified, an encrypted file is sent to the merchant server containing all of the payment information (#2). The merchant server then forwards the encrypted message to the merchant bank's clearinghouse for decryption and authorization (#3). The clearinghouse authenticates the merchant and cardholder and the transaction is processed like any other credit card purchase (#4, #5). The merchant receives authorization to ship, the product is sent to the consumer, and a debit for the purchase is reflected on the consumer's monthly statement (#6).

Although SET has not yet caught on, it is currently the most secure way to handle online payments. Most online merchants have not signed on with SET and continue to rely on traditional credit card procedures. Merchants have resisted the change because of the costs involved in integrating SET into existing systems, and the resistance—or lack of interest—among consumers who do not understand digital wallets or digital certificates, and who do not want to download these systems onto their computers.

6.3 E-COMMERCE DIGITAL PAYMENT SYSTEMS IN THE B2C ARENA

Traditional payment systems were never designed for use in the digital world. As Internet use and purchasing rises, the weaknesses of cash, checks, and credit and debit cards become more apparent. As a result, entrepreneurs and traditional financial institutions have created a bewildering array of digital payment options that promise to better meet the needs of both consumers and merchants. In this section, we will examine each of the five major types of digital payment systems: digital cash, online stored value payment systems, digital accumulated balance payment systems, digital credit card payment systems, and digital checking payment systems. But first we will discuss the concept of "digital wallets" (sometimes called *electronic wallets* or *e-wallets*) because many of the new digital payment systems require some kind of digital wallet.

DIGITAL WALLETS

digital wallet

authenticates the consumer through the use of digital certificates or other encryption methods, stores and transfers value, and secures the payment process from the consumer to the merchant

A regular wallet—let's call it your "analog wallet"—resides in your pants pocket or in your purse. Analog wallets are pretty universal; just about every transaction-based culture has some form of portable value storage and identifying device. A wallet typically contains your IDs, cash, phone cards, credit/debit cards, old receipts and records, photos of those close to you, and other miscellaneous items. A **digital wallet** seeks to emulate the functionality of an analog wallet. The most important functions of a digital wallet are to (a) authenticate the consumer through the use of digital certificates or other encryption methods, (b) store and transfer value, and (c) secure the payment process from the consumer to the merchant.

Ideally, you could go online to any Web site, use your digital wallet to authenticate yourself, pay for anything you wanted to buy using any of several payment systems with a single click, and keep a record of your transactions that would be instantly available for your review. You would also be able to use the same digital wallet on a wireless Internet device (such as your cell phone or Palm) to pay for gasoline, clothing, or other items. Your digital wallet would support payments using a regular credit card, digital cash, digital credit card, or digital check.

The major advantage of digital wallets is convenience for the consumer and lower transactions costs because order entry can be expedited. With a digital wallet, you no longer have to fill out forms to purchase online. Instead you just click on your digital wallet and the software fills out the billing and shipping information. Not only does this hasten the order process but also it potentially reduces the risk of fraud and the use of stolen credit cards. Merchants benefit from digital wallets through lower transaction costs, expanded marketing and branding opportunities, easier customer retention and conversion of visitors into buyers, and some reduction in fraud. Financial intermediaries who establish digital wallets benefit from processing fees on every transaction. Some of the many potential uses of digital wallets are listed in Table 6.2.

TABLE 6.2	**PROMISED FUNCTIONALITY OF DIGITAL WALLETS**
FUNCTION	DESCRIPTION
Authentication	Confirms identities via digital certificates, SET, or other forms of encryption.
Processing of payments	Pays bills via alliances with credit card associations and banks.
Privacy/password management	Helps customers control their digital environments, PINs, card numbers, and passwords in a secure product.
Receipt management	Reviews all transactions at a single source.
Bill presentment	Presents and pays bills at a single location.
Loyalty programs	Participates in and manages loyalty points at a single location.
Coupon delivery/discounts	Coordinates merchant promotions through a single wallet.
Spending allowances	Establishes e-allowances.
Micropayments	Makes payments under $5 anywhere on the Web based on credit cards.
Integration with other software	Links to taxation software, personal budgets, personal devices, and wireless software

This is the concept, although the reality falls short at this time. There are many unanswered questions such as who will supply the digital wallet, who owns the wallet and its information (and related privacy issues), where will the digital wallet reside (on the desktop or some remote server), and what standards will define a digital wallet so that it is universally accepted.

Currently, there are two different major categories of digital wallets: client-based wallets and server-based wallets. (See Figure 6.6.)

Client-based digital wallets such as Gator.com and MasterCard Wallet are software applications that consumers install on their computers. They offer consumers convenience by automatically filling out forms at online stores. Merchants install software on their servers to receive information from the client-based wallet. When a consumer clicks the relevant button at a participating merchant's site, the merchant's server queries the consumer's browser for information from her or his digital wallet.

The business model of client-based wallet vendors is to sell millions of wallets, establish a de facto proprietary industry standard, and reap the rewards of network economics by becoming the single, viable solution for consumers to shop online. The revenue model for these vendors is to collect multiple revenue streams from sales of the software as well as from all parties in an online transaction. Wallet vendors would like to collect fees from merchants for promoting merchant products, sell personal

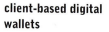

client-based digital wallets

software applications that consumers install on their computers, and that offer consumers convenience by automatically filling out forms at online stores

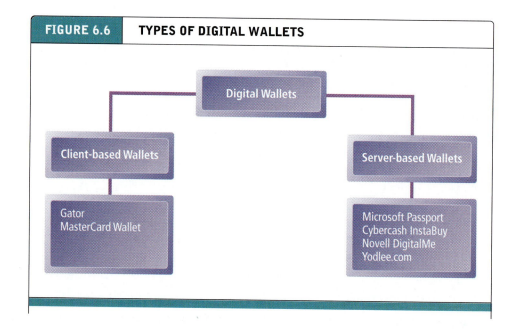

FIGURE 6.6   TYPES OF DIGITAL WALLETS

transaction information to merchants and intermediaries, and rent their systems to other financial intermediaries such as banks.

Client-based digital wallets have had low adoption rates since their inception in the mid-1990s. **Server-based digital wallets** have been more successful. These are software-based authentication and payment services and products sold to financial institutions that market the systems to merchants either directly or as a part of their financial service package. Vendors may provide both technology services (infrastructure needed to process payments) and wallet services. Merchants and financial institutions use the digital wallet products and services to provide easy, secure shopping, using whatever payment methods the customer desires. Server-based wallets typically offer online merchants a product/service that handles all aspects of online customer payments and offers lower transaction costs, lower customer acquisition and retention costs, and a branded online payment service. Server-based wallets do not require consumers to install special software. Server-based wallets can be dynamically updated as merchant forms change, whereas client-based wallets are more difficult to update because they require a download.

Perhaps the fastest growing server-based digital wallet system is Microsoft's Passport. Passport is one part of Microsoft's emerging .NET platform and strategy. Passport offers customers Single Sign-In service (SSI), and as an option, Express Purchase (EP). With Single Sign-In service, the customer can sign into a Web site with a single click of the Passport logo displayed at participating sites. Likewise, using EP, with a single click, the customer's payment preferences are communicated to the merchant's shopping cart. There are no more forms to fill out at every Web site.

Passport is unique among digital wallet schemes in that it dispenses with digital certificates. Early digital wallet schemes relied on digital certificates to authenticate the transactions between merchant and client.

A user obtains a Passport by opening an e-mail account at MSN.com or Hotmail.com, by registering at a merchant Web site, or by registering at www.passport.com. To obtain a unique sign-in profile, the user is required to submit a sign-in login name, password, and general background information. This exchange of information is encrypted using standard SSL. The user has the option of creating a "wallet" profile containing credit card payment information that can be used at merchants supporting the Express Payment option. Once the profiles are created, the user is issued a 64-bit Passport Unique Identifier (PUID). The PUID is the authentication credential sent to merchant sites when a Passport user signs in. Participating sites never receive the user's actual password. Figure 6.7 illustrates what happens when a registered user clicks on the Microsoft Passport logo at a participating merchant.

When a registered user clicks the Passport logo at a participating site, the site displays a Passport sign-in page where the user must enter his or her Passport sign-in name and password (#1) . The sign-in page redirects to Microsoft's Passport server to

server-based digital wallets
software-based authentication and payment services and products sold to financial institutions that market the systems to merchants either directly or as a part of their financial service package

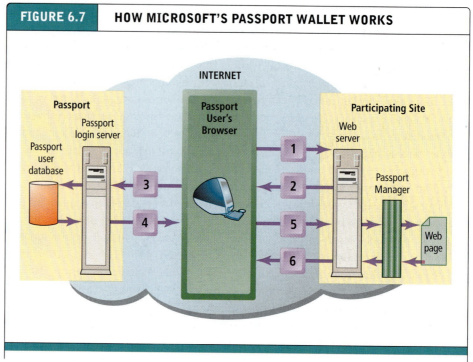

FIGURE 6.7	HOW MICROSOFT'S PASSPORT WALLET WORKS

SOURCE: Microsoft, 2001.

authenticate the user (#2, # 3). Passport authenticates the user and writes a cookie to the user's browser containing encrypted authentication and Passport profile information. The Passport Manager at the participating site decrypts the information (# 4, #5). The Passport Manager then caches the user's authentication and profile information in cookies on the user's browser and silently reverifies them as the user moves from page to page at the site (#6). Express Payment service is handled similarly.

The typical business model of server-based wallet vendors is to market their products directly to merchants and large financial intermediaries such as Visa, Master-Card, and Discover Card, and to develop a branded payment service and service trademark that will give consumers confidence and reduce their fear of credit card fraud. Server-based wallet vendors point to the fact that over 60% of online credit card purchases are terminated before the order is submitted because of consumer confusion in the order process and consumer fear of giving out credit card information. Wallet vendors also have developed partnerships with major credit card associations, and card issuing banks such as Wells Fargo, Citibank, and Chase, which are seeking quick solutions to online credit card fraud and consumer confusion.

The revenue model for these server-based digital wallet vendors is to generate revenue by charging merchants a setup fee, monthly minimum fees, and fees on every transaction. Some vendors also collect consumer transaction information and sell the data to marketing firms.

Microsoft's Passport system is currently available free of charge to merchants and consumers. Moreover, Microsoft promises never to sell either personally identifiable consumer information or transaction information to advertising and marketing firms. As a part of Microsoft's .NET strategy, Passport is targeted at becoming a universally accepted means of authentication and payment support system for the Internet.

It is apparent that the benefits of digital wallet technology will arrive only when there is widespread use by merchants and consumers, making the marginal benefits quite high for everyone. Consumers have resisted downloads, relying instead on their credit cards because of their existing advantages described above. Consumers distrust server-based merchant wallets; they fear loading all their personal information onto a remote server. It is uncertain at this time if Microsoft's Passport can clear this hurdle. Consumers continue to prefer to fill out forms manually rather than use any kind of digital wallet technology. Moreover, all digital wallets remove from consumers one of the most important consumer protections afforded by the existing online use of a credit card: the ability to repudiate a transaction, and/or refuse to pay the merchant for shoddy goods or non-delivery of goods. It is difficult for consumers to repudiate digital wallet transactions because these transactions are authenticated.

Merchants have found SET standards too difficult and expensive to implement although they have adopted the technology services of merchant wallet vendors (namely payment infrastructure services) while experimenting with the wallet services that consumers do not want to use.

Efforts to develop a standard for digital wallets have largely failed. A consortium formed by Dell, AOL, American Express, Sun Microsystems, Brodia, MasterCard, IBM, and Microsoft to develop a standard called **Electronic Commerce Modeling Language (ECML)** has made little collective progress since 1999, although Microsoft's Passport does comply with ECML. Other competing standards groups, such as Open Trading Protocol (OTP) and Open Buying on the Internet (OBI), have also made little progress.

Electronic Commerce Modeling Language (ECML)
a standard for digital wallets

Given the conflicting platforms being adopted by vendors and marginal benefits to consumers who would have to adopt many different digital wallets to shop online effectively, it is clear that the vision of a digital wallet will require many years to achieve. Many of the original consumer wallet companies either have disappeared completely or have been taken over by merchant wallet and payment services software firms. For instance, DigiCash, one of the earliest companies using a consumer-based digital wallet, withdrew its products from the market, but the brand name is being used to sell a suite of payment products to merchants. Until wallet technology is embedded in the technology platform—either in the operating system or the browser—such standards will not arise, and the benefits of the technology cannot be developed.

DIGITAL CASH

digital cash (e-cash)

as currently available, digital forms of value storage and value exchange that have limited convertibility into other forms of value and require intermediaries to convert

Digital cash (sometimes called *e-cash*) was one of the first forms of alternative payment systems developed for e-commerce. The name digital cash is in fact something of a misnomer. Recall our original definition of cash: legal tender (called *currency*) created by national authorities that is instantly convertible to other forms of value (goods and services) without the intermediation of any third parties. So far, neither the Federal Reserve Bank of the United States, nor the government regulators or any other country have created an electronic form of legal tender. If they did, we would really have "e-cash." Instead, what we do have are some interesting forms of value storage and value exchange that have limited convertibility into other forms of value, and that do require intermediaries to convert. Although most of the early examples of digital cash have failed, many of the ideas have survived today as a part of P2P (peer-to-peer) payment systems. Table 6.3 lists some examples of digital cash.

The early generations of digital cash were quite complex and required the creation of an entirely new set of payment industry standards and practices. For example, see Figure 6.8 for a description of how DigiCash, a first-generation digital cash payment system, worked.

TABLE 6.3	EXAMPLES OF DIGITAL CASH
NAME OF SYSTEM	**YEAR FOUNDED/DESCRIPTION**
First Virtual	1994. First secure stored value system based on credit cards, pre-use deposits, and PIN numbers. Ceased operations in 1998.
DigiCash (now e-Cash)	1996. Encryption-based prepaid stored value system requiring digital wallet on hard drive to store e-coins. Ceased operations in 1998, returned as e-cash.
Millicent	1996. Digital Equipment Corporation's entry into micropayment e-cash. Now a Compaq platform product with multiple options.
Peer-to-Peer Payment Systems	
PayPal	1999. Free P2P micropayment system.
Yahoo PayDirect	1999. Free Yahoo P2P payment service.
MoneyZap	1999. Western Union fee-based money transfer system.

As shown in Figure 6.8, to use DigiCash, a consumer first had to establish an account at a bank that was using the DigiCash system (#1). Once the account was established, the consumer then downloaded digital wallet software onto his or her computer's hard drive (#2). Then the consumer could request a transfer of digital cash (#3, #4). Once the digital wallet had cash, the consumer could spend that cash at merchants who were willing to accept it (#5). The software would deduct the cash from the digital wallet and transfer it to the merchant. The merchant could then transfer the cash back to the bank to confirm that it had not been double spent (#6). The bank would then cancel the e-coins and credit the merchant's account at the bank (#7).

These early concepts were not market successes, proving too complicated for both consumers and merchants. Both DigiCash and First Virtual, another early pioneer in digital cash, no longer offer services in the form originally envisioned.

The growth of eBay, the online auction site, into one of the most frequently visited and most active e-commerce Web sites, created the demand for payment services that would allow millions of individuals to pay for items, as well as receive payments from customers. In addition, there was substantial market demand for a service that would allow people to send small amounts of money over the Web. Beginning in 1998, a

---

FIGURE 6.8   **DIGICASH: HOW FIRST GENERATION DIGITAL CASH WORKED**

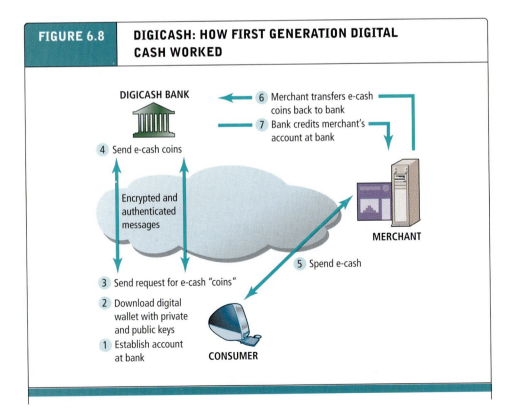

DIGICASH BANK

6 Merchant transfers e-cash coins back to bank

7 Bank credits merchant's account at bank

4 Send e-cash coins

Encrypted and authenticated messages

MERCHANT

5 Spend e-cash

3 Send request for e-cash "coins"

2 Download digital wallet with private and public keys

1 Establish account at bank

CONSUMER

number of P2P payment systems emerged, the most popular of which is PayPal, described at the beginning of the chapter. Other P2P payment systems include Yahoo's PayDirect, AOL's QuickCash, Western Union's MoneyZap, and Citibank's C2it.

As a form of cash, PayPal and the other P2P payments systems noted above have limitations. The systems require an intermediary and payments can be accepted only by people who have an e-mail account. Notwithstanding these limitations, PayPal and other forms of P2P payment have significant cash-like qualities that will make them successful over the longer term for small payments.

One variation on the digital cash concept is *gift cash*, which is a form of e-cash that is earned as "points." Two of the best known providers of gift cash, Beenz.com (which issued points as a reward for making a purchase) and Flooz.com (which could be purchased as a form of gift certificate), both ceased operations in August 2001. MyPoints.com, which issues points that can be redeemed for merchandise or gift certificates (but not cash) at partner sites in exchange for viewing ads or trying special offers, is still in business as of August 2001, however. MyPoints.com can be considered a gift cash provider, although the primary focus of its efforts is developing loyalty programs for clients rather than providing an online currency.

Online Stored Value Systems

online stored value payment systems

permit consumers to make instant, online payments to merchants and other individuals based on value stored in an online account

Online stored value payment systems permit consumers to make instant, online payments to merchants and other individuals based on value stored in an online account. Some stored value systems require the user to download a digital wallet (for example, Monetta's debit service and eCharge's prepaid service), whereas others require users to simply sign up and transfer money from their existing credit card accounts into an online stored value account. Online stored value systems rely on the value stored in a consumer's bank, checking, or credit card account. Table 6.4 describes some of the better known stored value systems. Ecount, for example, offers a prepaid debit account. Figure 6.9 illustrates how Ecount works. As shown in Figure 6.9, to use Ecount, a consumer must first establish an account with Ecount, funded by a credit or debit card. Account information is transferred via the Web using SSL (#1). Once Ecount has verified the account and its balance with the consumer's card issuing bank (#2), consumers can shop anywhere on the Web where MasterCard is accepted (Ecount is treated as if it were a MasterCard), and e-mail payments to individuals (recipients must sign up with Ecount to access the payment) (#3). Ecount immediately debits the consumer's account and transfers the funds to the merchant or individual (#4). At the end of the month, the consumer's card issuing bank sends a statement showing the debit to Ecount (#5). Real-time transaction history is available online directly from Ecount.

Rocketcash is another company that offers an online stored value system, in this case aimed at teenagers. Read *Insight on Business: Rocketcash.com* for a further look.

TABLE 6.4	ONLINE STORED VALUE SYSTEMS
NAME OF SYSTEM	**YEAR FOUNDED/DESCRIPTION**
Ecount	1998. Prepaid debit account.
Monetta Prepaid	2000. Prepaid virtual card that allows consumers to make online payments without using a credit card or bank account. Digital wallet.
Monetta Debit	2000. Account that allows users to pay from existing checking, savings, or line of credit accounts. Digital wallet.
eCharge	1997. Prepaid account with digital wallet.
Millicent	1998. Prepaid cards purchased at convenience stores (Japan only).
Smart Cards	
Mondex	1994. Smart card, stored value system in which value is stored on a chip on the card.
American Express Blue	1999. Combined credit and smart card.

FIGURE 6.9	HOW ECOUNT.COM WORKS: A STORED VALUE SYSTEM

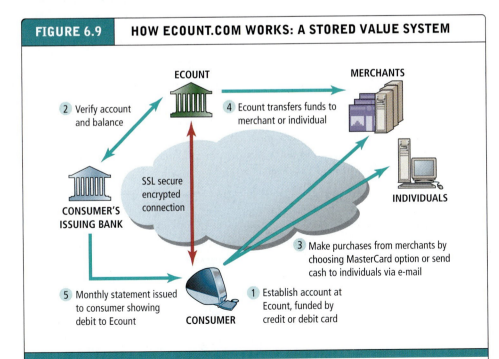

ECOUNT

MERCHANTS

2 Verify account and balance

4 Ecount transfers funds to merchant or individual

CONSUMER'S ISSUING BANK

SSL secure encrypted connection

INDIVIDUALS

3 Make purchases from merchants by choosing MasterCard option or send cash to individuals via e-mail

5 Monthly statement issued to consumer showing debit to Ecount

1 Establish account at Ecount, funded by credit or debit card

CONSUMER

Smart Cards as Stored Value Systems

smart card

a stored value system based on credit-card-sized plastic cards that have embedded chips that store personal information

Smart cards are another kind of stored value system based on credit-card-sized plastic cards that have embedded chips that store personal information. Whereas credit cards store a single charge account number in the magnetic strip on the back, smart cards can hold 100 times more data, including multiple credit card numbers and information regarding health insurance, transportation, personal identification, bank accounts, and loyalty programs, such as frequent flyer accounts. This capacity makes them an attractive alternative to carrying a dozen or so credit and ID cards in a physical wallet. Smart cards can also require a password, unlike credit cards, adding another layer of security.

There are actually two types of smart cards—*contact* and *contactless*—depending on the technology embedded. In order for contact cards to be read, they must be physically placed into a card reader, while contactless cards have an antenna built in that enables transmission of data without direct contact. A stored-value smart card, such as retail gift card purchased in a certain dollar value, is an example of a contact card because it must be swiped through a smart card reader in order for payment to be processed. A highway toll payment system such as EZPass is an example of a contactless smart card because the EZPass device in the card is read by a remote sensor, with the appropriate toll automatically deducted from the card at the end of the trip.

Smart card technology was initially developed by the French public telephone network as a convenient form of stored value and public telephone payment. They are not as prevalent in the United States because of the widespread adoption of credit cards.

The Mondex card is one of the original smart cards, invented in 1990 by NatWest Bank in England. The card contains a 20 mm square integrated circuit with an 8-bit CPU running at 10 MHz, with 512 K of RAM. Launched in 1994 as a commercial product, it is currently still on trial in Canada, the United States, the United Kingdom, and New Zealand. The card allows users to download cash from a bank account to the card via a Mondex-compatible telephone or a card reader attached to a PC, and spend large or small amounts. It can carry five different currencies simultaneously and can be accepted by merchants who have readers installed. Thus far, the card has not been a commercial success.

Interest in smart cards in the United States was rekindled somewhat in 1999 when American Express introduced its smart card American Express Blue. Blue is a combined credit card and smart card. American Express created a special Web site for Blue from which consumers can download a digital wallet and obtain special services such as free online bill payment, financial tools, entertainment content, and forthcoming event information. The digital wallet enables one-click shopping and automatic form completion. Physical world merchants can swipe the card at the point of sale, like any credit card. Users can also store their digital wallet on a chip located on

INSIGHT ON BUSINESS

ROCKETCASH.COM

The average teen spends somewhere between $85 and $100 a week on clothing, CDs, books, software, toys, and bedroom décor. And while most of that money has been spent in traditional retail outlets, new Web sites are trying to entice teens to spend more online. Part of the problem, however, is that most teens don't have regular access to a credit card — typically a necessity for online purchases.

Rocketcash.com is a site that enables teens to buy popular products online through an online account. Parents and teens can deposit money in a Rocketcash account, which functions like a credit card and allows the teen to buy products online at over 140 sites that accept rocketcash in payment.

As of early 2001, Rocketcash had signed up close to 500,000 customers — a small percentage of the estimated 35 million children and teens who are eager to spend. Jupiter Media Metrix believes this market segment will spend $1.3 billion online by 2002.

Kids like the freedom to buy whatever they want online without having to bug parents for a credit card and parents like giving their children the chance to learn fiscal responsibility within a controlled setting — teens can't spend more than is in their Rocketcash account.

Although the Rocketcash concept appears to serve an untapped market, competitors have either gone out of business (iCanBuy.com), or are struggling (DoughNet.com). This makes one wonder how Rocketcash will survive long term.

The site makes money from commissions of 5% to 15% on purchases at its merchant partner sites and earns additional fees for helping develop incentive programs that benefit the merchants. Once customers are signed up, the system seems to work. Its biggest challenge, however, is attracting new customers, so it has undertaken a new marketing partnership with soft drink Sprite in which 1 billion bottles will have caps imprinted with a code that can be redeemed for points worth between 20 cents and $1 at Rocketcash.

A new threat to Rocketcash, however, is major credit card companies that are debuting new stored value cards that work like phone cards with prepaid limits. Although they solve the credit card dilemma for teens wanting to shop online, they also give access to Web sites that parents might not approve of, such as porn sites. American Express and Visa are two companies that recently entered the fray, but more are expected. Can start-up Rocketcash hope to compete with the likes of these well-funded cards?

SOURCES: "Kids Get Freedom to Spend, But Parents Keep Control," by Marilyn Kennedy Melia, *Chicago Tribune*, February 20, 2001; "Where's My e-llowance," by Adam Bryant, *The Standard*, January 16, 2001; "Teenagers Fit Prime Consumer Profile for Online Retailers," by Joelle Tessler, *Knight Ridder Tribune Business News*, June 14, 2000.

the card. American Express gave away smart card readers for free. Using a card reader attached to their PCs, users can shop online in a secure, encrypted, and authenticated environment. American Express distributed more than 4 million cards to consumers. Offline merchants need to install readers in their stores to use the smart card features. Online merchants were required to develop new infrastructure that could accept information from consumer card readers. The cost to convert U.S. merchants from credit to American Express smart cards was estimated at $11 billion. Wal-Mart estimated it would take ten years to convert the point-of-purchase system used in its stores to read the cards (Branscum, 2001). As a result, American Express Blue is used currently primarily as a credit card; its smart card features are not widely used by consumers or merchants (Hansell, 2001).

DIGITAL ACCUMULATING BALANCE PAYMENT SYSTEMS

digital accumulating balance payment systems

allow users to make micropayments and purchases on the Web, accumulating a debit balance for which they are billed at the end of the month

Digital accumulating balance payment systems allow users to make micropayments and purchases on the Web, accumulating a debit balance for which they are billed at the end of the month. Like a utility or phone bill, consumers are expected to pay the entire balance at the end of the month using a checking or credit card account. Digital accumulating balance systems are ideal for purchasing intellectual property on the Web such as single music tracks, chapters of books, or articles from a newspaper. Table 6.5 lists some digital accumulating balance payment systems.

One of the most popular digital accumulating balance systems is qPass. qPass is an integrated platform for the marketing, sale, distribution, and transaction processing of digital content. It is the leading micropayment solution for media companies such as the *New York Times*, *Wall Street Journal*, and many other newspapers and journals that are seeking to convert their analog content into easily sold digital content, ranging in price from a few cents to thousands of dollars. Currently qPass has over 500,000 registered users.

To use qPass, users download a digital wallet that encrypts and authenticates their transactions. Thus, their transactions cannot be repudiated. Once the digital wallet is installed, users can purchase a wide variety of digital content at participating e-commerce sites. Consumers pay for this content by clicking a qPass icon at the site and authorizing the charge. At the end of the month, qPass bills the consumer's credit card or other account.

iPIN is a newer entrant to the micropayment accumulated balance marketspace. iPin provides its services either as an application service provider or as a merchant-owned solution (Johnson, 2000). With iPIN, merchants can choose the level of security and authentication they want, from simple login and password protection to digital wallet protection. iPIN relies on existing consumer billing services such as telephone utilities, ISPs, wireless service companies, and banks to invoice and collect consumer charges. The company's services become very competitive for purchases less than $20. It has been widely adopted at music sites that sell music tracks for 99 cents.

TABLE 6.5	DIGITAL ACCUMULATING BALANCE PAYMENT SYSTEMS
SYSTEM	**YEAR FOUNDED/DESCRIPTION**
qPass	1997. Integrated micropayment platform aimed at digital content providers. Digital wallet used.
iPIN	1997. Integrated payment platform with accumulated balance capability and flexible authentication procedures.
Millicent	1998. Compaq's platform optimized for buying and selling digital content. Users can fund accounts through ISP, telephone, or utility payments.

DIGITAL CREDIT CARD PAYMENT SYSTEMS

Digital credit card payment systems seek to extend the functionality of existing credit cards for use as online shopping payment tools. Even though many, if not all, of the new digital payment systems involve the use of the existing credit and checking payment infrastructure, digital credit card payment systems are focused specifically on making the use of credit cards safer and more convenient for both merchants and consumers. Digital credit card payment systems seek to address several limitations of online credit card payment for merchants including lack of authentication, repudiation of charges, and credit card fraud. Digital credit card systems also seek to address consumer fears about using credit cards such as having to reveal credit information at multiple sites and repeatedly having to communicate sensitive information over the Internet. They also seek to lower transaction costs by enabling automatic form completion. Table 6.6 lists some digital credit card payment systems.

digital credit card payment systems
seek to extend the functionality of existing credit cards for use as online shopping payment tools

TABLE 6.6	DIGITAL CREDIT CARD PAYMENT SYSTEMS
SYSTEM	**YEAR FOUNDED/DESCRIPTION**
eCharge Credit	1997. eCharge allows consumers to charge online payments to a credit card account. Digital wallet download required.
BillPoint Online Payments	1995/98. eBay, WellsFargo, and Visa's entry into P2P payment systems. BillPoint allows eBay sellers to accept credit card payments from buyers without having to have a merchant account. Does not require a digital wallet.

eCharge is a digital credit payment system that uses a client-based digital wallet. As shown in Figure 6.10, a consumer signs up for an eCharge account, passing personal and credit card account information to eCharge via an SSL secure encrypted connection (#1). After approving the consumer's application, eCharge downloads a digital wallet to the consumer's computer (#2). Consumers can then purchase online at participating merchants who accept eCharge by selecting the eCharge payment option (#3). eCharge then authenticates both the consumer and the merchant by verifying their digital certificates (#4), verifies the consumer's account and balance with the consumer's issuing bank (#5), and then authorizes the transaction. Consumers pay their bills electronically every month using an existing credit or debit account, any bank account, or eCharge Phone or any telephone company billing system (#6).

BillPoint is a digital credit card payment system that permits individuals and small merchants who use eBay to accept credit card payments without the expense of setting up a merchant server software or a merchant account with an issuing bank. In

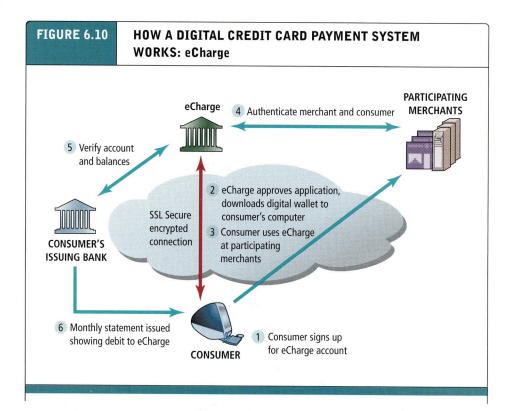

FIGURE 6.10 | **HOW A DIGITAL CREDIT CARD PAYMENT SYSTEM WORKS: eCharge**

essence, eBay and BillPoint become the merchant account bank and charge merchants credit card processing fees of 4.5% plus 75 cents per transaction. For consumers, BillPoint offers tracking of purchases, but still requires that they fill out credit information for every purchase.

American Express and Discover both offer a variation on traditional credit cards designed to allay consumers' fears about online credit card theft. Private Payments from American Express and deskshop from Discover Card both allow cardholders to create a "virtual" credit card based on a randomly generated account number linked to a real account number. The randomly generated number can be used only one time, so in effect it can never be stolen once it has been used. Thus far, however, consumers have not shown much interest in using these kinds of cards.

DIGITAL CHECKING PAYMENT SYSTEMS

The venerable check is not moving into retirement. On the contrary, checks are the fastest growing form of noncash payment: 65 billion checks were written in the United States in 2000, and the number is growing at about one billion a year—three times the growth rate in credit cards, debit cards, and other forms of electronic funds transfer (FSTC, 2001). Unfortunately, to process a check costs anywhere from $.75 to $3.00. The Federal Reserve Bank estimates that the cost to the U.S. economy each year is $44 billion. Checks are slow forms of payment and cumbersome, requiring an envelope and stamp to use. Digital checking payment systems offer some solutions.

Digital checking payment systems seek to extend the functionality of existing checking accounts for use as online shopping payment tools. You can think of them as extensions to the existing checking and banking infrastructure. Some of the simpler systems are used to electronically pay individuals and to settle accounts at online auction sites. More sophisticated systems are used by the Treasury Department to transfer billions of dollars electronically. Digital checking payment systems have many advantages: (1) they do not require consumers to reveal account information to other individuals when settling an auction, (2) they do not require consumers to continually send sensitive financial information over the Web, (3) they are less expensive than credit cards for merchants, and (4) they are much faster than paper-based traditional checking. Table 6.7 lists some of the more widely used digital checking payment systems.

One of the simplest digital checking systems is Achex. Achex is designed primarily as a P2P small payment mechanism for transferring funds among individuals. Users open an account at the Achex site and submit their traditional checking account number that they will use to pay checks. Once the account is verified, Achex subscribers can pay other individuals who have an e-mail address and a valid checking account into which they can transfer funds. Users access their Achex account using a

digital checking payment systems
seek to extend the functionality of existing checking accounts for use as online shopping payment tools

TABLE 6.7	DIGITAL CHECKING PAYMENT SYSTEMS
SYSTEM	**YEAR FOUNDED/DESCRIPTION**
eCheck	1998. Consortium of 15 banks, government agencies, and technology companies (Echeck.org.). Secure electronic checking system. Digital wallet required.
Achex Inc.	1999. Simple check-extension system. No digital wallet.
BillPoint Electronic Checks	2000. eBay, Wells Fargo entered into online digital checking for use at eBay only. No digital wallet.

login and password or PIN. Recipients receive an e-mail indicating that funds are available for transfer and requesting a valid checking account number to which the funds can be transferred. Achex transfers the funds to the recipient's checking account. The service is free to consumers, although merchants pay processing fees that are about half the price of credit card processing.

eCheck is a much more sophisticated system. A consortium of banks, government agencies, and technology companies began in 1996 to develop a plan for electronic checking that would use public key encryption and would not require a third party (such as Achex) to move funds. The goal was to replace paper checks altogether, and to extend electronic funds transfers that already exist among large institutions to all businesses and even consumers. Figure 6.11 illustrates how eCheck works.

As shown in Figure 6.11, eCheck requires users to obtain a hardware-based "electronic checkbook" from a traditional bank. The hardware could be a PCMCIA card, a standard PC card, or a specialized smart card reader external to the consumer's computer. The electronic checkbook contains the consumer's digital signature in the form of a private key. The electronic checkbook also contains the issuing bank's public key (#1). Using software provided with the checkbook, the consumer fills out an electronic check form and sends it to a merchant over the Internet (#2). The communication is encrypted and contains the consumer's digital signature, public key, and the issuing bank's digital signature. Upon receipt, the merchant authenticates the digital signatures of both the sender and the issuing bank using their respective public keys (#3A, #3B), and deposits the check at its bank (#4). A higher level certificate authority, such as the Federal Reserve Bank, certifies the issuing bank's public key (#5). eChecks can also contain invoice, remittance, and other information.

eChecks are currently being tested by the U.S. Department of the Treasury's Financial Management Service (FMS). FMS issues 857 million payments annually

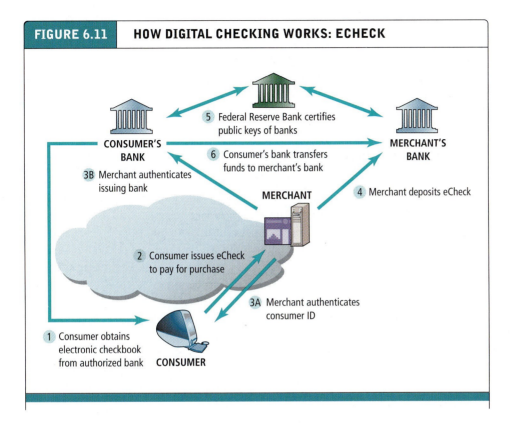

FIGURE 6.11   HOW DIGITAL CHECKING WORKS: ECHECK

5 Federal Reserve Bank certifies public keys of banks

CONSUMER'S BANK

MERCHANT'S BANK

6 Consumer's bank transfers funds to merchant's bank

3B Merchant authenticates issuing bank

4 Merchant deposits eCheck

MERCHANT

2 Consumer issues eCheck to pay for purchase

3A Merchant authenticates consumer ID

1 Consumer obtains electronic checkbook from authorized bank   CONSUMER

(about 494 million through electronic funds transfers and 363 million through paper checks), primarily to Social Security recipients and veterans.

eCheck is interesting because the electronic checkbook is a physical device. A physical device was chosen because it was thought to be more secure than creating accounts over the Internet. The device is portable and difficult to reverse engineer. Although intended to fit into the existing infrastructure of the checking system developed by the Federal Reserve and the commercial banks, eCheck itself requires significant investment in new infrastructure.

DIGITAL PAYMENT SYSTEMS AND THE WIRELESS WEB

Wireless device usage has exploded and is expected to continue as new products and services are introduced. From cellular phones to pagers and personal digital assistants (PDAs), wireless devices have spurred the creation of new Web sites to support them. One area in which there has been substantial interest is in financial services, including stock trading and money transfer. In fact, the number of people using wireless devices to transfer money is expected to climb from 4.6 million in 2001 to 60 million in 2004, according to Celent Communications (Trombly, 2001).

Insight on Technology: Do You Take Wireless? looks at some of the issues facing the development of digital payment systems that can be used on the wireless Web.

6.4 B2B PAYMENT SYSTEMS

Most of the payment systems we have discussed in this chapter are primarily used in B2C e-commerce. B2B payment systems pose special challenges and are much more complex than B2C payments, in large part because of the complexity involved in business purchasing. Sometimes a dozen or more documents may be needed to consummate the transaction, including a purchase order, invoice, bill of lading or shipping, insurance papers, financial documents, regulatory documents, credit verifications, escrow service documents (if any), authentication, letters of credit (foreign transactions), and payment methods or instruments. In addition, B2B payment systems must link into existing ERP (Enterprise Resource Planning) systems that integrate inventory, production, shipping, and other corporate data, and into EDI (Electronic Data Interchange) systems, which are systems that replace paper-based purchase orders with electronic equivalents. (We discuss EDI more fully in Chapter 12.) Table 6.8 describes some of the features of B2B payment systems.

The B2B payments market is actually much larger than the B2C market because of the larger size of transactions among businesses and the frequency of transactions. In the United States, most payments among companies are still handled by physical checks that are cleared through the Automated Clearing House (ACH) payments system operated by the Federal Reserve Bank. In a growing number of transactions, the settlement occurs through an electronic funds transfer. In Europe, physical checks are much less common, and in some countries, such as Holland, nearly all business payments are handled electronically within more tightly integrated national banking systems.

There are two main types of B2B payment systems that have risen to the challenge: systems that replace traditional banks and existing banking systems extending to the B2B marketplace. It is important to note that no system on the market today yet provides all of the features listed in Table 6.8 in one package.

Actrade is an example of an online B2B payment system that replaces the functionality provided traditionally by banks. Actrade serves as an international marketplace intermediary in the payment process by paying foreign sellers immediately and allowing domestic buyers a variable time period for repayment.

INSIGHT ON TECHNOLOGY

DO YOU TAKE WIRELESS?

Will your cell phone replace your credit card or change holder? Some analysts are predicting that within five years, it may, particularly for small payments of between $3 and $10.

Now that developers have had some experience creating "traditional" e-commerce payments systems, they are beginning to focus on the next frontier: m-commerce, and the technological building blocks needed to make wireless payments systems a reality.

In Europe, there are already a handful of phone-based transaction systems that have progressed beyond the pilot stage. For example, in London, you can buy Virgin Cola using a Virgin Mobile phone by simply dialing a number on the vending machine (the cost of the drink is simply charged to your cell phone account). In Germany, Brokat Technologies' mobile wallet (m-wallet) software allows users of Deutsche Telecom's wireless services to enter all their personal data just once, and then when they make purchases from vendors in the Deutsche Telecom network, the mobile wallet automatically fills in the blanks on the order form. In the United States, the development of technologies such as Bluetooth, a global standard for wireless connectivity, are also expected to help drive the movement. When two Bluetooth-equipped devices come within 30 feet of one another, they can establish a link, allowing you to point your phone at a vending machine or fast-food cash register and pay instantly.

As the history of the development of e-commerce payment shows, development of the technology is just the first step. There are many other necessary conditions before a payment system finds widespread acceptance.

First the technology must become widely available — as one analyst noted, "Bluetooth is like everything else — it needs ubiquity between devices and cash registers and phone. It needs to be almost universal."

Second, to become widely adopted, the technology needs the backing of most of the major stakeholders in payment systems — consumers, vendors, phone equipment manufacturers, wireless service providers, and financial industry participants. Another analyst points out: "Unless the banks and credit cards get behind a system like this and make it an adjunct of the services they are already offering, . . . it will be very difficult." At the Gartner Group, Mike McGuire notes that consumers won't be interested unless they can easily transfer funds from and to their bank and credit card accounts.

Some are looking to the wireless service providers to act as financial intermediaries, pointing out that cell phone users already have a billing relationship with them, and that those companies already have billing software in place to handle transactions. Others say, however, that cell phone carriers may be reluctant to become bankers — essentially what this model assumes — with all the associated administrative and technical overhead.

(continued)

Despite the existence of a number of common protocols such as WAP (Wireless Application Protocol), WTSL (Wireless Transport Security Layer, the wireless equivalent to SSL) and others that are supposed to smooth the way for development, getting all the players to agree on a common, secure platform for wireless e-commerce payment systems is likely to be very difficult.

SOURCES: "Paying for Stuff (Part Two): Out Micro, in Mini," by Adam Katz-Stone, *M-commerce Times*, April 30, 2001; "Paying for Stuff (Part One): Whip Out Your Mobile Wallet," by Adam Katz-Stone, *M-commerce Times*, April 4, 2001; "Dial Up a Soda," by Scott Spanbauer, *Business2.0*, December 21, 2000; "Mobile Heavyweights Vow Common Mobile E-commerce Framework," Internet.com, April 12, 2000.

TABLE 6.8	KEY FEATURES OF B2B PAYMENT SYSTEMS
FEATURE	**DESCRIPTION**
Credit verification and guarantee	Provides an assessment of creditworthiness and payment guarantee
Escrow service	Helps assure that both parties will perform their obligations
Nonrepudiation	Ensures that purchases are not reversible; allows unknown parties to trade with one another more confidently
Funds collection for seller	Handles funds transfer, transmittal, and storage
Financing	Provides "float" or variable payment delay to buyers in return for a fee
Integration with other business documents	Integrates purchase orders, invoices, shipping documents, and payments
Fraud detection	Helps seller trade more securely
Accounting	Provides account summary and invoice details
Dispute handling	Provides a method for adjudicating disputes
Integration to back-end corporate systems	Links payment systems with shipping, accounting, and other corporate systems
Online bill presentment	Has the ability to generate and present electronic bills
Multiple payment options	Ensures that buyers may pay with credit card, debit card, ACH check, electronic funds transfer, or other means

Actrade handles the credit risk for sellers by paying them immediately. The transactions are entirely digital and secured with digital certificates. Other competing B2B payment firms include TradeCard (handles procurement, fulfillment, risk management, and settlement), eRevenue, eFinance, and eCheck for handling small business transactions.

While traditional banks have been slow to enter this market, they now offer a wider variety of banking services entirely online. Orbian is a joint venture between Citigroup and SAP (the German enterprise software giant). Orbian offers financial credit instruments similar to Actrade, but also includes credit verification, nonrepudiation, financing, and integration with large-scale corporate back-end systems (provided by SAP). Another giant entrant is FinancialSettlementMatrix.com (FSM) formed by many large banks including Wells Fargo and Citigroup, plus technology companies such as i2 Technologies and S1. FSM is the only payment system that can work with multiple banks and offers letters of credit, escrow, international wire transfers, financing, and creditworthiness checks. For handling smaller transactions, traditional credit card companies such as MasterCard and American Express have developed "P-cards" or procurement cards. Currently limited to transactions of less than $2,500, some credit companies envisage P-card transactions up to $100,000. P-cards do not have purchase order or invoice tracking and therefore are not used for larger transactions.

ELECTRONIC BILLING PRESENTMENT AND PAYMENT

In the $9.2 trillion U.S. economy with a $6.7 trillion consumer sector, there are a lot of bills to pay. In fact, there are an estimated 30 billion monthly bills to be paid by over 200 million individual consumers and several million business establishments. No one knows for sure, but some experts believe the life-cycle cost of a bill for a business, from point of issuance to point of payment, ranges from $3 to $7. This calculation does not include the time value of consumers who must open bills, read them, write checks, address envelopes, stamp, and then mail remittances. Not including consumer costs, the overall societal cost for billing ranges conservatively from $360 to $840 billion, or from 4% to 8% of GDP. The billing market represents an extraordinary opportunity for using the Internet as an electronic billing and payment system that potentially could greatly reduce both the cost of paying bills and the time consumers spend paying them. As consumers increasingly go online, it is reasonable to believe they will want to use the Internet as a means of efficiently paying their bills.

Electronic billing presentment and payment (EBPP) systems are new forms of online payment systems for monthly bills. EBPP services allow consumers to view bills electronically and pay them through electronic funds transfers from bank or credit card accounts. More and more companies are choosing to issue statements and

electronic billing presentment and payment (EBPP) systems
new forms of online payment systems for monthly bills

bills electronically, rather than mailing out paper versions. But even those businesses that do mail paper bills are increasingly offering online bill payment as an option to customers, allowing them to immediately transfer funds from a bank account to pay a bill somewhere else. Although there were just three million households using online bill payment in 1999, analysts believe that figure will rise to 15 million by 2002 (Schwartz, 2000).

Although more than 90% of all EBPP takes place in B2C relationships, such payment systems are rapidly spreading to B2B commerce. Businesses in the United States currently generate approximately 12 billion bills for other businesses, costing an average of $3 to simply process and print the bill—versus just 33 cents to process and present an electronic version. The challenges involved in requesting and receiving electronic payment from customers are essentially the same for both consumers and businesses, except that business transactions generally involve larger amounts. Although start-up costs to implement an EBPP system can approach $100,000, the payback can be quick. One company—North Pittsburgh Telephone—estimates it will save 80% on billing after the up-front costs are taken care of. With such substantial

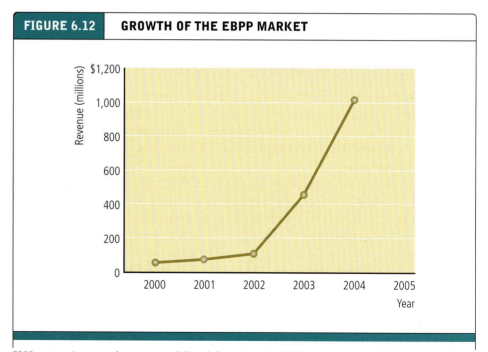

| FIGURE 6.12 | GROWTH OF THE EBPP MARKET |

EBPP revenue is expected to grow to a billion dollar industry by 2004.
SOURCE: Schwartz, 2000.

cost savings, B2B EBPP is expected to grow from 14% of B2B transaction value in 1999 to more than 60% by 2009 (Schwartz, 2000).

MARKET SIZE AND GROWTH

Paying bills electronically is expected to become a $1 billion market by 2004 according to market researchers at International Data Corp, although in 2000 it was just $59 million. See Figure 6.12 for a view of the growth of EBPP revenue.

One major reason for the surge in EBPP usage is that companies are starting to realize how much money they can save through online billing. Not only is there the savings in postage and processing, but payments can be received more quickly, thereby improving cash flow. Ferris Research estimates that companies can save anywhere from 10 cents to $1.50 per invoice by sending it using EBPP (Gaskin, 2000). The nation's utilities in particular could save $1.2 billion annually by switching to EBPP (Paul, 1999).

Growth in Internet usage, however, is the key driver, pushing many companies to explore online billing and payment. The more online users, the larger the market for EBPP.

Financials don't tell the whole story, however. Companies are discovering that a bill is a sales opportunity, and the electronic medium provides many more options when it comes to marketing and promotion. Rebates, savings offers, cross- and up-selling are all possible in the digital realm.

TYPES OF EBPP SYSTEMS

Although the concept of online billing and payment is simple, there are a number of competing business models in the marketspace. The most common is the biller-direct system, originally created by large utilities that send millions of bills each month. Their purpose is to make it easier for their customers to pay their utility and—increasingly—other bills routinely online. Telephone, utility, and credit card companies often offer this service, as well as a number of individual stores. Biller-direct systems often use a service bureau such as BillServ.com to provide the infrastructure necessary to implement the system. The second major type of EBPP is the consolidator model. Consolidators aggregate all bills for consumers and ideally permit one-stop bill payment (pay anyone). Portals are similar to consolidators but offer a variety of other financial management services as well. Figure 6.13 illustrates the major types of EBPP systems.

Companies can use EBPP to present bills to individual customers electronically, or contract with a service to handle all the billing and payment collection. Customers

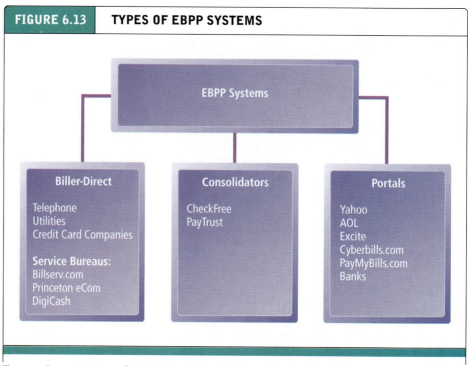

FIGURE 6.13 | **TYPES OF EBPP SYSTEMS**

There are three major types of EBPP systems: biller-direct, consolidator, and portal.

can then choose to pay the bill directly, use a bill consolidator to collect bills for them, or hire a payment service to collect and pay bills as directed by the customer. BlueGill Technologies is a direct billing company that allows customers to visit the Web site to review and pay a bill. CheckFree is a consolidator that will collect and present bills from multiple sources, so that the customer only has to log into one site to pay several bills at once. CyberBills works much like CheckFree, but is different in that invoices are sent from billers to the service, rather than to the consumer directly. And MessagingDirect issues e-mail invoices and payments with a direct link to the biller's Web site, for easy payment.

The bill payment process involves the customer, the bank, and potentially a third-party processor. Customers can e-mail an e-check drawn on their bank account, and the funds will be transferred via e-mail to the vendor's bank account (this is similar to the e-checking systems described in the previous section).

In the competition for market dominance in the consumer EBPP market, some institutions are clearly advantaged. Utility companies, Web portals, and traditional banks already have parts of the infrastructure required to build powerful EBPP systems. The strongest players are Web portals such as AOL and Yahoo. Through alliances with software service firms such as CheckFree and traditional banks, they are able to offer consumer bill payment and invoicing as part of a package of financial management services.

CheckFree—
On Top of Electronic Billing, For Now

Before there was an Internet there was CheckFree, an entrepreneurial firm started in 1981 by Peter Kight. Kight, a health club employee, started Check-Free in his mother's kitchen after thinking about how enrollment at his Nautilus health club might improve if a way could be found for patrons to easily pay their monthly bills. Kight began to build an electronic system in which patrons didn't even see their bills. Working with banks and the Automated Clearing House (ACH) that clears interbank transfers, Kight arranged for patrons to have their monthly health club bills automatically paid through the existing ACH electronic funds transfer system every month. Such automatic bill payment systems of the pre-Internet era became the foundation for an entire e-commerce industry: electronic bill presentation and payment (EBPP).

Flash forward twenty years to 2001: CheckFree is the market leader of online billing and payment with 5.2 million online subscribers, over 300 Internet sites offering CheckFree-based services, and 156 companies using CheckFree to present bills to their customers over the Internet. CheckFree is in three businesses: online billing and payment, investment services, and software services. Forty of the top fifty banks in the United States use CheckFree software to handle electronic billing services for their customers. CheckFree went on a tear in 2000 and 2001, buying up competitors and others offering complementary technology and relationships, and striking new strategic relationships with financial institutions. In the past few months, CheckFree has bought BlueGill Technologies (a specialist Internet billing company) and its largest competitor TransPoint (a joint venture of Microsoft and First Data Corporation) and has struck strategic relationships with Bank of America (BoA bought 16% of CheckFree, giving CheckFree access to 2.1 million online banking customers) and Wells Fargo (CheckFree is building Wells Fargo's electronic payment system).

The vision for EBPP (for consumers and bill consolidators such as CheckFree) is that consumers will be able to visit a single Web site, see all of their routine bills presented, and pay all of these bills, using any of several different payment methods, regardless of any other banking relationship they may have. And, of course, if the consumer wants more detail on a specific bill, simply clicking on the item will bring up all the relevant background data on any given purchase. Moreover, the site will keep a database of all bills, payments, and details for an indeterminate time. Currently, EBPP is far from achieving this ideal, and it is unclear just how long it will take to get there. CheckFree can present consumers with some of their bills, but it has been unable to consolidate all routine bills into a single site.

Although CheckFree dominates the industry of electronic bill payment, the industry itself is changing very fast and its leadership is precarious. Consumers have resisted online bill payment for more than twenty years. Even though the benefits to billers are clear—billing costs can decline by as much as 50%—consumers are charged $4 per month to use CheckFree, and banks charge $5 to $8 a month to pay bills online. A Gartner study found that 50% of Internet users do not want to use the Internet for bill payment. There are 90 million banking households, but only 3 million do any kind of online banking in 2001 according to the American Banking Association.

Online bill presentation has been delayed indefinitely because of conflicting strategic goals of merchants, banks, credit card companies, and billing firms such as CheckFree. Currently, consumers cannot go to a single Web site and find a listing of all the bills they need to pay, along with complete transaction detail. CheckFree can provide this for just a small portion of a consumer's bills (generally utility bills).

Merchants are opposed to consolidators such as CheckFree because they want to be "direct billers." Merchants such as Saks Fifth Avenue or Sears want customers to come to their Web sites to pay their merchant-specific bills. While visiting, they can be sold other services and products. Banks want customers to use bank Web sites for bill payment as a part of the financial services package they offer. Likewise with credit card companies: They have scaled up to handle upwards of thirty million customers with detailed credit card statements, and they can relatively easily broaden their offerings to include presenting bills from other merchants as well. Of course, EBPP firms want consumers to come to their single dedicated EBPP sites so they can charge hefty fees for the privilege.

While the EBPP industry participants work out their differences, technology changes. CheckFree uses proprietary technology for its software and builds custom linkages between its bill presentation software and the merchant's back-end legacy systems that keep track of consumers' detailed transaction data. But new competitors have entered the marketspace using XML-based solutions built on open Web standards. These open systems can be purchased for much lower costs than CheckFree's software, and can be easily integrated into the merchant's existing transaction systems. For instance, Princeton's eCom EBPP software is available on an application service provider (ASP) basis for $20,000 to $30,000 compared to CheckFree's price of millions of dollars for a merchant or banking EBPP system. In other words, prices for this software are falling, threatening CheckFree's margins and cash flow.

CheckFree's dominance is also threatened by new entrants to the market. In the last year, a number of alternative forms of digital payment have emerged—from eCheck to BillPoint and PayPal. The growth of these new payment services is astounding: PayPal gained one million customers in its first six months. It took CheckFree six

SOURCES: "CheckFree Loss Widens, Subscriber Numbers Up," *Reuters*, August 14, 2001; "E-Commerce Report: Online Billing" by Bob Tedeschi, *New York Times*, June 4, 2001; CheckFree Corp. Report on 10-K for the fiscal year ended June 30, 2000 filed with the Securities Exchange Commission on September 26, 2000; "EBPP Vendors Jockey for Big Payoff" by Jeetu Patel and Joe Fenner, *Network Computing*, September 18, 2000; "The Check's (Still) in the Mail" by Loren Fox, *Business 2.0*, August 22, 2000; "CheckFree Rules the World of Online Bill Paying" by Rivka Tadjer, *InformationWeek*, May 8, 2000.

years to attract one million customers. Once customers are accustomed to PayPal's easy-to-use interface, they can be introduced to additional services such as bill presentation.

Yet the potential market size for EBPP and electronic banking is huge. Although currently only 3 million households (3% of banking households) bank online in 2001, this is expected to grow to over 50 million by 2005. Gartner estimates that in 2005 fully 25 million consumers will want to pay all their bills online. How to capture the potential value in this marketspace remains open to question, however.

Case Study Questions

1. What business challenges does CheckFree face as it attempts to maintain its dominance in the EBPP market? Who are its main competitors?

2. What new technologies are posing a threat to CheckFree's leadership?

3. What social factors can you identify that might either inhibit or encourage use of CheckFree's services?

6.6 REVIEW

KEY CONCEPTS

■ **Describe the features of traditional payment systems.**

Traditional payment systems include:
- *Cash*, whose key feature is that it is instantly convertible into other forms of value without the intermediation of any other institution.
- *Checking transfers*, which are funds transferred directly through a signed draft or check from a consumer's checking account to a merchant or other individual; these are the second most common form of payment.
- *Credit card accounts*, which are accounts that extend credit to a consumer and allow consumers to make payments to multiple vendors at one time.
- *Stored value systems*, which are created by depositing funds into an account and from which funds are paid out or are withdrawn as needed. Stored value payments systems include debit cards, phone cards, and smart cards.
- *Accumulating balance systems*, which accumulate expenditures and to which consumers make periodic payments.

■ **Discuss the current limitations of online credit card payment systems.**

The most pervasive limitations involve:
- *Security*. Neither the merchant nor the consumer is authenticated. The existing system offers very poor security. The merchant could be a criminal organization designed to collect credit card numbers, and the consumer could be using stolen or fraudulent cards.
- *Merchant risk*. The risk facing merchants is high—consumers can repudiate charges even though the goods have been shipped or the product downloaded.
- *Cost*. Costs for merchants are also significant—roughly 3.5% of the purchase plus a transaction fee of 20 to 30 cents per transaction, plus other set-up fees. The high costs make it undesirable to sell goods on the Web for less than $10.
- *Social equity*. Not everyone has access to credit cards; millions of young people between the ages of 10 and 25 years of age do not have credit cards, along with 70 to 100 million other adult Americans who cannot afford cards or who are considered poor risks because of low incomes.

■ **Understand the features and functionality of digital wallets.**

The most important functions of a digital wallet are to:
- secure the payment process from the consumer to the merchant,
- authenticate the consumer through the use of digital signatures, and
- store and transfer value from the consumer to the merchant.

The major advantages of digital wallets are:
- Convenience for the consumer and lower transactions costs because order entry can be sped up.

- Reduction of risk of fraud and the use of stolen credit cards.
- Lower transaction costs, expanded marketing and branding opportunities, easier customer retention, and smoother conversion of visitors into buyers for merchants.

■ **Describe the features and functionality of the major types of digital payment systems in the B2C arena.**

The major types of digital payment systems include:

- *Digital cash*, which as currently available, provides a form of value storage and value exchange that has limited convertibility into other forms of value and requires intermediaries to convert. The idea of digital cash is to provide consumers with the ability to conveniently and safely pay other consumers or institutions for smaller purchases, generally under $200. While many of the early examples of digital cash have failed, many of the ideas have survived today as a part of P2P (peer-to-peer) payment systems.
- *Online stored value systems*, which permit consumers to make instant, online payments to merchants and other individuals based on value stored in an online account. Some stored value systems require the user to download a digital wallet, while others require users to simply sign up and transfer money from their existing credit card accounts into an online stored value account.
- *Digital accumulating balance systems*, which allow users to make purchases on the Web, accumulating a debit balance for which they are billed at the end of the month; consumers are then expected to pay the entire balance using a checking or credit card account. Accumulating balance systems are ideal for purchasing intellectual property on the Web such as single music tracks, chapters of books, or articles from a newspaper.
- *Digital credit card payment systems*, which seek to address the limitations of online credit card payment for merchants such as lack of authentication, repudiation of charges, and credit card fraud, as well as allaying consumer fears about using credit cards (repeatedly revealing credit information at multiple sites, and repeatedly communicating sensitive information over the Internet) and lowering transaction costs by enabling automatic form completion.
- *Digital checking payment systems*, which are extensions to the existing checking and banking infrastructure. Advantages include that they do not require consumers to reveal account information to other individuals when settling an auction, they do not require consumers to continually send sensitive financial information over the Web, they are less expensive than credit cards for merchants, and they are much faster than paper-based traditional checking.

■ **Describe the features and functionality of the major types of digital payment systems in the B2B arena.**

The key features required for B2B payment systems include:

- *Credit verification and guarantee*: provides an assessment of the buyer's credit worthiness and payment guarantee.

- *Escrow service*: helps assure both parties that the other will perform their obligations.
- *Non-repudiation*: ensures that purchases are not reversible, allowing unknown parties to trade with one another more confidently.
- *Funds collection*: provides a mechanism for funds transfer, transmittal, and storage.
- *Financing*: provides float to buyers in return for a fee.
- *Integration with other business documents*: allows payments to be integrated with purchase orders, invoices, and shipping documents.
- *Fraud detection*: enables sellers to trade more securely.
- *Accounting*: provides account summary and invoice details.
- *Dispute handling*: provides a method for dealing with disputes.
- *Integration with back-end corporate systems*: links payment systems to shipping, accounting, and other corporate systems.
- *Online bill presentment*: can generate and present electronic bills.
- *Multiple payment options*: allows purchasers to choose from among a variety of payment options.

To date, two main types of B2B payment systems have developed:
- Systems that replace the functionality traditionally provided by banks.
- Existing banking systems extending to the B2B marketplace.

No system on the market today yet provides all of the features listed above in one package.

■ Describe the features and functionality of electronic billing presentment and payment systems.

Electronic billing presentment and payment (EBPP) systems are a new form of online payment systems for monthly bills. EBPP services allow consumers to view bills electronically and pay them through electronic funds transfers from bank or credit card accounts. Major types of EBPP systems include:
- *Biller-direct systems*, which were originally created by large utilities to facilitate routine payment of utility bills, but which are increasingly being used by other billers.
- *Consolidators*, which attempt to aggregate all bills for consumers in one place and ideally permit one-stop bill payment.
- *Portals*, which are similar to consolidators, but which also typically offer a variety of other financial management services as well.

QUESTIONS

1. How do the interests of the four major payment systems stakeholders impact each other?
2. Which of these stakeholders currently carries the most risk in online payment transactions?

3. Compare and contrast stored value payment systems and checking transfers.
4. Why is a credit card not considered an accumulating balance payment system?
5. Name six advantages and six disadvantages of using cash as a form of payment.
6. Describe the relationship between credit card associations and issuing banks.
7. What is Regulation Z, and how does it protect the consumer?
8. Briefly discuss the disadvantages of credit cards as the standard for online payments. How does requiring a credit card for payment discriminate against some consumers?
9. Describe the major steps involved in an online credit card transaction.
10. What are the primary differences between the SSL (Secure Sockets Layer) protocol and the SET (Secure Electronic Transaction) protocol?
11. Name the most important functions of a digital wallet. What are the major advantages a digital wallet provides?
12. How are client-based and server-based digital wallets different? Why have server-based digital wallets been more successful at being adopted?
13. Describe PayPal's business model. Why has it become such a success when other forms of digital cash have failed? What are the main drivers of that success?
14. Compare and contrast smart cards and traditional credit cards.
15. What are the advantages of digital checking payment systems over traditional checking accounts? Name one major digital checking system.
16. How is money transferred in transactions using wireless devices?
17. Name two of the conditions that must be present in order for a payment system to become widely accepted.
18. Discuss why EBPP systems are becoming increasingly popular both in the B2C and B2B sectors.
19. How are the three types of EBPP systems both alike and different from each other?

PROJECTS

1. Prepare an overhead presentation that compares two online payment companies: Visa Buxx (www.visabuxx.com) and Rocketcash (www.rocketcash.com). How do they operate? What are the advantages and disadvantages of each? Which do you think is more popular and why?

2. Research the challenges associated with payments across international borders and prepare a brief presentation of your findings. Do most e-commerce companies conduct business internationally? How do they protect themselves from repudiation? How do exchange rates impact online purchases? What about shipping charges? Summarize by describing the differences between a U.S. customer and an international customer who each make a purchase from a U.S. e-commerce merchant.

3. Choose a digital payment system described in this chapter and prepare a table similar to that shown in Table 6.1 identifying the attributes of the system.

WEB SITE RESOURCES www.LearnE-commerce.net

- News: Weekly updates on topics relevant to the material in this chapter
- Video: Lecture: Professor Ken Laudon summarizes the key concepts of the chapter
- Research: Abstracts and links to articles referenced in the chapter, as well as other relevant research
- International Spotlight: More information about e-commerce payment systems outside the United States
- PowerPoint slides: Illustrations from the chapter and more
- Additional projects and exercises

Business Concepts and Social Issues

CHAPTER 7

E-commerce Marketing Concepts

MyPoints.com
Loyalty and Brands

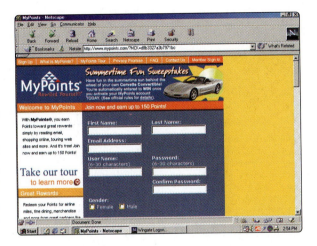

People who enjoy getting something for free love MyPoints.com, an online reward program and affiliate marketer. Registered members of MyPoints earn points for visiting and shopping at partner Web sites, reading and responding to targeted e-mail offers, and taking surveys. Those points can then be redeemed for free gift certificates or specific goods and services at more than 70 brand name companies, including Target, Macy's, Blockbuster, Carnival Cruises, and Barnes & Noble.

MyPoints affiliates, or partners, gain access to the company's 16 million-member database, enabling them to target offers to particular market segments or demographic groups. MyPoints claims it can deliver a targeted offer with a reward attached to a base of consumers very likely to respond, potentially driving hundreds of thousands of users to an affiliate's site in a matter of days. Once potential customers are at the site, partners can then hopefully make a sale. Companies pay MyPoints on a per click-through basis and/or a percentage of resulting purchases.

Are referrals from an incentive program site such as MyPoints the best way for e-commerce companies to market their products and services? Do such sites really build loyalty to a specific brand, which, as you will learn in this chapter, is what marketing is all about, or do they simply appeal to consumers who want to be rewarded for their actions? According to MyPoints, referred visitors have a much higher than average chance of returning to those partner sites when compared to visitors referred by other media. A Jupiter Media Metrix study indicates that they are as much as 50% more likely to return. The MyPoints referrals were also more loyal in the long run than visitors referred by other media.

MyPoints does allow companies to quickly begin building a relationship with a large customer base. For companies without established brands, rewards programs such as MyPoints can help create awareness and build critical mass. Rewards can entice consumers to gamble on an unknown product, which lets the company gather information on its prospective audience.

Another question has to do with the nature of the audience attracted by MyPoints. Consumers interested in free offers can probably be characterized as price-sensitive. In the E-commerce II era, with more emphasis on profits and premium pricing, the idea of attracting millions of price-sensitive shoppers to a site may not lead to a profitable outcome. In the E-commerce II period, one challenge for Internet marketing companies such as MyPoints may be how to attract millions of visitors willing to pay premium prices for added value.

MyPoints faces other challenges. Large corporations such as Wal-Mart, Sears, JC Penney, airlines, and others increasingly want to develop and control their own reward and loyalty programs at their own Web sites. For these companies, MyPoints has private-labeled its infrastructure technology — the Digital Loyalty Engine — and licensed or sold it to power other customer reward and loyalty programs at leading Internet sites, including About.com and ZDNet.

Perhaps the biggest challenge for MyPoints has been to remain afloat itself. MyPoints went public during the heyday of E-commerce I, successfully raising over $140 million. Its stock reached a high near $100 per share before plummeting to less than a dollar in early 2001. In June 2001, MyPoints agreed to be acquired by the investment arm of United Airlines, which intends to continue running the company as a separate subsidiary. United hopes to use MyPoints technology to better communicate special offers, upgrades, and fares to its customers through the airline's united.com and Mileage Plus program as well as to reach out to new customers.

SOURCES: "UAL Corp. Unit to Acquire Mypoints.com," *Reuters*, June 4, 2001; "Incentive Sites: Love Them or Leave Them," by Shawn Collins, adsGuide.com, May 18, 2001; "Loyalty Marketing: Loyal to What?" by Matthew Kinsman, *Promo*, July 2000; "Media Metrix Study Finds MyPoints.com Drives Higher Quality Traffic as Members Display More Loyalty to Client Sites," *PR Newswire*, May 21, 2000; "Rewards Bonanza," by Dennis Callaghan, *MC Technology Marketing Intelligence*, May 2000; "Money Magazine Names MyPoints Web's No. 1 Loyalty Program," *PR Newswire*, January 31, 2000.

Rewards and loyalty programs such as the one offered by MyPoints are certainly not new: S & H Green Stamps, frequent flier programs, and supermarket frequent shopper cards are all examples of these kinds of marketing programs, which aim to establish a relationship with a customer and encourage the customer to purchase goods by rewarding them with extra bene-fits. On the Internet, however, a rewards/loyalty program can scale to hundreds of millions of users at very low cost, and the impact of the program (from the cus-tomer's visit to a site such as MyPoints.com to view an advertisement, all the way through the purchase of a product at a partner site) can be precisely tracked and evaluated dynamically, in real time, using the Internet technologies described in previous chapters. The number of "points" given, the price of the product, and the messages delivered in ads can all be adjusted and optimized dynamically. Even better, from a consumer's point of view, points can be redeemed quickly from the comfort of one's home.

In the next two chapters, we will discuss avenues for marketing and adver-tising on the Internet. This chapter focuses on the basic marketing concepts you will need to understand and evaluate e-commerce marketing programs. Here we will examine consumer behavior on the Web, brands, the unique features of elec-tronic markets, and special technologies that support the new kinds of branding activities. Chapter 8 discusses e-commerce marketing communications, such as advertising and other tools.

7.1 CONSUMERS ONLINE: THE INTERNET AUDIENCE AND CONSUMER BEHAVIOR

Before firms can begin to sell their products online, they first must understand what kinds of people they will find online and how those people behave in the online mar-ketplace. In this section, we will be focusing primarily on individual consumers in the B2C arena. However, many of the factors discussed apply to the B2B arena as well, insofar as purchasing decisions by firms are made by individuals.

THE INTERNET AUDIENCE

We will start with an analysis of some basic background demographics of Web con-sumers in the United States. The first principle of marketing and sales is to "know thy customer." Who uses the Web, who shops, and what do they buy?

INTERNET TRAFFIC PATTERNS: THE ONLINE CONSUMER PROFILE

At mid-year 2001, around 170 million people (almost 60% of the total population) in United States had access to the Internet. This number is expected to grow to around 215 million users by 2005 (Nielsen/Net Ratings, 2001; Computer Industry Almanac,

2001). That corresponds to an online market penetration rate of around 75% by 2005. By comparison, 98% of all U.S. households currently have televisions and 94% have telephones (Rainie and Packel, 2001).

Although the number of new online users has been increasing at a double-digit rate over the last several years, this growth rate is slowing. Because of the cost and complexity of computer use required for Internet access, it is unlikely that Internet use will equal that of television or radio use in the near future, although this may change as computers become less expensive and complex. Nevertheless, e-commerce businesses can no longer count on an annual 50% growth rate in the online population to fuel their revenues. The days of extremely rapid growth in the U.S. Internet population are over.

Intensity of Usage

The slowing rate of growth in the U.S. Internet population is compensated for in part by an increasing intensity and scope of use. Several studies show that a greater amount of time is being spent online by Internet users. Overall, users are going online more frequently, with 56% of adult users in the United States logging on in a typical day. The more time users spend online, becoming more comfortable and familiar with Internet features and services, the more services they are likely to explore, according the Pew Report. Table 7.1 illustrates this trend over a six-month period in 2000. In each category, the frequency of daily use increased.

Scope of Use

People who go online are engaging in a wide set of activities. While e-mail remains the most-used Internet service, other popular activities include using search engines, researching products and services, sending greeting cards, catching up on news, gathering hobby-related information, seeking health information, conducting work-

TABLE 7.1	FREQUENCY OF DAILY USE OF VARIOUS INTERNET FEATURES	
	MAY–JUNE 2000	NOV.–DEC. 2000
Go online	52%	56%
Use e-mail	44%	49%
Browse for fun	18%	23%
Get news	18%	22%

SOURCE: Rainie and Packel, 2001

related research, and reviewing financial information (Jupiter Media Metrix, 2000a; Rainie and Packel, 2001). Table 7.2 illustrates the wide range of activities Internet users engage in when going online.

Demographics and Access

Some demographic groups have much higher percentages of online usage than other groups. Table 7.3 summarizes some of the major intergroup differences and their pace of change. All groups increased their use of the Internet over the period surveyed, although some groups increased their participation at a greater rate.

TABLE 7.2	A GROWING RANGE OF ONLINE ACTIVITIES		
E-mail	93%	Viewed job classifieds	26%
Used search engine	79%	Played board, card, or trivia games	26%
Researched products and services	78%	Visited TV program sites	24%
Viewed local content	59%	Visited sports sites	24%
Sent electronic greeting/post cards	57%	Viewed car classifieds	21%
Entered contests or sweepstakes	57%	Did homework/research for school	20%
Sent instant message	50%	Downloaded music	19%
Read daily news	49%	Viewed video online	18%
Consulted online directory	49%	Viewed real estate classifieds	18%
Downloaded free software	49%	Viewed adult entertainment	18%
Visited health sites	48%	Visited movie sites	16%
Did travel research	43%	Visited movie information sites	16%
Chatted online	35%	Paid a bill online	15%
Checked stocks and quotes	34%	Personalized a Web site	15%
Visited music sites	32%	Obtained investment/financial news or advice	15%
Obtained online coupons	31%	Read magazines online	14%
Visited newspaper Web site	31%	Created own Web page	13%
Did work research	31%	Posted classified ads	10%
Visited message boards	31%	Made voice-to-voice call over the Internet	10%
Listened to audio online	29%	Performed stock market trade	9%
Engaged in online banking	28%	Used online dating service/personal ads	7%
Played action, fantasy games	27%	Gambled online	4%
Viewed personal web pages	27%		

The scope of Internet usage measured by the number of online activities is growing rapidly.
SOURCE: Jupiter Media Metrix, 2001a; Jupiter Media Metrix, 2000a.

TABLE 7.3	CHANGING DEMOGRAPHIC DIFFERENCES IN INTERNET ACCESS	
The percent of each group online:		
	MAY–JUNE	NOV.–DEC.
All adults	47%	56%
Men	50%	58%
Women	45%	54%
Whites	49%	57%
Blacks	35%	43%
Hispanics	40%	47%
Parents of children under 18	55%	66%
Non-parents	43%	50%
Age cohorts		
18–29	61%	75%
30–49	57%	65%
50–64	41%	51%
65+	12%	15%
Income brackets		
Under $30,000	28%	38%
$30,000–$50,000	60%	64%
$50,000–$75,000	67%	72%
$75,000+	79%	82%
Educational attainment		
High school or less	28%	39%
Some college	62%	71%
College degree or more	76%	82%

SOURCE: Rainie and Packel, 2001.

The demographic profile of the Internet — and e-commerce — has changed greatly since 1995. Up until 1999, single, white, young, college-educated males with high incomes dominated the Internet. In recent years, there has been a marked increase in Internet usage by females, minorities, and families with modest incomes.

As can be seen in Table 7.3, 82% of households with income levels above $75,000 have Internet access compared to only 38% of households earning less than $30,000. However, those with lower earnings are rapidly gaining Internet access, with the under-$30,000 income segment improving from 28% to 38% online penetration in less than a year.

Teens and college students also comprise a larger share of the online audience, representing 23% of all online users but only 14% of the total U.S. population. Of the 12-to-17-year-old age group, 73% have Internet access, with 29% of those under age 12 having been online. This segment is also growing dramatically, in part due to increased access to computers and the Internet both at school and at home.

At the other end of the age spectrum, only 15% of the adults aged 65 and over have Internet access, compared with 51% for ages 50 to 64, and 75% for those aged 18 to 29. One of the biggest increases in the last year was observed in the 50-to-64- age group, which improved from 41% online usage to 51%, suggesting that more seniors are beginning to explore the Internet (Rainie and Packel, 2001).

Ethnicity

Variation across ethnic groups is not as wide as across age groups. Whites have the highest Internet usage rates, with 57%, but Hispanics have 47% and African Americans have 43%. The growth rates for Hispanics and African Americans was more than 17% and 22%, respectively, resulting in substantial gains for these demographic segments.

Education

Amount of education also seems to make a difference when it comes to online access. Of those individuals with a high school education or less, only 39% were online as of year-end 2000, compared to 82% of individuals with a college degree or more. Even some college education boosted Internet usage, with that segment reaching 71% penetration.

Gender

Finally, although men accounted for the majority of Internet users just a few short years ago, women have caught up and now outnumber men online. Of American adults with Internet access, 50.6% are women and 49.4% are men. Women are also almost as likely to use the Internet on a daily basis as men are.

Lifestyle Impacts

There are some worrisome impacts to intensive Internet use. The Internet may be causing a decline in traditional social activities — such as talking with neighbors and family members. It may be encouraging users to spend less time with family and friends, and more time working, whether at home or at the office. According to a study performed at Stanford University by a group of political scientists, Internet users lose touch with those around them; individuals spending just two to five hours a week online spend far less time talking with friends and family face-to-face and on the phone. Users who spend up to five hours a week online frequently experience an increase in time spent working while at home, while those who spend more than five hours a week online find themselves working more at work as well; the Internet is taking up a larger portion of what used to be free time for some workers. On the other hand, e-mail, instant messaging and chat groups, all decidedly social activities, albeit not face-to-face ones, are among the most popular uses of the Internet. While Internet use involves a single user sitting in front of a screen — much like television — it is very different from television because of the high levels of social interaction possible on the Internet. The impact on children is also worrisome and needs more research. Insofar as Internet use deters children from face-to-face interaction or from undirected "play" out of doors, undesirable effects on child social development may result (Nie and Erbring, 2000).

Media Choices

What may be of even more interest to marketers, however, is that the more time individuals spend using the Internet, "the more they turn their back on traditional media," according to the Stanford study. For every additional hour users spend online, they reduce their corresponding time spent with traditional media, such as TV, newspapers, and radio. Traditional media are competing with the Internet for consumer attention and so far, the Internet appears to be gaining.

CONSUMER BEHAVIOR MODELS

consumer behavior
a social science discipline that attempts to model and understand the behavior of humans in a marketplace

Once firms have an understanding of who is online, they need to focus on how consumers behave online. The study of **consumer behavior** is a social science discipline that attempts to model and understand the behavior of humans in a marketplace. Several social science disciplines play roles in this study, including sociology, psychology, and economics. Models of consumer behavior attempt to predict or "explain" what consumers purchase and where, when, how much, and why they buy. The expectation is that if the consumer decision-making process can be understood, firms will have a much better idea how to market and sell their products. Figure 7.1 illustrates a general consumer behavior model that takes into account a wide range of factors that influence a consumer's marketplace decisions.

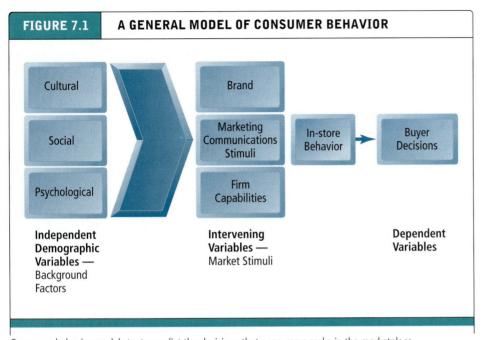

FIGURE 7.1   **A GENERAL MODEL OF CONSUMER BEHAVIOR**

Consumer behavior models try to predict the decisions that consumers make in the marketplace.
SOURCE: Adapted from Kotler and Armstrong, 2001.

Consumer behavior models seek to predict the wide range of decisions that consumers make on the basis of background demographic factors, and on a set of intervening, more immediate variables that shape the consumer's ultimate decisions.

Background factors are cultural, social, and psychological in nature. Firms must recognize and understand the behavioral significance of these background factors and adjust their marketing efforts accordingly. **Culture** is the broadest factor in consumer behavior because it shapes basic human values, wants, perceptions, and behaviors. Culture creates basic expectations that consumers bring to the marketplace such as what should be bought in different markets, how things should be bought, and how things should be paid for. Generally, culture affects an entire nation, and takes on major significance in international marketing. For instance, an American-style e-commerce site that sells cooking spices might have difficulty in a culture such as China or Japan, where food and spice shopping takes place at local neighborhood markets, large food stores do not exist, and shoppers tend to pick out and smell each spice before purchasing it.

Within nations, subcultures are extremely important in consumer behavior. **Subcultures** are subsets of cultures that form around major social differences such as

culture
shapes basic human values, wants, perceptions, and behaviors

subcultures
subset of cultures that form around major social differences

ethnicity, age, lifestyle, and geography. In the United States, ethnicity plays a very large role in consumer behavior. There are 31 million African Americans with a total annual purchasing power of $218 billion; 28 million Hispanics with a total purchasing power of $228 billion; and 11 million Asian Americans with a total purchasing power of $320 billion. Each of these ethnic groups represents a significant market segment that firms can target. For instance, in December 2000, Fingerhut Companies, Inc., one of the nation's largest direct marketing and online retailers, launched a special catalog aimed at the Hispanic market, accompanied by a Spanish language Web site (Wellner, 2000).

Among the important social factors that shape consumer behavior are the many reference groups to which all consumers "belong," either as direct participating members, or as indirect members by affiliation, association, or aspiration. **Direct reference groups** include one's family, profession or occupation, religion, neighborhood, and schools. **Indirect reference groups** include one's life-cycle stage, social class, and lifestyle group (discussed later). For instance, the concept of community-based Web sites is based on the notion that people choose to be members of groups and subgroups that express and reflect their interests, such as the home-schooling community, personal health-related-issues communities, and recreational activity communities.

Within each of these reference groups, there are **opinion leaders** (or **viral influencers**, as they are termed by Jupiter Media Metrix), who because of their personality, skills, or other factors, influence the behavior of others (Jupiter Media Metrix, Inc., 2001a). Marketers seek out opinion leaders in their communications and promotional efforts because of their influence over other people. For instance, many Web sites include testimonials submitted by successful adopters of a product or service. Generally, those giving the testimonials are portrayed as opinion leaders — "smart people in the know." At Procter & Gamble's Web site, for example, testimonials come from "P&G Advisors," who are consumers who take an active interest in Procter & Gamble products.

A unique kind of reference group is a **lifestyle group**, which can be defined as an integrated pattern of activities (hobbies, sports, shopping likes and dislikes, social events typically attended), interests (food, fashion, family, recreation), and opinions (social issues, business, government).

Lifestyle group classification systems — of which there are several — attempt to create a classification scheme that captures a person's whole pattern of living, consuming, and acting. The theory is that once you understand a consumer's lifestyle, or the lifestyles typical of a group of people — such as college students, for instance, then you can design products and marketing messages that appeal specifically to that lifestyle group. Lifestyle classification then becomes another method of segmenting the market.

In addition to lifestyle classification, marketers are interested in a consumer's psychological profile. A **psychological profile** is a set of needs, drives, motivations,

direct reference groups
one's family, profession or occupation, religion, neighborhood, and schools

indirect reference groups
one's life-cycle stage, social class, and lifestyle group

opinion leaders (viral influencers)
influence the behavior of others through their personality, skills, or other factors

lifestyle group
an integrated pattern of activities, interests, and opinions

psychological profile
set of needs, drives, motivations, perceptions, and learned behaviors

perceptions, and learned behaviors — including attitudes and beliefs. Marketers attempt to appeal to psychological profiles through product design, product positioning, and marketing communications. For instance, many health e-commerce sites emphasize that they help consumers achieve a sense of control over their health destiny by providing them with information about diseases and treatments. This message is a powerful appeal to the needs of a wealthy, educated, professional, and technically advanced set of Web users for self-control and mastery over what might be a complex, health-threatening situation.

Marketers cannot influence demographic background factors, but they can adjust their branding, communications, and firm capabilities to appeal to demographic realities. For instance, the National Basketball Association's Web site, NBA.com, appeals to a variety of basketball fan subgroups from avid fans interested in specific team statistics, to fashion-conscious fans who can purchase clothing for specific NBA teams, to fans who want to auction memorabilia.

PSYCHOGRAPHIC PROFILES OF ONLINE CONSUMERS

While they are helpful, baseline demographics do not give a very detailed picture or understanding of the "typical" e-commerce consumer. A **psychographic profile** combines both demographic and psychological data and divides a market into different groups based on social class, lifestyle, and/or personality characteristics. Research on the psychographic profile of active e-commerce shoppers attempts to understand the various lifestyle factors that lead to online buying behavior. For instance, in a study by the Wharton Forum on Electronic Commerce, a panel of 2500 people was surveyed to understand the factors that predict e-commerce purchases. As shown in Figure 7.2, the survey found that the most important factors in predicting buying behavior were (1) looking for product information online, (2) leading a "wired lifestyle" (one where consumers spend a considerable amount of their working and home lives online) and (3) recently ordering from a catalog.

psychographic profile
divides a market into different groups based on social class, lifestyle, or personality characteristics

THE PURCHASING DECISION

Now that you have an understanding of the various factors that affect consumers, you need to consider how buyers make the actual decision to purchase. There are five stages in the consumer decision process: awareness of need, search for more information, evaluation of alternatives, the actual purchase decision, and post-purchase contact with the firm (Kotler and Armstrong, 2001). Figure 7.3 shows the consumer decision process and the types of offline and online marketing communications that support this process and seek to influence the consumer before, during, and after the purchase decision.

As shown in Figure 7.3, traditional mass media, along with catalogs and direct mail campaigns, are used to drive potential buyers to Web sites. What's new about

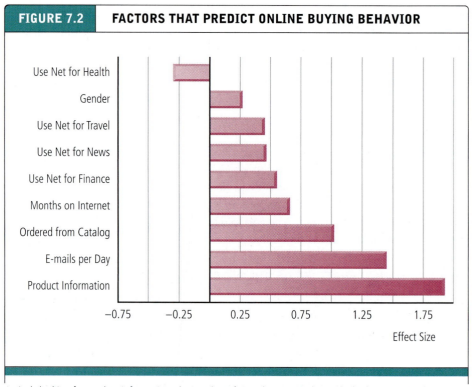

| FIGURE 7.2 | **FACTORS THAT PREDICT ONLINE BUYING BEHAVIOR** |

Actively looking for product information, the number of e-mails sent per day and whether someone has recently ordered from a catalog are the most significant variables in predicting whether someone will purchase online (variables are listed from lowest to highest effect).

SOURCE: Lohse, Bellman, and Johnson, 2000.

online purchasing is the new media marketing communications capabilities afforded by the Web: community bulletin boards, chat rooms, listservs, banner ads, targeted permission e-mail, search engines, and online product reviews. Simply put, the Web offers marketers an extraordinary increase in marketing communications tools and power, and the ability to envelop the consumer in a very rich information and purchasing environment. In Chapter 8, we describe these new communications techniques and gauge their effectiveness in greater detail.

A MODEL OF ONLINE CONSUMER BEHAVIOR

Is online consumer behavior fundamentally different from offline consumer behavior? Consumer behavior online and offline has both similarities and differences. The e-commerce world is not quite so revolutionary as some would have us believe. For instance, the stages of the consumer decision process are basically the same whether the consumer is online or offline. On the other hand, the general model of consumer

| FIGURE 7.3 | THE CONSUMER DECISION PROCESS AND SUPPORTING COMMUNICATIONS |

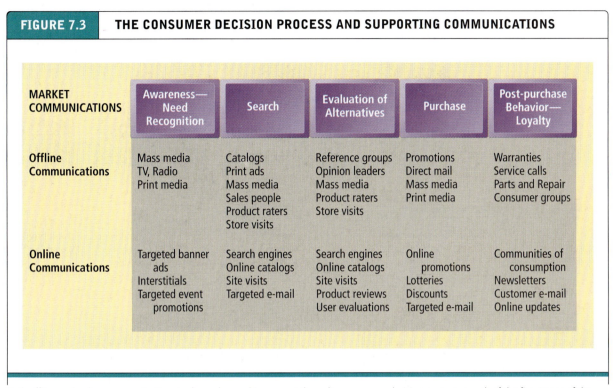

MARKET COMMUNICATIONS	Awareness— Need Recognition	Search	Evaluation of Alternatives	Purchase	Post-purchase Behavior— Loyalty
Offline Communications	Mass media TV, Radio Print media	Catalogs Print ads Mass media Sales people Product raters Store visits	Reference groups Opinion leaders Mass media Product raters Store visits	Promotions Direct mail Mass media Print media	Warranties Service calls Parts and Repair Consumer groups
Online Communications	Targeted banner ads Interstitials Targeted event promotions	Search engines Online catalogs Site visits Targeted e-mail	Search engines Online catalogs Site visits Product reviews User evaluations	Online promotions Lotteries Discounts Targeted e-mail	Communities of consumption Newsletters Customer e-mail Online updates

Both offline and online communications tools can be used to support the online consumer decision process at each of the five stages of the process.

behavior requires modification to take into account new factors. In Figure 7.4, we have added two new independent factors to the general model: Web site capabilities and consumer clickstream behavior.

Web site features include the content, design, and functionality of the site. We examine Web site design issues as they relate to marketing more fully in the next chapter. **Clickstream behavior** refers to the transaction log that consumers establish as they move about the Web. Each of these factors has independent predictive and explanatory power, and, for some Web marketers, they have replaced the traditional emphasis on background factors and intervening variables.

There are parallels in the analog world. For instance, it is well known that consumer behavior can be influenced by store design, and that understanding the precise movements of consumers through a physical store can enhance sales if goods and promotions are arranged along the most likely consumer tracks. For instance, because consumers almost invariably enter a store and move to the right, high margin items — jewelry and cosmetics — tend to be located there. And because it is known that consumers purchase fresh dairy products frequently, they are put at the back of grocery stores. Wal-Mart uses consumer-tracking databases within its stores to optimize

clickstream behavior
the transaction log that consumers establish as they move about the Web.

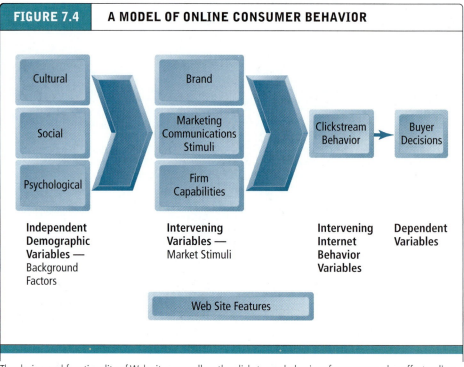

| FIGURE 7.4 | A MODEL OF ONLINE CONSUMER BEHAVIOR |

The design and functionality of Web sites as well as the clickstream behavior of consumers also affect online consumer behavior.

the convenience to consumers — putting clothing nearest the entry, and electronics and cameras toward the back. Proper store design and precision tracking of consumers is not new — but its technical implementation on the Web, its lowered cost, its ubiquity, and its comprehensiveness on the Web are new.

With respect to clickstream behavior, a number of researchers have argued that understanding the background demographics of Internet users is no longer necessary, and not that predictive in any event. In most studies of consumer behavior, background demographics account usually for less than 10% of the observed behavior. Many believe instead that the most important predictors of online consumer behavior are the session characteristics and the clickstream behavior of people online. The theory is that this information will enable marketers to understand what the consumer was looking for at each moment, and how much they were willing to pay, allowing the marketers to precisely target their communications.

For instance, a study by Booz Allen & Hamilton and NetRatings found that background demographics alone, even background demographics with attitudinal and lifestyle factors, fail to take into account the different types of user sessions and different clickstream patterns (see Table 7.4). Analyzing the clickstream behavior of 2,466

TABLE 7.4	SEVEN TYPES OF ONLINE SESSIONS			
ONLINE BEHAVIOR	SESSION LENGTH (MIN)	TIME PER PAGE (MIN)	SITE FAMILIARITY*	CATEGORY CONCENTRATION**
Quickies (finding sports, reading e-mail)	1	0.25	90%	90%
Just the Facts (finding and evaluating information from related sites)	9	0.5	88%	47%
Single Mission (going to un-familiar sites in same category, e.g., sports to real estate to find what they need)	10	1.5	11%	85%
Do It Again (going to favorite sites e.g., banking and chat rooms)	14	2	95%	87%
Loitering (leisurely visiting favorite sites, news, gaming)	33	2	90%	87%
Information Please (researching all aspects of a topic from many sites)	37	1	14%	41%
Surfing (exploring attention-grabbing sites such as news and shopping)	70	1	14%	26%

The researchers discovered that purchasing behavior was highest in Loitering, Information Please, and Surfing sessions. These types of sessions were the longest: Customers spent more time on each Web page, and thus were more receptive to advertising.

*Site Familiarity: the percent of time in a session that users spent at familiar sites they had visited four or more times.

**Category Concentration: the percent of time in a session users spent at sites that belong to the most frequented category. For example, if a user spent 10 minutes in a session, 5 minutes in sports, 3 minutes in news, and 2 minutes in entertainment, then the user had a 50% concentration in that session.

SOURCE: Rozanski, Bollman, and Lipman, 2001.

individuals engaged in 186,797 user sessions, the study identified seven categories of user sessions: "Quickies," "Just the Facts," "Single Mission," "Do It Again," "Loitering," "Information Please," and "Surfing." Researchers called these segments "occasions," and suggested "occasion-based" marketing is more effective than static market segmentation based on demographics and/or consumer attitudes. Segmenting the market in this way, they found that in some types of sessions, users are more likely to buy, whereas in other sessions, they appear to be immune to online advertising.

Clickstream marketing takes maximum advantage of the Internet environment. It presupposes no prior knowledge of the customer (and in that sense is "privacy-regarding"), and can be developed dynamically as customers use the Internet. For instance, Google places "sponsored" listings on the top of its search results screens when users enter specific search criteria.

SHOPPERS: BROWSERS AND BUYERS

The picture of Internet use sketched in the previous section emphasizes the complexity of behavior online. Although the Internet audience is still concentrated among the well educated, affluent, and youthful, increasingly the audience is becoming more diverse. Clickstream analysis shows us that people go online for many different reasons. Online shopping is similarly complex. Beneath the surface of the $65 billion B2C e-commerce market are substantial differences in how users shop online.

For instance, as shown in Figure 7.5, about 40% of online users are "buyers" who actually purchase something entirely online. Another 40% of online users research products on the Web ("browsers"), but purchase them offline. This combined group, referred to as "shoppers," constitutes approximately 80% of the online Internet audience. With the U.S. Internet audience estimated at about 170 million in 2001, online shoppers (the combination of buyers and browsers) add up to a market size of over 135 million consumers. Most marketers find this number exciting.

The significance of online browsing for offline purchasing is illustrated in Figure 7.6. In a Jupiter Media Metrix survey, over 80% of consumers indicate that online product research either often or sometimes impacts their offline purchase decisions. According to this study, online buyers and browsers together are expected to purchase almost $270 billion worth of products in 2001 through offline channels.

E-commerce is a major conduit and generator of offline commerce. The reverse is also true: Online traffic is driven by offline brands and shopping. This suggests strongly that e-commerce and traditional commerce are coupled and should be viewed by merchants (and researchers) as part of a continuum of consuming behavior and not as radical alternatives to one another. Commerce is commerce; the customers are often the same people.

FIGURE 7.5   **ONLINE SHOPPERS**

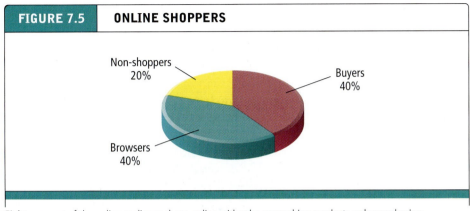
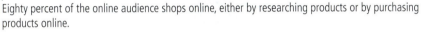

Eighty percent of the online audience shops online, either by researching products or by purchasing products online.

SOURCE: Jupiter Media Metrix, 2001a.

The significance of both these findings for marketers is very clear. Online merchants should build the information content of their sites to attract browsers looking for information, put less attention on selling per se, and offer products in offline settings where some users feel more secure and comfortable.

FIGURE 7.6   **IMPACT OF ONLINE PRODUCT RESEARCH ON OFFLINE PURCHASE DECISIONS**

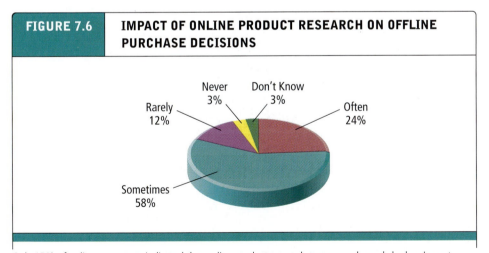
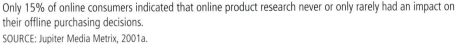

Only 15% of online consumers indicated that online product research never or only rarely had an impact on their offline purchasing decisions.

SOURCE: Jupiter Media Metrix, 2001a.

WHAT CONSUMERS SHOP FOR AND BUY ONLINE

Most online purchases involve small ticket items (see Figure 7.7). Among the top categories are books, music, apparel and accessories, software, and toys. These top cate-

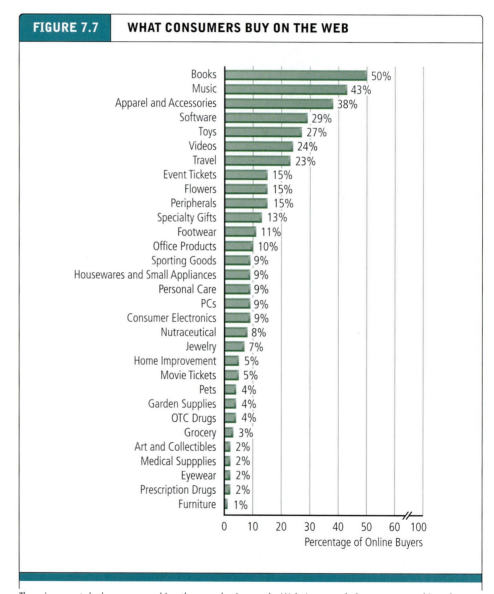

FIGURE 7.7 | **WHAT CONSUMERS BUY ON THE WEB**

There is a great deal more researching than purchasing on the Web. In general, the more researching, the more purchasing within each category.

SOURCE: Jupiter Media Metrix, 2001a.

gories have certain similar characteristics: First-movers on the Web sold these products early on, the purchase price is small (reduced consumer risk), the items are physically small (shipping costs are low), margins are high (at least on CDs and software), and there is a broad selection of products (e-commerce vendors can compete on scope when compared to traditional offline stores). In comparison, most consumers want to view goods such as furniture in person before purchasing it, and furniture typically is expensive, and hence high risk. Other products, such as home improvement supplies, pet supplies, and garden equipment, may be perceived as too bulky.

INTENTIONAL ACTS: HOW SHOPPERS FIND VENDORS ONLINE

Given the prevalence of "click here" banner ads, one might think customers are "driven" to online vendors by spur-of-the-moment decisions. In fact, only a tiny percentage of shoppers click on banners to find vendors. As shown in Figure 7.8, over 85% of shoppers direct themselves to vendor sites by typing a product into a search engine, going directly to the merchant's site, or entering a store or brand name into a search engine.

The notion that shoppers are highly intentional is strengthened by Figure 7.9, which shows that over 80% of shoppers are shopping on the Web for specific products or items.

E-commerce shoppers are not browsing aimlessly, looking for something to buy, likely targets for banner ads and impulse purchases. Instead, they are focused

| FIGURE 7.8 | **HOW SHOPPERS FIND VENDORS AND STORES ONLINE** |

For the most part, shoppers use search engines to find vendors or products they are looking for.

SOURCE: Jupiter Media Metrix, 2001a.

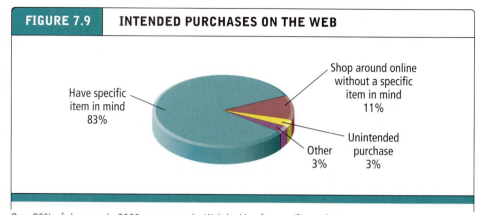

FIGURE 7.9 INTENDED PURCHASES ON THE WEB

Over 80% of shoppers in 2000 went onto the Web looking for specific products.
SOURCE: Jupiter Media Metrix, 2001a.

browsers looking for specific products, companies, and services. Merchants can convert these "goal-oriented," intentional shoppers into buyers if they can target their communications to them and design their sites in such a way as to provide easy-to-access and use product information, full selection, and customer service (Wolfinbarger and Gilly, 2001).

Wolfinbarger and Gilly also note, however, that while it is true that goal-oriented shopping is the most common type of online shopping behavior, more and more online consumers are engaging in "experiential" shopping ("shopping for fun"), which is valuable behavior for marketers since it is associated with increased impulse purchases and more frequent visits. The challenge for e-commerce companies is to appeal to these consumers without alienating their goal-oriented customers, who have very different motivations.

WHY MORE PEOPLE DON'T SHOP ONLINE

A final consumer behavior question to address is: Why don't more online Web users shop online? Table 7.5 lists some concrete actions that e-commerce vendors could take to increase the likelihood that shoppers and non-shoppers would purchase online more frequently.

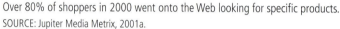

7.2 BASIC MARKETING CONCEPTS

marketing
the strategies and actions firms take to establish a relationship with a consumer and encourage purchases of its products or services

In Section 7.1 we discussed who's on the Web and online behavior as it relates to purchase decisions; in this section we will expand our focus to look at the broader topic of **marketing** — the strategies and actions firms take to establish a relationship with a consumer and encourage purchases of its products or services. The key objective of

TABLE 7.5	FACTORS THAT WOULD ENCOURAGE MORE ONLINE PURCHASING		
FACTORS	**BUYERS**	**BROWSERS**	**NON-SHOPPERS**
Better prices	74.0	58.9	31.2
Easier to comparison shop	46.4	36.6	6.2
Ability to return merchandise easily	42.4	45.7	4.7
Better security for credit card and/or personal information	40.9	62.2	37.4
Easier to find items	37.1	30	15.4
Ability to get answers to questions or advice from a merchant	36.8	40.3	2.9
Better information about products (descriptions, reviews, etc.)	31.7	29	9.6
Faster delivery	30.4	4.9	3.8
Better presentation of products	23.6	14.5	6.2
Easier to order	22.2	20.0	13.5
Availability of loyalty rewards (such as frequent flier points)	22.0	13.7	8.5
Greater trust in particular online merchants	21.4	32.0	17
Quicker to complete buying process within an Internet store	17.3	13.5	5.9
Greater familiarity with the Internet and online purchasing	6.5	18.6	15
Other	7.4	6.1	4.7
Nothing	7.2	11.2	44.1

Better prices, easier comparison shopping, simpler returns, and better security are the leading factors that would facilitate more online purchasing.

SOURCE: Jupiter Media Metrix, 2001a.

Internet marketing is to use the Web — as well as traditional channels — to develop a positive, long-term relationship with customers (who may be online or offline) and thereby create a competitive advantage for the firm by allowing it to charge a higher price for products or services than its competitors can charge.

To begin, you must first be familiar with some basic marketing concepts. Recall from Chapter 2 (Section 2.3) that the profitability of an industry depends on (1) the ease with which substitute products or services can enter the market, (2) the ease with which new entrants can enter the industry, (3) the power of customers and suppliers to influence pricing, and (4) the nature of competition within the industry. Competitive markets are ones that have lots of substitutes, easy entry, and customers and suppliers who possess strong bargaining power.

Marketing directly addresses the competitive situation of industries and firms. Marketing seeks to create unique, highly differentiated products or services that are

Internet marketing
using the Web — as well as traditional channels — to develop a positive, long-term relationship with customers, thereby creating a competitive advantage for the firm by allowing the firm to charge a higher price for products or services than its competitors can charge

feature set

the bundle of capabilities and services offered by the product or service

commodity

a good or service for which there are many dealers supplying the same product and all products in the segment are essentially identical

core product

the core benefit the customer receives from the product

actual product

the set of characteristics designed to deliver the product's core benefits

augmented product

a product with additional benefits to customers beyond the core benefits embodied in the actual product

brand

a set of expectations that consumers have when consuming, or thinking about consuming, a product or service from a specific company

produced or supplied by one trusted firm ("little monopolies"). There are few, if any, substitutes for an effectively marketed product or service, and new entrants have a difficult time matching the product or service's **feature set** (the bundle of capabilities and services offered by the product or service). When successful, these little monopolies reduce the bargaining power of consumers because they are the sole sources of supply; they also enable firms to exercise significant power over their suppliers.

Marketing is designed to avoid pure price competition and to create markets where returns on investment are above average, competition is limited, and consumers are willing to pay premium prices for products that have no substitute because they are perceived as unique. Marketing encourages customers to buy on the basis of nonmarket (i.e., nonprice) qualities of a product. Firms use marketing to prevent their products and services from becoming commodities. A **commodity** is a good or service for which there are many dealers supplying the same product and all products in the segment are essentially identical. Price and delivery terms are the only basis for consumer choice. Examples of commodities include wheat, corn, or steel.

FEATURE SETS

A central task of marketing is to identify and then communicate to the customer the unique, differentiated capabilities and services of a product or service's feature set. Figure 7.10 illustrates the three levels of a product or service: core, actual, and augmented. Although the example given is for a physical product, the concept applies equally to a digital product or service.

The core product is at the center of the feature set. The **core product** is the core benefit the customer receives from the product. Let's say, for example, that the core product is a washing machine. The **actual product** is the set of characteristics designed to deliver the product's core benefits. Marketers must identify the features of the washer that differentiate it from those of other manufacturers. In the case of a Maytag washing machine, the actual product is a washing machine carrying the Maytag name and with certain features and capabilities, such as durability and ease of use. The **augmented product** is a product with additional benefits to customers beyond the core benefits embodied in the actual product. In the case of Maytag, the augmented product is a Maytag washing machine with a five-year warranty, free delivery, factory-trained support service, and low-cost installation fees. The augmented product forms the basis for building the Maytag brand (a process known as *branding*) described below.

PRODUCTS, BRANDS, AND THE BRANDING PROCESS

What makes products truly unique and differentiable in the minds of consumers is the product's brand. A **brand** is a set of expectations that a consumer has when con-

---

FIGURE 7.10 **FEATURE SET**

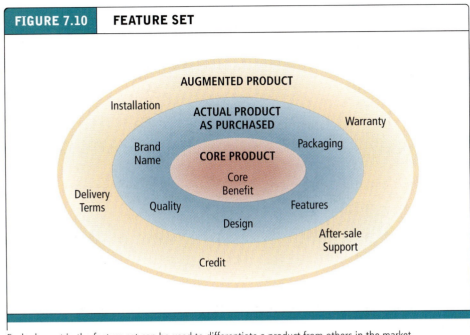

Each element in the feature set can be used to differentiate a product from others in the market.
SOURCE: Kotler and Armstrong, 2001.

---

suming, or thinking about consuming, a product or service from a specific company. These expectations are based in part on past experiences the consumer has had actually using the product, on the experiences of trusted others who have consumed the product, and on the promises of marketers who extol the unique features of the product in a variety of different channels and media.

The most important expectations created by brands are quality, reliability, consistency, trust, affection, loyalty, and ultimately, reputation. Marketers create promises, and these promises engender consumer expectations. As Charles Revson, the founder of Revlon noted, "In the factory we make cosmetics; in the store we sell hope" (Kotler and Armstrong, 2001). The promise made by cosmetic manufacturers to consumers is: "if you use this product, you will perceive yourself to be more beautiful."

Figure 7.11 illustrates the process of brand creation or **branding**.

Marketers identify the differentiating features of the actual and augmented product. They engage in a variety of marketing communications activities to transmit the feature set to the consumer. Based on the consumers' experiences and the promises made by marketers in their communications, consumers develop expectations about a product. For instance, when a consumer purchases a Maytag washer, the consumer expects to receive a durable, high quality, easy-to-use machine that cleans clothes

branding
process of brand creation

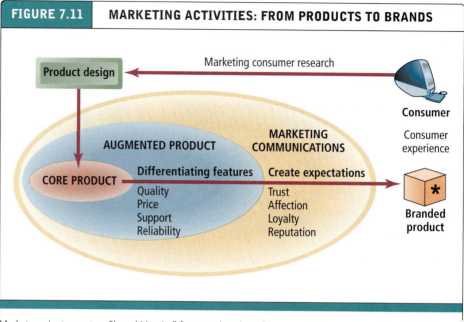

FIGURE 7.11 **MARKETING ACTIVITIES: FROM PRODUCTS TO BRANDS**

Marketers aim to create a "brand identity" for a product, based on consumer perceptions of trust, affection, loyalty, and reputation.

well. Consumers are willing to pay a premium price in order to obtain these qualities. If Maytag washers did not in fact perform according to these expectations, the brand would be weakened and consumers would be less willing to pay a premium price. In other words, a strong brand requires a strong product. But if Maytag machines do perform according to expectations, then customers will feel loyal to (they would purchase again or recommend to others), trust, feel affection for, and ascribe a good reputation to, both the product and the company that makes it.

Ideally, marketers directly influence the design of products to ensure the products have desirable features, high quality, correct pricing, product support, and reliability. When marketers are able to directly influence the design of a core product based on market research and feedback, this is called **closed loop marketing**. While ideal, it is more often the case that marketers are hired to "sell" a product that has already been designed. E-commerce — as we see below — offers some unique opportunities to achieve closed loop marketing.

Marketers devise and implement brand strategies. A **brand strategy** is a set of plans for differentiating a product from its competitor, and communicating these differences effectively to the marketplace. In developing new e-commerce brands, the ability to devise and develop a brand strategy has been crucial in the success and failure of many companies, as described throughout this book.

closed loop marketing
when marketers are able to directly influence the design of the core product based on market research and feedback from the market

brand strategy
a set of plans for differentiating a product from its competitors, and communicating these differences effectively to the marketplace

What kinds of products can be branded? According to many marketing specialists, there is no limit. Every product can potentially be branded. Sneakers that make you soar from Nike, cars from Volvo that make you feel safe on dark rainy nights, shirts from Polo that make you appear as if you were on the way to a country club — these are all examples of products with extraordinary brand names for which consumers pay premium prices.

How much is a brand worth? Brands differ in their power and value in the marketplace. **Brand equity** is the estimated value of the premium customers are willing to pay for using a branded product when compared to unbranded competitors (Feldwick, 1996). According to Interbrand' s 2001 World's Most Valuable Brands survey, the top five brands and their estimated equity value are Coca-Cola ($69 billion), Microsoft ($65 billion), IBM ($53 billion), General Electric ($42 billion), and Nokia ($35 billion) (Interbrand, 2001). Brand equity also affects stock prices insofar as brands strengthen future revenue streams.

brand equity
the estimated value of the premium customers are willing to pay for using a branded product when compared to unbranded competitors

SEGMENTING, TARGETING, AND POSITIONING

Markets are not unitary, but in fact are composed of many different kinds of customers with different needs. Firms seek to *segment* markets into distinct groups of customers who differ from one another in terms of product needs. Once the segments are established, each segment can be *targeted* with differentiated products. Within each segment, the product is *positioned* and branded as a unique, high-value product, especially suited to the needs of segment customers.

By segmenting markets, firms can differentiate their products to more closely fit the needs of customers in each segment. Rather than charge one price for the same product, firms can maximize revenues by creating several different variations on the same product and charging different prices in each market segment.

Once markets are segmented, the branding process proceeds within each segment by appealing to the segment members. For instance, automobile manufacturers segment their markets on many dimensions: demographics (age, sex, income, and occupation), geographic (region), benefits (special performance features), and psychographics (self-image and emotional needs). For each market segment, they offer a uniquely branded product.

ARE BRANDS RATIONAL?

Coca-Cola is one of the most enduring, powerful brands in U.S. commercial history. The core product is colored, flavored, carbonated sugar water. The augmented branded product is a delightful, refreshing, reputable, unique-tasting drink available worldwide, based on a secret formula that consumers willingly pay up to twice as much for when compared to unbranded store brands of cola. Coca-Cola is a marketing-created micro-monopoly: There is only one Coke and only one supplier. Why would consumers pay twice as much for Coke when compared to unbranded cola drinks? Is this rational?

The answer is a qualified yes. Brands introduce market efficiency by reducing the search costs and decision-making costs of consumers. Strong brands signal strong products that work. Brands carry information. Confronted with many different drinks, the choice of Coke can be made quickly, without much thought, and with the assurance that you will have the drinking experience you expect based on prior use of the product. Brands reduce consumer risk and uncertainty in a crowded marketplace. Brands are like an insurance policy against nasty surprises in the marketplace for which consumers willingly pay a premium — better safe than sorry.

The ability of brands to become a corporate asset — to attain brand equity — based on future anticipated premiums paid by consumers also provides an incentive for firms to build products that serve customer needs better than other products. Therefore, although brands create micro-monopolies, increase market costs, and lead to above-average returns on investment (monopoly rents), they also introduce market efficiencies for the consumer.

For business firms, brands are a major source of revenue and are obviously rational. Brands lower customer acquisition costs and increase customer retention. The stronger the brand reputation, the easier it is to attract new customers. **Customer acquisition costs** refer to the overall costs of converting a prospect into a consumer, and include all marketing and advertising costs. **Customer retention costs** are those costs incurred in convincing an existing customer to purchase again. In general, it is much more expensive to acquire a new customer than to retain an existing customer. For instance, Reichheld and Schefter calculated that e-commerce sites lose from $20 to $80 on each customer in the first year because of the high cost of acquiring a customer, but potentially can make up for this loss in later years by retaining loyal customers (Reichheld and Schefter, 2000). In some instances, however, e-commerce companies have gone out business before they ever reached that point.

A successful brand can constitute a long-lasting, impregnable unfair competitive advantage. As we discussed in Chapter 2, a competitive advantage is considered "fair" when it is based on innovation, efficient production processes, or other factors that theoretically can be imitated and/or purchased in the marketplace by competitors. An "unfair competitive advantage" cannot be purchased in the factor markets and includes such things as patents, copyrights, secret processes, unusually skilled or dedicated employees and managers, and, of course, brand names. Brands cannot be purchased (unless one buys the entire company).

customer acquisition costs

the overall costs of converting a prospect into a consumer

customer retention costs

costs incurred in convincing an existing customer to purchase again

DO BRANDS LAST FOREVER?

Brands, however, do not necessarily last forever, and the micro-monopolies they create may not be stable over the long term. In a study of brand endurance, Golder found that between 1923 and 1997, only 23% of the firms that ranked first in market share in 1923 were still in the market-leading position in 1997, while 28% of the leaders failed altogether (Golder, 2000). Less than 10% of the Fortune 500 of 1917 still exists (Starbuck and Nystrom, 1997). Life at the top is sweet, but often short, and market efficiency is restored long-term as entrepreneurs exploit new technologies and new public tastes at a faster rate than the incumbent market leaders.

CAN BRANDS SURVIVE THE INTERNET?

As we noted in Chapter 1, during the E-commerce I period, many academics and business consultants postulated that the Web would lead to a new world of information symmetry and "frictionless" commerce. In this world, newly empowered customers, using intelligent shopping agents and the near infinite product and price information available on the Internet, would shop around the world (and around the clock) with minimal effort, driving prices down to their marginal cost and driving intermediaries out of the market as customers began to deal directly with producers (Wigand and Benjamin, 1995; Rayport and Sviolka, 1995; Evans and Wurster, 1999; Sinha 2000).[1] The result was supposed to be an instance of the **"Law of One Price"**: With complete price transparency in a perfect information marketplace, one world price for every product would emerge. "Frictionless commerce" would, of course, mean the end of marketing based on brands.

law of one price
with complete price transparency in a perfect information marketplace, there will be one world price for every product

But it didn't work out this way. Price has not proven to be the only determinant of consumer behavior. E-commerce firms continue to rely heavily on brands to attract customers and charge premium prices. Internet technologies can be used to infinitely differentiate products by using personalization, customization, and community marketing techniques (described in the next section), thereby overcoming the price-lowering effects of lower search costs and a large number of worldwide suppliers for goods. For instance, Bailey and Brynjolfsson (1997) found that prices for books, music CDs, and software were not substantially lower at e-commerce sites than in traditional stores or catalogs (see also Clay et al., 1999 for similar results). Later studies found that prices at e-commerce sites were 9% to 16% lower than at conventional retail outlets for musical CDs (depending on whether taxes and shipping costs were included in the price), but also found substantial price dispersion — nearly as much as in traditional markets for the same goods (Brynjolfsson and Smith, 2000). **Price dispersion** refers to the difference between the highest and lowest prices in a market. In a perfect market, there is not supposed to be any price dispersion. Other evidence suggests that so many suppliers and price comparisons can overwhelm consumers, and that consumers achieve efficiencies by quickly purchasing from a trusted, high-price provider. For instance, Amazon, which has one of the strongest brand names on the Web, charges premium prices when compared to other e-tailers or even retail stores

price dispersion
the difference between the highest and lowest prices in a market

[1]The theory of frictionless commerce is not unique to the Internet. Computerized stock and options markets over the last 20 years have also attempted to achieve low-friction transactions.

(Clay et al., 1999). In general, the most frequently visited and used e-commerce sites are not the lowest-price sites (Smith et al., 1999).

We can conclude from the research evidence that brands are alive and well on the Web, that consumers are willing to pay price premiums for products and services they perceive as differentiated, and that in many instances Web prices may be higher than those available in retail stores because of the premium consumers will pay for convenience.

Now that we have covered these basic concepts, we move on in the next section to describe what makes Internet marketing different from ordinary marketing.

7.3   INTERNET MARKETING TECHNOLOGIES

Internet marketing has many similarities to and differences from ordinary marketing. The objective of Internet marketing — as in all marketing — is to build customer relationships so that the firm can achieve above average returns (both by offering superior products or services and by communicating the feature set to the consumer). But Internet marketing is also very different from ordinary marketing because the nature of the medium and its capabilities are so different from anything that has come before. In order to understand just how different Internet marketing can be and in what ways, you first need to become familiar with some basic Internet marketing technologies.

THE REVOLUTION IN INTERNET MARKETING TECHNOLOGIES

In Chapter 1, we described seven unique features of e-commerce technology. Table 7.6 describes how marketing has changed as a result of these new technical capabilities.

On balance, the Internet has had three very broad impacts on marketing. The Internet, as a communications medium, has broadened the scope of marketing communications — in the sense of the number of people who can be easily reached. Second, the Internet has increased the richness of marketing communications by combining text, video, and audio content into rich messages. Arguably, the Web is richer as a medium than even television or video because of the complexity of messages available, the enormous content accessible on a wide range of subjects, and the ability of users to interactively control the experience. Third, the Internet has greatly expanded the information intensity of the marketplace by providing marketers (and customers) with unparalleled fine-grained, detailed real-time information about consumers as they transact in the marketplace.

WEB TRANSACTION LOGS

transaction log
records user activity at a Web site

How can e-commerce sites know more than, say, a department store about consumer behavior? A primary source of consumer information on the Web is the transaction log maintained by all Web servers. A **transaction log** records user activity at a Web

TABLE 7.6	IMPACT OF UNIQUE FEATURES OF E-COMMERCE TECHNOLOGY ON MARKETING
E-COMMERCE TECHNOLOGY DIMENSION	**SIGNIFICANCE FOR MARKETING**
Ubiquity	Marketing communications have been extended to the home, work, and mobile platforms; geographic limits on marketing have been reduced. The marketplace has been replaced by "marketspace" and is removed from a temporal and geographic location. Customer convenience has been enhanced, and shopping costs have been reduced.
Global reach	Worldwide customer service and marketing communications have been enabled. Potentially hundreds of millions of consumers can be reached with marketing messages.
Universal standards	The cost of delivering marketing messages and receiving feedback from users is reduced because of shared, global standards of the Internet.
Richness	Video, audio, and text marketing messages can be integrated into a single marketing message and consuming experience.
Interactivity	Consumers can be engaged in a dialog, dynamically adjusting the experience to the consumer, and making the consumer a co-producer of the goods and services being sold.
Information density	Fine-grained, highly detailed information on consumers' real-time behavior can be gathered and analyzed for the first time. "Data mining" Internet technology permits the analysis of terabytes of consumer data everyday for marketing purposes.
Personalization/Customization	This feature potentially enables product and service differentiation down to the level of the individual, thus strengthening the ability of marketers to create brands.

site. The transaction log is built into Web server software. Figure 7.12 shows a few minutes of the Web transaction log for azimuth-interactive.com, a Web-based software training site. The log has been edited to eliminate the names of real persons and show only a few entries for each visitor. In fact, visitors usually create tens or hundreds of entries in the log, one entry for each page or object they request.

Table 7.7 lists the data elements contained in a Web transaction log and how these elements can be used in marketing, using the first entry in the transaction log in Figure 7.12 as an example.

WebTrends, discussed in Chapter 3, is a leading log file analysis tool. Transaction log data becomes even more useful when combined with two other visitor-generated data trails: registration forms and the shopping cart database. Users are enticed through various means (such as free gifts or special services) to fill out registration forms. **Registration forms** gather personal data on name, address, phone, zip code, e-mail address (usually required), and other optional self-confessed information on interests and tastes. When users make a purchase, they also enter additional information into the shopping cart database. The **shopping cart database** captures all the item selection, purchase, and payment data. Other potential additional sources of

registration forms
gather personal data on name, address, phone, zip code, e-mail address, and other optional self-confessed information on interests and tastes

shopping cart database
captures all the item selection, purchase, and payment data

> **FIGURE 7.12** **A WEB TRANSACTION LOG FROM AZIMUTH-INTERACTIVE.COM**
>
> 64.212.128.3 - - [14/May/2001:15:01:18 -0500] "GET /images/traininglibraryart.gif HTTP/1.1" 200 1966 "http://www.azimuth-interactive.com/office97text.htm" "Mozilla/4.0 (compatible; MSIE 4.01; Windows 95)"
>
> 64.212.128.3 - - [14/May/2001:15:01:18 -0500] "GET /images/office97fullbox.gif HTTP/1.1" 200 30377 "http://www.azimuth-interactive.com/office97text.htm" "Mozilla/4.0 (compatible; MSIE 4.01; Windows 95)"
>
> 64.212.128.3 - - [14/May/2001:15:01:18 -0500] "GET /images/interface1.gif HTTP/1.1" 200 26251 "http://www.azimuth-interactive.com/office97text.htm" "Mozilla/4.0 (compatible; MSIE 4.01; Windows 95)"
>
> 208-226-120-232.amazon.com - - [14/May/2001:15:21:43 -0500] "GET /images/win95fullbox.gif HTTP/1.0" 200 30958 "-" "aranhabot"
>
> 208-226-120-232.amazon.com - - [14/May/2001:15:21:43 -0500] "GET /images/word97fullbox.gif HTTP/1.0" 200 32866 "-" "aranhabot"
>
> ubr-33.65.143.sanford.cfl.rr.com - - [14/May/2001:15:30:51 -0500] "GET /interactivecomputing/icheader.htm HTTP/1.1" 200 1798 "http://www.azimuth-interactive.com/icmain.html" "Mozilla/4.0 (compatible; MSIE 5.5; Windows 98; Win 9x 4.90)"
>
> ubr-33.65.143.sanford.cfl.rr.com - - [14/May/2001:15:30:52 -0500] "GET /interactivecomputing/cont.htm HTTP/1.1" 200 988 "http://www.azimuth-interactive.com/icmain.html" "Mozilla/4.0 (compatible; MSIE 5.5; Windows 98; Win 9x 4.90)"
>
> ubr-33.65.143.sanford.cfl.rr.com - - [14/May/2001:15:30:52 -0500] "GET /interactivecomputing/ictext2.htm HTTP/1.1" 200 6019 "http://www.azimuth-interactive.com/icmain.html" "Mozilla/4.0 (compatible; MSIE 5.5; Windows 98; Win 9x 4.90)"

A few minutes of a Web transaction log.

information are information users submit on product forms, contribute to chat groups, or send via e-mail messages using the "Contact Us" option on most sites.

For a Web site that has a million visitors per month, and where, on average, a visitor makes 15 page requests per visit, there will be fifteen million entries in the log each month. These transaction logs, coupled with data from the registration forms and shopping cart database, represent a treasure trove of marketing information for both individual sites and the online industry as a whole. Nearly all the new Internet marketing capabilities are based on these data-gathering tools. For instance, here are just a few of the interesting marketing questions that can be answered by examining a site's Web transaction logs, registration forms, and shopping cart database:

- What are the major patterns of interest and purchase for groups and individuals?
- After the home page, where do most users go first, and then second and third?
- What are the interests of specific individuals (those we can identify)?

| TABLE 7.7 | MARKETING USES OF DATA FROM WEB TRANSACTION LOGS |

DATA ELEMENT	MARKETING USE
IP address of the visitor: 64.212.128.3	Can be used to send return e-mails for marketing when the visitor is using a dedicated URL as opposed to a dial-in modem. Dial-in modems use temporary IPs and cannot be used for return mail.
Date and time stamp: [14/May/2001:15:01:18 -0500]	Used to understand patterns in the time of day and year of consumer activity.
Pages and objects requested and visited ("Get" statements): GET /images/traininglibraryart.gif	Used to understand what this specific consumer was interested in finding (the clickstream). Can be used later to send "personalized" messages, "customized products," or simply return mail regarding related products.
Response of site server: 200 "(usually HTTP/1.1." "HTTP/1.1" 304 is a code to send users to a different source for the page or object)	Used to monitor for broken links, pages not returned.
Size of pages sent (bytes of information): 1966	Used to understand capacity demands on servers and communications links.
Name of page or site from which the consumer came to this site: "http://www.azimuth-interactive.com/office97text.htm"	Used to understand how consumers come to a site, and once there, their patterns of behavior.
Name and version of the browser used: Mozilla/4.0 compatible; MSIE 4.01 ("Mozilla" is a Netscape standard. MSIE is Microsoft Internet Explorer).	Useful for understanding target browsers, ensuring your site is compatible with browsers being used.
Name and version of the operating system of the consumer's client machine: Windows 95	Useful for understanding the capabilities of target client machines; more recent operating systems indicates new machine, or technically savvy user.
History of all the pages and objects visited during a session at the site.	Used to establish personal profiles of individuals, analyze site activity, and understand the most popular pages and resources.

- How can we make it easier for people to use our site so they can find what they want?
- How can we change the design of the site to encourage visitors to purchase our high margin products?
- Where are visitors coming from (and how can we optimize our presence on these referral sites)?
- How can we personalize our messages, offerings, and products to individual users?

Answering these questions requires some additional technologies. As noted by Jupiter Media Metrix, businesses can choke on the massive quantity of information found in a typical site's log file. We describe some technologies that help firms more effectively utilize this information below.

SUPPLEMENTING THE LOGS: COOKIES AND WEB BUGS

While transaction logs create the foundation of online data collection, they are supplemented by two other data collection techniques: cookies and Web bugs. As described in Chapter 3, a cookie is small text file that Web sites place on the hard disk of visitors' client computers every time they visit, and during the visit, as specific pages are visited. Cookies allow a Web site to store data on a user's machine and then later retrieve it. Typically, a Web site generates a unique ID number for each visitor and stores that ID number on the user's machine using a cookie file. The cookie may also (but is not required to) include an expiration date, a path that specifies the associated Web pages that can access the cookie, a domain that specifies the associated Web servers/domains that can access the cookie (which cannot, however, be the domain of anything other than the server setting the cookie), and a security setting that provides that it may only be transmitted by a secure protocol. Figure 7.13 shows a typical cookie file on a client machine.

A TYPICAL NETSCAPE COOKIE FILE

Taking the first cookie listed as an example, a typical cookie includes the domain name of the server placing the cookie (amazon.com); a true or false statement followed by a forward slash, indicating if all machines within a given domain can access the cookie, and the path within the domain that the cookie is valid for; a true or false statement indicating whether the cookie is secure (if False, the cookie does not require a secure protocol); a 10-digit number indicating the time the cookie expires (date and time expressed in the Unix programming language); and the name of the cookie (ubid-main) and an associated value, in this case, a user ID number.

A cookie provides Web marketers with a very quick means of identifying the customer and understanding his or her prior behavior at the site. Web sites use cookies to determine how many people are visiting the site, whether they are new or repeat visitors, and how often they have visited, although this data may be somewhat inaccurate because people share computers, they often use more than one computer, and cookies may have been inadvertently or intentionally erased. Cookies make shopping carts and "quick checkout" options possible by allowing a site to keep track of a user as he or she adds to the shopping cart. Each item added to the shopping cart is stored in the site's database along with the visitor's unique ID value.

Cookie files on a computer using Microsoft's Internet Explorer can typically be found in a directory called c:\windows\cookies. Cookie files on a computer with the Netscape browser can be found at c:\ProgramFiles\Netscape\Users\Default\cookies. Both Internet Explorer and Netscape now offer users the option of being notified when a Web site wants to send them a cookie and allow them to accept or reject the cookie.

Although cookies are site-specific (a Web site can only receive the data it has stored on a client machine and cannot look at any other cookie), when combined with

FIGURE 7.13 COOKIES PLACED BY AMAZON.COM

```
cookies - Notepad
File  Edit  Search  Help
*# Netscape HTTP Cookie File
# http://www.netscape.com/newsref/std/cookie_spec.html
# This is a generated file! Do not edit.

.amazon.com       TRUE    /    FALSE  2082794688    ubid-main      077-5856495-5508330
.yahoo.com        TRUE    /    FALSE  1271369085    B              b5n4p1gtmh2ep&b=2
.b2bmarketingbiz.com      TRUE  /  FALSE  2137630415  PREVENT_POPUP  1
.google.com       TRUE    /    FALSE  2147375933    PREF           ID=31a7b20218407e37:TM=996890867:LM=996890867
.bfast.com        TRUE    /    FALSE  1628387455    UID            2|4980464748|20210807
.doubleclick.net  TRUE    /    FALSE  1920510222    id             8000000bd25becd
.advertising.com  TRUE    /    FALSE  1154930584    ACID           ee040009971597910016!
.hitbox.com       TRUE    /    FALSE  1028775502    WSS_GW         U1AQ@
www.thestandard.com      FALSE  /   FALSE  1312563906    auid           129.37.115.166.686997192825307
www.ecommercetimes.com   FALSE  /   FALSE  1028757090    Apache         166.72.133.237.10673997210009776
.internet.com     TRUE    /    FALSE  1293851081    RMID           a64885ed3b7037f0
.adobe.com        TRUE    /    FALSE  1312591094    AVID           129.37.76.22.2659997220007941
.zdnet.com        TRUE    /    FALSE  1041321881    cgversion      4
.avenuea.com      TRUE    /    FALSE  1312599903    AA002          997240055-67392125/998449754
www.business2.com        FALSE  /   FALSE  1028788635    wtCookie       8710223371548699
.timeinc.net      TRUE    /    FALSE  2051233482    PFUID          cdbcee543b70b2d80fbc1000Fffffff9d
.pathfinder.com   TRUE    /    FALSE  2051233482    PFUID          cdbcee423b70b2e114761002ffffff9d
cookies.cmpnet.com       FALSE  /   FALSE  1043910042    Apache         32.103.44.65.15006997242961885
.wired.com        TRUE    /    FALSE  2145927881    p_uniqid       7AXuU3NLY91AJx79CC
.salon.com        TRUE    /    FALSE  1293851080    RMID           20672c413b70bc30
.marketwatch.com         TRUE   /   FALSE  1293851080    RMID           812574833b717ab0
.spinbox.net      TRUE    /    FALSE  1060385851    SBID           E32B672002AC2888&S=47248 0CC
.office.com       TRUE    /    FALSE  1155022982    UTC            UT99733223670219890 4
.mediaplex.com    TRUE    /    FALSE  1245628800    svid           99733221849540028921667 04995
www.businessweek.com     FALSE  /   FALSE  2145812682    NGUserID       a646515-13599-997333030-5
.cnet.com         TRUE    /    FALSE  2145841482    aid            D8C8F7013B721E14000076f2 000065 03
.msn.com          TRUE    /    FALSE  1065305100    MC1            V=2&GUID=4AA7FD1069A44E5EADAEE679A5BC12A3
.expedia.com      TRUE    /    FALSE  1065305102    MC1            V=2&GUID=4AA7FD1069A44E5EADAEE679A5BC12A3
.mycereal.com     TRUE    /    FALSE  2051233759    SITESERVER     ID=ed12ef6f2b870ef998511fe29b1b3a0f
.bcg.com          TRUE    /    FALSE  2051233304    SITESERVER     ID=187afb7d865a997bf07846b1179a7bbb
```

Web bugs, they can be used to create cross-site profiles. We discuss this practice further in the section on Advertising Networks.

Web bugs are tiny (1 pixel) graphic files embedded in e-mail messages and on Web sites. Web bugs are used to automatically transmit information about the user and the page being viewed to a monitoring server. For instance, when a recipient opens an e-mail in HTML format or opens a Web page, a message is sent to a server calling for graphic information. This tells the marketer that the e-mail was opened, indicating at least that the recipient was interested in the subject header. Web bugs are often clear or colored white so they are not visible to the recipient. You may be able to determine if a Web page is using Web bugs by using the "View Source" option of your browser and examining the "IMG" (image) tags on the page. As noted above, Web bugs are typically 1 pixel in size and contain the URL of a server that differs from the one that served the page itself (see Web Bugs FAQ, www.privacyfoundation.org). *Insight on Society: Should Web Bugs Be Illegal?* considers whether the use of Web bugs should be regulated.

INSIGHT ON SOCIETY

SHOULD WEB BUGS BE ILLEGAL?

Images called "clear GIFs," "Web beacons," and "invisible GIFs" don't sound too threatening. But when they're referred to as "Web bugs," Internet users begin to get a better sense of the true purpose of these devices.

Marketers using Web bugs claim their sole purpose is to aid in collecting statistics about Web usage, including how many visitors a particular site has had, which pages on a site are most popular, and which banner ads are providing the best results. Companies such as Microsoft, AOL, and Barnesandnoble.com use Web bugs to track millions of monthly advertising promotions. Without such data, they argue, they would be unable to determine which marketing techniques to use. All information collected is anonymous and, on its own, cannot be linked back to any particular individual. For that reason, Web bugs are innocuous, they say.

So why go to the trouble of hiding them?

That's what privacy advocates are asking. And what they've learned is that although Web bugs may have been designed to simply provide traffic counts, when combined with information from third-party sources, bugs can give marketers an all too complete picture of an individual consumer — right down to home address and online account balances.

Web bugs work by being inserted on a Web page or in an e-mail message as a tiny, virtually invisible image. Most Web bugs are only one pixel by one pixel in size, enabling them to remain transparent. However, once a user visits a Web page with a Web bug on it, or reads an e-mail with a bug inserted, unbeknownst to them, data about their online activities is forwarded to a third party information collector, usually a marketing firm.

Web bugs can report a user's IP address, referring URL, and cookie information from a visit to a site, and from an e-mail can link an e-mail address to previously set cookie data. The security firm Intelytics has identified several different types of Web bugs. The simplest and most common bug is the clear GIF that works with cookies to transmit information to third parties about a user's online travels. "Executable bugs" can install a file onto someone's hard drive to collect information whenever they go online; such bugs can scan a computer and send information on all documents containing key words, such as *medical* or *finance*. "Script-based executable bugs" can actually take documents from a computer without notice. So while the majority of bugs may be used simply to track a user's movements, there appears to be great potential for abuse.

Bugs enable marketers to know who's online, which Web sites they've visited, where they've spent money, what their address is, and more. When the technology is used by a network of sites linked to a third-party, such as DoubleClick or Linkexchange, consumer profiling becomes even more detailed, leading to a potentially significant loss of privacy.

Use of Web bug technology has risen sharply. An August 2001 report by Cyveillance found Web bugs on almost 20% of personal Web pages (compared to less than .5% in 1998) and over 15% of corporate home pages. Personal pages that AOL and Geocities (a company owned by Yahoo) allow members to create for free are the most common source of bugs. For example, someone who agrees to place an advertisement for a free AOL trial membership on their personal Web site receives $50 from AOL for any new member generated by the ad. However, such users may not realize that when they place the AOL ad on their site, they are also receiving a Web bug that forwards information to Be Free Inc., an Internet marketing company, about every individual who clicks on the AOL ad. Neither AOL nor Yahoo explicitly inform users that they insert Web bugs into personal Web pages created at their sites, according to an August 2001 Web Bug Report issued by Security Space.

Collecting information on consumers is nothing new, but the extent to which data can now be accumulated and combined to form very specific profiles of Internet users has led to calls for regulation. A bipartisan congressional group, Congressional Privacy Congress, has indicated that it will look into the Web bug phenomenon with an eye toward introducing legislation that will curtail use of such devices without consumer notification. Giving Internet users the opportunity to opt-in or opt-out is a necessary first step, some Congress members feel.

The Privacy Foundation has issued guidelines for Web bug usage. The guidelines suggest that Web bugs should be visible as an icon on the screen, the icon should be labeled to indicate its function, and it should identify the name of the company that placed the Web bug on the page. In addition, if a user clicks on the Web bug, it should display a disclosure statement indicating what data is being collected, how the data is used after it is collected, what companies receive the data, what other data the Web bug is combined with, and whether or not a cookie is associated with the Web bug. Users should be able to opt-out of any data collection done by the Web bug, and the Web bug should not be used to collect information from Web pages of a sensitive nature such as medical, financial, job-related, or sexual matters. The Privacy Foundation is also currently beta testing software that will notify consumers both visually and aurally of a Web bug's presence as well as a browser plug-in that will detect bugs. Several commercial firms are also in the process of developing software to identify and potentially disable such devices.

Currently, however, Internet users have little protection against such devices — technological or legislative. Most users probably have no idea that Web bugs are in use, and how they can or may be used.

SOURCES: "Web Bugs" Are Tracking Use of Internet," by John Schwartz, *New York Times*, August 14, 2001; "A Call to Regulate Web Bugs," by Jim Welte, *Business 2.0*, March 14, 2001; "Reversal of Fortune — Tracking Web Trackers," by Stefanie Olsen, ZDNet, March 5, 2001; "Congressional Group to Study Web Bugs," by Christopher Saunders, *InternetNews*, February 9, 2001; "New Proposal: Make Web Bugs Visible," Privacy Foundation, www.privacyfoundation.org, September 13, 2000.

DATABASES, DATA WAREHOUSES, AND DATA MINING: DEVELOPING PROFILES

Databases, data warehouses, data mining, and the variety of marketing decision-making techniques loosely called *profiling* are at the heart of the revolution in Internet marketing. Together these techniques attempt to identify precisely who the online customer is and what they want, and then, to fulfill the customer's criteria exactly. These techniques are more powerful and far more precise and fine-grained than the gross levels of demographic and market segmentation techniques used in mass marketing media or by telemarketing.

In order to understand the data in transaction logs, registration forms, shopping carts, cookies, Web bugs, and other sources, Internet marketers need massively powerful and capacious databases, database management systems, and data modeling tools. Just examine the transaction log in Figure 7.12 again, and then imagine trying to find the patterns in millions of entries each day!

database
a software application that stores records and attributes

database management system (DBMS)
a software application used by organizations to create, maintain, and access databases

SQL (structured query language)
an industry-standard database query and manipulation language used in relational databases

relational databases
represent data as two-dimensional tables with records organized in rows and attributes in columns; data within different tables can be flexibly related so long as the tables share a common data element

data warehouse
a database that collects a firm's transactional and customer data in a single location for offline analysis

Databases

The first step in interpreting huge transaction streams is to store the information systematically. A **database** is a software application that stores records and attributes. A telephone book is a physical database that stores records of individuals and their attributes such as names, addresses, and phone numbers. A **database management system** (**DBMS**) is a software application used by organizations to create, maintain, and access databases. The most common DBMS are DB2 from IBM and a variety of SQL databases from Oracle, Sybase, and other providers. **SQL** (**structured query language**) is an industry-standard database query and manipulation language used in relational databases. **Relational databases** such as DB2 and SQL represent data as two-dimensional tables with records organized in rows, and attributes in columns, much like a spreadsheet. The tables — and all the data in them — can be flexibly related to one another as long as the tables share a common data element.

Relational databases are extraordinarily flexible and allow marketers and other managers to view and analyze data from different perspectives very quickly. Figure 7.14 illustrates a relational database view of customers. The data are organized into four tables: customer, order, product, and supplier. The tables all share at least one data element. Using this model, it would be possible to query the database for a list of all customers who bought a certain product, or to message a supplier when the inventory falls below a certain level (and message a customer automatically via e-mail that the product is temporarily out of stock).

Data Warehouses and Data Mining

A **data warehouse** is a database that collects a firm's transactional and customer data in a single location for offline analysis by marketers and site managers. The data originate in many core operational areas of the firm, such as Web site transaction logs,

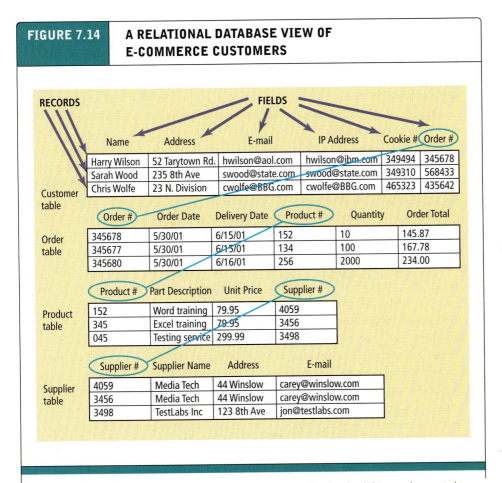

| FIGURE 7.14 | **A RELATIONAL DATABASE VIEW OF E-COMMERCE CUSTOMERS** |

RECORDS

FIELDS

Customer table

Name	Address	E-mail	IP Address	Cookie #	Order #
Harry Wilson	52 Tarytown Rd.	hwilson@aol.com	hwilson@ibm.com	349494	345678
Sarah Wood	235 8th Ave	swood@state.com	swood@state.com	349310	568433
Chris Wolfe	23 N. Division	cwolfe@BBG.com	cwolfe@BBG.com	465323	435642

Order table

Order #	Order Date	Delivery Date	Product #	Quantity	Order Total
345678	5/30/01	6/15/01	152	10	145.87
345677	5/30/01	6/15/01	134	100	167.78
345680	5/30/01	6/16/01	256	2000	234.00

Product table

Product #	Part Description	Unit Price	Supplier #
152	Word training	79.95	4059
345	Excel training	79.95	3456
045	Testing service	299.99	3498

Supplier table

Supplier #	Supplier Name	Address	E-mail
4059	Media Tech	44 Winslow	carey@winslow.com
3456	Media Tech	44 Winslow	carey@winslow.com
3498	TestLabs Inc	123 8th Ave	jon@testlabs.com

In a relational database, data gathered from an e-commerce site is stored on hard drives and presented to managers of sites in the form of interrelated tables.

shopping carts, point-of-sale terminals (product scanners) in stores, warehouse inventory levels, field sales reports, external scanner data supplied by third parties, and financial payment data. The purpose of a data warehouse is to gather all the firm's transaction and customer data into one logical repository where it can be analyzed and modeled by managers without disrupting or taxing the firm's primary transactional systems and databases. Data warehouses grow quickly into storage repositories containing terabytes of data (trillions of bytes) on consumer behavior at a firm's stores and Web sites. With a data warehouse, firms can answer such questions as: What products are the most profitable by region and city? What regional marketing campaigns are working? How effective is store promotion of the firm's Web site? According to a Data Warehousing Institute survey of more than 1,600 companies, most found

data mining
a set of analytical techniques that look for patterns in the data of a database or data warehouse, or seek to model the behavior of customers

customer profile
a description of the typical behavior of a customer or a group of customers at a Web site

query-driven data mining
data mining based on specific queries

model-driven data mining
involves the use of a model that analyzes the key variables of interest to decision makers

rule-based data mining
examines demographic and transactional data of groups and individuals at a Web site and attempts to derive general rules of behavior for visitors

collaborative filtering
site visitors classify themselves into affinity groups characterized by common interests; products are then recommended based on what other people in the group have recently purchased

major benefits in the successful implementation of a data warehouse, such as better segmentation and increased revenues because business managers had a more complete awareness of customers through data that could be accessed quickly (Jupiter Media Metrix, 2001b).

Data mining is a set of different analytical techniques that look for patterns in the data of a database or data warehouse, or seek to model the behavior of customers. Web site data can be "mined" to develop profiles of visitors and customers. A **customer profile** is simply a description of the typical behavior of a customer or a group of customers at a Web site. Customer profiles help to identify the patterns in group and individual behavior that occur online as millions of visitors use a firm's Web site.

There are many different types of data mining. The simplest type is **query-driven data mining** — data mining based on specific queries. For instance, based on hunches of marketers who suspect a relationship in the database or who need to answer a specific question, such as "What is the relationship between time of day and purchases of various products at the Web site?" marketers can easily query the data warehouse and produce a database table that rank orders the top ten products sold at a Web site by each hour of the day. Marketers can then change the content of the Web site to stimulate more sales by highlighting different products over time or placing particular products on the home page at certain times of day or night.

Another form of data mining is model-driven. **Model-driven data mining** involves the use of a model that analyzes the key variables of interest to decision makers. For example, marketers may want to reduce the inventory carried on the Web site by removing unprofitable items that do not sell well. A financial model can be built showing the profitability of each product on the site so that an informed decision can be made.

A more interesting kind of data mining is rule-based. **Rule-based data mining** examines demographic and transactional data of groups and individuals at a Web site and attempts to derive general rules of behavior for visitors. There are factual and behavioral approaches as well as different levels of granularity, from market segments down to individuals. In the *factual approach,* used by companies such as Engage Technologies and Personify, factual demographic and transactional data (purchase price, products purchased) and material viewed at the site are analyzed and stored in a customer profile table in order to segment the marketplace into well-defined groups. For instance, female customers who purchased items worth more than $50 in an average visit and who viewed travel articles might be shown a vacation travel advertisement. The rules are specified by marketing managers as a set of *filters* based on their expert opinions, as well as trial and error, and are applied to aggregate groups of visitors or market segments. There can be thousands of different types of visitors, and hence thousands of marketing decisions or filters that marketers have to make.

A different *behavioral approach* to data mining is **collaborative filtering** (see *Insight on Technology: Collaborative Filtering*). Behavioral approaches try to "let the data speak for itself" rather than impose rules by expert marketers. Collaborative filtering was first developed at the MIT Media Lab and commercialized by an MIT Media Lab-backed start-up company, Firefly. Here, rather than have expert marketers make decisions based on their own "rules of thumb," experience, and corporate needs (a need to move old inventory, for instance), site visitors collaboratively classify themselves based on common selections. The idea is that people classify themselves into "affinity groups" characterized by common interests. A query to the database can isolate the individuals who all purchased the same products. Later, based on purchases by other members of the affinity group, the system can recommend purchases based on what other people in the group have bought recently. For example, visitors who all purchased books on amateur flying could be pitched a video that illustrates small plane flying techniques. And then later, if it was discovered that several members of this "amateur flying interest group" were purchasing books on, say, parachuting, then all members of the group would be pitched a recommendation to buy parachuting books based on what other people "like themselves" are purchasing. This pitch would be made regardless of demographic background of the individuals.

A more fine-grained behavioral approach that seeks to deal with individuals as opposed to market segments or affinity groups derives rules from individual consumer behavior (along with some demographic information) and seeks to deal specifically with individuals (Adomavicious and Tuzhilin, 2001; Fawcett and Provost, 1996, 1997; Chan, 1999). Here, the pages actually visited by specific users are stored as a set of conjunctive rules. For example, if an individual — let's say William Wilson — visits a site and typically ("as a rule") moves from the home page to the financial news section to the Asian report section, and then often purchases articles from the "Recent Developments in Banking" section, then this person — based on purely past behavioral patterns — might be shown an advertisement for a book on Asian money markets. These rules can be constructed to follow an individual across many different Web sites.

There are many drawbacks to all these techniques, not least of which is that there may be millions of rules, many of them nonsensical, and many others of short-term duration. Hence, the rules need extensive validation and culling (Adomavicious and Tuzhilin, 2000). Also, there can be millions of affinity groups and other patterns in the data that are temporal or meaningless. The difficulty is isolating the valid, powerful (profitable) patterns in the data and then acting on the observed pattern fast enough to make a sale you would otherwise not have made. As we see later, there are practical difficulties and trade-offs involved in achieving these levels of granularity, precision, and speed.

ADVERTISING NETWORKS

Specialized marketing firms called *advertising networks* have appeared to help e-commerce sites take advantage of the powerful tracking and marketing potential of

INSIGHT ON TECHNOLOGY

COLLABORATIVE FILTERING

One of the biggest complaints users have about the Internet is the overwhelming amount of information available. Many individuals express frustration regarding the amount of time it takes to track down relevant information that meets their needs. Of course, users who have technologically savvy friends or family have an advantage: They can turn to such experts for advice and recommendations regarding where to go online. Being able to ask opinions of people like themselves is what collaborative filtering is all about.

Collaborative filtering essentially automates the process of collecting and distributing recommendations from other users. The software enables users to rely on feedback from others with similar tastes or buying habits in order to find what they are looking for. Software programs developed by Firefly (now owned by Microsoft), NetPerceptions, and LikeMinds (now owned by Macromedia) are among the best known, with Web sites such as Amazon.com (books), Media Unbound.com, and Mubu.com (music) and many others relying on such technology to provide visitors with product and service recommendations.

Collaborative filtering systems work by gathering information regarding purchases or preferences from a large group of people; the more input, the better the technology works. Using a similarity metric, which is a means of segmenting the user base, a subsegment of users are selected whose behavior or preferences are similar to the user seeking recommendations. An average of that subsegment is calculated, with a recommendation made based on that average.

In many cases, recommendations are made based on past purchasing behavior, which may or may not reflect the needs or preferences of the user today. The ability to narrow down the list of potential options, however, makes the information gathering process more efficient and, for many users, very helpful.

The weakness of the technology, however, is that in averaging the input and feedback provided, the process may skew the recommendations further away from the user's own individual interests or behavior. In effect, averaging results from a large group of people may actually result in recommendations that are not in tune with what the user would have chosen for himself or herself.

Another downside is that Web sites relying on this technology to recommend additional product or service purchases may actually prefer to recommend different options altogether. That is, some products and services may be less desirable for that e-commerce business to sell, perhaps because they are difficult to procure or because the profit margins are small. Most collaborative filtering systems do not take these factors into account — only the averaged preferences of the consumer base. NetPerceptions however, is in the process of expanding its system to include rules-based decision making, which will provide merchants with more options for controlling the kind of content that is driven by collaborative filtering.

For example, a merchant can write a rule that limits the types of items prompted by collaborative filtering to only the two most profitable possibilities in its inventory.

Cass Sunstein, a professor of law at the University of Chicago, has another, broader problem with collaborative filtering. In Sunstein's view, the effect of collaborative filtering systems is to reduce an individual's exposure to random or unwanted information. Although this might be efficient, Sunstein worries that this ultimately may be dangerous for society, because part of the function of news and other types of digital content is to for people to become aware of things they might not otherwise realize they were interested in, and part of the basis of democracy is having people see and understand people who are different from them. Collaborative filtering taken to its extremes might mean that users see nothing by accident, a frightening prospect to Sunstein. Although given the current state of collaborative filtering, this is probably not an imminent development, consider the implications.

SOURCES: "Personalize Me, Baby," by Janelle Brown, Salon.com, April 6, 2001; *Republic.com*, by Cass Sunstein, Princeton University Press, 2001; "Collaborative Filtering," by F. Heylighen, *Principia Cybernetica Web*, January 31, 2001; "CRM Makes Online Shopping Personal," by Charles Waltner, www.informationweek.com, January 29, 2001; "Personalization: The Tailor-Made Web," by Cade Metz, *PC Magazine*, June 26, 2000; "One to (N)one?" by Susan Kuchinskas, *Business 2.0*, September 12, 2000; "Technology Note: Collaborative Filtering," by Jean-Claude Charlet and Erik Brynjolfsson, Stanford University, March 1998; "From Dating to Voting, Collaborative Filtering Will Make Our Choices Easier," by Bob Metcalfe, *InfoWorld.com*, March 18, 1996.

the Internet. **Advertising networks** offer a number of services, from targeted e-mail campaigns to brand awareness programs, but they are best known for their ability to present users with banner advertisements based on a database of user behavioral data. Advertising networks represent the most sophisticated application of Internet database capabilities to date, and illustrate just how different Internet marketing is from traditional marketing.

> **advertising networks**
> present users with banner advertisements based on a database of user behavioral data

Perhaps the best-known advertising network is DoubleClick, which released its first generation tracking system, DART, in 1996. Realmedia Inc.'s Open Ad Stream, and L90 Inc.'s Admonitor are two other tracking systems. DoubleClick claims to "serve" 30 billion banner ads per month (in round numbers, about 12,000 ads per second) and maintains over 100 million user profiles on individual Web consumers. Specialized ad servers are used to store and send to users the appropriate banner ads. All these systems rely on cookies, Web bugs, and massive back-end user profile databases to pitch banner ads to users and record the results, including sales. This process allows feedback from the market to be entered into the database. DoubleClick has even invented a new service called Boomerang that traces the long-term purchasing behavior of all people who have ever been exposed to a banner ad. Figure 7.15 illustrates how these systems work. Advertising networks begin with a consumer requesting a page from a member of the advertising network (#1). A connection is established with the third-party ad server (#2) . The ad server identifies the user by reading the cookie file on the user's hard drive and checks its user profile database for the user's profile (#3) .

The ad server selects an appropriate banner ad based on the user's previous purchases, interests, demographics, or other data in the profile (#4). Whenever the user later goes online and visits any of the network member sites, the ad server recognizes the user and serves up the same or different ads regardless of the site content. The advertising network follows users from site to site through the use of Web bugs (#5).

Advertising networks have become controversial among privacy advocates because of their ability to track individual consumers across the Internet. We discuss privacy issues further in Chapter 9.

CUSTOMER RELATIONSHIP MANAGEMENT (CRM) SYSTEMS

customer relationship management system (CRM)

a repository of customer information that records all of the contacts that a customer has with a firm and generates a customer profile available to everyone in the firm with a need to "know the customer"

Customer relationship management (CRM) systems are another important Internet marketing technology. A **customer relationship management system** is a repository of customer information that records all of the contacts that a customer has with a firm (including Web sites) and generates a customer profile available to everyone in the firm with a need to "know the customer." CRM systems also supply the analytical software required to analyze and use customer information. Customers come to firms

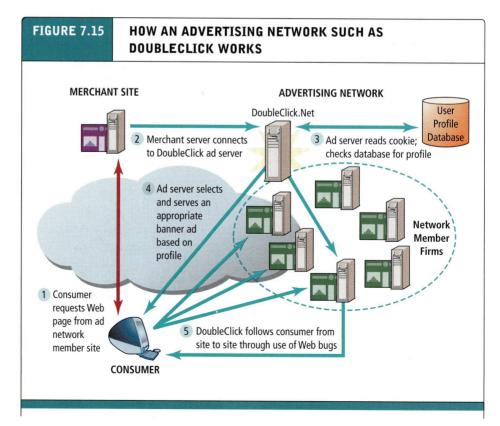

FIGURE 7.15 | **HOW AN ADVERTISING NETWORK SUCH AS DOUBLECLICK WORKS**

MERCHANT SITE

ADVERTISING NETWORK

DoubleClick.Net

User Profile Database

2 Merchant server connects to DoubleClick ad server

3 Ad server reads cookie; checks database for profile

4 Ad server selects and serves an appropriate banner ad based on profile

Network Member Firms

1 Consumer requests Web page from ad network member site

5 DoubleClick follows consumer from site to site through use of Web bugs

CONSUMER

not just over the Web but also through telephone call centers, customer service representatives, sales representatives, automated voice response systems, ATMs and kiosks, in-store point-of-sale terminals, and mobile devices (m-commerce). In the past, firms generally did not maintain a single repository of customer information, but instead were organized along product lines, with each product line maintaining a customer list (and often not sharing it with others in the same firm).

In general, firms did not know who their customers were, how profitable they were, or how they responded to marketing campaigns. For instance, a bank customer might see a television advertisement for a low-cost auto loan that included an 800-number to call. However, if the customer came to the bank's Web site instead, rather than calling the 800- number, marketers would have no idea how effective the television campaign was because this Web customer contact data was not related to the 800-number call center data. Figure 7.16 illustrates how a CRM system integrates customer contact data into a single system.

CRMs, like the advertising networks described above, are part of the evolution of firms toward a customer-centric and marketing-segment–based business, and away from a product-line-centered business. Also, like advertising networks, CRMs are essentially a database technology with extraordinary capabilities for addressing the needs of each customer and differentiating the product or service on the basis of treating each customer as a unique person. Customer profiles can contain the following information:

- A map of the customer's relationship with the institution
- Product and usage summary data
- Demographic and psychographic data
- Profitability measures
- Contact history summarizing the customer's contacts with the institution across most delivery channels
- Marketing and sales information containing programs received by the customer and the customer's responses

With these profiles, CRMs can be used to sell additional products and services, develop new products, increase product utilization, reduce marketing costs, identify and retain profitable customers, optimize service delivery costs, retain high lifetime value customers, enable personal communications, improve customer loyalty, and increase product profitability.

For instance, the National Basketball Association is in the process of rolling out a customer relationship management system from E.piphany that will serve the league and its 29 basketball teams. The system will take in data on basketball fans around the world from a variety of sources, including the NBA's Web site, e-mail marketing responses, direct mail marketing responses, individual team databases, the NBA store

FIGURE 7.16	A CUSTOMER RELATIONSHIP MANAGEMENT SYSTEM

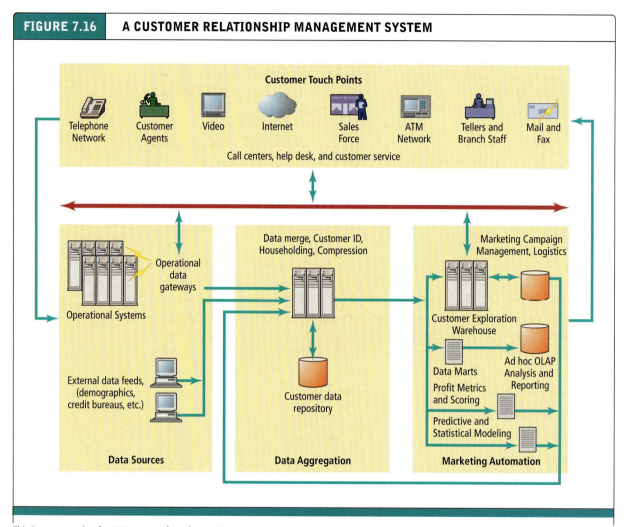

This is an example of a CRM system for a financial services institution. The system captures customer information from all customer "touch" points as well as other data sources, merges the data, and aggregates it into a single customer data repository or data warehouse where it can be used to provide better service, as well as to construct customer profiles for marketing purposes. Online Analytical Processing (OLAP) allows managers to dynamically analyze customer activities to spot trends or problems involving customers. Other analytical software programs analyze aggregate customer behavior to identify profitable and unprofitable customers as well as customer activities.
SOURCE: Compaq Inc. 1998.

in New York City, All-Star nomination ballots, and even the Home Shopping Network (which sells NBA memorabilia). One of the NBA's primary goals is to create personalized promotions for NBA teams, merchandise, and other products (Songini, 2001).

In addition to E.piphany, other leading CRM vendors include Siebel, Oracle, PeopleSoft, Kana, and eGain.

7.4   B2C AND B2B E-COMMERCE MARKETING AND BRANDING STRATEGIES

The new marketing technologies described above have spawned a new generation of marketing techniques and added power to some traditional techniques (such as direct mail campaigns with Web site addresses displayed). In this section we describe a variety of Internet marketing strategies for market entry, customer acquisition, customer retention, pricing, and dealing with channel conflict. It is important to note that although B2C and B2B e-commerce do have differentiating features (for instance in B2C e-commerce, marketing is aimed at individual consumers, whereas in B2B e-commerce, typically more than just one individual is involved with the purchase decision), the strategies discussed in this section in most instances can be, and are, applied in both the B2C and B2B arena.

MARKET ENTRY STRATEGIES

Both new firms and traditional existing firms have choices about how to enter the market, and establishing the objectives of their online presence. Figure 7.17 illustrates four basic market entry strategies.

Let's examine the situation facing new firms — quadrants 1 and 2 in Figure 7.17. In the E-commerce I era, the typical entry strategy was pure clicks/first mover advantage, utilized by such companies as Amazon, eBay and e-Trade (quadrant 1). Indeed, this strategy was at the heart of the so-called new economy movement, and provided the capital catch basin into which billions of investment dollars flowed. The ideas are beguiling and simplistic: Enter the market first and experience "first mover" advantages — heightened user awareness, followed rapidly by successful consumer transactions and experiences — and grow brand strength. According to leading consultants of this era, first movers would experience a short-lived mini-monopoly. They would be the only providers for a few months, and then other copycats would enter the market because entry costs were so low. To prevent new competitors from entering the market, growing audience size very rapidly became the most important corporate goal rather than profits and revenue. Firms following this strategy typically spent the majority of their marketing budget (which in and of itself may have constituted a large part of their available capital) on building brand (site) awareness by purchasing high visibility advertising in traditional mass media such as television (Super Bowl game ads), radio, newspapers, and magazines. If the first mover gathered most of the customers in a particular category (pets, wine, gardening supplies, and so forth), the belief was that new entrants would not be able to enter because customers would not be willing to pay the switching costs. Customers would be "locked in" to the first mover's interface. Moreover, the strength of the brand would inhibit switching even though competitors were just a click away.

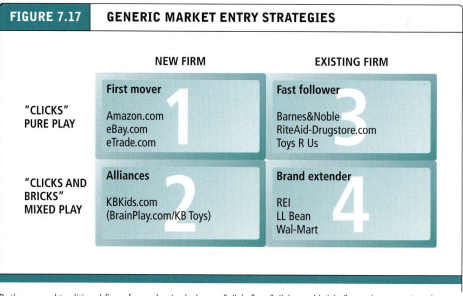

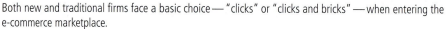

Both new and traditional firms face a basic choice — "clicks" or "clicks and bricks" — when entering the e-commerce marketplace.

In retrospect, it is now clear that pursuing first mover advantage as a marketing strategy was not particularly successful for most firms. Although first movers may have interesting advantages, they also have significant liabilities. The history of first movers in most areas of business is that statistically, they are losers for the most part because they lack the complementary assets and resources required to compete over the long term. While innovative, first movers usually lack financial depth, marketing and sales resources, loyal customers, strong brands, and production or fulfillment facilities needed to meet customer demands once the product succeeds (Teece, 1986). Research on Internet advertising conducted at the end of E-commerce I discovered that while expensive ad campaigns may have increased brand awareness, the other components of a brand such as trust, loyalty, and reputation did not automatically follow, and more important, site visits did not necessarily translate into purchases (Ellison, 2000).

Another possibility for new firms is to pursue a mixed clicks and bricks strategy, coupling an online presence with other sales channels (quadrant 2). However, few new firms can afford the "bricks" part of this strategy. Therefore, firms following this entrance strategy often ally themselves with established firms that have already developed brand names, production and distribution facilities, and the financial resources needed to launch a successful Internet business. For instance, BrainPlay, Inc., an e-tailer of children's goods, entered into an alliance with the established Consolidated Stores Corporation KB Toys unit to form a new online presence called KBkids.com.

Now let's look at traditional firms. Traditional firms face some similar choices, with of course one difference: They have significant amounts of cash flow and capital to fund their e-commerce ventures over a long period of time. For example, Barnes & Noble, the world's largest book retailer, formed Barnesandnoble.com, a follower site, when faced with the success of upstart Amazon.com (quadrant 3). The Web site was established as an independent firm, a Web pure play, although obviously making use of the Barnes & Noble brand name. Likewise, Rite-Aid followed the success of online pharmacies by establishing its own Web site (riteaid.com) and then forming an alliance with Drugstore.com to fulfill and service prescriptions ordered online at Drugstore.com (and perform back-end processing of insurance payments).

The most common strategy for existing firms is to extend their businesses and brands by using a mixed "clicks and bricks" strategy in which online marketing is closely integrated with offline physical stores (quadrant 4). These "brand extension" strategies characterize REI, L.L. Bean, Wal-Mart, and many other established retail firms. Like fast followers, they have the advantage of existing brands and relationships. However, even more than fast followers, the brand extenders do not set up separate pure-play online stores, but instead typically integrate the online firm with the traditional firm from the very beginning. L.L. Bean and Wal-Mart saw the Web as an extension of their existing order processing and fulfillment, marketing, and branding efforts.

Each of the market entry strategies discussed above has seen its share of successes and failures. While the ultimate choice of strategy depends on a firm's existing brands, management strengths, operational strengths, and capital resources (Gulati and Garino, 2000; Tedeschi, 1999), today most firms are opting for a mixed "clicks and bricks" strategy in the hope that it will enable them to reach profitability more quickly.

ESTABLISHING THE CUSTOMER RELATIONSHIP

Once a firm chooses a market entry strategy, the next task is establishing a relationship with the customer. Traditional public relations and advertising media (newsprint, direct mail, magazines, television, and even radio) remain vital for establishing awareness of the firm. However, a number of unique Internet marketing techniques have emerged that have proven to be very powerful drivers of Web site traffic and purchases. Here we discuss three of these new techniques: permission marketing, affiliate marketing, and viral marketing.

Permission Marketing

The phrase **permission marketing** was coined by author and consultant Seth Godin to describe the strategy of obtaining permission from consumers before sending them

permission marketing
marketing strategy in which companies obtain permission from consumers before sending them information or promotional messages

information or promotional messages (Godin, 1999). Godin's premise is that by obtaining permission to send information to consumers up front, companies are much more likely to be able to develop a customer relationship. When consumers agree to receive promotional messages, they are *opting-in*; when they decide they do not want to receive such messages, they *opt-out*.

Most consumers need an incentive to spend time reading promotional material, or to provide personal information companies can use to improve their own marketing. Godin's former company, Yoyodyne, pioneered the creation of online sweepstakes and games that gathered information from participants in return for the chance to win money and prizes. Another company, portal Iwon.com, gives users the chance to win money each week for visiting the site; each month the company offers special bonus prizes to users who are willing to complete a more in-depth survey about their personal life. The site gains useful personal information and the user earns the chance to win a free prize.

A key component of permission marketing is e-mail. In addition to being one of the most widely used Internet applications, e-mail has become a very effective marketing tool. Companies request e-mail addresses from customers and then send marketing messages of potential interest; some marketers issue such messages regularly, even weekly, while others do so only when something relevant comes up. Not only is it inexpensive to send, but it is also targeted, measurable, and effective. We will discuss e-mail as a marketing communication tool in greater detail in Chapter 8.

Affiliate Marketing

affiliate marketing

one Web site agrees to pay another Web site a commission for new business opportunities it refers to the site

In the offline world, referrals are one of the best sources of qualified leads. **Affiliate marketing** is the online application of this marketing method, where one Web site agrees to pay another Web site a commission for new business opportunities it refers to the site. The affiliate adds a link to the company's Web site on its own site and encourages its visitors to patronize its marketing partner. Some affiliates are paid a commission based on any sales that are generated, while others may be paid a fee based on number of click-throughs or new registrations, or a flat fee, or some combination of these.

For instance, Amazon.com has a strong affiliate program consisting of more than 500,000 participant sites, called Associates, which receive up to 15% on sales their referrals generate. Ebay's Affiliates Program pays $4.00 for each visitor who becomes a registered user. Amazon and eBay and other large e-commerce companies with affiliate programs typically administer such programs themselves. Smaller e-commerce firms who wish to use affiliate marketing often decide to join an *affiliate network* (sometimes called an *affiliate broker*), which acts as an intermediary. The affiliate network brings would-be affiliates and merchants seeking affiliates together, helps affiliates set up the necessary links on their Web site, tracks all activity, and arranges all payments. Leading affiliate networks include Commission Junction,

BeFree, and LinkShare. In return for their services, affiliate networks typically take about 20% of any fee that would be payable to the affiliate.

A key benefit of affiliate marketing is the fact that it typically operates on a "pay for performance" basis. Affiliates provide qualified sales leads in return for pre-agreed upon compensation. Another advantage, however, is the existence of an established user base that a marketer can tap into through an affiliate immediately. For affiliates, the appeal is a steady income — potentially large — that can result from such relationships. In addition, the presence of another company's logo or brand name can provide a measure of prestige and credibility.

Affiliate marketing can have some drawbacks, however, if not managed carefully. Too many links that are not relevant to a firm's primary focus can lead to brand confusion, for instance. Affiliate marketing works best when affiliates choose products and services that match and supplement the content of their own Web site. Web sites with affiliate links also risk "losing" those customers who click on a link and then never return, unless the Web site takes action to prevent this, such as by having the link open a new window that when closed returns the customer to the original site.

Viral Marketing

Just as affiliate marketing involves using a trusted Web site to encourage users to visit other sites, **viral marketing** is the process of getting customers to pass along a company's marketing message to friends, family, and colleagues. It's the online version of word-of-mouth advertising, which spreads even faster than in the real world. In addition to increasing the size of a company's customer base, customer referrals also have other advantages: They are less expensive to acquire since existing customers do all the acquisition work and they tend to use online support services less, preferring to turn back to the person who referred them for advice. Also, because they cost so little to acquire and keep, referred customers begin to generate profits for a company much earlier than customers acquired through other marketing methods (Reichheld and Schefter, 2000).

Half.com's Refer-a-Friend program is an example of viral marketing, where registered users at the site selling used books, music, movies, and games are given an incentive to tell their friends about the site — $5 if the friends buy something. Users clicking on the Refer-a-Friend icon at the Half.com site are asked to enter the first name and e-mail address of friends and family they want to tell about the site. Half then sends out a brief e-mail inviting the friends to visit the site and enjoy a $5 coupon off their first order of $10. When any friend spends $10, the first user gets a $5 referral fee. Because its business is growing by word of mouth, Half.com's customer acquisition cost is less than $10 per customer (Reichheld and Schefter, 2000), which is impressive since online customer acquisition can cost 1.5 to 2.5 times what it costs in the physical world (Kenny and Marshall, 2000).

viral marketing
the process of getting customers to pass along a company's marketing message to friends, family, and colleagues

The process of viral marketing can also involve users who do not know each other. When a consumer decides to make a major purchase, such as a new mountain bike, getting advice and opinions from people who own such bikes is usually the first step. And with the Internet, it is fairly easy to find and read reviews of various bike models written by knowledgeable consumers. Sites such as Epinions.com and ConsumerReports.org provide objective product reviews by people who have bought and used a long list of products and services. Armed with feedback and input from online aficionados, consumers can then click through to an e-commerce site and make a purchase. Epinions has links to a number of affiliate e-tailers who pay a fee back to the site for each purchase that originates there. CNET does the same thing, providing high tech product reviews and links to online retailers who can immediately ship the desired item.

Leveraging Brands

brand leveraging

using the power of an existing brand to acquire new customers for a new product or service

Perhaps the most successful online customer acquisition strategy in the E-Commerce II period is brand leveraging (Carpenter, 2000). **Brand leveraging** refers to the process of using the power of an existing brand to acquire new customers for a new product or service. For instance, while Tab was the first to discover a huge market for diet cola drinks, Coca-Cola ultimately succeeded in dominating the market by leveraging the Coke brand to a new product called Diet Coke.

In the online world, some researchers predicted that offline brands would not be able to make the transition to the Web because customers would soon learn who was offering products at the cheapest prices and brand premiums would disappear (price transparency) (Sinha, 2000). But this has not occurred. In retail, firms such as Kmart, Wal-Mart and JCPenney have leaped into the top ten online retail firms in a very short period in large part because of the strength of their offline brand, which gave them the ability to attract millions of their offline customers to their Web sites. In the financial service industry sector, firms such as Wells-Fargo, Citibank, Fidelity, and Merrill Lynch have all succeeded in acquiring millions of online customers based on their large offline customer bases and brands. In the content provider industry, the *Wall Street Journal* and *Consumer Reports* have become among the most successful subscription-based content providers. In manufacturing and retail, Dell Computer has been very successful in leveraging its brand of custom-built computers ordered by telephone into a made-to-order computer ordered over the Internet (Kraemer et al., 2000). A major advantage of brand leveraging — when compared to a start-up venture with no brand recognition — is that it significantly reduces the costs of acquiring new customers (Kotler and Armstrong, 2001).

In addition to leveraging offline brands into the online world, it is also possible to leverage established online brands to new products and product lines. As you saw in the opening case in Chapter 1 on Amazon.com, this has been one of Amazon.com's primary marketing strategies. However, as evident from the case study on Priceline in Chapter 2, this strategy is not always a successful one.

CUSTOMER RETENTION: STRENGTHENING THE CUSTOMER RELATIONSHIP

The Internet offers several extraordinary marketing techniques for building a strong relationship with customers and for differentiating products and services.

Personalization and One-to-One Marketing

No Internet-based marketing technique has received more popular and academic comment that "one-to-one" or "personalized marketing." **One-to-one marketing** means segmenting the market on the basis of individuals (not groups), based on a precise and timely understanding of their needs, targeting specific marketing messages to these individuals, and then positioning the product vis-à-vis competitors to be truly unique (Peppers and Rogers, 1997). One can think of one-to-one marketing as the ultimate form of market segmentation, targeting, and positioning — where the segments are individuals.

The movement toward market segmentation has been ongoing since the development of systematic market research and mass media in the 1930s. However, e-commerce and the Internet are different in that they enable personalized one-to one-marketing to occur on a mass scale. Figure 7.18 depicts the continuum of marketing — from mass marketing of undifferentiated products, where one size and one price fits all, to personalized one-to-one marketing.

Mass marketing, based on national media messages aimed at a single national audience and with a single national price, is appropriate for products that are relatively simple and attractive to all consumers in a single form. Think of Coke and Tide and McDonalds. *Direct marketing*, which is based on direct mail or phone messages and aimed at segments of the market likely to purchase and which has little variation in price (but special offers to loyal customers), is most often used for products that can be stratified into different categories. *Micromarketing*, which is aimed at geographical units (neighborhoods, cities) or specialized market segments (technology buffs), is the first form of true database marketing. Frito Lay, for instance, maintains a national sales database for each of 10,000 route sales personnel and over 50,000 store outlets. Frito Lay marketers know precisely at the end of every day how many small bags of Salsa Chips sell in Los Angeles, and how many bags of Ranch Chips sell in Cambridge, Massachusetts, neighborhoods, store by store. Although seemingly simple, the corn chip can take on fairly complex and nuanced taste experiences that attract different customers in different neighborhoods. Using its database, Frito dynamically adjusts prices to market conditions and competitor product and pricing, every day.

Personalized one-to-one marketing is suitable for products (1) that can be produced in very complex forms, depending on individual tastes, (2) whose price can be

one-to-one marketing
segmenting the market based on a precise and timely understanding of an individual's needs, targeting specific marketing messages to these individuals, and then positioning the product vis-à-vis competitors to be truly unique

FIGURE 7.18	THE MASS MARKET-PERSONALIZATION CONTINUUM

MARKETING STRATEGIES	MARKETING ATTRIBUTES			
	Product	Target	Pricing	Techniques
Mass Marketing	Simple	All consumers	One nation, one price	Mass media
Direct Marketing	Stratified	Segments	One price	Targeted communications, e.g., mail and phone
Micromarketing	Complex	Micro-segments	Variable pricing	Segment profiles
Personalized, One-to-one Marketing	Highly complex	Individual	Unique pricing	Individual profiles

Personalized one-to-one marketing is part of a continuum of marketing strategies. The choice of strategy depends on the nature of the product as well as the technologies that are available to enable various strategies.

adjusted to the level of personalization, and (3) where the individual's tastes and preferences can be effectively gauged.

Personalization has become a very common marketing technique. For instance, of the 375 business and IT managers who participated in the 2000 *InformationWeek* Research's E-Business Agenda Study, 74% personalized communications with customers. The survey also showed that businesses that use personalization are seeing real benefits in return. Of those that personalize all communication, 39% say revenue has increased significantly. Among companies that personalize only some of their communication, 25% report a significant increase in revenue (Bachelder, 2000). eVineyard.com (formerly wine.com), for example, created a highly targeted, personalized e-mail campaign by merging internal behavioral, transaction, and demographic data and lifted its average order size 60% over a pervious e-mail marketing effort (Jupiter Media Metrix, Inc., 2001b).

A good example of personalization at work is Amazon.com or Barnesandnoble.com. Both sites greet registered visitors (based on cookie files), recommend recent books based on user preferences (based on a user profile in their database), and expedite checkout procedures based on prior purchases.

Is Web-based personalization as good as the personal attention you would receive from a local, independent bookstore owner? Can a Web site such as eVineyards.com really know you and advise you in the same way that a local wine merchant can? Probably not. Nevertheless, these Web-based techniques use more individual knowledge and personalization than traditional mass media, and more than a direct mail post card.

However, personalization is not necessarily an unmitigated good. Research indicates that most consumers appreciate personalization when it increases their sense of control and freedom, such as through personalized order tracking, purchase histories, databases of personalized information to ensure quicker transactions during future sessions, and opt-in email notification of new products and special deals. The online buyers participating in Wolfinbarger and Gilly's focus groups saw personalization as negative, however, when it resulted in unsolicited offers or in reducing anonymity; such features are perceived to take away user control and freedom (Wolfinbarger and Gilly, 2001). Furthermore, although personalization technologies have made significant advances over the past several years, it is still difficult for a computer to accurately understand and anticipate the interests and needs of a customer. "Personalized" offers that miss the mark can lead to more customer disdain than satisfaction (Waltner, 2001).

Customization and Customer Co-Production

Customization is an extension of personalization. **Customization** means changing the product — not just the marketing message — according to user preferences. **Customer co-production** in the Web environment takes customization one step further by allowing the customer to interactively create the product.

Many leading companies are starting to offer "build-to-order" customized products on the Internet on a large scale, creating product differentiation and hopefully customer loyalty. Customers appear to be willing to pay a little more for a unique product. The key to making the process affordable is to build a standardized architecture that lets consumers combine a variety of options. For example, Nike has been offering customized sneakers through its Nike iD program on its Web site since 1999. Consumers can choose the type of shoe, colors, material and even a logo of up to eight characters. Nike transmits the orders via computers to specially equipped plants in China and Korea. The sneakers cost only $10 extra and take about three weeks to reach the customer. General Mills has recently concluded a successful test of its mycereal.com Web site with a limited audience and plans to open it to the public soon. At mycereal.com, consumers will be able to design their own cereal, such as

customization
changing the product, not just the marketing message, according to user preferences

customer co-production
in the Web environment, takes customization one step further by allowing the customer to interactively create the product

Chocolate Cheerios or Mango Total, choosing from among 100 different ingredients, and have it delivered to their homes. Reflect.com, a cosmetics company with over 1 million registered users, gathers information from women and then formulates makeup to meet their specific needs. Customers can select their own packaging and even create their own label. The cost of the products is comparable to department store makeup prices since the company profits from being both a manufacturer and a distributor (Lorek, 2001).

Information goods — goods whose value is based on information content — are also ideal for this level of differentiation. For instance, the *New York Times* — and many other content distributors — allows customers to select the news they want to see on a daily basis. Many Web sites, particularly portal sites such as Yahoo, MSN, Netscape, and AOL, allow customers to create their own customized version of the Web site. Such pages frequently require security measures such as usernames and passwords to ensure privacy and confidentiality.

Transactive Content

According to several studies, the most common reasons people go online are to communicate (e-mail) and to find information. As we noted in Section 7.1, shopping is not the primary Internet consumer activity.

transactive content
results from the combination of traditional content, such as articles and product descriptions, with dynamic information culled from product databases, tailored to each user's profile

Marketers have adjusted their Web marketing strategies accordingly. The result is "transactive content," a term originally coined by Forrester Research, a Web research firm (Forrester Research, 1997). **Transactive content** results from the combination of traditional content, such as articles and product descriptions, with dynamic information — such as new product announcements — culled from product databases, tailored to each user's profile. Such applications dynamically respond to user needs and preferences, for instance, by featuring a product within a price range typically preferred by the customer on the order page. You might be reading an article on travel to Africa at Iexplore.com, a travel company with an extensive Web site for adventure-travel advice, products, and services. Based on data drawn from your user profile as well as real-time clickstream behavior (for instance, you had previously expressed an interest in water sports), you might be served a link, among other content, to information on kayaking safaris in Africa (Waltner, 2001). Transactions, content, and interactivity are combined into a seamless experience.

Customer Service

A Web site's approach to customer service can significantly help or hurt its marketing efforts. Online customer service is more than simply following through on order fulfillment; it has to do with users' ability to communicate with a company and obtain desired information in a timely manner. Customer service can help reduce consumer frustration, cut the number of abandoned shopping carts, and increase sales (Bannan, 2000).

According to Wolfinbarger and Gilly, most consumers want to, and will, serve themselves as long as the information they need to do so is relatively easy to find. Online buyers largely do not expect or desire "high touch" service unless they have questions or problems, in which case they want relatively speedy answers that are responsive to their individual issue. According to a recent Jupiter Media Metrix survey, the majority of online consumers expect a resolution to their e-mail inquiry within six hours (Jupiter Media Metrix, 2001c). Wolfinbarger and Gilly noted that participants in their study said that the first opportunity to cement them to an online brand came when they had a problem with the order; customer loyalty increased substantially when online buyers learned that customer service representatives were available online or at a 1-800 number and were willing and able to resolve the situation quickly. Conversely, online buyers who did not receive satisfaction at these critical incidents terminated their relationship and became willing to do business with a site that might charge more, but offered better customer service (Wolfinbarger and Gilly, 2001).

There are a number of tools that companies can use to encourage interaction with prospects and customers and provide customer service, including the customer relationship management systems described in the preceding section, FAQs, customer service chat systems, intelligent agents, and automated response systems.

Frequently Asked Questions (FAQs), a text-based listing of common questions and answers, provide an inexpensive way to anticipate and address customer concerns. Adding an FAQ page on a Web site linked to a search engine helps users track down needed information more quickly, enabling them to help themselves resolve questions and concerns. By directing customers to the FAQs page first, Web sites can give customers answers to common questions. If a question and answer do not appear, it is important for sites to make contact with a live person simple and easy. Offering an e-mail link to customer service at the bottom of the FAQs page is one solution.

Real-time customer service chat systems (in which a company's customer service representatives interactively exchange text-based messages with one or more customers on a real-time basis) is an increasingly popular way for companies to assist online shoppers during a purchase. Chat with online customer service representatives can provide direction, answer questions, and trouble-shoot technical glitches that can kill a sale. Leading vendors of customer service chat systems include LivePerson, FaceTime, and NetCustomer (Bannan, 2000). Vendors claim that chat is significantly less expensive than telephone-based customer service; however, Jupiter Media Metrix believes that this may be based on optimistic assumptions that chat representatives can assist three or four customers at once and that chat sessions are shorter than phone sessions. According to Jupiter's research, representatives can effectively (with prompt response) serve only one or two customers at a time. The same research indicates that average chat sessions often run longer than comparable telephone sessions. Jupiter advises companies evaluating the cost benefits of chat as a third support

frequently asked questions (FAQs)
a text-based listing of common questions and answers

real-time customer service chat
a company's customer service representatives interactively exchange text-based messages with one or more customers on a real-time basis

channel to carefully compare them to those of telephone service and e-mail (Jupiter Media Metrix, 2000b).

Chat has also been reported to raise per-order sales figures, providing sales assistance by allowing companies to "touch" customers during the decision-making process. According to Jupiter Media Metrix, anecdotal evidence suggests that chat can lower shopping cart abandonment rates, increase the number of items purchased per transaction, and increase the dollar value of transactions. For instance, mobile technology retailer iGo.com added customer service chat to its site and watched its average sale jump from $108 to $168 — more than 50% — because of more completed sales and add-on sales.

Intelligent agent technology, described in Chapter 3, is another way customers are providing assistance to online shoppers. Intelligent agents are part of an effort to reduce costly contact with customer service representatives.

automated response system

sends e-mail order confirmations and acknowledgments of e-mailed inquiries

Automated response systems send e-mail order confirmations and acknowledgments of e-mailed inquiries, in some cases letting the customer know that it may take a day or two to actually research an answer to their question. Automating shipping confirmations and order status reports are also common. Although the upfront cost to install and implement automated systems may be costly, the potential reduction in calls to live telephone operators and online help centers is an incentive for companies to increasingly automate as many aspects of the online shopping experience as possible. Firms must use and monitor automated response systems carefully, however, or they may backfire. Many customers still resent automated communications, even if they appear personalized. If automated replies are not useful, they may drive consumers to use live support even more.

NET PRICING STRATEGIES

pricing

putting a value on goods and services

In a competitive market, firms compete for customers through price as well as product features, scope of operations, and focus. **Pricing** (putting a value on goods and services) is an integral part of marketing strategy. Together, price and quality determine customer value. Pricing of e-commerce goods has proved very difficult for both entrepreneurs and investors to understand.

demand curve

the quantity of goods that can be sold at various prices

In traditional firms, the prices of traditional goods — such as books, drugs, and automobiles — are usually based on their fixed and variable costs as well as the market's **demand curve** (the quantity of goods that can be sold at various prices). *Fixed costs* are the costs of building the production facility. *Variable costs* are costs involved in running the production facility — mostly labor. In a competitive market, with undifferentiated goods, prices tend toward their *marginal costs* (the incremental cost of producing the next unit) once manufacturers have paid the fixed costs to enter the business.

Firms usually "discover" their demand curves by testing out various price and volume bundles, closely watching their cost structure. Normally, prices are set to maximize profits. A profit-maximizing company sets its prices so that the *marginal revenue* (the revenue a company receives from the next unit sold) from a product just equals its marginal costs. If a firm's marginal revenue is higher than its marginal costs, it would want to lower prices a bit and sell more product (why leave money on the table when you can sell a few more units?). If its marginal revenue for selling a product is lower than its marginal costs, then the company would want to reduce volume a bit and charge a higher price (why lose money on each additional sale?).

During the E-commerce I era, something unusual happened: Sellers were pricing their products far below their marginal costs. Some sites were losing money on every sale. How could this be? New economics? New technology? The Internet Age? No. Internet merchants could sell below their marginal costs (even giving away products for free) simply because a large number of entrepreneurs and their venture capitalist backers thought this was a worthwhile activity — at least in the short term. The idea in E-commerce I was to attract "eyeballs" with free goods and services, and then later, once the consumer was part of a large, committed audience, charge advertisers enough money to make a profit, and (maybe) charge customers subscription fees for value-added services (the so-called *"piggy-back" strategy* in which a small number of users can be convinced to pay for premium services that are piggy-backed upon a larger audience that receives standard or reduced value services). To understand the behavior of E-commerce I entrepreneurial firms, it is helpful to examine a traditional demand curve (see Figure 7.19).

A small number of customers are willing to pay a great deal for the product — far above P_1. A larger number of customers would happily pay P_1, and an even larger number of customers would pay less than P_1. If the price were zero, the demand might approach infinity! Ideally, in order to maximize sales and profits, a firm would like to pick up all the money in the market by selling the product at the price each customer is willing to pay. This is called **price discrimination** — selling products to different people and groups based on their willingness to pay. If some people really want the product, sell it to them at a high price. But sell it to indifferent people at a much lower price; otherwise, they will not buy. This only works if the firm can (a) identify the price each individual would be willing to pay, and (b) segregate the customers from one another so they cannot find out what the others are paying. Therefore, most firms adopt a fixed price for their goods (P_1), or a small number of prices for different versions of their products.

E-commerce I firms were willing to charge far below their costs, sometimes giving away valuable services, in order to attract huge audiences. Millions of visitors accepted free or nearly free services and products being sold below their cost.

What if the marginal cost of producing a good is zero? What should the price be for these goods? It would be impossible then to set prices based on equalizing marginal revenue and marginal cost — because marginal cost is zero. The Internet is primarily filled with information goods — from music to research reports, to stock

price discrimination
selling products to different people and groups based on their willingness to pay

---

FIGURE 7.19 | **A DEMAND CURVE**

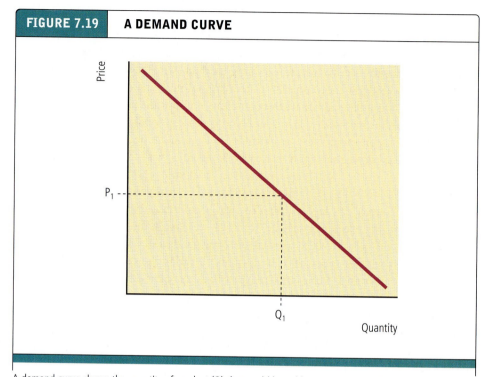

A demand curve shows the quantity of product (Q) that could be sold at various prices (P).

---

quotes, stories, weather reports, articles, pictures, and opinions — whose marginal cost of production is zero when distributed over the Internet. Thus another reason certain goods — such as information goods — may be free on the Internet is that they are "selling" for what it costs to produce them — zero.

It's Free!

Let's examine free pricing of Internet services. Everyone likes a bargain and the best bargain is something for free. In its heyday, E-commerce I businesses gave away free PCs, free data storage, free music, free Web sites, free photo storage, and free Internet connections. There can be a sensible economic logic to giving away things for free. Free content can help build market awareness (such as the free online *New York Times* that contains only the daily stories — not the archived stories) and can lead to sales of other follow-on products; widely dispensing one's software for free also builds network effects (millions use the free version of WinZip bundled with Windows to compress and share files); finally, free products and services knock out potential and actual competitors (as the free browser Internet Explorer from Microsoft spoiled the market for Netscape's browser) (Shapiro and Varian, 1999).

"Free" as a pricing strategy does have its limits. Many E-commerce I businesses were unable to convert the eyeballs into paying customers. Free sites attracted hundreds of thousands of price-sensitive "free loaders" who had no intention of ever paying for anything, and who switched from one free service to another at the very mention of charges. The piggyback strategy has not been a great success. The Web's largest subscription service is the *Wall Street Journal*, which charges 574,000 subscribers from $29–$59 a year, but the largest free financial news sites have over five million daily visitors. Many companies started offering their services for free, but now charge an annual subscription fee. For instance, PhotoPoint, the Web's largest photo storage site, recently began charging $20 per year for its service and hopes to shed 80% of its freeloading customers.

Versioning

One solution to the problem of free information goods is **versioning** — creating multiple versions of the good and selling essentially the same product to different market segments at different prices. Here, the price depends on the value to the consumer. Consumers will segment themselves into groups that are willing to pay different amounts for various versions (Shapiro and Varian, 1998). Versioning fits well with a modified "free" strategy. A reduced-value version can be offered for free, while premium versions can be offered at higher prices. What makes a "reduced-value version?" Low priced — or in the case of information goods, even "free" versions — might be less convenient to use, less comprehensive, slower, less powerful, and offer less support than the high-priced versions. Just as there are different General Motors car brands appealing to different market segments (Cadillac, Buick, Chevrolet, and Pontiac), and within these divisions, hundreds of models from the most basic to the more powerful and functional, so can information goods be "versioned" in order to segment and target the market and position the products. In the realm of information goods, online magazines, music companies, and book publishers offer sample content for free, but charge for more powerful content. The *New York Times*, for instance, offers free daily content for several days after publication, but then charges per article for access to the more powerful archive of past issues. Writers, editors, and analysts are more than willing to pay for access to archived, organized content. Some Web sites offer "free services" with annoying advertising, but turn off the ads for a monthly fee.

versioning
creating multiple versions of the good and selling essentially the same product to different market segments at different prices

Bundling

"Ziggy" Ziegfeld, a vaudeville entrepreneur at the turn of the century in New York, noticed that nearly one-third of his theater seats were empty on some Friday nights, and during the week, matinee shows were often half empty. He came up with an idea for bundling tickets into "twofers": pay for one full price ticket and get the next ticket free. Twofers are still a Broadway theater tradition in New York. They are based on the idea that (a) the marginal cost of seating another patron is zero, and (b) a great many people who would not otherwise buy a single ticket would buy a "bundle" of tickets for the same or even a slightly higher price.

bundling

offers consumers two or more goods for one price

Bundling of information goods online extends the concept of a twofer. **Bundling** offers consumers two or more goods for one price. The key idea behind the concept of bundling is that although consumers typically have very diverse ideas about the value of a single product, they tend to agree much more on the value of a bundle of products offered at a fixed price. In fact, the per product price people are willing to pay for the bundle is often higher than when the products are sold separately. Bundling reduces the variance (dispersion) in market demand for goods. Figure 7.20 illustrates how the demand curve changes when information goods are offered in a bundle.

Examples of bundling abound in the information goods marketplace. Microsoft bundles its separate Office tools (Word, Excel, PowerPoint, and Access) into a single MS Office package. Even though many people want to use Word and Excel, far fewer want Access, or PowerPoint. However, when all products are put into a single bundle, a very large number of people will agree that about $300 (or around $75 per tool) is a "fair" price for so many products. Likewise, the more software applications that Microsoft bundles with its basic operating system, the more the marketplace agrees that as a package of functionality, it is reasonably priced. On the Web, many content

FIGURE 7.20 | **THE DEMAND FOR BUNDLES OF 1–20 GOODS**

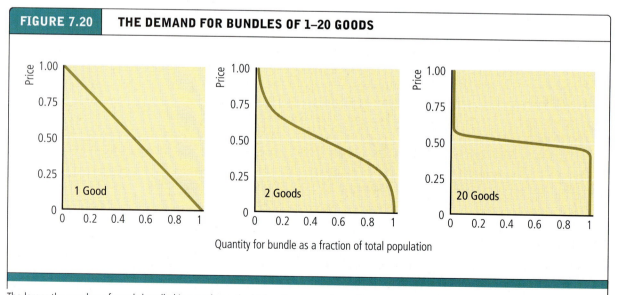

Quantity for bundle as a fraction of total population

The larger the number of goods bundled in a package, the higher the per product price consumers are willing to pay.

SOURCE: Bakos and Brynjolfsson, 1999.

sites bundle as opposed to charge individual prices. Electronic libraries such as E-Library.com and Net Library.com offer access to thousands of publications for a fixed annual fee. Theoretically, bundlers have distinct competitive advantages over those who do not or cannot bundle. Specifically, on the supply side, bundler firms can pay higher prices for content, and on the demand side, bundlers can charge higher prices for their bundles than can single-good firms (Bakos and Brynjolfsson, 2000).

Dynamic Pricing

The pricing strategies we have discussed so far are all fixed price strategies. Versions and bundles are sold for fixed prices based on the firm's best effort at maximizing its profits. But what if there is product still left on the shelf along with the knowledge that someone, somewhere, would be willing to pay something for this product? It might be better to obtain at least some revenue from the product, rather than let it sit on the shelf, or even perish. In other situations, such as for an antique, the value of the product has to be discovered in the marketplace (usually because there is a belief that the marketplace would value the product at a much higher price than its owner paid as a cost). In other cases, the value of a good is equal to what the market is willing to pay (and has nothing to do with its cost). Here is where dynamic pricing mechanisms come to the fore, and where the strengths of the Internet can be seen.

There are generally two kinds of *dynamic pricing* mechanisms: auctions and yield management. *Auctions* have been used for centuries to establish the instant market price for goods. Auctions are flexible and efficient market mechanisms for pricing unique or unusual goods, as well as commonplace goods such as computers and cameras.

Yield management is quite different from auctions. In auctions, thousands of consumers establish a price by bidding against one another. In *yield management*, managers set prices in different markets, appealing to different segments, in order to sell excess capacity. Airlines exemplify yield management techniques: Every few minutes during the day, they adjust prices of empty airline seats to ensure at least some of the 50,000 empty airline seats are sold at some reasonable price — even below marginal cost of production. Frito Lay, as mentioned earlier, also uses yield management techniques to ensure products move off the shelf in a timely fashion.

Yield management works under a limited set of conditions. Generally, the product is perishable (an empty airline seat perishes when the plane takes off without a full load); there are seasonal variations in demand; market segments are clearly defined; markets are competitive; and market conditions change rapidly (Cross, 1997). In general, only very large firms with extensive monitoring and database systems in place have been able to afford yield management techniques.

We discuss dynamic pricing, auctions, and yield management techniques in greater detail in Chapter 13 (www.LearnE-commerce.net).

CHANNEL STRATEGIES: MANAGING CHANNEL CONFLICT

channel
refers to different methods by which goods can be distributed and sold

channel conflict
occurs when a new venue for selling products or services threatens to destroy existing venues for selling goods

In the context of commerce, the term **channel** refers to different methods by which goods can be distributed and sold. Traditional channels include sales by manufacturers both directly and through intermediaries such as manufacturer representatives, distributors, and retailers. The emergence of e-commerce on the Web has created a new channel and has led to channel conflict. **Channel conflict** occurs when a new venue for selling products or services threatens to destroy existing venues for selling goods. Channel conflict is not new, but the Web creates incentives for producers of goods and services to establish direct relationships with consumers and thereby eliminate "middle persons" such as distributors and retailers. In the music business, for instance, two of the leading top five record companies — Universal Music Group and BMG Entertainment — have formed an online venture called GetMusic.com that offers more than 250,000 musical titles for downloading. Some retail sales will no doubt be cannibalized as a result (Hibbard, 2000).

In some cases, manufacturers have withdrawn from direct channel confrontation. For instance, Levi Strauss & Co. decided in 1998 to begin selling Levi's jeans and Dockers over its recently started Levi.com and Dockers.com sites. At the same time, it forbade retailers (such as Macy's — one of Levi's largest retailers) from selling Levi products on the Web. However, by the beginning of 2000, the storm of protest from retailers, falling sales, and drooping profits forced Levi to stop sales on its own sites and allow retailers to sell through their Web channels (King, 2000). Ford and General Motors have similarly withdrawn plans to purchase dealerships from which they could make direct sales (Gilbert and Bachelder, 2000).

In many cases, however, the opening of direct Web channels succeeds and the traditional distribution network is also strengthened. For instance, in travel services, online airline and travel reservation systems such as Expedia and Travelocity, as well as the airlines' own reservation site Orbitz have been real Web success stories. But most travel agents have demonstrated strong survival skills. Almost 50% of travel agencies have their own Web sites, and 56% of travelers report shopping online for the lowest fares (if they have time), but then book through travel agents "just to be sure its right." A large percentage of travelers continue to ask their travel agents — 76% of whom have Web access — to find the lowest fares and book them in return for a fee (McDowell, 1999).

Rather than engage in direct confrontation with alternative channels, many manufacturers have turned toward a partnership model. For instance, Ethan Allen furniture developed its own Web site for direct sales of its entire line of furniture. At the same time, Ethan Allen recognizes the importance of its 310 independent retail stores for delivery, service, and support and pays dealers in a local area 25% of the Internet sale for delivery and service, and 10% of the Internet sale even if the dealer does not participate in any way (Guthrie, 2000).

7.5 ONLINE MARKET RESEARCH: KNOWING YOUR CUSTOMER

Market research involves gathering information that will help a firm identify potential products and customers. There are two general types of market research. **Primary research** involves gathering first-hand information using techniques such as surveys, personal interviews, and focus groups. This type of research is typically used to gain feedback on brands, products, or new marketing campaigns where no previous study has been done. **Secondary research** relies on existing, published information as the basis for analyzing the market. Both primary and secondary research can be completed online more efficiently, less expensively, and often more accurately than offline (Grossnickle and Raskin, 2001; Rao, 2000).

In addition to two different approaches to market research, there are two types of data to be studied. *Quantitative data* is data that can be expressed as a number, such as a percentage. Quantitative data can be analyzed using statistical programs that identify relationships between certain *variables*, or factors that affect how someone responds. *Qualitative data* is data that cannot easily be quantified, such as opinions. Survey questions that yield qualitative responses are analyzed by grouping responses into similar subsegments based on the answer given. One type of analysis is *content analysis*, which tries to identify the major categories of responses given.

PRIMARY RESEARCH

Surveys and questionnaires are the most popular and frequently used market research tools. Using a *survey instrument*, which is a list of questions, researchers can approach groups of people to ask their views on virtually any imaginable topic. Table 7.8 lists the types of survey questions commonly used, along with the associated kinds of responses.

Online surveys typically can be administrated more quickly and less expensively than traditional mail or telephone surveys. E-commerce companies can either hire an outside market research firm to conduct the survey or create and administer their own. For instance, survey sites such as Zoomerang.com allow companies to use existing survey templates or edit them for their own use and distribute them to Zoomerang's built-in panel of consumers (see *Insight on Business: Zoomerang*).

Online surveys also make it possible to track respondents and to follow up with those who haven't yet completed the survey, which helps to improve *response rates*, the percentage of people who complete a survey. A low response rate can damage the validity, or believability, of a survey's results.

Feedback forms, which ask users to provide input regarding a site's operations in a set format, are another type of online survey. Requesting regular input from site vis-

market research
involves gathering information that will help a firm identify potential products and customers

primary research
involves gathering first-hand information using techniques such as surveys, personal interviews, and focus groups

secondary research
relies on existing, published information as the basis for analyzing the market

TABLE 7.8	TYPES OF SURVEY QUESTIONS
FORMAT	INFORMATION GATHERED
Yes–No: "Have you made an online purchase in the last 30 days?"	Forces respondent to choose between a Yes and a No response.
Open-ended: "Has using a PDA improved your productivity? How?"	Allows individual to express an opinion in own words.
Ranking: "Rank the following ice cream flavors from your most to least favorite."	Researcher gets a sense of individual preferences and satisfaction levels.
Likert scale: "How satisfied are you with the selection of used textbooks available at textbooks.com; rate from 1 to 5, with 1 being extremely satisfied and 5 being extremely dissatisfied."	Permits customer to rate satisfaction levels using a scale from 1 to 5, or 1 to 10.
Demographic: "How many children under age 18 are in your household?"	Collects personal information regarding gender, education level, income, etc.

itors may provide more qualitative than quantitative data, which is more difficult to analyze, but the resulting information can assist in improving and enhancing site performance.

Personal interviews are another primary research tool. The interview is generally guided by a set of questions very similar to a survey instrument. Although it is more difficult to incorporate personal interviews within Web sites, it is possible to conduct research online via live chat or e-mail, with a trained researcher interacting with the study participants. Personal interviews offer an opportunity to gather more in-depth information on a topic. In some cases, personal interviews are used as a second phase of a research project, following initial information gathering by survey. In-depth interviews with a target market segment can yield more specific answers to issues and questions brought up in the survey research phase. However, the amount of time required to gather information and the low response rate are both disadvantages; it is more difficult to convince someone to participate in an extended interview than in a short survey.

Focus groups, like personal interviews, allow researchers to gather more specific responses to questions and to probe some issues more deeply. However, focus groups are less structured in order to allow participants to voice their opinions and feelings. Focus groups generally consist of 8 to 12 participants who are members of a particu-

INSIGHT ON BUSINESS

ZOOMERANG

Before the Web, conducting market research was a time-consuming, often arduous task. Creating and conducting a survey, for example, could take weeks, if not months to complete and finalize results. Fortunately, the reach and immediacy of the Web has made online surveys virtually instantaneous and far less expensive than traditional phone or mail surveys. One company even provides such survey services for free.

Zoomerang.com, a product of MarketTools, Inc., is an online service for creating and managing surveys, enabling users to choose from dozens of prebuilt survey templates, edit them as needed, distribute the finished product to a preselected list of recipients, or use Zoomerang's consumer panel, and collect responses—all online. Whether the need for a survey is personal, such as gathering input from family members regarding a proposed family reunion or collecting ideas for wedding gifts from friends, or business, such as implementing a new customer satisfaction survey or developing an advertising performance study, Zoomerang has a wide range of already-created surveys ready to be issued.

The cost to use the basic service is free and the program is run from the Zoomerang server, rather than locally on the user's computer. For more advanced research features, such as the ability to upload corporate graphics, cross-tabulate results, and download data into spreadsheets, users can sign up for the premium service, which costs $199 per year. Access to larger lists of Zoomerang panel members also involves a fee.

Zoomerang makes money by encouraging registered users to actually use the service and then upgrade to the annual $199 subscription. When the company decided it needed assistance in building its base of customers, it turned to MyPoints.com (see the opening case in this chapter). Zoomerang paid MyPoints for 300,000 guaranteed click-throughs, which generated nearly a 40% response rate, bringing close to 120,000 people to the site over the course of the next few months. By working with MyPoints to continue giving their members incentives to use the service, thereby becoming more reliant on it, Zoomerang bumped the number of surveys issued per month from 6,000 in January to approximately 40,000 per month by September 2000.

The question, however, is whether Zoomerang can sustain this growth. With MyPoints' assistance, the company acquired more than 100,000 new members who were given an incentive to issue surveys on a regular basis—25 points per survey. Now that the MyPoints contract has ended, can Zoomerang sustain such usage without incentives? To try and ensure that the answer is yes, Zoomerang is partnering with small business-related companies, such as Staples, to target a market segment most likely to need access to a low-cost survey-generating tool. But can such alliances build demand for survey services? That remains to be seen. MarketTools has recently shifted its focus to marketing higher-end products, such as zTelligence, an enterprise-wide research and knowledge management tool. That may be a sign that Zoomerang isn't the cash cow MarketTools had hoped for.

SOURCES: "Net Freebies," by John Yaukey, *Gannett News Service*, April 24, 2001; "Zoomerang Gets Great Results from MyPoints.com," by Heidi Anderson, Clickz.com, October 5, 2000; "Zoomerang," by Sheryl Canter, *PC Magazine*, January 18, 2000.

lar market segment or target market. A third-party facilitator leads the group in expressing opinions and stating preferences regarding products, services, or other issues. Online focus groups typically run for one hour and have participants log into a chat room, where opinions and ideas can be expressed within a group. The advantage of focus groups is that many views and opinions can be learned in a short period of time. However, more extroverted individuals can overshadow more timid participants so that only a few opinions are heard. This concern is less of an issue online because participants cannot see each other and feel more confident expressing themselves through typing.

Observation is another traditional market research method. *Observation* involves simply watching consumers as they make a purchase, or while they engage in some activity that is being studied. Online customer tracking is the Internet equivalent to observation. It, too, involves simply observing — rather than interacting with — consumers as they navigate a Web site and consider various purchase options. Using cookies and other session monitoring tools, Web site marketers can easily collect data on consumer preferences, dislikes, and challenges in order to improve future experiences at the site.

SECONDARY RESEARCH

Secondary research involves gathering information using Web sites as the information source. Table 7.9 lists some popular secondary research tools.

The key to being efficient and effective as a researcher is identifying the Web sites most likely to provide answers to the questions posed in the research. By establishing and agreeing on the key question to be answered through market research, as well as why that information will be useful, researchers can zero in on their information needs. Understanding how the information will impact other decisions also helps to further refine information collection.

Effective marketing begins with solid research, helping to define and target the most lucrative market segments with a marketing message that encourages customers to buy. However, research is not a one-time event, at least in successful companies. Ongoing research assists in improving and refining products, services, brand image, and marketing messages to continually improve sales results.

When it comes to reports about consumers and e-commerce, leaders include Jupiter Media Metrix, Forrester Research, and Cyber Dialogue. These companies are frequently cited in the press as the source of the latest data on trends in Internet activity. Jupiter Media Metrix and Forrester primarily rely on experienced analysts. Cyber Dialogue, in contrast, uses online panels of consumers — Internet users who are willing to participate in online focus groups and surveys in exchange for being paid between $5 and $30 for up to an hour of their time.

Although online market research is a fairly new phenomenon, Cyber Dialogue has been in business since 1993. In 2000, however, the company shifted away from

TABLE 7.9	SOME POPULAR SECONDARY RESEARCH TOOLS
factiva.com	Source for international articles; headline free, articles cost $2.95
businesswire.com	Free company news
hoovers.com	Free corporate profiles
localeyes.com	Free guide to local Web sites
thomasregister.com	Free directory of industrial products and companies
corporateinformation.com	Free global database of sources
sec.gov	Free source of corporate financial filings

pure Internet research and toward the customer relationship management (CRM) sector; it is now applying its online research expertise to assist companies in identifying their best current customers, researching potentially lucrative new markets, and solidifying long-term relationships with those groups in order to yield bigger profit margins.

America Online

Given America Online's (AOL) huge customer base — now well over 30 million — and virtual ownership of the online portal category, it's hard to picture a struggling upstart with just 200,000 subscribers a few years ago. And yet, that's the position AOL was in during the early 1990s. Prodigy and CompuServe were the clear leaders in the commercial online world, while AOL was in a distant third place. But that was before the Internet, before technology shifts created a wide open market that AOL was determined to dominate.

Yes, the experts scoffed, says *U.S. News & World Report*, when AOL chairman Steve Case proclaimed in the mid-1990s that AOL would be as big a force on the Internet as Microsoft was in software by the year 2005. They clearly underestimated Case's business acumen. His savvy use of marketing and strategic alliances have catapulted AOL far beyond Prodigy, CompuServe, and almost all other competitors. Fifty-four percent of U.S. consumers access the Internet through AOL reported an early-2000 *New York Times* article, indicating the company's dominance. The company's recent merger with Time Warner only serves to fortify its resources and expand its customer base. Yet a short while ago, few would have believed AOL capable of partnering with such a media behemoth.

AOL's transformation from also-ran to leader began with its adoption of a marketing technique that had been little-used in the online world — sampling. Formerly relegated primarily to consumer products and a few services, AOL decided that the best means of increasing the size of its customer base was to entice consumers to try the service for free. And once consumers were connected, the company hoped it could create disincentives to switch to the competition.

Starting with a direct mail campaign of 250 million free trial AOL floppy diskettes in 1993, the company hit 600,000 subscribers that year and its goal of 1,000,000 by mid-1994 — a dramatic increase in just a few months. But the sampling campaign became much more ubiquitous in years to come, transitioning to compact discs as the technology evolved, with free CDs appearing almost everywhere: as inserts in magazine wrappers, in bookstore bags, and as point-of-purchase giveaways. The disks were so visible that jokes cropped up regarding potential uses for the millions of trial media that were being distributed.

Changing its pricing structure was another marketing strategy AOL employed to lure new users. Until 1996, like its competitors, AOL charged a monthly access fee and an hourly fee for connection time; customers paid $9.95 per month for access, which included five free hours of usage, and $3.50 for each hour above five per

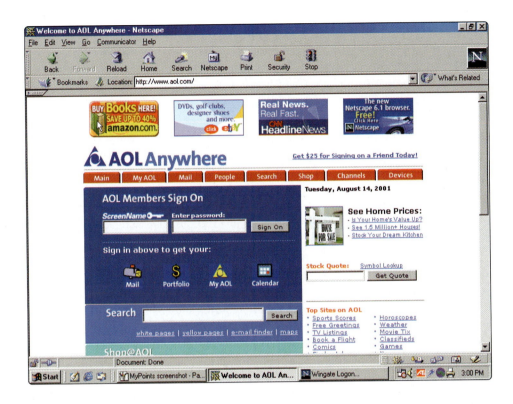

month. But in 1996, other online service companies began switching to a flat-rate pricing plan of $19.95 for unlimited system access, forcing AOL to rethink its own rate structure.

At the same time, use of the Internet was growing in popularity and forcing proprietary online systems, such as AOL, to find a way to provide access to both. By becoming an Internet Service Provider (ISP) in addition to continuing to offer its own licensed content, AOL aimed to meet the needs of its existing customers while attracting new customers who were interested in Internet content. By making its service easy to obtain and use, AOL attracted mainstream consumers that other services had given up on.

To remain competitive, the company also decided to introduce a flat-rate policy in December 1996 and planned to automatically switch existing customers over on the first of the month. Low-volume users could request a special payment plan of $4.95 per month, which included three hours of usage, with additional time costing $2.50 a hour.

The good news was that on December 2, 1996, AOL's stock price surged nearly $5 as a result of its move to flat-rate pricing. The bad news was that many of its subscribers couldn't access the system, leading to class-action suits against the company by frustrated customers who had paid for connection time they couldn't get.

AOL's system capacity was not keeping pace with demand for access to its network and the company quickly earned a reputation for busy signals, frozen computer screens, and e-mail delivery cycles that lasted days, not minutes. "America On Hold" became the company's new moniker. As a result, it actually lost many customers to its competitors; Prodigy reported a substantial jump in new users the following month, January 1997.

To remedy the situation, AOL began adding 30,000 modems a month to expand its capacity. Its goal was to support 400,000 simultaneous users by July 1997, and the company spent $350 million to do so. Unfortunately, that investment nearly broke the bank and caused AOL to raise its flat fee to $21.95 in 1998 while its competitors stuck with $19.95 a month.

At that point, however, AOL had begun acquiring many of its competitors, such as CompuServe's consumer business and Netscape, significantly boosting its subscriber base. Its earlier acquisition of ICQ, an e-mail messaging pioneer, would serve the company well as it rolled out innovative features such as the Buddy List, which enabled users to keep track of the comings and goings of online friends, and Instant Messenger (IM), which remains the most popular service for instantaneously communicating with fellow users.

Alliances are another strategy AOL has used to build its business. Early on, partnering with well-known brands gave the company credibility strong enough to entice potential users to sign on with the lesser-known service. By the time AOL had established itself as one of the strongest brands in cyberspace, partners were paying the company millions for prime placement on the site. Starting with Tel-Save Holdings in 1997, which paid $100 million to market its long distance services on AOL, investment firms such as e*Trade and Waterhouse Investor Services each paid $12.5 million for ad space the following year. Other companies bartered technology for visibility, such as AOL's alliance with Kodak that enabled users to get digitized versions of their photos e-mailed to them, and Dell's deal to bundle AOL software on its computers for two years. Later alliances involved CBS News, Banc One, Supermarkets Online, NBC, ABC, and SBC Communications.

Partnering with such a wide array of companies and information providers has helped AOL succeed in using another winning marketing strategy — value bundling. The concept of value bundling involves aggregating multiple offerings, such as products, information, and/or services for a price that is far less than what the individual services would cost on their own. Although AOL's subscribers may only use one or two of the features offered, the availability of so many others makes the company's $21.95 monthly fee seem like a pittance.

By focusing on consumer interests rather than the technology itself, AOL positioned itself as a one-stop shop for Internet access. And for the masses unfamiliar with

SOURCES: *How to Think Like the World's Greatest New Media Moguls*, by Marcia Layton Turner, McGraw-Hill, 2001; "The New Media Colossus," by Julia Angwin and Martin Peers, *Wall Street Journal*, December 15, 2000; "Value of a Bundle," by Evan Schwartz, *Business 2.0*, April 1, 2000; "America Online Agrees to Buy Time Warner for $165 Billion," by Saul Hansell, *New York Times*, January 11, 2000; "How America Online Became a Superpower," by Jim Hu et al., *CNET News.com*, January 10, 2000; "Now, AOL Everywhere," by Saul Hansell, *New York Times*, July 4, 1999; "America Online Inc.: The Portal Era," by Edward Stohr, S.Viswanathan and Larry White, NYU Case Study, July 1999.

browsers, ISPs, and modems, AOL was an appealing option. Keeping its marketing message simple was part of the recipe for success that has led to AOL be the most-visited site for many months, hitting 38 million visitors in early 1999, as well as one of the stickiest. In fact, 39% of Americans' time spent online is with services AOL controls — ten times the share of its nearest competitor, Microsoft.

AOL's 2000 revenues of $6.8 billion are a far cry from its humble beginnings as Quantum Computer Services 1985, which was renamed America Online in 1991. When AOL acquired 55% of Time Warner in 2001 in a $183 billion deal (rather than the other way around), many analysts were shocked. Access to Time Warner's vast media channels was a big draw for AOL, as well as its broadband capabilities — a direction AOL sees the market going in but which, until now, it couldn't tap into without a significant investment of resources to develop a broadband initiative.

Joining forces with an old media leader also makes sense for AOL, which wants to leverage its huge customer base into new revenue channels, which are delivered by Time Warner. Now, in addition to Internet services, AOL Time Warner has a $6.1 billion cable network, a $3.8 billion music profit center, publishing avenues with $4.66 billion in revenue, filmed entertainment valued at $8.07 billion, and $5.37 billion worth of cable systems.

Case Study Questions

1. Describe how AOL has utilized the following marketing strategies:
   (a) branding
   (b) pricing
   (c) alliances

2. What is AOL's core product? What is its augmented product?

3. AOL's merger with Time Warner opens the door for new marketing strategies. How might AOL Time Warner best exploit its combined resources to market its products?

7.7 REVIEW

KEY CONCEPTS

■ **Identify the key features of the Internet audience.**

Key features of the Internet audience include:
- *The number of users online in the United States.* At mid-year 2001, around 170 million, a number that is expected to grow to about 215 million users by 2005. However, the rate of growth in the U.S. Internet population has begun to slow.
- *Intensity and scope of use.* Both are increasing, with over 56% of adult users in the United States logging on in a typical day and engaging in a wider set of activities, including sending and reading e-mail, gathering hobby-related information, catching up on news, browsing for fun, buying products, seeking health information, conducting work-related research, and reviewing financial information.
- *Demographics and access.* Although the Internet population is growing increasingly diverse, some demographic groups have much higher percentages of online usage than other groups, and different patterns of usage exist across various groups.
- *Ethnicity.* Variation across ethnic groups is not as wide as across age groups. At year-end 2000, whites had the highest Internet usage rates, with 57%, but Hispanics had 47% and African Americans 43%, and both of these groups are going online at higher rates than whites.
- *Education.* Amount of education seems to make a difference when it comes to online access. Of those individuals with a high school education or less, 39% were online as of year-end 2000, while 82% of individuals with a college degree or more were online.
- *Gender.* Although men accounted for the majority of Internet users just a few short years ago, women have caught up and now outnumber men online.
- *Lifestyle impacts:* Intensive Internet use may cause a decline in traditional social activities. The social development of children who use the Internet intensively instead of engaging in face-to-face interactions or undirected play out of doors may also be negatively impacted.
- *Media choices.* The more time individuals spend using the Internet, the less time they spend using traditional media.

■ **Understand the basic concepts of consumer behavior and purchasing decisions.**

Models of consumer behavior attempt to predict or explain what consumers purchase, and where, when, how much, and why they buy. Factors that impact buying behavior include:
- cultural factors,
- social factors, and
- psychological factors.

There are five stages in the consumer decision process:
- awareness of need,
- search for more information,
- evaluation of alternatives,
- the actual purchase decision, and
- post-purchase contact with the firm.

The online consumer decision process is basically the same, with the addition of two new factors:
- *Web site capabilities* — the content, design, and functionality of a site.
- *Consumer clickstream behavior* — the transaction log that consumers establish as they move about the Web and through specific sites. Analysts believe the most important predictors of online consumer behavior are the session characteristics and the clickstream behavior of people online, rather than demographic data.

■ **Understand how consumers behave online.**

Clickstream analysis shows us that people go online for many different reasons, at different times, and for numerous purposes.
- About 40% of online users ("buyers") purchase something entirely online. Another 40% of online users ("browsers") research products on the Web, but purchase them offline.
- Most online purchases involve small ticket items, with the top categories being books, music, apparel and accessories, software, and toys.
- More than 85% of shoppers go directly to vendor sites by typing a product into a search engine, going straight to the merchant's site, or entering a store or brand name into a search engine.
- More than 80% of shoppers are shopping on the Web for specific products or items.
- There are a number of actions that e-commerce vendors could take to increase the likelihood that shoppers and non-shoppers would purchase online more frequently. These include better prices, easier comparison shopping, easier returns, and better security.

■ **Describe the basic marketing concepts needed to understand Internet marketing.**

The key objective of Internet marketing is to use the Web — as well as traditional channels — to develop a positive, long-term, relationship with customers (who may be online or offline) and thereby create a competitive advantage for the firm by allowing the firm to charge a higher price for products or services than its competitors can charge.
- Firms within an industry compete with one another on four dimensions: differentiation, cost, focus, and scope. "Competitive markets" are ones with lots of substitute products, easy entry, low differentiation among suppliers, and strong bargaining power of customers and suppliers.

- Marketing is an activity designed to avoid pure price competition, and to create imperfect markets where returns on investment are above average, competition is limited, and consumers are convinced to pay premium prices for products that have no substitute because they are unique. Marketing encourages customers to buy on the basis of perceived and actual nonmarket, i.e., non-price, qualities of products.

- A product's brand is what makes products truly unique and differentiable in the minds of consumers. A brand is a set of expectations, such as quality, reliability, consistency, trust, affection, and loyalty, that consumers have when consuming, or thinking about consuming, a product or service from a specific company.

- Marketers devise and implement brand strategies — a set of plans for differentiating a product from its competitors and communicating these differences effectively to the marketplace. Segmenting the market, targeting different market segments with differentiated products, and positioning products to appeal to the needs of segment customers are key parts of brand strategy.

- Brand equity is the estimated value of the premium customers are willing to pay for using a branded product when compared to unbranded competitors. Consumers are willing to pay more for branded products in part because they reduce consumers' search and decision-making costs. The ability of brands to attain brand equity also provides incentive for firms to build products that serve customer needs better than other products. Brands also lower customer acquisition cost and increase customer retention.

- Although some predicted that the Web would lead to "frictionless commerce" and the end of marketing based on brands, recent research has shown that brands are alive and well on the Web and that consumers are still willing to pay price premiums for products and services they perceive and differentiate.

■ **Identify and describe the main technologies that support online marketing.**

- *Web transaction logs* — records that document user activity at a Web site.

- *Transaction logs* — coupled with data from the registration forms and shopping cart database, these represent a treasure trove of marketing information for both individual sites and the online industry as a whole.

- *Cookies* — a small text file that Web sites place on visitors' client computers every time they visit, and during the visit, as specific pages are visited. Cookies provide Web marketers with a very quick means of identifying the customer and understanding his or her prior behavior at the site.

- *Web bugs* — tiny (1 pixel) graphic files hidden in marketing e-mail messages and on Web sites. Web bugs are used to automatically transmit information about the user and the page being viewed to a monitoring server.

- *Databases, data warehouses, data mining, and "profiling"* — technologies that allow marketers to identify exactly who the online customer is and what they want, and then to present the customer with exactly what they want, when they want it, for the right price.

- *Advertising networks* — best known for their ability to present users with banner advertisements based on a database of user behavioral data. Specialized ad servers are used to store and send to users the appropriate banner ad. Advertising networks rely on cookies and massive back-end user profile databases to pitch banner ads to users and record the results, including sales.

- *CRM systems* — a repository of customer information that records all of the contacts that a customer has with a firm and generates a customer profile available to everyone in the firm who has a need to "know the customer."

■ **Identify and describe basic e-commerce marketing and branding strategies.**

The marketing technologies described above have spawned a new generation of marketing techniques and added power to some traditional techniques.

- Internet marketing strategies for market entry for new firms include pure clicks/first mover and mixed "clicks and bricks"/alliances; and for existing firms include pure clicks/fast follower and mixed "clicks and bricks"/brand extender.
- Online marketing techniques to online customers include permission marketing, affiliate marketing, viral marketing, and brand leveraging.
- Online techniques for strengthening customer relationships include one-to-one marketing; customization and customer co-production; transactive content; and customer service (CRMs, FAQs, live chat, intelligent agents, and automated response systems).
- Online pricing strategies include offering products and services for free, versioning, bundling, and dynamic pricing.
- Companies operating in the e-commerce environment must also have marketing strategies in place to handle the possibility of channel conflict.

■ **Explain how online market research is conducted.**

Market research involves gathering information that will help a firm identify potential products and customers. There are two general types. Primary research involves gathering first-hand information, and secondary research relies on existing, published information as the basis for analyzing the market.

- Online primary research is conducted by using online surveys, feedback forms, interviews, focus groups, and observation.
- Online secondary research involves gathering information using Web sites as the information source.

QUESTIONS

1. Is growth of the Internet, in terms of users, expected to continue indefinitely? What will cause it to slow, if anything?
2. Other than search engines, what are some of the most popular uses of the Internet?
3. Would you say that the Internet fosters or impedes social activity? Explain your position.
4. Why would the amount of experience someone has using the Internet likely increase future Internet usage?

5. Research has shown that many consumers use the Internet to investigate purchases before actually buying, which is often done in a physical storefront. What implication does this have for online merchants? What can they do to entice more online buying, rather than pure research?

6. Name four improvements Web merchants could make to encourage more browsers to become buyers.

7. Name the five stages in the buyer decision process and briefly describe the online and offline marketing activities used to influence each.

8. Why are "little monopolies" desirable from a marketer's point of view?

9. Describe a perfect market from the supplier's and customer's perspective. Explain why an imperfect market is more advantageous for businesses.

10. What are the components of the core product, actual product, and augmented product in a feature set?

11. List some of the major advantages of having a strong brand. How does a strong brand positively influence consumer purchasing?

12. How are product positioning and branding related? How are they different?

13. List the differences among databases, data warehouses, and data mining.

14. Name some of the drawbacks to the four data mining techniques used in Internet marketing.

15. Why have advertising networks become controversial? What, if anything, can be done to overcome any resistance to this technique?

16. Which of the four market entry strategies is most lucrative?

17. Compare and contrast the four marketing strategies used in mass marketing, direct marketing, micromarketing, and one-to-one marketing.

18. What pricing strategy turned out to be deadly for many e-commerce ventures during E-commerce I? Why?

19. Is price discrimination different from versioning? If so, how?

20. What are some of the reasons that freebies, such as free Internet service and giveaways, don't work to generate sales at a Web site?

21. Explain how versioning works. How is this different from dynamic pricing?

22. Why do companies that bundle products and services have an advantage over those that don't or can't offer this option?

23. What are the two types of market research? How are they different?

24. How is online survey-taking and analysis different from the traditional process of mailing surveys?

25. Compare and contrast the various types of online primary research — surveys, personal interviews, focus groups, and observation.

PROJECTS

1. Go to the SRI site (www.future.sri.com/VALS/VALSindex.shtml). Click on "Survey." Take the survey to determine what lifestyle category you fit into. Then write a brief two-page paper describing how your lifestyle and values impact

your use of the Web for e-commerce. How is your online consumer behavior affected by your lifestyle?

2. Find an example of a Web site that you feel does a good job appealing to both goal-directed and experiential consumers. Explain your choice.

3. Choose a digital content product available on the Web and describe its feature set.

4. Visit www.eluxury.com and create an Internet marketing plan for it that includes each of the following:

   market research
   one-to-one marketing
   viral marketing
   affiliate marketing

   Describe how each plays a role and create a PowerPoint or other form of presentation of your marketing plan.

5. Create a 10-question online survey to assess customer satisfaction with a popular Web site of your choosing, using the five types of survey questions from the chapter. (Be sure and select a site that is well-known to ensure you'll get enough responses to your survey.) After developing the survey, go to Zoomerang.com to input the survey questions and to distribute the survey to your own list of at least 10 recipients or to the Zoomerang panel. Collect the responses and analyze the data, preparing a brief overhead presentation summarizing your findings.

WEB SITE RESOURCES   www.LearnE-commerce.net

- News: Weekly updates on topics relevant to material in this chapter
- Video Lecture: Professor Ken Laudon summarizes the key concepts of the chapter
- Research: Abstracts and links to articles referenced in the chapter, as well as other relevant research
- International Spotlight: More information about e-commerce marketing outside the United States
- PowerPoint slides: illustrations from the chapter and more
- Additional projects and exercises

CHAPTER 8

E-commerce Marketing Communications

NextCard

Effective Impressions

Banner ads may be falling out of favor with online marketers, but not for NextCard, Inc., an online credit card issuer and one of the biggest Internet advertisers. In fact, the company has consistently achieved impressive marketing results through the use of banner ads—lots of them. Each month the company runs an estimated 100 different banner ad designs on about 200 different Web sites, spending $3 million to generate a whopping three billion impressions, or views of its ads. It also tests another 200,000 banner ads on more than 500 Web sites, comparing and contrasting response rates and the corresponding profitability of new customers.

A major factor in NextCard's online advertising success is its Internet Database Marketing system, IDM. NextCard's software engineers created a proprietary, patent-pending system, using standard hardware from vendors such as Dell Computer and software from Oracle and Microsoft, that enables NextCard to learn quickly and accurately which advertising investments are paying off and which are not. IDM then shows the company where to shift its advertising money to improve results. NextCard boasts that in the past year it has reduced the cost of acquiring a customer using banner ads by 40%, down to $65. In addition, IDM gives the company substantial bargaining power with advertisers.

Although banner ad rates are falling, hitting a median rate of $25 per 1,000 viewers by the end of 2000, NextCard can frequently negotiate even better deals by using results supplied by its IDM system. NextCard's marketers know precisely how much they should spend for placement of a banner or button ad at a particular site, based on the historical response rate NextCard has been able to achieve at the site and the corresponding revenue generated. Sites charging more than their ads are worth risk losing NextCard's business.

By applying many of the tricks of the direct mail trade to the online medium, NextCard has become a credit card standout. By July 2001, the company had about 1 million cardholders, and had issued $1.3 billion in credit card loans, with the expectation that the company would hit $2 billion in loans by year end. Its secret seems to be constant testing and placement of online ads.

Not content to repeatedly use the same old banner ad, NextCard constantly changes minor aspects of ads, just as direct mail pros do. Exact wording of the offer, placement, font size, color, and positioning of various elements, such as the Visa logo, are moved and changed in an effort to raise response rates from more profitable applicants.

Some of the company's other smart moves include designing a short online application, delivering credit decisions in less than 30 seconds, and developing new card features and benefits it can offer its customers, such as the ability to put custom images on their cards and an online "concierge" service that automatically completes online shopping forms. In the future, NextCard plans to pre-approve consumers, displaying banner ads announcing pre-approval only to the individuals it wants as customers.

NextCard's success has some advertisers worried, however. The size of its marketing budget and timely access to data regarding advertising results has given the company significant negotiating weight. Historically, popular sites could charge whatever the market would bear for advertising space, even when advertisers could not measure whether they were getting any value from that placement. But NextCard's IDM system signals that those days may be over, as marketers gain access to information that places a value on those ads — a value that may be lower than what they have been paying.

SOURCES: "NextCard Bucks the Trend of Web, Credit-Card Stocks," by Peter Edmonston, *Wall Street Journal*, July 11, 2001; "Pay for Performance," by Peter Loftus, *Wall Street Journal*, April 23, 2001; "Tips from NextCard on Selling Cards Online," by W.A. Lee, *American Banker*, March 29, 2001; "Dot-Com Rarity: NextCard Finds Online Ads Work," by Paul Beckett, *Wall Street Journal*, January 29, 2001; "NextCard Results Dazzle — As Do Its Projections," by David Breitkopf, *American Banker*, November 6, 2000.

N extCard illustrates how traditional mass marketing techniques are brought to the Web. Banner ads are not very different from 15- or 30-second spots on television, or advertisements in newspapers. Minor variations in content and design can produce large variations in consumer behavior. However, the Internet is quite different from mass marketing media in other key respects. Internet marketing technologies such as NextCard's IDM system provide an entirely new set of tracking and measurement techniques that allow marketers to understand in a few hours precisely how effective various banner ads are in generating new purchases. Marketers must understand both the Internet audience and the new forms of marketing communications and measurement made possible by the Web.

In Chapter 7, we described brands as a set of expectations that consumers have about products offered for sale. We described some of the marketing activities that companies engage in to create those expectations. In this chapter we will focus on understanding **online marketing communications** — all the methods that online firms use to communicate to the consumer and create strong brand expectations. What are the best methods for attracting people to a site and converting them into customers? We will also examine the Web site as a marketing communications tool. How does the design of a Web site affect sales?

online marketing communications
methods used by online firms to communicate to the consumer and create strong brand expectations

8.1 ONLINE MARKETING COMMUNICATIONS

Marketing communications have a dual purpose: branding and sales. One purpose of marketing communications is to develop and strengthen a firm's brands by informing consumers about the differentiating features of the firm's products and services. In addition, marketing communications are used to promote sales directly by encouraging the consumer to buy products (the sooner, the better). The distinction between the branding and sales purposes of marketing communications is subtle but important because branding communications differ from promotional communications. **Promotional sales communications** almost always suggest that the consumer "buy now," and they make offers to encourage immediate purchase. **Branding communications** rarely encourage consumers to buy now, but instead focus on extolling the differentiable benefits of consuming the product or service.

There are many different forms of online marketing communications, including online advertising, e-mail marketing, and public relations. Even the Web site itself can be viewed as a marketing communications tool.

promotional sales communications
suggest the consumer "buy now" and make offers to encourage immediate purchase

branding communications
focus on extolling the differentiable benefits of consuming the product or service

ONLINE ADVERTISING

Advertising is the most common and familiar marketing communications tool. Companies will spend an estimated $185 billion on advertising in 2001, and an estimated

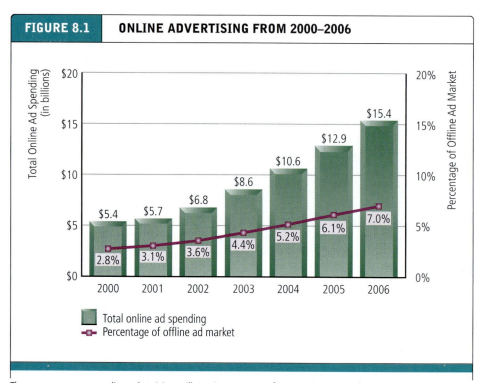

| FIGURE 8.1 | ONLINE ADVERTISING FROM 2000–2006 |

The amount spent on online advertising will continue to grow, from approximately $5.4 billion in 2000 to $15.4 billion in 2006.

SOURCE: Jupiter Media Metrix, 2001a.

online advertising

a paid message on a Web site, online service, or other interactive medium

$5.7 billion of that amount on **online advertising** (defined as a paid message on a Web site, online service, or other interactive medium, such as instant messaging).[1] Although the growth rate of online advertising slowed significantly from 2000 to 2001 (growing only about 5.3%), Jupiter Media Metrix (2001a) still expects total online advertising to reach about $15 billion by 2006 (see Figure 8.1).

Online advertising has both advantages and disadvantages when compared to advertising in traditional media, such as television, radio, and print (magazines and newspapers). The biggest advantages of online advertising are the ability to target ads to narrow segments and to track performance of advertisements in almost real time. Online advertisements also provide greater opportunities for interactivity — two-way communication between advertiser and the potential customer. The primary disadvantages of online advertising are concerns about its cost versus its benefits as well as about how to adequately measure its results. These disadvantages illustrate why

---

[1]Estimated amounts of total advertising spending vary greatly depending on the definitions and methodologies used. For example, eMarketer forecasts online advertising at approximately $7.6 billion for 2001 (eMarketer, August 2001).

online advertising still comprises a very small portion of the total advertising pie — approximately 3% in 2001. We will examine the costs and benefits of online advertising as well as research on its effectiveness in Section 8.2.

Currently, the heaviest online advertisers on a percentage basis are computer hardware and media companies, followed closely by financial services companies (see Figure 8.2). The Internet's ability to deliver information-rich messages lends itself well to high consideration, information-intensive products (i.e., products that consumers typically research before purchasing). Packaged goods (which buyers typically purchase based on brand rather than research) are expected to have smaller shares of online advertising until significant broadband and alternative ad platforms are widespread enough to allow rich media advertising. Product categories with large online commerce potential (i.e., financial and travel services) or a natural link to the Internet (media) also command significant shares.

There are a number of different forms of online advertisement including:

- banner and rich media ads,
- paid search engine inclusion and placement,
- sponsorships, and
- affiliate relationships.

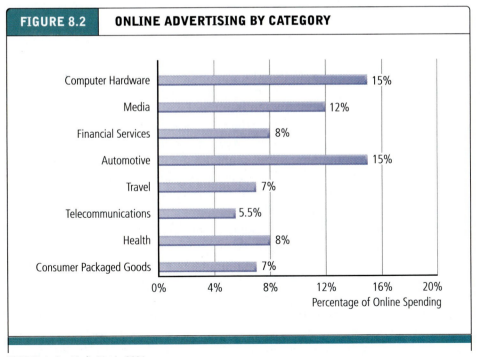

FIGURE 8.2 | **ONLINE ADVERTISING BY CATEGORY**

SOURCE: Jupiter Media Metrix, 2001a.

Banner and Rich Media Ads

banner ad
displays a promotional message in a rectangular box at the top or bottom of a computer screen

Banner ads were the first Internet advertisements. A **banner ad** displays a promotional message in a rectangular box at the top or bottom of a computer screen. A banner ad is similar to a traditional ad in a printed publication, but has some added advantages. If clicked on, it can bring a potential customer directly to the advertiser's Web site. It also is much more dynamic than a printed ad: It can present multiple images or otherwise change its appearance.

Banner ads typically feature animated GIFs, which display different images in relatively quick succession, creating an animated effect. The Interactive Advertising Bureau (IAB), an industry organization, has established voluntary industry guidelines for banner ads. A full banner, the most common, is 468 pixels wide by 60 pixels high with a resolution of 72 dpi (dots per inch) and a maximum file size of 13K.

button
a permanent banner ad

The IAB's original guidelines listed specifications for four types of banner ads (full, half, vertical, and micro bar) and three types of buttons. (A **button** is essentially a permanent banner ad.) In February 2001, the IAB added specifications for a variety of new types of ads, including skyscrapers (a tall, narrow banner ad almost three times the height of the traditional vertical banner ad), rectangles of various sizes, and a square pop-up (which opens in a separate window), to allow marketers to develop ads featuring enhanced interactivity as well as expanded creativity. The new types of ads (including the new rich media ads discussed below) are designed to help advertisers break through the "noise" and clutter created by the growing number of banner ad impressions that a typical user is exposed to within a given day (in 2001, estimated at about 600 per day; increasing to over 900 a day by 2006, according to Jupiter Media Metrix, 2000b). Figure 8.3 shows some examples of the different types of banners, as specified by the IAB.

pop-under ad
opens underneath a user's active browser window and does not appear until the user closes the active window

A new variety of banner ad not approved by the IAB has recently surfaced. This is the pop-under ad, best exemplified by the x10.com wireless camera ad that seemed omnipresent during the summer of 2001. **Pop-under ads** open underneath a user's active browser window and do not appear until the user closes the active window. The ad remains visible until the user takes action to close it. The technique has sparked strong debate as to whether such ads are viewed as so intrusive by consumers that they result in negative branding (Hansell, 2001d).

rich media ads
ads employing Flash, DHTML, and Java, and streaming audio and/or video

While traditional banner ads will undoubtedly remain the dominant form for some time to come, the use of **rich media ads** (ads employing Flash, DHTML, and Java, and streaming audio and/or video) has been increasing. Jupiter Media Metrix predicts that by 2005, almost 30% of all online advertising will be some form of rich media (Jupiter Media Metrix, 2000b). Interactive rich media ads seek to involve the user even more deeply by forcing him or her to interact with ad in some fashion. For instance, three-dimensional imagery helps users envision the product in use, rather than seeing it flat, in two-dimensions only. The IAB added voluntary guidelines for

FIGURE 8.3	TYPES OF BANNER ADS

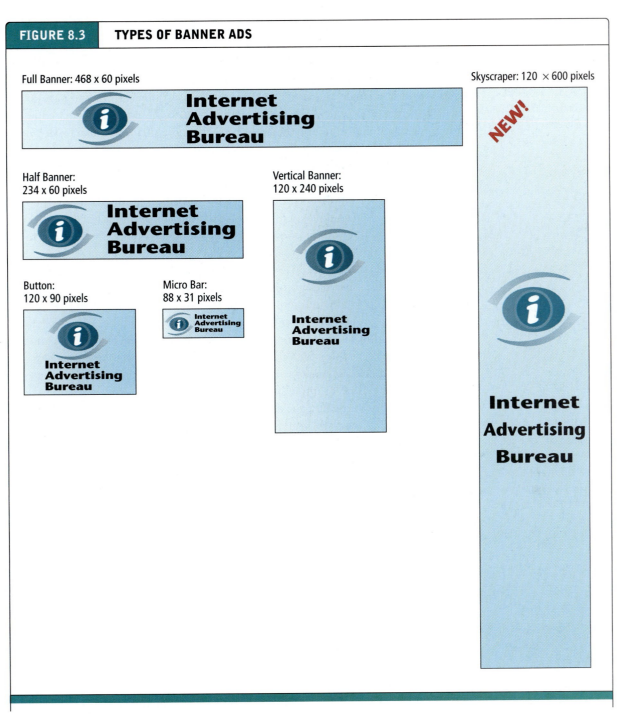

Full Banner: 468 x 60 pixels

Half Banner: 234 x 60 pixels

Button: 120 x 90 pixels

Micro Bar: 88 x 31 pixels

Vertical Banner: 120 x 240 pixels

Skyscraper: 120 × 600 pixels

SOURCE: Interactive Advertising Bureau, 2001.

rich media advertising formats for banners, rectangles, pop-ups, and interstitials (discussed below) in August 2001.

interstitial ad

a way of placing a full page message between the current and destination pages of a user

An **interstitial ad** (interstitial means "in between") is a way of placing a full page message between the current and destination pages of a user. Interstitials are usually inserted within a single site, and displayed as the user moves from one page to the next. The interstitial typically moves automatically to the page the user requested after allowing enough time for the ad to be read. Interstitials can also be deployed over an advertising network and appear as users move among sites.

Since the Web is such a busy place, people have to find ways to cope with over-stimulation. One means of coping is known as sensory *input filtering*. This means that people learn to filter out the vast majority of the messages coming at them. Internet users quickly learn at some level to recognize banner ads or anything that looks like a banner ad and to filter out most of the ads that are not exceptionally relevant. Interstitial messages, like TV commercials, attempt to make viewers a captive of the message. Typical interstitials last ten seconds or less and force the user to look at the ad for that time period. To avoid boring users, interstitials typically use animated graphics and music to entertain and inform them. A good interstitial will also have a "skip through" or "stop" option for users who have no interest in the message. One disadvantage of interstitials is that users may not understand that the ad they see on their screen while they're waiting for a page to load is using "dead time"; instead they may think the interstitial is slowing the arrival of the page they have requested and become annoyed. For an online example of an interstitial ad see Internet Marketing Solution's Interstitial Advertising page at http://marketingsolutions.com/interstitial.htm (scroll to the end of the page, and click "see sample interstitial again").

superstitial

a rich media ad that is pre-loaded into a browser's cache and does not play until fully loaded and the user clicks to another page

A **superstitial** is a rich media ad that can be any screen display size up to 550 × 480, and with a file size of up to 100 KB. Superstitials were created by Unicast Communications, and differ from interstitials in that they are pre-loaded into a browser's cache and do not play until fully loaded. When the file is finished downloading, like an interstitial, it waits until the user clicks to another page before popping up in a separate window.

Since the format's marketplace debut in May 1999, superstitial ads have been used by more than 150 companies, including global brand-name advertisers American Express, Intel, Jack Daniels, Johnson &Johnson, Microsoft, Nike, Nissan Motor Corp., SmithKline Beecham, Time Warner, Unilever, Universal Pictures, and Visa, among others. Visit www.unicast.com/superstitial to see a superstitial ad in action.

Superstitials enable the simultaneous pursuit of multiple advertising goals, including branding, direct response, entertainment, and commerce. Both qualitative and quantitative research have shown that superstitials are much more effective than simple banner ads in driving browsers to Web sites (Millward Brown Interactive, 1999).

An advertiser who wants to place a banner or rich media advertisement on the Web has several options: via banner swapping, banner exchange programs, ad networks or by dealing directly with the publisher (the Web site that will post the advertisement). **Banner swapping** arrangements among firms allow each firm to have its banners displayed on other affiliate sites for no cost. **Banner exchanges** (such as Microsoft's bCentral Banner Network) arrange for banner swapping among firms, usually small firms that cannot afford expensive ad networks such as DoubleClick. By displaying the banners of other firms, the firm can earn credits toward the display of its banner on other Web sites. The bCentral Banner Network has over 300,000 firms signed up in 33 languages, and claims to have exposure to over 40 million Web viewers worldwide. Ad networks such as DoubleClick and Flycast act as brokers between advertisers and publishers, placing the ads and tracking all activity related to the ad.

There is a widespread impression that banner ads are the most common form of marketing communications in the online e-commerce world. This is not true. According to ActivMedia Research, other techniques such as search engine optimization and public relations are more popular, while purchasing banner ads is at the bottom of the list. Table 8.1 illustrates the rank order of online marketing communications methods.

Paid Search Engine Inclusion and Placement

Search engine sites originally performed unbiased searches of the Web's huge collection of Web pages and derived most of their revenue from advertisements. Since 1998, search engine sites have slowly been transforming themselves into digital yellow pages, where firms pay for inclusion in the search engine index (which were formerly free and based on "objective" criteria) — paid inclusion — and/or a guarantee that their firm will appear prominently in the results of relevant searches — paid placement. For instance, Overture.com, a Web search engine and provider of search results to Lycos, AltaVista, and other portals, charges all firms for a listing and placement in search results. Merchants who wish to be at or near the top of particular search results bid for position based on how much they are willing to pay Overture on a "per-click" basis. Overture collects a fee any time someone clicks through to the

banner swapping
an arrangement among firms that allows each firm to have its banners displayed on other affiliate sites for no cost

banner exchanges
arrange for banner swapping among firms

TABLE 8.1	**MOST POPULAR ONLINE MARKETING METHODS**
1. Search engine and directory positioning
2. Online public relations and press releases
3. Buttons and links
4. Reciprocal ads and links (banner swapping)
5. Affiliate programs
6. Paid banner ads

SOURCE: *Entrepreneur Magazine*, June 2001, based on ActivMedia Research, July 2000.

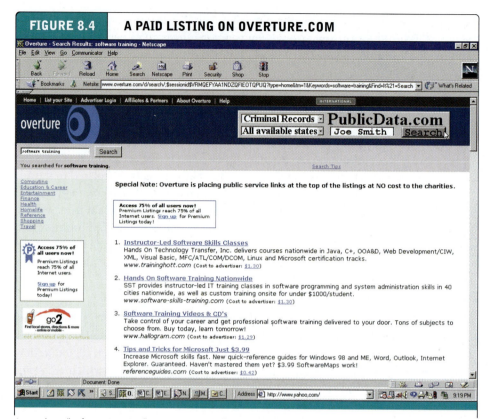

FIGURE 8.4 | **A PAID LISTING ON OVERTURE.COM**

A search on "software training" at Overture.com (formerly GoTo.com) brings up a list of companies that have paid for their inclusion and placement on the search results list. The amount each company has agreed to pay per clickthrough is shown.

merchant's site. The amount the advertiser has agreed to pay is displayed next to the listing (see Figure 8.4).

Inktomi and LookSmart, two of the largest suppliers of search engine technology to other Web sites, have also begun charging for inclusion. Yahoo offers an option called Business Express for faster review of a site for possible inclusion in its directories. Even Google, a search engine known for its dedication to objectivity, has begun to include "text ads" at the top and right of search results pages. Table 8.2 lists the policies of major search engine sites with respect to paid placement and inclusion.

In some cases, search engines do not inform the user that the results of a query have been paid for by participating firms. Some analysts argue that users don't care if merchants pay for listings — just as they don't care when they use the yellow pages — so long as the searches produce relevant results. Some have even argued that informing the user about the commercial nature of placement and listings would harm e-commerce because users have been trained by the industry to "avoid anything that

TABLE 8.2	SEARCH ENGINE POLICIES ON PAID PLACEMENT AND INCLUSION	
SEARCH ENGINE	PAID PLACEMENT POLICY	PAID INCLUSION POLICY
AltaVista	Paid links sold by AltaVista or from GoTo appear in the Featured Site section at the top of the results page.	Yes, in "Directories" results provided by LookSmart.
AOL	Paid links from GoTo appear in Sponsored Links section at top of results page.	Yes, since results are provided by Inktomi, which offers paid inclusion.
Excite	Paid links sold by Excite or from FindWhat appear at the top and bottom of the results page.	No.
Google	Sponsored links ("text ads") sold by Google appear at the top and right of the results page.	No.
Inktomi	No.	Yes, paid inclusion provides for more frequent, extensive "crawling" of the site.
LookSmart	Yes, paid links appear as featured listings at the top of the results page.	Yes, all commercial sites are required to pay to be considered for listing.
Lycos	Paid links from GoTo appear in the Featured Listings section at the top and in the middle of the results page.	No.
MSN	Featured sites have ads placed on search result pages.	Yes, in Web Directory results from LookSmart or Web Pages information from Inktomi.
Overture	Position on results page determined by amount bid.	Yes, with the cost to the advertiser noted.
Yahoo	Paid links appear as sponsored listings in various commercial categories.	Business Express option.

looks commercial." Users might actually not pursue appropriate and relevant links if they thought the listing was commercially influenced (Hansell, 2001c). In July 2001, Commercial Alert, a consumer advocacy group founded by Ralph Nader, filed a complaint with the FTC that search engines that fail to clearly indicate they accept payments for higher search ranking are engaging in deceptive practices (Tate, 2001).

Paid search engine inclusion and placement is arguably one of the most effective marketing communications tools on the Web, given the large percentage of shoppers who use search engines to find products (43%). Overture, for instance, has been very helpful to small businesses that cannot afford large marketing campaigns. Because shoppers are looking for a specific product or service when they use search engines, they are what marketers call "hot prospects" — people who are looking for information and often intending to buy. Moreover, in many cases the search engines charge only for clickthroughs to a site.

Sponsorships

sponsorship

a paid effort to tie an advertiser's name to information, an event, or a venue in a way that reinforces its brand in a positive, yet not overtly commercial manner

A **sponsorship** is a paid effort to tie an advertiser's name to particular information, an event, or a venue in a way that reinforces its brand in a positive, yet not overtly commercial manner. Sponsorships typically are more about branding than immediate sales. A common form of sponsorship is an *advertorial* (in which editorial content is combined with an ad message to make the message more valuable and attractive to its intended audience), such as Crayola's sponsorship of an arts and crafts column on a parenting site.

Affiliate Relationship

affiliate relationships

permit a firm to put its logo or banner ad on another firm's Web site from which users of that site can click through to the affiliate's site

An **affiliate relationship** permits a firm to put its logo or banner ad on another firm's Web site from which users of that site can click through to the affiliate's site. Such relationships are often called *tenancy deals* because they allow a firm to become a "tenant" on another site without charge. Affiliate relationships are essentially strategic partnerships in which the interests of both parties are advanced and there is no direct exchange of money. Several types of affiliate relationships are common. In some cases, the firms share a single corporate parent or investor group that is seeking to optimize the performance of all its sites by creating links among its "children" sites. In other cases, two sites may sell complementary products and the firms may strike an affiliate relationship to make it easier for their customers to find the products they are looking for.

Perhaps the largest and best known affiliate relationship involves Amazon and ToysRUs. Amazon, seeking to become a general merchandiser, recognized that it did not have the expertise to purchase, warehouse, and fulfill orders for toys, one of the fastest growing product categories on the Web. ToysRUs — at the time in a pitched battle with eToys.com — recognized it did not have the Web presence to compete with eToys. Amazon and ToysRUs struck an affiliate deal. The ToysRUs logo and front-end ordering machinery is available as a button on the Amazon site. ToysRUs accepts and fulfills orders for toys, and performs all the back-end purchasing and warehousing. Amazon receives a commission on sales. Both firms benefit, as do their customers. *Insight on Society: Targeting Children* considers some of the social issues that marketing to children on the Web present.

Direct E-mail Marketing

direct e-mail marketing

e-mail marketing messages sent directly to interested users

spam

unsolicited commercial e-mail

E-mail marketing messages sent directly to interested users (**direct e-mail marketing**) has proven to be one of the most effective forms of marketing communications. The key to effective direct e-mail marketing is "interested users." Direct e-mail marketing is not spam. **Spam** involves sending unsolicited e-mail to a mass audience of Internet users who have expressed no interest in the product. Instead, direct e-mail marketing messages are sent to an "opt in" audience of Internet users who have

INSIGHT ON SOCIETY

TARGETING CHILDREN

Children as young as three or four years old can often recognize brands and status items before they can even read, and 73% of four-year-olds generally ask their parents for specific brands. These findings are cause for celebration for some marketers. In the United States, 57 million school-age children spend approximately $100 billion annually of their own and their family's money on food, drinks, video and electronic products, toys, and clothing, and they influence family spending decisions valued at another $165 billion. In order to capture a portion of this spending and position themselves for future purchases as the child ages, marketers are becoming increasingly interested in advertising aimed at children.

In addition to investing in television advertising, which accounts for 70% of the total amount spent on advertising to children in the United States, marketers are now migrating to the Web, where an estimated four million children are active worldwide. Using custom banner ads, product characters, games, and surveys, marketers are both influencing behaviors and gathering valuable data about purchasing preferences and family members. Other companies are retaining child psychologists to help them more effectively target children.

While such moves may be savvy marketing, are they ethical? Some people say no. Experts argue that since children don't understand persuasive intent until they are eight or nine years old, it is unethical to advertise to them before they

can distinguish between advertising and the real world. Others believe that fair advertising is an important, and necessary, process of the maturation process for future adults in today's society. But does that argument hold when children are gaining increased access to information about unhealthy activities, such as beer drinking, for example, through Web sites geared to a younger audience?

Although brewers admit they are targeting a younger market segment — twenty-somethings — they have set up warning screens and registration pages that require users to enter a birth date proving they are of legal drinking age. Of course, there is no process to verify such data, making it easy for underage consumers to gain access to, and be influenced by, entertaining content at drinking-oriented sites.

Most experts agree such access is bad; the sticking point is where to draw the line. There is also dissent among psychologists about whether colleagues are helping to exploit children by assisting companies, such as consumer product manufacturers and toy retailers, in improving their marketing. Those involved argue that psychology itself is merely a tool and that there is nothing wrong with helping companies use such a tool wisely.

What just about everyone agrees on is that advertising can have a major impact on child development. Unfortunately, the result is that some children feel inferior if they don't have "an endless array of new products." Migrating marketing activities to the Web, where children are

(continued)

apt to be in the future, will serve to influence children even more. Currently, there is no voluntary industry code governing child advertising on the Web, and no government regulations on content or access, although the Children's Online Privacy Protection Act (COPPA) (discussed more fully in Chapter 9) regulates the collection of personal information by commercial Web sites and online services from children under the age of 13.

■■■ SOURCES: "Here's to the Net," by David Armstrong, *Wall Street Journal*, April 23, 2001; 2000–2001 Toy Industry Fact Book, www.toy-tia.org/industry/publications/fbcurrent/advertising.htm; "Advertising to Children: Is It Ethical?" by Rebecca Clay, *Monitor on Psychology*, American Psychological Association, September 2000; "Marketing to Children," by Sharon Beder; "A Community View, Caring for Children in the Media Age, Papers from a National Conference," edited by John Squires and Tracy Newlands, New College Institute of Values Research, 1998, www.uow.edu.au/arts/sts/sbeder/children.html.

expressed at one time or another an interest in receiving messages from the advertiser. By sending e-mail to an opt-in audience, advertisers are targeting interested consumers. Response rates to e-mail campaigns range from 3% to 10%, depending on the targeting. Because of the comparatively high response rates and low cost, direct e-mail marketing is the fastest growing form of online marketing.

The primary cost of e-mail marketing is for the purchase of the list of names to which the e-mail will be sent. This generally costs anywhere from 15 to 50 cents a name, depending on how targeted the list is. Sending the e-mail is virtually cost-free. In contrast, a direct mail 5x7-inch post card mailing costs about 15 cents per name, but printing and mailing costs raise the overall cost to around 75 to 80 cents a name.

Due to the cost savings possible with e-mail, the short time to market, and high response rates, companies are expected to increasingly use e-mail to communicate directly with consumers. Jupiter Media Metrix forecasts that commercial e-mail will grow from a $1.3 billion industry in 1999 to a $7.3 billion industry by 2005, with commercial e-mail message volume soaring from approximately 44 billion messages in 2001 to 268 billion messages in 2005 (Jupiter Media Metrix, 2000a).

The downside of this growth is that e-mail response rates are expected to decline as competition for consumer attention becomes more fierce, and as users become annoyed by their bulging e-mail in-boxes. Users can employ software filter programs to eliminate many e-mail messages (Jupiter Media Metrix, 2000a).

Online Catalogs

Online catalogs are the equivalent of a paper-based catalog. The basic function of a catalog is to display the merchant's wares (see Figure 8.5). The electronic version typically contains a color image of each available product, a description of the item, as well as size, color, material composition, and pricing information. While simple catalogs are, technically, hard-coded HTML pages and graphics displaying wares, most

| FIGURE 8.5 | BEVAL'S ONLINE CATALOG |

Beval Saddlery Ltd.'s site offers a variety of riding apparel and equipment. Customers can click on one of the product categories listed on the left side of the screen and are taken to a page listing products within that category. Clicking on a particular product takes the customer to a page with a description and photo of the product and an order button.

sites with more than 15–20 products generate catalog pages from a product and price database that can be easily changed. Simply by clicking on an order button at the site, customers can make a purchase instantaneously.

Public Relations

Another marketing communications tool used to increase awareness of a site, and potentially boost traffic, is public relations. **Public relations (PR)** involves communicating with target audiences, or publics, using methods other than advertising. Some of these methods include publicity (media coverage); special events, such as a grand opening celebration or press conference; and publications, such as newsletters and customer bulletins. Half.com, for instance, convinced an Oregon town to rename

public relations (PR)
involves communicating with target audiences, or publics, using methods other than advertising

itself, becoming Half, Oregon, for a full year in return for some economic development funds and a donation of computers, among other things. This publicity stunt netted the company plenty of media coverage and improved awareness of the site among book and music buyers, which was its aim.

Beyond publicity stunts, which have a high risk of not paying off, pursuing media coverage via the Internet is a smart use of online technology. Whereas traditional public relations techniques required writing and distribution of offset printed press releases and press kits through the U.S. Postal Service, Web sites and e-mail frequently replace such costly efforts in the online realm. Companies such as PR Newswire and Bacon's can provide a list of media contacts, called a *media list*, as well as manage the process of distributing press kits to ensure that key media representatives receive a company's information in a timely manner. A free online press release distribution service also exists at PRWeb.com, where companies can post and distribute press releases at no charge.

Public relations firms can also support a Web site by creating promotional strategies, developing relationships with reporters and producers of interest to the client company, proposing articles and TV program subjects, and generally keeping the press aware of any good news regarding an online company. Some firms specialize in dot-coms or have an online media specialty. The major advantage of public relations is the low cost relative to other media exposure.

MIXING OFFLINE AND ONLINE MARKETING COMMUNICATIONS

During the E-commerce I era, many believed that the traditional world of marketing based on mass media was no longer relevant to the exploding online commercial world. In the "New Economy," nearly all marketing communications would be online. As it turned out, this did not happen.

The marketing communications campaigns most successful at driving traffic to a Web site have incorporated both online and offline tactics, rather than relying too heavily on one or the other. The objective is to draw the attention of people who are already online and persuade them to visit a new site, as well as attract the attention of people who will be going online in the near future in order to suggest that they, too, visit the site. Several research studies have shown that the most effective online advertisements were those that used consistent imagery with campaigns running in other media at the same time. (Briggs, 1999). Offline mass media such as television and radio have nearly a 100% market penetration into the 140 million households in the United States. More than 35 million adults read a newspaper everyday. It would be foolish not to use these more popular media to drive traffic to the online world of commerce. In the early days of e-commerce, the Internet audience was quite different from the general population, and perhaps was best reached by using online marketing alone. This is no longer true as the Internet population becomes much more like the general population.

Many online ventures have used offline marketing techniques to drive traffic to their Web sites, increase awareness, and build brand equity. For instance, Martha Stewart includes ads in her magazine, *Martha Stewart Living*, directing readers to the Martha Stewart Web site. A picture in the magazine may show a recently redesigned kitchen with a listing of the manufacturers of the kitchen's appliances. For more detailed information and Web links to the manufacturers, readers are directed to www.marthastewart.com. Such "tie-ins" between a print product and its Web site have proven to be very successful in driving Web traffic.

Another example of the online/offline marketing connection is the use of print catalogs by heretofore entirely online ventures. Some online ventures have created paper catalogs and mailed them to their customers to improve their relationship with that group. Amazon has one, and so does consumer products company Unilever. In 2000, Unilever took its database of customer addresses, which had been collected online, and mailed a paper magazine filled with cooking and cleaning tips to that list (Hansell, 2001b). Although an electronic magazine would have been less costly, Unilever believed a paper publication to be better suited for providing the information.

Insight on Business examines how Tiffany & Co. uses online marketing in conjunction with its offline marketing efforts.

8.2 UNDERSTANDING THE COSTS AND BENEFITS OF ONLINE MARKETING COMMUNICATIONS

As we saw in Section 8.1, online marketing communications still comprise only a very small part of the total marketing communications universe. While there are several reasons why this is the case, two of the main ones are concerns about whether online advertising really works and about how to adequately measure the costs and benefits of online advertising. We will address both these topics in this section. But first, we will define some important terms used in looking at the effectiveness of online marketing.

ONLINE MARKETING METRICS: LEXICON

In order to understand the process of attracting prospects to your firm's Web site via marketing communications and converting them into customers, you will need to be familiar with Web marketing jargon. Table 8.3 lists some terms commonly used to describe the impacts and results of online marketing.

The first nine metrics focus primarily on the success of a site in achieving audience or market share by "driving" shoppers to the site. In the E-commerce I period, these measures often substituted for solid information on sales revenue as e-commerce

INSIGHT ON BUSINESS

TIFFANY & CO.

Developing an online marketing approach that increases a company's access to consumers while retaining an image of exclusivity was the challenge faced by the world-renowned jeweler Tiffany & Co. when it redesigned its Web site in 1999. The company was in the enviable position of being perhaps the most famous jewelry company in the United States. Tiffany's offline marketing communications sought to engender feelings of beauty, quality, and timeless style — all hallmarks of the Tiffany brand. How could Tiffany maintain its approach on the Web, a medium that often emphasizes speed and flashy graphics over grace and elegance?

Tiffany's Web designers, Oven Digital Inc., responded with a Web site that uses soft, neutral colors throughout, sparse wording, and pictures that fade slowly onto the screen. The shopping portion of the Web site shows just one large item, with some smaller photos that can be enlarged by clicking at the bottom of the screen. The Web site also includes information on buying and caring for jewelry. Caroline Naggiar, Tiffany's senior vice president of marketing characterizes the site "as an enormous exercise in reserve."

Tiffany's efforts to promote the Web site are also reserved. The company alerts people that it has a Web site, but feels little need to do much more. Its Web address is included in the fine print at the bottom of most of the company's general ads, and from time to time it highlights the site in its daily 4 × 7-inch, page 3 ad in the *New York Times*. Tiffany also limits its online advertising to just a few Web sites, such as the online version of the *New York Times* and the *Wall Street Journal*. Its online ads are as understated as the rest of its marketing efforts, simply including the Tiffany & Co. logo over the familiar blue background.

Despite its low-key marketing approach, the site is helping Tiffany achieve its objectives. Its worldwide operations are growing at a double-digit pace, reaching $1.67 billion for the fiscal year ending January 21, 2001, up 13%, while the division that includes Web operations, a print catalog, and corporate gift-giving also rose 13% to $156 million. Tiffany has also learned that a large percentage of its online purchasers are new customers and that many are located in cities that have a brick-and-mortar Tiffany & Co. storefront. Far from cannibalizing store sales, Tiffany's Web site has proved to be an excellent place for shoppers to find information on new products and designs that they later purchase in local stores.

SOURCES: "Keeping the Cachet," by Lisa Vickery, *Wall Street Journal*, April 23, 2001; "Tradition Meets Technology," by Waheeda Harris, *National Post* (*Toronto*), February 17, 2001; "Old-Line Charlotte, NC-based Retailer Puts Bridal Registry Online," by Samantha Thompson Smith, *The News & Observer*, January 24, 2001; "Tiffany's Brings a Touch of Class to the Web," by Jeff Pelline and Stefanie Olson, CNET News.com, November 16, 1999.

TABLE 8.3	MARKETING METRICS LEXICON

COMMON MARKETING E-METRICS	DESCRIPTION
Impressions	Number of times an ad is served
Clickthrough rate (CTR)	Number of times an ad is clicked
Hits	Number of http requests
Page views	Number of pages viewed
Stickiness (duration)	Average length of stay at a site
Unique visitors	Number of unique visitors in a period
Loyalty	Measured variously as the number of page views, frequency of single user visits to the site, or percentage of customers who return to the site in a year to make additional purchases
Reach	Percentage of site visitors who are potential buyers; or the percentage of total market buyers who buy at a site
Recency	Time elapsed since the last action taken by a buyer, such as a site visit or purchase
Acquisition rate	Percentage of visitors who indicate an interest in the site's product by registering or visiting product's pages
Conversion rate	Percentage of visitors who become customers
Attrition rate	Percentage of customers who do not return during the next year after an initial purchase
Abandonment rate	Percentage of shoppers who begin a shopping cart purchase but then leave the site without completing a purchase
Retention rate	Percentage of existing customers who continue to buy on a regular basis (similar to loyalty)

entrepreneurs sought to have investors and the public focus on the success of the site in "attracting eyeballs" (viewers).

Impressions are the number of times an ad is served. **Clickthrough rate (CTR)** measures the percentage of people exposed to an online advertisement who actually click on the advertisement. **Hits** are the number of http requests received by a firm's server. Hits can be misleading as a measure of site activity because a "hit" does not equal a page: a single page may account for several hits if the page contains multiple images or graphics. A single site visitor can generate hundreds of hits. For this reason, hits are not an accurate representation of Web traffic or visits, even though they are

impressions
number of times an ad is served

clickthrough rate (CTR)
the percentage of people exposed to an online advertisement who actually click on the banner

hits
number of http requests received by a firm's server

page views

number of pages requested by visitors

stickiness (duration)

average length of time visitors remain at a site

unique visitors

the number of distinct, unique visitors to a site

loyalty

percentage of purchasers who return in a year

reach

percentage of the total number of consumers in a market who will visit a site

recency

average number of days elapsed between visits

acquisition rate

measures of the percentage of visitors who register or visit product pages

conversion rate

percentage of visitors who purchase something

attrition rate

percentage of customers who purchase once, but do not return within a year

abandonment rate

percentage of shoppers who begin a shopping cart form, but then fail to complete the form

generally easy to measure; the sheer volume of hits can be huge — and sound impressive, but not be a true measure of activity. **Page views** are the number of pages requested by visitors. However, with increased usage of Web frames that divide pages into separate sections, a single page that has three frames will generate three page views. Hence, page views per se are also not a very useful metric.

Stickiness (sometimes called *duration*) is the average length of time visitors remain at a site. Stickiness is important to marketers because the longer the amount of time a visitor spends at a site, the greater the probability of a purchase. For instance, eBay, which is one of the stickiest and most profitable sites on the Web, is often held up as evidence that stickiness correlates with success. However, experience at other sites counters this argument, calling into question the relevance of stickiness as a measure. Search engine Google.com, for example, is a very popular destination and yet reports very low stickiness ratings (Weber, 2001). Its founders take this as a sign that they have achieved their objective — sending users to their desired destination almost instantaneously.

The number of unique visitors is perhaps the most widely used measure of a site's popularity. The measurement of **unique visitors** counts the number of distinct, unique visitors to a site, regardless of how many pages they view. **Loyalty** measures the percentage of visitors who return in a year. This can be a good indicator of a site's Web following, and perhaps the trust shoppers place in a site. **Reach** is typically a percentage of the total number of consumers in a market who visit a site; for example, 10% of all book purchasers in a year will visit Amazon at least once to shop for a book. This provides an idea of the power of a site to attract market share. **Recency** — like loyalty — measures the power of a site to produce repeat visits and is generally measured as the average number of days elapsed between shopper or customer visits. For example, a recency value of 25 days means the average customer will return once every 25 days.

The metrics described so far do not say much about commercial activity or help understand the conversion from visitor to customer. Five other measures are more helpful. **Acquisition rate** measures of the percentage of visitors who register or visit product pages (indicating interest in the product). **Conversion rate** measures the percentage of visitors who actually purchase something. **Attrition rate** measures the percentage of customers who purchase once, but never return within a year (the opposite of loyalty and retention rates). **Abandonment rate** measures the percentage of shoppers who begin a shopping cart form but then fail to complete the form and leave the site. Abandonment rates can signal a number of potential problems — poor form design, lack of consumer trust, or consumer purchase uncertainty caused by other factors. Marketing firms estimate that 65% to 75% of online shopping carts are abandoned before completion (Ernst and Young, 2001; Jupiter Media Metrix, 2001b). Given that more than 80% of online shoppers generally have a purchase in mind when they visit a Web site, a high abandonment rate signals many lost sales. **Retention rate** indicates the percentage of existing customers who continue to buy on a regular basis.

There is a lengthy path from simple online ad impressions, site visits, and page views to the purchase of a product and the company making a profit (see Figure 8.6). You first need to make customers aware of their needs for your product and somehow drive them to your Web site. Once there, you need to convince them you have the best value — quality and price — when compared to alternative providers. You then must persuade them to trust your firm to handle the transaction (by providing a secure environment and fast fulfillment). Based on your success, a percentage of customers will remain loyal and purchase again or recommend your site to others.

retention rate
percentage of existing customers who continue to buy on a regular basis

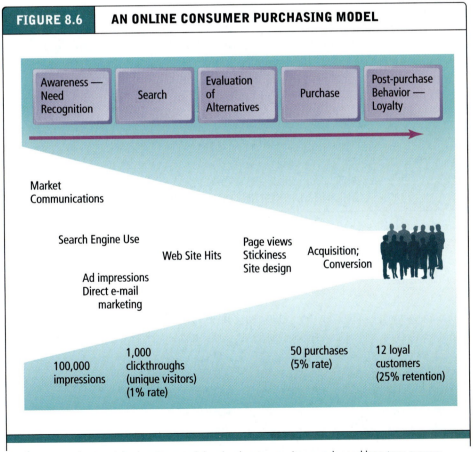

| FIGURE 8.6 | AN ONLINE CONSUMER PURCHASING MODEL |

The conversion of visitors into customers, and then loyal customers, is a complex and long-term process.

DOES ONLINE ADVERTISING WORK?

Table 8.4 lists the clickthrough rates for various types of online marketing communications tools. Many point to low clickthrough rates as evidence that online advertising does not work. However, clickthrough rates are just one measure of the effectiveness of online advertising, and do not, in and of themselves, tell the whole story. In fact, some Web publishers are no longer even reporting clickthrough rates to advertisers on the grounds that they are a misleading statistic that is not indicative of the true impact of online advertising (Saunders, 2001).

One of the first studies on the impact of banner advertisements was conducted in 1996 by Millward Brown Interactive on behalf of Hotwired. The study found that advertising communications occurred even when users did not directly respond by clicking on an ad (Briggs and Hollis, 1997). This study has been replicated a number of times and applied to other online marketing communications tools, in each instance finding that online advertising in its various forms can boost brand awareness and brand recall, create positive brand perceptions, and increase intent to purchase (IAB and Millward Brown Interactive, 1997; Briggs, 1999; IAB, 2001). The IAB/Millward Brown Interactive Study found that clickthrough was usually motivated by a consumer believing that an immediate need would be satisfied by clicking on the banner, but that failure to click was not necessarily an indication of lack of commercial impact.

TABLE 8.4	ONLINE MARKETING COMMUNICATIONS
ONLINE MARKETING METHODS	**TYPICAL CLICKTHROUGH RATES**
Advertising	
Banner ads	.5%–1%
Interstitials	2%
Superstitials	Up to 10%
Search engine paid inclusion/placement	10%–30%
Sponsorships	1.5%
Affiliate relationships	Variable
Direct e-mail marketing	3%–10%
Online catalogs	Variable
Public relations	Variable

Banner ads can be made far more effective if they are targeted to specific occasions (occasion-based marketing), particular keyword search arguments (described below), or users who have an identified user profile and can be pitched the ad at just the right moment. Usually this kind of precision ad pitching requires the services of an advertising network firm such as DoubleClick or 24/7 Media. For instance, companies such as IBM have had success using banners as part of highly targeted occasion-based marketing campaigns. When IBM held entry-level job interviews in Boston in 1999, it alerted local college students by inserting custom banners on its own Web site, tailored to the college from which the student was accessing the Internet. Students at Boston University, for example, saw a banner ad that read "Boston University students, please click here." That strategy paid off for IBM, which achieved a 25% response rate — substantially higher than the less than 1% response most banners obtain (Miles, 2001).

THE COSTS OF ONLINE ADVERTISING

Effectiveness cannot be considered without an analysis of costs. Initially, most online ads were sold on a barter or **cost per thousand (CPM)** (M is the symbol for thousand in Latin) basis, with advertisers purchasing impressions in 1,000-unit lots. Today, other pricing models have developed, including **cost per click (CPC)**, where the advertiser pays a prenegotiated fee for each click an ad receives, **cost per action (CPA)**, where the advertiser pays a prenegotiated amount only when a user performs a specific action, such as a registration or a purchase, and hybrid arrangements, combining two or more of these models (see Table 8.5).

cost per thousand (CPM)
advertiser pays for impressions in 1,000 unit lots

cost per click (CPC)
advertiser pays prenegotiated fee for each click an ad receives

cost per action (CPA)
advertiser pays only for those users who perform a specific action

TABLE 8.5	DIFFERENT PRICING MODELS FOR ONLINE ADVERTISEMENTS
PRICING MODEL	DESCRIPTION
Barter	Exchange of ad space for something of equal value
Cost per thousand (CPM)	Advertiser pays for impressions in 1,000 unit lots
Cost per click (CPC)	Advertiser pays prenegotiated fee for each click ad receives
Cost per action (CPA)	Advertiser pays only for those users who perform a specific action, such as registering, purchasing, etc.
Hybrid	Two or more of the above models used together
Sponsorship	Term-based; advertiser pays fixed fee

E-commerce Web sites spend an average of $250 on marketing and advertising to acquire one customer. The average customer spends about $24.50 during the first quarter at a site and $52.50 in every quarter thereafter that he or she remains a customer. Unfortunately, less than 5% of all site visitors on average ever become customers (Mowrey, 2000). These numbers suggest the central marketing and business challenges for all online sites hoping to make a profit.

However, in addition to sales, there are other benefits to online marketing, such as increasing the brand awareness of your products and firm. Increasing your brand equity may not result in immediate sales, but ultimately, brand equity translates into sales revenue and profits.

One of the advantages of online marketing is that online sales can generally be directly correlated with online marketing efforts. The online merchant can measure precisely just how much revenue is generated by specific banners or e-mail messages sent to prospective customers. One way to measure the effectiveness of online marketing is by looking at the ratio of additional revenue received divided by the cost of the campaign (Revenue/Cost). Any positive whole number means the campaign was worthwhile.

A more complex situation arises when both online and offline sales revenues are affected by an online marketing effort. As we have seen above, 40% of the online audience uses the Web to "shop" but not buy. These shoppers buy at physical stores. Moreover, in the E-commerce II period, existing merchants such as Sears and Wal-Mart will use e-mail to inform their registered customers of special offers available for purchase either online or at stores. Unfortunately, purchases at physical stores cannot be tied precisely with the online e-mail campaign. In these cases, merchants have to rely on less precise measures such as customer surveys at store locations to determine the effectiveness of online campaigns.

In either case, measuring the effectiveness of online marketing communications — and specifying precisely the objective (branding versus sales) — is critical to profitability. To measure marketing effectiveness, you will need to understand the costs of various marketing media and the process of converting online prospects into online customers.

In general, online marketing communications are less costly than traditional mass media marketing. Table 8.6 shows costs for typical online and offline marketing communications. For instance, a local television spot (30 seconds) can cost from $4,000 to $40,000 to run the ad and an additional $40,000 to produce the ad, for a total cost of $44,000 to $80,000. The ad may be seen by a population of, say, 250,000 thousand persons in a local area for a CPM ranging from $176 to $320. A Web site banner ad costs virtually nothing to produce and can be purchased at Web sites for a cost of from $5 to $50 per thousand impressions. Direct mail can cost 80 cents per household drop, but e-mail lists that can be sent for virtually nothing cost only 25 cents per targeted name.

TABLE 8.6	TRADITIONAL AND ONLINE ADVERTISING COSTS COMPARED
Traditional Advertising	
Local television	$4,000 for a 30-second commercial during a movie; $45,000 for a highly rated show.
Network television	$80,000–$600,000 for a 30-second spot during prime time; the average is $120,000 to $140,000.
Cable television	$5,000–$8,000 for a 30-second ad during prime time.
Radio	$200–$1,000 for a 60-second spot, depending on the time of day and program ratings.
Newspaper	$120 per 1,000 circulation for a full-page ad.
Magazine	$50 per 1,000 circulation for an ad in a regional edition of a national magazine, versus $120 per 1,000 for a local magazine.
Direct mail	$15–$20 per 1,000 delivered for coupon mailings; $25–$40 per 1,000 for simple newspaper inserts.
Billboard	$5,000–$25,000 for a 1–3 month rental of a freeway sign.
Online Advertising	
Banner ads	$5–$50 per 1,000 impressions on a site, depending on how targeted the ad is (the more targeted, the higher the price).
Rich media	$40–$50 per 1,000 ads, depending on the site's demographics.
E-mail	$15–$25 per 1,000 e-mail addresses targeted for content sponsored by an advertiser; $100–$300 per 1,000 for an ad.
Sponsorships	$30–$75 per 1,000 viewers, depending on the exclusivity of the sponsorship (the more exclusive, the higher the price).

SOURCE: Rewick, 2001.

SOFTWARE FOR MEASURING ONLINE MARKETING RESULTS

A number of software programs are available to automatically calculate activities at your site. Figure 8.7 illustrates a Web site activity report available from the WebTrends software program.

Other software programs and services assist marketing managers in identifying exactly which marketing initiatives are paying off and which are not. WebSideStory.com is one such service. See *Insight on Technology: WebSideStory.*

FIGURE 8.7	**WEB SITE ACTIVITY ANALYSIS**

Shopping Cart Executive Summary	
Total visits	24,134
Engagement rate	16.7%
Total shoppers	4,031
Abandonment rate	97.4%
Conversion rate	0.4%
Total buyers	103

Shopping Cart Executive Summary – Help Card

Abandonment rate — The percentage of **shoppers** who did not become **buyers**. This includes both **cart abandoners** and **checkout abandoners**.

Conversion rate — Percentage of visitors who became **buyers**.

Engagement rate — Percentage of visitors who become **shoppers**.

Total buyers — Number of buyers who visited your site. Buyers are visitors who reached a page that you configured as an **order complete page**.

Total shoppers — Number of shoppers who visited your site. A shopper is a visitor who reached a page that you configured as a **shopping page**.

Total visits — Number of times a visitor came to your site.

SOURCE: www.webtrends.com, June 2001.

INSIGHT ON TECHNOLOGY

WEBSIDESTORY

In an industry where the players cannot seem to agree on standards for measuring site performance, WebSideStory.com is working to create consensus. This Web site auditing firm provides both free and fee-based software to Webmasters to help collect visitor intelligence and monitor behavior in real time, enabling faster adjustments to underperforming pages. It is also seeking to provide most, if not all, of the answers Web sites want to questions about performance and return on investment (ROI).

WebSideStory's major product is HitBox, a Web tool that provides real-time traffic analysis through close to 100 statistical categories and almost 400 statistics, including traffic counts, number of unique visitors, content, navigation, and page views, among many others. Those individual statistics can then be more closely examined. HitBox can evaluate a page-by-page navigation path a visitor has taken through a site. HitBox works by imbedding a small piece of code into each HTML page a client wants to track and analyze. One benefit to clients is that HitBox eliminates the need to capture, store, and process log files, which are expensive to run and maintain and consume a good bit of a company's time and resources.

Established in San Diego in 1996, WebSideStory now has more than 200,000 clients worldwide, as well as enterprise customers such as Cisco, Sun Microsystems, AT&T, and Hewlett-Packard. It also monitors close to seven billion page views per month for its clients.

A variety of different subscription models exists for HitBox: a free version available for customers who place a banner ad on their site in exchange for the service, a small business version called HitBox Professional for sites that have fewer than 500,000 page views a month and costs $19.95 per month, and two higher volume business versions, one for online retail sites called HitBox Commerce, and another called HitBox Enterprise that starts at $2,000 per month and is scaled up by page views. WebSide Story also offers StatMarket, statistics on global Internet user trends. The statistics at StatMarket are culled from the collective surfing behavior of more than 50 million daily unique visitors to more than 150,000 sites using WebSideStory's HitBox technology. StatMarket statistics provide daily and historical data on Web browser versions, installed Netscape plug-ins, referring search engines, operating system versions, peak Internet traffic hours, and more.

Given that its competitors, such as ABC Interactive, charge anywhere from $1,000 to tens of thousands of dollars each month, WebSideStory could easily corner the market on real-time Web traffic audits. One challenge, however, will be convincing marketers that such data is valuable. Media buyers do not currently place great stock in Web audits, making such services a harder sell to advertising-based Web sites.

SOURCES: "Web-Based Businesses Seek to Measure Up," by Anne Stein, *Crain's Chicago Business*, April 30, 2001; "WebSideStory: Directing Traffic Right To Your Desktop," by Debra Estock, *Application Planet*, March 29, 2001; "WebSideStory Reels in $3M Investment," by Donna Balancia, LocalBusiness.com/San Diego, April 9, 2001; "WebSideStory Deal Should Ease Auditing of Web Traffic," by Patricia Riedman, *Advertising Age*, January 29, 2001.

8.3 THE WEB SITE AS A MARKETING COMMUNICATIONS TOOL

One of the strongest online marketing communications tools is a functional Web site that customers can find. In some ways, a Web site can be viewed as an extended online advertisement. An appropriate domain name, search engine optimization, and proper Web site design are integral parts of a coordinated marketing communications strategy and ultimately, necessary conditions for e-commerce success.

DOMAIN NAMES

One of the first communications an e-commerce site has with a prospective customer is via its URL. Domain names play a important role in reinforcing an existing brand and/or developing a new brand. There are a number of considerations to take into account in choosing a domain name. Ideally, a domain name should be short, memorable, not easily confused with others, and difficult to misspell. If possible, the name should also reflect the nature of the company's business. Companies that choose a name unrelated to their business must be willing to spend extra time, effort, and money to establish the name as a brand. Dot.com domain names are still considered the most preferable, especially in the United States.

Today, however, it may be difficult to find a domain name that satisfies all of the above criteria. Many of the "good" dot.com domain names have already been taken. During E-commerce I, some firms viewed particular domain names as so valuable that they were willing to spend millions to acquire them (for example, business.com, which was purchased for over $7 million, loans.com, which was purchased for $3 million, and bingo.com, which was sold for $1 million). A number of companies exist that list domain names for sale (such as GreatDomains.com and BuyDomains. com). There are also a number of tools to help companies discover domain names that are appropriate for them, such as Network Solutions' NameFetcher and E-gineer's Dominator.

SEARCH ENGINE OPTIMIZATION

Despite the fact that major search engines are moving toward a "pay for inclusion/ranking" model, it is still advisable to take the steps needed to objectively improve a site's visibility to search engines. The major search engines still accept non-paying sites, and still send crawler programs around the Web to index and include pages in their databases free of charge. There are hundreds of search engines in the world, most of which do not charge for inclusion or placement (www. searchenginewatch.com, 2001). Also, given that 42% of shoppers find a vendor by entering the name of a product into a search engine, optimizing the firm's ranking in search engines becomes an important element in a Web site marketing campaign. Search engines produce lists of "hits," sometimes hundreds of them. A hit is the result of a search engine's investigation of its database of indexed Web pages. Web sites appearing at the top of these lists, especially on the first page, are more likely to be visited than those further down the list because they are assumed to be more relevant to the searcher. Consumers may never become aware of sites that are listed later in a search engine report: Only 7% of consumers look any further than the first three pages of results (Dahm, 2000).

The first step in improving a firm's search engine ranking is to register with as many search engines as possible, so that a user looking for similar sites has a chance of coming across that particular site.

The second step is ensuring that keywords used in the Web site description match keywords likely to be used as search terms by prospective customers. Using a keyword of "lamps," for example, will not help your search engine ranking if most prospective customers are searching for "lights." Search engines differ, but most search engines read home page title tags, metatags, and other text on the home page in order to understand and index the content of the page. Keywords are contained in a site's metatag; as described earlier, this is an HTML tag containing a list of words describing the site. Metatags are heavily used by search engines to determine the relevance of sites to search terms used frequently by users. The title tag provides a brief description of the site's content. The words in both the metatags and the title tags should match words on the home page.

A third step in optimizing a firm's ranking on search engines is to link the site to as many other sites as possible. Some search engines, such as google.com, rank sites based on the number of links from other sites. Recall from Chapter 3 that the Internet is a highly interconnected series of sites, surrounded by a set of isolated sites that are not well connected. Search engines such as Google are guessing that when you enter a query for a product, chances are good that the product is located at one of the highly connected Web sites. The assumption is the more links there are to a site, the more useful the site must be. How can a firm increase links to its site? Placing advertising is one way: banner ads, buttons, interstitials, and superstitials are all links to a firm's site. Entering into affiliate relationships with other sites is another method.

While the three steps listed above are a beginning, increasing a firm's ranking is still a bit of an art form and usually requires a full-time professional effort to tweak metatags, keywords, and network links before solid results are obtained. The task often requires several months and is complicated by the fact that each search engine

TABLE 8.7	SEARCH ENGINE RANKING CRITERIA
SEARCH ENGINE	**CRITERIA**
Google	Uses weighted link popularity and analyzes link content to determine site rankings. Recently partnered with Yahoo, the largest directory.
AltaVista	Uses link analysis and ranks sites based on "good" link popularity. Tends to ignore links generated through link exchange programs. Title tags are also important.
Excite	Uses link popularity and quality data to determine relevancy.
Northern Light	Ranks sites based on frequency of the search terms in the text on the page (does not index META tags or ALT tag content), context of search terms in the page, natural language analysis of the search terms, and link popularity.
DirectHit	Based on search activity at Web sites. Sites that are clicked on more frequently will be ranked higher.
Inktomi	Link popularity is one ranking criteria.

SOURCES: Dahm, 2000; www.northernlight.com; www.google.com. www. webdevelopersjournal.com; www.searchenginewatch.com

uses slightly different indexing methods. Search engines fail to find millions of Web pages, and are biased toward large firms that place advertising on other sites (Dahm, 2000).

A recent survey by CyberAtlas Research found that over half of the firms polled work on search engine optimization monthly (Nua Internet Surveys, 2001). Many commercial sites rely on ranking specialists who, for a fee, will create metatags and descriptions that will push a site's ranking toward the top. Some specialists even guarantee a top position, although how near the top is the key question. Being in the top 100 isn't as valuable as being in the top 10, or even top 25. Table 8.7 describes the criteria used by several leading search engines. Most search engines use a combination of keywords and links to rank sites.

TABLE 8.8	SITE DESIGN FEATURES THAT IMPACT ONLINE PURCHASING	
DESIGN FEATURE	**DESCRIPTION**	
Compelling experience	Provide interactivity, entertainment, human interest; site is fun to use.	
Fast download times	Quicker is better; if longer, provide amusement.	
Easy product list navigation	Consumers can easily find the products they want.	
Few clicks to purchase	The shorter the click list, the greater the chance of a sale.	
Customer choice agents	Recommendation agents/configurators help the consumer make quick, correct choices.	
Responsiveness	Automated e-mail response; 1-800 phone capability shown on Web site.	

WEB SITE FUNCTIONALITY

Attracting users to a company's site is the objective of marketing, but once a consumer is at a site, the sales process begins. This means that whatever brought the individuals to the site becomes much less relevant, and what they find at the site will ultimately determine whether they will make a purchase or return.

In Chapter 4 (Section 4.4), we identified seven basic design features that were necessary from a business point of view to attract and retain customers. The site must be informative, employ simple navigation (ease of use), use redundant navigation, make it easy for customers to purchase, and feature multi-browser functionality, simple graphics, and legible text.

Researchers have also found a number of other design factors that marketing managers should be aware of (see Table 8.8).

Sites that offer a "compelling experience" in the sense of providing entertainment with commerce or interactivity, or that are perceived as "fun" to use, are more successful in attracting and keeping visitors (Novak et al., 2000). Long download times frustrate consumers and lead to high rates of abandonment, although this can be mitigated with online amusement to distract the consumer (Dellaert and Khan, 1999). While simplicity of design is hard to define, Lohse et al. (2000) found that the most important factor in predicting monthly sales was product list navigation and choice features that save consumers time. Thus, Amazon's "one click" purchase capability is a powerful tool for increasing sales. Increasingly, sites are using interactive consumer decision aids to help the consumer make choices. *Recommendation agents* are programs that can recommend a product based on either a consumer's completing a survey or a review of a consumer's profile. Dell Computer users an *online configurator* to help consumers decide what computer to order (Haubl and Trifts, 2000). Responsiveness to consumer inquiries through automated customer response systems has been found to affect return visits and purchases.

No matter how successful the offline and online marketing campaign, a Web site that fails to deliver information and customer convenience spells disaster. Attention to site design features will help ensure success.

CASE STUDY

Ad Bombs, Ambush Marketing
and Other Invasive Marketing Techniques Grow on the Internet

The Holy Grail of advertising and marketing is to deliver the right message to the right person at the right time. If this were possible, no one would receive ads they did not want to see and then no advertising dollars would be wasted. One vision of E-commerce I was a trade-off between privacy and efficiency: Let us know a little more about you and we will show you only the advertising and products you are interested in seeing. E-commerce was supposed to end the mass advertising that exploded in the television era. But if you have a DSL or cable modem connection to the Web, you will quickly learn that your permanent Internet address can easily be discovered by marketing firms — who often share your address with one another — and thereafter you are treated to hundreds of e-mail messages a week offering "free" credit cards, cash prizes, businesses that require no work, and other get-rich quick schemes.

Instead of achieving the Holy Grail of advertising, sometimes the technology can lead aggressive marketers in the opposite direction, increasing the chances that you will see the wrong ads at the wrong time without your consent.

Consider the following scenario. A ten-year-old visits your house (she could be a friend of your children or a relative) and wants to "play with the computer" as adults go about their business. You have a DSL or cable modem service with a permanent IP address. Surfing to a game site, she sees an offer for $100 in "free" prizes. She clicks and up pops the following proposition: "Click Here to Get Your Free Prizes." She clicks and up pops pictures of ten free prizes, ranging from free CDs to free clothing. But in the background a program is loaded onto your machine that automatically — without your intervention — requests that pop-up advertisements served by the L90 advertising network be displayed every few minutes whenever you are using your computer. It is not even necessary to have launched your browser because the program automatically launches your browser whenever it wants to serve up an ad. Thankfully, however, most of the ads served up are appropriate for a ten-year-old (more offers of free prizes, CDs for children, and clothing), although there are some inappropriate advertisements, such as those for credit cards.

Following one of these ads back to its originator, you discover a marketing firm called colonize.com that specializes in putting together e-mail marketing lists. There, in order to actually obtain your free gift, you are required to enter your name and e-mail address. Colonize.com adds your name to its 35 million other e-mail addresses,

and then re-sells this list to firms who want to market to you. Firms hire colonize.com to create the unwanted ads, and L90 is used as the ad serving mechanism.

This "ad bomb" is just one of many examples of pernicious and invasive advertising techniques being developed by aggressive marketing firms that operate without the user's consent to deliver unwanted, poorly targeted, and inappropriate ads. We define an ad bomb as any computer program that is surreptitiously downloaded on a client machine for the purpose of calling for unwanted advertising without the user's consent or intervention.

In an effort to rid your machine of the offending ad bomb, you contact L90. L90 technicians explain in an e-mail that they are just serving the ads and bear no responsibility for the downloaded program. They explain that "you may have unknowingly downloaded an application from one of these sites. An application downloaded from one of these sites may be requesting an advertisement from our ad server. Please note that L90 does not download any applications to your computer. L90 does not control these web sites or ISPs." L90 technical support fails to mention that L90 is paid by the advertisers involved to respond to the ads. L90 does offer to help, however. Technical support advises you to close down ad windows as they appear, or press ctrl + n to display the URL of the advertisers and then send the URLs to L90, which will, in turn notify the advertisers to unsubscribe you from their lists.

In the meantime, you click one of ads that leads you the colonize.com's Web site and request to unsubscribe from their list, but this does not take effect immediately. Ads from many other companies appear, making the task of visiting each one to unsubscribe very time-consuming. Finally, you open Windows' Add/Remove Programs utility in the hope of identifying the program and removing it. After scanning the list of programs, you discover an unfamiliar program. Guessing this oddly named program is the offender, you remove it, and finally the ad bomb event is over.

Another company called Gator.com has developed a technique called ambush advertising. Gator originally started business as a provider of a client-side digital wallet that would store personal information and automatically fill out forms for some eight million current users. From there, Gator added a new product called the Offer-Companion. Now when users download the digital wallet program, a pair of green eyes appear on the screen — your "smart" online companion.

But Gator's OfferCompanion is pernicious: The program follows your movements on the Web, and when you arrive at a site, say Staples.com, the OnlineCompanion notifies Gator's servers, which search their ad database for an ad purchased by a Staples competitor such as OfficeMax. Then the Gator server serves up a "mini-billboard" that appears directly over the Staples Web site, asking you to go the OfficeMax site. Dozens of firms are running these so-called "ambush" ads at rival sites.

On August 28, 2001, the Interactive Advertising Bureau (IAB) — a trade group that represents Internet advertising agencies — announced its opposition to Gator's OnlineCompanion, charging that Gator was infringing on the trademark, copyright, and intellectual property rights of Web site publishers and other advertisers whose ads were being covered up by the Gator mini-billboard. IAB is considering filing a complaint with the Federal Trade Commission, and demanded Gator cease use of the program. Gator has in turn sued the IAB in a California Federal Court for IAB's "malicious disparagement" of its products and "to protect the right to utilize Gator's newest advertising vehicle, the Companion Pop-up Banner." Gator's Chief Executive said "We refuse to allow the IAB to falsely claim that pop-up banners are illegal or to interfere in any way with our advertisers' right to deliver relevant advertising, or our consumers' right to decide for themselves what is or isn't displayed on their own computer screens."

Taking the technology one step further, the ad network firm L90 signed an exclusive arrangement in February 2001 with peer-to-peer network Aimster in one of the first partnerships to promote goods to consumers via instant messaging. Here's how it will work. L90 will scour the musical postings of Aimster members who freely and willingly post songs on their client machines for others in the Aimster network to download. By posting these songs, they are simultaneously letting the world know

SOURCES: "Shooting Back at Gator's 'Ambush Ads,'" by Leslie Walker, *Washington Post*, August 30, 2001; "IAB Asserts Gator.com's Business Practices Violate the Contract, Trademark and Copyright Interests of Web Publishers and Advertisers," Interactive Advertising Bureau Press Release, August 28, 2001; "Get Ready for IM Spam!" www.zdnet.com, February 18, 2001.

what their musical tastes are. L90 hopes to identify the musical listening habits of Aimster members, and then send instant commercial advertisements to users via Aimster's buddy lists.

Commenting on these developments, Jim Nail, advertising analyst at Forrester Research, said this was "really a bad idea — like instant spam — because instant messaging is like a private conversation. This is like you're talking to your boyfriend over the phone and 1-800-Flowers jumps in and says 'I see you're having an argument, why don't you buy some flowers.'"

Given the falling clickthrough rates on Internet banner advertising and the declining advertising revenues experienced by many Web sites, there is tremendous pressure to invent new forms of marketing that stand out, get the user's attention, and if necessary, intrude on the average Web user's activities. If history is any guide, demands will increase on federal regulatory agencies to pass laws and set standards regulating the online marketing industry.

Case Study Questions

1. Do you believe L90 bears any responsibility for ad bombs placed on your machines? How about www.colonize.com? Why or why not?

2. Do these programs results in greater "targeting" of advertising, or are they just as mass market in nature as television ads?

3. What types of industry or government regulations might be needed to control these forms of advertising?

4. If you use instant messaging services, how would you feel about advertisements delivered via instant messaging? What kind of controls do you think your instant messaging provider should implement?

| 8.5 | **REVIEW** |

KEY CONCEPTS

■ **Identify the major forms of online marketing communications.**

Marketing communications include promotional sales communications that encourage immediate purchases and branding communications that focus on extolling the differentiable benefits of consuming a product or service. There are a number of different forms of marketing communications, including:

- *Banner and rich media ads* are promotional messages that users can respond to by clicking on the banner and following the link to a product description or offering. Variations include different size banners, buttons, skyscrapers, pop-ups, and pop-unders. Rich media ads use Flash, DHTML, Java, and streaming audio and/or video and typically seek to involve users more deeply than static banner ads.

- *Interstitial ads* are a way of placing full page messages between the current and destination pages of a user. They are usually inserted within a single site, and are displayed as the user moves from one page to the next; they can also be made to appear as users move among sites.

- *Superstitials* are rich media ads developed by Unicast that pre-load into a browser's cache and do not play until fully loaded and the user clicks to another page.

- *Paid search engine inclusion and placement* is a relatively recent phenomenon. Firms now pay search engines for inclusion in the search engine index (formerly free and based on "objective" criteria), receiving a guarantee that their firm will appear in the results of relevant searches.

- *Sponsorships* are paid efforts to tie an advertiser's name to particular information, an event, or a venue in a way that reinforces its brand in a positive, yet not overtly commercial manner. Advertorials are a common form of online sponsorship.

- *Affiliate relationships* permit a firm to put their logo or banner ad on another firm's Web site from which users of that site can click through to the affiliate's site.

- *Direct e-mail marketing* sends e-mail directly to interested users, and has proven to be one of the most effective forms of marketing communications. The key to effective direct e-mail marketing is "interested users" — Internet users who, at one time or another, have expressed an interest in receiving messages from the advertiser (people who have "opted in").

- *Online catalogs* are the online equivalent of paper-based catalogs. Their basic function is to display an e-commerce merchant's wares.

- *Public relations* involves pursuing media coverage and exposure to target audiences without buying advertising space. Publicity, special events, and newsletters are examples of ways to encourage the media to report on a site, thereby attracting more traffic.

- *Offline marketing combined with online marketing communications* are typically the most effective. Although many e-commerce ventures want to rely heavily on online communications, marketing communications campaigns most successful at driving traffic to a Web site have incorporated both online and offline tactics.

■ **Understand the costs and benefits of online marketing communications.**

Key terms that one must know in order to understand evaluations of online marketing communications' effectiveness and its costs and benefits include:

- *Impressions* — the number of times an ad is served.
- *Clickthrough rate* — the number of times an ad is clicked.
- *Hits* — the number of http requests received by a firm's server.
- *Page views* — the number of pages viewed by visitors.
- *Stickiness (duration)* — the average length of time visitors remain at a site.
- *Unique visitors* — the number of distinct, unique visitors to a site.
- *Loyalty* — the percentage of purchasers who return in a year.
- *Reach* — the percentage of total consumers in a market who will visit a site.
- *Recency* — the average number of days elapsed between visits.
- *Acquisition rate* — the percentage of visitors who indicate an interest in the site's product by registering or visiting product's pages.
- *Conversion rate* — the percentage of visitors who purchase something.
- *Attrition rate* — the percentage of customers who purchase once, but do not return within a year.
- *Abandonment rate* — the percentage of shoppers who begin a shopping cart form but then fail to complete the form.
- *Retention rate* — the percentage of existing customers who continue to buy on a regular basis.

Studies have shown that low clickthrough rates are not indicative of a lack of commercial impact of online advertising, and that advertising communication does occur even when users do not directly respond by clicking. Online advertising in its various forms has been shown to boost brand awareness and brand recall, create positive brand perceptions, and increase intent to purchase.

Effectiveness cannot be considered without analysis of cost. Typical pricing models for online marketing communications include:

- *Barter* — the exchange of ad space for something of equal value.
- *Cost per thousand (CPM)* — the advertiser pays for impressions in 1,000 unit lots.
- *Cost per click (CPC)* — the advertiser pays a prenegotiated fee for each click an ad receives.
- *Cost per action (CPA)* — the advertiser pays only for those users who perform a specific action.
- *Hybrid models* — combines two or more other models.
- *Sponsorships* — the advertiser pays a fixed fee for a particular term.

Online marketing communications are typically less costly than traditional mass media marketing. Also, online sales can generally be directly correlated with online marketing efforts, unlike with traditional marketing communications tactics. The online merchant can measure precisely just how much revenue is generated by specific banners or specific e-mail messages sent to prospective customers.

■ Discuss the ways in which a Web site can be used as a marketing communications tool.

A functional Web site that customers can find is one of the strongest online communications tools. The following are all integral parts of a coordinated marketing communications strategy:

- *Appropriate domain name* — companies should choose a domain name that is short, memorable, hard to confuse or misspell, and indicative of a firm's business functions, and that preferably uses dot.com as its top level domain.
- *Search engine optimization* — companies should register with all the major search engines so that a user looking for similar sites has a better chance of finding that particular site; ensure that keywords used in the Web site description match keywords likely to be used as search terms by prospective customers; and link the site to as many other sites as possible.
- *Web site functionality* — once at a Web site, visitors need to be enticed to stay and to buy. Web site design features that impact online purchasing include how compelling the experience of using the Web site is, download time, product list navigation, the number of clicks required to purchase, the existence of customer choice agents, and the Web site's responsiveness to customer needs.

QUESTIONS

1. Explain the difference between marketing and marketing communications.
2. Explain the difference between branding communications and sales/promotional communications.
3. What are some reasons why online advertising constitutes less than 5% of the total advertising market?
4. What kinds of products are most suited to being advertised online?
5. What is the difference between an interstitial ad and a superstitial?
6. What are some of the reasons for the decline in clickthrough rates on banner ads today? How can banner ads be made more effective?
7. Why are some affiliate relationships called "tenancy" deals? How do they differ from pure affiliate arrangements?
8. There is some controversy surrounding paid placements on search engines — What are the issues surrounding paid placement search engines? Why might consumers object to this practice?
9. What are some of the advantages of direct e-mail marketing?
10. Why is offline advertising still important?

11. What is the difference between hits and page views? Why are these not the best measurements of Web traffic? Which is the preferred metric for traffic counts?
12. Define CTR, CPM, CPC, and CPC.
13. What are the key attributes of a good domain name?
14. What are some of the steps a firm can take to optimize its search engine rankings?
15. List and describe some Web site design features that impact online purchasing.

PROJECTS

1. Use the Online Consumer Purchase Model (Figure 8.6) to assess the effectiveness of an e-mail campaign at a small Web site devoted to the sales of apparel to the ages 18–26 young adult market in the United States. Assume a marketing campaign of 100,000 e-mails (at 25 cents per e-mail address). The expected clickthrough rate is 15%, the conversion to customer rate is 10%, and the loyal customer retention rate is 25%. The average sale is $60, and the profit margin is 50% (the cost of the goods is $30). Does the campaign produce a profit? What would you advise doing to increase the number of purchases and loyal customers? What Web design factors? What communications messages?

2. Surf the Web for at least 15 minutes. Visit at least two different sites. Make a list describing in detail all the different marketing communication tools you see being used. Which do you believe is the most effective and why?

3. Do a search for a product of your choice on at least 5 of the search engines listed in Table 8.2. Examine the results page carefully. Can you discern which results, if any, are a result of a paid placement? If so, how did you determine this? What other marketing communications related to your search appear on the page?

4. Examine the use of rich media in advertising. Find and describe at least two examples of advertising using streaming video, sound, or other rich media technologies (hint: check the sites of Internet advertising agencies for case studies or examples of their work). What are the advantages and/or disadvantages of this kind of advertising? Prepare a short 3- to 5-page report on your findings.

WEB SITE RESOURCES   www.LearnE-commerce.net

- News: Weekly updates on topics relevant to the material in this chapter
- Video Lecture: Professor Ken Laudon summarizes the key concepts of the chapter
- Research: Abstracts and links to articles referenced in the chapter, as well as other relevant research
- International Spotlight: More information about the use of e-commerce marketing communications outside the United States
- PowerPoint Slides: Illustrations from the chapter and more
- Additional projects and exercises

C H A P T E R 9

Ethical, Social, and Political Issues in E-commerce

After reading this chapter, you will be able to:

- Understand why e-commerce raises ethical, social, and political issues.
- Recognize the main ethical, social, and political issues raised by e-commerce.
- Identify a process for analyzing ethical dilemmas.
- Identify the practices of e-commerce companies that threaten privacy.
- Understand basic concepts related to privacy.
- Describe the different methods used to protect online privacy.
- Understand the various forms of intellectual property and the challenge of protecting it.
- Understand how governance of the Internet has evolved over time.
- Explain why taxation of e-commerce raises governance and jurisdiction issues.
- Identify major public safety and welfare issues raised by e-commerce.

Hacker to the Slammer
Piracy and Free Speech

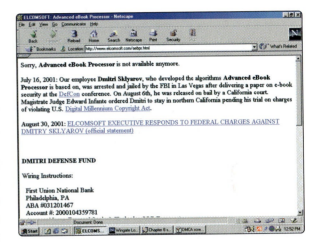

Dmitri Sklyarov, a PhD student at Moscow State Technical University, spent his first night in a Las Vegas jail on July 16, 2001. His crime: presenting a paper entitled "eBook Security: Theory and Practice" at Def-Con, a conference of computer hackers. The paper described software created by Sklyarov that can decrypt Adobe Systems electronic books. Sklyarov was arrested by the FBI and charged with four counts of trafficking in software that circumvents copyrightable and encrypted materials, and one count of conspiracy to aid and abet such trafficking. Each count carries a possible penalty of up to five years in jail and/or a $500,000 fine. Sklyarov has pleaded not guilty. His case will be tried in federal criminal court in San Jose, California.

No matter the verdict, there will undoubtedly be an appeal, and ultimately a test of the constitutionality of the new law he violated: the Digital Millennium Copyright Act of 1998 (the "DMCA"). Sklyarov is the first person to be indicted under the criminal provisions of the DMCA. In a previous civil action in May 2001, the Motion Picture Industry Association succeeded in obtaining an injunction against the Web magazine www.2600.com for publishing DcCSS, a program that unlocks the DVD encryption scheme used by Hollywood studios. Copyright owners of intellectual property such as movies, trade books, and textbooks are all seeking to prevent the "Napsterization" of their property.

Until Congress passed the DMCA, Dmitri Sklyarov's activities would have been perfectly legal. But the DMCA makes it a criminal offense for anyone to disseminate—either by selling or by giving away—a scheme that breaks the encryption scheme publishers use to protect their copyrighted works. In addition, under the DMCA, federal prosecutors can also seek to hold the company for which Dmitri works (ElcomSoft, a Moscow-based small software company with 200 employees) liable for up to $500,000 in additional fines. ElcomSoft develops and sells, and in some cases gives away, software specifically designed to break the e-book encryption scheme developed by Adobe Systems and other firms. ElcomSoft, in other words, is in the business of code-breaking of commercial encryption schemes for the purpose of allowing its customers to pirate copyrighted works.

Adobe recently released a much improved version of its encryption software that it is marketing to publishing companies interested in developing e-books for college and mass market sales. Obviously, publishing companies would never buy Adobe's encryption product if it could easily be defeated by hackers such as Dmitri, or by firms such as ElcomSoft. Many other software firms such as NetLibrary and RSA Security are seeking to sell similar encryption systems to publishing companies. Should these firms succeed, thousands of copyrighted titles, including college textbooks, would be available for distribution over the Web at potentially much lower prices than is true of books today — perhaps 50% less than physical books.

In his defense, Mr. Sklyarov declared the Adobe encryption system was inherently flawed and could be easily broken. Bruce Schneier, a cryptographer, said that "trying to secure this [e-book PDF files] is like trying to make water not wet. Bits are inherently copyable by definition." Even a representative of Adobe Systems said "No software on the market is 100 percent secure to determined hackers." Adobe changed its encryption scheme in June 2001 to defeat the ElcomSoft decryption software, but ElcomSoft issued a new release in a few days that broke the new Adobe code. Moreover, using the highest levels of security would slow the performance of e-books to a crawl.

Sklyarov's case raises several dilemmas for which there are no easy solutions. The First Amendment declares that Congress shall pass no laws limiting the freedom of expression. However, rights are not absolute. The First Amendment does not protect speech that harms people, or speech used for illegal conduct. Should Dmitri's actions be protected by the First Amendment? However, if ElcomSoft succeeds in routinely breaking e-book encryption, publishers will withhold their copyrighted materials from the market, and this will keep the price of books high, denying millions of readers access to inexpensive books. A second question concerns the ability of a U.S. court to hold ElcomSoft, a Russian company, liable for its actions under a U.S. law that has no force outside the United States. Like Sklyarov, ElcomSoft has pleaded not guilty, maintaining that its program is legal in Russia.

SOURCES: "Russian Programmer Enters Plea," by Jennifer Lee, *New York Times*, August 31, 2001; "Russian Programmer and Employer Indicted," *Reuters*, August 29, 2001; "Arrest Raises Stakes in Battle Over Copyright," by Amy Harmon and Jennifer S. Lee, *New York Times*, July 23, 2001; "U.S. Arrests Russian Cryptographer as Copyright Violator," by Jennifer Lee, *New York Times*, July 18, 2001; "Judges Weigh Copyright Suit on Unlocking DVD Shield," by Amy Harmon, *New York Times*, May 2, 2001; "Does Anti-Piracy Plan Quash the First Amendment?" by Carl S. Kaplan, *New York Times*, April 27, 2001; "Banned Code Lives in Poetry and Song," by David P. Hamilton, *Wall Street Journal*, April 12, 2001.

D efining the rights of people to express their ideas and the property rights of copyright owners are just two of many ethical, social, and political issues raised by the rapid evolution of e-commerce. These questions are not just ethical questions that we as individuals have to answer; they also involve social institutions such as family, schools, and business firms. And these questions have obvious political dimensions because they involve collective choices about how we should live and what laws we would like to live under.

In this chapter we discuss the ethical, social, and political issues raised in e-commerce, provide a framework for organizing the issues, and make recommendations for managers who are given the responsibility of operating e-commerce companies within commonly accepted standards of appropriateness.

9.1 UNDERSTANDING ETHICAL, SOCIAL, AND POLITICAL ISSUES IN E-COMMERCE

The Internet and its use in e-commerce have raised pervasive ethical, social and political issues on a scale unprecedented for computer technology. Entire sections of daily newspapers and weekly magazines are devoted to the social impact of the Internet. But why is this so? Why is the Internet at the root of so many contemporary controversies? Part of the answer lies in the underlying features of Internet technology itself, and the ways in which it has been exploited by business firms. Internet technology and its use in e-commerce disrupts existing social and business relationships and understandings.

Consider for instance the table we presented in Chapter 1 listing the unique features of Internet technology. Instead of considering the business consequences of each unique feature, here we examine the actual or potential ethical, social, and/or political consequences of the technology (see Table 9.1).

We live in an "information society," where power and wealth increasingly depend on information and knowledge as central assets. Controversies over information are often in fact disagreements over power, wealth, influence, and other things thought to be valuable. Like other technologies such as steam, electricity, telephones, and television, the Internet and e-commerce can be used to achieve social progress, and for the most part, this has occurred. However, the same technologies can be used to commit crimes, despoil the environment, and threaten cherished social values. Before automobiles, there was very little interstate crime and very little federal jurisdiction over crime. Likewise with the Internet: Before the Internet, there was very little "cybercrime."

Many business firms and individuals are benefiting from the commercial development of the Internet, but this development also exacts a price from individuals,

TABLE 9.1	UNIQUE FEATURES OF E-COMMERCE TECHNOLOGY AND THEIR POTENTIAL ETHICAL, SOCIAL, AND/OR POLITICAL IMPLICATIONS
E-COMMERCE TECHNOLOGY DIMENSION	**POTENTIAL SIGNIFICANCE**
Ubiquity	Work and shopping can invade family life; shopping can distract workers at their jobs, lowering productivity; the use of mobile devices can lead to automobile and industrial accidents; ubiquity also presents confusing issues of "nexus" to taxation authorities.
Global reach	May reduce cultural diversity in products and weaken local, small firms while strengthening large global firms; manufacturing production may be moved to low-wage areas of the world; also weakens the ability of all nations—large and small—to control their information destiny.
Universal standards	Increase vulnerability to viruses and hacking attacks worldwide, affecting millions of people at once; also increase the likelihood of "information" crime, crimes against systems, and deception.
Richness	Makes very persuasive messages that may reduce reliance on multiple independent sources of information possible.
Interactivity	The nature of interactivity at commercial sites can be shallow and meaningless. Customer e-mails are frequently not read by human beings. Customers do not really "co-produce" the product so much as they "co-produce" the sale. The amount of customization of products that occurs is minimal, occurring within predefined platforms and plug-in options.
Information density	While the total amount of information available to all parties increases, so does the possibility of false and misleading information, unwanted information, and invasion of solitude. Trust, authenticity, accuracy, completeness, and other quality features of information can be degraded. The ability of individuals and organizations to make sense of out of this plethora of information is limited.
Personalization/Customization	Opens up an unprecedented possibility of intensive invasion of privacy for commercial and governmental purposes.

organizations, and societies. These costs and benefits must be carefully considered by those seeking to make ethical and socially responsible decisions in this new environment. The question is: How can you as a manager make reasoned judgments about what your firm should do in a number of e-commerce areas — from securing the privacy of your customer's clickstream to ensuring the integrity of your company's domain name?

A MODEL FOR ORGANIZING THE ISSUES

E-commerce — and the Internet — have raised so many ethical, social, and political issues that it is difficult to classify them all, and hence complicated to see their relationship to one another. Clearly, ethical, social, and political issues are interrelated. One way to organize the ethical, social, and political dimensions surrounding e-commerce is shown in Figure 9.1. At the individual level, what appears as an ethical issue — "What should I do?" — is reflected at the social and political levels — "What should we as a society and government do?" The ethical dilemmas you face as a manager of a business using the Web reverberate and are reflected in social and political debates. The major ethical, social, and political issues that have developed around e-commerce over the past seven to eight years can be loosely categorized into four major dimensions: information rights, property rights, governance, and public safety and welfare.

Some of the ethical, social, and political issues raised in each of these areas include the following:

- **Information rights:** What rights to their own personal information do individuals have in a public marketplace, or in their private homes, when Internet technologies make information collection so pervasive and efficient? What rights do individuals have to access information about business firms and other organizations?

- **Property rights:** How can traditional intellectual property rights be enforced in an Internet world where perfect copies of protected works can be made and easily distributed worldwide in seconds?

- **Governance:** Should the Internet and e-commerce be subject to public laws? And if so, what law-making bodies have jurisdiction — state, federal, and/or international?

- **Public safety and welfare:** What efforts should be undertaken to ensure equitable access to the Internet and e-commerce channels? Should governments be responsible for ensuring that schools and colleges have access to the Internet? Is certain online content and activities — such as pornography and gambling — a threat to public safety and welfare? Should mobile commerce be allowed from moving vehicles?

To illustrate, imagine that at any given moment society and individuals are more or less in an ethical equilibrium brought about by a delicate balancing of individuals, social organizations, and political institutions. Individuals know what is expected of them, social organizations such as business firms know their limits, capabilities, and roles, and political institutions provide a supportive framework of market regulation, banking, and commercial law that provides sanctions against violators.

Now, imagine we drop into the middle of this calm setting a powerful new technology such as the Internet and e-commerce. Suddenly individuals, business firms, and political institutions are confronted by new possibilities of behavior. For instance, individuals discover that they can download perfect digital copies of music tracks, something which, under the old technology of CDs, would have been impossible. This can be done, despite the fact that these music tracks still "belong" as a legal mat-

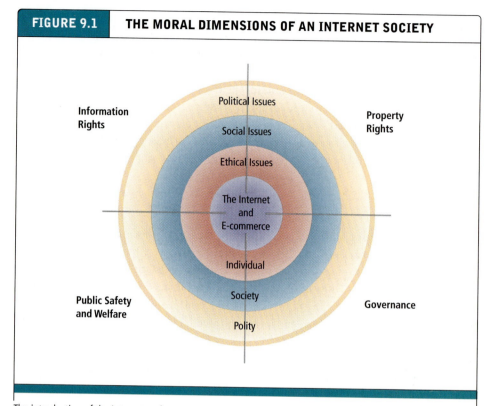

FIGURE 9.1 | **THE MORAL DIMENSIONS OF AN INTERNET SOCIETY**

The introduction of the Internet and e-commerce impacts individuals, societies, and political institutions. These impacts can be classified into four moral dimensions: property rights, information rights, governance, and public safety and welfare.

ter to the owners of the copyright — musicians and record label companies. Then, business firms discover that they can make a business out of aggregating these digital musical tracks — or creating a mechanism for sharing musical tracks — even though they do not "own" them in the traditional sense. This, of course, is the story of Napster described in Chapter 1. The record companies, courts, and Congress were not prepared at first to cope with the onslaught of online digital copying. Courts and legislative bodies will have to make new laws and reach new judgments about who owns digital copies of copyrighted works and under what conditions such works can be "shared." It make take years to develop new understandings, laws, and acceptable behavior in just this one area of social impact. In the meantime, as an individual and a manager, you will have to decide what you and your firm should do in legal "grey" areas, where there is conflict between ethical principles, but no clear-cut legal or cultural guidelines. How can you make good decisions in this type of situation?

Before reviewing the four moral dimensions of e-commerce in greater depth, we will briefly review some basic concepts of ethical reasoning that you can use as a guide to ethical decision making, and provide general reasoning principles about the social and political issues of the Internet that you will face in the future.

BASIC ETHICAL CONCEPTS: RESPONSIBILITY, ACCOUNTABILITY, AND LIABILITY

Ethics is at the heart of social and political debates about the Internet. **Ethics** is the study of principles that individuals and organizations can use to determine right and wrong courses of action. It is assumed in ethics that individuals are free moral agents who are in a position to make choices. When faced with alternative courses of action, what is the correct moral choice? Extending ethics from individuals to business firms and even entire societies can be difficult, but it is not impossible. As long as there is a decision-making body or individual (such as a Board of Directors or CEO in a business firm, or a governmental body in a society), their decisions can be judged against a variety of ethical principles.

If you understand some basic ethical principles, your ability to reason about larger social and political debates will be improved. In western culture, there are three basic principles that all ethical schools of thought share: responsibility, accountability, and liability. **Responsibility** means that as free moral agents, individuals, organizations, and societies are responsible for the actions they take. **Accountability** means that individuals, organizations, and societies should be held accountable to others for the consequences of their actions. The third principle — liability — extends the concepts of responsibility and accountability to the area of law. **Liability** is a feature of political systems in which a body of law is in place that permits individuals to recover the damages done to them by other actors, systems, or organizations. **Due process** is a feature of law-governed societies and refers to a process in which laws are known and understood and there is an ability to appeal to higher authorities to ensure that the laws have been applied correctly.

You can use these concepts immediately to understand some contemporary Internet debates. For instance, consider the case of Napster and the sharing of digital copies of copyrighted musical tracks. Napster claimed that it was not responsible for the actions of its members who were widely sharing musical tracks — even though it provided the mechanism for this exchange of files. Napster claimed it could not be held accountable for the action of its members, and therefore it could not be held liable for any damages that may have been done to the copyright holders — the record label companies and artists. The courts have disagreed with Napster's reasoning and have found that by providing a mechanism for widespread sharing of music files, Napster was in fact responsible for the sharing and should be held accountable and liable for the damages done. The courts relied on copyright laws to arrive at their deci-

ethics
the study of principles that individuals and organizations can use to determine right and wrong courses of action

responsibility
as free moral agents, individuals, organizations, and societies are responsible for the actions they take

accountability
individuals, organizations, and societies should be held accountable to others for the consequences of their actions

liability
a feature of political systems in which a body of law is in place that permits individuals to recover the damages done to them by other actors, systems, or organizations

due process
a process in which laws are known and understood and there is an ability to appeal to higher authorities to ensure that the laws have been applied correctly

sions, but these laws reflect some basic underlying ethical principles of responsibility, accountability, and liability.

Underlying the Napster decision and others like it is an even more fundamental rejection of the E-commerce I notion that the Internet is an ungoverned "Wild West" environment that cannot be controlled. No organized civilized society has ever accepted the proposition that technology can flaunt basic underlying social and cultural values. Through all of the industrial and technological developments that have taken place, societies have intervened through legal and political decisions to ensure that the technology serves socially acceptable ends without stifling the positive consequences of innovation and wealth creation. The Internet in this sense is no different, and in the E-commerce II period we can expect societies around the world to exercise more regulatory control over the Internet and e-commerce in an effort to arrive at a new balance between innovation and wealth creation, on the one hand, and other socially desirable objectives on the other. This is a difficult balancing act, and reasonable people will arrive at different conclusions.

ANALYZING ETHICAL DILEMMAS

dilemma

a situation in which there are at least two diametrically opposed actions, each of which supports a desirable outcome

Ethical, social, and political controversies usually present themselves as dilemmas. A **dilemma** is a situation in which there are at least two diametrically opposed actions, each of which supports a desirable outcome. When confronted with a situation that seems to present ethical dilemmas, how can you analyze and reason about the situation? The following is a five-step process that should help.

1. **Identify and describe clearly the facts.** Find out who did what to whom, and where, when, and how. In many instances, you will be surprised at the errors in the initially reported facts, and often you will find that simply getting the facts straight helps define the solution. It also helps to get the opposing parties involved in an ethical dilemma to agree on the facts.

2. **Define the conflict or dilemma and identify the higher-order values involved.** Ethical, social, and political issues always reference higher values. Otherwise, there would be no debate. The parties to a dispute all claim to be pursuing higher values (e.g., freedom, privacy, protection of property, and the free enterprise system). For example, DoubleClick and its supporters argue that their tracking of consumer movements on the Web increases market efficiency and the wealth of the entire society. Opponents argue this claimed efficiency comes at the expense of individual privacy, and DoubleClick should cease its activities or offer Web users the option of not participating in such tracking.

3. **Identify the stakeholders.** Every ethical, social, and political issue has stakeholders: players in the game who have an interest in the outcome, who have invested in the situation, and usually who have vocal opinions. Find out the identity of these groups and what they want. This will be useful later when designing a solution.

4. **Identify the options that you can reasonably take.** You may find that none of the options satisfies all the interests involved, but that some options do a better job than others. Sometimes, arriving at a "good" or ethical solution may not always be a balancing of consequences to stakeholders.

5. **Identify the potential consequences of your options.** Some options may be ethically correct, but disastrous from other points of view. Other options may work in this one instance, but not in other similar instances. Always ask yourself, "What if I choose this option consistently over time?"

Once your analysis is complete, you can refer to the following well established ethical principle to help decide the matter.

CANDIDATE ETHICAL PRINCIPLES

Although you are the only one who can decide which among many ethical principles you will follow and how you will prioritize them, it is helpful to consider some ethical principles with deep roots in many cultures that have survived throughout recorded history.

- **The Golden Rule:** Do unto others as you would have them do unto you. Putting yourself into the place of others and thinking of yourself as the object of the decision can help you think about fairness in decision making.

- **Universalism:** If an action is not right for all situations, then it is not right for any specific situation (Immanuel Kant's categorical imperative). Ask yourself, "If we adopted this rule in every case, could the organization, or society, survive?"

- **Slippery Slope:** If an action cannot be taken repeatedly, then it is not right to take at all (Descartes' rule of change). An action may appear to work in one instance to solve a problem, but if repeated, would result in a negative outcome. In plain English, this rule might be stated as "once started down a slippery path, you may not be able to stop."

- **Collective Utilitarian Principle:** Take the action that achieves the greater value for all of society. This rule assumes you can prioritize values in a rank order and understand the consequences of various courses of action.

- **Risk Aversion:** Take the action that produces the least harm, or the least potential cost. Some actions have extremely high failure costs of very low probability (e.g., building a nuclear generating facility in an urban area) or extremely high failure costs of moderate probability (speeding and automobile accidents). Avoid the high-failure cost actions and choose those actions whose consequences would not be catastrophic, even if there were a failure.

- **No Free Lunch:** Assume that virtually all tangible and intangible objects are owned by someone else unless there is a specific declaration otherwise. (This is the ethical "no free lunch" rule.) If something someone else has created is useful to you, it has value and you should assume the creator wants compensation for this work.

• **The *New York Times* Test (Perfect Information Rule):** Assume that the results of your decision on a matter will be the subject of the lead article in the *New York Times* the next day. Will the reaction of readers be positive or negative? Would your parents, friends, and children be proud of your decision? Most criminals and unethical actors assume imperfect information, and therefore they assume their decisions and actions will never be revealed. When making decisions involving ethical dilemmas, it is wise to assume perfect information markets.

• **The Social Contract Rule:** Would you like to live in a society where the principle you are supporting would become an organizing principle of the entire society? For instance, you might think it is wonderful to download illegal copies of music tracks, but you might not want to live in a society that did not respect property rights, such as your property rights to the car in your driveway, or your rights to a term paper or original art.

None of these rules is an absolute guide, and there are exceptions and logical difficulties with all these rules. Nevertheless, actions that do not easily pass these guidelines deserve some very close attention and a great deal of caution because the appearance of unethical behavior may do as much harm to you and your company as the actual behavior.

Now that you have an understanding of some basic ethical reasoning concepts, let's take a closer look at each of the major types of ethical, social, and political debates that have arisen in e-commerce.

9.2 PRIVACY AND INFORMATION RIGHTS

The Internet and the Web provide an ideal environment for invading the personal privacy of millions of users on a scale unprecedented in history. Perhaps no other recent issue has raised as much widespread social and political concern as protecting the privacy of over 160 million Web users in the United States alone. The major ethical issues related to e-commerce and privacy include the following: Under what conditions should we invade the privacy of others? What legitimates intruding into others' lives through unobtrusive surveillance, market research, or other means? The major social issues related to e-commerce and privacy concern the development of "expectations of privacy" or privacy norms, as well as public attitudes. In what areas of life should we as a society encourage people to think they are in "private territory" as opposed to public view? The major political issues related to e-commerce and privacy concern the development of statutes that govern the relations between record keepers and individuals. How should organizations — public and private — who are reluctant to remit the advantages that come from the unfettered flow of information on individuals — be restrained, if at all? In the following section, we will look first at the various practices of e-commerce companies that pose a threat to privacy.

INFORMATION COLLECTED AT E-COMMERCE SITES

Almost all (97%) Web sites collect personally identifiable information and use cookies to track the clickstream behavior of visitors on the site. **Personally identifiable information (PII)** is any data that can be used to identify, locate, or contact an individual (FTC, 2000a). As described below, advertising networks track the behavior of consumers across thousands of popular sites, not just at one site. In addition, most sites collect **anonymous information** composed of demographic and behavioral information that does not include any personal identifiers. For instance, sites collect information about age, occupation, income, zip code, ethnicity, and other data that characterizes your life without identifying who you are. These sites will, however, place a cookie on your hard drive to identify you by number — but not by name. Table 9.2 lists many of the personal identifiers routinely collected by online e-commerce sites.

Table 9.3 illustrates some of the major ways online firms gather information about consumers.

PROFILING: PRIVACY AND ADVERTISING NETWORKS

A majority (57%) of all Web sites, and 78% of the most popular 100 sites allow third parties — including advertising networks such as Adforce, Avenue A, DoubleClick, Engage, L90, MatchLogic, and 24/7 Media (these firms constitute about 90% of the network advertising industry) — to place cookies on a visitor's hard drive in order to engage in profiling. **Profiling** is the creation of digital images that characterize online individual and group behavior. An advertising network such as 24/7 Media maintains over 60 million anonymous profiles and more than 20 million personal profiles. DoubleClick maintains over 100 million anonymous profiles. **Anonymous profiles** identify people as belonging to highly specific and targeted groups, for example, 20–30-year-old males, with college degrees and incomes greater than $30,000 a year, and interested in high-fashion clothing. **Personal profiles** add a personal e-mail

personally identifiable information (PII)
any data that can be used to identify, locate, or contact an individual

anonymous information
demographic and behavioral information that does not include any personal identifiers

profiling
the creation of digital images that characterize online individual and group behavior

anonymous profiles
identify people as belonging to highly specific and targeted groups

personal profiles
add a personal e-mail address, postal address, and/or phone number to behavioral data

TABLE 9.2	PERSONAL INFORMATION COLLECTED BY E-COMMERCE SITES	
Name	Bank account	Browser type
Address	Credit card accounts	Preference data
Phone number	Gender	Transaction data
E-mail address	Age	Clickstream data
Social security number	Occupation	Education

SOURCE: Federal Trade Commission, 2000a; 1998.

TABLE 9.3	THE INTERNET'S MAJOR PERSONALLY IDENTIFIABLE INFORMATION GATHERING TOOLS
INTERNET CAPABILITY	**IMPACT ON PRIVACY**
Search engines	Can be used to trace user statements and views on newsgroups, chat groups, and other public forums on the Web, and profile users' social and political views.
Site transaction logs	Can be used to collect and analyze detailed information on page content viewed by users.
Cookies	Can be used to track individuals at a single site, or across thousands of sites that belong to an advertising network.
Shopping carts	Can be used to collect detailed payment and purchase information.
Forms	PII from forms that users voluntarily fill out can be linked with clickstream or other behavioral data to create a personal profile.

address, postal address, and/or phone number to behavioral data. Increasingly, online firms are attempting to link their online profiles to offline consumer data collected by established retail and catalog firms.

In the past, individual stores collected data on customer movement through a single store in order to understand consumer behavior and alter the design of stores accordingly. Also, purchase and expenditure data was gathered on consumers purchasing from multiple stores — usually long after the purchases were made — and the data was used to target direct mail and in-store campaigns, and mass media advertising.

The online advertising networks have added several new dimensions to established offline marketing techniques. First, they have the ability to precisely track not just consumer purchases but *all browsing behavior* on the Web at thousands of the most popular member sites, including browsing book lists, filling out preference forms, and viewing content pages. Second, they create the ability to dynamically adjust what the shopper sees on screen — including prices. Third, they create the ability to build and continually refresh high-resolution data images or behavioral profiles of consumers (Laudon, 1996). What's different about advertising networks is the scope and intensity of the data dragnet, and the ability to manipulate the shopping environment to the advantage of the merchant. Most of this activity occurs in the background without the knowledge of the shopper, and it occurs dynamically online in less than a second. Arguably, no other Web-based technique comes so close to being a real-world implementation of George Orwell's novel *1984* and its lead character, Big Brother. Here's an illustration of online profiling from "Online Profiling: A Report to Congress," an FTC report.

> Online consumer Joe Smith goes to a Web site that sells sporting goods. He clicks on the pages for golf bags. While there, he sees a banner ad, which he ignores as it does not interest him. The ad was placed by USAad Network. He then goes to a travel site and enters a search on "Hawaii." The USAad Network serves ads on this site, and Joe sees an ad for rental cars there. Joe then visits an online bookstore and browses through books about the world's best golf courses. USAad Network serves ads there as well. A week later, Joe visits his favorite online news site, and notices an ad for golf vacation packages in Hawaii. Delighted, he clicks on the ad, which was served by USAad Network. Later, Joe begins to wonder whether it was a coincidence that this particular ad appeared and, if not, how it happened. (Federal Trade Commission, 2000(b))

The sample online profile illustrates several features of such profiles. First, the profile created for Joe Smith was completely anonymous and did not require any personal information such as a name, e-mail address, or social security number. Obviously, this profile would be more valuable if the system did have personal information because then Joe could be sent e-mail marketing. Second, ad networks do not know who is operating the browser. If other members of Joe's family used the same computer to shop the Web, they would be exposed to golf vacation ads, and Joe could be exposed to ads more appropriate to his wife or children. Third, profiles are usually very imprecise, the result of "best guesses" and just plain guesses. Profiles are built using a product/service scoring system that is not very detailed, and as a result the profiles are crude (www.doubleclick.net, 2001).

In the above example, Joe is obviously interested in golf and travel because he intentionally expressed these interests. However, he may have wanted to scuba dive in Hawaii, or visit old friends, not play golf. The profiling system in the example took a leap of faith that a golf vacation in Hawaii is what Joe really wants. Sometimes these guesses work, but there is considerable evidence to suggest that simply knowing Joe made an inquiry about Hawaii would be sufficient to sell him a trip to Hawaii for any of several activities and the USAad Network provided little additional value. As a result of the crudeness of the profiles, marketers have been unwilling to pay premium prices for highly targeted, profile-based ads, preferring instead to use more obvious and less expensive techniques such as placing travel ads on travel sites and golf ads on golf sites (Hansell, 2000).

Network advertising firms argue that Web profiling benefits both consumers and businesses. Profiling permits targeting of ads, ensuring that consumers see advertisements mostly for products and services in which they are actually interested. Businesses benefit by not paying for wasted advertising sent to consumers who have no interest in their product or service. The industry argues that by increasing the effectiveness of advertising, more advertising revenues go to the Internet, which in turn subsidizes free content on the Internet. Last, product designers and entrepreneurs benefit by sensing demand for new products and services by examining user searches and profiles.

Critics argue that profiling undermines the expectation of anonymity and privacy that most people have when using the Internet, and change what should be a private experience into one where an individual's every move is recorded. As people become aware that their every move is being watched, they will be far less likely to explore sensitive topics, browse pages, or read about controversial issues. In most cases, the profiling is invisible to users, and even hidden. Consumers are not notified that profiling is occurring. Profiling permits aggregating data on hundreds or even thousands of unrelated sites on the Web. The cookies placed by ad networks are persistent. Their tracking occurs over an extended period of time and resumes each time the individual logs on to the Internet. This clickstream data is used to create profiles that can include hundreds of distinct data fields for each consumer. Associating so-called anonymous profiles with personal information is fairly easy, and companies can change policies quickly without informing the consumer. Some critics believe profiling permits **weblining** — charging some customers more money for products and services based on their profiles (Stepanek, 2000).

weblining

charging some customers more money for products and services based on their profiles

Although the information gathered by network advertisers is often anonymous (non-PII data), in many cases, the profiles derived from tracking consumers' activities on the Web are linked or merged with personally identifiable information. DoubleClick and other advertising network firms have attempted to purchase offline marketing firms that collect offline consumer data for the purpose of matching offline and online behavioral data at the individual level. However, public reaction was so negative that no network advertising firms publicly admit to matching offline PII with online profile data. Nevertheless, client Web sites encourage visitors to register for prizes, benefits, or content access in order to capture personal information such as e-mail addresses. Anonymous behavioral data is far more valuable if it can be linked with offline consumer behavior, e-mail addresses, and postal addresses. This consumer data can also be combined with data on the consumers' offline purchases, or information collected directly from consumers through surveys and registration forms. As the technology of connection to the Internet for consumers moves away from telephone modems where IP addresses are assigned dynamically, and toward static assigned IP addresses used by DSL and cable modems, then connecting anonymous profiles to personal names and e-mail addresses will become easier and more prevalent.

From a privacy protection perspective, the advertising network raises issues about who will see and use the information held by private companies, the absence of consumer control over the use of the information, the lack of consumer choice, the absence of consumer notice, and the lack of review and amendment procedures.

The pervasive and largely unregulated collection of personal information online has raised significant fears and opposition among consumers. In recent surveys, 92% of online households said they do not trust online companies to keep their personal information confidential, and 82% agreed that the government should regulate how online companies use personal information. One result of the lack of trust toward online firms and specific fears of privacy invasion is a reduction in online purchases. An estimated $3 billion was lost in 2000 sales, and $18 billion will be lost in 2002 online sales if nothing is done to allay consumer fears (Columbus Group, 2001; *New York Times*, 2000).

The Internet and e-commerce — as we have seen in previous chapters — strengthens the ability of governments and private firms to collect, store, and analyze personal information at a level never envisioned by privacy thinkers and legislators. With Web technologies, the invasion of individual privacy is low-cost, profitable, and effective.

Concerns about online privacy have led to two types of regulatory efforts: governmental regulation by federal and state agencies and private self-regulation efforts led by industry groups. But before considering these efforts to preserve and maintain privacy, we should first take a more in-depth look at the concept of privacy.

THE CONCEPT OF PRIVACY

Privacy is the moral right of individuals to be left alone, free from surveillance or interference from other individuals or organizations, including the state. Privacy is a girder supporting freedom: Without the privacy required to think, write, plan, and associate independently and without fear, social and political freedom is weakened, and perhaps destroyed. Information privacy is a subset of privacy. The right to **information privacy** includes both the claim that certain information should not be collected at all by governments or business firms, and the claim of individuals to control the use of whatever information that is collected about them. Individual control over personal information is at the core of the privacy concept.

Due process also plays an important role in defining privacy. The best statement of due process in record keeping is given by the Fair Information Practices doctrine developed in the early 1970s and extended to the online privacy debate in the late 1990s (described below).

Privacy claims — and thinking about privacy — mushroomed in the United States at the end of the nineteenth century as the technology of photography and tabloid journalism enabled the invasion of the heretofore private lives of wealthy industrialists. For most of the twentieth century, however, privacy thinking and legislation focused on restraining the government from collecting and using personal

privacy

the moral right of individuals to be left alone, free from surveillance or interference from other individuals or organizations, including the state

information privacy

includes both the claim that certain information should not be collected at all by governments or business firms, and the claim of individuals to control the use of whatever information that is collected about them information. With the explosion in the collection of private personal information by Web-based marketing firms since 1995, privacy concerns are increasingly directed toward restraining the activities of private firms in the collection and use of information on the Web. Claims to privacy are also involved at the workplace: Millions of employees are subject to various forms of electronic surveillance that in many cases is enhanced by firm Intranets and Web technologies. For instance, 38% of employers monitor employee e-mail, and 30% monitor employee computer files (Congressional Research Service, 2001).

Informed Consent

informed consent

consent given with knowledge of all material facts needed to make a rational decision

The concept of **informed consent** (defined as consent given with knowledge of all material facts needed to make a rational decision) plays an important role in protecting privacy. In the United States, business firms (and government agencies) can gather transaction information generated in the marketplace and then use that information for other marketing purposes, without obtaining the informed consent of the individual. For instance, in the United States, if a Web shopper purchases books about baseball at a site that belongs to an advertising network such as DoubleClick, a cookie can be placed on the consumer's hard drive and used by other member sites to sell the shopper sports clothing without the explicit permission or even knowledge of the user. This online preference information may also be linked with personal identifying information. In Europe, this would be illegal. A business in Europe cannot use marketplace transaction information for any purpose other than supporting the current transaction, unless of course it obtains the individual's consent in writing or by filling out an on-screen form.

opt-in

requires an affirmative action by the consumer to allow collection and use of consumer information

There are traditionally two models for "informed consent": "opt-in" and "opt-out." The **opt-in** model requires an affirmative action by the consumer to allow collection and use of information. For instance, using opt-in, consumers would first be asked if they approved of the collection and use of information, and then directed to check a selection box if they agreed. Otherwise, the default is not to approve the collection of data. In the **opt-out** model, the default is to collect information unless the consumer takes an affirmative action to prevent the collection of data by checking a box, or by filling out a form.

opt-out

the default is to collect information unless the consumer takes an affirmative action to prevent the collection of data

Up until recently, most U.S e-commerce companies have rejected "informed consent" and instead have simply published their information use policy on their site. U.S. businesses argue that informing users how the information will be used is sufficient to obtain the users' informed consent. Some sites have an opt-out selection box at the very bottom of their Information Policy statements where the consumer is unlikely to see it. Privacy advocates counter that most information policy statements on Web sites are obscure, difficult to read, and legitimate just about any use of personal information. Table 9.4 contains excerpts from Kmart's BlueLight.com privacy policy.

| **TABLE 9.4** | **EXCERPTS FROM KMART'S BLUELIGHT.COM PRIVACY POLICY** |

COLLECTING YOUR INFORMATION

This section explains what information we collect through the BlueLight.com Website and ISP Services. Please note that we correlate and supplement this data with both aggregate and personally identifiable information gathered by other companies. For example, Kmart collects personally identifiable information and information relating to customer purchases in its retail stores, and then shares this information with us.

Important: Children under the age of 18 should use our Website under the supervision of their parents or guardians.

INFORMATION COLLECTED THROUGH OUR WEBSITE

When you use our Website we may collect a variety of technical data, which we store in both aggregate and, if you are registered with BlueLight [ISP], personally identifiable forms. This data includes (but is not limited to) your IP address (a unique number that identifies your access account on the Internet), domain, and Web browser information. We may track the page you visited before coming to BlueLight, and the page you link to when you leave BlueLight, which of our pages you access, and how long you spend on each page.

We allow third parties to collect aggregate and other anonymous information about our visitors through the BlueLight.com Website. Should we enter into agreements that allow third parties to collect personally identifiable information about our visitors, we will inform visitors of these activities at the location of the collection.

USING YOUR INFORMATION

We do not intentionally share your personally identifiable information, except: (a) with our ISP Service Partners (including start page and home page providers for the ISP Services); (b) with Kmart and our other corporate affiliates; (c) with Martha Stewart Living Omnimedia Inc.; (d) with other companies with whom we have substantial strategic or marketing relationships (including our ISP Partners); (e) with companies to whom we outsource certain functions of our Website and the ISP Services; (f) as required by law; and (g) in event of BlueLight.com's insolvency, with another entity in connection with the sale of BlueLight.com assets. In addition, if you indicate your desire to receive a particular service or information from another company (e.g., catalogs), BlueLight will share your personally identifiable information with that particular company. Note finally that we share aggregate data about our customers with third parties.

If you supply us with your telephone numbers, you will only receive telephone contact from us regarding your BlueLight.com Website or ISP Services accounts, or orders you have placed online. Except as specified above, we will not share your telephone number with other organizations.

Please note that the date of the most recent opt in/out request will supersede prior requests.

Upon your reasonable request via the contact information below (and subject to our security practices), we will provide you with access to your contact information (for example, name, address, phone number), financial information, unique identifier information (for example, customer number or password), and transaction information (for example, when and what you purchased from our Website). If you're a registered BlueLight.com Website member, you can sign in and access your Website account information from the Website My Account page.

SOURCE: www.bluelight.com/helpdesk/index.jsp?display=safety&subdisplay=privacy (September 7, 2001)

Note that Kmart's "privacy policy" never mentions the word *privacy* (except in the title), and there are few limitations on how it will use the information it collects about consumers. Kmart will merge offline store information with online information, will share information with any business with which it has an important business relationship, and will sell its personally identifiable information as an asset should the company become bankrupt.

LEGAL PROTECTIONS

In the United States, Canada, and Germany, rights to privacy are explicitly granted in, or can be derived from, founding documents such as constitutions, as well as in specific statutes. In England and the United States, there is also protection of privacy in the common law, a body of court decisions involving torts or personal injuries. For instance, in the United States, four privacy-related torts have been defined in court decisions involving claims of injury to individuals caused by other private parties: intrusion on solitude, public disclosure of private facts, publicity placing a person in a false light, and appropriation of a person's name or likeness (mostly concerning celebrities) for a commercial purpose (Laudon, 1996). In the United States, the claim to privacy against government intrusion is protected primarily by the First Amendment guarantees of freedom of speech and association and the Fourth Amendment protections against unreasonable search and seizure of one's personal documents or home, and the Fourteenth Amendment's guarantee of due process.

In addition to common law and the Constitution, there are both federal laws and state laws that protect individuals against government intrusion and in some cases define privacy rights vis-à-vis private organizations such as financial, educational, and media institutions (cable television and video rentals) (see Table 9.5).

STATUTORY AND REGULATORY PROTECTIONS OF ONLINE PRIVACY

Governments around the world are reacting to growing public concerns about online privacy. For the most part, governments have extended well understood concepts of privacy from the offline world to the online world. In the United States, the Federal Trade Commission (FTC) has taken the lead in conducting research on online privacy and recommending legislation to Congress. The FTC is a cabinet-level agency charged with promoting the efficient functioning of the marketplace by protecting consumers from unfair or deceptive practices and increasing consumer choice by promoting competition. In addition to reports and recommendations, the FTC enforces existing legislation by suing corporations it believes are in violation of federal fair trade laws.

In 1995, the FTC began a series of investigations of online privacy based on its belief that online invasion of privacy potentially involved deceit and unfair behavior. In 1998, the FTC issued its Fair Information Practice (FIP) Principles on which it based its assessments and recommendations for online privacy. Table 9.6 describes

TABLE 9.5	FEDERAL PRIVACY LAWS
NAME	**DESCRIPTION**
General Federal Privacy Laws	
Freedom of Information Act of 1966	Gives people the right to inspect information about themselves held in government files; also allows other individuals and organizations the right to request disclosure of government records based on the public's right to know.
Privacy Act of 1974, as amended	Regulates the federal government's collection, use, and disclosure of data collected by federal agencies. Gives individuals a right to inspect and correct records.
Electronic Communications Privacy Act of 1986	Makes conduct that would infringe on the security of electronic communications illegal.
Computer Matching and Privacy Protection Act of 1988	Regulates computerized matching of files held by different government agencies.
Computer Security Act of 1987	Makes conduct that would infringe on the security of computer-based files illegal.
Driver's Privacy Protection Act of 1994	Limits access to personal information maintained by state motor vehicle departments to those with legitimate business purposes. Also gives drivers the option to prevent disclosure of driver's license information to marketers and the general public.
Privacy Laws Affecting Private Institutions	
Fair Credit Reporting Act of 1970	Regulates the credit investigating and reporting industry. Gives people the right to inspect credit records if they have been denied credit and provides procedures for correcting information.
Family Educational Rights and Privacy Act of 1974	Requires schools and colleges to give students and their parents access to student records and to allow them to challenge and correct information; limits disclosure of such records to third parties.
Right to Financial Privacy Act of 1978	Regulates the financial industry's use of personal financial records; establishes procedures that federal agencies must follow to gain access to such records.
Privacy Protection Act of 1980	Prohibits government agents from conducting unannounced searches of press offices and files if no one in the office is suspected of committing a crime.
Cable Communications Policy Act of 1984	Regulates the cable industry's collection and disclosure of information concerning subscribers.
Video Privacy Protection Act of 1988	Prevents disclosure of a person's video rental records without court order or consent.

the FTC's five fair information practice principles. Two of the five are designated as basic, "core" principles that must be present to protect privacy, whereas the other practices are less central. The FTC's FIP restates and strengthens in a form suitable to deal with online privacy the Fair Information Practices doctrine developed in 1973 by a government study group (USDHEW, 1973).

The FTC's FIP principles set the ground rules for what constitutes due process privacy protection procedures at e-commerce and all other Web sites — including government and nonprofit Web sites — in the United States.

At this point, the FTC's FIP practices are guidelines, not laws. They have stimulated private firms and industry associations to develop their own private guidelines (discussed below). However, the FTC's FIP guidelines are being used as the basis of new legislation. The most important online privacy legislation to date that was directly influenced by the FTC's FIP guidelines is the Children's Online Privacy Pro-

TABLE 9.6	FEDERAL TRADE COMMISSION FAIR INFORMATION PRACTICE PRINCIPLES
PRINCIPLE	**DESCRIPTION**
Notice/Awareness (Core principle)	Sites must disclose their information practices before collecting data. Includes identification of collector, uses of data, other recipients of data, nature of collection (active/inactive), voluntary or required, consequences of refusal, and steps taken to protect confidentiality, integrity, and quality of the data.
Choice/Consent (Core principle)	There must be a choice regime in place allowing consumers to choose how their information will be used for secondary purposes other than supporting the transaction, including internal use and transfer to third parties. Opt-in/Opt-out must be available.
Access/Participation	Consumers should be able to review and contest the accuracy and completeness of data collected about them in a timely, inexpensive process.
Security	Data collectors must take reasonable steps to assure that consumer information is accurate and secure from unauthorized use.
Enforcement	There must be in place a mechanism to enforce FIP principles. This can involve self-regulation, legislation giving consumers legal remedies for violations, or federal statutes and regulation.

SOURCE: Federal Trade Commission, 1998; 2000a.

TABLE 9.7	**FTC RECOMMENDATIONS REGARDING ONLINE PROFILING**
PRINCIPLE	DESCRIPTION OF RECOMMENDATION
Notice	Complete transparency to user by providing disclosure and choice options on the host Web site.
	"Robust" notice for PII (time/place of collection; before collection begins).
	Clear and conspicuous notice for non-PII.
Choice	Opt-in for PII, opt-out for non-PII.
	No conversion of non-PII to PII without consent.
	Opt-out from any or all network advertisers from a single page provided by the host Web site.
Access	Reasonable provisions to allow inspection and correction.
Security	Reasonable efforts to secure information from loss, misuse, or improper access.
Enforcement	Done by independent third parties, such as seal programs and accounting firms.
Restricted collection	Advertising networks will not collect information about sensitive financial or medical topics, sexual behavior or sexual orientation, or use social security numbers for profiling.

tection Act (1998) (COPPA), which requires Web sites to obtain parental permission before collecting information on children under 13 years of age.

In July 2000, the FTC recommended legislation to Congress to protect online consumer privacy from the threat posed by advertising networks. Table 9.7 summarizes the Commission's recommendations. The FTC profiling recommendations significantly strengthen FIP principles of notification and choice, while also including restrictions on information that may be collected.[1] Although the FTC supports industry efforts at self-regulation, it nevertheless recommended legislation to ensure that all Web sites using network advertising and all network advertisers comply. (Currently 10% of network advertisers are not members of the Network Advertising Initiative, an industry association, discussed below.)

---

[1]Much general privacy legislation affecting government, e.g., the Privacy Act of 1974, precludes the government from collecting information on political and social behavior of citizens. The FTC restrictions are significant both because they are the FTC's first effort at limiting the collection of certain information, and also because they fail to mention important categories like political attitudes, affiliation, and activity, religious views, or social views.

TABLE 9.8	SUMMARY OF PROPOSED E-COMMERCE PRIVACY LEGISLATION IN 2001
NAME AND YEAR	**OBJECTIVE**
H.R. 89 Online Privacy Protection Act (2001)	Would require the FTC to prescribe regulations to privacy of PII not covered by COPPA.
H.R. 91 Social Security Online Protection Act (2001)	Regulates the use by interactive services of SSN and other personal identifiers such as driver license numbers.
H.R. 112 Electronic Privacy Protection Act (2001)	Makes it illegal for persons to sell, install, or use "spyware" programs that trace online user activities without their permission or knowledge.
H.R. 220 Identity Theft Prevention Act (2001)	Protects use of SSNs online, and prohibits establishment of uniform national identifying numbers on protection of privacy grounds.

SOURCE: Congressional Research Service, 2001. For more current information, see the Center for Democracy and Technology (www.cdt.org).

Table 9.8 lists some other recent federal legislation that has been introduced to Congress and is under consideration.

PRIVATE INDUSTRY SELF-REGULATION

The online industry in the United States has historically opposed privacy legislation, arguing that industry can do a better job of protecting privacy than government. The online industry formed the Online Privacy Alliance (OPA) in 1998 to encourage self-regulation in part as a reaction to growing public concerns and the threat of legislation being proposed by FTC and privacy advocacy groups.

Private industry in the United States has created the idea of safe harbors from government regulation. A **safe harbor** is a private self-regulating policy and enforcement mechanism that meets the objectives of government regulators and legislation, but does not involve government regulation or enforcement. The government plays a role in certifying safe harbors, however. For instance, COPPA includes a provision enabling industry groups or others to submit for the Commission's approval self-regulatory guidelines that implement the protections of the FIP guidelines and Com-

safe harbor
a private self-regulating policy and enforcement mechanism that meets the objectives of government regulators and legislation but does not involve government regulation or enforcement

FIGURE 9.2	**PERCENTAGE OF WEB SITES WITH PRIVACY SEALS**

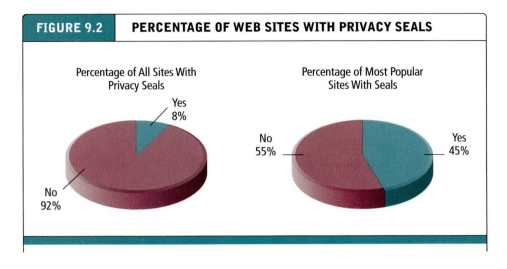

Percentage of All Sites With Privacy Seals

Percentage of Most Popular Sites With Seals

mission rules. In May, 2001, the FTC approved the TRUSTe Internet privacy protection program under the terms of COPPA as a safe harbor.[2]

OPA has developed a set of privacy guidelines that members are required to implement. The primary focus of industry efforts has been the development of online "seals" that attest to the privacy policies on a site. The Better Business Bureau (BBB), TRUSTe, WebTrust, and major accounting firms — among them PriceWaterhouse-Coopers's BetterWeb — have established "seals" for Web sites. To display a seal, Web site operators must conform to certain privacy principles, a complaint resolution process, and monitoring by the seal originator. Over 1200 sites now display the TRUSTe seal. Nevertheless, online privacy seal programs have had a limited impact on Web privacy practices. A recent survey found that 92% of a random sample of online sites did not subscribe to any of the seal programs in 2000. Of those sites with a seal, only half implemented all five FIP principles. Although 45% of the most popular sites did have a privacy seal, fully 37% of these sites did not implement the notice and consumer choice "core" FIP principles, but instead simply declared their policies of sharing information (FTC, 2000a). (See Figure 9.2.) Critics argue that the seal programs are evidence of sites having a privacy policy, without there actually being any such policies. For these reasons, the FTC has not deemed the seal programs as "safe harbors" yet (with the exception of TRUSTe's children's privacy seal under COPPA), and the agency continues to push for legislation to enforce privacy protection principles.

[2]Another long-standing industry group with a safe harbor program for children online is CARU (Children's Advertising Review Unit) founded in 1974 as the advertising industry's self-regulation program for the protection of children.

The advertising network industry has also formed an industry association, the Network Advertising Initiative (NAI), to develop privacy policies. NAI member companies include Adforce, Avenue A, DoubleClick, Engage, L90, MatchLogic, and 24/7 Media, which together represent about 90% of the network advertising industry. The NAI has developed a set of privacy principles in conjunction with the Federal Trade Commission. The NAI policies have two objectives: to offer consumers a chance to opt-out of advertising network programs, and to provide consumers redress from abuses. In order to opt-out, NAI has created a Web site — networkadvertising.org — where consumers can go to obtain cookies — one for each of the participating network advertisers (six cookies are available as of July 2001). These cookies will prevent network advertising agencies from placing their cookies on a user's computer. If consumers have complaints, NAI has worked with Andersen Accounting to create a Web site where users can make complaints (andersencompliance.com). Based on the NAI initiative and FTC reports, DoubleClick has recently unveiled a new privacy policy summarized in Table 9.9.

Read *Insight on Business: Chief Privacy Officers — New Execs on the Job* to see a different approach to industry self-regulation.

THE EUROPEAN DIRECTIVE ON DATA PROTECTION

In Europe, privacy protection is much stronger than in the United States. In the United States, private organizations and businesses are permitted to use personally identifiable information gathered in commercial transactions for other business purposes without the prior consent of the consumer (so-called secondary uses of PII). In the United States, there is no federal agency charged with enforcing privacy law. Instead, privacy law is enforced largely through self-regulation by businesses, and by individuals who must sue agencies or companies in court to recover damages. This is expensive and rarely done. The European approach to privacy protection is more comprehensive and regulatory in nature. European countries do not allow business firms to use PII without the prior consent of consumers. They enforce their privacy laws by creating data protection agencies to pursue complaints brought by citizens and to actively enforce privacy laws.

On October 25, 1998, the European Commission's Directive on Data Protection went into effect, standardizing and broadening privacy protection in the European Union (EU) nations. The Directive is based on the Fair Information Practices doctrine, but extends the control individuals can exercise over their personal information. The Directive requires companies to inform people when they collect information about them and to disclose how it will be stored and used. Customers must provide their informed consent before any company can legally use data about them, and they have the right to access that information, correct it, and request that no further data be collected. Further, the Directive prohibits the transfer of PII to organizations or

TABLE 9.9	A SUMMARY OF DOUBLECLICK'S PRIVACY POLICY
PRIVACY DIMENSION	DOUBLECLICK POLICY
Notice	Disclosure of collection and use; works with client companies to disclose and provide notice. Transparency to user.
Choice	Opt-out options are clearly displayed; opt-out for e-mail.
Access	Reasonable access to personal information.
Security	Reasonable business practices to protect data.
Enforcement	NAI self-regulatory mechanism including use of Andersen to monitor compliance.
Data retention	"Market decay" in value of information causes deletion in 45 days. Long-term logs are not easily searched and not used.
Policy changes	Notification; no retroactive changes without consent.
Sensitive data	Anonymous browser data only. No attempt is made to link profiles to persons, only to browsers. Personal information collected for clients is not used for profiling. No data collected on health, detailed financial information, sexual orientation or behavior, child-related data, racial and ethnic origin, political opinions, religious or philosophical views, trade union membership, or visits to sites outside of the United States.
Changes in corporate structure	In the event of a corporate merger or sale, the company will take steps to ensure data is used only for purposes for which it was gathered and under the policies in operation at the time of collection.
Disclosure of information	Service companies assisting DoubleClick are bound by limits on use of information. Third-party users are bound by the same limits on use as DoubleClick.

SOURCE: www.doubleclick.com/privacy, July 2001.

countries that do not have similarly strong privacy protection policies. This means that data collected in Europe by American business firms cannot be transferred or processed in the United States (which has weaker privacy protection laws). This would potentially interfere with a $350 billion annual trade flow between the United States and Europe.

The Department of Commerce, working with the European Commission, developed a safe harbor framework for U.S. firms. Organizations that decide to participate in the safe harbor program must develop policies that meet European standards, and they must publicly sign on to a Web-based register maintained by the Department of

INSIGHT ON BUSINESS

CHIEF PRIVACY OFFICERS — NEW EXECS ON THE JOB

How can you tell if your own corporate practices actually conform to the privacy policy stated on your Web site? How can your business keep track of all the new privacy legislation and changes in European policies? The answer for many corporations is to create a new executive position — Chief Privacy Officer (CPO). Firms such as IBM, AT&T, Eastman Kodak, DoubleClick and many others have recently added this new position to senior management ranks. There are now over 100 privacy chiefs in the United States, making $125,000–$150,000 a year, according to Alan Westin, who runs a training program for CPOs.

What does a Chief Privacy Officer do? According Richard Purcell, CPO for Microsoft, the job has three aspects: coming up with privacy policies for the firm to follow, monitoring the development of new technology to ensure it respects consumer privacy, and informing and educating the company's employees about privacy. Another job is helping the company avoid privacy "landmines," which are mistakes in policy or technology that, had any one thought about it, would obviously be embarrassing to the company because of the potential for a storm of protest from privacy protection groups. Some recent examples include U.S. Bancorp's decision to sell personal financial data to a direct-marketing company in violation of its own stated policies. This cost Bancorp $3 million in a legal settlement in Minnesota. RealNetworks recently had to apologize to users and change its data collection policies after a disclosure that the company's RealJukebox Internet music software captured data about users' preferences.

The new corporate emphasis on privacy has also created a new business for the big accounting firm PriceWaterhouseCoopers called the Privacy Audit Practice. Headed by Dr. Larry Ponemon, PriceWaterhouseCoopers conducted over 200 firm audits in 2000. Companies are taking this issue very seriously, Ponemon noted, to avoid class action suits, Internet-based protests, and shareholder enmity. And what do the auditors find? About 80% of the companies audited by Ponemon's group do not follow their own stated privacy policies. Most of the time this is the result of poor training and human error.

After Expedia completed a privacy audit led by PriceWaterhouseCoopers, they changed their information collection policy from "opt-out" to "opt-in." Now Expedia's customers have to actively click a button and ask to be informed of new offers from the travel site. The result is that far fewer customers ask to unsubscribe from mailing solicitations. Expedia executives believe trust and privacy are major concerns of their customers, and anything they can do to enhance trust is good for their business.

Chief Privacy Officers often have a difficult time getting business sales and production units to pay attention to their concerns. Coordinating the activities of an entire firm can be challenging. One solution used by EarthLink's new CPO was to form an internal privacy council with representatives from all the major company departments. The council has the responsibility for coming up with new privacy policies, and, more important, implementing them within the operating units of the company. CPOs and internal corporate privacy councils are even extending their reach to business partners. The message: Either live up to strict privacy standards or we will find another partner. For instance, IBM has recently announced it will no longer advertise on Web sites that do not have acceptable privacy policies.

SOURCES: "Chief Privacy Officers," by Shelly Escalante-Cone, *Silicon 2.0*, August 2001; "First Line of Defense; Chief Privacy Officers Forge Evolving Corporate Roles," by John Schwartz, *New York Times*, February 12, 2001; "Private Matters: It Seems That Trust Equals Revenues," by Andrea Petersen, *Wall Street Journal*, February 12, 2001.

Commerce. Enforcement occurs in the United States and relies to a large extent on self-policing and regulation, backed up by government enforcement of fair trade statutes. For more information on the safe harbor procedures and the EU Data Directive, see www.export.gov/safeharbor/sh-workbook.html.

PRIVACY ADVOCACY GROUPS

There are a number of privacy advocacy groups on the Web that monitor developments in privacy. Some of these sites are industry-supported, while others rely on private foundations and contributions. Some of the better known sites are listed in Table 9.10.

TABLE 9.10	PRIVACY ADVOCACY GROUPS
ADVOCACY GROUP	FOCUS
Epic.org	Washington-based watch-dog group
Privacyinternational.org	Tracks international privacy developments
Cdt.org (Center for Democracy and Technology)	Foundation- and business-supported group with a legislative focus
Privacy.org	Clearinghouse sponsored by EPIC and Privacy International
Privacyrights.org	Educational clearinghouse
Privacyalliance.org	Industry-supported clearinghouse

TECHNOLOGICAL SOLUTIONS TO PRIVACY INVASION ON THE WEB

Privacy-enhancing technologies for protecting user privacy during interactions with Web sites are being developed (Vijayan, 2000; Reiter and Rubin, 1999; Goldschlag, Reed, and Syverson, 1999; Gabber et al. 1999). Most of these tools emphasize security — the ability of individuals to protect their communications and files from illegitimate snoopers. This is just is one element of privacy. The other is the development of private and public policies that enable consumers to control the collection and use of information that is gathered in the course of market transactions. Table 9.11 describes some ways in which technology can be used to protect privacy.

P3P (Platform for Privacy Preferences)
a standard designed to communicate to Internet users a Web site's privacy policy, and to compare that policy to the user's own preferences, or to other standards such as the FTC's FIP guidelines or the EU Data Protection Directive

Perhaps the most comprehensive technological privacy protection effort is **P3P**, the Platform for Privacy Preferences sponsored by W3C (the World Wide Web Consortium — an international, nonprofit, industry-supported Web standards group). P3P is a standard designed to communicate to Internet users a Web site's privacy policy, and to compare that policy to the user's own preferences, or to other standards such as the FTC's FIP guidelines or the EU Data Protection Directive. P3P does not establish privacy standards and relies on government and industry to develop them.

P3P works through a user's Web browser. On the server side, P3P enables sites to translate their privacy policies into a standardized machine-readable XML format that can be read either by the browser or by installed software plug-ins. On the user client side, the browser automatically fetches a Web site's privacy policy and informs the user. Figure 9.3 illustrates how this could work.

TABLE 9.11	TECHNOLOGICAL PROTECTIONS FOR ONLINE PRIVACY	
TECHNOLOGY	PRODUCTS	PROTECTION
Secure e-mail	Ziplip.com; SafeMessage.com; Hushmail.com; Pretty Good Privacy (PGP)	E-mail and document encryption
Anonymous remailers	World Wide Web Anonymous Remailer; Jack B. Nymble	Send e-mail without trace
Anonymous surfing	Freedom; Anonymizer.com	Surf without a trace
Cookie managers	CookieCrusher; Magic Cookie Monster	Prevents client computer from accepting cookies
Disk/file erasing programs	FileWiper; Eraser; DiskVac	Completely erases hard drive and floppy files
Policy generators	OECD Privacy Policy Generator	Automates the development of an OECD privacy compliance policy
Privacy Policy Reader	P3P	Software for automating the communication of privacy policies to users

FIGURE 9.3	HOW P3P WORKS

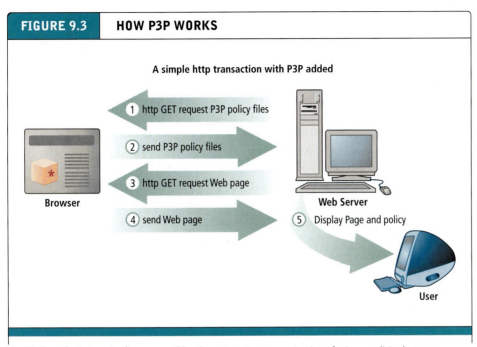

The Platform for Privacy Preferences enables the automatic communication of privacy policies between e-commerce sites and consumers.

SOURCE: www.W3.org/p3p/brochure.html World Wide Web Consortium.

Insight on Technology: Tug of War describes some other new technologies being used to both invade and protect privacy.

9.3 INTELLECTUAL PROPERTY RIGHTS

> *Congress shall have the power to "promote the progress of science and useful arts, by securing for limited times to authors and inventors the exclusive right to their respective writings and discoveries."*
>
> — Article I, Section 8, Constitution of the United States, 1788.

Next to privacy, the most controversial ethical, social, and political issue related to e-commerce is the fate of intellectual property rights. *Intellectual property* encompasses all the tangible and intangible products of the human mind. As a general rule, in the United States, the creator of intellectual property owns it. For instance, if you personally create an e-commerce site, it belongs entirely to you, and you have exclusive rights to use this "property" in any lawful way you see fit. But the Internet

INSIGHT ON TECHNOLOGY

TUG OF WAR

Mark Hochhauser refuses to shop online anymore. The Golden Valley, Minnesota research psychologist did something unusual: He read Amazon's privacy policy. Most people just ignore it, at their peril. Amazon's privacy policy says it will not sell customer information to third parties, but in the event of bankruptcy, it reserves the right to sell its customer database — including all the data on user preferences and actual books purchased — to the purchasing company. Hochhauser, who refers to his personal information at Amazon as his "online DNA," cannot get Amazon to expunge his personal information now (rather than wait for Amazon to go bankrupt), nor will Amazon let him even see his own data.

It seems as though we are in a technological tug of war between technologies that make invading customer privacy very easy versus other technologies that make protecting privacy easier. On the privacy invasion side, Experian.com links Web sites to its database and provides the names and addresses of visitors to the sites in real time. ThinkDirectMarketing.com provides similar services. Other companies such as Acxiom.com combine offline and online purchasing and behavioral data into one central database. TIAN monitors online behavior of visitors from 16 different perspectives, and then, depending on the rules selected by managers, alters the content delivered to appeal to what the system believes is the user's intention and interest. TeaLeaf's TeaCommerce Platform captures customers' entire online ses-

sions exactly as it looked to them. This exact tracking of customer experiences allows managers to see just where customers visit, what they see, and under what circumstances they leave the site. From this, managers may be able to infer why people leave a site without purchasing.

On the privacy protection side, iPrivacy.com provides a proxy server that you visit first before shopping. Then as sites look at your behavior and try to understand you, all they see is the iPrivacy server. Cookies are all dropped off at iPrivacy and discarded later. iPrivacy is working with the U.S. Postal Service to develop an encrypted shipping address scheme so that only the post office knows where you live.

Companies such as Persona and McAfee, the well-known security company, offer programs that allow users to control and manage cookies downloaded while shopping. Even more powerful technology from Microsoft — such as MS Passport described in the Case Study at the end of the chapter — will be available in the next few years that allows online consumers to determine the level of privacy they want to achieve and manages the privacy relationship with Web sites.

The problem with privacy-protecting software is that fewer than 5% of Internet users have used "anonymizing" software that can hide their identity, 56% of users do not know what a cookie is or where to expunge it, and only 10% of Internet users set their browsers to reject cookies. The advantage of privacy-invading software used by merchants is that they have an economic incentive to use it. Many fear a "privacy Chernobyl" or meltdown in which people begin to realize how serious their loss of control over personal information really is. Individuals may be denied insurance if they're suspected of having cancer because they sought information about cancer on Web sites, and others could lose child custody cases if they visited porn sites and that information was subpoenaed in court.

▬ **SOURCES:** "Spy on Your Customers (They Want You To)," by Bob Tedeschi, *SmartBusiness,* August 2001; "Shoppers Have Defenses to Protect Their Privacy Online," by Leslie Brooks Suzukamo, *Knight Ridder Newspapers*, January 8, 2001.

potentially changes things. Once intellectual works become digital, it becomes difficult to control access, use, distribution, and copying. These are precisely the areas that intellectual property seeks to control.

Digital media differ from books, periodicals, and other media in terms of ease of replication, transmission, and alteration; difficulty in classifying a software work as a program, book, or even music; compactness — making theft easy; and difficulty in establishing uniqueness. Before widespread use of the Internet, copies of software, books, magazine articles, or films had to be stored on physical media, such as paper, computer disks, or videotape, creating some hurdles to distribution.

The Internet technically permits millions of people to make perfect digital copies of various works — from music to plays, poems, and journal articles — and then to distribute them nearly cost-free to hundreds of millions of Web users. The proliferation of innovation has occurred so rapidly that few entrepreneurs have stopped to consider who owns the patent on a business technique or method their site is using. The spirit of the Web has been so free-wheeling that many entrepreneurs ignored trademark law and registered domain names that could easily be confused with another company's registered trademarks. In short, the Internet has demonstrated the potential for destroying traditional conceptions and implementations of intellectual property law developed over the last two centuries.

The major ethical issue related to e-commerce and intellectual property concerns how we (both as individuals and as business professionals) should treat property that belongs to others. From a social point of view, the main questions are: Is there continued value in protecting intellectual property in the Internet age? In what ways is society better off, or worse off, for having the concept of property apply to intangible ideas? From a political perspective we need to ask how the Internet and e-commerce can be regulated or governed to protect the institution of intellectual property while at the same time encouraging the growth of e-commerce and the Internet.

TYPES OF INTELLECTUAL PROPERTY PROTECTION

There are three main types of intellectual property protection: copyright, patent, and trademark law. In the United States, the development of intellectual property law begins in the U.S. Constitution in 1788, which mandated Congress to devise a system of laws to promote "the progress of science and the useful arts." Congress passed the first copyright law in 1790 to protect original written works for a period of 14 years. Since then, the idea of copyright has been extended to include music, films, translations, photographs, and most recently (1998), the designs of vessels under 200 feet (Fisher, 2000).

The goal of intellectual property law is to balance two competing interests — the public and the private. The public interest is served by the creation and distribution of inventions, works of art, music, literature, and other forms of intellectual expression. The private interest is served by rewarding people for creating these works through the creation of a time-limited monopoly granting exclusive use to the creator.

Maintaining this balance of interests is always challenged by the invention of new technologies. In general, the information technologies of the last century — from radio and television to CD-ROMs and the Internet — have at first tended to weaken the protections afforded by intellectual property law. Owners of intellectual property have usually been successful in pressuring Congress and the courts to strengthen the intellectual property laws to compensate for any technological threat, and even to extend protection for longer periods of time and to entirely new areas of expression. In the case of the Internet and e-commerce technologies, once again, intellectual property rights are severely challenged. Below we discuss the significant developments in each area: copyright, patent, and trademark.

COPYRIGHT: THE PROBLEM OF PERFECT COPIES AND ENCRYPTION

copyright law

protects original forms of expression such as writings, art, drawings, photographs, music, motion pictures, performances, and computer programs from being copied by others for a minimum of 50 years

In the United States, **copyright law** protects original forms of expression such as writings (books, periodicals, lecture notes), art, drawings, photographs, music, motion pictures, performances, and computer programs from being copied by others for a minimum of 50 years. Copyright does not protect ideas — just their expression in an tangible medium such as paper, cassette tape, or handwritten notes.

Since the first federal Copyright Act of 1790, the congressional intent behind copyright laws has been to encourage creativity and authorship by ensuring that creative people receive the financial and other benefits of their work. Most industrial nations have their own copyright laws, and there are several international conventions and bilateral agreements through which nations coordinate and enforce their laws.

In the mid-1960s, the Copyright Office began registering software programs, and in 1980, Congress passed the Computer Software Copyright Act, which clearly provides protection for source and object code and for copies of the original sold in commerce, and sets forth the rights of the purchaser to use the software while the creator retains legal title. For instance, the HTML code for a Web page — even though easily available to every browser — cannot be lawfully copied and used for a commercial purpose, say, to create a new Web site that looks identical.

Copyright protection is clear-cut: It protects against copying of entire programs or their parts. Damages and relief are readily obtained for infringement. The drawback to copyright protection is that the underlying ideas behind a work are not protected, only their expression in a work. A competitor can view the source code on your Web site to see how various effects were created and then reuse those techniques to create a different Web site without infringing on your copyright.

Look and Feel

"Look and feel" copyright infringement lawsuits are precisely about the distinction between an idea and its expression. For instance, in 1988, Apple Computer sued Microsoft Corporation and Hewlett-Packard Inc. for infringing Apple's copyright on the Macintosh interface. Among other claims, Apple claimed that the defendants copied the expression of overlapping windows. Apple failed to patent the idea of overlapping windows when it invented this method of presenting information on a computer screen in the late 1960s. The defendants counterclaimed that the idea of overlapping windows could only be expressed in a single way and, therefore, was not protectable under the "merger" doctrine of copyright law. When ideas and their expression merge (i.e., if there is only one way to express an idea), the expression cannot be copyrighted, although the method of producing the expression might be patentable (*Apple* v. *Microsoft*, 1989). In general, courts appear to be following the reasoning of a 1992 case — Brown Bag Software vs. Symantec Corp. — in which the court dissected the elements of software alleged to be infringing. There, the Federal Circuit Court of Appeals found that neither similar concept, function, general functional features (e.g., drop-down menus), nor colors were protectable by copyright law (*Brown Bag* vs. *Symantec Corp.*, 1992).

Fair Use Doctrine

Copyrights, like all rights, are not absolute. There are situations where strict copyright observance could be harmful to society, potentially inhibiting other rights such as the right to freedom of expression and thought. As a result the doctrine of fair use has been created. The **doctrine of fair use** permits teachers and writers to use copyrighted materials without permission under certain circumstances. Table 9.12 describes the five factors that courts consider when assessing what constitutes fair use.

The fair use doctrine draws upon the First Amendment's protection of freedom of speech (and writing). Journalists, writers, and academics must be able to refer to, and cite from, copyrighted works in order to criticize or even discuss copyrighted works. Professors are allowed to clip a contemporary article just before class, copy it, and hand it out to students as an example of a topic under discussion. However, they are not permitted to add this article to the class syllabus for next semester without compensating the copyright holder.

doctrine of fair use
under certain circumstances, permits use of copyrighted material without permission

TABLE 9.12	FAIR USE CONSIDERATIONS TO COPYRIGHT PROTECTIONS
FAIR USE FACTOR	**INTERPRETATION**
Character of use	Nonprofit or educational use versus for-profit use.
Nature of the work	Creative works such as plays or novels receive greater protection than factual accounts, e.g., newspaper accounts.
Amount of work used	A stanza from a poem or a single page from a book would be allowed, but not the entire poem or a book chapter.
Market effect of use	Will the use harm the marketability of the original product? Has it already harmed the product in the marketplace?
Context of use	A last minute, unplanned use in a classroom versus a planned infringement.

The Digital Millennium Copyright Act of 1998

Digital Millennium Copyright Act (DMCA)

the first major effort to adjust the copyright laws to the Internet Age

The **Digital Millennium Copyright Act (DMCA)** of 1998 is the first major effort to adjust the copyright laws to the Internet Age. This legislation was the result of a confrontation between the major copyright holders in the United States (publishing, sheet music, record label, and commercial film industries), Internet service providers, and users of copyrighted materials such as libraries, universities, and consumers. While social and political institutions are sometimes thought of as "slow" and the Internet as "fast," in this instance, powerful groups of copyright owners anticipated Web music services such as Napster by several years. Napster was formed in 1999, but work by the World Intellectual Property Organization — a worldwide body formed by the major copyright-holding nations of North America, Europe, and Japan — began work in 1995. Table 9.13 summarizes the major provisions of the DMCA.

The penalties for willfully violating the DMCA include restitution to the injured parties of any losses due to infringement. Criminal remedies are available to federal prosecutors that include fines up to $500,000 or five years imprisonment for a first offense, and up to $1 million in fines and ten years in prison for repeat offenders. These are serious remedies.

The DMCA attempts to answer two vexing questions in the Internet age. First, how can society protect copyrights online when any practical encryption scheme imaginable can be broken by hackers and the results distributed worldwide? Second, how can society control the behavior of thousands of Internet Service Providers (ISPs), who often host infringing Web sites, or who provide Internet service to individuals who are routine infringers? ISPs claim to be like telephone utilities — just car-

TABLE 9.13	THE DIGITAL MILLENNIUM COPYRIGHT ACT
SECTION	**IMPORTANCE**
Title I, WIPO Treaty Implementation	Makes it illegal to circumvent technological measures to protect works for either access or copying or to circumvent any electronic rights management information.
Title II, Online Infringement Liability Limitations	Requires ISPs to "take down" sites they host if they are infringing copyrights, and requires search engines to block access to infringing sites. Limits liability of ISPs and search engines.
Title III, Computer Maintenance and Repair	Permits users to make a copy of a computer program for maintenance or repair of the computer.
Title IV, Miscellaneous Provisions	Requires the copyright office to report to Congress on the use of copyright materials for distance education; allows libraries to make digital copies of works for internal use only; extends musical copyrights to include "webcasting."

SOURCE: www.loc.gov/copyright/legislation.

rying messages — and they do not want to put their users under surveillance or invade the privacy of users.

The DMCA implements a World Intellectual Property Organization (WIPO) treaty of 1996, which declares it illegal to make, distribute, or use devices that circumvent technology-based protections of copyrighted materials, and attaches stiff fines and prison sentences for violations. WIPO is an organization within the United Nations. Recognizing that these provisions alone cannot stop hackers from devising circumventions, DMCA makes it difficult for such inventors to reap the fruits of their labors by making the ISPs (including universities) responsible and accountable for hosting Web sites or providing services to infringers once the ISP has been notified. ISPs are not required to intrude on their users. However, when copyright holders inform the ISP that a hosted site or individual users are infringing, they must "take down" the site immediately to avoid liability and potential fines. ISPs must also inform their subscribers of their copyright management policies. Copyright owners can subpoena in federal court the personal identities of any infringers using an ISP. There are important limitations on these ISP prohibitions that are mostly concerned with the transitory caching of materials for short periods without the knowledge of the ISP. However, should the ISP be deriving revenues from the infringement, it is as liable as the infringer, and is subject to the same penalties.

There are a number of exceptions to the strong prohibitions against defeating a copyright protection scheme outlined above. There are exceptions for libraries to examine works for adoption, for reverse engineering to achieve interoperability with other software, for encryption research, for privacy protection purposes, and security testing.

No one knows if the DMCA will prevent widespread online violations of copyright protections. In fall 2000, the Secure Digital Music Initiative (SDMI) — a record industry trade group — offered a prize of $10,000 to groups of computer scientists who could remove any of four different music encryption ("watermarking") standards developed by the industry without harming the quality of the sound. Professor Edward Felten of Princeton University, along with colleagues at Rice University, broke several of the watermarks, and French researchers broke the rest. However, the Recording Industry Association of America (RIAA) and the SDMI threatened to invoke the penalties available to them under the DMCA and thereby prevented the professors from publicly presenting their papers at two academic conferences held at Georgetown University and Carnegie Mellon University in January and April 2001. The industry argued that despite the contest they had sponsored, publishing the results of breaking the encryption standard would violate the Digital Millennium Copyright Act's prohibition on creating and distributing any method of circumventing a technology-based copyright protection scheme (Markoff, 2001). On June 6, 2001, the Electronic Freedom Frontier and the professors filed a lawsuit against the RIAA, asking a federal court for a declaratory judgment that Felten and his research team had a First Amendment right to present their research (*Felten et al.* v. *RIAA et al.*, 2001). On August 15, 2001, with the permission of RIAA and SDMI, researchers on Felten's team presented their research at the Usenix Security Conference. They are continuing to pursue the lawsuit against RIAA and SDMI, however, because, according to Felten, RIAA and SDMI are continuing to insist on veto power over the researcher's ongoing work and future publications.

PATENTS: BUSINESS METHODS AND PROCESSES

> *"Whoever invents or discovers any new and useful process, machine, manufacture, or composition of matter, or any new and useful improvement thereof, may obtain a patent therefore, subject to the conditions and requirements of this title."*
>
> Section 101, U.S. Patent Act

patent

grants the owner an exclusive monopoly to the ideas behind an invention for 20 years

A **patent** grants the owner an exclusive monopoly to the ideas behind an invention for 20 years. The congressional intent behind patent law was to ensure that inventors of new machines, devices, or industrial methods would receive the full financial and other rewards of their labor and yet still make widespread use of the invention possible by providing detailed diagrams for those wishing to use the idea under license from the patent's owner. Patents are obtained from the United States Patent and Trademark Office (USPTO), created in 1812. Obtaining a patent is much more difficult and time-consuming than obtaining copyright protection (which is automatic with the creation of the work). Patents must be formally applied for, and the granting of a patent is determined by Patent Office examiners who follow a set of rigorous rules. Ultimately, federal courts decide when patents are valid and when infringement occurs.

Patents are very different from copyrights because patents protect the ideas themselves and not merely the expression of ideas. There are four types of inventions for which patents are granted under patent law: machines, man-made products, compositions of matter, and processing methods. The Supreme Court has determined that patents extend to "anything under the sun that is made by man" (*Diamond* v. *Chakrabarty*, 447 US 303 (1980)) as long as the other requirements of the Patent Act are met. There are three things that cannot be patented: laws of nature, natural phenomena, and abstract ideas. For instance, a mathematical algorithm cannot be patented unless it is realized in a tangible machine or process that has a "useful" result (the mathematical algorithm exception).

In order to be granted a patent, the applicant must show that the invention is new, original, novel, nonobvious, and not evident in prior arts and practice. As with copyrights, the granting of patents has moved far beyond the original intent of Congress's first patent statute that sought to protect industrial designs and machines. Patent protection has been extended to articles of manufacture (1842), plants (1930), surgical and medical procedures (1950), and software (1981). The Patent Office did not accept applications for software patents until a 1981 Supreme Court decision that held that computer programs could be a part of a patentable process. Since that time, thousands of software patents have been granted. Virtually any software program can be patented as long as it is novel and not obvious.

Essentially, as technology and industrial arts progress, patents have been extended to both encourage entrepreneurs to invent useful devices and promote widespread dissemination of the new techniques through licensing and artful imitation of the published patents (the creation of devices that provide the same functionality as the invention but use different methods) (Winston, 1998). Patents encourage inventors to come up with unique ways of achieving the same functionality as existing patents. For instance, Amazon's patent on one-click purchasing caused Barnesandnoble.com to invent a simplified two-click method of purchasing.

The danger of patents is that they stifle competition by raising barriers to entry into an industry. Patents force new entrants to pay licensing fees to incumbents, and thus slow down the development of technical applications of new ideas by creating lengthy licensing applications and delays.

E-commerce Patents

Much of the Internet's infrastructure and software was developed under the auspices of publicly funded scientific and military programs in the United States and Europe. Unlike Samuel F. B. Morse, who patented the idea of Morse Code, and made the telegraph useful, most of the inventions that make the Internet and e-commerce possible were not patented by their inventors. The early Internet was characterized by a spirit of worldwide community development and sharing of ideas without consideration of personal wealth (Winston, 1998).

This early Internet spirit changed in the mid-1990s with the commercial development of the World Wide Web. Business firms began applying for "business methods" and software patents. Figure 9.4 illustrates the growth in e-commerce patents.

"Business Methods" Patents

In 1998, in a landmark decision that paved the way for Internet business methods patents, a Federal Circuit Court of Appeals in the *State Street Bank & Trust* v. *Signature*

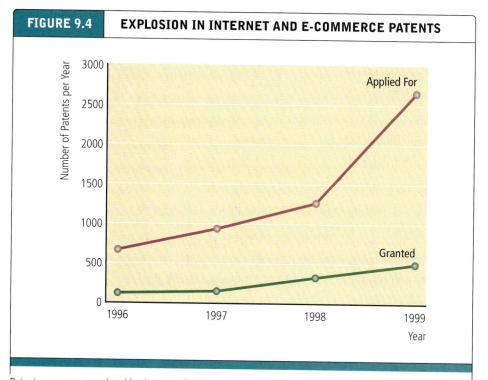

FIGURE 9.4 **EXPLOSION IN INTERNET AND E-COMMERCE PATENTS**

Patents on computer-related business methods are increasing. Bolstered by a 1998 legal decision, new applications for such patents have leapt dramatically.

SOURCE: United States Patent and Trademark Office, 2000.

Financial Group, Inc. case upheld the claims of Signature Financial to a valid patent for a business method that allows managers to monitor and record financial information flows generated by a partner fund (a "hub and spoke" system). In hub and spoke financial systems, mutual funds (the spokes) pool their funds into a single portfolio to achieve greater financial leverage, diversification, and higher returns. Signature Financial had invented and obtained a patent ("Data Processing System for Hub and Spoke Financial Services Configuration") on such a system in 1993. State Street Bank & Trust attempted to license the system from Signature Financial, but when negotiations broke down, State Street sought to have the patent declared invalid and unenforceable because business methods could not be patented. However, the Federal Appeals Court threw out the so-called business methods exception under which it was thought business methods could not be patented.

The court concluded that business methods should be treated like any process and that Signature Financial had invented a business method that could be patented. The court ruled there was no reason to disallow business methods from patent protection, or any "step by step process, be it electronic or chemical or mechanical, [that] involves an algorithm in the broad sense of the term." (*State Street Bank & Trust Co.* v. *Signature Financial Group*, 149 F. 3d 1368 (1998)).

The State Street decision led to an explosion in applications for e-commerce "business methods" patents, with about three thousand applications per year and four hundred granted. Table 9.14 lists some of the better known e-commerce patents.

Reviewing the patent claims in Table 9.14, you can understand the concerns of commentators and corporations. Some of the patent claims are very broad (for example, hyperlinks and "name your price" sales methods), have historical precedents in the pre-Internet era (shopping carts and affiliate marketing), and seem "obvious" (one-click purchasing). Critics of online business methods patents argue that the Patent Office has been too lenient in granting such patents and that in most instances, the supposed inventions merely copy pre-Internet business methods and thus do not constitute "inventions" (Thurm, 2000a; Chiappetta, 2001). In other cases, critics argue, the Patent Office has failed to understand the history of the Internet and has granted patents for practices that were in the public domain and that had been invented long before by others. To complicate matters, the European Patent Convention and the patent laws of most European countries do not recognize business methods per se unless the method is implemented through some technology (Takenaka, 2001). In response, the Patent Office is strengthening its Internet examination process and consulting with outside technology experts before granting patents (Matthews, 2000). Amazon Chief Executive, Jeff Bezos, has argued for shorter patent terms and inclusion of more outside experts in the examination process, but has refused calls for Amazon to give up its patents to one-click purchasing and online affiliate marketing (Thurm, 2000b).

TABLE 9.14	SELECTED E-COMMERCE BUSINESS METHODS PATENTS	
COMPANY	SUBJECT	UPDATE
Amazon	One-click purchasing	Amazon.com has used its patent to force changes to Barnes & Noble's Web site. In February 2000, a federal court overturned an earlier injunction against B&N's Express Lane checkout, calling the Amazon patent's validity into question.
Amazon	Online affiliate marketing	A method that allows owners of other Web sites to refer customers to Amazon in return for a fee (February 2000). Rejected by the Japanese Patent Office in 2001.
CyberGold	Attention brokerage	Patent covers rewarding Web surfers for paying attention to online advertisements.
E-Data	Download-based sales	A judge blocked E-Data's attempts to enforce this pre-Internet era patent.
Netcentives	Online incentives	One of several recently issued patents covering reward systems for Internet purchasing.
Open Market	Electronic shopping carts	This patent is probably being infringed by many e-commerce sites on the Internet.
Priceline	Buyer-driven "name your price" sales	Priceline sued Microsoft and its Expedia travel site for copying its patented business method. Expedia settled and agreed to pay a royalty in January 2001.
Sightsound	Music downloads	Sightsound is demanding a 1% royalty from all online music sellers, and has sued Time Warner's CDNow.com music site for infringing its patent.
Accompany	Internet group buying and dynamic pricing	A method for individuals to obtain lower prices by aggregating into groups and negotiating online with suppliers (August 1998).
DE Technologies	Computer-mediated international trading system	A broad patent for any system that automatically calculates prices based on real-time currency fluctuations.
Akamai	Internet content delivery Global Hosting System	A broad patent covering techniques for expediting the flow of information over the Internet.
NetZero	Display of third-party advertisements in floating windows	NetZero won a court order against rival Juno Online Services for displaying third-party ads in windows in January 2001.
MuniAuction	System for holding online municipal bond auctions	Broad patent could apply to all fixed-income online trading.
British Telecom	Hyperlinks	In 1989 British Telecom received a U.S. patent for a hyperlink system developed as part of a videotext telephone system.
24/7 Media	Dynamic delivery of online advertising	A patent (February 2000) underlying 24/7 Media's method for delivering banner advertising online.
DoubleClick	Dynamic delivery of online advertising	The patent (September, 2000) underlying DoubleClick's business of online banner ad delivery.
Jupiter Media Metrix	A method for tracking and analyzing online user activity	A patent (September 2000) protecting Jupiter's method of using panels of PC users around the world to track their Internet activities. Pursuing actions against NetValue SA and NetRatings Inc.

TRADEMARKS: ONLINE INFRINGEMENT AND DILUTION

> *Trademark is "any word, name, symbol, or device, or any combination thereof ... used in commerce ... to identify and distinguish ... goods ... from those manufactured or sold by others and to indicate the source of the goods."*
>
> ▬▬ The Trademark Act, 1946

Trademark law is a form of intellectual property protection for **trademarks** — a mark used to identify and distinguish goods and indicate their source. Trademark protections exist at both the federal and state levels in the United States. The purpose of trademark law is twofold. First, the trademark law protects the public in the marketplace by ensuring that it gets what it pays for and wants to receive. Second, trademark law protects the owner — who has spent time, money, and energy bringing the product to the marketplace — against piracy and misappropriation. Trademarks have been extended from single words to pictures, shapes, packaging, and colors. Some things may not be trademarked: common words that are merely descriptive ("clock"), flags of states and nations, immoral or deceptive marks, or marks belonging to others. Federal trademarks are obtained, first, by use in interstate commerce, and second, by registration with the U.S. Patent and Trademark Office (USPTO). Trademarks are granted for a period of ten years, and can be renewed indefinitely.

trademark
a mark used to identify and distinguish goods and indicate their source

Disputes over federal trademarks involve establishing *infringement*. The test for infringement is twofold: market confusion and bad faith. Use of a trademark that creates confusion with existing trademarks, causes consumers to make market mistakes, or misrepresents the origins of goods is an infringement. In addition, the intentional misuse of words and symbols in the marketplace to extort revenue from legitimate trademark owners ("bad faith") is proscribed.

In 1995, Congress passed the Federal Trademark Dilution Act, which created a federal cause of action for dilution of famous marks. This new legislation dispenses with the test of market confusion (although that is still required to claim infringement), and extends protection to owners of famous trademarks against **dilution,** which is defined as any behavior that would weaken the connection between the trademark and the product. Dilution occurs through *blurring* (weakening the connection between the trademark and the goods) and *tarnishment* (using the trademark in a way that makes the underlying products appear unsavory or unwholesome).

dilution
any behavior that would weaken the connection between the trademark and the product

Trademarks and the Internet

The rapid growth and commercialization of the Internet have provided unusual opportunities for existing firms with distinctive and famous trademarks to extend their brands to the Internet. These same developments have provided malicious individuals and firms the opportunity to squat on Internet domain names built upon famous marks, as well as attempt to confuse consumers and dilute famous or distinctive marks (including your personal name or a movie star's name). The conflict between legitimate trademark owners and malicious firms was allowed to fester and grow because Network Solutions Inc. (NSI), the Internet's sole agency for domain name registration, for many years, had a policy of "first come, first served." This meant anyone could register any domain name that had not already been registered, regardless of the trademark status of the domain name. NSI was not authorized to decide trademark issues (Nash, 1997).

In response to a growing number of complaints from owners of famous trademarks who found their trademark names being appropriated by Web entrepreneurs, Congress passed the **Anticybersquatting Consumer Protection Act (ACPA)** in November 1999. The ACPA creates civil liabilities for anyone who attempts in bad faith to profit from an existing famous or distinctive trademark by registering an Internet domain name that is identical, confusingly similar, or "dilutive" of that trademark. The Act does not establish criminal sanctions. The Act proscribes using "bad faith" domain names to extort money from the owners of the existing trademark (cybersquatting), or using the bad faith domain to divert Web traffic to the bad faith domain that could harm the good will represented by the trademark, create market confusion, tarnish, or disparage the mark (cyberpiracy). The Act also proscribes the use of a domain name that consists of the name of a living person, or a name confusingly similar to an existing personal name, without that person's consent, if the registrant is registering the name with the intent to profit by selling the domain dame to that person.

Trademark abuse can take many forms on the Web. Table 9.15 lists the major behaviors on the Internet that have run afoul of trademark law, and the court cases that resulted.

Cybersquatting

Cybersquatting involves the registration of an infringing domain name, or other Internet use of an existing trademark, for the purpose of extorting payments from the legitimate owner. In one of the first cases involving the ACPA, E. & J. Gallo Winery, owner of the registered mark "Ernest and Julio Gallo" for alcoholic beverages, sued Spider Webs Ltd. for using the domain name "ernestandjuliogallo.com". Spider Webs Ltd. was a domain name speculator that owned numerous domain names consisting of famous company names. The ernestandjuliogallo.com Web site contained information on the risks of alcohol use, anticorporate articles about E. & J. Gallo Winery, and was poorly constructed. The court concluded that Spider Webs Ltd. was in violation of the ACPA and that its actions constituted dilution by blurring because the "ernestandjuliogallo.com" domain name appeared on every page printed off the Web site accessed by that name, and that Spider Webs Ltd. was not free to use this particular mark as a domain name. The court also appeared to find dilution by tarnishment, based on the negative content and poor quality of the defendant's Web site. The court

Anticybersquatting Consumer Protection Act (ACPA)

creates civil liabilities for anyone who attempts in bad faith to profit from an existing famous or distinctive trademark by registering an Internet domain name that is identical, or confusingly similar, or "dilutive" of that trademark

cybersquatting

involves the registration of an infringing domain name, or other Internet use of an existing trademark, for the purpose of extorting payments from the legitimate owners

TABLE 9.15	INTERNET AND TRADEMARK LAW	
ACTIVITY	DESCRIPTION	EXAMPLE CASES
Cybersquatting	Registering domain names similar or identical to trademarks of others to extort profits from legitimate holders.	*E. & J. Gallo Winery* v. *Spider Webs Ltd.*, 129 F. Supp. 2d 1033 (S.D. Tex. 2001)
Cyber piracy	Registering domain names similar or identical to trademarks of others to divert Web traffic to their own sites.	*Ford Motor Co.* v. *Lapertosa*, 2001 U.S. Dist. LEXIS 253 (E.D. Mich. Jan. 3, 2001) *PaineWebber Inc.* v. *Fortuny*, Civ. A. No. 99-0456-A (E.D. Va. Apr. 9, 1999) *Playboy Enterprises, Inc.* v. *Global Site Designs, Inc.*, 1999 WL 311707 (S.D. Fla. May 15, 1999)
Metatagging	Using trademark words in a site's metatags.	*Bernina of America, Inc.* v. *Fashion Fabrics Int'l, Inc.*, 2001 U.S. Dist. LEXIS 1211 (N.D. Ill. Feb. 8, 2001). *Nissan Motor Co., Ltd.* v. *Nissan Computer Corp.*, 289 F. Supp. 2d 1154 (C.D. Cal.), aff'd, 2000 U.S. App. LEXIS 33937 (9th Cir. Dec. 26, 2000).
Keywording	Placing trademarked keywords on Web pages, either visible or invisible.	*Playboy Enterprises, Inc.* v. *Netscape Communications, Inc.*, 55 F. Supp. 2d 1070 (C.D. Cal.), aff'd, 1999 U.S. App. LEXIS 30215 (9th Cir. 1999). *Nettis Environment Ltd.* v. *IWI, Inc.*, 46 F. Supp. 2d 722 (N.D. Ohio 1999).
Linking	Linking to content pages on other sites, bypassing the home page.	*Ticketmaster* v. *Tickets.com*, C.D. Cal. August 2000
Framing	Placing the content of other sites in a frame on the infringer's site.	*The Washington Post, et al.* v. *TotalNews, Inc., et al.*, S. D. N. Y., Civil Action Number 97-1190. (February 1997)

ordered Spider Webs Ltd. to transfer the domain name to E. & J. Gallo Winery and enjoined it from using any domain name containing the word "Gallo" or the words "Ernest" and "Julio" in combination (*E. & J. Gallo Winery* v. *Spider Webs Ltd.*, 2001).

Cyberpiracy

Cyberpiracy involves the same behavior as cybersquatting, but with the intent of diverting traffic from the legitimate site to an infringing site. In *Ford Motor Co.* v. *Lapertosa*, Lapertosa had registered and used a Web site called www.fordrecalls.com as an adult entertainment Web site. The court ruled that www.fordrecalls.com was in

cyberpiracy
involves the same behavior as cybersquatting, but with the intent of diverting traffic from the legitimate site to an infringing site

violation of the ACPA in that it was a bad faith attempt to divert traffic to the Lapertosa site and diluted Ford's wholesome trademark (*Ford Motor Co.* v. *Lapertosa,* 2001).

The Ford decision reflects two other famous cases of cyberpiracy. In the *Paine Webber Inc.* v. *Fortuny* case, the court enjoined Fortuny from using the domain name "wwwpainewebber.com" — a site that specialized in pornographic materials — because it diluted and tarnished Paine Webber's trademark and diverted Web traffic from Paine Webber's legitimate site — www.painewebber.com (*PaineWebber Inc.* v. *Fortuny,* 1999). In the *Playboy Enterprises, Inc.* v. *Global Site Designs, Inc.* case, the court enjoined the defendants from using the "Playboy" and "Playmate" marks in their domain names "playboyonline.net" and "playmatesearch.net" and from including the Playboy trademark in their metatags. In these cases, the defendants' intention was diversion for financial gain (*Playboy Enterprises, Inc.* v. *Global Site Designs, Inc.,* 1999).

Metatagging

The legal status of using famous or distinctive marks as metatags is more complex and subtle. The use of trademarks in metatags is permitted if the use does not mislead or confuse consumers. Usually this depends on the content of the site. A car dealer would be permitted to use a famous automobile trademark in its metatags if the dealer sold this brand of automobiles, but a pornography site could not use the same trademark, nor a dealer for a rival manufacturer. A Ford dealer would most likely be infringing if it used "Honda" in its metatags, but would not be infringing if it used "Ford" in its metatags. (Ford Motor Company would be unlikely to seek an injunction against one of its dealers.)

In the *Bernina* case, the court enjoined Fashion Fabrics International, an independent dealer of sewing machines, from using the trademarks "Bernina" and "Bernette," which belonged to the manufacturer Bernina, as metatags. The court found the defendant's site contained misleading claims about Fashion Fabrics International's knowledge of Bernina products that were likely to confuse customers. The use of the Bernina trademarks as metatags per se was not a violation of ACPA, according to the court, but in combination with the misleading claims on the site would cause confusion and hence infringement (*Bernina of America, Inc.* v. *Fashion Fabrics Int'l, Inc.,* 2001).

In the *Nissan* case, Uzi Nissan had used his surname "Nissan" as a trade name for various businesses since 1980, including Nissan Computer Corp. He registered Nissan.com in 1994 and Nissan.net in 1996. Nissan.com had no relationship with Nissan Motor, but over the years began selling auto parts that competed with Nissan Motor. Nissan Motor Company objected to the use of the domain name Nissan.com and the use of "Nissan" in the metatags for both sites on grounds it would confuse customers and infringe on Nissan Motor's trademarks. Uzi Nissan offered to sell his sites to Nissan Motor for several million dollars. Nissan Motor refused. The court ruled that

Nissan Computer's behavior did indeed infringe on Nissan Motor's trademarks, but it refused to shut the site down. Instead, the court ruled Nissan Computer could continue to use the Nissan name, and metatags, but must post notices on its site that it is not affiliated with Nissan Motor (*Nissan Motor Co., Ltd.* v. *Nissan Computer Corp,* 2000).

Keywording

The permissibility of using trademarks as keywords on search engines is also subtle and depends both on the extent to which such use causes "initial customer confusion" and on the content of the search results. In *Playboy Enterprises, Inc.* v. *Netscape Communications, Inc.,* Playboy objected to the practice of Netscape and Excite search engines to display banner ads unrelated to *Playboy Magazine* when users entered search arguments such as "playboy," "playmate," and "playgirl." Here the court ruled in favor of the defendants, arguing that the trademark words were being used as ordinary English language words, and, even if they were not, no consumer confusion resulted, and no dilution or tarnishment of Playboy Enterprises trademarks occurred (*Playboy Enterprises, Inc.* v. *Netscape Communications, Inc.,* 1999).

However, in the *Nettis* case, Nettis and IWI Inc. were competitors in the ventilation business. IWI had registered the trademarks "nettis" and "nettis environmental" on over 400 search engines, and in addition, used these marks as metatags on its site. The court required IWI to remove the metatags and de-register the keywords with all search engines because consumers would be confused — searching for Nettis products would lead them to an IWI Web site (*Nettis Environment Ltd.* v. *IWI, Inc.,* 1999).

Linking

Linking refers to building hypertext links from one site to another site. This is obviously a major design feature and benefit of the Web. **Deep linking** involves bypassing the target site's home page and going directly to a content page. In *Ticketmaster Corp.* v. *Tickets.com,* Tickets.com — owned by Microsoft — competed directly against Ticketmaster in the events ticket market. Ticketmaster is a long-time participant in this market and had a much larger inventory of tickets than Tickets.com. When Tickets.com did not have tickets for an event, it would direct users to Ticketmaster's internal pages, bypassing the Ticketmaster home page. Even though its logo was displayed on the internal pages, Ticketmaster objected on the grounds that such "deep linking" violated the terms and conditions of use for its site (stated on a separate page altogether and construed by Ticketmaster as equivalent to a shrink-wrap license), and constituted false advertising, as well as the violation of copyright. The court found, however, that deep linking per se is not illegal, no violation of copyright occurred because no copies were made, the terms and conditions of use were not obvious to users, and users were not required to read the page on which the terms and

linking
building hypertext links from one site to another site

deep linking
involves bypassing the target site's home page, and going directly to a content page

conditions of use appeared in any event. The court refused to rule in favor of Ticket-master, but left open further argument on the licensing issue. In an out-of-court set-tlement, Tickets.com nevertheless agreed to stop the practice of deep linking (*Ticketmaster* v. *Tickets.com,* 2000).

Framing

framing

involves displaying the content of another Web site inside your own Web site within a frame or window

Framing involves displaying the content of another Web site inside your own Web site within a frame or window. The user never leaves the framer's site and can be exposed to advertising while the target site's advertising is distorted or eliminated. Framers may or may not acknowledge the source of the content. In *The Washington Post, et al.* v. *TotalNews, Inc.* case, the *Washington Post*, CNN, Reuters, and several other news organizations filed suit against TotalNews Inc., claiming that TotalNews's use of frames on its Web site, TotalNews.com, infringed upon the respective plaintiffs' copy-rights and trademarks, diluted the content of their individual Web sites, and misap-propriated the content of those Web sites. The plaintiffs claimed additionally that TotalNews's framing practice effectively deprived the plaintiffs' Web sites of advertis-ing revenue.

TotalNews's Web site employed four frames: The TotalNews logo appeared in the lower left frame, the various links were located on a vertical frame on the left side of the screen, TotalNews's advertising was framed across the screen bottom, and the "news frame," the largest frame, appeared in the center and right. Clicking on a spe-cific news organization's link allowed the reader to view the content of that particu-lar organization's Web site, including any related advertising, within the context of the "news frame." In some instances, the framing distorted or modified the appearance of the linked Web site, including the advertisements, while the appearance of Total-News's advertisements, in a separate frame, remained unchanged. In addition, the URL remained fixed on the TotalNews address, even though the content in the largest frame on the Web site was from the linked Web site. The "news frame" did not, how-ever, eliminate the linked Web site's identifying features.

The case was settled out of court. The news organizations allowed TotalNews to link to their Web sites, but prohibited framing and any attempt to imply affiliation with the news organizations (*The Washington Post, et al.* v. *TotalNews, Inc.,* 1997).

E-COMMERCE II: BALANCING THE PROTECTION OF PROPERTY WITH OTHER VALUES

In the areas of copyright, patent law, and trademark law, societies have moved quickly to protect intellectual property from challenges posed by the Internet. In each of these areas, traditional concepts of intellectual property have not only been upheld, but even strengthened. The DMCA seems to restrict journalists and academ-ics from even accessing copyrighted materials if they are encrypted, a protection not true of traditional documents. Patents have been extended to Internet business methods, and trademarks are more strongly protected than ever because of fears of cyber-squatting. In the E-commerce I period, many commentators believed that Internet technology would sweep away the powers of corporations to protect their property (Dueker, 1996). The case of Napster and digital sound files was a powerful example. However, as we enter the E-commerce II period, it is apparent that existing corporations have some very powerful legal tools for protecting their digital properties. In addition, there are now four arbitration panels established to hear trademark disputes: WIPO, ICANN, the National Arbitration Forum (Minneapolis), eResolutions Consortium (Amherst, Massachusetts), and C.P.R. Institute for Dispute Resolutions in New York. Of the approximately 1,000 cases heard so far, trademark owners have prevailed in 75% of the cases (Flynn, 2000).

The difficulty now may be in going too far to protect the property interests of the powerful and the rich, preventing parody sites or parody content from receiving wide distribution and recognition, and in this sense interfering with the exercise of First Amendment guarantees of freedom of expression.

9.4 GOVERNANCE

Governance has to do with social control: Who will control e-commerce, what elements will be controlled, and how will the controls be implemented? A natural question arises and needs to be answered: "Why do we as a society need to 'control' e-commerce?" Because e-commerce and the Internet are so closely intertwined (though not identical), controlling e-commerce also involves regulating the Internet.

governance
has to do with social control: Who will control e-commerce, what elements will be controlled, and how will the controls be implemented?

WHO GOVERNS E-COMMERCE AND THE INTERNET?

Governance of both the Internet and e-commerce has gone through four stages. Table 9.16 summarizes these stages in the evolution of e-commerce governance.

Prior to 1995, the Internet was a government program. Beginning in 1995, private corporations were given control of the technical infrastructure as well as the process of granting IP addresses and domain names. However, the NSI monopoly created in this period did not represent international users of the Internet, and was unable to cope with emerging public policy issues such as trademark and intellectual property protection, fair policies for allocating domains, and growing concerns that a small group of firms was benefiting from growth in the Internet.

President Clinton, using funds from the Department of Commerce, encouraged the establishment of an international body called the Internet Corporation for Assigning Numbers and Names (ICANN) that hopefully could better represent a wider range of countries and a broad range of interests, and begin to address emerging public

TABLE 9.16	THE EVOLUTION OF GOVERNANCE OF E-COMMERCE
INTERNET GOVERNANCE PERIOD	**DESCRIPTION**
Government Control Period 1970–1994	DARPA and the National Science Foundation control the Internet as a fully government-funded program.
Privatization 1995–1998	Network Solutions Inc. is given a monopoly to assign and track high-level Internet domains. Backbone is sold to private telecommunications companies. Policy issues are not decided.
Self-Regulation 1995–present	President Clinton and the Department of Commerce encourage the creation of a semiprivate body, the Internet Corporation for Assigning Numbers and Names, to deal with emerging conflicts and establish policies.
Governmental Regulation 1998–present	Executive, legislative, and judicial bodies worldwide begin to implement direct controls over the Internet and e-commerce.

policy issues in the E-commerce I period. ICANN was intended to be an Internet/e-commerce industry self-governing body, not another government agency.

However, the explosive growth of the Web and e-commerce created a number of issues over which ICANN had no authority. Content issues such as pornography, gambling, and offensive written expressions and graphics, along with commercial issue of intellectual property protection ushered in the current era of growing governmental regulation of the Internet and e-commerce throughout the world. Currently, we are in a mixed-mode policy environment where self-regulation through a variety of Internet policy and technical bodies co-exists with limited government regulation.

Can the Internet Be Controlled?

Early Internet advocates argued that the Internet was different from all previous technologies. They argued that the Internet could not be controlled, given its inherent decentralized design, its ability to cross borders, and its underlying packet switching technology that made monitoring and controlling message content impossible. The slogans were "Information wants to be free," and "the Net is everywhere" (but not in any central location). The implication of these slogans was that the content and behavior of e-commerce sites — indeed Internet sites of any kind — could be not "controlled" in the same way as traditional media such as radio and television.

In fact, the Internet is technically very easily controlled, monitored, and regulated from central locations. For instance, in China, Malaysia, and Singapore, access to the Web is controlled from government-owned centralized routers that direct traffic across their borders and within the country, or via tightly regulated ISPs operating within the countries. This permits governments to block access to U.S. or European Web sites. In addition, Web ISPs and search engines operating in Asia such as Yahoo, MSN, and Lycos self-censor their Asian content by using only government-approved news sources. In China, all ISPs need a license from the Ministry of Information Industry (MII), and they are prohibited from disseminating any information that may harm the state or permit pornography, gambling, or the advocacy of cults. Yahoo's Chinese Web page — unlike Yahoo's domestic U.S. and European Web pages — never mention the harvesting of organs from Chinese prisoners or the Falun Gong spiritual movement because of fears of offending the Chinese government and disrupting their business objectives in China. Likewise, under pressure from European governments, both eBay and Yahoo have dropped the sale of Nazi memorabilia from their sites (Yee, 2001; Uimonen and Lawson, 2000). In the United States, as we have seen in our discussion of intellectual property, e-commerce sites can be put out of business for violating existing laws, and ISPs can forced to "take down" offending content. Government security agencies such as the Federal Bureau of Investigation can obtain court orders to monitor ISP traffic, and the FBI's DSC1000 (formerly called Carnivore) gives the FBI the ability to engage in widespread monitoring of millions of e-mail messages.

In the United States, efforts to control media content have run up against equally powerful social and political values that protect freedom of expression. The U.S. Constitution's First Amendment says "Congress shall make no law . . . abridging the freedom of speech, or of the press." As it turns out, the 200-year-old Bill of Rights has been a powerful brake on efforts to control twenty-first-century e-commerce content.

PUBLIC GOVERNMENT AND LAW

The reason we have governments is ostensibly to regulate and control activities within the borders of the nation. What happens in other nations, for the most part, we ignore, although clearly environmental and international trade issues require multinational cooperation. E-commerce and the Internet pose some unique problems to public government that center on the ability of the nation-state to govern activities within its borders. Nations have considerable powers to shape the Internet.

Taxation

Few questions illustrate the complexity of governance and jurisdiction more potently than taxation of e-commerce sales. In both Europe and the United States, governments rely on sales taxes based on the type and value of goods sold. In Europe, these taxes are collected along the entire value chain, including the final sale to the consumer, and are called "value-added taxes" (VAT), whereas in the United States, taxes are collected on final sales to consumers and are called consumption taxes. In the United States, there are fifty states, 3,000 counties, and 12,000 municipalities, each with unique tax rates and policies. Cheese may be taxable in one state as a "snack food," but not taxable in another state (such as Wisconsin), where it is considered a basic food. Consumption taxes are generally recognized to be regressive because they disproportionately tax poorer people, for whom consumption is a larger part of total income.

Sales taxes were first implemented in the United States in the late 1930s as a Depression era method of raising money for localities. Ostensibly, the money was to be used to build infrastructure such as roads, schools, and utilities to support business development, but over the years the funds have been used for general government purposes of the states and localities. In most states, there is a state-based sales tax, and a smaller local sales tax. The total sales tax ranges from zero in some states (North Dakota) to as much as 13% in New York City.

The development of "remote sales" such as mail order/telephone order retail (MOTO) in the United States in the 1970s broke the relationship between physical presence and commerce, complicating the plans of state and local tax authorities to tax all retail commerce. States sought to force MOTO retailers to collect sales taxes for them based on the address of the recipient, but Supreme Court decisions in 1967 and 1992 established that states had no authority to force MOTO retailers to collect state taxes unless the businesses had a "nexus" of operations (physical presence) in the state. Congress could however create legislation giving states this authority. But every congressional effort to tax catalog merchants has been beaten back by a torrent of opposition from catalog merchants and consumers, leaving intact an effective tax subsidy for MOTO merchants (Swisher, 2001).

The explosive growth of e-commerce, the latest type of "remote sales," has once again raised the issue of how — and if — to tax remote sales. E-commerce has bene-fited from a tax subsidy since its inception of up to 13% for goods shipped to high sales-tax areas. Local retail merchants have complained bitterly about the e-commerce tax subsidy. E-commerce merchants have argued that this new form of commerce needs to be nurtured and encouraged in its early years, and that in any event, the crazy quilt of sales and use tax regimes would be difficult to administer for Internet merchants. State and local governments meanwhile see a potential source of new revenue slipping from their reach.

In 1998, Congress passed the Internet Tax Freedom Act that placed a moratorium on any taxation of e-commerce sales for three years until October 2001. As of September 2001, bills to extend the moratorium were being considered by the both the House and Senate, with passage considered likely, although not definite. During this moratorium period, a number of competing plans have emerged. The Multistate

Streamlined Sales Tax Project, supported by state tax administrators, proposes to make uniform definitions of taxable goods across all states, and uniform tax rates within any single state (permitting states to tax at different rates). The National Council of State Legislators has rejected this approach as too ambitious. They propose another three-year moratorium and further congressional deliberation. The National Governors' Association proposes a single state sales tax rate for all e-commerce, regardless of product type, that could differ from existing sales tax rates. For instance, the sales tax for a digitally downloaded book could be 5% for all states, while in some states the physical book sales tax rate might be 8% (or zero).

The merger of online e-commerce with offline commerce further complicates the taxation question. For instance, Wal-Mart, which has a nexus in all 50 states, charged sales tax on purchases at its Internet site. Customers objected, claiming Internet sales are "supposed to be tax-free." Wal-Mart responded by spinning off its online e-commerce site to a separate company with a venture capital partner. Now it charges sales tax only on sales in four states where the online store has a physical presence (warehouses and transshipment facilities). These facilities are located in states where sales taxes are very low.

The taxation situation in Europe, and trade between Europe and the United States, is similarly complex. The Organization for Economic Cooperation and Development (OECD), the economic policy coordinating body of European, American, and Japanese governments, is currently investigating different schemes for applying consumption and business profit taxes for e-commerce digitally downloaded goods. The European Union (the EU, the supra-national body representing 15 European nations) is considering how to collect VAT taxes on digital goods such as music and software delivered to consumers by foreign companies (Brown and Gruenwald, 2001). Currently, European Union companies are required to collect taxes on VAT sales to EU customers, but U.S. companies are not required to collect VAT taxes on goods sent or downloaded to EU customers. This gives the Americans a huge tax edge, and the EU is considering ways to force foreign companies to collect VAT taxes for them. The EU already collects VAT taxes for physical goods ordered online and digital goods delivered online to business customers within the EU.

Thus, there is no integrated rational approach to taxation of domestic or international e-commerce (Varian, 2001). The national and international character of Internet sales is wreaking havoc on taxation schemes in the United States that were built in the 1930s and based on local commerce and local jurisdictions. Although there appears to be acquiescence among large Internet retailers such as Amazon to the idea of some kind of sales tax on e-commerce sales, their insistence on uniformity will delay taxation for many years, and any proposal to tax e-commerce will likely incur the wrath of 60 million U.S. e-commerce consumers. Congress is not likely to ignore their voices.

9.5	**PUBLIC SAFETY AND WELFARE**

Governments everywhere claim to pursue public safety, health, and welfare. This effort produces laws governing everything from weights and measures to national highways, to the content of radio and television programs. Electronic media of all kinds (telegraph, telephone, radio, and television) have historically been regulated by governments seeking to develop a rational commercial telecommunications environment and to control the content of the media — which may be critical of government or offensive to powerful groups in a society. Historically, in the United States, newspapers and print media have been beyond government controls because of constitutional guarantees of freedom of speech. Electronic media such as radio and television have, on the other hand, always been subject to content regulation because they use the publicly owned frequency spectrum. Telephones have also been regulated as public utilities and "common carriers," with special social burdens to provide service and access, but with no limitations on content.

In the United States, critical issues in e-commerce center around the protection of children, strong sentiments against pornography in any public media, efforts to control gambling, and the protection of public health through restricting sales of drugs and cigarettes.

PROTECTING CHILDREN

Pornography is an immensely successful Internet business. Oddly, given this success, it is very difficult to find solid data on the size of the Internet pornography market. There were an estimated 92,000 pornography sites on the Web in 1997, generating an estimated $62 million in revenue (www.levelbest.com). By 2000, there were an estimated 200,000–300,000 sites selling pornography, generating revenues estimated by various industry sources of from $175 million to $1 billion. According to Jupiter Media Metrix, online porn is "the single biggest category of paid online content" (Bushkin, 2000). Pundits have quipped — only half in jest — that it is the only truly successful e-commerce model. Prior to self-censorship in April 2001, about 10% of Yahoo's revenue came from purchases of pornographic materials and links to adult sites. Web sites such as AOL offer special search engines for pornographic materials, and others refer users entering pornographic search arguments to WebPower, which operates several adult content and chat Web sites.

Online porn sites are also major players in the FBI's 2,856 online pedophilia cases opened in 2000 (Nordland and Bartholet, 2001). An estimated 20% of youth ages 10–17 received an online sexual solicitation in 2000 from pedophiles hanging out on these sites (National Center for Missing and Exploited Children, 2000). According to Net-

Value, children spent 64.9% more time at pornography sites than they did at game sites in 2000, and over one quarter of children online had visited an adult content site (NetValue, 2000). Child pornography is outlawed in the United States, Western Europe, and Eastern Europe.

To control the Web as a distribution medium for pornography, in 1996 Congress passed the Communications Decency Act (CDA). This act made it a felony criminal offense to use any telecommunications device to transmit "any comment, request, suggestion, proposal, image or other communications which is obscene, lewd, lascivious, filthy, or indecent" to anyone, and in particular, to persons under the age of 18 years of age (Section 502, Communications Decency Act of 1996). In 1997, the Supreme Court struck down the CDA as an unconstitutional abridgement of freedom of speech protected by the First Amendment. While the government argued the CDA was like a zoning ordinance designed to allow "adult" Web sites for people over 18 years of age, the Court found the CDA was a blanket proscription on content and rejected the "cyberzoning" argument as impossible to administer.

In 1998, Congress passed the Children's Online Protection Act (COPA). This act made it a felony criminal offense to communicate for "commercial purposes" "any material harmful to minors." Harmful material was defined as prurient, depicting sexual acts, and lacking value for minors. The act differed from CDA by focusing on "commercial speech" and minors exclusively. In February 1999, however, the Federal District Court in Pennsylvania struck down COPA as an unconstitutional restriction on Web content that was protected under the First Amendment. The court nevertheless recognized the interest of Congress and society to protect children on the Internet and in e-commerce. The Justice Department is appealing this ruling.

Although Congress has had a difficult time framing constitutionally acceptable legislation to protect children and other consumers from pornography, in the Children's Online Privacy Protection Act (COPPA) (1998) (described in Section 9.2), it appears to have been successful in preventing e-commerce sites from collecting information on minors without parental consent. Pornographers who collect information on children without parental consent are potential felons. Because COPPA does not regulate e-commerce content, to date it has not been challenged.

In addition to government regulation, private pressure from organized groups has also been successful in forcing some Web sites to eliminate the display of pornographic materials. For instance, in April 2001, Yahoo agreed to take down its "Adult and Erotica" section that listed thousands of adult video and content sites, along with Yahoo's trademark short descriptions of each site. Following a *Los Angeles Times* article on Yahoo's promotion of pornographic material, the portal had received over 100,000 e-mails from irate parents. Yahoo estimated the pornography sites contributed no more than 10% of its annual revenue (Hansell, 2001).

GAMBLING, CIGARETTES, AND DRUGS: IS THE WEB REALLY BORDERLESS?

In the United States, both the states and federal government have adopted legislation to control certain activities and products in order to enhance public health and welfare. Gambling, cigarettes, medical drugs, and of course addictive recreational drugs, are either banned or tightly regulated by federal and state laws. Yet these products and services are ideal for distribution over the Internet through e-commerce sites (see *Insight on Society: Cat Orders Viagra — The Internet Drug Bazaar*). Because the sites can be located offshore, they can operate beyond the jurisdiction of the state and federal prosecutors. Or so it seemed in the E-commerce I period. Gambling provides an interesting example of the clash between traditional jurisdictional boundaries and claims to a "borderless Web."

There are more than 1,400 wagering sites on the Web that generate over $1.5 billion a year in revenue. Gambling sites are expected to generate over $5 billion in 2003. Every day about one million Americans gamble online, with additional millions worldwide (Richtel, 2000a; Rainie and Packel, 2001). It appears that gambling is a very successful e-commerce business model.

Because online wagering is illegal in most states in the United States, along with unregulated gambling of any kind, most wagering sites are located offshore in Costa Rica or Antigua. It is unclear if online gambling is illegal under U.S. federal law. The Justice Department believes online gambling violates the Wire Act of 1960, but federal judges have refused to find online gambling illegal. MSNBC, Yahoo, and Google accept advertising from Internet gambling sites, and according to several states attorneys general, they are technically aiding and abetting illegal acts. So far, these companies have not been prosecuted. States such as New Jersey and Florida have recently sued offshore Internet casinos in St. Kitts and South Africa, and California has passed legislation (in the Assembly only) that permits its Attorney General to prosecute offshore and out-of-state online casinos. However, state prosecutors have been unable to enforce their state laws over an international phenomenon (McGuire, 2001).

Several bills have been introduced in Congress to regulate online gambling, but each has failed to find sufficient support. The traditional gaming industry in the United States originally opposed any form of online wagering, but in 2001 switched positions and now sees significant opportunities to extend their brand names into e-commerce. The Interactive Gaming Council, an industry trade group, argues that the Web is borderless and cannot be controlled by state legislatures. Federal and state legislators and judges argue the Internet does not change laws.

geolocation software
attempts to identify the geographical location of Web users

New technologies, called generically "Internet zoning" and "geolocation" software, offer some interesting solutions. **Geolocation software** attempts to identify the geographical location of Web users. Originally designed to target ads to regional areas, start-up firms such as RealMapping, Quova, and BorderControl, as well as Akamai — the Internet expediter — are selling products that can identify roughly where an Internet user lives. It was the possibility of geolocation software that influenced a French judge named Jean Jacques Gomez to rule that Yahoo would be required to prevent French citizens from viewing Nazi memorabilia on its Web portal (Richtel, 2000 (b)). Gomez, and others, believe national boundaries do indeed apply to a virtual world as well as to a physical world (Guernsey, 2001). Geolocation software could lead to a kind of Internet zoning, where users would be required to submit a digital passport before they are allowed access to sites containing proscribed content. At this point, it is not clear that the Web will remain borderless or that e-commerce can continue to flaunt national, state, and local laws with impunity.

EQUITY AND THE DIGITAL DIVIDE

In 1998, a U.S. Department of Commerce report, "Falling through the Net II: New Data on the Digital Divide," found that although more Americans now own computers, certain groups are still far less likely to have computers or online access. Other studies by the Pew Foundation have confirmed the **digital divide:** large differences in Internet access and e-commerce access among income, ethnic, and age groups (Rainie and Packel, 2001). Lack of such access affects the ability of children to improve their learning with educational software, of adults to acquire valuable technology skills, and of families to benefit from online connections to important health and civic information. A follow-up study, released in July 1999, documented that the digital divide was continuing to grow. Similar data gathered by the U.S. Department of Education highlighted a digital divide in our nation's schools, with children attending high poverty schools less likely to have access to computers, the Internet, or high quality educational technology programs.

digital divide
large differences in Internet access and e-commerce access among income, ethnic, and age groups

More recent studies focus on digital inclusion and the fact that the share of households with Internet access in 2000 has soared to 41% from 26% in 1998. More than half of households — 51% — now have computers, up from 42% in 1998, and more than 116 million Americans are online at work or at home, up from 86 million in 1998 (Howard et al., 2001).

Still, the rapid rate of inclusion has not reduced the digital divide that separates income, ethnic, rural, and handicapped groups, from the rest of society. People with disabilities are only half as likely to use the Internet, the gap between white and black household Internet use actually expanded from 15% to 18% in 2000, and for Hispanics, a similar widening of the gap occurred. About half of the gap among ethnic groups is accounted for by income differences. Income is still a very powerful factor preventing people from gaining access to e-commerce and the Internet. For the poorest one-quarter of families, the digital divide has become even wider, as wealthy families posted extraordinary gains in Internet use (U.S. Department of Commerce, 2000).

Governments have an interest in ensuring that everyone in society can participate in commerce. And as this commerce becomes increasingly electronic, govern-

CAT ORDERS VIAGRA — THE INTERNET DRUG BAZAAR

In 2001, there were over 500 online pharmacies dispensing prescription medicines in what is currently a $510 million industry that is expected to grow to $4 billion by 2004. According to the 1938 Food, Drug, and Cosmetic Act, prescription drugs may not be bought without the involvement of a physician, and must be dispensed by a state licensed pharmacy. However, e-commerce has challenged this traditional method of controlling medicines that can kill people if they are not properly dispensed and supervised.

For instance, in 1997 Dr. Pietr Hitzig filled an Internet prescription request received from Alvin Chernov in Arizona. After Chernov filled out an online questionnaire, Hitzig diagnosed Chernov's problem as stress-related depression and prescribed two powerful muscle relaxants and fen-phen, a diet drug. Six months later, Chernov committed suicide after experiencing wild mood swings. In another case, Michigan reporter used his cat's name, acknowledged under "prior surgeries" that it was neutered, but still successfully ordered Viagra for the cat!

Generally, online pharmacies are using questionnaires to diagnose disease and are supposedly having these questionnaires reviewed by doctors. Internet pharmacies are bypassing traditional safeguards. In some cases, Internet pharmacies are fly-by-night operations dispensing counterfeit drugs.

The federal government plays a role in regulating prescription medicine, but states play a much larger role in licensing physicians and pharmacies. The Food, Drug, and Cosmetic Act provides that prescription drugs cannot be sold without the involvement of a physician, and gives the Food and Drug Administration (FDA) authority to enforce that provision. However, the FDA has been slow to respond to the e-commerce sales of prescriptions or to investigate the extent of the problem.

In 1999, the Clinton administration proposed a strengthening of the FDA's powers to force compliance with existing laws, create civil penalties for illegal pharmaceutical sales, and launch a public education campaign. Congress is considering the Internet Pharmacy Consumer Protection Act, which would require Web pharmaceutical sites to identify their location, register their pharmacists, and list the states where they are licensed to practice and ship drugs. If the Web site provides medical diagnoses, doctors and other health care professionals would have to be similarly identified. The legitimate online pharmacy industry has also taken steps to protect consumers. The National Association of Boards of Pharmacy has developed a Verified Internet Pharmacy Practice Sites Program (VIPPS). This program gives a "seal of approval" for display on a site if it meets the Boards' prescribing standards. The American Medical Association has developed a similar program for self-regulation of online diagnosis.

So far, however, Congress has not passed any legislation regulating online diagnosis or prescription drug sales. Consumers could be pur-

chasing from foreign sites and not know it, and they could be purchasing bogus medicines. In this environment, the FDA urges consumers to check with the National Association of Boards of Pharmacy (www.nabp.net) before purchasing any prescription drugs from an online pharmacy.

SOURCES: "E-Drug Sales Face Scrutiny by FDA, States, and Congress," by Bob Enteen, *Internet Review*, 2001; "A Cat Can Order Viagra?" by Michael Towle, *WebMD Medical News*, May 1, 2001; "Clinton Seeks Regulation of Online Pharmacies," by Kristen Wedell, *Internet Law Journal*, March 8, 2000.

ments have taken steps to make sure that everyone can participate. In the United States, the Department of Education has undertaken programs to ensure that rural and poor urban schools receive funds to purchase computer equipment, and to train teachers in the use of the Internet. The Department of Education is spending $65 million on Community Technology Centers to develop computer learning facilities in poor communities. The National Science Foundation Advanced Networking Project is spending $6 million in 2001 to assist minority-serving schools in developing infrastructure and links to surrounding higher education institutions. There are no short-term solutions to the digital divide, but long-term efforts will be challenged to overcome longstanding and persistent wealth and educational differences between large groups in society.

9.6 CASE STUDY

There's a HailStorm
in Your Future

A social and political e-commerce issue likely to persist into the foreseeable future is Microsoft's dominance of the computer platform, including operating systems and browsers for now, but also extending in the future to e-commerce media players, text readers, authentication and payment services, content, and business services. In this book, we have identified the major areas of e-commerce as retail, services, B2B, auctions, portals, communities, and digital content. In each of these areas Microsoft will play a significant role, perhaps even a monopolistic role in some areas. It is also clear how this will occur: Microsoft has a 91% share of the PC operating system market, a 41% share of server operating systems, a 92% share of the office productivity market through its Microsoft Office products, and a 66% share of the Internet browser market. Using this foundation — one which a Federal Appeals Court in the case of operating systems recently affirmed is a monopoly attained through illegal market behavior — Microsoft plans to extend its technical platform and e-commerce applications through its .NET MyServices (formerly code-named HailStorm).

INFORMATION SILOS: NOTHING IS CONNECTED

.NET and HailStorm are responses to a common observation about the e-commerce and Internet experience: Nothing is connected to anything particularly well. E-commerce devices — from laptops to mainframes to handheld computers — can't talk to each other. Applications such as your personal calendar and Travelocity's travel booking service cannot talk to each other, and neither can your online bank and your online brokerage accounts. At every e-commerce site you visit, you need to identify yourself and fill out information about yourself. And then you instantly lose control over that information to online companies that believe they can do anything with your personal information that they want because they "own" the information about you.

.NET AND HAILSTORM

Microsoft has a solution to the Information Silo problem. .NET is Microsoft's platform for XML Web services that will allow applications to communicate and share data over the Internet regardless of operating system, programming language, or client device. .NET is a set of operating systems, Web services, Web servers, and development tools, all of which support the breakdown of information silos and the integration of diverse elements of online use and e-commerce. The .NET operating systems (such as XML-enabled Windows XP, Windows CE, Windows Embedded, and Windows 2000) will operate on diverse client devices such as game machines, laptop computers, tablet computers, handheld devices, televisions, and Internet telephones, permitting these different client machines to communicate easily. Microsoft's .NET services will allow corporate mainframes and PalmPilots to communicate with each other and any other device on the Internet. Microsoft's .NET servers will make it possible to implement and deliver XML services over the Web. And a new programming environment called VisualStudio allows programmers to develop XML applications using any of several different languages.

HailStorm is Microsoft's code name for a set of applications and saleable services built on the .NET architecture and operated online by Microsoft through a variety of venues such as MSN, Hotmail, bCentral, and future planned Web sites. There are 14 services planned now (see Table 9.17).

HailStorm services will run on Microsoft servers and Web sites. The centerpiece of HailStorm services is MS Passport (described earlier in this chapter and in Chapter 6), which acts primarily as a user-centered authentication service, but also has powerful capabilities to provide individuals greater control over their personal information. Passport stores all your personally identifiable information, and payment

TABLE 9.17	**PLANNED HAILSTORM APPLICATIONS AND SERVICES**
.Net Address	Electronic and geographic address for an identity of a business or person.
.Net Profile	Name, nickname, special dates, pictures.
.Net Contacts	Electronic relationships/address book.
.Net Location	Electronic and geographical location and rendezvous.
.Net Notifications	Notification, subscription, management, and routing.
.Net Inbox	E-mail, voice mail.
.Net Calendar	Time and task management services.
.Net Documents	Raw document storage.
.Net ApplicationSettings	Application settings.
.Net Favorite Web Sites	Favorite URLs.
.Net Wallet (Passport)	Receipts, payment instruments, coupons, transaction records.
.Net Devices	Device settings, capabilities.
.Net Services	Services provided for an identity.
.Net Usage	Usage report for above services.

method information if you choose, on Microsoft servers. Passport is the key to the kingdom, required for access to HailStorm services. Microsoft plans to bundle Passport with its XP operating system, and in order to use any of the new Web-based services available with XP, such as additional PowerPoint slide templates or clip art, you will need to obtain a Microsoft Passport. In the current version of XP, for instance, the first time a user connects to the Web, the following message appears: "You've just connected to the Internet. You need a Passport to use Windows XP Internet communications features (such as instant messaging, voice chat, and video) and to access .Net enabled features. Click here to set up your Passport."

HailStorm services authenticated by Passport are intended to create a "user-centric" model of computing and Internet services that focuses on integration of user services, one-stop identity, shopping, and purchasing, and far greater privacy protection than existing e-commerce technology provides.

THE SUBSCRIPTION BUSINESS MODEL

Microsoft will operate HailStorm as a business using a subscription revenue model similar to AOL or cable television. Microsoft has clearly decided that it is much more lucrative to receive, say, $21.95 per month from every HailStorm user, than to receive $250 every second or third year from every user of MS Office who wants to upgrade. In addition, Microsoft plans to license these capabilities to other Web sites and businesses that will integrate these capabilities into their site, rather than build them themselves. So, for instance, an online book store can add a gift service allowing customers to purchase gifts for their friend's birthdays using Microsoft's .Net Profile Web service. The bookstore would simply build a simple XML query to Microsoft's .Net Profile Web site and database.

SOCIAL AND POLITICAL ISSUES: OVERSIGHT AND CONTROL OF MONOPOLIES

Monopolies can have many social and economic benefits. Obviously, it is much better for society if there is a single set of telephone system standards, a single railroad standard, and a single electricity standard. In certain areas of economic life, "natural monopolies" occur — such as water companies — and often regulated monopolies are granted rights to operate in the public interest. When this happens in the United States, as in the case of public utilities, special state and federal commissions are established to ensure that monopolies do not engage in predatory pricing behavior and consumers and society will benefit from network economies — the fact that everyone is using the same standard utility.

Monopolies also have social costs, and in the United States they have been officially frowned upon since the Sherman Anti-Trust Act of 1890 broke up the steel monopoly of J.P. Morgan and later the oil monopoly of John Rockefeller. Monopolies can engage in predatory pricing behavior to drive competitors out of business, threaten new entrants to the marketplace, and raise prices above what a competitive marketplace would produce. As a result, they can stifle innovation. The Sherman Anti-Trust Act does not declare monopolies illegal, but it does proscribe monopolistic anticompetitive behavior intended to either create or sustain a monopoly.

Since the early 1990s, the U.S. Department of Justice has been monitoring Microsoft's market behavior. It has found a consistent pattern of monopolistic and anticompetitive behavior. In 1994, Microsoft consented to a Justice Department decree that it stop tying the purchase of one product to that of another — say, the operating system to an office productivity suite. In 1996, the Justice Department began investigating Microsoft's dominance of the operating system and browser markets, and in particular the tying together of the operating system and the browser. In October 1997, the Justice Department filed a petition against Microsoft, alleging it was violating the 1994 consent decree by forcing PC manufacturers to install the Internet Explorer browser as a condition of offering Windows. In May 1998, the Justice Department and various state attorneys filed an antitrust lawsuit against Microsoft, claiming it was engaging in illegal, anticompetitive practices to destroy competition. In June 2000, a U.S. District Judge found Microsoft guilty of violating antitrust laws in the operating system and browser markets, and recommended breaking up the company into two parts. A U.S. Court of Appeals court in June 2001 accepted the finding on operating systems, but rejected the charge of monopolizing the browser market. Microsoft has recently abandoned its anticompetitive licensing practices that forced PC manufacturers to display Microsoft icons on the desktop, and discarded plans for the XP operating system to use SmartTags to link users of MS Office tools to Microsoft Web sites and services.

The question is: Do we, as a society, want Microsoft to dominate the e-commerce environment just as it has dominated the operating system and browser marketplace? If .NET and HailStorm succeed, Microsoft will not only supply the operating system of all your devices, the browser, and office productivity tools, but will also supply all the vital e-commerce and personal information management tools required to lead a digital life. The centerpiece of these strategies — Passport — will supply your digital ID and will handle the payment process as well for much of B2C e-commerce. Microsoft will become the repository of personal identifiable information for tens of millions of e-commerce consumers.

Some extraordinary consumer benefits will result from these services. Many of the digital information silos will disappear, e-commerce transactions costs will fall, and consumers will have greater control over their personal information.

However, .NET and HailStorm raise some very interesting questions. If .NET and HailStorm succeed, it is likely that other firms will not be able to compete with Microsoft in providing similar services because Microsoft already controls the operating system and the browser. Microsoft can simply integrate .NET and HailStorm

SOURCES: "Privacy Group Taking Issue With Microsoft," by Steve Lohn, *New York Times*, July 25, 2001; "Appeals Court Voids Order For Breaking Up Microsoft But Finds It Abused Power," by Stephen Labaton, *New York Times*, June 29, 2001; "Making A Judgment On a Moving Target," by John Markoff, *New York Times*, June 29, 2001; "Microsoft Backs Off Plan to Add Its Links to Other's Web Sites," by Walter S. Mosberg, *Wall Street Journal*, June 28, 2001; www.microsoft.com/net/ hailstorm.asp; www.microsoft.com/ net/whatis.asp.

services into its browser and operating system platforms where few other firms — if any — can compete. Microsoft may, as it has in the past, engage in monopolistic anti-competitive behavior through its licensing process. For instance, it may refuse to license .NET and HailStorm services to Web sites that also use competing services from AOL.

Do we want a single company to dominate e-commerce authentication and payment services? Passport stores your vital personal and payment information on Microsoft servers, but who watches over Microsoft? If Microsoft is allowed to establish a dominant position in providing Web-based personal services such as those described in Table 9.17, what kinds of regulatory or oversight mechanisms can control this much power? Can market forces and consumer opinion work by themselves to keep Microsoft in check?

In July 2001, a privacy advocacy group, Electronic Privacy Information Center (EPIC), announced it would file a formal complaint about Passport with the Federal Trade Commission under Section 5 of the Federal Trade Commission Act, which prohibits unfair or deceptive trade practices. The Microsoft executive in charge of Passport said: "We totally acknowledge that we have a perception problem ... And we understand that the key challenge we face with HailStorm and Passport is trust. For Passport and these services to gain any success any adoption, we have to gain the trust of both end users and industry partners."

Case Study Questions

1. There are "structural" and "conduct" remedies for dealing with the potential for Microsoft's future dominance of e-commerce. Structural remedies generally break up monopolies into small units. Conduct remedies generally proscribe certain conduct and involve continued oversight by courts and the Justice Department. What kinds of remedies do you think are best for ensuring Microsoft does not stifle competition and engage in monopolistic behavior that might harm e-commerce? Do you think consumers and market forces can contain Microsoft's behavior? Is any regulation necessary?

2. Examine Microsoft's planned HailStorm services in Table 9.17. Would you be interested in using these services? What benefits and dangers do you see in each service?

3. If you were to build an e-commerce B2C Web site, how could you use HailStorm services to help your business? What value propositions would you offer your customers based on HailStorm services?

4. If trust is so important to the success of Passport, what measures do you recommend Microsoft take to build trust among e-commerce customers?

5. Can Microsoft be trusted as a repository for personal information for millions of consumers? Who should provide oversight and ensure that abuses do not occur?

9.7 REVIEW

KEY CONCEPTS

■ **Understand why e-commerce raises ethical, social, and political issues.**

Internet technology and its use in e-commerce disrupts existing social and business relationships and understandings. Suddenly, individuals, business firms, and political institutions are confronted by new possibilities of behavior for which understandings, laws, and rules of acceptable behavior have not yet been developed. Many business firms and individuals are benefiting from the commercial development of the Internet, but this development also has costs for individuals, organizations, and societies. These costs and benefits must be carefully considered by those seeking to make ethical and socially responsible decisions in this new environment, particularly where there are as yet no clear-cut legal or cultural guidelines.

■ **Recognize the main ethical, social, and political issues raised by e-commerce.**

The major issues raised by e-commerce can be loosely categorized into four major dimensions:

- *Information rights:* What rights do individuals have to control their own personal information when Internet technologies make information collection so pervasive and efficient?
- *Property rights:* How can traditional intellectual property rights be enforced when perfect copies of protected works can be made and easily distributed worldwide via the Internet?
- *Governance:* Should the Internet and e-commerce be subject to public laws? If so, what law-making bodies have jurisdiction — state, federal, and/or international?
- *Public safety and welfare:* What efforts should be undertaken to ensure equitable access to the Internet and e-commerce channels? Do certain online content and activities pose a threat to public safety and welfare?

■ **Identify a process for analyzing ethical dilemmas.**

Ethical, social, and political controversies usually present themselves as dilemmas. Ethical dilemmas can be analyzed via the following process:

- Identify and describe clearly the facts.
- Define the conflict or dilemma and identify the higher-order values involved.
- Identify the stakeholders.
- Identify the options that you can reasonably take.
- Identify the potential consequences of your options.
- Refer to well-established ethical principles, such as the Golden Rule, Universalism, Descartes' Rule of Change, the Collective Utilitarian Principle, Risk Aversion, the No Free Lunch Rule, the *New York Times* Test, and the Social Contract Rule to help you decide the matter.

■ **Identify the practices of e-commerce companies that threaten privacy.**

Almost all e-commerce companies collect personally identifiable information and use cookies to track clickstream behavior of visitors. A majority of all Web sites and over 75% of the most popular 100 sites allow third parties such as advertising networks to place cookies on a visitor's hard drive in order to engage in profiling and track visitor browsing behavior on the Web.

■ **Understand basic concepts related to privacy.**

To understand the issues concerning online privacy, you must first understand some basic concepts:

- *Privacy* is the moral right of individuals to be left alone, free from surveillance or interference from others.
- *Information privacy* includes both the claim that certain information should not be collected at all by governments or business firms, and the claim of individuals to control the use of information about themselves.
- *Due process* as embodied by the Fair Information Practices doctrine, informed consent, and opt-in/opt-out policies also play an important role in privacy.

■ **Describe the different methods used to protect online privacy.**

There are a number of different methods used to protect online privacy. They include:

- *Legal protections* deriving from constitutions, common law, federal law, state laws, and government regulations. In the United States, rights to online privacy may be derived the U.S. Constitution, tort law, federal laws such as the Children's Online Privacy Protection Act, the Federal Trade Commission's Fair Information Practice Principles, and a variety of state laws. In Europe, the European Commission's Directive on Data Protection has standardized and broadened privacy protection in the European Union nations.
- *Industry self-regulation* via industry alliances such as the Online Privacy Alliance and the Network Advertising Initiative that seek to gain voluntary adherence to industry privacy guidelines and safe harbors. Some firms also hire chief privacy officers.

- *Privacy-enhancing technological solutions* include secure e-mail, anonymous remailers, anonymous surfing, cookie managers, disk file erasing programs, policy generators, and privacy policy readers.

■ **Understand the various forms of intellectual property and the challenge of protecting it.**

There are three main types of intellectual property protection: copyright, patent, and trademark law.

- *Copyright law* protects original forms of expression such as writings, drawings, and computer programs from being copied by others for a minimum of 50 years. It does not protect ideas — just their expression in a tangible medium. "Look and feel" copyright infringement lawsuits are precisely about the distinction between an idea and its expression. If there is only one way to express an idea, then the expression cannot be copyrighted (*Apple* v. *Microsoft* and *Brown Bag Software* v. *Symantec Corp*). Copyrights, like all rights, are not absolute. The doctrine of fair use permits certain parties under certain circumstances to use copyrighted material without permission. The Digital Millennium Copyright Act (DMCA) is the first major effort to adjust the copyright laws to the Internet Age. The DMCA implements a World Intellectual Property Organization treaty, which declares it illegal to make, distribute, or use devices that circumvent technology-based protections of copyrighted materials, and attaches stiff fines and prison sentences for violations.

- *Patent law* grants the owner of a patent an exclusive monopoly to the ideas behind an invention for twenty years. Patents are very different from copyrights in that they protect the ideas themselves and not merely the expression of ideas. There are four types of inventions for which patents are granted under patent law: machines, man-made products, compositions of matter, and processing methods. In order to be granted a patent, the applicant must show that the invention is new, original, novel, non-obvious, and not evident in prior arts and practice. Most of the inventions that make the Internet and e-commerce possible were not patented by their inventors. This changed in the mid-1990s with the commercial development of the World Wide Web. Business firms began applying for "business methods" and software patents.

- *Trademark protections* exist at both the federal and state levels in the United States. The purpose of trademark law is twofold. First, trademark law protects the public in the marketplace by ensuring that it gets what it pays for and wants to receive. Second, trademark law protects the owner who has spent time, money, and energy bringing the product to market against piracy and misappropriation. Federal trademarks are obtained, first, by use in interstate commerce, and second, by registration with the U.S. Patent and Trademark Office (USPTO). Trademarks are granted for a period of ten years and can be renewed indefinitely. Use of a trademark that creates confusion with existing trademarks, causes consumers to make market mistakes, or misrepresents the origins of goods is an infringement. In addition, the intentional misuse of words and symbols in the marketplace to extort revenue from legitimate trademark owners ("bad faith") is proscribed. The Anticybersquatting Consumer Protection Act (ACPA) creates civil liabilities for anyone who attempts in bad faith to profit from an existing famous or distinctive trademark by registering an Internet domain name that is identical, confusingly similar, or "dilutive" of that trademark. Trademark abuse can take many forms on the Web. The major behaviors on the Internet that have run afoul of trademark law include cybersquatting, cyberpiracy, metatagging, keywording, linking, and framing.

■ **Understand how governance of the Internet has evolved over time.**

Governance has to do with social control: who will control e-commerce, what elements will be controlled, and how the controls will be implemented. Governance of both the Internet and e-commerce has gone through four stages:

- *Government control* (1970–1994). During this period, DARPA and the National Science Foundation control the Internet as a fully government funded program.
- *Privatization* (1995–1998). Network Solutions is given a monopoly to assign and track high-level Internet domain names. The backbone is sold to private telecommunications companies and policy issues are undecided.
- *Self-regulation* (1995–present). President Clinton and the Department of Commerce encourage creation of ICANN, a semi-private body, to deal with emerging conflicts and to establish policies.
- *Governmental regulation* (1998–present). Executive, legislative, and judicial bodies worldwide begin to implement direct controls over the Internet and e-commerce.

We are currently in a mixed-mode policy environment where self-regulation, through a variety of Internet policy and technical bodies, co-exists with limited government regulation.

■ **Explain why taxation of e-commerce raises governance and jurisdiction issues.**

E-commerce raises the issue of how — and if — to tax remote sales. The national and international character of Internet sales is wreaking havoc on taxation schemes in the United States that were built in the 1930s and based on local commerce and local jurisdictions. E-commerce has benefited from a tax subsidy since its inception. E-commerce merchants have argued that this new form of commerce needs to be nurtured and encouraged in its early years, and that in any event, the crazy quilt of sales and use tax regimes would be difficult to administer for Internet merchants. In 1998, Congress passed the Internet Tax Freedom Act that placed a moratorium on any taxation of e-commerce sales for three years until October 2001. As of September 2001, bills to extend the moratorium were being considered by the both the House and Senate, with passage considered likely, although not definite. Although there appears to be acquiescence among large Internet retailers to the idea of some kind of sales tax on e-commerce sales, insistence on uniformity will delay taxation for many years, and any proposal to tax e-commerce will likely incur the wrath of 60 million U.S. e-commerce consumers.

- Identify major public safety and welfare issues raised by e-commerce.

Critical public safety and welfare issues in e-commerce include:

- *The protection of children and strong sentiments against pornography.* The Children's Online Protection Act (COPA) of 1998 made it a felony criminal offense to communicate for commercial purposes any material harmful to minors. This law has been struck down by a federal district court as an unconstitutional restriction on Web content that was protected under the First Amendment. The ruling is currently being appealed. In addition to government regulation, private pressure from organized groups has also been successful in forcing some Web sites to eliminate the display of pornographic materials.

- *Efforts to control gambling and restrict sales of drugs and cigarettes.* In the United States, gambling, cigarettes, medical drugs, and addictive recreational drugs are either banned or tightly regulated by federal and state laws. Yet these products and services are often distributed via offshore e-commerce sites operating beyond the jurisdiction of federal and state prosecutors. However, the development of geolocation software could lead to a kind of Internet zoning, where users would be required to submit a digital passport before they are allowed access to sites containing proscribed content. At this point, it is not clear that the Web will remain borderless or that e-commerce can continue to flaunt national, state, and local laws with impunity.

QUESTIONS

1. What basic assumption does the study of ethics make about individuals?
2. What are the three basic principles of ethics? How does due process factor in?
3. Explain Napster's position that it is a legitimate business, based on the three principles of ethics.
4. Define universalism, slippery slope, the *New York Times* test, and the social contract rule as they apply to ethics.
5. Explain why someone with a serious medical condition might be concerned about researching his or her condition online, through medical search engines or pharmaceutical sites, for example. What is one technology that could prevent one's identity from being revealed?
6. Name some of the personal information collected by Web sites about their visitors.
7. How does information collected through online forms differ from site transaction logs? Which potentially provides a more complete consumer profile?
8. How is the opt-in model of informed consent different from opt-out? In which type of model does the consumer retain more control?
9. What are the two core principles of the FTC's Fair Information Practice Principles?
10. How do safe harbors work? What is the government's role in them?

11. Name three ways online advertising networks have improved on, or added to, traditional offline marketing techniques.

12. Explain how Web profiling is supposed to benefit both consumers and businesses.

13. What are some of the challenges that Chief Privacy Officers face in their jobs?

14. How could the Internet potentially change protection given to intellectual property? What capabilities make it more difficult to enforce intellectual property law?

15. What does the Digital Millennium Copyright Act attempt to do? Why was it enacted? What types of violations does it try to prevent?

16. Define cybersquatting. How is it different from cyberpiracy? What type of intellectual property violation does cybersquatting entail?

17. What is deep linking and why is it a trademark issue? Compare it to framing — how is it similar and different?

18. What are some of the tactics illegal businesses, such as betting parlors and casinos, successfully use to operate outside the law on the Internet?

19. What kind of technology could be used to create Internet zones to limit access to certain parts of the Web based on geographic location?

20. Why are Microsoft's .NET and HailStorm projects considered potential threats to privacy? What are the key issues at stake in the development of these products?

PROJECTS

1. Go to www.aol.com or www.lycos.com and activate the parental controls option. Now surf the Web in search of content that could be considered objectionable for children, to see how the parental controls function works. What are the pros and cons of such restrictions? Are there terms that could be considered inappropriate to the software but be approved by parents? Name five questionable terms. Prepare a brief PowerPoint or other form of presentation to report on your experiences and to explain the positive and negative aspects of such filtering software.

2. Consider the case of Dmitri Sklyarov and ElcomSoft discussed at the beginning of the chapter. Prepare a list of reasons why code breakers such as Sklyarov should and should not be permitted to publish the results of their research. What moral dilemmas present themselves? What higher order values, and what kinds of value conflicts, are revealed in these lists? How do you propose that we as a society resolve these dilemmas? You might conclude by applying each of the Candidate Ethical Principles described in Section 9.1.

3. Develop a list a privacy protection features that should be present if a Web site is serious about protecting privacy. Then, visit at least four well-known Web sites and examine their privacy policies. Write a report that rates each of the Web sites on the criteria you have developed.

4. Review the provisions of the Digital Millennium Copyright Act of 1998. Examine each of the major sections of the legislation and make a list of the protections afforded property owners and users of copyrighted materials. Do you believe this legislation balances the interests of owners and users appropriately? Do you have suggestions for strengthening "fair use" provisions in this legislation?

5. Visit at least four Web sites that take a position on e-commerce taxation beginning with The National Conference of State Legislatures (www.ncsl.org) and The National Governor's Association (www.nga.org). You might also include national associations of local businesses or citizen groups opposed to e-commerce taxation. Develop a reasoned argument for, or against, taxation of e-commerce.

WEB SITE RESOURCES **www.LearnE-commerce.net**

- News: Weekly updates on topics relevant to the material in this chapter
- Video Lecture: Professor Ken Laudon sumarizes the key concepts of the chapter
- Research: Abstracts and links to articles referenced in the chapter, as well as other relevant research
- International Spotlight: More information about ethical, social, and political issues related to e-commerce outside the United States
- PowerPoint Slides: Illustrations from the chapter and more
- Additional projects and exercises

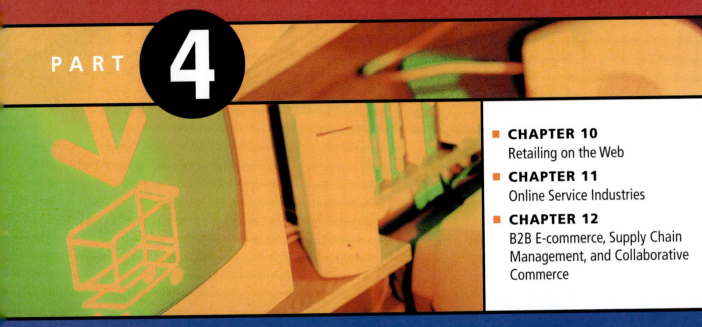

E-commerce in Action

CHAPTER 10

Retailing on the Web

After reading this chapter, you will be able to:

- Identify the major features of the retail sector.
- Describe the vision of online retailing in the E-commerce I period.
- Understand the environment in which the online retail sector operates today.
- Explain how to analyze the economic viability of an online firm.
- Identify the challenges faced by the different types of online retailers.

Wal-Mart Moves Online

Although Bentonville, Arkansas-based Wal-Mart is the world's largest retailer, with sales of more than $191 billion in 2000 generated through its 4,189 locations worldwide, its Web site ranks only in the top 50 — somewhat surprising given its huge customer base. Offline, Wal-Mart dwarfs JCPenney ($31 billion in sales), Sears ($32 billion), Target ($36 billion), and Kmart ($36 billion). About 100 million Americans shop at its 2,295 U.S. stores each week. Wal-Mart is so large and successful that its sales revenues equal the combined sales of the top ten other national retail chains in the United States. However, its performance on the Web is another matter.

Wal-Mart created a Web storefront in 1995, but has redesigned and redeveloped it several times since then in an attempt to improve its performance. The site was relaunched with a new design that more closely reflected the "look and feel" of its retail facilities in January 2000. The product mix was also changed to include toys and electronics, and customization technology from Broadvision was adopted that allows visitors from different geographical locations to see special promotions on local items. Airline tickets and travel packages were added in 2001. Some 2.2 million people visited the Walmart.com Web site in April 2001, a big improvement from April 2000, but Wal-Mart's Web traffic is still lagging far behind the impressive 18.2 million people who shopped at Amazon.com in April 2001. Why isn't Wal-Mart doing as well online as it is offline?

Increasingly, established "multichannel" retailers are winning a larger share of the online retail market when pitted against "pure plays" such as the now-defunct Pets.com and eToys. But in order to be successful on the Web, brick-and-mortar retailers need to create an integrated shopping environment that allows customers to move from one channel to another seamlessly. Wal-Mart needs to erase the line between its physical storefronts and their online equivalent in order to succeed in the long term. That means allowing customers to return online purchases at offline stores, to make online purchases while visiting physical stores, and to return products purchased in stores to online product service centers. Trying to make a product return without a receipt today requires a call to the customer service center to check on pricing. Synchronizing online and offline pricing will also be required because in-store prices don't always match online prices. And making the Wal-Mart site even easier and more exciting to use will help boost sales.

Wal-Mart also faces competition from other established multichannel online retailers such as Kmart, JCPenney, Target, and Sears. For instance, using T-1 lines already installed in 1,100 brick-and-mortar stores, Kmart installed 3,500 in-store kiosks directly connected to its BlueLight.com Web site. Previously, its kiosks had been attached to in-store CD-ROMs or to a corporate Intranet. Store staffs were retrained to direct shoppers unable to find a product in the store to look for it online using the kiosks. Then Kmart relaunched its free ISP services program. Anyone can get 12 hours of Internet access for free, but if you purchase anything at BlueLight.com, you get six 100-hour months of Internet access. Kmart also places sales inserts in 72 million Sunday newspapers that advertise bargains both at stores and at BlueLight.com.

The results of Kmart's efforts have been impressive. BlueLight.com jumped to the number two destination retail site with 2.8 million visitors (following Sears at 2.9 million visitors) in April 2001. A remarkable 20% of BlueLight.com's traffic came from in-store kiosks. The ISP rewards program also worked better than expected: BlueLight.com's sales to ISP customers jumped 56%.

Although the competition may be stiff, Wal-Mart has some strong advantages, including an extremely strong brand name and the world's most efficient retailing distribution system, coupled with extraordinary financial muscle and resources. These assets provide both a loyal customer base that is increasingly going online to shop and purchase, and the cash to nurture and develop its growing online enterprise. Wal-Mart has laid a strong foundation for future online growth, starting with its impressive logistics system that enables the company and its suppliers to track merchandise sales by unit, store, or region, as well as to review inventory levels and returns in real time. However, successfully leveraging its capabilities and considerable financial assets to the Web will require careful planning and insight.

SOURCES: Wal-Mart 2001 Annual Report; "Traditional Retailers Gaining Online Market Share as Web-Only Brands Falter," by Todd Pack, *The Orlando Sentinel*, June 10, 2001; "Once Ridiculed, He's Now Carving Out Dot-Com Niche," by Kevin Maney, *USA Today*, April 4, 2001; "Selling Strategies — People Like Us: The Net Takes Customized Marketing to a Whole New Level," by Stephanie Miles, *Wall Street Journal*, April 23, 2001; "E-Business Credo: Meet Commitments to Customers," by Robert Preston, *InternetWeek*, March 5, 2001; "Many Hands Make Site Work," by Jacqueline Emigh, *E-Business*, February 16, 2000.

The Wal-Mart case illustrates the advantages of traditional offline merchants for becoming powerful e-commerce retailers. Established offline retailers such as Wal-Mart, JCPenney, Sears, and Target have established brand names, a loyal customer base, and, in the case of Wal-Mart, extraordinarily efficient inventory control and fulfillment systems. As we shall see in this chapter, traditional offline catalog merchants are even more advantaged. Yet the Wal-Mart case also illustrates that in order to leverage their assets and core competencies, established offline retailers need to cultivate new competencies and a carefully developed business plan.

In this chapter, we review the recent experience of online retail e-commerce and place online retail commerce in the context of all retail commerce (including offline retail). In the process, we will analyze six online retail companies that exemplify the major types of online retailing.

10.1 THE RETAIL SECTOR

By any measure, the size of the U.S. retail market is huge. In a $9.2 trillion economy, personal consumption of retail goods and services accounts for about $6.2 trillion (about 63%) of total gross domestic product (GDP) — or nearly two-thirds of all economic activity (see Figure 10.1).

If we examine the personal consumption sector more closely, we find that 56% of personal consumption is for services, 14% is for durable goods, and 30% is for nondurable goods. Services include medical, educational, financial, and food services. **Durable goods** are those that are consumed over a longer period of time (generally more than a year), such as automobiles, appliances, and furniture. **Nondurable goods** are consumed quickly and have shorter life spans, and include general merchandise, clothing, music, drugs, and groceries.

The distinction between a "good" and a "service" is not always clear cut, and is becoming more ambiguous over time. Increasingly, manufacturers and retailers of physical goods sell support services that add value to the physical product. It is difficult to think of a sophisticated physical good that does not include significant services in the purchase price. The movement toward "product-based services" can be seen in the packaged software market. Microsoft's new Windows XP and Office XP, and its forthcoming .NET product line, offer purchasers of the products additional value-added services from a variety of Microsoft Web sites. Charging for services, particularly on a monthly subscription basis, can be highly profitable. For instance, warranties, insurance policies, after-sale repairs, and purchase loans are increasingly a large source of revenue for manufacturers and retailers. Nevertheless, in this chapter, *retail goods* refer to physical products, and *retailers* refer to firms that sell physical

durable goods
goods that are consumed over a longer period of time (generally more than a year)

nondurable goods
goods that are consumed quickly and have shorter life spans

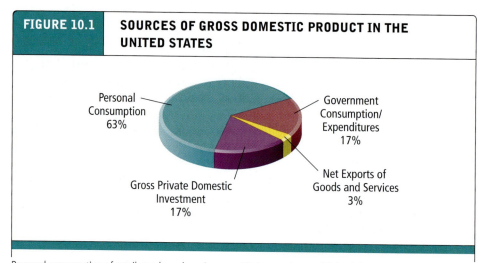

FIGURE 10.1

SOURCES OF GROSS DOMESTIC PRODUCT IN THE UNITED STATES

Personal Consumption 63%

Government Consumption/ Expenditures 17%

Net Exports of Goods and Services 3%

Gross Private Domestic Investment 17%

Personal consumption of retail goods and services constitutes nearly two-thirds of the U.S. economy.
SOURCE: Table 715, Statistical Abstract of the United States, 2000.

goods to consumers, recognizing that retail goods include many services. We focus on the retail services industries in Chapter 11.

THE RETAIL INDUSTRY

The retail industry is composed of many different types of firms. Figure 10.2 divides the retail industry into eight major types of firms based on the kinds of products sold: durable goods, general merchandise, groceries, specialty stores, gasoline and fuel, eating and drinking, MOTO (mail order/telephone), and online retail firms.

Each of these segments offers opportunities for online retail, and yet in each segment the uses of the Internet may differ. Some eating and drinking establishments use the Web to inform people of their physical locations and menus, while others offer delivery via Web orders (although this has not been a successful model). Given that consumers primarily purchase small-ticket nondurable items on the Web (as described in Chapter 7), retailers of durable goods typically use the Web as an informational tool rather than as a direct purchasing tool. For instance, automobile manufacturers still do not sell cars over the Web, but they do provide information to assist customers in choosing among competing models.

The biggest opportunities for direct online sales are within those segments that sell small-ticket items (generally less than $100). This includes specialty stores (apparel, shoes, sporting goods), general merchandisers, mail order catalogs, and groceries. There seem to be few online opportunities for gasoline and fuel dealers,

---

FIGURE 10.2 **COMPOSITION OF THE U.S. RETAIL INDUSTRY**

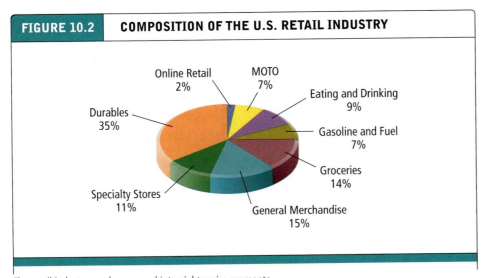

The retail industry can be grouped into eight major segments.

SOURCE: Estimated Monthly Retail Sales, by Kinds of Business, U.S. Census, January 2000 to December 2000.

although Priceline did attempt to enter this market in 1999 by offering discounted gasoline coupons at subscribing gas stations. This model did not work and was discontinued.

The largest segments of the U.S. retail market are general merchandisers and grocery stores. Both segments, particularly general merchandise, are highly concentrated with large firms dominating sales (see Table 10.1). These very large firms have developed highly automated real-time inventory control systems (systems that collect point-of-sale data from cash registers, update inventory records, and inform vendors of stock levels), large national customer bases, and customer databases containing detailed purchasing information.

The mail order/telephone order (MOTO) sector is the most similar to the online retail sales sector. In the absence of physical stores, MOTO retailers distribute millions of physical catalogs (their largest expense) and operate large telephone call centers to accept orders. They have developed extraordinarily efficient order fulfillment centers that generally ship customer orders within 24 hours of receipt. MOTO was the fastest growing retail segment throughout the 1970s and 1980s. It grew as a direct result of improvements in the national toll-free call system, falling long distance telecommunications prices, and of course, the growth of the credit card industry and associated technologies without which neither MOTO nor e-commerce would be possible on a large national scale. MOTO was the last "technological" retailing revolution that preceded e-commerce. See Table 10.2 for a list of the leading MOTO retailers in 2000.

TABLE 10.1	THE TOP TEN GENERAL MERCHANDISERS
NAME	**2000 REVENUES**
Wal-Mart	$191,329,000,000
Kmart	$ 37,028,000,000
Target	$ 36,728,000,000
Costco	$ 33,702,000,000
Sears	$ 32,164,296,000
JCPenney	$ 31,846,000,000
Federated Department Stores	$ 17,716,000,000
Fred Meyer	$ 14,878,771,000
May Department Stores	$ 13,869,000,000

SOURCE: Form 10-K filings with the Securities and Exchange Commission, 2000.

TABLE 10.2	THE TOP TEN MOTO RETAILERS (2000)
NAME	**2000 REVENUES**
Spiegel Inc.	3,724,778,000
Lands' End Inc.	1,462,283,000
PC Connection	1,449,908,000
Blair Corp.	619,388,739
Hanover Direct Inc.	603,014,000
Coldwater Creek Inc.	458,445,000
ValueVision International Inc.	385,940,000
Lillian Vernon Corp.	287,094,000
J Jill Group Inc.	250,281,000
E4L Inc.	241,111,000
Sportsmans Guide Inc.	154,938,000

SOURCE: Form 10-K filings with the Securities and Exchange Commission, 2000.

Like general merchandisers, MOTO retailers have sophisticated inventory control systems, substantial customer databases, and large scale, giving them significant market power over vendors. In addition, MOTO retailers are advantaged in online retailing because they also have very effective order fulfillment systems and procedures — something with which general merchandisers have little experience. For these reasons, MOTO retailers are among the fastest growing online retail firms in the E-commerce II period.

ONLINE RETAILING

Online retail is perhaps the most high-profile sector of e-commerce on the Web. Over the past seven years, this sector has experienced both explosive growth and spectacular failures.

Many of the new firms that pioneered the retail marketspace have failed, and many others are struggling to stay afloat. Entrepreneurs and their investors seriously misjudged the factors needed to succeed in this market. Despite those failures, online retail remains an important part of the e-commerce story.

E-commerce I: The Vision

In the E-commerce I period, literally thousands of entrepreneurial Web-based retailers were drawn to the $2.7 trillion marketplace for retail goods simply because it was one of the largest market opportunities in the U.S. economy. Many entrepreneurs initially believed it was easy to enter the retail market. Early writers predicted that the retail industry, the largest single segment in the U.S. economy, would be revolutionized, literally "blown to bits" — as prophesized by two consultants in a famous Harvard Business School book (Evans and Wurster, 2000). The basis of this revolution would be fourfold. First, because the Internet greatly reduced both search costs and transaction costs, consumers would use the Internet to find the lowest cost products. Several results would follow. Consumers would increasingly drift to the Web for shopping and purchasing, and only low-cost, high-service, quality online retail merchants would survive. Economists assumed the Web consumer was rational and cost-driven — not perceived-value or brand-driven, both of which are nonrational factors.

Second, it was assumed that the entry costs to the online retail market were much less than those needed to establish physical store fronts, and that online merchants were inherently more efficient at marketing and order fulfillment than offline stores. The costs of establishing a powerful Web site were thought to be minuscule compared to the costs of warehouses, fulfillment centers, and physical stores. There would be no difficulty building sophisticated order entry, shopping cart, and fulfillment systems because this technology was well known, and the cost of technology was falling by 50% each year. Even the cost of acquiring consumers was thought to be much lower on the Web because of search engines that could almost instantly connect customers to online vendors.

Third, as prices fell, traditional offline physical store merchants would be forced out of business. New entrepreneurial companies — such as Amazon — would replace the traditional stores. It was thought that if online merchants grew very quickly, they would have first mover advantages and lock out the older traditional firms that were too slow to enter the online market.

Fourth, in some industries — such as electronics, apparel, and digital content — the market would be disintermediated as manufacturers or their distributors entered to build a direct relationship with the consumer, destroying the retail intermediaries or middlemen. In this scenario, traditional retail channels — such as physical stores, sales clerks, and sales forces — would be replaced by a single dominant channel: the Web.

Many predicted, on the other hand, a kind of hypermediation based on the concept of a virtual firm in which online retailers would gain advantage over established offline merchants by outsourcing the warehousing and order fulfillment functions — the original concept of Amazon and Drugstore.com.

As it turned out, few of these assumptions were correct, and the structure of the retail marketplace in the United States has not been blown to bits, disintermediated, or revolutionized in the traditional meaning of the word revolution. Online retail has not been successful as an independent platform on which to build a successful "pure play" Web-only business. However, the Internet has created an entirely new venue for multichannel firms that have a strong offline brand. The Web has created a new marketplace for consumers to conveniently shop. The new online channel can compete with other channels such as direct sales forces, physical stores, and mail order, but this multichannel competition can be managed.

E-commerce II: The Online Retail Sector Today

Although online retailing is the smallest segment of the retail industry, constituting about 2% of the total retail market today, it is continuing to grow at an exceptionally fast rate, with new functionality and product lines being added every day (see Figure 10.3). Despite the high failure rate of online retailers, more consumers than ever are shopping online. As of April 2001, 100.2 million people (nearly half of the total U.S. population over 18 years of age) and over 80% of all individuals with Internet access had purchased something online (Nielsen/NetRatings, 2001). Also, as noted in Chapter 7, millions of additional consumers research products on the Web and are influenced in their purchase decisions at offline stores.

The primary beneficiaries of this growing consumer support are not the first-mover dot.com companies, but rather the established offline retailers who have the brand name recognition, supportive infrastructure, and financial resources to fill the gaps left by failed online retailers. Gone are the innovative, brash, young entrepreneurs and their upstart niche companies backed by much older venture capitalists and pension fund managers. In are the offline giants who are reaping the financial value from methods pioneered by the now-departed innovators.

FIGURE 10.3	ONLINE RETAIL IS ALIVE AND WELL

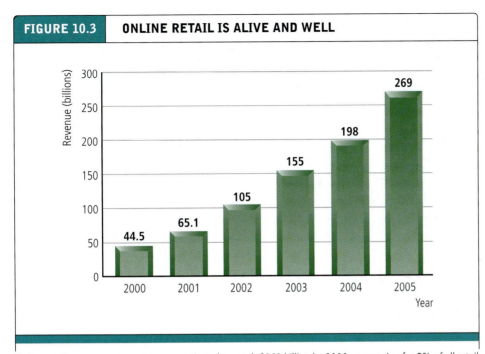

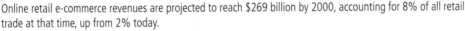

Online retail e-commerce revenues are projected to reach $269 billion by 2000, accounting for 8% of all retail trade at that time, up from 2% today.

SOURCE: Boston Consulting Group, 2001; Dykema, 2000.

Table 10.3 lists some top online retail success stories based on share of the online purchasing audience. (Note that although they have been categorized as "e-tailers" by the firm compiling the report, we would place some of these firms, such as travelocity.com, southwest.com, and others into other categories, such as service firms.) Many of these firms are not yet profitable. Yet these sites are successful in the sense that they have attracted large audiences. Their challenge is to convert this audience share into a profitable business. Amazon and eBay together account for almost a third of all online shopping and have the strongest brand names (note that because Half.com is owned by eBay, eBay actually has a larger audience share than shown), and the top ten online retailers together account for more than half of all purchasing online.

As the E-commerce II period begins, established offline retailers are rapidly gaining market share. The new challengers in E-commerce II are the awakening general merchandising giants such as Wal-Mart, Target, JCPenney, and the catalog-based retailers such as L.L. Bean, Lands' End, and Columbia House (retailer of music). JCPenney, for instance, has rocketed from no online presence two years ago to a ranking in the top ten retail sites today (Table 10.3). Increasingly, consumers are

TABLE 10.3	TOP TEN E-TAILERS RANKED BY SHARE OF ONLINE PURCHASING AUDIENCE (MARCH 2001)	
COMPANY	UNIQUE AUDIENCE (IN MILLIONS)	SHARE OF ONLINE PURCHASING AUDIENCE
Amazon.com	22,751	15.10%
eBay.com	18,987	14.50%
BMG.com	4,762	4.30%
Barnes&Noble.com	5,948	3.80%
ColumbiaHouse.com	2,723	3.70%
Half.com	4,939	3.10%
JCPenney.com	3,339	3.00%
Travelocity.com	7,966	2.50%
CDNow.com	5,295	2.20%
Southwest.com	3,954	2.00%
TOTAL		54.20%

SOURCE: Nielsen/Net Ratings and Harris Interactive eCommercePulse, March 2001.

attracted to stable, well-known retail brands and retailers. The online audience is very sensitive to brand names (as we described in Chapter 7) and is not primarily cost-driven. Other factors such as reliability, trust, fulfillment, and customer service are equally important. Rather than demonstrate disintermediation, online retailing provides an example of the powerful role that intermediaries continue to play in retail trade.

One prediction of the E-commerce I era has proven true, however, namely that online retailing would become an important channel. Table 10.4 shows the online retail market product penetration rate for various types of products. Three categories of online retail — computer hardware/software, books, and travel — have surpassed the 10% level, and the top eleven categories are all above the 1% level and growing quickly. Products marked with an asterisk have a penetration rate that is growing annually at 50% or more.

The product categories with the highest market penetration growth rates (greater than 50% annually), such as home/office supplies, sporting goods, flowers/gifts, and health/beauty products, underscore the fact that for many non-necessity products, e-commerce will become a major channel. *Insight on Business: eVineyard Is a Survivor — for Now* looks at the online prospects for one purveyor of a non-necessity — wine.

TABLE 10.4	ONLINE RETAIL MARKET PRODUCT PENETRATION RATE (%)		
CATEGORY	2000	2001	GROWTH
Computer hardware/software	17.7	22.6	28
Books	11.3	13	15
Travel	10.8	14.9	38
Music/Video	6.3	9.3	48
Collectibles/antiques	4.6	6.1	33
*Toys	3.7	6.2	68
Event Tickets	3.5	4.9	40
*Flowers/cards/gifts	3.4	5.7	68
*Consumer electronics	3.2	4.9	53
*Sporting	1.4	2.9	107
*Apparel	1.1	1.7	55
*Home/office	0.7	1.4	100
*Jewelry	0.6	1	67
*Mass merchants/stores	0.6	0.9	50
*Health/beauty	0.5	0.9	80
Automotive	0.3	0.4	33
*Food/beverage	0.2	0.3	50
Garden/hardware	0.1	0.1	0

SOURCE: Boston Consulting Group, 2001.

10.2 ANALYZING THE VIABILITY OF ONLINE FIRMS

In this and the following chapters, we will be analyzing the viability of a number of online companies that exemplify specific e-commerce models. We are primarily interested in understanding the near-to-medium term (1–3 years) economic viability of these firms and their business models. **Economic viability** refers to the ability of firms to survive during the specified period as profitable business firms. To answer the question of economic viability, we take two business analysis approaches: strategic analysis and financial analysis.

economic viability
means these firms can survive during the specified period as profitable business firms

EVINEYARD IS A SURVIVOR—FOR NOW

Many new companies are encouraged to break the rules, think "outside the box," and do things differently in order to succeed online. Unfortunately, when it comes to the wine industry, breaking the rules appears to be a strategy for failure.

Online wine retailer eVineyard, based in Portland, Oregon, is one of the very few wine retailers left standing after hundreds of millions of dollars were invested in competing online wine merchants by leading venture capital firms. VirtualVineyard, which garnered the supposedly impenetrable first mover advantage, became Wine.com, which merged with Wineshopper, only to be bought in early 2001 by eVineyard for an unimpressive $10 million. In the end, it came down to playing by the rules: eVineyard took the time to apply for and receive state retail liquor licenses that allow it to sell wine directly to customers in 27 states. Its former competitors—in a hurry to achieve first-mover advantages—took orders online from their Web sites, but then fulfilled the orders through local wholesalers and retailers. With each middleman taking a cut of the sale, profits were meager.

In contrast, eVineyard is doing well. Started in 1999 with just $20 million in financial backing and 48 workers, versus Wine.com's $200 million and 265 employees, eVineyard has experienced 1,000% growth in customers and revenues from 1999 to 2000, even before the acquisition of the nearly defunct Wine.com. The addition of Wine's 400,000 customers and $28 million in sales will significantly boost the operations and bottom line for eVineyard, which itself had just $10 million in sales in 2000.

Although analysts estimate the size of the wine market to be around $18 billion, with premium wines accounting for $9 billion of that, they also project that online wine retailers will comprise just 10% of that total market by 2003. eVineyard, however, claims to have captured 75% of the domestic market for off-premise wine sales through transactions with 27 states and Japan. Those 27 states are estimated to comprise more than 85% of the wine-buying public.

While eVineyard can't offer the personalized counseling an on-site sommelier can in a corner wine store, it does offer more than 5,000 premium wines and hundreds of wine accessories. Customers can search for wines by brand, vintage, vineyard, rating, price, name, or variety as well as view winemakers' notes, learning which wines go best with different foods; they can even query a wine expert in eVineyard's Live Talk chat room. For many wine buyers, such convenience appears to be winning them over. eVineyard expects to be profitable in 2001.

This takes us to eVineyard's business model. By making the effort to obtain state licenses and operating within the established structure for wine sales, eVineyard is racking up gross margins of 32%. That's significant given that the company does not carry inventory and does not have to split its take with retailers, as many former wine online retailers did. Working through retailers and paying a fee to use their licenses, VirtualVineyard,

Wine, and Wineshopper earned a much smaller percentage on each sale, ultimately causing their financial undoing.

eVineyard must still be mindful of its increasing competition from the wineries themselves, which are aiming to sell directly to con-sumers. In doing so, wineries can increase their per-bottle revenue from $3 to as much as $12 on the sale of a $20 bottle of wine. Whether eVineyard survives in spite of the new onslaught of manufacturer-direct competitors remains to be seen.

SOURCES: "Acquisitions Have Made eVineyard the Top Online Wine Seller, But It Still Must Show That the Concept Can Succeed," by Bob Tedeschi, *New York Times*, May 7, 2001; Susan Stellin. "eVineyard Takes over Larger Rival," by Susan Stellin, *New York Times*, May 1, 2001; "Online Wine Industry Hit by Economic Slowdown, Internal Squabbles," by Beth Healy, *Boston Globe*, April 16, 2001; eVineyard Web site, www.evineyard.com.

STRATEGIC ANALYSIS

Strategic approaches to economic viability focus on both the industry in which a firm operates and the firm itself (see Chapter 2, Section 2.4). The key industry strategic factors are:

- **Barriers to entry:** Can new entrants be barred from entering the industry through high capital costs or intellectual property barriers (such as patents and copyrights)?
- **Power of suppliers:** Can suppliers dictate high prices to the industry or can vendors choose from among many suppliers? Have firms achieved sufficient scale to bargain effectively for lower prices from suppliers?
- **Power of customers:** Can customers choose from many competing suppliers and hence challenge high prices and high margins?
- **Existence of substitute products:** Can the functionality of the product or service be obtained from alternative channels or competing products in different industries? Are substitute products and services likely to emerge in the near future?
- **Industry value chain:** Is the chain of production and distribution in the industry changing in ways that benefit or harm the firm?
- **Nature of intra-industry competition:** Is the basis of competition within the industry based on differentiated products and services, price, scope of offerings, or focus of offerings? How is the nature of competition changing? Will these changes benefit the firm?

The strategic factors that pertain specifically to the firm and its related businesses include:

- **Firm value chain:** Has the firm adopted business processes and methods of operation that allow it to achieve the most efficient operations in its industry? Will changes in technology force the firm to realign its business processes?

- **Core competencies:** Does the firm have unique competencies and skills that cannot be easily duplicated by other firms? Will changes in technology invalidate the firm's competencies, or strengthen them?

- **Synergies:** Does the firm have access to the competencies and assets of related firms either owned outright or through strategic partnerships and alliances?

- **Technology:** Has the firm developed proprietary technologies that allow it to scale with demand? Has the firm developed the operational technologies (e.g., customer relationship management, fulfillment, supply chain management, inventory control, and human resource systems) to survive?

- **Social and legal challenges:** Has the firm put in place policies to address consumer trust issues (privacy and security of personal information)? Is the firm the subject of lawsuits challenging its business model, such as intellectual property ownership issues? Will the firm be liable to changes in Internet taxation laws or other foreseeable statutory developments?

FINANCIAL ANALYSIS

Strategic analysis helps us comprehend the competitive situation of the firm. Financial analysis helps us understand how in fact the firm is performing, and is best illustrated by an example. Table 10.5 shows the Consolidated Statements of Operations and Summary Balance Sheet Data for Amazon.com for the years 1998–2000. This is essentially a profit-and-loss statement showing how Amazon generated revenue and how it spent the money.

Here are some of the key factors to look for in a firm's Statement of Operations:

- **Revenues:** Are revenues growing and at what rate? Amazon's revenues have increased from about $600 million to $2.7 billion, or 400%, in three years. This is very impressive, explosive revenue growth.

- **Cost of sales:** What is the cost of sales compared to revenues? Cost of sales typically includes the cost of the products sold and related costs. The lower the cost of sales compared to revenue, the higher the gross profit. In Amazon's case, cost of sales increased from $476 million in 1998 to $2.1 billion in 2000, about the same rate that revenue increased (400%) during the same time period.

- **Gross margin:** What is the firm's gross margin (gross profit divided by net sales), and is it increasing or decreasing? Amazon's improved slightly, from 22% in 1998 to 24% in 2000, and improved greatly over 1999 (18%).

- **Operating expenses:** What are the firm's operating expenses, and are they increasing or decreasing? In Amazon's case, total operating expenses mushroomed from $252 million to $1.5 billion, or about 600%, in three years. Losses from operations increased from $109 million to $863 million. The reasons are clear: Marketing, technology, and administrative costs (which include salaries) rose very rapidly

TABLE 10.5	AMAZON'S CONSOLIDATED STATEMENTS OF OPERATIONS AND SUMMARY BALANCE SHEET DATA, 1998–2000

AMAZON.COM
CONSOLIDATED STATEMENTS OF OPERATIONS
(in thousands)

	2000	1999	1998
Revenue			
Net sales	$ 2,761,983	$1,639,839	$609,819
Cost of sales	2,106,206	1,349,194	476,155
Gross profit	655,777	290,645	133,664
Gross margin	24%	18%	22%
Operating expenses			
Marketing and fulfillment	594,489	413,150	132,654
Technology and content	269,326	159,722	46,424
General and administrative	108,962	70,144	15,618
Stock-based compensation	24,797	30,618	1,889
Amortization of goodwill and other intangibles	321,772	214,694	42,599
Impairment-related and other	200,311	8,072	3,535
Total operating expenses	1,519,657	896,400	242,719
Loss from operations	(863,880)	(605,755)	(109,055)
Other income/expense			
Net interest expense and other	(242,797)	(37,444)	(12,586)
Loss before equity in losses of equity-method investees, net	(1,106,677)	(643,199)	(121,641)
Equity in losses of equity-method investees, net	(304,596)	(76,769)	(2,905)
Net loss	**($1,411,273)**	**($719,968)**	**($124,546)**
Net margin	**–51%**	**–43%**	**–20%**

SUMMARY BALANCE SHEET DATA
(in thousands)

At December 31	2000	1999	1998
Current assets			
Cash and cash equivalents	$822,435	$133,309	$71,583
Marketable securities	278,087	572,879	301,862
Inventories	174,563	220,646	29,501
Total assets	2,135,169	2,465,850	648,460
Current liabilities	974,956	733,234	161,575
Long-term debt	2,127,464	1,466,338	348,140

SOURCE: Amazon.com, Inc. Form 10-K for the fiscal year ended December 31, 2000, filed with the Securities and Exchange Commission on March 23, 2001.

as Amazon built warehouses, hired thousands of employees, and marketed its site heavily during this period. Once additional financial transactions are added into the equation, Amazon's net loss was about $1.4 billion in 2000.

- **Net margin:** What is the firm's net margin, and is it increasing or decreasing? Net margin (net income or loss divided by net sales/revenue) sums up in one number how successful a company has been at the business of making a profit on each dollar of sales. In Amazon's case, net margin for 2000 was a negative 51%. In other words, for every dollar in net sales in the year 2000, Amazon was losing 51 cents.

The prospect for Amazon based on this financial analysis of its operations does not look very good. How can Amazon survive these losses? A look at the Summary Balance Sheet Data shows how Amazon plans to survive in the short term. A **balance sheet** provides a financial snapshot of a company on a given date, and shows its financial assets and liabilities. **Assets** refer to stored value. **Current assets** are those assets such as cash, securities, accounts receivable, inventory, or other investments that are likely to be able to be converted to cash within one year. **Liabilities** are outstanding obligations of the firm. **Current liabilities** are debts of the firm that will be due within one year. Liabilities that are not due until the passage of a year or more are characterized as **long-term debt**. For a quick check of a firm's short-term financial health, compare its current assets to its current liabilities. If current assets are less or not much more than current liabilities, the firm will likely have trouble meeting its short-term obligations.

Amazon's balance sheet shows that at the end of December 2000, it had about $1 billion in cash and marketable securities, with current assets in excess of its current liabilities, and total assets of around $2 billion. The cash and securities were obtained from venture capital investors and institutional investors such as mutual funds, insurance companies, and pension funds in return for equity (shares) in the company. This should be enough to cover another deficit year in 2001 equal in size to that of 2000 (about $1.4 billion). However, Amazon has already gone into long-term debt for $2.1 billion, and with share prices low, it will not be able to raise much money in further public offerings of shares. Institutional investors similarly are wary of investing more in Amazon. It is fair to conclude that Amazon's management is under a great deal of pressure to become a profitable company soon.

10.3   E-COMMERCE IN ACTION: E-TAILING BUSINESS MODELS

So far we have been discussing online retail as if it was a single entity. In fact, as we briefly discussed in Chapter 2, there are five major types of online retail business models: virtual merchant, clicks and mortar, catalog merchant, online mall, and

---

balance sheet

provides a financial snapshot of a company on a given date and shows its financial assets and liabilities

assets

refers to stored value

current assets

assets such as cash, securities, accounts receivable, inventory, or other investments that are likely to be able to be converted to cash within one year

liabilities

outstanding obligations of the firm

current liabilities

debts of the firm that will be due within one year

long-term debt

liabilities that are not due until the passage of a year or more manufacturer direct. Each of these different types of online retailers faces a different strategic environment, as well as different industry and firm economics.

Perhaps the best way to understand the challenges facing online retailers is to examine both the strategies and the operating results of actual online firms. We have enough experience now with online commerce to move beyond speculation and look at real-world performance. In this section, we analyze the strategic and financial situation of real online retail companies that exemplify the five types of online business models described below.

VIRTUAL MERCHANTS

Virtual merchants are single-channel Web firms that generate almost all their revenue from online sales. Virtual merchants face extraordinary strategic challenges: They must build a business and brand name from scratch, quickly, in an entirely new channel and confront many virtual merchant competitors (especially in smaller niche areas). These firms typically do not have to bear the costs associated with building and maintaining physical stores, but they face large costs in building and maintaining a Web site and for marketing. Customer acquisition costs are also high, and the learning curve is steep. Like all retail firms, their margins (the difference between the retail price of goods and the cost of goods to the retailer) are very low. Therefore, virtual merchants must achieve highly efficient operations in order to preserve a profit, while building a brand name as quickly as possible in order to attract sufficient customers to cover their costs of operations.

We'll now analyze two different virtual merchants with different strategies: Buy.com and Ashford.com. Buy.com is a general merchandiser, while Ashford.com is focused niche player.

General Merchandiser: Buy.com

Buy.com offers customers 11 online specialty stores: computer hardware and peripherals, software, books, videos and DVDs, computer games, music, clearance products, electronics, sporting goods, office products, and wireless products and services. These product lines were selected based on market potential and the existence of a dominant distributor with whom Buy could partner for inventory. Sales of computers have accounted for more than 80% of the company's revenues. What makes Buy a standout, however, is its product breadth; its more than 1,000,000 product SKUs dwarf those of traditional offline retailers of these products.

Business Model The company makes money mainly through product sales (94%), with a small amount being derived from advertising revenue (6%). Its business model is based on outsourcing virtually all activities associated with its operating infrastructure — including distribution and fulfillment, customer service, order processing,

virtual merchants
single-channel Web firms that generate almost all their revenue from online sales

and hosting and server functioning and maintenance. While such a model allows Buy to eliminate many significant capital investments, as well as inventory purchasing and storage costs, it puts the company at the mercy of its suppliers. So far, the company has not experienced substantial difficulties with suppliers. Nevertheless, if Buy fails to purchase a contracted amount of merchandise from its distribution partners, such as Ingram Micro, its favorable pricing schedules could change, further hampering its efforts to reach profitability and potentially limiting its product selection.

Buy's 3.5 million customers spent $788 million at the site in 2000, and earned Buy several e-commerce awards and honors, including "Best of the Web" in the computer and electronics category by Forbes, and "Best Overall Place to Buy" by Computer Shopper. Buy was also ranked the top electronics e-tailer by Forrester Research. Many of those kudos, however, were based on the company's top-notch phone and e-mail customer support crew, employees who have since been terminated, leaving customers now with e-mail-only service and support as Buy has struggled with financial pressures.

Financial Analysis Table 10.6 shows Buy's results of operations and summary balance sheet data for 1998–2000. The company's revenue has grown explosively from $125 million in 1998 to $787 million in 2000, although revenue growth slowed from this torrid pace in the 1999–2000 period to a 31% increase. Cost of goods sold as a proportion of sales has decreased slightly and remained under control as a result of Buy's favorable contractual relationships with suppliers from whom it purchases a large volume of goods. Gross margin in 2000 was a very thin 5.9%, although it has improved markedly from the losing margins of the prior years.

Although Buy.com's investment in sales and marketing increased in 2000 to more than $92 million, in continued support of strong brand building, sales and marketing as a percentage of total revenue remained close to 12%, as in previous years. A 12% investment in marketing is above average for an existing business, but somewhat below that of other dot.com companies seeking near instant recognition. General and administrative expenses also increased slightly. Buy's overall expenses resulted in a negative net margin of 16.8%, with Buy losing about 17 cents for every dollar of net revenue and a total net loss of $133 million. Nevertheless, these results are an improvement over previous years.

Examining its balance sheet, we can see that at December 31, 2000, Buy had about $66 million in liquid assets, only enough to cover losses at the current rate for about three quarters of a year. When Buy.com went public in February 2000, less than three years after its founding, the stock began trading at $13.00 per share and quickly rose to a high of $27.50 in the hope that this multi-category online superstore would be another Amazon. As of August 2001, Buy's stock price had sunk to 17 cents per share and it was delisted from the NASDAQ. Clearly, the public market is no longer

TABLE 10.6	BUY.COM'S CONSOLIDATED STATEMENTS OF OPERATIONS AND SUMMARY BALANCE SHEET DATA, 1998–2000

BUY.COM INC.
CONSOLIDATED STATEMENTS OF OPERATIONS
(in thousands)

At December 31	2000	1999	1998
Revenue			
Net revenues	$ 787,670	$596,848	$125,290
Cost of goods sold	740,977	603,695	123,527
Gross profit/(loss)	46,693	(6,847)	1,763
Gross margin	**5.9%**	**−1.1%**	**1.4%**
Operating expenses			
Sales and marketing	92,425	71,189	13,430
Product development	25,280	7,617	950
General and administrative	49,076	42,692	5,425
Total operating expenses	166,781	121,498	19,805
Operating loss	(120,088)	(128,345)	(18,042)
Other income/expense			
Total other income/(expense)	6,500	(988)	198
Net loss before equity in losses of joint ventures	(113,588)	(129,333)	(17,844)
Equity in losses of joint ventures, net	(19,434)	(835)	—
Net loss	**($133,022)**	**($130,168)**	**($17,844)**
Net margin	**−16.8%**	**−21.8%**	**−14.2%**

SUMMARY BALANCE SHEET DATA
(in thousands)

	2000	1999	1998
Current assets			
Cash and cash equivalents	$56,656	$24,693	$9,221
Marketable securities	10,769	—	—
Accounts receivable	19,424	17,882	4,986
Total assets	136,504	119,606	26,837
Current liabilities	52,948	94,820	19,027
Long-term debt	324	1,738	1,175

SOURCE: Buy.com Inc. Form 10-K for the year ended December 31, 2000, filed with the Securities and Exchange Commission on March 29, 2001.

open to Buy.com for new fund raising and venture capitalists are not making further investments in this type of e-commerce venture. Buy.com's management is under significant pressure to stem the losses.

Strategic Analysis — Business Strategy Recognizing the company's dire situation, management reorganized the business in early 2001, cutting its employee base from 258 to 146 full-time employees and reducing its marketing and advertising budget for the year. Earlier, in 2000, Buy severed its relationships with several joint venture partners outside the United States and decided to focus its attention solely on its domestic market. As a result, the company currently has no international operations with the exception of one alliance in the United Kingdom.

Buy's merchandising and pricing strategy has been to heavily promote popular products with high brand awareness at lower prices in order to entice consumers to the site. Its motto is "Lowest Prices on Earth." Once they are at the Web site, customers increasingly receive cross-marketing promotions on higher margin products and services. Buy has also been experimenting with raising prices across the board among less price-sensitive items as another means of improving profitability. Raising prices, however, is expected to negatively affect the company's bottom line in future years.

Strategic Analysis — Competition Each of Buy's 11 specialty stores has both online and traditional competitors, few of which can compete on product breadth. They can, however, compete on price, causing Buy's margins to be squeezed even tighter. From Amazon.com for books to CompUSA for computers and Beyond.com for software, the list of competitors is long. And with few barriers to entry, it could get longer.

Strategic Analysis — Technology Buy's business model puts the responsibility for its technology infrastructure in the hands of third-party professionals, who maintain and host its Web site, in addition to providing the back-end transactional support the company requires. This helps achieve operating efficiencies, but Buy may be paying more than it should for inventory management and fulfillment as a result.

Strategic Analysis — Social and Legal Challenges The company is currently involved in the early stages of a class action lawsuit filed in California that alleges Buy collected, used, and disclosed private customer information without the knowledge or consent of its customer base. The suit seeks $10,000 per class member per violation and could be disastrous if the company loses. Buy is also suing, and being sued by, the PGA related to its sponsorship of the Buy.com golf tour. While resolution of this suit is unlikely to ruin the company, it could damage its reputation and marketing ability.

Future Prospects In August 2001, Buy's founder, Scott Blum, offered to purchase all the outstanding shares of Buy's stock for 17 cents a share in cash. The Board of Directors of Buy have approved the transaction, and it is expected to occur by November 30, 2001. As a result, Buy will no longer be a public company. As a part of the agreement, Blum agreed to immediately provide Buy with interim financing of up to $9 million.

Buy's future rests on its ability to meet its current operating plan, which calls for price increases and reduced investment in marketing. As offline established retailers move into online retailing and extend their brand, Buy will face growing challenges from well-endowed competitors. The slowing U.S. economy may also dampen sales in the future. However, more people are going online for shopping and this may mean more potential new customers for Buy.com.

Niche Merchandiser: Ashford.com

Ashford.com is a Web retailer specializing in luxury goods, such as new and vintage watches, clocks, diamonds, jewelry, leather goods, writing instruments, fragrances, sunglasses, clothing accessories, home décor, and lifestyle products. From its founding in Houston in 1998 as premium watch purveyor, NewWatch Corporation, Ashford has changed its name and expanded its product offerings to create a portfolio of both frequently purchased luxury items, such as sunglasses and leather goods and higher-priced but seldom-purchased items such as watches and diamonds. The company currently employs 248 people and has available more than 20,000 products from over 400 leading luxury brands.

In March 2000, Ashford launched a corporate gifts division that offers an additional 800 items appropriate for business gift-giving, including crystal, silver, and pewter goods. Designed to even out the seasonality of its core business, which provides 50% of the company's sales in the fourth quarter alone, the corporate gifts division is expected to deliver sales more consistently throughout the year.

Business Model Ashford's business plan was to become the Web's premiere luxury goods site, a market Ashford estimated to be worth $130 billion worldwide. Ashford's founders believed today's luxury goods customer was too time-starved to shop in luxury stores and would prefer a more efficient Web shopping experience. Traditional store retailers were forced to pay high rents in luxury malls, offer fewer products from small stores, endure high labor costs, and deal with poorly trained employees. Ashford's solution was to offer a broader selection of products online, convenient 24x7 shopping, superb service, and competitive prices. Ashford also offers a search capability for unusual products, on-site interaction, gift and wish lists, price notifications, and personalized Web pages so customers can view a number of objects together.

Financial Analysis Table 10.7 presents Ashford's results of operations and summary balance sheet data for 1999–2001. Ashford's net sales increased by nearly 70% from 2000 to 2001. The cost of goods sold also increased by nearly 70%. Gross margins remained flat at 16% in this period.

| TABLE 10.7 | ASHFORD.COM'S CONSOLIDATED STATEMENTS OF OPERATIONS AND SUMMARY BALANCE SHEET DATA, 1998-2000 |

ASHFORD.COM, INC.
CONSOLIDATED STATEMENTS OF OPERATIONS
(in thousands)

For the fiscal year ended March 31	2001	2000	1999
Revenue			
Net sales	$ 67,195	$ 39,931	$ 5,938
Cost of sales	56,348	33,487	5,110
Gross profit	10,847	6,444	828
Gross margin	**16%**	**16%**	**14%**
Operating expenses			
Marketing and sales	105,895	60,806	1,013
General and administrative	27,929	17,093	1,019
Restructuring charge	622	—	—
Impairment loss	1,094	—	—
Depreciation and amortization	13,460	3,277	67
Total operating expenses	149,040	81,176	2,099
Loss from operations	(138,193)	(74,732)	(1,271)
Other income/(expense)			
Interest income	1,644	2,677	13
Interest expense	(132)	(7)	(6)
Net loss	**(136,681)**	**(72,062)**	**(1,264)**
Net margin	**−203%**	**−180%**	**−21.2%**

SUMMARY BALANCE SHEET DATA
(in thousands)

At March 31	2001	2000	1999
Current assets			
Cash and equivalents	$ 7,095	46,474	893
Restricted cash	1,500	120	100
Accounts receivable	2,559	4,527	
Total assets	56,266	177,608	5,108
Current liabilities	12,894	6,221	2,300
Long-term debt	104	117	—
Stockholders' equity	43,268	171,270	2,808

SOURCE: Ashford.com, Inc. Form 10-K for the fiscal year ended March 31, 2001, filed with the Securities and Exchange Commission on June 29, 2001.

Unfortunately, operating expenses in this period mushroomed by almost 200% as well, due in part to an increase in the number of employees hired to service Ashford's growing customer base, but also because of depreciation of merchandise in inventory and the writing off of purchases that could not be sold. Net margin sank to a –203%. For every dollar in sales, Ashford was losing $2.03, and Ashford's net loss for 2001 was $136 million on net sales of $67 million.

A look at the balance sheet shows the strain these losses placed on Ashford. On March 31, 2000, Ashford had $46 million in cash and equivalents, provided mostly by sales of preferred stock to institutions and the sale of shares on the public market, and total assets of $177 million. One year later, on March 31, 2001, Ashford's cash had dropped precipitously to only $7 million, and total assets had been depleted to $56 million. By March 31, 2001, it had become clear that Ashford would have to act quickly to reduce its losses to a more manageable level.

Strategic Analysis — Business Strategy To improve its profitability, Ashford significantly expanded its product base to include a broader range of high-end goods, including items that are purchased more frequently. Its new home and lifestyle category contains gift and specialty items, for example. The introduction of its corporate gifts business was another tactic to increase sales while evening out the seasonality of its regular business. Ashford also negotiated with suppliers to try and buy products directly from the brand owners, rather than distributors, as a means of reducing its cost.

Ashford invested heavily in marketing and advertising in order to attract Web traffic and establish a credible online brand, but has recently cut back on its traditional print and media marketing, redirecting funds toward Internet and online media, which it believes is a more efficient and economical means of attracting customers. Ashford spent more than $32 million in the three-month period from April 1 to June 30, 2000; in the corresponding period in 2001, the company cut back its marketing spending to just $3 million.

Strategic Analysis — Competition Ashford's competitors include traditional retailers of luxury goods such as Bloomingdales, Saks Fifth Avenue, and Neiman Marcus; manufacturers that sell directly to the public either offline or online, such as Gucci and Prada; catalog retailers of luxury goods such as Spiegel and Talbots; and other online sites such as Miadora.com, Adornis.com, and eluxury.com.

Strategic Analysis — Technology Ashford has developed its Web sites internally and operates and maintains all aspects of its operations in-house, including transaction processing, customer profiling, and order verification. While helping to keep Web consulting costs down, maintaining a Web site internally has posed challenges for Ashford.

Ashford has experienced periodic systems interruptions due to server failure, which the company believes will continue to occur from time to time. If the volume of traffic on the Ashford Web site significantly increases, Ashford will need to further expand and upgrade its technology, transaction processing systems, and network infrastructure. Ashford has experienced and expects to continue to experience temporary capacity constraints due to sharply increased traffic during sales or other promotions, which cause unanticipated system disruptions, slower response times, degradation in levels of customer service, impaired quality, and delays in reporting accurate financial information. Ashford's Web site architectures cannot scale easily with expansion. Continuing to upgrade and expand capacity is a prerequisite for success online.

Strategic Analysis — Social and Legal Challenges

Ashford does not currently have litigation pending against it. However, Ashford faces two social challenges: keeping the personal information of its wealthy customers private, and maintaining the integrity of its brand name and intellectual property. Ashford has developed a strong privacy policy and does not sell information about customers or purchases to outsiders. To protect its Web brand name, Ashford currently holds, among others, the "Ashford. com," "newwatch.com," "sunglasses.com," "TimeZone.com," "Paris1925.com," "Jasmin. com" and "Ashfordcorporategifts.com" domain names and may seek to acquire additional domain names.

Future Prospects

The purchase of luxury goods, including fine artwork, can be affected by the state of the economy, with purchases of some luxury items falling during economic downturns. On the other hand, high-priced items such as watches, original art, and jewelry are remarkably resistant to economic downturns.

The most important risk Ashford faces is financial. Management must take steps in the short run to stem Ashford's losses and implement a strategy that will produce a profitable business.

In pursuit of financial stability and real earnings, management has taken a number of sometimes confusing steps. In 2001, Ashford cut its employee base by 20%, and, as noted above, sharply reduced its use of traditional print and media in marketing, focusing instead on Internet marketing and "pay for performance" marketing relationships.

In February 2001, Ashford merged with an online watch retailer to broaden its Web presence. However, after continuing disagreements between Ashford and the former principals of the online watch retailer, the agreement was dissolved and Ashford took a charge against earnings of $2.3 million. In May 2001, Ashford closed a merger with an online art dealer. Shortly after closing, Ashford determined that the art dealer's operating cost structure did not fit Ashford's objectives (i.e., to make a profit) and as a result, it spun off the newly acquired entity as a separately capitalized company in return for a 5% ownership stake and a share of gross sales revenues from the new company.

In September 2001, Ashford agreed to be acquired by Global Sports Inc. Global Sports develops and operates e-commerce sporting goods sites for traditional, established sporting goods retailers; general merchandisers; Internet companies; professional sports teams; and media companies under exclusive agreements. Global Sports is, in other words, an outsourcer of Web services with a special focus on sporting goods. Global Sports's revenue comes from sales of sporting goods through its partner Web sites, Web site development and operation fees, fulfillment fees, and direct 800-sales. Global Sports has also entered into an agreement with Kmart to operate Kmart's BlueLight.com.

Ashford shareholders will receive 12.5 cents per share in cash plus .0076 shares of Global Sports common stock in a deal estimated to be worth $14.5 million overall (about 25 cents per share overall). This is a long way from the approximate $12.85 per share Amazon paid for 7 million shares of Ashford stock in January 2000 in a deal estimated at the time to be worth $90 million. Amazon's shares are now worth only $1.7 million.

Global Sports purchased Ashford to extend its e-commerce platform to the luxury goods market; it also hopes to begin offering proprietary solutions to other purveyors of luxury goods. Ashford will become the twenty-fourth e-commerce Web site to run on Global Sports' platform.

Global Sports itself posted a net loss of $16 million for the first half of 2001, roughly half the loss in the previous year. However, its share price had risen to $16.51 at the time of the Ashford deal from a low of $2.37, as Global Sports has grown aggressively and achieved some success in attracting other Web site operations business such as Kmart.

CLICKS AND MORTAR

Also called "store-based" retailers, **clicks and mortar** companies have a network of physical stores as their primary retail channel, but also have introduced online offerings. These are multichannel firms such as Wal-Mart, JCPenney, Sears, and other brand name variety merchants. While clicks and mortar merchants face high costs of physical buildings and large sales staffs, they also have many advantages such as a brand name, a national customer base, warehouses, large scale (giving them leverage with suppliers), and a trained staff. Acquiring customers is less expensive because of their brand names, but these firms face challenges in coordinating prices across channels and handling returns of Web purchases at their retail outlets. However, these retail players are used to operating on very thin margins and have invested heavily in purchasing and inventory control systems to control costs, and in coordinating returns from multiple locations. Clicks and mortar companies face the challenge of leveraging their strengths and assets to the Web, building a credible Web site, hiring

clicks and mortar
companies that have a network of physical stores as their primary retail channel, but also have introduced online offerings

new skilled staff, and building rapid response order entry and fulfillment systems. JCPenney.com is a prime example of a clicks and mortar company on the Web.

JCPenney.com

JCPenney was founded in 1902 by James Cash Penney and has grown since then to include more than 1,100 department stores in the United States, Puerto Rico, and Mexico, as well as 49 Renner department stores and 2,640 Eckerd Drugstores. In addition, JCPenney has a substantial and well-established catalog business and a recently formed online retail Web site. The Plano, Texas-based company's annual revenues are $32.6 billion. Its department stores, catalog, and Internet channels all primarily serve the same target market: "modern spenders" and "starting-outers," or two-income families with median annual incomes of $48,000.

At jcpenney.com, customers can buy family clothing, jewelry, shoes, accessories, and home furnishings. And whether they buy merchandise in a brick-and-mortar store, through the catalog, or on the Internet, customers can return items at a store or through the mail, a convenience that few retailers offer. Most retailers separate the operations of traditional and online channels, making it difficult for customers to make returns.

Business Model JCPenney started out as a traditional general merchandiser with a strong catalog operation. This model still describes most of Penney's revenues and operations, but its growing Web business is slowly changing Penney's business model. Although Internet sales currently account for just 1% of the company's revenues, that figure is climbing rapidly. The Web is Penney's fastest growing channel. JCPenney has been struggling to improve the financial performance of all of its marketing channels and has succeeded only in one area — Internet operations. Internet merchandise sales increased from $102 million in the fiscal year ending January 29, 2000 to $294 million in the fiscal year ending January 27, 2001. The company draws on its existing inventory, merchandising it through the online medium just as it does in its stores and mail-order catalog.

Financial Analysis Table 10.8 shows Penney's consolidated results of operations and summary balance sheet data for fiscal 1999–2001. JCPenney's revenue growth has been relatively flat for several years, reaching $31.8 billion in the fiscal year ending January 27, 2001. Cost of goods has risen slightly, forcing a decline in gross margins from 31% to 28%.

Like all physical retail stores, JCPenney suffers from very high operating expenses to maintain its 1,100 stores nationwide, a large labor force, and huge inventories. In fiscal 2001, Penney went into the red and had a net loss of $705 million. Its net margin shrank from a positive 1% in fiscal 2000 to a negative 2%. Penney's was losing two cents on every dollar of net sales.

TABLE 10.8	**JCPENNEY'S CONSOLIDATED STATEMENTS OF OPERATIONS AND SUMMARY BALANCE SHEET DATA, 1998–2000**

JCPENNEY COMPANY, INC. AND SUBSIDIARIES
CONSOLIDATED STATEMENTS OF OPERATIONS
(in millions)

For the fiscal year ended	January 27, 2001	January 29, 2000	January 30, 1999
Revenue			
Net retail sales	$31,846	$31,743	$29,761
Cost of goods sold	23,031	22,286	20,621
Gross profit	8,815	9,457	9,140
Gross margin	28%	30%	31%
Operating expenses			
Selling, general and administrative expenses	8,637	8,604	7,966
Other unallocated	27	(13)	(18)
Net interest expense and credit operations	427	294	387
Acquisition amortization	122	125	112
Restructuring and other charges, net	488	169	(22)
Total costs and expenses	32,732	31,465	29,046
(Loss)/income from continuing operations before income taxes	(886)	278	715
Income taxes	(318)	104	277
(Loss)/income from continuing operations	(568)	174	438
Other income			
Income from discontinued operations	159	162	156
Loss on sale of discontinued operations (including income taxes)	(200)	(296)	—
Net (loss)/income	(705)	336	594
Net margin	−2%	1%	1.9%

SUMMARY BALANCE SHEET DATA
(in millions)

At	January 27, 2001	January 29, 2000	January 30, 1999
Current assets (cash, receivables, inventory, etc).	$ 7,257	$8,177	$11,007
Total assets (land, buildings, equipment, goodwill, etc.)	19,742	20,908	23,508
Current liabilities	4,235	4,272	5,912
Long-term debt	5,448	5,844	7,143

SOURCE: JC Penney Company, Inc. Form 10-K for the fiscal year ended January 27, 2001, filed with the Securities and Exchange Commission on April 24, 2001.

However, like other large established offline retailers, JCPenney has extraordinary assets to finance its operating losses. At January 27, 2001, Penney had $7.2 billion in current liquid assets (more than seven times its net loss), and total assets (including stores and real estate) of $19.7 billion. Even though JCPenney cannot go on losing money forever, it has extraordinary financial assets that can be utilized to stage a comeback.

Strategic Analysis — Business Strategy Much of the company's focus in 2000 was on shutting down 92 underperforming department stores, which cost JCPenney $206 million on top of the lost $950 million in sales that would have been generated. Reducing the number of employees has been another cost-cutting measure, as well as centralizing the merchandizing process in department stores and catalog operations.

JCPenney has spent $200 million since 1994 to set up its e-commerce site, a vast sum in comparison to other retailers, such as Canadian Hudson Bay, which spent $15 million, and the now defunct eToys, which spent $80 million to set up a distribution system (Hunt 2001). Penney's move into online retail e-commerce is a major strategy of the company to shore up its poorly performing catalog and store operations and to stay competitive with other large retailers such as Wal-Mart, Sears, and Kmart, who have developed online sites as well.

In 1998, JCPenney finally made the commitment to put its entire catalog inventory online. Penney's strong brand and advertising program has vaulted the company into one of the top ten online retail sites. Although the Internet operations have not yet turned a profit, the company expects its Web operations to be profitable in fiscal 2002 when sales are predicted to reach $400 million.

The company has achieved online success through some savvy decisions: putting approximately 200,000 of its products online, from lingerie to home furnishings, surpassing the competition in terms of selection, targeting women as the primary consumer, and making it easy to move from one category to the next on the site. In doing so, online sales are attracting new, younger JCPenney shoppers, 25% of whom have never bought anything in a JCPenney store. Online sales are complementing, rather than cannibalizing, store and catalog sales. Shoppers who buy through all three channels spend four times more — $1,000 — than the shopper who makes purchases only at the retail store (Koenig, 2001).

Strategic Analysis — Competition JCPenney competes primarily with traditional retail department stores focused on the cost-conscious consumer, such as Wal-Mart, Kmart, Sears, and Target. That competitive environment carries over into the electronic realm, where most competitors have similar e-commerce storefronts.

Strategic Analysis — Technology JCPenney was one of the first national retailers in the 1970s to develop point-of-sale data capture using bar coding. The point-of-sale system was linked to a national inventory management system, and then to suppliers. In addition, throughout the 1980s, Penney had developed customer management systems to operate the catalog division, allowing customers to return catalog items to any store in the nation. Converting these substantial systems to support the new Web operations has involved major expenses to handle the increased sales on the Web.

Strategic Analysis — Social and Legal Challenges JCPenney has no material legal matters pending against it at this time. Historically, the company has been conservative in its use of marketing data that it collects from point-of-sale terminals.

Future Prospects Continued poor financial performance will jeopardize JCPenney's future, potentially forcing the company to close more of its brick-and-mortar stores. Strong results by competitors Wal-Mart and Target suggest that retail growth is possible, and that JCPenney may simply have not hit on the right product mix or marketing strategy. Risks inherent in the retailing world include quickly changing consumer appetites for trendy products, which can cause significant losses. While management is clearly under pressure from investors to improve its profits, Penney has substantial financial assets that will permit management sufficient time to extend the Penney brand to the Web and improve its store operating efficiency.

CATALOG MERCHANTS

Catalog merchants such as Lands' End, L.L. Bean, Eddie Bauer, and Victoria's Secret are established companies that have a national offline catalog operation that is their largest retail channel, but who have recently developed online capabilities. JCPenney could also be included here, given the large scale of its catalog operation. Catalog merchants face very high costs for printing and mailing millions of catalogs each year — many of which have a half-life of 30 seconds after the customer receives them. Nevertheless, catalog merchants have the highest margins in the retail sector because they have achieved very efficient operations. They generally have few, if any, physical stores. They also typically have developed centralized fulfillment and call centers, extraordinary service, and excellent fulfillment in partnership with package delivery firms such as FedEx and UPS.

Catalog merchants face many of the same challenges as brick-and-mortar stores — they must leverage their existing assets and competencies to a new technology environment, build a credible Web presence, and hire new staff. Catalog firms are uniquely advantaged, however, because they already possess very efficient, fast response order entry and fulfillment systems.

catalog merchants
established companies that have a national offline catalog operation that is their largest retail channel, but who have recently developed online capabilities

Landsend.com

Lands' End, Inc. is a leading direct marketer of traditionally styled casual clothing for men, women, and children, as well as accessories, shoes, luggage, and housewares. Its promotional catalogs arrive in millions of customer mailboxes each month. The company's total customer mailing list consists of 31 million names, with 6.7 million current buyers. And while the company may not be the largest catalog marketer, the National Retail Federation believes that landsend.com, the company's e-commerce site, is the largest seller of apparel online. Its Internet sales have jumped from $61 million in fiscal 1999 to $218 million in fiscal 2001 — more than a 250% increase in just two years.

In addition to its Internet sales channel, Lands' End sells its products through its catalogs and retail outlet stores. The company has three operating segments: core, specialty, and international. The core business segment consists of adult apparel. The specialty business segment consists of corporate sales, including Lands' End merchandise that is custom-embroidered with organization or special event logos and symbols, the *Lands' End Kids* and *Coming Home* catalogs. Lands' End's international segment is composed of foreign-based operations located in Japan, Germany, and the United Kingdom. Catalogs mailed within these countries are written in the local language and feature local currency denominations. In fiscal year 2001, three new international Web sites were launched in Ireland, France, and Italy, which will begin to build customer bases in those areas.

Customers can place orders via phone through a toll-free number, by mail, fax, or Web site, although phone orders through the catalog still comprise 80% of Lands' End's sales, with the remainder coming through mail, fax, or Internet.

Business Model Lands' End is a direct marketer, selling primarily through printed catalogs, with ancillary retail and Internet operations. Worldwide, the company mailed an estimated 269 million catalogs in the last year.

Since 1963, Lands' End's operations in Dodgeville, Wisconsin, have been growing to keep up with demand for casual, conservative clothing. Revenue is generated through both product sales and shipping charges, which provided $107 million to the bottom line and were up more than 10% over the previous year due to higher merchandise sales and increased shipping rates.

Financial Analysis Table 10.9 shows Lands' End's consolidated results of operations and summary balance sheet data. Lands' End sales revenues have grown 3% in the fiscal year ending January 26, 2001, but still have not exceeded 1999 sales. Gross margins have remained around 42%, far higher than typical general merchandisers such as JCPenney and Sears. Many catalog merchants are able to charge premium prices for house label goods that are produced under contract for them around the world, thus eliminating the profits earned by proprietary designer label manufacturers such as Calvin Klein or Nike.

Operational expenses have expanded faster than revenues, reducing net margins to 2.4% for Lands' End fiscal year ending January 26, 2001. Selling, general, and administrative (SG&A) expenses were up close to 10%, mainly due to higher catalog

TABLE 10.9	LANDS' END'S CONSOLIDATED STATEMENTS OF OPERATIONS AND SUMMARY BALANCE SHEET DATA, 1999-2001

LANDS' END, INC.
CONSOLIDATED STATEMENTS OF OPERATIONS
(in thousands)

For the fiscal year ended	January 26, 2001	January 28, 2000	January 29, 1999
Revenue			
Net sales	1,462,283	1,416,886	1,466,121
Cost of sales	840,604	827,082	850,029
Gross profit	621,679	589,804	616,092
Gross margin	42.5%	41.6%	42.0%
Expenses			
Selling, general and administrative	560,019	512,647	543,824
Non-recurring charge (credit)	—	(1,774)	12,600
Total operating expenses			
Income from operations	61,660	78,931	59,668
Other income/expense:			
Total other income(expense), net	(6,649)	(2,687)	(10,168)
Income before income taxes	55,011	76,244	49,500
Income tax provision	20,354	28,210	18,315
Net income	34,657	48,034	$31,185
Net margin	2.4%	3.4%	2.1%

SUMMARY BALANCE SHEET DATA
(in thousands)

At	January 26, 2001	January 28, 2000	January 29, 1999
Current assets			
Cash and cash equivalents	$75,351	$76,413	6,641
Receivables, net	19,808	17,753	21,083
Inventory	188,211	162,193	219,686
Total assets	507,629	456,196	455,919
Current liabilities	178,874	150,872	205,283
Long-term debt	—	—	—

SOURCE: Lands' End Inc. Form 10-K for the fiscal year ended January 26, 2001, filed with the Securities and Exchange Commission on April 23, 2001.

production costs — which accounted for 39% of SG&A — and higher information services expenses. The number of catalogs mailed increased by 14%, with the total number of pages mailed also climbing 18%. Expenses have also expanded as Lands' End invested in its Web site and added additional employees to operate the site. Lands' End earned $34 million, and for every dollar in net sales, it was earning about 3 cents.

A look at the balance sheet summary shows a healthy company. At January 26, 2001, Lands' End had $321 million in current assets, compared to $178 million of current liabilities, total assets of $507 million and no long-term debt. With these kinds of resources available, Lands' End is in a very good position to extend its brand to new channels such as e-commerce.

Strategic Analysis — Business Strategy
The company's growth strategy has three key elements. First, the company is seeking to increase sales through its multiple selling channels, both by expanding its customer base and by increasing sales to its existing customers through improvements in its merchandise offerings and creative presentations. Second, the company is attempting to generate additional sales by making targeted mailings of its specialty catalogs to existing and prospective customers and by offering its products on the Internet. Third, the company is actively pursuing opportunities to expand the customer base through its operations in Japan, Germany, and the United Kingdom.

Lands' End's online business is growing substantially. Approximately 17% of Internet buyers are new customers for Lands' End, with an additional 7% representing individuals on the company's mailing list who are making their first purchase. In addition to increasing the company's reach, its Web operations also help even out the very seasonal nature of its sales cycle: a disproportionate amount of the company's sales occur during the winter season (nearly 37%). Even though a paper catalog has space limitations, the online Lands' End catalog can carry out-of-season inventory and clearance items without significant additional cost. In the future, Lands' End expects that growth of its e-commerce business will reduce lead times that are required by catalogs, help to improve inventory turnover, and decrease operating costs incurred in designing, printing, and distributing paper catalogs.

Strategic Analysis — Competition
Lands' End's principal competitors are other catalog marketers and retail stores, although television shopping channels and online retailing are further intensifying the competitive nature of the business. Lands' End competes primarily on the basis of merchandise quality and price, its established customer list, and customer service, including 24-hour order fulfillment and an unconditional guarantee of its merchandise. The key to much of this competitive advantage is its well-honed technology infrastructure and systems.

Strategic Analysis — Technology
Lands' End has invested heavily in its technology infrastructure in an effort to establish a strong Web presence that keeps pace with

growing demand for its products. The company has been repeatedly cited by the media and industry experts as having one of the most effective and innovative Web sites in the world, due to its innovations and continued dedication to customer service. Last year, Fortune's Technology Guide for the 2000/2001 holiday season named Landsend.com as one of the notable Web sites to shop. Notable Web sites were chosen based on their level of comfort and convenience offered to shoppers.

For the fiscal year ending January 26, 2001, the company spent $31 million on computer hardware and software, on top of money spent on Web functioning. Lands' End anticipates spending another $45–$50 million in fiscal 2002 on information technology and completion of a new production facility.

Part of its technology expenditure was on two new Web capabilities designed to enhance the customer shopping experience. Lands' End has frequently been heralded for its leading edge approach to selling on the Web. Recent innovations included Lands' End Live and Shop with a Friend. Lands' End Live allows customers to shop online with real-time assistance from a company customer service representative who is connected either by phone or electronic chat. With both customer and service representative viewing the same Web page, questions and concerns can be dealt with immediately before an order is placed. Shop with a Friend enables two people in different locations to view Lands' End Web pages simultaneously.

This year, the company debuted My Virtual Model and MyPersonal Shopper, which give customers the opportunity to load personal physical information into a database in order to create a 3-D online electronic model and to create a shopping bot based on stated personal preferences for styles and fabrics, essentially replicating a live professional shopper's services.

Strategic Analysis — Social and Legal Challenges Although Lands' End is not party to any significant litigation, it may face a major battle regarding sales tax in the not-too-distant future. A 1992 Supreme Court ruling prevents states from collecting sales tax unless a mail order company has a physical presence in the state, but that was before the emergence of the Internet as a new sales tool. In 1998, the Internet Tax Freedom Act was signed, applying a three-year moratorium on charging sales tax on e-commerce transactions, with the Advisory Committee recommending an extension of that moratorium until 2006. Lands' End realizes, however, that with enough pressure from states, beginning in 2006, the company may be required to start charging sales tax on Internet purchases. Such a move could hamper further growth of that sales channel. (See *Insight on Society: Internet Taxation*.)

Future Prospects Lands' End believes the factors that create the greatest risk for the company include customer response to its merchandise and the shift from catalog to e-commerce purchases. Increasing costs associated with production of its catalogs could significantly affect the business as well. Notwithstanding these risk factors,

INSIGHT ON SOCIETY

INTERNET TAXATION

Since 1998, with the passing of the federal Internet Tax Freedom Act, online retailers have been exempt from charging customers sales tax as long as the customer is not located in a state where the company has a physical presence—the same rules that apply to direct mail catalog operations. That Act placed a moratorium on taxes until October 2001, but kept the door open for a five-year extension beyond that date.

From the consumer's perspective, not having to pay sales tax on a purchase amounts to as much as a 13% discount over a product bought locally. Local brick-and-mortar businesses believe this policy is unfair.

Physical storefronts argue that freeing online retailers from the vexing process of collecting sales tax amounts to an unfair subsidy of their operations. And given the sophistication of the technology used to power retail Web sites, such businesses should be forced to accurately calculate and collect sales tax from every consumer, just as local merchants do.

This perspective is wholeheartedly supported by state and local governments, which have been losing revenue from every Internet purchase (just as they lose out on most mail order and catalog purchases). State and local governments believe they will lose $13.7 billion in e-commerce-related taxes by 2004, according to Jupiter Media Metrix. Currently, as much as one-third of local government revenue comes from sales tax.

Online retailers, on the other hand, have complained from the start that it is unreasonable for governments to ask them to determine the appropriate tax rate from among the 7,600 different state and local taxing jurisdictions. Moreover, they argue that many of the goods they sell—such as apparel and food—are exempt from sales taxes in many states.

Another issue, argue online retailers, is determining which taxing authority gets the collected money. The answer depends on which nexus, or physical location, is used to calculate sales tax: Is it the location of the customer, the warehouse where the inventory is stored, the point from which it is shipped to the customer, or the location of the company's headquarters?

For companies with both physical storefronts and Internet operations, sales tax calculations could be even more complicated. Wal-Mart, for example, has stores nationwide and was therefore required to collect sales tax from customers in those states who ordered from Wal-Mart's online storefront. But customers complained loudly about being taxed, so Wal-Mart restructured its Internet business, creating a separate company, and formed a joint venture with a Web firm to operate it. Now Wal-Mart need only collect sales tax in the four states where the Web company has physical locations. But what should be done about in-store kiosk sales?

Bills have been introduced in both the House and the Senate to extend the moratorium on Internet taxes until 2006, but they open the door to increased taxation at the end of that term if states can simplify their sales tax collection systems. It remains to be seen whether states are actually capable of creating uniform definitions for goods and services and agreeing on a single tax rate per state within that timeframe. But the bills suggest that pressure from state governments is taking precedence over fueling continued Internet growth. Perhaps the spate of e-commerce failures has local officials turning their attention back to the stability and longevity of the brick-and-mortar revenue base.

The issue of Internet taxation has also spread beyond U.S. borders. India's government, for instance, has recently released a report recommending a uniform sales tax system and has encouraged all Internet purchases to be taxed once, thereby eliminating the double taxation that occurs with purchases by businesses in India who are taxed for both purchases of raw materials and sales of finished products. Shipments overseas, however, would not be taxed.

This brings up the issue of international commerce: Who receives the tax on an item shipped out of the country?

SOURCES: "Senators Reach Internet Tax Deal: States May Get Chance to Collect After 5 Years," by Tom Squitieri, *USA Today*, June 14, 2001; "CII Backs Taxing Trade on Net," *The Times of India*, June 14, 2001; "Boom Town: E-Tailers Faced Death, Now Can They Handle Taxes?" by Kara Swisher, *Wall Street Journal*, April 9, 2001; "Forget Taxing Internet Sales. In Fact, Just Forget Sales Taxes Altogether," by Hal Varian, *New York Times*, March 8, 2001.

Lands' End management is in a very strong position to extend the Lands' End brand to the e-commerce channel, which may offer higher margins and greater profitability than the catalog channel.

ONLINE MALLS

Online malls are a variation on the virtual merchant business model. Like offline shopping malls, these online companies generate revenue from "rents" and services paid by retailers who sell under the mall's umbrella. Firms such as FashionMall.com, eLuxury.com, Mall.com, and MaternityMall.com exemplify the concept. Online malls also face difficult strategic challenges: They must build a "centrally located" category Web site from scratch, quickly, in an entirely new channel. Essentially, online malls face all the challenges of virtual merchants plus some additional ones. These online malls benefit from not having to spend millions on physical malls, but they face large costs in building a Web site and marketing. Online malls are also dependent on the underlying success of retail merchants who have a presence at the mall. These online merchants may vary in quality. The malls may offer participating merchants a number of order entry, fulfillment, and inventory services as an additional source of revenue for the mall. Online malls are uniquely advantaged, however, because they can offer consumers a wide array of products — more than typical catalog merchants — and they do not face the direct costs of inventory, order entry, and fulfillment that are handled and paid for by participating retailers.

online malls

a variation on the virtual merchant business model; they generate revenue from "rents" and services paid for by retailers who sell under the mall's umbrella

Fashionmall.com

Fashionmall.com, Inc. operates three Internet properties specializing in fashion and lifestyle content and merchandise: Fashionmall.com, a general fashion mall with links to online retailers; Outletmall.com, which provides similar links to fashion bargains; and newly acquired Boo.com, a global style guide for the Web, whose clients include traditional and online retailers, catalogs, apparel manufacturers, and fashion magazines seeking to drive traffic from Fashionmall's customer base to their own sites. In return for providing access to its fashion-conscious Internet visitors, Fashionmall earns a per-click fee.

Based in New York City and formed originally in 1995 by several entrepreneurs, the 23-employee company has been operating at a significant loss since its initial public offering in 1999, through which it raised $35 million. To date, the company has an accumulated loss of more than $16.1 million and shows no sign of turning that trend around. It has acquired four new companies in an effort to expand its market share and increase client advertising options. It has added significantly to its sales force to shore up its weakening ad revenue base. Still, company management expresses serious doubt that "an advertising and tenant fee-based business model on the Internet can generate revenues in excess of its expenses." And in fact, since its inception, Fashionmall has been financed almost exclusively through private investments and its IPO, rather than through earnings from operations.

Business Model Fashionmall views its Web sites as vertical portals for the category of "fashion." Fashionmall defines fashion as apparel, accessories, footwear, beauty products, eyewear, jewelry, watches, home furnishings, and related lifestyle products and accessories. The Fashionmall concept combines an online shopping mall with fashion content merchandized from multiple clients to provide a centralized site for manufacturers, retailers, catalogs, e-commerce sites, and magazines to advertise, display, and sell their products on the Web. Boo.com, purchased in 2000 and re-launched in the fourth quarter of 2000, acts as a style guide and virtual "cool hunter." Boo.com's off-site "style scouts" search for cutting edge merchandise around the world and profile it with commentary and direct links to the merchants offering the products. The site is in its early stages of development, and Fashionmall managers hope to achieve revenue from the Boo.com site by pursuing advertising, sponsorship, and slotting fees. What makes Fashionmall's sites different from those of other e-tailers is that they provide links to sites where shopping can occur, rather than direct purchase opportunities, such as at jcpenney.com and Dell.com. Fashionmall has no need for an order entry system, or inventory.

Initially, Fashionmall charged its advertising clients a fixed or variable fee for site placements that were tied to the location and/or amount of traffic generated by its three sites. Advertisers lease space on Fashionmall sites as a means of driving traffic to their own Web sites, where they can market and sell merchandise to the visitor.

However, in late 1999, the company switched to a "cost-per-click" model, where clients pay according to the amount of traffic Fashionmall delivers to its site. The fee is paid to Fashionmall regardless of whether the consumer actually makes a purchase from the advertiser. Traditional banner ads and sponsorships are also available using a CPM (cost per thousand impressions) model, based on the amount of exposure provided to the advertisements.

Unfortunately, increased customer turnover and lapsed contracts are driving down Fashionmall's revenues. A larger percentage of the company's sales is being generated by a smaller pool of advertisers, with one client accounting for 25% of the company's revenues at year-end 2000. Part of the reason for the cutback is the economic downturn and across-the-board budget-cutting. However Fashionmall's inability to directly link sales to traffic from advertising on its sites is another major reason cited by clients for discontinuing their association with the company.

Financial Analysis Table 10.10 shows Fashionmall's consolidated results of operations and summary balance sheet data for 1999-2000. Revenues for 2000 were 46% higher than 1999, a sign, says the company, of increased industry acceptance of its model, resulting in increased traffic and rates for space. The company has no "cost of goods sold" since it just provides a service to vendors and customers. Therefore, gross margins are not applicable (N/A).

Expenses increased just 22% in this period, including an 18% increase in site development, merchandise, and content expenses, to $722,000. Much of that increase was attributed to the acquisition of Boo.com and the rapid re-launch of the site. Advertising and marketing expenses increased 24%, to $4.7 million, primarily due to increased branding activities in traditional and online media. One of the largest jumps was in the selling expense category, where Fashionmall saw a 256% increase, to $1.3 million, as a result of hiring eight new sales representatives — bringing the total number of sales reps to ten.

Strategic Analysis — Business Strategy To help keep its costs in check, Fashionmall has frequently bartered ad space for Web creation services and print advertising space, which has generated revenue on paper but not real income. It has also paid for online banner advertising and public relations services in this manner.

Fashionmall's strategic focus during the past two years since going public has been to invest in advertising and marketing to increase the strength of its brand as a means of driving traffic to its sites, thereby generating client fees and increasing advertising and sponsorship revenue.

Strategic Analysis — Competition Fashionmall competes against other retail fashion sites including giants such as JCPenney and Sears. Other "mall" concepts on the Web such as Amazon's Z Shops and Yahoo's Yahoo Stores stores are not directly competitive

TABLE 10.10	FASHIONMALL.COM'S CONSOLIDATED STATEMENTS OF OPERATIONS AND SUMMARY BALANCE SHEET DATA, 1999–2000

FASHIONMALL.COM INC.
CONSOLIDATED STATEMENTS OF OPERATIONS

	2000	1999
Revenue	$5,386,000	$3,690,000
Gross margin	N/A	N/A
Costs and expenses		
Site development, merchandise and content	722,000	612,000
Advertising and marketing	4,728,000	3,805,000
Selling expense	1,386,000	389,000
General and administrative	6,208,000	5,862,000
Total costs and expenses	13,044,000	10,668,000
Loss from operations	(7,658,000)	(6,978,000)
Other income/expense		
Interest and dividend income	2,570,000	1,433,000
Interest expense and other financing costs	—	(737,000)
Total other income	2,570,000	696,000
Net loss	($5,088,000)	($6,282,000)
Net margin	−94.4%	−170%

SUMMARY BALANCE SHEET DATA

At December 31	2000	1999
Current assets		
Cash and cash equivalents	$26,512,000	$34,114,000
Marketable securities	7,503,000	7,452,000
Accounts receivable	1,198,000	797,000
Total assets	38,132,000	43,541,000
Current liabilities	2,649,000	3,118,000
Long-term debt	—	—

SOURCE: Fashionmall.com, Inc. Form 10-K for the fiscal year ended December 31, 2000, filed with the Securities and Exchange Commission on April 11, 2001.

because they do not have the niche focus on leading edge fashion. Fashionmall's primary competitors for advertising and traffic dollars consist of other Web sites, specifically the apparel shopping areas of other Internet portals. Dedicated fashion sites, portals, and advertising networks, such as DoubleClick, comprise another set of competitors who vie with Fashionmall for the advertising dollars of fashion vendors. The company expects that new competitors will continue to arrive due to lack of barriers to entry.

Strategic Analysis — Technology Fashionmall's systems combine proprietary technology with commercially available products, augmenting internally developed solutions with off-the-shelf technology. Its investment in developing its infrastructure internally may mean continued higher-than-average technology costs, as well as higher-than-average service interruptions.

Strategic Analysis — Social and Legal Challenges Fashionmall's biggest legal fight has to do with its acquisition of the assets of Boo.com in early 2000. Boo Inc., a Minneapolis clothing vendor who also claims use of the term "boo," has argued that Fashionmall's use of certain Boo trademarks infringes on its own ability to differentiate and market its product. The case is currently in federal court. The company is also involved in a dispute, expected to be resolved, with a former vendor, Teknowledge Corp., which Fashionmall alleges failed to live up to its contract. As a result, Fashionmall has refused to pay its invoice for $452,204.

Although the company has no other pending litigation, its involvement in global Web site Boo.com means that issues of international e-commerce activity will inevitably arise. Since Internet rules and regulations vary by country, a Web site seeking to serve consumers worldwide may ultimately clash with a foreign regulatory body that has conflicting guidelines regarding Internet commerce.

Future Prospects The greatest risk facing Fashionmall is e-commerce competition from general merchandisers such as JCPenney and catalog companies such as Lands' End. There are few barriers to entry in the specialized fashion marketplace. Given the substantial loss from operations of $5 million, management is under pressure to significantly raise revenues while keeping costs under control. However, given its good fortune in going public in May 1999 — at the height of the dot.com boom in which it raised $34 million, Fashionmall has a substantial cushion of cash and marketable securities. At the current rate of loss, this would give management about five years to grow its brand awareness and profitability.

MANUFACTURER-DIRECT

Manufacturer-direct firms are either single or multichannel manufacturers who sell directly online to consumers without the intervention of retailers. Manufacturer-

manufacturer-direct
single or multichannel manufacturers who sell directly online to consumers without the intervention of retailers

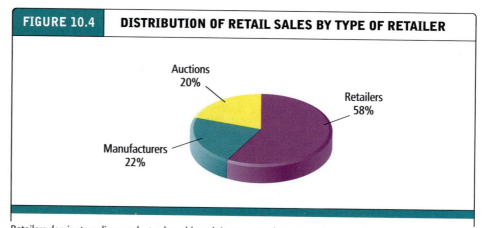

| FIGURE 10.4 | DISTRIBUTION OF RETAIL SALES BY TYPE OF RETAILER |

Retailers dominate online product sales, although in some product categories — such as computer equipment — manufacturers have made a large impact.

direct firms were predicted to play a very large role in e-commerce, but this has generally not happened (see Figure 10.4). The primary exception is computer hardware, where firms such as Dell, Compaq, Hewlett-Packard, Gateway, and IBM account for 67% of computer retail sales online. Some of these firms had retail experience prior to the Web (Dell was built on the direct sales model) whereas others — such as Compaq — had no prior direct sales experience.

As discussed in Chapter 7, manufacturer-direct firms face channel conflict challenges. Channel conflict occurs when physical retailers of products must compete on price and currency of inventory directly against the manufacturer, who does not face the cost of maintaining inventory, physical stores, or sales staffs. Firms with no prior direct marketing experience face the additional challenges of developing a fast-response online order and fulfillment system, acquiring customers, and coordinating their supply chains with market demand. Dell has avoided many of these challenges because it never had a retail channel, and long before the Web, Dell had developed a "produce on demand" custom computer business model with supporting supply chain management, call center, and manufacturing capabilities. Switching from a **supply-push model** (where products are made prior to orders received based on estimated demand) to a **demand-pull model** (where products are not built until an order is received) has proved extremely difficult for traditional manufacturers. Yet for many products, manufacturer-direct firms have the advantage of an established national brand name, an existing large customer base, and a lower cost structure than even catalog merchants because they are the manufacturer of the goods and thus do not pay profits to anyone else. Therefore, manufacturer-direct firms should have higher margins.

supply-push model

products are made prior to orders received based on estimated demand

demand-pull model

products are not built until an order is received

Dell.com

Dell Computer Corporation is the world's largest direct computer systems supplier, providing corporations, government agencies, small-to-medium businesses, and individuals with computer products and services ordered straight from the manufacturer's headquarters in Austin, Texas. Although sales representatives support corporate customers, individuals and smaller businesses buy direct from Dell by phone, fax, and via the Internet, with approximately half of the company's fiscal 2001 revenues of $31.9 billion generated online.

When Michael Dell started the company in 1984 in his college dorm room, his idea was to custom-build computers for customers, to eliminate the middleman and more effectively meet the technology needs of his customers. Today, the company sells more than individual computer systems; it offers enterprise systems, desktop, and laptop computers, as well as installation, financing, repair, and management services.

Dell operates internationally, dividing the company into three geographic segments: the Americas, Europe, and Asia-Pacific and Japan. To supply these markets, the company has manufacturing facilities strategically located worldwide, in addition to its Austin, Texas, corporate headquarters. By relying on a build-to-order manufacturing process, the company achieves faster inventory turnover, and reduced component and finished goods inventory levels; this strategy virtually eliminates the chance of product obsolescence.

Business Model The direct model simplifies the company's operations, eliminating the need to support a wholesale and retail sales network, as well as cutting out the costly associated mark-up, and gives Dell complete control over its customer database. In addition, Dell can build and ship custom computers nearly as fast as a mail order supplier can pull a computer out of inventory and ship it to the customer. Industry rivals Compaq, Gateway, and IBM typically carry 50 to 90 days of inventory, while Dell carries 5 days inventory and is aiming for 2.5 days, further reducing the capital tied up in unsold product (Perman, 2001).

To extend the benefits of its direct sales model, Dell has been aggressively moving sales, service, and support online. Each quarter, the company receives more than 500 million page visits at www.dell.com, where it maintains an estimated 80 country-specific Web sites. During the 2000 holiday season, Dell's Web site was the third most-visited site in the United States.

For corporate customers, however, the push online has been even stronger. By developing and making available Premier Pages, Dell has made it possible for companies to investigate product offerings, complete order forms and purchase orders, track orders in real time, and review order histories all online. To date, Dell has developed more than 60,000 Premier Pages for its corporate clientele worldwide. For its small business customers, it has created an online virtual account executive, as well as a spare-parts ordering system and virtual help desk with direct access to technical support data.

Financial Analysis

Financial Analysis Table 10.11 shows Dell's consolidated statements of operations and summary balance sheet data for 1998-2001. Through strong sales of servers, which showed a 39% increase in unit shipments over 2000, a jump of 52% in notebook unit sales, as well as solid revenues from its "beyond the box" services, Dell's revenues have grown impressively over the past three years. Dell's revenues were up 38% in 2000, and up a further 26% for its fiscal year ending February 2, 2001. However, its gross margins have been falling, down to 20%, as prices of computers have plunged. Average revenue per unit shipped declined 2%.

Dell's operating expenses nearly doubled over the last three years to $3.7 billion, growing faster than revenue from sales. This growth in expenditures was due primarily to increases in headcount and marketing expenses. Overall net margin remained stable at around 6%–7% over the three-year period. Dell's net margin is about seven times larger than JCPenney's, and nearly twice as large as a catalog retail firm such as Lands' End. The manufacturer-direct model, in other words, is quite profitable (at least for Dell) when compared to alternative investments in retail

With margins on PCs hitting a low of 2% in recent months, however, Dell's ability to maintain these respectable figures may be further challenged. The introduction of a new automated communication and management information system in 2000 is one step the company is taking to further shave its manufacturing costs; so far, Dell believes it is saving $40–$50 per order through the use of the new system (Perman, 2001).

Strategic Analysis — Business Strategy

Strategic Analysis — Business Strategy Recognizing that slower sales of PCs could significantly impact its revenue base, Dell has continued to broaden its offerings beyond pure product sales, adding warranty services, product integration and installation services, Internet access, software, peripherals, and technology consulting, referring to them as "beyond the box" offerings. These include nearly 30,000 software and peripheral products from leading manufacturers that can be bundled with Dell products. Dell's "beyond the box" revenues increased 37% in fiscal 2001, accounting for 18% of net revenues — a sign of their increasing importance as hardware sales slide.

Dell's sales and marketing efforts are similar for all target markets, based on the theory that demand levels for each customer group are primarily driven by similar changes in market prices and conditions. In addition to its Internet sales channel, Dell maintains a global field sales force focused on the business and institutional markets. The company also advertises on TV and online, as well as in trade and business publications, and regularly mails promotional information, catalogs, and customer newsletters to its database of prospects and customers. Dell's customer base is fairly diverse, with no one customer accounting for more than 10% of the company's net revenues during the past three years.

| TABLE 10.11 | **DELL'S CONSOLIDATED STATEMENTS OF OPERATIONS AND SUMMARY BALANCE SHEET DATA, 1999-2001** |

DELL COMPUTER CORPORATION CONSOLIDATED STATEMENTS OF OPERATIONS
(in millions)

For the fiscal year ended	February 2, 2001	January 28, 2000	January 29, 1999
Revenue			
Net revenue	$31,888	$25,265	$18,243
Cost of revenue	25,445	20,047	14,137
Gross profit	6,443	5,218	4,106
Gross margin	20%	21%	23%
Operating expenses			
Selling, general and administrative	3,193	2,387	1,788
Research, development and engineering	482	374	272
Special charges	105	194	—
Total operating expenses	3,780	2,955	2,060
Operating income	2,663	2,263	2,046
Investment and other income, net	531	188	38
Income before income taxes and cumulative effect of change in accounting principle	3,194	2,451	2,084
Provision for income taxes	958	785	624
Income before cumulative effect of change in accounting principle	2,236	1,666	1,460
Cumulative effect of change in accounting principle, net	59	—	—
Net income	2,177	1,666	1,460
Net margin	6.8%	6.6%	8%

SUMMARY BALANCE SHEET DATA
(in millions)

At	February 2, 2001	January 28, 2000	January 29, 1999
Current assets			
Cash	$4,910	$3809	$1,726
Short-term investments	528	323	923
Accounts receivable	2,895	2,608	2,094
Inventories	400	391	273
Total assets	13,435	11,471	6,877
Current liabilities	6,543	5,192	3,695
Long-term debt	509	508	512

SOURCE: Dell Computer Corporation Form 10-K for the fiscal year ended February 2, 2001, filed with the Securities and Exchange Commission on May 2, 2001.

Strategic Analysis—Competition Dell's competition consists of traditional computer retailers, such as CompUSA and Gateway, as well as corporate systems integrators and computer dealers. Although the number of competitors is not expected to increase dramatically in the near future, price wars among existing vendors could have a negative effect on Dell's profitability.

Strategic Analysis—Technology Dell's impressive manufacturing capabilities, including its virtually unheard of shipping speed, is due in good measure to its sophisticated management information system, which enables the company to track each unit sold from the initial sales contact to any post-sales support and service. Linking manufacturing facilities and operations worldwide, Dell's information system makes its direct sales model possible by coordinating component parts shipments and deliveries, order configurations, inventory levels, marketing, and deliveries. Although Dell's sales efforts are increasingly moving to the Internet as the central point of contact, its management information system is perhaps an even more critical piece of its operations.

Strategic Analysis: Social and Legal Challenges Although Dell is not currently party to any material litigation, the company is staunchly protective of its intellectual property and patents. The company currently holds 605 U.S. patents and has an additional 512 U.S. patents pending, in addition to a number of foreign patents pending as well. Dell has registered approximately 700 domain names and 300 country-specific domain names as it looks to its future on the Internet.

Future Prospects Continued reliance on the PC architecture and product model for personal computing is a long-term risk factor for Dell. Dell has not participated in the development of personal handheld computers, Internet telephony, game machines, or other forms of computing aside from Web servers. With prices of PC products likely to continue falling, Dell is under pressure to find replacement revenue streams. Cost-cutting measures such as the company's recent announcement that, for the first time, it would let go of approximately 5,700 of its 40,000 employees worldwide, may stem the slide in net margins for a short period.

10.4 COMMON THEMES IN E-COMMERCE II ONLINE RETAILING

We have looked at some very different companies in the preceding section, from entrepreneurial Web-only merchants to established offline giants. Online retail e-commerce is indeed alive and well for some retailers, particularly for established offline retailers with existing brands. Online retail is the fastest growing channel in retail on

TABLE 10.12	**PROFITABILITY PER ORDER BY ONLINE RETAIL CATEGORY**						
	BOOKS	PRE-SCRIPTION DRUGS	DRUG-STORE	APPAREL MANU-FACTURER	MULTILABEL APPAREL RETAILER	GROCERY	TOYS
Average per-order revenue	$37.82	$63.27	$19.50	$85.00	$61.82	$81.30	$52.00
Shipping revenue	$7.18	$0.80	$4.00	$9.70	$0.00	$0.00	$10.00
Total per-order revenue	$45.00	$64.07	$23.50	$94.70	$61.82	$81.30	$62.00
Cost of product	$27.92	$60.29	$20.75	$43.60	$47.01	$66.20	$40.04
Shipping costs	$7.18	$0.80	$4.88	$7.80	$9.01	$0.00	$12.00
Gross margin*	$9.90	$2.98	−$2.13	$43.30	$5.80	$15.10	$9.96
Gross margin % of revenue	22%	5%	−9%	46%	9%	19%	16%
Fulfillment costs**	$5.00	$14.29	$14.29	$10.70	$11.00	$28.00	$14.00
Contribution margin	$4.90	−$11.30	−$16.42	$32.60	−$5.20	−$12.90	−$4.04

Most online retail product categories are showing losses on each transaction. The exceptions are books and apparel.

Figures for fourth quarter 1999

*Gross margin equals total per-order revenue, less cost of product, less shipping costs.

**Included customer-service and credit card processing costs.

SOURCE: Mowry, 2000.

a revenue basis, has the fastest growing consumer base, and has growing penetration across many categories of nonessential goods. Nevertheless, online retailers are facing difficult times. The primary difficulty is the absence of profits. Table 10.12 shows that only two categories of retail e-commerce goods typically are profitable: books and apparel. For other major online product categories, there are losses, with some categories such as drugstores losing over $16 on each order.

The reasons for the absence of profits are also now clear. The path to success in any form of retail involves having a central location in order to attract a larger number of shoppers, charging high enough prices to cover the costs of goods as well as marketing, and developing highly efficient inventory and fulfillment systems so that the company can offer goods at lower costs than competitors and still make a profit. Many online merchants failed to follow these fundamental ideas, and lowered prices below the total costs of goods and operations, failed to develop efficient business processes, or spent far too much on customer acquisition and marketing.

For the most part, disintermediation did not occur and the retail middleman did not disappear. Indeed, virtual merchants, along with powerful offline merchants who moved online, maintained their powerful grip on the retail customer, with some notable exceptions in electronics and software. Manufacturers — with the exception of electronic goods — have used the Web primarily as an informational resource, driving consumers to the traditional retail channels for transactions.

In E-commerce II, the most significant online growth has been that of offline giants such as Wal-Mart and JCPenney and catalogers such as Lands' End and L.L. Bean. Many of the first mover, Web pure-play merchants failed to achieve profitability and closed their doors en masse in 2000 and 2001 as their venture capital funds were depleted. Traditional retailers are the fast followers (although many of them cannot be characterized as particularly "fast") most likely to succeed on the Web by extending their traditional competencies and assets. In this sense, e-commerce technological innovation is following the historical pattern of other technology-driven commercial changes, from automobiles and radio to television (Rigdon, 2000; Tellis and Golder, 1996).

To succeed online, established merchants need to create an integrated shopping environment that combines their catalog, store, and online experiences into one. Established retailers have significant fulfillment, inventory management, supply chain management, and other competencies that apply directly to the online channel. And although established merchants have moved online, their e-commerce operations are not always profitable. To succeed online, established retailers will need to extend their brands, incentivize consumers to use the online channel, avoid channel conflict, and build partnerships with online portals such as AOL, Amazon, and Yahoo.

Virtual merchants — young start-up ventures — need to build alliances with powerful offline branded retailers quickly in order to survive. Many virtual merchants have developed large, online customer bases, as well as the online tools required to market to their customer base. These online brands can be strengthened further through alliances and partnerships that add the required competencies in inventory management and fulfillment services. Virtual merchants need to build operational strength and efficiency before they can become profitable.

Both Web-only and established offline retailers wishing to strengthen their e-commerce revenues will be favorably affected in the future by new retailing technologies — from mobile commerce to software that gives marketers a better chance of anticipating exactly what the customers want and when. Predictive modeling, described in *Insight on Technology: Predictive Modeling Builds on CRM*, is a new Web-based software tool that will help online retailers achieve this goal.

PREDICTIVE MODELING BUILDS ON CRM

When CVS.com launched its online site in 1999, its goal was to rapidly increase market share to become an online pharmacy industry leader. Although CVS is the largest drugstore chain—with 4,100 stores and $20.1 billion in net sales—its online business at that point trailed the competition. By building a robust e-commerce infrastructure, the company hoped to win new customers and to do more business with existing customers by providing a new shopping vehicle. Its clicks and mortar strategy appears to be paying off, with CVS winning the "2000 Best in E-commerce Systems Award" in recognition of building a complete online pharmacy.

CVS has a better e-commerce system in part because of predictive modeling software the company uses to learn more about its site visitors. Predictive modeling works by studying and recognizing patterns and trends in data stored in company databases, helping to forecast sales, identify market opportunities, and manage retail inventory levels. In addition to monitoring how many people visit the site, and, of those, how many arrived there through online ads, CVS can also learn why those people visited the site, how to attract more buying visitors, and which online ads actually generated purchases rather than just traffic.

Its predictive modeling system, which builds on the basic tenets of customer relationship management (CRM), aggregates multiple data sources, combining the data with an analytical capability in order to assess which customers to target, with what message, during what time period, and through which channel, in order to reap the greatest benefits. Basic CRM systems simply keep track of customer purchases, orders, addresses, and points of contact with the company. They lack the analytical power of predictive modeling systems. Good predictive modeling software helps businesses adjust to what they expect their customers will do, rather than having to wait to see how they react to a new marketing initiative or change in marketing program.

Four key areas in which predictive modeling can impact customer behavior predictions include retention, ROI, risk, and response, according to predictive modeling developer Quadstone. Retention measures help companies gauge how likely each customer is to stop doing business with them during a certain period of time, based on data regarding past behavior and preferences stored in its databases. Predictive modeling software, however, can also help companies understand the likely effect of certain types of marketing responses to retain each customer. Based on that information, companies can target those customers most likely to stay when presented with the right marketing message. By looking at historical revenue patterns, potential future revenue patterns, net revenue, and margin for customer segments, as well as likely responses to marketing promotions, companies can improve their return on marketing investment by targeting the most lucrative customers.

(continued)

Predictive modeling can also be used to estimate the potential risk a company faces by granting credit to a particular customer. Evaluating how likely a customer is to default on a loan, as well as the customer's potential profit contribution, helps companies assess how much risk they are willing to take with each customer, based on the potential reward.

By creating a model of the potential response to a marketing campaign, companies can apply those results to various market segments and predict up front whether the program is worth implementing, or whether only certain market segments should receive it.

The growing popularity of predictive modeling software, such as that produced by Quadstone, is perhaps a reaction to the lack of solid evidence that customer relationship management systems — so-called CRM — actually work. Many companies that jumped on the CRM bandwagon have yet to demonstrate measurable results from their sizeable investments. Research from the Gartner Group seems to bear this out, stating that "Through 2006, 55 percent of CRM initiatives will fail to meet measurable benefit objectives and will fail to positively affect ROI." IDC projects, however, that the market for analytic applications, such as predictive modeling, will grow from $2 billion in 1999 to more than $6 billion in 2004. Exactly how this progress in software will square with efforts to protect consumer privacy and financial privacy is not clear at this time.

SOURCES: "On Best Behavior, PREDICT! From Quadstone," June 2001; "E-commerce Case Study: CVS.com Prescribes Quadstone to Better Understand Customer Behavior," www.quadstone.com/customer/studies/CVS.html; "Quadstone Launches Predictive Marketing Solutions for Vertical Markets and Customer Touchpoints," Quadstone Press Release, May 23, 2001; "Quadstone Picks Up CRM Solution of the Year Award," Quadstone Press Release, May 8, 2001.

L.L. Bean
Webward Bound

The president of catalog retailer L.L. Bean admits his company has been reactive when it comes to an e-commerce strategy. Although the company created a Web site in 1995, it provided more information on enjoying the outdoors than on buying L.L. Bean products. Within a year, however, L.L. Bean quickly became more aggressive in its online plans in response to growing demand from international customers.

Based in Freeport, Maine, L.L. Bean is a veteran catalog retailer that has been slowly adding retail stores and outlet shops — it now has nine nationwide — to supplement its core catalog business, as well as focusing more intently on building its Web business. More than 4.5 million customers worldwide spent about $1.2 billion at L.L. Bean in 2000, with almost 17% of that revenue resulting from international sales. But catalog sales have been relatively flat for several years. Before the mid-1990s, L.L. Bean sales were soaring at times to 20% year-to-year growth rates. But the collapse of the yen, the rise in paper and postage costs, and competition from other catalog merchants slowed Bean's growth. L.L. Bean is looking to its online site to boost sales growth by developing a new channel that complements its catalog operation.

Boosting its Web presence makes a lot of sense for L.L. Bean, the company that has been open all day and night, 365 days a year since 1951, when the company founder decided that would be company policy. The 24/7 availability of the Internet complements L.L. Bean's continuous operations nicely. Bean's staff will not need extensive new training on around-the-clock operations.

Adding an Internet sales channel also creates a new potential revenue stream without requiring a significant capital investment. The company already has the infrastructure in place to fulfill and service online orders as a result of its well-honed catalog business. Customers can order products at the Web site and return them through catalog sales, and vice versa. Coordinating prices and special promotions can cause issues, however. The Web sales effort also could potentially allow the company to cut back on catalog production and mailing, further reducing costs.

On average, catalogs cost between 50 cents and $1 to print and mail to each household, according to the Direct Marketing Association. This cost is fairly economical given the amount of information that can be provided. L.L. Bean prints 200 million such catalogs a year, its largest single expense. But putting the same catalog online costs far less, with little to no incremental cost per customer; once the catalog has been loaded, it costs the same for 100 or 100,000 customers to access the information.

Given the fact that catalog and online consumers are "a similar breed," branching out into online sales makes perfect sense for Bean. Both segments prefer to browse through merchandise at their leisure, without the help of salespeople unless specifically requested. They are also comfortable taking chances with sizes and colors based on what they see on-screen or on the page. Applying its well-honed back-office operations to the Internet has fortified Bean's sales and further expanded its distribution channels.

Since it revamped its site in 1996, Bean has carved out a strong niche in the $100,000+ household income market segment, with 22.9% of that online bracket visiting its site in August 2000, according to Jupiter Media Metrix. That puts the company in fifth place among online catalog merchants in terms of traffic, behind Nordstrom, Banana Republic, JCrew, and Coldwater Creek. In 2001, the Web site will account for about $218 million in sales, 16% of L.L. Bean's overall sales.

Catalog marketers such as Bean are finding that Internet sales are less predictable than catalog responses; most catalogs generate 75% to 80% of the sales within 40 days of mailing, making it easier to schedule inventory shipments and gauge which products are in hot demand. On the Internet, however, sales are not bunched around a particular catalog mailing, making them much less predictable and placing additional demands on the company's inventory management and logistics technology.

The biggest challenges facing L.L. Bean's online store have been maintaining customer service at its traditional high level, avoiding technological bells and whistles that interfere with customer shopping, and learning how to satisfy Web customers without alienating catalog customers. In its catalog operations, L.L. Bean does not evaluate customer service representatives based on average length of calls or on the revenue they generate. Following the founder's commitment to complete customer satisfaction, all calls are treated as unique events that should take whatever time is required to solve the problem. On the Web site, this policy translates into a person responding to all e-mails personally within four hours. As a result of its dedication to customer service, the lifetime value of L.L. Bean's online customers are about 30% greater than the industry average according to company executives.

Fortunately, Bean upgraded its fulfillment center in 1997, spending $38 million on a 650,000-square-foot warehouse consisting of four-and-a-half miles of conveyor belts and enough storage space for 4 million items. Its process for picking orders — pulling together the components of an individual's purchase, packing, and shipping them — is legendary. Today, most orders, whether by Internet or by phone, are processed and ready for shipment within 2 hours.

L.L. Bean's catalog customer is 50 years old on average, but its Web customer is 40 years old on average. This means the catalog and Web site product and promotional mixes need to be different, with the Web site emphasizing more active sports gear and different fashions. The company is still learning how to do this effectively.

SOURCES: L.L. Bean Web site, www.llbean.com; "Reality Bytes," *Wall Street Journal*, October 9, 2000; "E-retailers Turn to the Printed Page to Put Their Wares Before Consumers," by Bob Tedeschi, *New York Times*, July 10, 2000; "L.L. Bean and Net.commerce Bring the Great Outdoors to Cyberspace," IBM Case Study, July 1999; "L.L. Bean Delivers the Goods," by Kate Kane, *Fast Company*, August 1997;

Critics argue that L.L. Bean's Web site is stodgy, without many features adopted by other merchants such as online telephone contact with sales representatives. Indeed, Wall Street critics argue the company is a retail laggard, adding only 12 new stores by 2005, a "marginal effort" according to one investment analyst compared to other fast growth retailers. L.L. Bean executives counter that the company is a "meat and potatoes" company that would prefer to grow slowly and avoid hyperexpansion, as well as technology experiments that might alienate customers. L.L. Bean will add an online telephone service and companion shopper capability in 2001, but only after the technology provider demonstrates that online telephone service will equal the company's ordinary telephone service.

L.L. Bean may not be the prototypical multichannel retailer, since it prefers to extend its brand to the Web slowly over a long period of time. The L.L. Bean Web site of 2001 is far different from the site of 1995, but it has retained the emphasis on outdoor products and guidance, helping visitors choose products based on their interests and offering assistance in selecting just the right fly-rod or sleeping bag for a particular use. Now, however, visitors can browse the company's inventory of 16,000-plus pieces of outdoor gear, clothing, footwear, and gifts at the site. Although the private company does not release specific figures, this combination seems to be working.

Case Study Questions

1. What do you think are some of the customer loyalty issues that L.L. Bean managers face as they grow online sales?

2. How can L.L. Bean best pursue a multichannel retailing strategy? Is the current management making the right judgment about developing online capabilities slowly over a long period of time?

3. Critics argue that L.L. Bean should be expanding its total retail operations — including stores — at a much faster rate in order to meet the competition. Do you agree? Why or why not?

KEY CONCEPTS

■ Identify the major features of the retail sector.

Personal consumption of retail goods and services comprise 63% (nearly two-thirds) and account for about $6.2 trillion of total gross domestic product (GDP). The retail sector can be broken down into three main categories:
- *Services,* which account for 56% of total retail sales,
- *Durable goods,* which account for 14% of total retail sales, and
- *Nondurable goods,* which account for 30% of total retail sales.

Although the distinction between a good and a service is not always clear-cut and "product-based services" are becoming the norm, we use the term *retail goods* to refer to physical products and *retailers* to refer to firms that sell physical goods to consumers.

The retail industry can be further divided into eight major firm types:
- General merchandise
- Groceries
- Durable goods
- Specialty stores
- Eating and drinking
- Gasoline and fuel
- MOTO (mail order/telephone)
- Online retail firms

Each type offers opportunities for online retail. The biggest opportunities for direct online sales are within those segments that sell small-ticket items (less than $100). This includes specialty stores, general merchandisers, mail order cataloguers, and grocery stores. The mail order/telephone sector is the most similar to the online retail sales sector, and MOTO retailers are among the fastest growing online retail firms in the E-commerce II period.

■ Describe the vision of online retailing in the E-commerce I period.

During E-commerce I, some predicted that the retail industry would be revolutionized, based on the following beliefs:
- Greatly reduced search costs on the Internet would encourage consumers to abandon traditional marketplaces in order to find the lowest prices for goods. First movers who provided low-cost goods and high-quality service would succeed.
- Market entry costs would be much lower than those for physical storefront merchants, and online merchants would be more efficient at marketing and order fulfillment than their offline competitors because they had command of the technology (technology prices were falling sharply).

- Online companies would replace traditional stores as physical store merchants were forced out of business. Older traditional firms that were too slow to enter the online market would be locked out of the marketplace.
- In certain industries, the "middleman" would be eliminated (disintermediation) as manufacturers or their distributors entered the market and built a direct relationship with the consumer. This cost savings would ensure the emergence of the Web as the dominant marketing channel.
- In other industries, online retailers would gain the advantage over traditional merchants by outsourcing functions such as warehousing and order fulfillment, resulting in a kind of hypermediation, in which the online retailer gained the upper hand by eliminating inventory purchasing and storage costs.

■ **Understand the environment in which the online retail sector operates today.**

As we enter the E-commerce II period, it has become clear that few of the E-commerce I assumptions about the future of online retail were correct. Also, the structure of the retail marketplace in the United States has not been revolutionized. The reality is that:

- Online consumers are not primarily cost-driven — instead, they are as brand-driven and influenced by perceived value as their offline counterparts.
- Online market entry costs were underestimated, as was the cost of acquiring new customers.
- Older traditional firms such as the general merchandising giants and the established catalog-based retailers are taking over as the top online retail sites.
- Disintermediation did not occur. On the contrary, online retailing has become an example of the powerful role that intermediaries play in retail trade.

■ **Explain how to analyze the economic viability of an online firm.**

The economic viability, or ability of a firm to survive during a specified time period, can be analyzed by examining the key industry strategic factors, the strategic factors that pertain specifically to the firm and the financial statements for the firm. The key industry strategic factors include:

- *Barriers to entry,* which are expenses that will make it difficult for new entrants to join the industry.
- *Power of suppliers,* which refers to the ability of firms in the industry to bargain effectively for lower prices from suppliers.
- *Power of customers,* which refers to the ability of the customers for a particular product to shop among the firm's competitors, thus keeping prices down.
- *Existence of substitute products,* which refers to the present or future availability of products with a similar function.
- *The industry value chain,* which must be evaluated to determine if the chain of production and distribution for the industry is changing in ways that will benefit or harm the firm.
- *The nature of intra-industry competition,* which must be evaluated to determine if the competition within the industry is based on differentiated products and

services, price, the scope of the offerings, or the focus of the offerings and whether any imminent changes in the nature of the competition will benefit or harm the firm.

The key firm strategic factors include:

- The *firm value chain*, which must be evaluated to determine if the firm has adopted business systems that will enable it to operate at peak efficiency and whether there are any looming technological changes that might force the firm to change its processes or methods.
- *Core competencies,* which refer to unique skills that a firm has that cannot be easily duplicated. When analyzing the economic viability of a firm, it is important to consider whether technological changes might invalidate these competencies.
- *Synergies,* which refer to the availability to the firm of the competencies and assets of related firms that it owns or with which it has formed strategic partnerships.
- The firm's current *technology,* which must be evaluated to determine if it has proprietary technologies that will allow it to scale with demand and if it has developed the customer relationship, fulfillment, supply chain management, and human resources systems that it will need in order to be viable.
- The *social and legal challenges* facing the firm, which should be examined to determine if the firm has taken into account consumer trust issues such as the privacy and security of personal information and if the firm may be vulnerable to legal challenges.

The key financial factors include:

- *Revenues,* which must be examined to determine if they are growing and at what rate.
- *Cost of sales,* which is the cost of the products sold, including all related costs. The lower the cost of sales compared to revenue, the higher the gross profit.
- *Gross margin,* which is calculated by dividing gross profit by net sales. If the gross margin is improving consistently, the economic outlook for the firm is enhanced.
- *Operating expenses,* which should be evaluated to determine if the firm's needs in the near interim will necessitate increased outlays. Large increases in operating expenses may result in net losses for the firm.
- *Net margin,* which is calculated by dividing net income or net loss by net sales. It evaluates the net profit or loss for each dollar of net sales. For example, a net margin of –24% indicates that a firm is losing 24 cents on each dollar of net sales.
- The firm's *balance sheet,* which is a financial snapshot of a company on a given date that displays its financial assets and liabilities. If current assets are less than or not much more than current liabilities, the firm will likely have trouble meeting its short-term obligations.

■ **Identify the challenges faced by the different types of online retailers.**

There are five major types of online retail business models, and each faces its own particular challenges:

- *Virtual merchants* are single-channel Web firms that generate all of their revenues from online sales. Their challenges include building a business and a brand name quickly, many competitors in the virtual marketplace, substantial costs to build and maintain a Web site, considerable marketing expenses, large customer acquisition costs, a steep learning curve, and the need to quickly achieve operating efficiencies in order to preserve a profit. Buy.com is an example of a general merchandiser virtual merchant and Ashford.com is an example of a niche merchandiser virtual merchant.

- *Clicks and mortar* companies have a network of physical stores as their primary retail channel, but have also begun online operations. Their challenges include high cost of physical buildings, high cost of large sales staffs, the need to coordinate prices across channels, the need to develop methods of handling cross-channel returns from multiple locations, building a credible Web site, hiring new skilled staff, and building rapid-response order entry and fulfillment systems. JCPenney.com is an example of a clicks and mortar company.

- *Catalog merchants* are established companies that have a national offline catalog operation as their largest retail channel, but who have recently developed online capabilities. Their challenges include high costs for printing and mailing, the need to leverage their existing assets and competencies to the new technology environment, the need to develop methods of handling cross-channel returns, building a credible Web site, and hiring new skilled staff. Landsend.com is an example of a catalog merchant.

- *Online malls* are a variation on the virtual merchant business model. Like their offline counterparts, they generate revenue by collecting "rent" and by charging for services they provide to merchants who sell on their site. Their challenges include building a "centrally located" Web site quickly and from scratch, substantial costs to build and maintain the Web site, many competitors in the virtual marketplace, building a business and a brand name quickly, considerable marketing expenses, large customer acquisition costs, a steep learning curve, the need to quickly achieve operating efficiencies in order to preserve a profit, and dependency on the success of the retail merchants they recruit to the mall. Fashionmall.com is an example of an online mall.

- *Manufacturer-direct* merchants are either single or multi-channel manufacturers who sell to consumers directly online without the intervention of retailers. They were predicted to play a very large role in e-commerce, but this has not generally happened. Their challenges include channel conflict, which occurs when physical retailers of a manufacturer's products must compete on price and currency of inventory with the manufacturer who does not face the cost of maintaining inventory, physical stores, and a sales staff, quickly developing a fast-response online order and fulfillment system, switching from a supply-push (products are made prior to orders being received based on estimated demand) to a demand-pull model (products are not built until an order is received), and creating sales, service and support operations online. Dell.com is an example of a manufacturer-direct merchant.

QUESTIONS

1. Why were so many entrepreneurs drawn to start businesses in the online retail sector initially?
2. What frequently makes the difference between profitable and unprofitable online businesses today?
3. Name four additional value-added services manufacturers are increasingly offering as part of product sales.
4. Which of the eight types of retail business is most like online retailing? Why?
5. Name the largest segment of U.S. retail sales. Explain why businesses in this segment have achieved and continue to dominate online retailing.
6. Describe the technological revolution that preceded the growth of e-commerce. What were some of the innovations that made later online retailing possible?
7. Name two assumptions e-commerce analysts made early on about consumers and their buying behavior that turned out to be false.
8. Why were customer acquisition costs assumed early on to be lower on the Web? What was supposed to reduce those costs?
9. Explain the distinction between disintermediation and hypermediation as it relates to online retailing.
10. How would you describe the top 10 online retailers as a group? Do they account for a small or large percent of online business, for example?
11. Name two retail product categories that have been demonstrating greater than 50% annual growth.
12. Compare and contrast virtual merchants and clicks and mortar firms. What type of online retailer is most like the virtual merchant?
13. What is the difference between a supply-push and a demand-pull sales model? Why do most manufacturer-direct firms have difficulty switching to one of these?
14. What are five strategic issues specifically related to a firm's capabilities? How are they different from industry-related strategic issues?
15. Which is a better measure of a firm's financial health: revenues, gross margin, or net margin? Why?

PROJECTS

1. Find the SEC Web site at www.sec.gov, and access the EDGAR archives, where you can review 10-K filings for all public companies. Search for the 10-K report for the most recent completed fiscal year for two online retail companies of your choice (preferably ones operating in the same area, such as Barnesandnoble.com and Borders.com). Prepare a PowerPoint or other form of presentation that compares the financial stability and prospects of the two businesses, focusing specifically on the performance of their respective Internet operations.

2. Examine the financial statements for Ashford.com and Fashionmall.com within the chapter. What observations can you make about the two businesses? Which one is stronger financially and why? Which one's business model appears to be weaker and why? If you could identify two major problem areas for each, what would they be? Prepare a PowerPoint or other form of presentation that makes your case.

3. Conduct a thorough analysis — strategic and financial — of one of the following companies: CDNow, OfficeDepot, or Victoria's Secret. Prepare a PowerPoint or other form of presentation that summarizes your observations about the company's Internet operations and future prospects.

4. Find an example not mentioned in the text of each of the five types of online retailing business models. Prepare a short report describing each firm and why it is an example of the particular business model.

5. Drawing on material in the chapter and your own research, prepare a short paper describing your views on the major social and legal issues facing online retailers.

WEB SITE RESOURCES   www.LearnE-commerce.net

- News: Weekly updates on topics relevant to the materials in this chapter
- Video Lecture: Professor Ken Laudon summarizes the key concepts of the chapter
- Research: Abstracts and links to articles referenced in the chapter as well as other relevant research
- International Spotlight: More information about retail e-commerce outside the United States
- PowerPoint Slides: Illustrations from the chapter and more
- Additional projects and exercises

CHAPTER 11

Online Service Industries

After reading this chapter, you will be able to:

- Describe the major features of the online service sector.
- Discuss the trends taking place in the online financial services industry.
- Identify the key features of the online banking and brokerage, insurance, and real estate industries.
- Explain why online travel services can be considered the most successful B2C segment.
- Describe the major trends in the online travel services industry today.
- Explain why career services online may be the ideal Web business.
- Identify current trends in the online career services industry.

One by Net, Two by Land
NetBank Expands

NetBank is the first federally insured bank to operate in the United States solely on the Internet. Formed in 1996 under the trade name Atlanta Internet Bank, the founders of NetBank believed it had first-mover advantages relative to other online banks and a cost advantage over traditional banks burdened by thousands of bricks-and-mortar branches and expensive ATM machines. NetBank is one of the few Internet banks to operate profitably over several years, and it continues to grow rapidly. By June 30, 2001, NetBank had over 230,000 accounts in all 50 states and 20 foreign countries (nearly double the number of accounts in the previous year) and $2.2 billion in assets. It has been able to offer its customers a full line of banking services — from checking to mortgages and loans, credit cards, online brokerage, insurance, IRAs, and free unlimited online bill payment. Because of its lower cost structure, it is also able to offer customers 3% interest on savings accounts and free checking — benefits that traditional banks, with their higher costs, cannot match.

Despite its success in branchless Internet banking, NetBank's future growth — like that of most other pure Internet financial services firms — will increasingly depend on developing a physical presence in neighborhoods across the United States, in addition to an aggressive expansion program in pure online ventures.

NetBank is not alone: Other pure Internet banking ventures have either failed or switched strategies to include building a physical presence. As it turns out, despite the advantage of having up to a 50% lower general and administrative cost structure, the Net-only banking business model does not work as a model for a major new sector of the financial services industry. Why not?

NetBank's early vision of first-mover advantage has turned out to be a mirage. Other online financial services firms such as E*Trade.com and Juniper.com successfully moved into online banking in 2001, and established bricks-and-mortar banks such as Wells Fargo, Citigroup, and Chase have entered the online market and grown far larger and faster than NetBank. In a year, E*Trade has opened over 400,000 accounts — almost twice the total number of NetBank's accounts — and has $12 billion in assets. Other formerly pure online financial services firms, such as E*Trade and Ameritrade.com, are rapidly developing networks of kiosks and investment centers around the country. But it has been much easier for established full-service banks to develop an online presence than it has been for pure online banks to develop the physical infrastructure that many customers demand from banks.

While the online banking market is huge — 22 million Internet users in the United States will use online banking services in 2001 — only 4% of them will use a pure Net-only bank as their primary bank. The other 96% use the Internet channel provided by their existing bank. The established banks might be second to market, or they might even be slow followers, but they have been successful in converting millions of offline banking customers to their Web services.

To counter the growth of its competitors, NetBank continues to expand online. It purchased a less successful online bank called Compubank in 2001. This added an additional 100,000 accounts. NetBank also developed a relationship with Intuit. When users install Intuit's accounting package Quicken, a NetBank icon will be placed on the user's computer screen.

The biggest change at NetBank is its purchase of Market Street Mortgage, a Florida-based mortgage lender with 43 bricks-and-mortar offices in 11 states. In addition, NetBank is involved in discussions with an automated teller machine network. Although NetBank customers can withdraw cash from thousands of ATMs operated by the large banking networks such as Cirrus, they cannot deposit money. Instead, NetBank customers must first have a checking account at a traditional physical bank and then use that checking account to transfer funds to their NetBank accounts. Or NetBank's customers mail funds to NetBank. In either event, without physical presence, using NetBank is inconvenient for many banking activities.

One would think given the higher interest rates, free services, and sheer online convenience, that millions of customers would flock to NetBank and its other online cousins. In England, for instance, the world's largest pure online bank, Egg.com, has over 1.5 million customers. But in the United States, customers have learned that using a pure online bank can be a lot less convenient than using a regular bank. To a large extent, the inconvenience factor is the main reason why NetBank has failed to grow into a sizable bank even though it is profitable. The future for NetBank — as most pure Internet financial services firms have also learned — is on land.

SOURCES: NetBank Inc. Form 10-Q for the six-month period ended June 30, 2001, filed with the Securities and Exchange Commission on August 14, 2001; "By Land and by Web, NetBank Expands Reach," by Tara Siegel Bernard, *Wall Street Journal*, August 9, 2001; "Round One Knockout," by Stan Draenos, *Upside Today*, July 2001; NetBank Inc. Form 10-K for the fiscal year ended December 31, 2000, filed with the Securities and Exchange Commission on March 28, 2001; "Don't Bank On It," by Sean Donahue, *Business 2.0*, January 2001.

T he promise of online service providers such as NetBank is that they can deliver superior quality service and greater convenience to millions of consumers at a lower cost than established bricks-and-mortar service providers, and still make a respectable return on invested capital. If e-commerce is going to succeed, it would appear that the service sector is the place where it will happen because so much of the value in services is based on collecting, storing, and exchanging information — something for which the Web is ideally suited. And, in fact, online services have been extraordinarily successful in attracting banking, brokerage, travel, and job hunting customers. The quality and amount of information online to support consumer decisions in finance, travel, and career placement is also extraordinary, especially when compared to what was available to consumers before e-commerce. However, translating these successes into profitable operations has proved far more difficult than anticipated.

In this chapter, we take a close look at the three most successful online services: financial services (including insurance and real estate), travel services, and career services.

11.1 THE SERVICE SECTOR: OFFLINE AND ONLINE

The online service sector — like online retail — has shown both explosive growth and some recent impressive failures. Despite the failures, online services have established a significant beachhead and they are continuing to grow, although more slowly than in the early years. In selected areas such as online brokerage and banking, online services are an extraordinary success story, and are transforming their industries. As with the retail sector, many of the early innovators — delivery services such as Kozmo and WebVan and consulting firms such as BizConsult.com — are gone. However, some early innovators such as E*Trade and Schwab have been successful, while many established service providers such as Citigroup, Wells Fargo, and Merrill Lynch, and the large airlines have developed successful online e-commerce service delivery sites.

The service sector is the largest and most rapidly expanding part of the economies in advanced industrial nations such as the United States, and in European and some Asian countries. In the United States, services employ 37% of the labor force and account for $1.8 trillion in Gross Domestic Product (GDP). If you add Finance, Insurance, and Real Estate (**FIRE**), about 44% of the labor force works in service delivery, and the combined group accounts for around $3.5 trillion of U.S. economic output or 40% of the entire U.S. economy (see Figures 11.1 and 11.2).

On the other hand, productivity in the service sector has lagged far behind productivity in factories and on farms. Productivity in the service sector over the last decade has averaged about 1%, while farm and factory productivity has averaged about 5% (U.S. Census Bureau, 2001). While the explosion in information technology

FIRE

finance, insurance, and real estate services

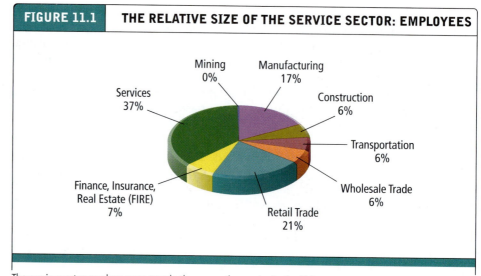

FIGURE 11.1 | **THE RELATIVE SIZE OF THE SERVICE SECTOR: EMPLOYEES**

The service sector employs more people than any other sector in the U.S. economy.

SOURCE: Table 715, Statistical Abstract of United States, 2000.

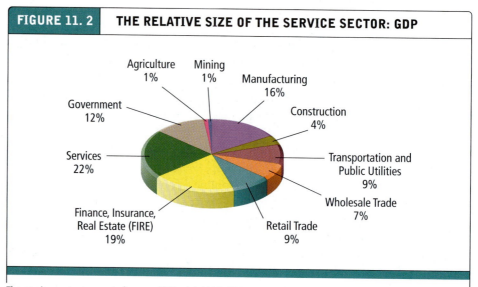

FIGURE 11. 2 | **THE RELATIVE SIZE OF THE SERVICE SECTOR: GDP**

The service sector accounts for over 40% of the U.S. GDP.

SOURCE: Table 715, Statistical Abstract of United States, 2000.

capital investment since 1995 has certainly added to overall productivity, "white collar" service sector employees did not benefit from this as much as factory employees. In part, this is because the very nature of services — performing activities for others in a highly personalized and customized manner — is somewhat immune to the beneficial aspects of computerization. The productivity of doctors, lawyers, accountants, and business consultants — all service occupations — has not been markedly affected in terms of unit output per unit time by the explosion in information technology, although the quality of their work has undoubtedly improved. What this means for e-commerce is that the service sector offers extraordinary opportunities insofar as e-commerce sites can deliver information, knowledge, and transaction efficiencies.

WHAT ARE SERVICES?

Just what are services? The U.S. Department of Labor defines **service occupations** as "concerned with performing tasks" in and around households, business firms, and institutions (U.S. Department of Labor, 1991). The U.S. Census Bureau defines **service industries** as those "domestic establishments providing services to consumers, businesses, governments and other organizations" (U.S. Census Bureau, 2001). Figure 11.3 lists the major service industry groups and their relative size.

FIRE (finance, insurance, and real estate) services, business services, and health services are the largest service industries. Business services include activities such as consulting, advertising and marketing, and information processing.

service occupations
occupations concerned with performing tasks in and around households, business firms, and institutions

service industries
establishments providing services to consumers, businesses, governments, and other organizations

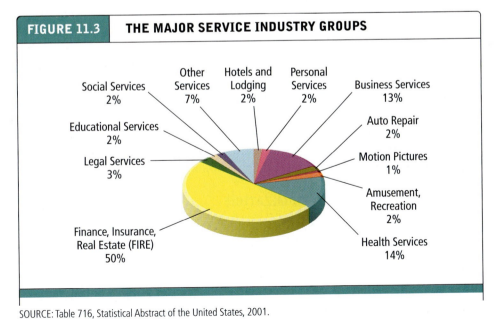

| FIGURE 11.3 | THE MAJOR SERVICE INDUSTRY GROUPS |

- Social Services 2%
- Educational Services 2%
- Legal Services 3%
- Finance, Insurance, Real Estate (FIRE) 50%
- Other Services 7%
- Hotels and Lodging 2%
- Personal Services 2%
- Business Services 13%
- Auto Repair 2%
- Motion Pictures 1%
- Amusement, Recreation 2%
- Health Services 14%

SOURCE: Table 716, Statistical Abstract of the United States, 2001.

CATEGORIZING SERVICE INDUSTRIES

transaction brokering

acting as an intermediary to facilitate a transaction

Within these service industry groups, companies can be further categorized into those that involve **transaction brokering** (acting as an intermediary to facilitate a transaction) and those that involve providing a "hands-on" service. For instance, one type of financial services involves stockbrokers who act as the middle person in a transaction between buyers and sellers. Online mortgage companies such as Mortgage-Ramp.com refer customers to mortgage companies that actually issue the mortgage. Employment agencies put a seller of labor in contact with a buyer of labor. The service involved in all these examples is brokering a transaction.

In contrast, legal, medical, accounting, and other such industries perform specific hands-on activities for consumers. In order to provide their service, these professionals need to interact directly and personally with the "client." For these service industries, the opportunities for e-commerce are somewhat different. Currently, doctors and dentists cannot treat patients over the Internet. However, the Internet can assist their services by providing consumers with information, knowledge, and communication.

KNOWLEDGE AND INFORMATION INTENSITY

With some exceptions (for example, providers of physical services, such as cleaning, gardening, and so on), perhaps the most important feature of service industries (and occupations) is that they are knowledge and information intense. In order to provide value, service industries process a great deal of information and employ a highly skilled, educated work force. For instance, to provide legal services, you need lawyers with law degrees. Law firms are required to process enormous amounts of textual information. Likewise with medical services. Financial services are not so knowledge intensive, but require much larger investments in information processing just to keep track of transactions and investments. In fact, the financial services sector is the largest investor in information technology, with over 80% of invested capital going to information technology equipment and services (Laudon and Laudon, 2001).

For these reasons, many services are uniquely suited to e-commerce applications and the strengths of the Internet, which are to collect, store, and disseminate high value information and to provide reliable, fast communication.

PERSONALIZATION AND CUSTOMIZATION

Services differ in the amount of personalization and customization required, although just about all services entail some personalization or customization. Some services, such as legal, medical, and accounting services, require extensive personalization — the adjustment of a service to the precise needs of a single individual or object. Others, such as financial services, benefit from customization by allowing individuals to choose from a restricted menu. The ability of Internet and e-commerce technology to personalize and customize service, or components of service, is a major factor under-girding the extremely rapid growth of e-commerce services. Future expansion of e-services will depend in part on the ability of e-commerce firms to transform their customized services — choosing from a list — into truly personalized services, such as providing unique advice and consultation based on a digital, yet intimate under-standing of the client (at least as intimate as professional service providers).

11.2 ONLINE FINANCIAL SERVICES

The online financial services sector is a shining example of an e-commerce success story, but the success is somewhat different than what had been predicted in the E-commerce I era. While the innovative, pure-online firms have been instrumental in transforming the brokerage industry, the impacts of e-commerce have been less pow-erful in banking, insurance, and real estate, where consumers are more likely to use the Web for research, but conduct transactions through traditional suppliers.

In addition, pure online financial services firms are, in general, not yet profitable. The costs of marketing and technology have far exceeded the early estimates of E-commerce I analysts. As in the retail marketspace, in E-commerce II, it is the mul-tichannel established financial services firms — the slow followers — who are showing the fastest growth and strongest prospects of long-term survival.

ONLINE ASSET GROWTH

Figure 11.4 illustrates the rapid growth of online financial services. At the present time, about $2 trillion is managed online by individuals, but by 2005, another $3 tril-lion will be added. Currently, about 33 million households (or about 30% of the 120 million households) in the United States use online banks or brokerages, and this number is expected to grow to about 75 million households by 2005, comprising more than half of all households (see Figure 11.5).

The movement toward online asset management is global, with Western Europe leading all regions (see Table 11.1). Western Europe has far fewer, but larger banks than the United States, and more extensive national banking institutions, whereas the United States has historically relied on many more local banking firms. By 2004, there are expected to be over 120 million individuals banking online worldwide.

ONLINE FINANCIAL CONSUMER BEHAVIOR

For many of the approximately 18 million online banking households, financial sites are among the first ones they visit on the Web. Financial institutions are increasingly encouraging their customers to visit their online sites. Surveys show that consumers are attracted to financial sites because of their desire to save time and access

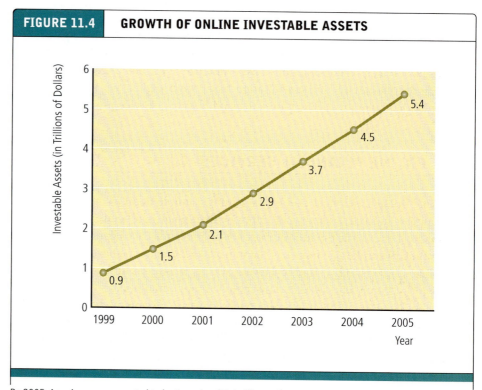

| FIGURE 11.4 | **GROWTH OF ONLINE INVESTABLE ASSETS** |

By 2005, Americans are expected to be investing $5.4 trillion online.
SOURCE: Jupiter Media Metrix, 2000a.

information rather than saving money, although saving money is an important goal among the most sophisticated online financial households. Most online consumers use financial services sites for mundane financial management, such as checking balances of existing accounts, most of which were established offline. Once accustomed to performing mundane financial management activities, consumers move on to more sophisticated capabilities such as using personal financial management tools, making loan payments, and considering offers from online institutions (Jupiter Media Metrix, 2000c). Table 11.2 shows the online financial activities of online financial households (not the entire online population).

Online stock trade execution — now around 7% of online consumers — is the most rapidly expanding financial activity. The number of online trading households is expected to grow from 15 million to 34 million by 2005.

The number of insurance quotes accessed online is also increasing, with most of this activity involving auto insurance. In general, online consumers have not shown

---

FIGURE 11.5 | **ONLINE INVESTING AND BANKING**

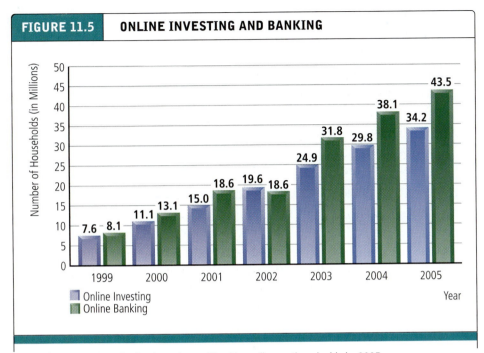

The market penetration of online investing and banking will more than double by 2005.

SOURCE: Jupiter Media Metrix, 2000a.

interest in life or property insurance. And even though consumers are seeking insurance information online, online sales have not become popular: Fewer than 5% of online consumers have purchased any kind of insurance online, preferring instead to purchase insurance through traditional agents.

TABLE 11.1 | **NUMBER OF INDIVIDUALS BANKING ONLINE (IN MILLIONS)**

	WESTERN EUROPE	UNITED STATES	JAPAN	ASIA PACIFIC	REST OF WORLD	TOTAL
2000	18.6	9.9	2.5	2.4	1	34.4
2001	28	14.7	6.5	4.4	1.7	55.3
2002	37.8	17.1	11.9	6.8	3.1	76.7
2003	47.7	20.4	19.6	9.8	5.1	102.6
2004	57.9	22.8	21.8	13.9	6.1	122.5

SOURCE: Hallford, 2001.

TABLE 11.2	ONLINE CONSUMERS' FINANCIAL ACTIVITIES	
Checked stock quotes	31%	
Conducted online banking	30%	
Searched for real estate information	24%	
Paid bill	21%	
Applied for car loan or credit card	20%	
Requested insurance quote	16%	
Executed stock trade	7%	

SOURCE: Jupiter Media Metrix, 2000c.

Online consumers are likely to have relationships with multiple financial institutions, and there is a positive relationship between personal wealth, age, and the number of financial institution relationships. In general, older, wealthier individuals accumulate financial relationships as they move through life.

FINANCIAL SERVICES INDUSTRY TRENDS

The financial services industry provides four generic kinds of services: storage and access to funds, protection of assets, means to grow assets, and movement of funds. Historically in the United States and elsewhere, these financial services were provided by separate institutions (see Table 11.3).

However, two important global trends in the financial services industry that have direct consequences for online financial services firms are changing the institutional structure of financial services. The first trend is industry consolidation (see Figure 11.6).

In the United States, the banking, finance, brokerage, and insurance industries were legally separated by the Glass-Steagall Act of 1934, which prohibited banks,

TABLE 11.3	TRADITIONAL PROVIDERS OF FINANCIAL SERVICES
FINANCIAL SERVICE	INSTITUTIONAL PROVIDER
Storage of and access to funds	Banking, lending
Protection of assets	Insurance
Growth	Investment firms, brokerage
Movement of funds (payment)	Banks, credit card firms

| FIGURE 11.6 | INDUSTRY CONSOLIDATION AND INTEGRATED FINANCIAL SERVICES |

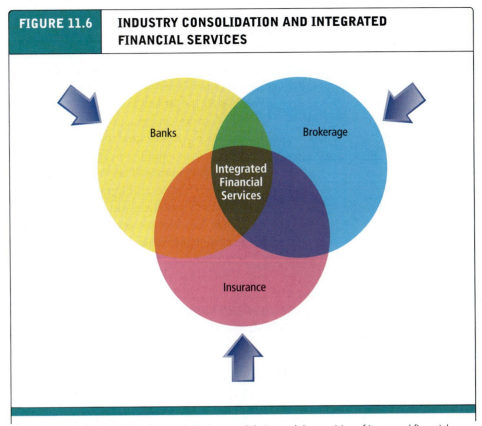

The major trends in financial services are industry consolidation and the provision of integrated financial services to consumers.

insurance firms, and brokerages from having significant financial interests in one another in order to prevent a repetition of the calamitous financial institution failures that followed the stock market crash of 1929 and the ensuing Depression. The Glass-Steagall Act also prevented large banks from owning banks in other states. This legal separation meant that financial institutions in the United States could not provide customers with integrated financial services, and could not operate nationwide. One result was the proliferation of small, inefficient, local banks in the United States, arguably the most "over-banked" country in the world with 11,420 banks (one bank for every 26,000 citizens compared to the United Kingdom's 420 banks — a 1:140,000 ratio — and 41 banks in Canada — a 1:600,000 ratio). West European and Japanese financial institutions did not face similar restrictions, putting the American industry at a disadvantage. The Financial Reform Act of 1998 amended Glass-Steagall and permitted banks, brokerages, and insurance firms to merge and to develop nationwide banks.

CitiBank, for instance, purchased Travelers Insurance in 1999, and E*Trade.com, an online brokerage firm, purchased Telebank to offer online banking services and 11 other companies such as LoansDirect and Card Capture Services (the third largest ATM network in the United States) and added 10,000 financial services kiosks in Target stores across the country. TD Waterhouse, another formerly pure online player, is opening 200 full-service financial centers around the United States in 2001.

A second related trend is the movement toward integrated financial services. Once banks, brokerages, and insurance companies are permitted to own one another, it becomes possible to provide consumers with what countless surveys have documented they really want: trust, service, and convenience. The movement toward financial service integration began in the 1980s when Merrill Lynch developed the first "cash management account" that integrated the brokerage and cash management services provided to Merrill Lynch's customers into a single account. Spare cash in each customer account was invested at the close of business each day into a money market fund. In the 1990s, CitiBank and other large money center banks developed

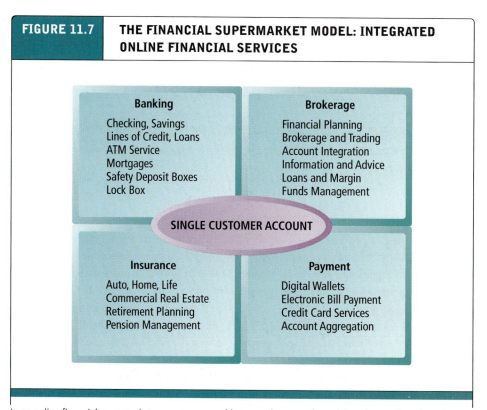

FIGURE 11.7 | **THE FINANCIAL SUPERMARKET MODEL: INTEGRATED ONLINE FINANCIAL SERVICES**

Banking
Checking, Savings
Lines of Credit, Loans
ATM Service
Mortgages
Safety Deposit Boxes
Lock Box

Brokerage
Financial Planning
Brokerage and Trading
Account Integration
Information and Advice
Loans and Margin
Funds Management

SINGLE CUSTOMER ACCOUNT

Insurance
Auto, Home, Life
Commercial Real Estate
Retirement Planning
Pension Management

Payment
Digital Wallets
Electronic Bill Payment
Credit Card Services
Account Aggregation

In an online financial supermarket, consumers are able to purchase any financial service product through a single account at one institution.

the concept of a **financial supermarket**, where consumers could find any financial product or service at a single physical center or branch bank (see Figure 11.7). Nearly all large national banks now provide some form of financial planning and investment service.

The Internet has created the technical foundations for an online financial supermarket to operate, but, for the most part, it has still not arrived. It is not yet possible to arrange for a car loan, obtain a mortgage, receive investment planning advice, and establish a pension fund at any single financial institution with one account. Nevertheless, this is the direction in which large banking institutions are attempting to move.

The promise of the Internet in the long term is to take the financial supermarket model one step further by providing a truly personalized, customized, and integrated offering to consumers based on a complete understanding of the consumer and his or her financial behavior, life cycle status, and unique needs. It will take many years to develop the technical infrastructure, as well as change consumer behavior toward a much deeper relationship with online financial services institutions.

financial supermarket
provides a variety of financial products and services at a single physical center or branch bank

ONLINE BANKING AND BROKERAGE

Online banking was pioneered in the United States by NetBank and Wingspan in 1996 and 1997, respectively. Traditional banks had developed earlier versions of telephone banking, but did not use online services until 1998. Although late by a year or two, the established brand name national banks have taken a substantial lead in market share as measured by the number of unique visitors. This is also true with brokerage firms. Early innovators such as E*Trade and Ameritrade have been displaced from their leadership positions by financial industry giant Fidelity (which has more mutual fund customers and more funds under management than any other U.S. firm) and discount broker pioneer Charles Schwab. Merrill Lynch, the largest stock brokerage firm in the United States, did not develop an online presence until 2000, but it is rapidly adding new clients from its established client base. Merrill has shot into the number six position among online brokerages (see Table 11.4). Following the market crash of technology and dot.com stocks in Spring 2000, trading at pure online firms such as Ameritrade, DLJ Direct, and E*Trade fell precipitously, while established brands such as Fidelity and Merrill Lynch remained fairly steady. We examine E*Trade's experience in depth in the section, E-commerce in Action: E*Trade.com.

Multichannel vs. Pure Online Financial Services Firms

Online consumers prefer to visit financial services sites that have physical outlets or branches. In general, multichannel financial services firms that have both physical branches or offices plus solid online offerings are growing faster than and assuming market leadership in competition with pure online firms that have no physical pres-

TABLE 11.4	THE LEADING FINANCIAL SERVICES FIRMS

Top Online Banking Firms: Unique Visitors (in thousands)

	NOV 2001	MAY 2001	% GROWTH
Wells Fargo	2030	3298	62.5%
Bank of America	1887	3109	64.8%
CitiBank	1954	2453	25.5%
NetBank	904	1252	38.5%
Chase	1008	1229	21.9%
BankOne	620	728	17.4%
Juniper.com	147	384	161.2%
EtradeBank	273	260	−4.8%
WingspanBank	297	239	−19.5%

Top Online Brokerage Firms: Market Share and Unique Visitors (in thousands)

	MARKET SHARE	UNIQUE VISITORS MARCH 2000	UNIQUE VISITORS AUGUST 2000	% DECLINE
E*Trade	23%	2882	2039	−29%
Fidelity	23%	1974	1978	0%
Charles Schwab	13%	1161	1095	−6%
Ameritrade	9%	1408	821	−42%
Datek	6%	651	565	−13%
Merrill Lynch	6%	470	500	6%
DLJDirect	6%	875	484	−45%
TD Waterhouse	5%	634	422	−33%
MSDW	4%	315	383	22%
Smith Barney	4%	397	350	−12%
Other	1%	135	100	−26%

SOURCES: Online Banking: Jupiter Media Metrix, 2001a; Online Brokerage: Mowrey, 2001 and Jupiter Media Metrix, 2000b.

ence. The three leading online banking firms — Wells Fargo, Bank of America, and Citigroup — have thousands of branches where customers can open accounts, deposit money, take out loans, find home mortgages, and rent a safety deposit box. Fidelity has service center branches, although it primarily relies on the telephone for interacting with investors, and Charles Schwab has decided to open investment centers around the country as an adjunct to its online strategy. Pure online banks and brokerages cannot provide customers with many services that still require a hands-on interaction.

Customer Acquisition, Conversion, and Retention

Internet-only banks and brokerages lack physical client acquisition channels and therefore they must rely on their Web sites and advertising to acquire customers, whereas established multichannel institutions can convert existing branch customers to online customers at a far lower cost. In 2000, online brokerage firms were paying up to $500 to acquire customers, whereas multichannel institutions were paying less than $50. Multichannel institutions draw nearly four times as many visitors as pure online institutions, and more than 86% of those visitors open a secure channel (indicating an interest in transacting) compared to only 50% of visitors to pure online institutions. In terms of loyalty and intensity, a different picture emerges. Users of pure online institutions utilize these sites more intensively for a wide variety of services that used to be performed at branches, whereas the established multichannel site users do less online and less often. However, customers of pure online institutions comparison shop more, are more price driven, and are less loyal than customers of established multichannel players (Jupiter Media Metrix, 2001b).

E-Commerce in Action: E*Trade.com

Menlo Park-based E*Trade Group, Inc. provides an estimated 3.7 million customers with online personal financial services, including domestic brokerage (its core service with 2.9 million accounts), banking (400,000 accounts), and global and institutional brokerage (100,000 accounts). E*Trade started business in 1996 — at the dawn of E-commerce I — the same year as its main online competitors Schwab (a bricks-and mortar-discount broker), DLJDirect, and CDFBdirect. They all were following in the footsteps of PC Financial Network (a spin-off of the Donaldson Lufkin Jenrette brokerage firm), which began electronic brokerage on the Prodigy proprietary network in 1988.

The Vision In 1996, the new Internet-based brokerages such as E*Trade promised to revolutionize the domestic brokerage business by offering low, flat-rate discount commissions on stock trades, free online price feeds, free stock quotations, online order entry, more efficient order execution, and better customer service than traditional bricks-and-mortar brokers. Some of the new online companies also promised high-quality, free stock research and market analysis — services for which traditional firms charged. The online brokers of E-commerce I promised to revolutionize the way people bought and sold stocks and other financial instruments. Instead of having to call brokers to check prices and make transactions, the customer would be immersed in a totally new online, dynamic environment where information and transactions flowed continuously and instantly around the clock, and where expensive research services could be unbundled from transactions.

To a large extent, companies such as E*Trade have delivered on the promise. The online trading companies have driven down the cost of the average 100-share, $10,000 trade from an average of 3% of the transaction value in 1995 at a traditional broker ($300 in this case) to $29.00 (Schwab and Merrill Lynch) and even lower — $7 — at some online firms that do not offer research services. More high-quality, free information is available to stock traders, transaction costs have fallen, information asymmetry has been reduced through the greater speed of information flow, and the search costs for suitable investment instruments have fallen dramatically (Bakos et al., 2000).

Brokerage customers have responded to the superior customer value proposition offered by online brokers. Online brokerage industry growth has been torrid since 1996. Today, nearly a third of all stock market trades occur over the Internet. Growth at E*Trade mirrored the industry's growth. In the two-year period of 1998–2000, total accounts grew by a factor of five — from 600,000 to 3.3 million . In 2000, E*Trade had revenue of $1.9 billion. The success of the online brokerage firms in attracting customers forced established firms such as Merrill Lynch to develop an online presence, drastically reduce commissions, unbundle service charges from transaction charges, and change their own business models to those of a multichannel financial services firm.

Despite the extraordinary growth and success of E*Trade, the pure online model of domestic brokerage has not been profitable. It is clear that E*Trade will have to expand its scope of operations and depth of product and build strategic alliances rapidly in order to survive in the long term. It has become clear that the consumer occasionally wants physical contact with a financial services provider, and that pure online companies cannot ignore traditional channels, especially since established bricks-and-mortar firms are rapidly building an online presence. The collapse of the stock market in 2001 and its impact on trading volumes and revenues have demonstrated the fragility of E*Trade's reliance on pure online domestic brokerage.

Business Model E*Trade's business model is to provide online delivery of financial and investing services to individuals and corporations worldwide. E*Trade's revenue is based on commissions and fees that it charges for stock trades and retail and corporate banking services. The company divides its business into four categories: domestic retail brokerage, banking, global and institutional, and asset gathering/ other. The domestic retail brokerage business provides online investing services; the banking business offers FDIC-insured and other banking products, including a network of more than 9,600 ATMs; the global and institutional category serves institutional investors and international affiliates; and the asset gathering business provides 401(k) programs, college savings plans, mutual fund operations, and other money management services to both individuals and institutions.

Financial Analysis There are really two periods to consider when examining E*Trade's business results: before January 2001, and after that time. Table 11.5 reports the three-year period 1998–2000. E-Trade's gross revenues for fiscal 2000 were $1.9 billion, with 86% of this revenue coming from brokerage revenues and interest income from banking and margin accounts. This represents an incredible fourfold growth in gross revenue since 1998. Like most services companies, gross margins (in this case net revenue minus cost of services divided by gross revenue) are a healthy 43% of gross revenue.

As of September 30, 2000, the company had nearly 3 million active brokerage accounts, up 90% for the year, with assets held in those accounts valued at nearly $60 billion. The average daily transaction volume was 167,000 in 2000, up 144% from the year before. During 2000, E*Trade worked to establish alliances with leading wireless service providers, such as Sprint PCS, Verizon, and AT&T Wireless, in order to offer its services to the more than 50 million wireless subscribers nationwide.

In its banking division, approximately 87% of customer contacts occur via the Internet, although telephone and ATM access is also available. By eschewing bricks-and-mortar facilities, E*Trade eliminated a significant portion of traditional operating expenses associated with retail banking. Since 1997, bank deposits have grown at a compound annual growth rate of 140%, in part due to emphasis on cross-selling. During the fourth quarter of 2000, 40% of E-Trade's new banking accounts were from cross-sold customers. Expanding internationally, however, is an important aspect of E*Trade's growth strategy, with new retail sites being launched in Japan, Korea, Denmark, and Norway, boosting its non-U.S. Web sites to a total of nine.

Commission revenues, transaction revenues, and interest income all increased substantially during 2000. And while the company's cost of services and operating expenses were also up, they declined as a percentage of net revenues.

In 2000, E*Trade saw across-the-board growth in virtually all areas, including gross and net revenues, active brokerage and banking accounts, global and institutional accounts, and total assets. However, two figures suggest increasing competition in its market: E*Trade's cost per new account rose 7% to $263, up from $245 in 1999 and $219 in 1998, and its average domestic commission shrank to $15.52 from $18.35 in 1999 and $19.53 in 1998.

Operating costs — marketing, technology and operations, and other costs — are typically high in service organizations. At E*Trade, operating costs have grown five-fold since 1998, nearly doubling from 1999–2000. Marketing has expanded fourfold,

TABLE 11.5	E*TRADE'S CONSOLIDATED STATEMENTS OF OPERATIONS AND SUMMARY BALANCE SHEET DATA 1998–2000

E*TRADE GROUP, INC.
CONSOLIDATED STATEMENTS OF OPERATIONS
(in thousands)

For the fiscal year ended September 30	2000	1999	1998
Revenues			
Transaction revenues	$ 739,078	$ 355,830	$ 162,097
Interest income	960,358	369,074	186,123
Global and institutional	166,061	124,233	105,851
Other	107,686	40,546	28,173
Gross revenues	1,973,183	889,683	482,244
Interest expense	600,862	215,452	120,334
Provision for loan losses	4,003	2,783	905
Net revenues	1,368,318	671,448	361,005
Cost of services	515,571	302,342	151,329
Gross margin	**43%**	**41%**	**43%**
Operating expenses			
Sales and marketing	521,532	325,449	126,141
Technology development	142,914	79,935	36,203
General and administrative	209,436	102,826	51,346
Amortization of good will and intangibles	22,764	2,915	2,480
Acquisition expenses	36,427	7,174	1,167
Total operating expenses	933,073	518,299	217,337
Total cost of services and operating expenses	1,448,644	20,641	368,666
Operating loss	(80,326)	(149,193)	(7,661)
Non-operating income	184,775	65,787	10,504
Pre-tax income/(loss)	**104,449**	**(83,406)**	**2,843**
Net margin	**7.6%**	**−12.4%**	**.8%**

SUMMARY BALANCE SHEET DATA
(in thousands)

At September 30	2000	1999	1998
Cash and equivalents	$ 175,443	$ 157,705	$ 78,717
Brokerage receivables	6,542,508	2,982,076	1,365,247
Mortgage-backed securities	4,188,553	1,426,053	1,021,163
Loans receivable	4,172,754	2,154,509	904,854
Other assets	2,238,179	1,311,831	987,942
Total assets	17,317,437	8,032,174	4,348,923
Total liabilities	15,429,073	6,549,795	3,462,693

SOURCE: E*Trade Group, Inc. Form 10-K for the fiscal year ended September 30, 2000, filed with the Securities and Exchange Commission on November 9, 2000.

and technology spending has also expanded fourfold since 1998. Information technology is a core element in E*Trade's strategy to provide a superior customer experience and it has spent heavily to develop the capacity needed to service over three million accounts. Acquisition costs — a significant factor in E*Trade's growth has been acquisition of banking operations — have increased dramatically by a factor of 30 since 1998.

With costs growing at about the same pace as revenues, E*Trade had an operating loss of $80 million in 2000. Non-operating income (primarily from gains on its own investments, which are unlikely to be repeated in 2001) nevertheless created a small pre-tax income of $104 million, and a positive net margin of 7.6%, a profitable year. This is far better than 1999, when it experienced an $83 million loss and negative net margin of 12.4%.

On balance, it appears that E*Trade's business model does not scale well. Its spectacular growth in revenues and size has not led to scale economies produced by declining costs and increasing earnings. Instead, costs are growing about as fast as revenues.

Looking at E*Trade's balance sheet, at September 30, 2000 the company had $175 million in cash — much of it from public stock offerings and debt — enough to cover its operating losses for two years. The company also had considerable assets in the form of receivables, which could be converted to cash should that become necessary.

Beginning in January 2001, the story changed dramatically for E*Trade. The stock market decline in 2001, particularly the decline in technology stocks, has had a devastating impact on E*Trade and other pure online trading companies, but a much smaller impact on bricks-and-mortar giants such as Merrill Lynch and Fidelity. Table 11.6 provides an indication of problems facing E*Trade management in 2001.

Table 11.6 shows that E*Trade's acquisition of new brokerage accounts has slowed from the torrid pace of 216% annual growth in 1998 to –71% in the first six months of 2001. Those most likely to be attracted to pure online trading have already received the message, and many online traders have stopped trading altogether. Banking and global/institutional account growth, transaction volume, and assets under management all have slowed dramatically in 2001. Customer acquisition costs of $263 in 2000 have risen to $386 in 2001. Average commission revenues fell in 2000, and continue to decline in 2001. In the first quarter of 2001, E*Trade reported a 42% drop in trades (similar to that experienced by many other pure online trading companies, but a great deal larger than that reported by bricks-and-mortar established firms).

Strategic Analysis — Business Strategies In order to address the inevitable fall in the rate of growth of new online domestic brokerage and banking accounts, E*Trade's management has initiated five strategies: expansion to global markets, acquisition of domestic firms that could broaden the scope of E*Trade offerings, development of alliances with strong online and offline companies to reach new domestic clients,

TABLE 11.6	E*TRADE GROWTH MEASURES POST-2000

E*Trade Key Performance Indicators
Six Months Ended June 30
(In thousands except cost per new account and average commission per domestic brokerage transaction)

	2001	2000	% Change
Active domestic brokerage accounts	3,289,014	2,951,946	11%
Active banking accounts	434,804	288,073	51%
Active global and institutional accounts	104,792	75,416	39%
Total active accounts at period end	3,828,610	3,315,435	15%
Net new domestic brokerage accounts	176,646	817,881	–78%
Net new banking accounts	72,187	91,947	–21%
Net new global and institutional accounts	20,768	34,413	–40%
Total net new accounts	269,601	944,241	–71%
Total assets in global and institutional accounts	$ 1,202,718	$ 1,348,672	–11%
Total assets in domestic brokerage accounts	44,553,710	59,901,277	–26%
Total deposits in banking accounts	7,687,006	4,630,068	66%
Total assets/deposits in customer accounts	$53,443,434	$65,880,017	–19%
Total domestic brokerage transactions	15,233,084	24,733,340	–38%
Daily average domestic brokerage transactions	121,865	196,296	–38%
Average commission per domestic brokerage transaction	$13.44	$15.55	–14%
Cost per new account	$ 328	$ 269	22%

SOURCE: E*Trade Group, Inc. Form 10-Q for the six-month period ended June 30, 2001, filed with the Securities and Exchange Commission on August 14, 2001.

development of a multichannel "bricks-and-mortar" presence, and development of a "business to business to consumer" (B2B2C) strategy.

E*Trade has developed branded Web sites in nine countries, including Germany, Japan, Korea, Sweden, and South Africa. Since January 2000, the firm has acquired 11 companies to deliver online banking services (Telebanc), a mortgage firm (Loans-Direct), and the third largest ATM network in the United States (Card Capture Services). E*Trade also has developed alliances with Internet companies (AOL, Yahoo, and Microsoft); airlines and free-mile plans (United, Delta, Northwest, and TWA); and hotels (Hilton and Marriott). In addition to its 10,000 ATMs and full investment kiosks in Target stores, it is also opening ten full-service "mega stores." E*Trade's Business Services Group is developing a B2B2C model in which E*Trade supplies Fortune 500 firms with packaged financial services made available to employees. By broadening its financial products and services, E*Trade is attempting to move away from a volatile short-term day-trading customer with an average account balance of $15,000 and toward a more sophisticated long-term banking and investing customer with account balances greater than $100,000 (more typical of a Schwab or Merrill Lynch customer).

Strategic Analysis — Competition E*Trade's direct competitors include full commission brokerage firms, such as Merrill Lynch, discount brokerage firms such as Charles Schwab, online brokerage firms such as Datek, and both pure-play and bricks-and-mortar commercial banks. To separate itself from the competition, E*Trade aims to grow internationally while deepening its penetration of the domestic market. The firm will be focusing on delivering high-quality customer service through multiple channels, easy-to-use interfaces, and greater physical presence.

Strategic Analysis — Technology Since 1997, E*Trade has made significant investments in technology, including development, operations, transaction capacity, and its data center facilities, with technology development expenses totaling $142.9 million in 2000. At the core of its worldwide operations is a proprietary transaction enabling engine that provides its graphical user interface, session management, and transaction processing. E*Trade operates data centers in California, Georgia, and London. Its graphical user interface is based on Netscape's Secure Enterprise Server, and runs on Sun servers. E*Trade's engine handles 95% of the company's transactions without any manual intervention.

Strategic Analysis — Social and Legal Challenges E*Trade was expected to settle a suit in mid-2001 filed by the National Association of Securities Dealers (NASD) that claimed the company's aggressive ads were illegal. The Securities and Exchange Commission (SEC) has already dropped a similar suit. Questions had risen as far back as 1998 regarding as many as 2,400 print, radio, and TV ads regarding E*Trade's claims that a technology index mutual fund was the "lowest cost," when in fact there was no basis for such a claim. E*Trade blamed the problem on a clerical error and pulled the ad after the NASD voiced its objection.

Future Prospects E*Trade faces a number of challenges. Established offline branded brokerage and banking firms are developing competitive Web sites, cutting into E*Trade's market for online brokerage and banking. There has been a dramatic fall-off in the online small account trader marketplace, which will cut into E*Trade revenues severely. Expansion into Target kiosks and full-service physical branches will raises costs significantly, putting pressure on the company to reduce other marketing costs. E*Trade's stock price has fallen from a high of $25 to around $5 in Fall 2001, making the raising of new funds through the public market unlikely and expensive.

It is unclear at this time if E*Trade's new strategies will be able to overcome these factors. With such a low stock price, E*Trade may become an acquisition target for an established brokerage firm seeking to strengthen its online channel.

Financial Portals: Comparison Shopping, Planning, and Advice Sites

financial portals

sites that provide consumers with comparison shopping services, independent financial advice, and financial planning

The $3 trillion in assets that are expected to come online in the next four years has attracted non-financial institutions to the online financial services marketplace. **Financial portals** are sites that provide consumers with comparison shopping services, independent financial advice, and financial planning. Independent portals do not themselves offer financial services, but act as steering mechanisms to online providers. They generate revenue from advertising, referral fees, and subscription fees. For example, Yahoo's financial portal, Yahoo Finance, offers consumers credit card purchase tracking, market overviews, real-time stock quotes, news, financial advice, streaming video interviews with financial leaders, and a Yahoo! digital wallet. Other independent financial portals include Intuit's Quicken.com, MSN's Money-Central, and America Online's Personal Finance channel.

account aggregation

the process of pulling together all of a customer's financial (and even nonfinancial) data at a single personalized Web site

Financial portals are a major source of visitors to major established financial services sites. For instance, about one-third of visitors to Wells Fargo's online bank begin their sessions at a financial portal. About 20% of visitors to established sites exit to portal sites. Portals have become so important to established online service firms that some, such as CitiBank, Schwab, and others, have attempted to create their own portals such as myciti.com and myschwab.com that permit users to personalize their financial Web pages and provide account aggregation services (described below).

In general, the financial portals do not offer financial services (they make their money from advertising); instead, they add to the online price competition in the industry and run counter to the strategy of large banking institutions to ensnare consumers into a single branded, financial institutional system, with a single account and high switching costs.

Account Aggregation Sites

One of the most rapidly growing online financial services is **account aggregation.** Account aggregation is the process of pulling together all of a customer's financial (and even nonfinancial) data at a single personalized Web site — including brokerage, banking, insurance, loans, frequent flyer miles, personalized news, and much more. For example, a consumer can see his or her Merrill Lynch brokerage account, Fidelity 401k account, Travelers Insurance annuity account, and American Airlines frequent flyer miles all displayed on a single site. The idea is to provide consumers with a holistic view of their entire portfolio of assets, no matter what financial institution actually holds those assets.

A recent survey found that from January to December 2000, the number of online consumers using aggregation services exploded from 100,000 to 700,000. Industry projections call for 22 million online aggregation customers by 2003 (Altman et al., 2001).

The leading providers of account aggregation technology are Yodlee and VerticalOne. Both use screen-scraping technology and other software tools to pull information from up to one thousand different online financial sites. A smart mapping technology is also used so that if the underlying Web sites change, the scraping software can adapt and still find the relevant information (Massaro, 2000).

Financial portal sites were the first to adopt Yodlee and Vertical One's account aggregation technology. Established institutions such as Merrill Lynch, Citigroup, and Chase opposed independent account aggregators as a threat to their customer base. Why spend time at a Merrill Lynch Web site when all you can see are your Merrill Lynch accounts? But heeding customer demand, the major established financial institutions have recently signed deals with Yodlee and VerticalOne to provide account aggregation at their sites as well. Merrill Lynch, Chase, and Citigroup now offer Yodlee's account aggregation at their sites (McGeehan, 2000).

Account aggregation raises a number of issues. In order to use account aggregation services, consumers must release all their login and password information to the aggregator. If all account information is held by one institution, consumers face the privacy risk of losing control over their information, which heretofore was spread across many largely inaccessible sites. Financial aggregators will, of course, be tempted to "cross sell" products to consumers at their sites, raising the possibility of fairly intense marketing campaigns, although aggregator sites claim they will not use their customers' information to promote products without the customer's explicit permission. See *Insight on Technology: Screen Scraping* for a further look at the technology behind account aggregation and the issues it raises.

Online Mortgage and Lending Services

The U.S. home mortgage market is a $1.5 trillion market. In the E-commerce I period, hundreds of firms launched pure-play online mortgage sites to capture this rich prize. Early entrants hoped to radically simplify and transform the traditional mortgage value chain process, speed up the loan closing process dramatically, and share the economies with consumers by offering lower rates.

By 2001, over half of these early-entry, pure-online firms had failed. The largest failure was Mortgage.com in October 2000, which followed a year-long loss of over $100 million and left over $33 million in debts. Early pure-play online mortgage institutions had difficulties developing a brand name at an affordable price and failed to

INSIGHT ON TECHNOLOGY

SCREEN SCRAPING

Account aggregation allows you to see all of the financial relationships you have, all your current balances, and account transaction detail, all in one place. The service is so popular that over 800,000 online consumers have signed up for Yodlee's free account aggregation service—either at the Yodlee site or at one of the many financial services firms that license the software from Yodlee. When Citigroup offered account aggregation as a free service, about one-third of the people who signed up did not even have accounts at CitiBank. Account aggregation is now offered by Schwab, Fidelity, Morgan Stanley, and JP Morgan Chase, along with many other online banks.

Account aggregation uses screen scraping technology. Originally, screen scraping was used to convert data from mainframe legacy systems to new client/server systems using Windows. A software program intercepts messages sent to a display terminal, converts the messages to a Windows-readable format, and displays the information on a PC. The new breed of screen scrapers use HTML to pull information off one Web site and display it on another.

Here's how it works. First, you must register at a site offering account aggregation services (call it the "account aggregator"). Then you must give the account aggregator the login name and password of all Web sites you want to aggregate. The account aggregator passes that information along to an aggregator service such as Yodlee or VerticalOne. These services actually do the data mining for your information, and then pass the information back to your account aggregator for display.

Done right, screen scraping and account aggregating can deliver a new level of time saving and convenience. Sara Dods, 27, an attorney in Seattle who works 60 to 80 hours a week, keeps track of her airline miles and Amazon book orders, in addition to her savings and checking accounts, on Yodlee's site. The service is free. Account aggregators make money from advertising and by attracting customers to their sites, where they can sell them profitable financial services. Dods comments that "it comes down to laziness. Why not have it all in one place and not have to worry about all those passwords, and PINS, for all the places where I have a financial relationship?"

Critics point out, however, that using an account aggregator gives your financial holdings over to the aggregator. What if the aggregator goes bankrupt and sells the data as an asset? What if someone—such as a disgruntled employee—breaks into the aggregator's site and drains your account? Are your assets insured by the aggregators? Generally, account aggregators do not allow you to perform transactions, so there is little chance of hackers making changes in your account by intercepting your screen displays. The greatest issue appears to be trusting aggregators' management and employees with your account information. Traditionally, banks and brokerages

perform these information fiduciary roles, and can be held legally accountable through federal and state statutes should they make mistakes. However, account aggregators services such as Yodlee and VerticalOne are not subject to the same scrutiny or legal standards as banks or brokerage firms.

SOURCES: "Screen Scraping: Uglier Than It Sounds," by Andrea Bennett, *American Banker*, June 15, 2000; "Here Come the Screen Scrapers," by Bill Atkinson, *On Time Digital Archive*, April 2000; "Screen Scraping Lawsuit May Clarify Liability Issue," *American Banker*, January 27, 2000.

simplify the mortgage generation process. They ended up suffering from high start-up and administrative costs, high customer acquisition costs, rising interest rates, and poor execution of their strategies.

Nevertheless, the online mortgage market is growing rapidly, perhaps as much as 100% a year; it is dominated by established online banks and other online financial services firms, traditional mortgage vendors, and a few successful online mortgage firms. About 6% of all home mortgages were initiated online in 2000, but only 2% were completed totally online (Vaughan-Nichols and Schmutter, 2001). In 2001, about 3% of all U.S. mortgages were initiated online, but in 2004 this figure is expected to rise to 12% of all mortgages (Reuters, 2001). See Table 11.7.

There are four basic kinds of online mortgage vendors:

- Established online banks, brokerages, and lending organizations such as Chase Manhattan, Countrywide Credit Industries, Wells Fargo, and E*Trade.
- Pure online mortgage bankers/brokers such as E-loan.com, LoanCity.com, and Quicken's QuickenLoans.com. These companies aim to expedite the mortgage shopping and initiation process, but still require extensive paperwork to complete

TABLE 11.7	ONLINE MORTGAGES 1999–2004
YEAR	ONLINE MORTGAGE LENDING (IN BILLIONS OF DOLLARS)
1999	5
2000	20
2001	42
2002	86
2003	130
2004	180

SOURCES: Motoko, 2001; Reuters, 2001.

a mortgage. For example, QuickenLoans.com's primary service is to provide comparison loan shopping for consumers and professional advice at its 400-person call center. In addition, the site offers a loan calculator, rate updates, and market information.

- Mortgage brokers such as LendingTree.com and MortgageRamp.com that offer visitors access to hundreds of mortgage vendors who bid for their business.

- Mortgage service companies such as ABN AMRO Group's Mortgage.com (ABN AMRO purchased the name of the defunct Mortgage.com).

Consumer benefits from online mortgages include reduced application times, market interest rate intelligence, and process simplification that occurs when participants in the mortgage process (title, insurance, and lending companies) share a common information base. MortgageRamp.com, for instance, hopes to reduce the application time required to obtain a mortgage from the industry standard of 60–90 days down to 10–15 days. Mortgage lenders benefit from the 30% cost reduction involved in online processing of applications, while charging rates marginally lower than traditional bricks-and-mortar institutions (Rich, 2001).

Nevertheless, the online mortgage industry has not transformed the process of obtaining a mortgage. A significant break on market expansion is the complexity of the mortgage process, which requires physical signatures and documents, multiple institutions, and complex financing details — such as closing costs and points — that are difficult for shoppers to compare across vendors (Mullaney, 2001).

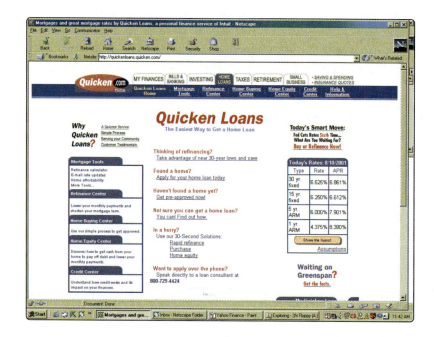

ONLINE INSURANCE SERVICES

In 1995, the price of a $500,000 term life policy for a healthy 40-year-old male was $995 a year. In 2001, the same policy cost $455 — a decline of 54% — while other prices have risen 15% in the same period. In a recent study of the term life insurance business, Brown and Goolsbee discovered that Internet usage led to an 8% to 15% decline in term life insurance prices industry-wide (both offline and online), and increased consumer surplus by about $115 million per year (and hence reduced industry profits by the same amount) (Brown and Goolsbee, 2000). Price dispersion for term life policies initially increased, but then fell as more and more people began using the Internet to obtain insurance quotes.

Unlike books and CDs, where online price dispersion is higher than offline, and in many cases online prices are higher than offline, term life insurance stands out as one product group supporting the conventional wisdom that the Internet will lower search costs, increase price comparison, and lower prices to consumers. Term life insurance is a commodity product, however, and in other insurance product lines, the Web offers insurance companies new opportunities for product and service differentiation and price discrimination.

The insurance industry is a $500 billion chunk of the $1.6 trillion financial services sector. It has four major segments: automobile, property and casualty, health, and life (see Table 11.8).

Insurance products are much more complex than Table 11.8 indicates. For instance, there are many different types of nonautomotive property and casualty insurance: liability, fire, homeowners, commercial, workers compensation, marine, accident, and other lines such as vacation insurance. Writing an insurance policy in any of these areas is very information intense, often requiring personal inspection of the properties, and requires considerable actuarial experience and data. The life

TABLE 11.8	THE INSURANCE INDUSTRY: SEGMENTS
INSURANCE INDUSTRY PREMIUMS	REVENUES (IN BILLIONS OF DOLLARS)
Automobile	138
Property and casualty	113.5
Life	119
Health	137
Total Premiums	507.5

SOURCES: Statistical Abstract of the United States, 2000. Tables 849 and 851.

insurance industry has also developed life insurance policies that defy easy comparison and can only be explained and sold by an experienced sales agent. Historically, the insurance industry has relied on thousands of local insurance offices and agents to sell complex products uniquely suited to the circumstances of the insured person and the property. Complicating the insurance marketplace is the fact that the insurance industry is not federally regulated, but rather is regulated by 50 different state insurance commissions that are strongly influenced by local insurance agents. Before a Web site can offer quotations on insurance, it must obtain a license to enter the insurance business in all the states where it provides quotation services or sells insurance.

Managing Channel Conflict in the Online Insurance Industry

Like the online mortgage industry, the online insurance industry has been very successful in attracting visitors to obtain prices and terms of insurance policies, but weak at getting customers to buy policies online. In large part this is a result of channel conflict: Major national insurance underwriting companies decided not to offer competitive products directly on the Web that might injure the business operations of their traditional local agents. However, this situation is changing rapidly.

Online insurance sites attract an estimated 150,000 unique visitors each month, but only 1% of insurance policies — about $5 billion worth — are purchased online (Bray, 2001a). On the other hand, 16% of online consumers — about 12 million consumers — checked a Web site for an insurance quote in 2000 (Jupiter Media Metrix, 2000). Hence, the Internet is a powerful influence over consumer insurance decisions. The Internet has dramatically reduced search costs and changed the price discovery process, but little else in the insurance industry value chain has been changed to date. The typical consumer behavior pattern is to check the Web for prices and terms, and then purchase insurance from local agents, using the Internet information to obtain a better bargain. See Table 11.9 for a list and description of some of the leading online insurance services companies.

Despite the slow evolution of online insurance sales, as opposed to information and quotes, a number of industry-wide consortia offer the prospect of significant change by 2005. Online banking and brokerage institutions such as E*Trade and Fidelity are beginning to offer insurance products online, pressuring traditional insurers to respond. Allstate Corporation, one of the United States' largest insurance writers, is planning to offer online insurance services including direct sales to 90% of the population by 2005. Three of the largest underwriters (American International Group, Kemper Insurance Companies, and Prudential Financial) formed an insurance supermarket called Fusura in 2001 to offer online personal insurance lines. Insurance.com, a unit of Fidelity, has linked up with Comparison Market, a consortium of five automobile insurers, to provide comparison auto insurance shopping and binding insurance quotes to 90% of the nation's drivers by 2005 (Bray, 2001b). Industry sources believe the prices of products at these emerging Web sites will be 15% to 20% lower

TABLE 11.9	LEADING ONLINE INSURANCE SERVICES	
COMPANY	REVENUES	DESCRIPTION
Answerfinancial.com	ND	Matchmaker. Holding company for Insurance Answer Center.
InsWeb.com	$25 million	Comparison shopping for consumers; insurance companies pay for client leads (90% of revenue). Acquired Intuit's Quicken Insurance. Term life, auto, and homeowner's insurance quotes. Public company.
Quotesmith.com	$15.8 million	Free quotes from 300 insurance companies on a full range of policies with no fee. Most popular Web site. Public company.
Progressive.com	$475 million	Fourth largest auto insurer in the United States with a long history of technological innovation. 15% of business is now online.
Accuquote.com	ND	Term life insurance site.
SelectQuote.com	ND	Term life insurance site.
Quickquote.com	ND	Free quotes on a full range of policies. Revenue from advertising and client leads.
eHealthinsurance.com	ND	Comparison shopping for individual health insurance.
health-insurance.com	ND	Information and quotes on health insurance.
digitalinsurance.com	ND	Health and other insurance for individuals. Limited quotations in some states.

ND = Not disclosed

than similar products purchased through agents. However, the online products will be simpler and more basic, and personally tailored and serviced products will be available through agents (Tergesen, 2001).

ONLINE REAL ESTATE SERVICES

Real estate is a $930 billion industry that seemed ripe in E-commerce I for an Internet revolution that would rationalize this historically local, complex, and local-agent-driven industry that monopolized the flow of consumer information. There are approximately 119 million housing units in the United States, and in 1999, the latest year for which we have data, about 900,000 new one-family houses came on the market, 5.2 million existing one-family homes were sold, and about 800,000 apartments, condos, and coops were rented or sold. Commercial real estate, which at $320 billion accounts for about one-third of the overall real estate market, involves 4.5 million commercial buildings with 58 billion square feet of floor space, about 10% of which is rented each year. Altogether, real estate transactions represent about 10% of the gross domestic product of the United States.

Potentially, the Internet and e-commerce might have disintermediated this huge marketspace, allowing buyers and sellers, renters and owners to transact directly, lower search costs to near zero, and dramatically reduce prices. However, this did not happen. What did happen, however, is extremely beneficial to buyers and sellers, as well as real estate agents.

Currently, there are an estimated 100,000 real estate sites on the Internet worldwide (see Table 11.10 for a small sampling of online real estate sites). Most real estate brokers in the United States have their own agency Web sites to deal with clients, in addition to participating with thousands of other agencies in Multiple Listing Services that list homes online.

About 50% of home buyers (including apartment renters) now consult real estate sites on the Web, and this percentage is expected to grow to 80% by 2005 (Jupiter Media Metrix, 2000d). Real estate differs from other types of online financial services because it is impossible to complete a property transaction online. A recent survey showed that only 2 out of 65 real estate sites permitted online bids for properties

TABLE 11.10	MAJOR ONLINE REAL ESTATE SITES
COMPANY	DESCRIPTION
homestore.com	Network of sites (including realtor.com) with 1.3 million listings. Significant ownership by National Association of Realtors.
homeadvisor.com (MSN)	Microsoft site with listings from 120 MLS.
homes.com	Over 900,000 home and apartment listings, plus a wide range of useful services.
homegain.com	Real estate agent selection and home valuation site.
ired.com	International Real Estate Directory links to 25,000 sites worldwide.
mlx.com	Manhattan site listing 3,000 coops and condominiums.
cityrealty.com	Manhattan apartment listings.
owners.com	Listings of "For sale by owner" homes.
thinkglink.com	Ilyce R. Glink, author and advisor on real estate.
cityfeet.com	Commercial and small business office rental in Manhattan.
MrOfficeSpace.com	Commercial office listings, Manhattan. Established by Yale Robbins Inc., a traditional real estate listing company.

(Jupiter Media Metrix, 2001c). Clearly, the major impact of Internet real estate sites is in influencing offline decisions. By 2005, online real estate research by consumers is expected to influence about $200 billion in offline purchases (Jupiter Media Metrix, 2000d).

The primary service offered by real estate sites is a listing of houses available. About 1.3 million housing units are now listed. The offerings have become sophisticated and integrated. Consumers can link to mortgage lenders, credit reporting agencies, house inspectors, and surveyors. There are also online loan calculators, appraisal reports, sale-price histories by neighborhood, school district data, crime reports, and social and historical information on neighborhoods.

Homestore.com, the Web's largest site with 1.3 million listings, also offers a "Find a Neighborhood" feature that allows users to choose the type of neighborhood they want to live in by weighing factors such as the quality (and tax costs) of schools, age of the population, number of families with children nearby, and available social and recreational services. See *Insight on Society: Is Homestore.com a Monopoly?* for a further look at Homestore.com.

Despite the revolution in available information, there has not been a revolution in the industry value chain. The listings available on Web sites are provided by local Multiple Listing Services supported by local real estate agents. Typically, addresses of the houses are not available and online users are directed to the local listing agent who is hired by the seller of house. Traditional hands-on real estate brokers will show the house and handle all transactions with the owner to preserve their fees, ranging from 4% to 6 % of the transaction.

In this sense, the Internet has benefited the traditional brokers as much as consumers. One agent reports, for instance, that Internet-informed customers ask to see only 6 apartments before deciding, whereas clients who do not use the Internet ask to see an average of 22 apartments before renting (Romano, 2000). Perhaps reflecting the limited impact of the Internet on the real estate value chain, the consumer price index for housing since 1995 has been rising on average about one-half of a percentage point faster than prices for all other items (Table 772, Statistical Abstract of the United States, 2000).

11.3 ONLINE TRAVEL SERVICES

Despite the economic downturn in 2001, online travel services revenues continue to grow briskly. Arguably, the online travel services segment is the single most successful B2C e-commerce segment in the sense that it attracts the largest single e-commerce audience and the largest slice of B2C revenues, surpassing PC hardware/software and peripherals combined. The Internet is becoming the most common channel used by consumers to research travel options, seek the best possi-

IS HOMESTORE.COM A MONOPOLY?

The promise of e-commerce is that it would create a fair, level playing field where thousands of suppliers and millions of consumers could negotiate prices and terms in a very efficient marketplace. These electronic markets would be more efficient in part because intermediaries — the distributors, wholesalers, and agents — would be eliminated by direct commerce between sellers and buyers.

Although these outcomes may have occurred in some e-commerce sectors, in many other sectors we see the emergence of oligopolies — near monopolies — characterized by three or four giant firms, or an even smaller number. Instead of disintermediation, e-commerce sometimes can cause a strengthening of existing intermediaries through exclusive market relationships. At times, the level of concentrated power and collusion online can become so strong that the U.S. Department of Justice opens an investigation to determine if antitrust laws are being broken.

Consider Homestore.com. Homestore.com lists more than 1.3 million homes based on local trade associations called Multiple Listing Services (MLS) that list homes for sale throughout the nation and represent over 122,000 real estate agents. The National Association of Realtors (NAR) aggregates all the homes listed by its member MLS into a single database at Realtor.com. Homestore.com has an exclusive agreement with NAR to be the exclusive distributor on the Web for the MLS listings on Realtor.com. No other e-commerce site can list homes offered by NAR local real estate agents in the United States.

In February 2001, Homestore.com eliminated its largest competitor by purchasing Cendant's Move.com. Currently, Homestore lists over 93% of the homes for sale on the Web, far outdistancing rivals Homeseekers.com and Microsoft's HomeAdvisor.com. The Move.com acquisition will give Homestore access to more than 25% of the industry's brokers and transactions, and tap into more than 200,000 local real estate agents. Perhaps the biggest jewel in the Move.com purchase is a 40-year exclusive listing agreement with Century 21, Coldwell Banker, and ERA, three of Cendant's prized national franchises, as well as 7-year exclusive listing pacts with the nation's largest rental market brokers (NRT and Rent.net). This means that Homestore.com will now have exclusive access to three of the largest bricks-and-mortar real estate firm listings in the United States.

Wall Street smells a winner here. Homestore's stock has shot up 50% since January 2001, running against the flood of dot.com stocks going the other direction. Even though Homestore has not been profitable in previous years, analysts believe it will post a profit this year given its exclusive relationships with NAR and its purchase of Move.com.

In April 2000, the Justice Department opened an investigation into Homestore.com, Realtor.com, and the NAR. At issue were the exclusive agreements that Homestore had with NAR and the fact that other Web-based competitors could not have access to the MLS listings around the country. Homestore executives argue they have not violated antitrust laws or "restrained trade" in any way, but they have simply been successful in growing quite large. Industry experts argue that competitor sites such as HomeAdvisor and Homeseeker could obtain local listings from sources other than local MLS agencies. For instance, competitors could obtain listings from local newspapers, although this clearly would not be as efficient as having access to local MLS listings.

In July 2001, the Justice Department ended its inquiry into Homestore.com without comment.

Some analysts believe antitrust actions of the Justice Department are heavily influenced by Washington politics, and the fact that the current administration is opposed to strong antitrust enforcement played a role in this decision. Clearly, in the instance of the online real estate business, it appears that e-commerce has strengthened the established players in the traditional value chain and restricted the number of suppliers and competitors to a very small number, which in turn allows the few suppliers to accrue higher profits, befitting their dominance of the marketplace.

SOURCES: "Government Ends Homestore.com Inquiry," *New York Times*, July 17, 2001; "Gut-Check Time for Homestore.com," by Amy Stone, *BusinessWeek Online*, April 24, 2001; "Homestore Builds Its Empire, Brick by Brick," by Larry Barrett, *CNETNews.com*, February 21, 2001; "Homestore.com Faces Antitrust Probe," by Keith Regan, *E-Commerce Times*, April 26, 2000.

ble prices, and book reservations for airline tickets, rental cars, hotel rooms, cruises, and tours. By 2006, online travel booking revenues are expected to grow to $63 billion from the current level of $24 billion (see Figure 11.8). This represents an increase in market share from 10% in 2001 to 21% of all travel services expenditures in 2006.

Although travel services is the largest single revenue source of consumer commerce, travel is an expensive item. In general, consumers purchase smaller items when first introduced to the Web, and later, when they have more experience, move on to purchasing higher priced items such as travel. A February 2001 survey found, for instance, that while 29% of U.S. online users have purchased travel services on the Web, another 29% have only used the Web to research travel products, and 42% of online consumers have never sought travel information or purchased products online (Jupiter Media Metrix, 2001d). Online travel services, therefore, have a huge untapped audience, and as the Internet population grows, an even larger population will be attracted to online travel services.

WHY ARE ONLINE TRAVEL SERVICES SO POPULAR?

Online travel sites offer consumers a one-stop, convenient, leisure and business travel experience where travelers can find content (descriptions of vacations and facilities), community (chat groups and bulletin boards), commerce (purchase of all travel elements), and customer service (usually through call centers). Online sites claim to offer much more information and travel options than traditional travel agents. For

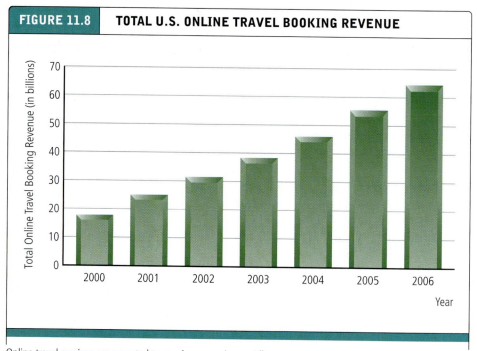

FIGURE 11.8 **TOTAL U.S. ONLINE TRAVEL BOOKING REVENUE**

Online travel services are expected to continue growing rapidly.
SOURCE: Jupiter Media Metrix, 2001d.

suppliers — the owners of hotels, rental cars, and airlines — the online sites aggregate millions of consumers into singular, focused customer pools that can be efficiently reached through onsite advertising and promotions. Online sites claim to create a much more efficient marketplace, bringing consumers and suppliers together in a low transaction cost environment.

Travel services appear to be an ideal service/product for the Internet, and therefore e-commerce business models should work well for this product. Travel is an information-intensive product requiring significant consumer research. It is an electronic product in the sense that travel requirements — planning, researching, comparison shopping, reserving, and payment — can be accomplished for the most part online in a digital environment. On the fulfillment side, travel does not require any "inventory": There are no physical assets. And the suppliers of the product — owners of hotels, airlines, rental cars, vacation rooms, and tour guides — are highly fragmented and often have excess capacity. Always looking for customers to fill vacant rooms and rent idle cars, suppliers will be anxious to lower prices and willing to advertise on Web sites that can attract millions of consumers. The online agencies — such as Travelocity.com, Expedia.com and others — do not have to deploy thousands of travel agents in physical offices across the country, but can instead concentrate on a single interface with a national consumer audience. Travel services may not require the kind of expensive multichannel "physical presence" strategy required of financial services (although they generally operate centralized call centers to provide personal customer service). Therefore, travel services might "scale" better, permitting earnings to grow faster than costs.

ONLINE TRAVEL SERVICES COMPONENTS

The expected growth in online travel services affects each of the major components of travel services differently. For instance, air reservations are expected to be the largest single component of the online travel market — tripling in size by 2006 — although hotel and car reservations are projected to grow at slightly faster rates (see Figure 11.9).

The huge size and continued robust growth in online airline reservations relative to other travel services reflects several factors. Airline reservations are largely a commodity; they can be easily described over the Web. The same is true with auto rentals; most people can reliably rent a car over the phone or the Web and expect to obtain what they ordered. However, hotels are somewhat more difficult to describe. Hotels have differing rates, discounts for group membership, different classifications (business vs. consumer travel vs. luxury), and different facilities and ambiance. This level of information complexity is difficult to portray over the Web. Cruises and tours suffer from the same problem. Therefore, we should expect that cruises and tours, along with hotels to some extent, will grow more slowly than airline reservations and auto rentals in the online environment.

Online Travel Industry Segments: Leisure and Managed Business Travel

There are two major segments in the online travel industry: leisure and unmanaged and managed business travel. The online travel industry has concentrated mostly on the leisure travel market (including unmanaged business travel), but this is expected to change considerably in the future as the managed travel segment grows even faster (see Figure 11.10). The managed travel business refers to mid-size and large corporations' efforts to control corporate travel costs by actively managing their employees' travel arrangements. In the past five years, corporate travel expenses have mushroomed, leading corporations to seek greater control over employee travel plans (Sharkey, 2001). Many corporations will not reimburse employee travel unless it is made through an approved in-house travel office or a contracted travel agency such as American Express, Rosenbluth International, Carlson Travel, or increasingly, through Web-based solutions such as Sabre's GetThere.com.

Increasingly, corporations are outsourcing their travel offices entirely to vendors who can provide Web-based solutions, high quality service, and lower costs. Online

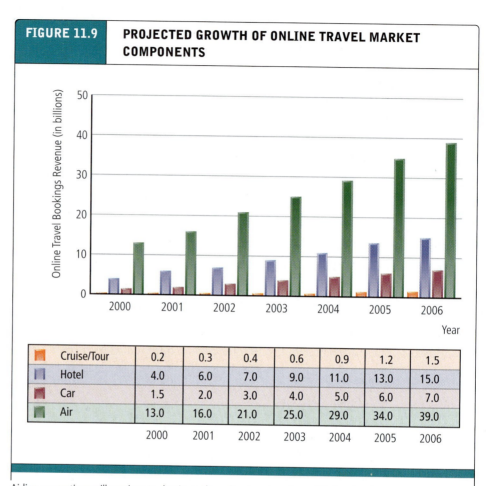

FIGURE 11.9 | **PROJECTED GROWTH OF ONLINE TRAVEL MARKET COMPONENTS**

	2000	2001	2002	2003	2004	2005	2006
Cruise/Tour	0.2	0.3	0.4	0.6	0.9	1.2	1.5
Hotel	4.0	6.0	7.0	9.0	11.0	13.0	15.0
Car	1.5	2.0	3.0	4.0	5.0	6.0	7.0
Air	13.0	16.0	21.0	25.0	29.0	34.0	39.0

Airline reservations will continue to dominate the online travel market, while hotel and car reservations will be growing at an even faster pace.
SOURCE: Jupiter Media Metrix, 2001d.

corporate online-booking solutions (COBS)

provide integrated airline, hotel, conference center, and auto rental services at a single site

vendors to corporations provide **corporate online-booking solutions (COBS)** that provide integrated airline, hotel, conference center, and auto rental services at a single site.

ONLINE TRAVEL INDUSTRY DYNAMICS

Because much of what travel agency sites offer is a commodity, and thus they face the same costs, competition among online providers is intense. Price competition is difficult because shoppers, as well as online site managers, can comparison shop easily.

FIGURE 11.10	PROJECTED GROWTH OF MANAGED AND LEISURE/BUSINESS TRAVEL

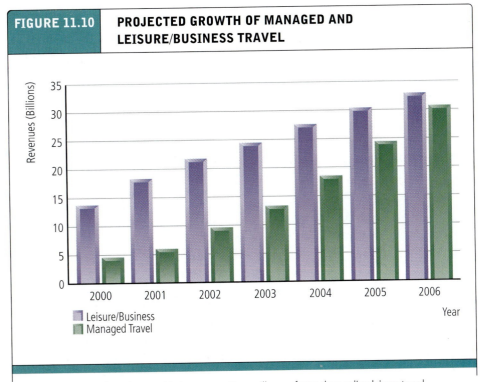

Online managed travel services provided to corporations will grow faster than online leisure travel.

SOURCE: Jupiter Media Metrix, 2001d.

Therefore, competition among sites tends to focus on scope of offerings, ease of use, payment options, and personalization. Some well-known travel sites are listed in Table 11.11.

Pure online travel sites are in general not yet profitable, as we shall see when we look at Expedia.com in more detail in the next section. While successful in attracting a large Internet audience share and influencing significant offline travel purchases, commodity products and competitive forces on the Internet have restricted the ability of online travel services to show strong profits. The online travel services industry is going through a period of consolidation as stronger offline, established agencies such as Cendant (which recently purchased Trip.com and Cheap Tickets) and USA Networks (which purchased a 70% controlling interest in Expedia) purchase weaker and relatively inexpensive online travel agencies in order to build stronger multichannel travel sites that combine physical presence, television sales outlets, and online sites.

TABLE 11.11	LARGE ONLINE TRAVEL SITES
NAME	**FOCUS**
Expedia.com	Second largest online provider; leisure focus.
Travelocity.com	Largest online travel provider; leisure focus.
Orbitz.com	Supplier-owned reservation system.
Priceline.com	"Name your price" model; leisure focus.
CheapTickets.com	Discount airline tickets, hotel reservations and auto rentals. Acquired by Cendant Corporation in Fall 2001.
Trip.com	Primary focus is business travel. Acquired by Cendant Corporation in Fall 2001.
Hotel Reservations Network (180096hotel.com)	Largest hotel reservation network; leisure and corporate focus.
Sabre's GetThere.com	Corporate online booking solution (COBS).
Etravel.com	Competitor in leisure market.
Travelpoint.com	Allows travelers to make their own air, hotel, and car reservations with all ticketing done by a Galileo or Apollo-network travel agent.
Sidestep.com	Surveys Web sites for lowest cost airfares, hotels and cars.
Hotwire.com	Seeks out discount fares based on airline excess inventory.
digitalcity.com/travel	Surveys last-minute bargain fares and cyberfares available only from airline Web sites. An AOL company.
11thhourvacations.com	Focuses on inexpensive last-minute vacation fares.
site59.com	Also focuses on inexpensive last-minute vacation travel.

SOURCE: Brown and Gasparino, 2001.

global distribution systems (GDS)

merchants who buy reservations from suppliers, and then resell the "inventory" to agencies, who then retail the inventory to consumers or create vacation packages that are then sold to retail agent

Opportunities for Disintermediation and Re-intermediation

The travel industry value chain is more complex than commonly realized (see Figure 11.11). Suppliers such as large national airlines, international hotel chains, auto rental companies, and cruise/tour operators generally must deal through a group of intermediaries such as **global distribution systems (GDS)** and travel agencies rather than directly with consumers. GDS are merchants who buy reservations from suppliers and then resell the "inventory" to agencies, who then retail the inventory to consumers or create vacation packages that are then sold to retail agents. In the past, it was difficult if not impossible for suppliers to have a direct relationship with the consumer. Merchants and GDS have far higher profit margins, with 50% markups not

---

FIGURE 11.11   **THE TRAVEL SERVICES VALUE CHAIN**

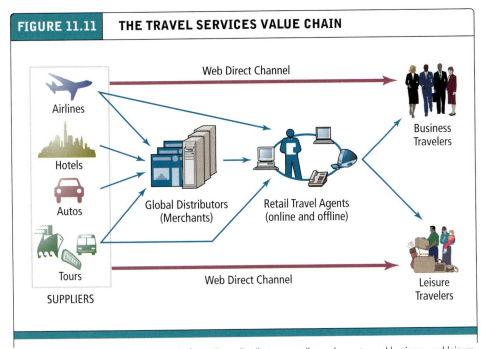

The travel services industry is composed of suppliers, distributors, retail travel agents, and business and leisure travelers. Internet travel sites are an example of how e-commerce can create new intermediaries while weakening existing intermediaries.

---

uncommon. Travel agencies, in contrast, receive fees and commissions that rarely rise above 10% to15% of the amount of the travel booked.

GDS and travel agencies are under pressure from both the supply side and the corporate demand side. Suppliers — such as airlines, hotels, and auto rental firms — would like to eliminate middlemen such as GDS and travel agencies, and develop a direct relationship with consumers. For instance, the seven major airlines have formed their own online reservation system called Orbitz to deal directly with corporations and leisure travelers (see *Insight on Business: Orbitz Takes Off*). The major auto rental firms have all opened direct-to-customer Web sites (Alamo.com, budget.com, and hertz.com) in part to reduce agency fees and to combat Priceline's sale of unused rental capacity.

At the same time, successful online travel agencies are attempting to turn themselves into merchants by purchasing large blocks of travel inventory and then reselling it to the public, eliminating the global distributors and earning much higher returns (while assuming greater risk).

INSIGHT ON BUSINESS

ORBITZ TAKES OFF

After years of planning and the expenditure of $145 million, the online travel site Orbitz opened its site and literally took off. In its first month of operation in June 2000, Orbitz attracted 2.1 million at-home visitors, and 1.6 million unique visitors, jumping from no place into third place, behind Expedia and Travelocity. Sales in June topped $100 million. Orbitz also picked up kudos from travel site aficionados who complimented Orbitz on its interface, which makes comparison shopping for the lowest fares exceptionally easy.

Orbitz is a joint venture between AMR Corporation's American Airlines, Continental Airlines, Delta Airlines, Northwest Airlines, and UAL Corporation's United Airlines. Using new technology that is different from any of the existing traditional computer reservations systems, Orbitz's search ("the Orbot") continuously scans its database of flight information provided by 455 airlines worldwide. In contrast, Travelocity searches the Sabre reservation system, and Expedia searches the Worldspan system. Neither of these traditional systems is as fast or comprehensive as the new Orbot engine.

The biggest advantage of Orbitz is that the suppliers of the air travel — the airlines themselves — own the retail distribution channel that goes directly to the consumer. There are only a few examples in the history of e-commerce where suppliers have sought to take advantage of the Web's ability to put suppliers in direct contact with consumers. Dell, Compaq, IBM Direct, and selected other computer equipment manufacturers come to mind. In the case of the airlines, Orbitz is flying directly into the strategies and business interests of its largest distributors: other online travel sites and, of course, traditional travel agents.

One of the advantages of being a coalition of suppliers is the ability to offer unique fares that other distributors do not even know about. For instance, Orbitz highlights discount Web fares from more than 20 major airlines, and gives consumers a simple table in which to compare the lowest Web fares available without having to go to every airline's site to find prices. Also, Orbitz has an agreement with 35 airlines requiring them to release last-minute low-price Web fares typically published on Wednesdays. These unique features of Orbitz translate into both the lowest prices on the Web and the largest selection.

Orbitz is still working out some of its problems. It does not have a good selection of international flights and it does not provide as complete a selection of hotels and car rentals as can be found on other sites. In the future, Orbitz may run afoul of consumer groups who believe it will lead to instant, online, efficient price collusion among airlines. Electronic marketplaces are ideal for coordinating prices among disparate suppliers. The Department of Transportation reviewed Orbitz' operations in May 2001 for signs of monopolistic pricing practices, but cleared the company in June. The Justice Department is conducting a separate probe and close monitoring of price competition.

The ultimate goal of Orbitz is to capture more of the revenue from airline travel by eliminating distributors and local agents. In August 2001, American Airlines announced a significant cut in travel agents' commissions to below 5%. Commissions used to be 8% up until the late 1990s.

SOURCES: "Airlines Hushed on Prospect of Commission Cuts," by Kaja Whitehouse and Kathy Chu, *Dow Jones Newswires*, August 20, 2001; "Orbitz Has Cool Technology, But Not For International Flights," by Jane Costello, *Wall Street Journal Online*, July 30, 2001; "Orbitz Takes Off, in the Spotlight," by Bob Tedeschi, *New York Times*, June 17, 2001.

E-commerce in Action: Expedia.com

Expedia.com is a Bellevue, Washington-based online travel services company that provides access to information on scheduling, pricing, and availability of flights, hotel accommodations, and rental cars. It had been an operating unit of Microsoft until late 1999. In 2001, USA Networks purchased a 70% interest in Expedia from Microsoft (Caney, 2001). Expedia is one of the top players in online travel services, generating revenues of $222 million for 2001 in an industry estimated to be $3.8 trillion worldwide, according to the World Travel and Tourism Council.

The Vision The vision behind Expedia was to create a global travel marketplace, enabling travel services suppliers to extend their marketing reach online, and giving consumers the ability to research, plan, and purchase travel services. Expedia's customer value proposition was to reduce customer transaction and search costs, and increase price transparency. By replacing many of the functions of local travel agents, Expedia potentially would change the industry structure.

To a large extent, Expedia has succeeded in achieving its vision. Through Expedia, consumers and business travelers can access real-time schedule and pricing information from 450 airlines, 65,000 lodging properties, and all major car rental agencies, 24 hours a day. Visitors can also consult extensive editorial content on more than 350 destinations, review travel information and advice from industry experts, and learn from other travelers through chat groups and community bulletin boards. After gathering needed information, customers can also make reservations at the site. With more than 8 million unique visitors headed to its site for travel information and reservations, Expedia is one of the most-visited sites on the Web.

Business Model Expedia generates revenue in much the same way as a traditional travel agent, by earning a commission or flat fee on each transaction. The company is migrating toward a merchant business model, however, in which Expedia purchases inventory from suppliers at discounted wholesale prices and then resells it to consumers at a retail price that it sets itself. This model will enable Expedia to offer consumers more competitive prices and will generate a higher gross profit per transaction than the commission-based agency model. In addition, Expedia earns revenue from paid advertising from suppliers such as airlines and hotels and licenses core parts of its technology platform to Continental Airlines, Northwest Airlines, and American Express.

Financial Analysis Expedia's gross revenues for its fiscal year ended June 30, 2001 were about $222 million, up substantially from $135 million in 2000 (see Table 11.12). About 55% of that revenue was generated through its agency operation selling airline tickets, booking hotel reservations, and renting cars ($122 million). Its recent expansion into merchant activities, reselling blocks of reservations to retail customers, has paid off very well, generating $64 million in revenues. The company's advertising revenue accounted for just 15% of total revenues in 2001. However, while gross revenues expanded by 5.8 times in the years 1999–2001, cost of revenues jumped nearly as fast, by a factor of 4.6. (Operating expenses have more than kept pace with the increased level of sales.) While product development costs are steady, sales and marketing is up by a factor of 6.2 over 1999. Several acquisitions of travel companies with unique technologies — such as the Best Fare Finder — also added to acquisition costs in 2000. Overall operating expenses are up by a factor of 5.4 since 1999, roughly the same as the growth in revenues in this same period.

The results of Expedia's operations in 2001 were a net loss of $78 million and a negative net margin of –52.7%. This means that for every dollar of net revenue, the company loses 53 cents, or put another way, it costs Expedia $1.53 to earn $1.00 of net revenue. Nevertheless, this is a significant improvement over its net margin in 2000.

Strategic Analysis — Business Strategies Expedia management is pursuing a number of strategies to improve its results.. Recognizing the importance of expanding beyond the U.S. borders, Expedia has developed localized versions of its core Web site in the United Kingdom, Canada, and Germany. These local sites reflect language and cultural differences, as well as purchasing preferences; in the United Kingdom, for example, negotiated fares are the norm, rather than published fares.

Mining its strong brand within the United States, Expedia has developed a number of marketing programs based on the application of traditional media: Expedia Radio broadcasts to more than 2.5 million listeners in more than 100 U.S. cities and *Expedia Travels* magazine is a bimonthly publication that extends the material available on the Expedia site. Launched in 2000, *Expedia Travels* is available on newsstands and by subscription.

The company has also grown through acquisition, having bought Travelscape.com and VacationSpot.com in 2000. In mid-2001, USA Networks announced that it was

TABLE 11.12	EXPEDIA.COM'S CONSOLIDATED STATEMENTS OF OPERATIONS AND SUMMARY BALANCE SHEET DATA, 1999–2001

EXPEDIA.COM, INC.
CONSOLIDATED STATEMENTS OF OPERATIONS
(in thousands)

For the fiscal year ended June 30	2001	2000	1999
Revenue			
Agency revenues	$122,987	$59,534	$24,677
Merchant revenues	64,548	10,912	
Advertising and other revenues	34,685	24,185	14,022
Gross revenues	222,220	94,631	38,699
Cost of revenues	74,274	40,148	15,950
Gross profit	147,946	54,483	22,749
Gross margin	**66%**	**58%**	**58%**
Operating expenses			
Product development	24,682	20,391	21,180
Sales and marketing	90,159	65,701	14,888
General and administrative	22,540	10,507	6,283
Amortization of goodwill	62,026	17,864	—
Recognition of stock-based compensation	31,183	60,689	—
Total operating expenses	230,590	175,151	42,351
Loss from operations	(82,644)	(120,668)	(19,602)
Net interest income and other	4,591	2,353	—
Net loss	**(78,053)**	**($118,315)**	**(19,602)**
Net margin	**−52.7%**	**−217%**	**−86%**

SUMMARY BALANCE SHEET DATA

At June 30	2001	2000	1999
Cash and cash equivalents	$182,161	$60,670	—
Accounts receivable	29,716	13,997	4,970
Prepaid merchant bookings and expenses	41,812	6,452	—
Total assets	389,844	273,050	5,756
Current liabilities	157,542	60,997	3,580
Long-term liabilities, net	1,303	4,557	3,851

SOURCE: Expedia.com, Inc. Form 10-K for the fiscal year ended June 30, 2001, filed with the Securities and Exchange Commission on August 22, 2001.

acquiring Microsoft's 70% stake in Expedia in order to extend its reach within the travel market, providing the media conglomerate with a new channel for travel information and a new advertising vehicle.

Expedia has also sought to use new information technologies to differentiate its product. The company purchased a proprietary price comparison engine and marketed it as Best Fare Search, allowing Expedia to show customers hundreds more priced itineraries than other Internet sites. Expedia has invested in software to personalize the travel planning experience, added a mobile commerce capability called ExpediaToGo, and invested heavily in infrastructure to increase response speed and avoid downtimes.

Strategic Analysis — Competition Expedia competes primarily with other online commercial travel Web sites, such as its main rival Travelocity, HotelReservationsNetwork, Cendant sites CheapTickets and Trip.com, TravelWeb, GetThere, TravelNow, and Worldres.com. Also, sites such as Priceline and Yahoo, which are not travel-focused but do offer travel services, are also competition. Finally, traditional travel agencies that have established their own commercial Web sites are targeting the same customers, and airlines intending to build direct-distribution Web sites such as Orbitz are also direct competitors.

Strategic Analysis — Technology To ensure reliability, security, and scalability as the site grows, with the help and support of Microsoft, Expedia developed a multi-layered platform capable of handling large transaction volumes. It also created several powerful search tools to assist consumers in finding and acting on a wide range of travel information.

Best Fare Search, a Windows-based reservation and price comparison engine, allows Expedia to show customers many more priced itineraries than other travel Web sites. Fare Tracker enables subscribers to select three travel routes and receive updates and alerts regarding special fares and offers via a weekly e-mail bulletin. My Trips and My Profile are two means of helping customers track travel itineraries and personal travel profiles online. Mileage Miner helps consumers manage their frequent flyer program memberships at the site as well. And its new mobile commerce initiative, called ExpediaToGo, provides customers with flight status, flight schedules, driving directions, hotel availability, and access to personal itineraries arranged through Expedia — all on a handheld device.

Strategic Analysis — Social and Legal Challenges In 1999, Priceline.com filed two lawsuits against Microsoft and Expedia, alleging that Expedia's Hotel Price Matcher and Flight Price Matcher infringed on Priceline patents, and accusing the companies of engaging in unfair and deceptive acts or practices. The suit has not yet been decided and is the only material legal challenge the company currently faces.

Future Prospects Unlike many other retail sites, Expedia's biggest risk lies not in whether it can attract enough traffic to be successful, but whether it can retain such customer relationships in the face of mounting competition from the airlines and other supplier-based sites. With American, Continental, Delta, Northwest, and United having launched their joint Web site, Orbitz, Expedia will need to develop new features to keep price-sensitive consumers using their site. Orbitz has been marketed as the only Web site where consumers can find unpublished weekly special fares. Hotwire.com, another direct-to-consumer Web site, also debuted in 2000 and is operated by other major airlines.

Moreover, since the World Trade Center disaster on September 11, 2001, the size of the entire travel market will shrink at least temporarily, and the effects will be most severe in the airline industry. Given the temporary decline in the size of the general travel market, online travel expenditures will also decline. Expedia's ability to maintain its leadership position will be challenged even more. Expedia has yet to prove that it can be a profitable operation even in a buoyant market, and it will have to move quickly into the fast expanding managed travel services market in order to achieve profitability.

11.4 CAREER SERVICES

Next to travel services, one of the Internet's most successful online services has been job hunting services (recruitment sites) that provide a free posting of individual resumes, plus many other related career services; for a fee, they also list job openings posted by companies. Forrester Research estimates that the total online recruitment industry revenues will be $7 billion by 2005, with about half of this revenue paid by employers advertising positions (see Figure 11.12). Job sites collect revenue from other sources as well by providing value-added services to users and collecting fees from related service providers (Bradford, 2001; Walker, 2000). There are an estimated 40,000 online recruitment sites including firm listings, and about 5,000 dedicated recruitment sites not affiliated with a firm.

Traditionally, companies have relied on five employee recruitment tools: classified and print advertising, career expos (or trade shows), on-campus recruiting, private employment agencies (now called "staffing firms"), and internal referral programs. By comparison to online recruiting, these tools have severe limitations. Print advertising usually includes a per-word charge that limits the amount of detail employers provide about a job opening, as well as a limited time period within which the job is posted. Career expos do not allow for pre-screening of attendees and are limited by the amount of time a recruiter can spend with each candidate. Staffing firms charge high fees and have a limited, usually local, selection of job hunters. On-campus recruiting also restricts the number of candidates a recruiter can speak with dur-

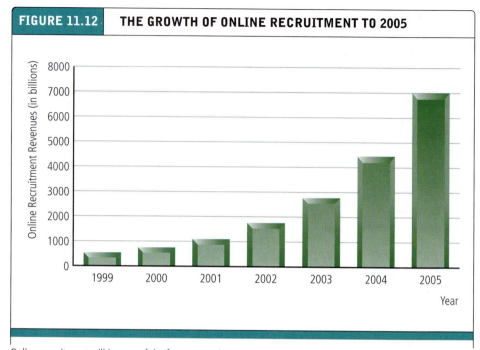

Online recruitment will be one of the fastest growing e-commerce services.
SOURCE: Forrester Research, as cited in Walker, 2000.

ing a normal visit and requires that employers visit numerous campuses. And internal referral programs may encourage employees to propose unqualified candidates for openings in order to qualify for rewards or incentives offered.

Online recruiting overcomes these limitations, providing a more efficient and cost-effective means of linking employers and potential employees, while reducing the total time-to-hire. Online recruiting enables job hunters to more easily build, update, and distribute their resumes while gathering information about prospective employers and conducting job searches.

IT'S JUST INFORMATION: THE IDEAL WEB BUSINESS?

Online recruitment appears to be ideally suited for the Web. The hiring process is an information-intense business process that involves discovering the skills and salary requirements of individuals and matching those with available jobs. Prior to the Internet, this information sharing was accomplished locally by human networks of friends, acquaintances, former employers and relatives, and also by employment agencies that developed paper files on job hunters. The Internet can clearly automate this flow of information, reducing search time and costs for all parties. Given the Internet-based advantages to both firms and job hunters, it seems that recruitment services should be able to become highly profitable.

WHY JOB SITES ARE SO POPULAR

Altogether, job recruitment sites in the United States generate about 12 million unique visitors a month, making them among the most popular Internet sites. The most popular online recruitment site in the United States is Monster.com, which currently generates about 8 million unique visitors each month. Table 11.13 lists some of the most popular recruitment sites.

TABLE 11.13	POPULAR ONLINE RECRUITMENT SITES
GENERAL RECRUITMENT SITES	**BRIEF DESCRIPTION**
TMP Sites	
Monster.com	General job searches.
HotJobs.com	General job searches.
Jobline.com	Primarily northern Europe.
FlipDog.com	Web bot scours employer sites; free service advertising model.
headhunter.net	Free resume posting or pay to play.
CareerWeb.com	One of the original recruiting sites on Web. Part of the Trader Publishing Network.
CareerBuilder.com (formerly CareerPath.com)	Joined forces with Tribune Company and Knight Ridder in August 2000. Features jobs from over 70 different career sites.
MBAGlobalNet.com	MBA-oriented community site.
Executive Search Sites	
FutureStep.com	Korn/Ferry site. Low-end executive recruiting.
Spencer Stuart Talent Network (spencerstuart.com)	Middle-level executive recruiting.
Leadersonline.com	Heidrick & Struggles site. Specializes in technology professionals.
execunet.com	Executive search firm.

Why are so many job hunters and employers using Internet job sites? Recruitment sites are popular largely because they save time and money for both job hunters and employers seeking recruits. For instance, Dow Chemical no longer accepts offline resumes. You must apply electronically at its web site. All new salaried workers hired (about 1500 per year) apply through its career site and through Internet job boards that Dow uses. This has shaved the time to fill a job from 90 days to 34 days, and costs per hire are down 26% on average. Dow's internal recruiter department shrunk from 100 to 60 people worldwide (Gill, 2001). In a recent survey of 400 job recruiters, 78% said Internet job postings were the most effective way to spend their tight job search budgets (compared to newspaper classified ads — 12%). Payroll services provider ADP recruits about one-third of its new staffers through the Internet (Gill, 2001).

For job seekers, online sites are popular not only because their resumes can be made widely available to recruiters but also because of a variety of other related job-hunting services. The service delivered by online recruitment sites has greatly expanded since their beginning in 1996. Originally, online recruitment sites just provided a digital version of newspaper classified ads. But today's sites offer many other services including skills assessment, personality assessment questionnaires, personalized account management for job hunters, organizational culture assessments, job search tools, employer blocking (prevents your employer from seeing your posting), employee blocking (prevents your employees from seeing your listings if you are their employer), and e-mail notification. For instance, Monster.com has a MyAgent service that sends e-mail messages to job hunters when an appropriate job is newly listed on a site. Online sites also provide a number of educational services such as resume writing advice, software skills preparation, and interview tips.

For the most part, online recruitment sites work, in the sense of linking job hunters with jobs, but they are just one of many ways people actually find a job. Figure 11.13 shows the results of a recent survey of members of the online population looking for a job. About 38% had posted a resume to the Web, but nearly 80% read the newspaper classifieds.

A recent survey by the Society for Human Resources found that job seekers still believe traditional methods are the best way to actually find a job: 80% of job seekers said personal contact and networking were the most effective (Armour, 2001). But for those who post resumes on the Web, the results are often positive. Figure 11.14 shows that 23% of those posting a resume had one interview, and 15% had five or more interviews. Given that the cost of posting a resume is zero, the marginal returns are very high.

Perhaps the most important function of online recruitment sites is not so much their capacity to actually match employees with job hunters, but their ability to establish market prices and terms. Notice that nearly 70% of online job hunters have searched Internet sites. Online recruitment sites identify salary levels for both employers and job hunters, and categorize the skill sets required to achieve those

FIGURE 11.13 | **MANY WAYS TO FIND A JOB**

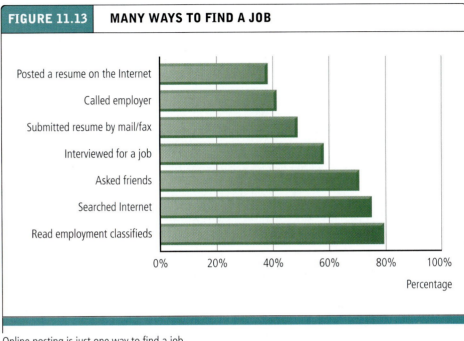

Online posting is just one way to find a job.
SOURCE: Mantz, 2000.

FIGURE 11.14 | **SURVEY RESULTS**

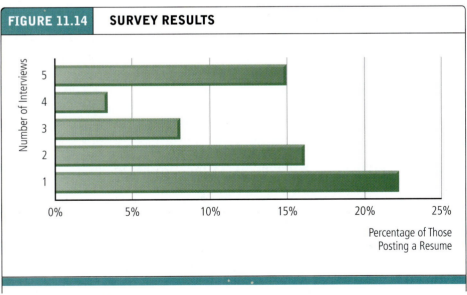

Online job postings are effective in producing interviews.
SOURCE: Mantz, 2000.

salary levels. In this sense, online recruitment sites are online national marketplaces establishing the terms of trade in the labor markets. The existence of these nation-wide sites should lead to a rationalization of wages, greater labor mobility, and higher efficiency in recruitment and operations because employers will be able to quickly find the people they need.

RECRUITMENT MARKET SEGMENTS

There are three segments to the recruitment business. General job recruitment is the largest segment and focuses on placing a wide range of individuals at all skill and salary levels. In the past, general job recruitment has been performed by govern-ment labor agencies and private placement firms, and through newspaper classified ads (a major source of revenue for newspapers). The executive search segment focuses on placing executives with annual salaries of $100,000 or more. Specialized executive placement firms conduct executive searches for employers, generally charging one-third of the first year's salary as a fee. Executive search firm revenues had been growing at over 20% annually since 1990, but their growth has slowed to only 14% since 1999. A third segment is specialized job placement services, which are often run by professional societies such as the Society for Plastic Engineers site, www.4spec.org, and the police recruiting site, www.policeemployment.com.

Online recruitment has focused primarily on the largest market for general job recruitment. However, many general sites — such as Monster — have begun listing lower- and middle-level management jobs. Indeed, the largest revenue potential for the general job online sites is in executive recruiting, where fees are currently very high. The traditional executive placement agencies such as Korn/Ferry and Spencer Stuart — seeing the threat from online sites — have also developed their own Web sites for lower- and middle-level managers seeking salaries above $100,000. Internet executive recruiting is expected to grow from $250 million this year to $5 billion in 2003, half the size of the traditional industry (Baig and Armstrong 2000). Pitney Bowes (PBI) and Accenture are just two firms hiring mid-level and even senior exec-utives through the Internet. They are saving $50,000 per hire by avoiding expensive executive search firms.

ONLINE RECRUITMENT INDUSTRY DYNAMICS: CONSOLIDATION

The online recruitment industry is going through a period of rapid consolidation led by TMP Worldwide Inc., a New York-based provider of yellow page advertising (referred to now as "directional marketing") and recruitment advertising (the place-ment of newspaper classified job ads for large firms), historically its primary busi-nesses. Despite the growth of online job services, traditional classified newspaper job ad revenues grew at a 12% annual compound rate in the 1995–2000 period. TMP has purchased more than 70 general and executive online recruiting sites worldwide, including Monster.com, Jobline.com, HotJobs.com (discussed in more detail in the next section), FlipDog.com, as well as executive recruiting agencies such as LAI Inc. and TASA International. In 1999, TMP paid $100 million to be the exclusive provider of online job listings for AOL for a four-year period.

Because of its acquisitions, TMP is now the world leader in online executive recruiting, executive moving and relocation, e-resourcing (placement of temporary managers and executives for limited periods of time), temporary contracting, and recruitment advertising. TMP Worldwide employs 9,500 people in 32 countries and generates commissions and fee revenues of $1.2 billion. In 2000, TMP had profits of $114 million (TMP Worldwide 10-K, 2000; Luh, 2001).

Through its acquisition strategy, TMP has been able to establish Monster.com as the leading brand in online recruitment. By rolling in the capabilities of firms in diverse segments of recruiting and placement, TMP has significantly added to Monster's functionality, software, and scope. Monster now commands a 53% U.S. market share in online recruiting. Nevertheless, local newspaper advertising remains a powerful factor in job markets because most job hunters are looking for work in their local areas, and local employers — especially smaller and medium-sized businesses — are looking for local recruits. As local newspapers develop online job sites, sometimes using software provided by major national players such as Monster.com, they remain a viable source of jobs and job information.

E-commerce in Action: HotJobs.com

HotJobs.com is a New York City-based online recruiter, linking employers, staffing firms, and job seekers through its Web site HotJobs.com. More than 9,100 employers pay an average of $870 per month to list job openings and direct potential candidates to their human resource departments, drawing on HotJobs' database of close to 3 million job seekers. Begun in 1997, HotJobs grew rapidly, hitting revenues of $96.5 million in 2000, up from $20.7 million during the prior year, and amassing several hundred thousand job postings. Still, the company remained unprofitable and generated an accumulated deficit of $83.5 million, in part due to acquisitions.

In July 2001, Monster.com's parent company, TMP Worldwide, announced plans to acquire HotJobs for $460 million in stock. Although the initial plan is to keep both Monster.com and HotJobs as independent entities, together they feature 14 million online resumes and more than 650,000 job postings, making them the clear industry leader. Currently, Hotjobs.com is the second largest recruitment destination site, after its sister company Monster.com.

The Vision HotJobs' vision was to become a leading provider of comprehensive recruiting solutions for employers and staffing firms who paid fees for listing their jobs. Solutions for job hunters would include posting of resumes plus tools for managing a job hunting campaign including market research, career planning, and advice. The belief was that HotJobs would enable job hunters to leverage the global reach of the Web, and lower the cost in time and money required for job placement, while retaining many of the personal attributes of traditional recruiting methods. By aggregating millions of job seekers at one Web site, employers could reduce their search costs by efficiently mining a single large pool of potential recruits. Transaction costs of job hunters would be reduced to zero — all fees are paid by employers. Price transparency would increase: It would be possible to review salaries being offered by employers for jobs requiring specific skills.

To a large extent, HotJobs succeeded in achieving its vision, but not as an independent or profitable company.

Business Model   The majority of HotJobs' revenue is derived from membership fees paid by employers and staffing firms, which allows them to access the HotJobs database of job seekers, as well as post, track, and manage job openings. HotJobs also generates revenue from 12 career expos it holds annually, online advertising by employers, and sales of recruitment management software to large firms.

HotJobs provides a flexible pricing model whereby employers can pay a flat fee in order to post openings and search the site database at no additional cost during their membership period. The company also recently added new *a la carte* payment options that allow employers to pay per database search or for a short-term job posting. The option to buy fixed-price packages based on length of commitment and usage may negatively impact the company's business model and revenue stream, however.

Financial Analysis   One of HotJobs' major accomplishments for 2000 was increasing revenue almost fivefold, from $20.7 million to $96.5 million, due to revenue jumps in all of its profit centers, but especially in e-recruitment fees (see Table 11.14). One analyst believes HotJobs' revenues will rise to $147 million in 2001 (Marcial, 2001).

Like so many dot.coms, HotJobs' revenues exploded in the period 1998–2000. About three-quarters of this revenue growth came from online recruitment fees paid by employers, with software licensing (primarily through the acquisition of Resumix) and career expos contributing the rest. However, its cost of revenues (largely direct labor costs) increased even faster, reducing gross margins to 78%, still a healthy margin.

Similarly, operating expenses in the 1998–2000 period expanded by a factor of 25. The leading cost has been marketing and advertising. The very rapid rise in expenditures for technology, and fast growing general and administrative expenses contributed to a $46 million loss in 2000. However, the negative net margin was decreased to –61.7% from even higher levels in earlier years. This suggests that HotJobs.com is experiencing some positive scale effects: Its losses are receding as revenues expand. Nevertheless, for every dollar HotJobs took in, it lost almost 62 cents.

Looking at the balance sheet, on December 31, 2000 HotJobs had a strong current asset position, with about $120 million in liquid assets available. These assets are the

TABLE 11.14	HOTJOBS.COM'S CONSOLIDATED STATEMENTS OF OPERATIONS AND SUMMARY BALANCE SHEET DATA, 1998–2000

HOTJOBS.COM LTD.
CONSOLIDATED STATEMENTS OF OPERATIONS
(in thousands)

	2000	1999	1998
Revenues			
e-Recruitment	$74,745	$15,606	$2,638
Software	12,941	1,527	873
Career expos	4,968	2,327	—
Other	3,881	1,214	1
Total revenues	96,535	20,674	3,512
Cost of revenues	21,490	3,750	505
Gross profit	75,045	16,924	3,007
Gross margin	78%	82%	86%
Operating expenses			
Product development	8,069	1,423	474
Sales and marketing	82,514	24,490	3,085
General and administrative	25,794	8,112	1,642
Non-cash compensation, net	1,860	2,012	—
Amortization of goodwill	10,211	—	—
Total operating expenses	128,448	36,037	5,201
Loss from operations	(53,403)	(19,113)	(945)
Net interest income/(expense)	7,072	1,297	–63
Net loss	**($46,331)**	**($17,816)**	**($2,257)**
Net margin	–61.7%	–105%	–75%

SUMMARY BALANCE SHEET DATA
(in thousands)

At December 31	2000	1999	1998
Current assets			
Cash and cash equivalents	$50,848	$88,372	$167
Marketable securities	48,248	49,897	—
Accounts receivable	22,202	6,456	1,553
Total assets	**190,736**	**152,541**	**3,653**
Current liabilities	52,477	15,189	6,457
Long-term debt	1,554	1,824	80

SOURCE: HotJobs.com, Inc. Form 10-K for the fiscal year ended December 31, 2000, filed with the Securities and Exchange Commission on March 30, 2001.

result of public stock offering, investor contributions, and other sources. At current rates of loss, HotJobs could continue in operation for several years, assuming it raised no new funds.

Between 1999 and 2000, the cost of revenues increased almost in sync with revenue growth: from $3.8 million to $21.5 million, or 22% of revenues. Product development expenses rose several-fold, to $8.1 million; general and administrative expenses increased more than 300%, to $25.8 million; and sales and marketing expenses increased an additional 300 + %, to $82.5 million. It was these mounting expenses that resulted in the company's $46.3 million net loss.

Strategic Analysis — Business Strategies Opening offices in local markets has been one strategy HotJobs has used to expand its market presence and accelerate site traffic. Since the company has found greater success in attracting employer members in markets where a local office is situated, new offices were established in Miami, Washington, D.C., and Toronto in 2000. These offices are in addition to existing sites in Austin, Texas; Boston; Chicago; New York; San Francisco; Santa Monica; and Sydney, Australia. To staff these offices, the direct sales force has grown from 85 sales executives to 196.

Creating new tools for job seekers to use in identifying potential job opportunities has been another strategy HotJobs has used to attract new candidates. Resume Builder enables seekers to create an HTML-formatted resume acceptable for submission to the site; MyHotJobs allows users to specify job openings of interest and receive customized career management information on a regular basis; and HotBlock permits seekers to choose which employers have access to their resume, thereby eliminating unwanted solicitations and preventing their current employer from knowing they are looking for a new opportunity.

For employers, HotJobs created HR Exchange, a forum where members can share experiences, ideas, and get expert advice from industry insiders, and *Req Sheet*, a bulletin of recent news stories of interest to human resource professionals.

During 2000, HotJobs developed a new B2B service by accepting job postings from staffing firms through a new service called AgencyExchange. Staffing firm postings appear on HotJobs just as employer listings do, but are identified as being listed by a staffing firm. Staffing firms can also market their services to HotJobs member companies through AgencyExchange.

HotJobs continued to build brand awareness and site traffic through 12 locally produced Career Expos that combine the applicant tracking and sorting capabilities available through HotJobs with a pool of local job applicants.

The acquisition of software developer Resumix was also completed in 2000, providing HotJobs with access to Resumix's applicant tracking software capabilities. By entering into several strategic partnerships with leading industry Web sites, HotJobs has been strengthening the quantity and quality of features it can offer its job seekers as well as creating new revenue opportunities. Its newest relationship with CMP Media, for example, gives HotJobs the responsibility of developing job boards for a number of CMP publications, such as *Internet Week* and *Dr. Dobbs' Journal*, with CMP advertising representatives reselling HotJobs' ad postings in exchange.

Recognizing the need to stem its growing expenses, however, HotJobs reorganized its workforce in early 2001, cutting its employee base from 665 to 581 at the end of the first quarter. The company also consolidated its software operations in Sunnyvale, California and New York City, thereby eliminating lease payments on several satellite offices.

Strategic Analysis — Competition HotJobs' competitors consist of online job boards, both general — such as industry leader and fellow subsidiary of TMP Worldwide, Monster.com, with 53% market share — and industry-focused — such as JournalismJobs.com, as well as newspapers, magazines, and traditional media companies that accept job postings. Large Internet portals, recruiting software companies, and career expo companies are additional competitors.

Strategic Analysis — Technology The acquisition of Resumix was designed to strengthen HotJobs' software development business, which licenses and sells an ASP software suite called Softshoe that enables companies to manage their own internal recruiting process, as well as create and manage their own job boards. Presumably, HotJobs resides on an internally developed and supported version of Softshoe.

Strategic Analysis — Social and Legal Challenges There are no legal proceedings or claims that HotJobs is currently a party to.

Future Prospects HotJobs is now a part of the TMP empire, but is still operating as a separate branded site. The losses of HotJobs are balanced by gains in other parts of TMP's portfolio of companies. Nevertheless, HotJobs' management is under pressure to develop real earnings and profits. Perhaps the biggest risk these managers face is the ability to manage the rapid growth the company is experiencing — to keep revenues growing but start reducing costs. Its managerial, operational, and financial resources, as well as its information systems, have been strained by trying to keep up with the exponential growth in employers and job seekers. Prior to its acquisition, HotJobs' management emphasized revenue growth and site visitor growth, but increasingly they will have to consider how to generate profits. Although increases in usage and traffic might bring HotJobs to profitability at some future date, management stated in HotJobs' 2000 Form 10-K that "We continue to expect to lose money in the foreseeable future" (HotJobs.com, 2000). At this point, HotJobs continues to operate at a loss within the TMP empire.

Why WebVan Failed
(and Britain's Tesco Succeeded)

In 1997, Louis Borders, founder of the Borders bookstore chain, founded a new company that he thought would revolutionize the grocery business. The idea was deceptively simple: Take orders for groceries over the Internet and use highly automated centralized warehouses and computerized logistics systems controlling a local fleet of trucks to efficiently deliver groceries to a customer's doorstep at a cost no more than if the customer had gone to the supermarket himself. This Web grocery business would be profitable, Borders figured, because it would save consumers time, millions would sign up for service, and the cost of providing the service would be no higher than the costs faced by traditional grocers. Efficiencies would be so great that there would be no need for a delivery charge. The higher costs of delivery would be offset by savings in physical store space. Rolling out in San Francisco first, the plan was to prove the concept in San Francisco, and then expand to 26 cities across the United States at a cost of $35 million for each city's warehouse and delivery vehicles.

After spending $1.2 billion, much of which was raised from Silicon Valley venture firms such as Benchmark Capital, Sequoia Capital, and Goldman Sachs and from a successful IPO (initial public offering), WebVan closed its doors on July 8, 2001 and dismissed its 2000 employees. To date, WebVan is the largest single e-commerce loss (the runner up was e-Toys, which had lost $478 million).

WebVan was thought to be an e-commerce "killer app" and could be found in most Internet stock portfolios. Like so many E-commerce I start-ups, the company's philosophy was to grow as fast as possible, achieve brand name recognition early to dominate the marketspace, and worry about the cost structure later. Its stock went from a one-day high of $34, to its low of 6 cents just before closing its doors.

WebVan joined a host of failed U.S. Internet-based delivery services such as UrbanFetch, Kozmo, and HomeGrocer. These free delivery services tried to save themselves by switching to traditional courier services and charging fees, and then faced steep declines in orders and declining revenues that were unable to support centralized delivery warehouses and fleets of delivery vehicles.

In contrast to WebVan is Britain's Tesco.com, the online arm of Britain's largest supermarket chain. Tesco.com is the world's largest online grocery delivery business. Tesco has one million online customers, makes an average delivery worth $123, generating $422 million in annual sales, and is profitable, according to the company, which does not break out physical store financial data from its online operation. Tesco adopted a go-slow, store-based business model of home grocery delivery. Instead of building huge, expensive, computerized central warehouses in each city, Tesco instead relied on its chain of 690 British grocery stores to pick, pack, and deliver groceries. Tesco hired local "pickers" (people) who walk the aisles of Tesco local stores as orders arrive over the Internet. The orders are placed in bins, and a store truck delivers orders throughout the day and evening in the local neighborhood for a fee of about $7. With its base of stores, Tesco can reach over 90% of the UK population within a few minutes — to be exact, 25 minutes in the worst case. Tesco has spent $56 million to develop its online grocery Web site and delivery service — a tiny fraction of WebVan's investment.

The idea of "pick, pack, and deliver" household consumer items is not new. In the 1940s and 1950s, dairy and bread companies routinely delivered groceries to consumers using fleets of trucks in cities. That service eventually declined with the growth of suburbs and mega-supermarkets, and the changing lifestyles of customers. As it turns out, moving this old business model to the Web did not change consumers' lives.

In hindsight, it is easy to see where WebVan and other similar "last mile" delivery services failed. WebVan clearly overestimated the size of the market. WebVan discovered, much too late, that there was a strong relationship between sales concentration (average order size per person), population density, and revenue. The home delivery business works only where average order size approaches $100, and where the population density is high (say in New York City or London, where density approaches 30,000 per square mile). High population densities reduce the time of delivery (but can also delay delivery due to traffic congestion). As it turns out, there are few cities that have the same characteristics as London and New York.

The central computerized warehouse model might have worked in WebVan's 26 cities if the average order size was large. But WebVan misunderstood its average customer. As it turned out, the size of the average order was only $30, the average profit on the groceries was only about 5% at best — $1.50 — and the cost of delivery was $10–$14. This was a money-losing proposition from the start. WebVan discovered that wealthy households where both spouses worked were increasingly eating out at restaurants, and that they tended to order small amounts of pre-cooked food when they did order.

WebVan also overestimated the consumer's dissatisfaction with grocery shopping. Grocery shopping takes time, but in crowded urban areas, there are several grocery stores in any given neighborhood. Surveys report that 75% of U.S. grocery shoppers "enjoy the experience" of going to the marketplace, meeting people, and seeing and touching food products. It was unclear what "problem" WebVan was the solution for. Initially, WebVan assumed someone would be home to receive the order. Later it discovered working men and women were not at home during the day to receive groceries. To accommodate its customers' busy schedules, it developed a "30 minute delivery window or we pay" policy. Unfortunately, WebVan could not deliver in that time window very often, and it ended losing even more sales revenue.

SOURCES: "Early Winner in Online Food," by Suzanne Kapner, *New York Times*, July 20, 2001; "Why WebVan Went Bust," by Roger Blackwell, *New York Times*, July 16, 2001; "An Ambitious Internet Grocer Is Out of Both Cash and Ideas," by Saul Hansell, *New York Times*, July 8, 2001; "The Last Mile to Nowhere: Flaws and Fallacies in Internet Home-Delivery Schemes," by Tim Laseter, Pat Houston, Anne Chung, Silas Byrne, Martha Turner, and Andrew Devendran, *Strategy and Business*, March 2000.

It also appears that WebVan misunderstood the industry. The grocery industry is increasingly dominated by huge national chains that can achieve extraordinary economies of scale in a business that even the best find challenging because profit margins are about 1.08%. This is not an industry where a young upstart company with a new technology can revolutionize the cost structure. The cost structure has already been squeezed to a minimal size. In fact, to succeed in this business, WebVan would have had to first develop the kinds of operational efficiencies in inventory management, transportation, sourcing, warehousing, and logistics that the large national store chains already have developed. This would take years of effort.

Internet home grocery services are still available in the United States and most likely will survive, although not at the revenue levels once envisioned by Louis Borders. Online grocery delivery will account for only 2% of all grocery sales in 2006, up from .2% in 2001. The largest survivor is Peapod, now controlled by Dutch grocer Royal Ahold, which owns several supermarket chains throughout the United States. Safeway Stores, along with GroceryWorks (a Dallas-based firm now partly owned by Tesco), is now testing home delivery from its local stores in Houston. Both Peapod and Safeway will be employing a mixed bricks and clicks strategy, using local stores in combination with central warehouses for their delivery operations, a business model with far lower costs than the approach pioneered by WebVan. Most important, as big players in the bricks-and-mortar grocery business, Peapod and GroceryWorks can obtain favorable prices from suppliers.

Case Study Questions

1. Do you think the founders of WebVan, and perhaps their venture capitalist investors, could have anticipated the response of consumers to WebVan's grocery service?

2. Why is a store-based model for Internet grocers more viable than computerized centralized warehouses?

3. If you were a manager at Peapod, what steps would you take to ensure a profitable outcome?

4. Compare and contrast WebVan's experience with other service companies discussed in this chapter. What are some common factors of success and failure?

11.6 REVIEW

KEY CONCEPTS

■ **Describe the major features of the online service sector.**

The service sector is the largest and most rapidly expanding part of the economy of advanced industrial nations. Service industries are companies that provide services (i.e., perform tasks for) consumers, businesses, governments, and other organizations. The major service industry groups are FIRE, business services, and health services. Within these service industry groups, companies can be further categorized into those that involve transaction brokering and those that involve providing a "hands-on" service. With some exceptions, the service sector is by and large a knowledge- and information-intense industry. For this reason, many services are uniquely suited to e-commerce and the strengths of the Internet. The rapid expansion of e-commerce services in the areas of finance, including insurance and real estate, travel, and job placement, can be explained by the ability of these firms to:
• collect, store, and disseminate high value information;

- provide reliable, fast communication; and
- personalize and customize service or components of service.

E-commerce offers extraordinary opportunities to improve transaction efficiencies and thus productivity in a sector where productivity has so far not been markedly affected by the explosion in information technology.

■   **Discuss the trends taking place in the online financial services industry.**

The online financial services sector is a good example of an e-commerce success story, but the success is somewhat different than what had been predicted in the E-commerce I era. Pure online financial services firms are in general not yet profitable. In E-commerce II, once again, it is the multichannel established financial firms that are growing the most rapidly and that have the best prospects for long-term viability. Other significant trends include the following:

- Management of financial assets online is growing rapidly. By 2005, it is projected that more than half of all households in the United States will be investing online; online banking is also expected to more than double by 2005; online stock trading is expected to grow from 15 million households today to 34 million households in 2005.
- In the insurance and real estate industries, consumers still generally utilize the Internet just for research and use a conventional transaction broker to complete the purchase.
- Historically, separate institutions have provided the four generic types of services provided by financial institutions. Today, as a result of the Financial Reform Act of 1998, which permitted banks, brokerage firms, and insurance companies to merge, this is no longer true. This has resulted in two important and related global trends in the financial services industry that have direct consequences for online financial services firms: the move toward industry consolidation and the provision of integrated financial services.

■   **Identify the key features of the online banking and brokerage, insurance, and real estate industries.**

Key features of the online banking and brokerage industries include the following:

- Multichannel firms that have both physical branches and solid online offerings are growing faster and assuming market leadership over the pure online firms that cannot provide customers with many services that still require hands-on interaction.
- Customer acquisition costs are significantly higher for Internet-only banks and brokerages that must invest heavily in marketing versus their established brand name clicks and mortar competitors, which can simply convert existing branch customers to online customers at a much lower cost.
- Multichannel institutions draw nearly four times the number of visitors, and significantly more of those visitors open a secure channel, indicating they are

interested in transacting. However, visitors to pure online firms use the sites more intensively and for a wider variety of services, while multichannel site users visit less frequently and perform fewer transactions online. Unfortunately for the pure online firms, their more active consumers are also more apt to comparison shop, are more cost driven, and are therefore less loyal than established multichannel users.

- The projected boom in online investment and banking has also attracted non-financial institutions. Financial portals provide comparison shopping services and steer consumers to online providers for independent financial advice and financial planning. They generate revenue from advertising, referral fees, and subscription fees. Financial portals add to the online price competition in the industry. They also thwart the ambitions of the large banking institutions that would like to ensnare consumers in a single branded financial supermarket in which the switching costs from a single, all-purpose account would be considerable.

- Account aggregation is another rapidly growing online financial service, which pulls together all of a customer's financial data on a single personalized Web site. Established financial institutions were originally opposed to these independent sites as a threat to their already established customer base, but consumer demand for this convenience has forced them to sign deals with the major account aggregation software providers in order to offer the service on their own sites. Privacy issues are raised by this new technology because in order to pull all of this data together in one place, consumers must release all of their login and password information to the account aggregator.

- In the E-commerce I period, a radically altered online mortgage and lending services market was envisioned in which the mortgage value chain would be simplified and the loan closing process speeded up, with the resulting cost savings passed on to consumers. Affordably building a brand name, the resulting high customer acquisition costs, and instituting these value chain changes proved to be too difficult. In E-commerce II, it is again the established banks and lenders who are reaping the benefits of a relatively small but rapidly growing market.

- There are four basic types of online mortgage lenders, including established online banks, brokerages, and lending organizations; pure online bankers/brokers; mortgage brokers; and mortgage service companies.

Key features of the online insurance industry include the following:
- Term life insurance stands out as one product group supporting the E-commerce I vision of lower search costs, increased price transparency, and the resulting consumer savings. Policy prices for term life insurance have fallen as much as 54% in the last six years. However, in other insurance product lines, the Web offers insurance companies new opportunities for product and service differentiation and price discrimination.

- The insurance industry has several other distinguishing characteristics that make it difficult for it to be completely transferred to the new online channel, such as policies that defy easy comparison and that can only be explained by an experienced sales agent; a traditional reliance on local insurance offices and agents to sell complex products uniquely suited to the circumstances of the insured person and/or property; and a marketplace that is coordinated by state insurance commissions in each state with differing regulations. The result is that consumers for the most part will check the Web for prices and terms, but will not buy policies online. Although search costs have been dramatically reduced and price comparison shopping is done in an entirely new way, the industry value chain has so far not been significantly impacted.

- A number of new industry-wide consortia may change this picture by 2005 as the nations' largest underwriting firms respond to the pressure from online banking and brokerage firms that are now offering insurance products. Insurance industry experts expect that the products offered by these consortia will be appreciably less expensive than those offered by local agents, but that they will also be more basic policies and that personalization and customization will remain in the hands of the local agents.

Key features of the online real estate services industry include the following:

- Although once again the vision of E-commerce I (that the historically local, complex, and agent-driven real estate industry would be transformed into a disintermediated marketplace where buyers and sellers could transact directly) has not been realized, what has happened has been beneficial to buyers, sellers, and real estate agents alike.
- About 50% of home buyers now consult real estate sites on the Web, and this percentage is expected to grow to 80% by 2005.
- Since it is not possible to complete a property transaction online, the major impact of the online real estate industry is in influencing offline purchases.
- The primary service is a listing of available houses, with secondary links to mortgage lenders, credit reporting agencies, neighborhood information, loan calculators, appraisal reports, sales price histories by neighborhood, school district data, and crime reports.
- The industry value chain however, has remained unchanged. Home addresses are not available online and users are directed back to the local listing agent for further information about the house.
- Buyers benefit because they can quickly and easily access a wealth of valuable information; sellers benefit because they receive free online advertising for their property; and real estate agents have reported that Internet-informed customers ask to see fewer properties.

■ **Explain why online travel services can be considered the most successful B2C segment.**

Online travel services attract the largest single e-commerce audience and the largest slice of B2C revenues. The Internet is becoming the most common channel used by consumers to research travel options. It is also the most common way for people to search for the best possible prices and book reservations for airline tickets, rental cars, hotel rooms, cruises and tours. Online travel services' market share is expected to increase from 10% to 21% of all travel service expenditures by 2006. Some of the reasons why online travel services have been so successful include the following:

- Online travel sites offer consumers a one-stop, convenient, leisure and business travel experience where travelers can find content, community, commerce, and customer service. Online sites offer more information and travel options than traditional travel agents, with such services as descriptions of vacations and facilities, chat groups and bulletin boards, and the convenience of purchasing all travel elements at one stop. They also bring consumers and suppliers together in a low transaction cost environment.

- Travel is an information-intensive product as well as an electronic product in the sense that travel requirements can be accomplished for the most part online. Since travel does not require any inventory, suppliers (which are highly fragmented) are always looking for customers to fill excess capacity. Also, travel services do not require an expensive multichannel physical presence. For these reasons, travel services appear to be particularly well suited for the online marketplace.

- It is important to note that various segments of the travel industry fit this description better than others — for instance, airline reservations, auto rentals, and to a lesser extent, hotels. Cruises and tours are more differentiated with varying quality and a more complex level of information required for the decision-making process. Therefore, cruises, tours, and hotels to some extent will probably not grow as quickly in the online environment.

- In the past five years, corporate travel expenses have mushroomed, leading corporations to seek greater control over employee travel plans. Corporations are outsourcing their travel offices entirely to vendors who can provide Web-based solutions, high-quality service, and lower costs.

■ Identify the major trends in online travel services.

The major trends include the following:

- The online travel services industry is going through a period of consolidation as stronger offline, established agencies purchase weaker and relatively inexpensive online travel agencies in order to build stronger multichannel travel sites that combine physical presence, television sales outlets, and online sites.

- Suppliers — such as airlines, hotels, and auto rental firms — are attempting to eliminate intermediaries such as GDS and travel agencies, and develop a direct relationship with consumers; an example is Orbitz, the online reservation system formed by seven major airlines to deal directly with corporations and leisure travelers. The major auto rental firms have also all opened direct-to-customer Web sites. At the same time, successful online travel agencies are attempting to turn themselves into merchants by purchasing large blocks of travel inventory and then reselling it to the public, eliminating the global distributors and earning much higher returns.

■ Explain why career services online may be the ideal Web business.

Next to travel services, job hunting services have been one of the Internet's most successful online services because they save money for both job hunters and employers. In comparison to online recruiting, traditional recruitment tools have severe limitations.

- Online recruiting provides a more efficient and cost-effective means of linking employers and job hunters and reduces the total time-to-hire.
- Job hunters can easily build, update, and distribute their resumes, conduct job searches, and gather information on employers at their convenience and leisure.
- It is an information-intense business process which the Internet can automate, and thus reduce search time and costs for all parties.

Online recruiting can also serve to establish market prices and terms, thereby identifying both the salary levels for specific jobs and the skill sets required to achieve those salary levels. This should lead to a rationalization of wages, greater labor mobility, and higher efficiency in recruitment and operations as employers are able to more quickly fill positions.

■ Identify current trends in the online career services industry.

Current trends in the online career services industry include the following:
- Although online recruitment has focused primarily on general job recruitment, many general sites have begun listing lower- and middle-level management jobs, which offer the largest revenue potential.
- The online recruitment industry is going through a period of rapid consolidation led by TMP Worldwide Inc, which because of its acquisitions, is now the world leader in online executive recruiting, executive moving and relocation, e-resourcing, temporary contracting, and recruitment advertising.

QUESTIONS

1. What are some of the difficulties in providing services in an online environment? What factors differentiate the services sector from the retail sector, for example?
2. Compare and contrast the two major types of online services industries. What two major features differentiate services from other industries?
3. What are the pros and cons of using account aggregation services?
4. Name and describe the four types of online mortgage vendors. What are the major advantages of using an online mortgage site? What factors are slowing the growth of such service businesses?
5. What is the biggest deterrent to growth of the online insurance industry nationally?

6. Define channel conflict and explain how it currently applies to the mortgage and insurance industries. Name two online insurance companies or brokers.

7. What is the most common use of real estate Web sites? What do most consumers do when they go there?

8. Name and describe the four types of services provided by financial services firms on the Web.

9. Who are the major players in the financial industry consolidation currently occurring worldwide?

10. Explain the two global trends impacting the structure of the financial services industry and their impact on online operations.

11. How have travel services suppliers benefited from consumer use of travel Web sites?

12. What are the two major segments of travel? Which one is growing the fastest and why?

13. Explain how global distribution systems (GDS) function.

14. Name and describe the five traditional recruitment tools companies have used to identify and attract employees. What are the disadvantages of such tools in light of new online sites?

15. In addition to matching job applicants with available positions, what larger function do online job sites fill? Explain how such sites can affect salaries and going rates.

16. Given the popularity of online job and career sites, why are classified ads still the preferred information source for so many job seekers and employers?

PROJECTS

1. Go to the SEC Web site at www.sec.gov, and access the Edgar archives, where you can review 10-K filings for all public companies. Find the Form 10-K report for the most recent completed fiscal year for schwab.com and datek.com. Prepare a PowerPoint or other presentation that compares the financial stability and prospects of the two businesses, focusing specifically on the performance of their Internet operations.

2. Conduct a thorough analysis — strategic and financial — of one of the following Web sites: progressive.com, quotesmith.com, or insweb.com. Prepare a Power-Point or other presentation that summarizes your observations about the company's operations and future prospects.

3. Choose a services industry not discussed in the chapter (such as legal services, medical services, accounting services, or another of your choosing). Prepare a 3- to 5-page report discussing recent trends affecting online provision of these services.

4. Together with a teammate, investigate the use of wireless applications in the financial services industries. Prepare a short joint presentation on your findings.

5. Find at least two examples of companies not mentioned in the text that act as transaction brokers and at least two examples of companies that provide a "hands-on" service. Prepare a short memo describing the services each company offers and why the company should be categorized as a transaction broker or a hands-on service provider.

WEB SITE RESOURCES www.LearnE-commerce.net

- News: Weekly updates of topics relevant to the materials in this chapter
- Video Lecture: Professor Ken Laudon summarizes the key concepts of the chapter
- Research: Abstracts and links to articles referenced in the chapter as well as other relevant research
- International Spotlight: More information about online service industries outside the United States
- PowerPoint Slides: Illustrations from the chapter and more
- Additional projects and exercises

CHAPTER 12

B2B E-commerce: Supply Chain Management and Collaborative Commerce

LEARNING OBJECTIVES

After reading this chapter, you will be able to:

- Define B2B commerce and understand its scope and history.
- Understand the procurement process, the supply chain, and collaborative commerce.
- Identify the main types of B2B commerce: Net marketplaces and private industrial networks.
- Understand the four types of Net marketplaces.
- Identify the major trends in the development of Net marketplaces.
- Identify the role of private industrial networks in transforming the supply chain.
- Understand the role of private industrial networks in supporting collaborative commerce.

Covisint LLC

The Mother of All Net Marketplaces

I n 1999, the Big Three automakers in Detroit — DaimlerChrysler, General Motors, and Ford Motor Company — joined by Nissan/Renault and PSA Peugeot Citroen, formed what today has become the largest Internet-based marketplace for B2B commerce: Covisint. With a $200 million investment from the founding partner firms, Covisint instantly became the largest industry-sponsored Net marketplace, and a direct competitor to several other attempts by third-party independent Internet market makers to capture the automobile industry's procurement dollars.

Collectively, the Big Three automakers purchase $240 billion in direct and indirect supplies each year. Direct supplies include raw materials used in production from steel, glass, plastic mold parts, and electronics to nuts and bolts. Indirect supplies include paper supplies, maintenance, repairs, and other operational goods. Worldwide, the automobile industry procures nearly $1 trillion in supplies annually. The procurement process is highly inefficient, involving the use of telephones, fax machines, and some older computer-based technologies. Covisint estimates that if they succeed, they will be able to lower procurement and product development costs by 16% over three years, resulting in a reduction in prices of about $1,000 per car.

Following a slow start, and with many industry skeptics doubting the slow-moving tradition-bound automobile industry would ever "get it," Covisint went live in October 2000. By the end of July 2001, Covisint had managed more than $129 billion in transactions — nearly 53% of the estimated $240 billion spent by the founders in 2001. GM alone purchased $96 billion in direct raw materials for current and future models, and $2.2 billion in auction and online catalog purchases of indirect supplies.

The largest single purchase to date has been a DaimlerChrysler purchase of $3 billion worth of highly engineered parts for future models. In order to derive more revenues from its technology investment, Covisint has established a new holding company, Covisint, Inc., to expand into other manufacturing industries.

By July 2001, Covisint had also qualified 1,700 supplier companies at the site, generated more than $37.6 billion in auction revenues, and hosted 26,000 transactions from more than 200 online supplier catalogs, involving over 2.5 million SKU (stocking units or separate parts). Ford Motor claims that it has saved $70 million in indirect procurement costs alone in 2001, and expects to save a total of $350 million by year's end. By any measure, Covisint has been an outstanding success story in B2B commerce.

Currently, Covisint suppliers are Tier 1 suppliers — the largest suppliers to the industry. The next step is to deploy Covisint to thousands of Tier 2 and Tier 3 suppliers — smaller suppliers who sell parts to the Tier 1 suppliers. The average Tier 1 supplier has about 1,300 smaller suppliers. Just as the large auto manufacturers have reduced the number of suppliers they work with, the Tier 1 suppliers are planning a 20% reduction in the number of their smaller suppliers to simplify their production processes and reduce costs. Covisint and the Tier 1 suppliers wield a big stick in this effort: Auto industry procurement officials will refuse to buy from any suppliers who do not participate in Covisint. The objective is to work with the auto manufacturers to reduce product development and procurement costs by almost 20% in the next two years.

Once the lower tiers of the industry supply chain are linked into Covisint and more sophisticated design and production software is in place, the auto industry will be prepared to attempt its final objective: demand-pull production. Instead of supply-push production — building millions of cars on speculation in the hope someone will purchase them — the auto industry plans to take orders for cars with precisely the features desired by each customer and deliver the vehicle within a few weeks. There are many obstacles yet to be overcome, primarily the integration of smaller suppliers and the development of a rich collaborative environment among product designers, parts producers, and manufacturers. It remains to be seen if Covisint itself will be profitable and sustainable as an independent entity as it expands. The arrival of "mass-customized" cars is many years off. Nevertheless, Covisint has in a short period achieved the first step in a long march.

SOURCES: "Ford Extends Covisint to Suppliers," by Demir Barlas, *Line56.com*, August 30, 2001; "Great Sites: Covisint," by Steve Konicki, *InformationWeek*, August 27, 2001; "GM Spends $98 Billion Via Covisint," by Richard Brown, *Line56.com*, August 21, 2001; "Big Auto Suppliers To Wield Tech Clout," by Chuck Moozakis, *InternetWeek*, August 13, 2001; "Covisint Poised for New Industries," by Richard Brown, *Line56.com*, August 10, 2001.

T he Covisint case illustrates the exciting potential for B2B e-commerce to lower production costs, speed up new product delivery, and ultimately revolutionize both the manufacturing process inherited from the early twentieth century and the way we purchase industrial products. Covisint is an example of just one type of Net marketplace, namely, industry-sponsored consortia, and there are many other equally promising efforts at using the Internet to change the relationships among manufacturers and their suppliers.

There are many failed efforts to consider as well; these provide important lessons to all managers.

In this chapter, we will examine the many different types of B2B commerce in detail. In Section 12.1, we define B2B commerce and place it in the context of trends in supply chain management, which, ultimately, is the objective of B2B commerce — to help businesses manage the flow of supplies needed for production. The next two sections describe the two fundamental types of B2B commerce: Net marketplaces and private industrial networks. We describe four major types of Net marketplaces, their biases (seller, buyer, and neutral), accessibility (private vs. public), and value creation dynamics, and then the emergence of private Internet-based industrial networks that tie a smaller number of organizations into a collaborative commercial system.

The field of B2B commerce can be very confusing because there are so many new terms, and the pace of evolution is very fast. There is little agreement among scholars about how to label things, and therefore there is much jargon that can easily confuse both students and scholars who are trying to understand the field. Ironically, B2B commerce began long before the Internet, and one would have hoped the basic conceptual framework for understanding it would be agreed on by now. But this is not the case. The Internet is just the latest digital technology to support B2B trade. The failure on the part of many entrepreneurs and venture capitalists to understand the history and evolution of B2B trade as well as the real needs of business firms, is one of the reasons why thousands of Internet-based B2B firms and business models in E-commerce I failed shortly after they emerged.

12.1 B2B E-COMMERCE AND SUPPLY CHAIN MANAGEMENT

The trade between business firms represents a huge marketplace; in 2001, B2B trade amounted to about $12 trillion in the United States, and by 2006, it is expected to exceed $16 trillion (Jupiter Media Metrix, 2001c). A significant part of this trade could be conducted over the Internet or assisted by it more efficiently and effectively than is currently the case.

The process of conducting trade among business firms is complex and requires significant human intervention, and therefore, it consumes significant resources.

Some firms estimate that the average cost of each corporate purchase order for support products costs them $100 in administrative overhead. Administrative overhead includes processing paper, approving purchase decisions, spending time using the telephone and fax machines to search for products and arrange for purchases, arranging for shipping, and receiving the goods (Aberdeen, 2001). Across the economy, this adds up to trillions of dollars annually being spent for procurement processes that might be automated. GE estimates that using B2B procurement methods might save it $10 billion in 2003 (General Electric Information Services, 2001). If only a portion of inter-firm trade could be automated, and if only parts of the entire procurement process could be assisted by the Internet, then literally trillions of dollars might be released for more productive uses, consumer prices potentially would fall, productivity would increase, and the economic wealth of the nation would expand. This is the promise of B2B commerce. The challenge of B2B commerce is changing existing patterns and systems of procurement, and designing and implementing new Internet-based B2B solutions.

DEFINING AND MEASURING THE GROWTH OF B2B COMMERCE

total inter-firm trade
the total flow of value among firms

Before the Internet, business-to-business transactions were referred to simply as *trade* or the *procurement process*. The term **total inter-firm trade** refers to the total flow of value among firms. Today, we use the term **B2B commerce** to describe all types of computer-enabled inter-firm trade, such as the use of the Internet and other networking technologies to exchange value across organizational boundaries. This definition of B2B commerce does not include digital transactions that occur within the boundaries of a single firm — for instance, the transfer of goods and value from one subsidiary to another, or the use of corporate intranets to manage the firm. We use the term **Internet-based B2B commerce** (or **B2B e-commerce**) to describe specifically that portion of B2B commerce that is enabled by the Internet.

B2B commerce
all types of computer-enabled inter-firm trade

Internet-based B2B commerce (B2B e-commerce)
that portion of B2B commerce that is enabled by the Internet

THE EVOLUTION OF B2B COMMERCE

automated order entry systems
involve the use of telephone modems to send digital orders

B2B commerce has evolved over a 35-year period through several technology-driven stages (see Figure 12.1). The first step in the development of B2B commerce in the mid-1970s was **automated order entry systems** that involved the use of telephone modems to send digital orders to health care products companies such as Baxter Health Care. Baxter, a diversified supplier of hospital supplies, placed telephone modems into its customers' procurement offices to automate re-ordering from Baxter's computerized inventory database (and to discourage re-ordering from competitors). This early technology was replaced by personal computers using private networks in the late 1980s and in the late 1990s by Internet workstations accessing electronic online catalogs. Automated order entry systems are **seller-side solutions**. They are owned by the suppliers and they are seller-biased markets — they show only goods from a single seller. Customers benefited from these systems because they

seller-side solutions
seller-biased markets that are owned by, and show only goods from, a single seller

---

| FIGURE 12.1 | THE EVOLUTION OF B2B COMMERCE |

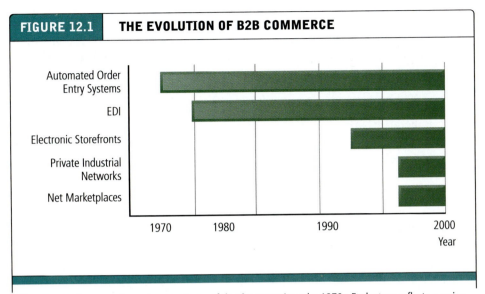

B2B commerce has gone through many stages of development since the 1970s. Each stage reflects a major change in technology platforms from mainframes to private dedicated networks, and finally to the Internet.

---

reduced the costs of inventory replenishment and they were paid for largely by the suppliers. Automated order entry systems continue to play an important role in B2B commerce.

By the late 1970s, a new form of computer-to-computer communication called **electronic data interchange (EDI)** emerged. We describe EDI in greater detail below, but at this point it is necessary only to know that EDI is a communications standard for sharing business documents such as invoices, purchase orders, shipping bills, product stocking numbers (SKUs), and settlement information among a small number of firms. Virtually all large firms have EDI systems, and most industry groups have industry standards for defining documents in that industry. EDI systems are owned by the buyers and hence they are **buyer-side solutions** and buyer-biased because they aim to reduce the procurement costs of supplies for the buyer. Of course, by automating the transaction, EDI systems also benefit the sellers by reducing costs of serving their customers. The topology of EDI systems is often referred to as a **hub-and-spoke system**, with the buyers in the center and the suppliers connected to the central hub via private dedicated networks.

EDI systems generally serve vertical markets. A **vertical market** is one that provides expertise and products for a specific industry, such as automobiles. In contrast, **horizontal markets** refer to markets that serve many different industries.

Electronic storefronts emerged in the mid-1990s along with the commercialization of the Internet. **B2B electronic storefronts** are perhaps the simplest and

electronic data interchange (EDI)
a communications standard for sharing business documents and settlement information among a small number of firms

buyer-side solutions
buyer-biased markets that are owned by buyers and that aim to reduce the procurement costs of supplies for buyers

hub-and-spoke system
suppliers connected to a central hub of buyers via private dedicated networks

vertical market
one that provides expertise and products for a specific industry

horizontal markets
markets that serve many different industries

B2B electronic storefronts
online catalogs of products made available to the public marketplace by a single supplier

easiest to understand form of B2B e-commerce because they are simply online catalogs of products made available to the public marketplace by a single supplier — similar to Amazon for the B2C retail market. Owned by the suppliers, they are seller-side solutions and seller-biased because they show only the products offered by a single supplier.

Electronic storefronts are a natural descendant of automated order entry systems, but there are two important differences: (1) the far less expensive and more universal Internet becomes the communication media and displaces private networks, and (2) electronic storefronts tend to serve horizontal markets — they carry products that serve a wide variety of industries. Although electronic storefronts emerged prior to Net marketplaces described below, they are usually considered a type of Net marketplace.

Net marketplaces emerged in the late 1990s as a natural extension and scaling-up of the electronic storefronts. There are many different kinds of Net marketplaces that we describe in detail in Section 12.2, but the essential characteristic of a Net marketplace is that they bring hundreds of suppliers — each with electronic catalogs and potentially thousands of purchasing firms — into a single Internet-based environment to conduct trade.

Net marketplaces can be organized under a variety of ownership models: Some are owned by independent third parties backed by venture capital, some are owned by established firms who are the main or only market players, and some are a mix of both. Net marketplaces establish the prices of the goods they offer in four primary ways — fixed catalog prices or more dynamic pricing, such as negotiation, auction, and bid/ask ("exchange" model). Net marketplaces earn revenue in a number of ways, including transaction fees, subscription fees, service fees, software licensing fees, advertising and marketing, and sales of data and information.

Although the primary benefits and biases of Net marketplaces have to be determined on a case-by-case basis depending on ownership and pricing mechanisms, it is often the case that Net marketplaces are biased against suppliers because they can force suppliers to reveal their prices and terms to other suppliers in the marketplace. Net marketplaces can also significantly extend the benefits of simple electronic storefronts by seeking to automate the procurement value chain of both selling and buying firms.

Private industrial networks also emerged in the late 1990s as natural extensions of EDI systems and the existing close relationships that developed between large industrial firms and their suppliers. Described in more detail in Section 12.3, **private industrial networks** are Internet-based communication environments that extend far beyond procurement to encompass truly collaborative commerce. Private industrial networks permit buyer firms and their principal suppliers to share product design and development, marketing, inventory, production scheduling, and unstructured communications. Like EDI, private industrial networks are owned by the buy-

---

Net marketplace
brings hundreds of suppliers into a single Internet-based environment to conduct trade

private industrial networks
Internet-based communication environments that extend far beyond procurement to encompass truly collaborative commerce

ers and are buyer-side solutions with buyer biases: These systems are directly intended to improve the cost position and flexibility of large industrial firms.

Naturally, private industrial networks have significant benefits for suppliers as well. Inclusion in the direct supply chain for a major industrial purchasing company can allow a supplier to increase both revenue and margins because the environment is not competitive — only a few suppliers are included in the private industrial network. Private industrial networks are the most prevalent form of Internet-based B2B commerce, and this will continue into the foreseeable future.

THE GROWTH OF B2B COMMERCE 2001–2006

In the period 2001–2006, all forms of B2B commerce are projected to grow from about 4% to 36% of total inter-firm trade in the United States, or from $466 billion in 2001 to more than $5.4 trillion in 2006 (see Figure 12.2). As shown in Figure 12.2, Net mar-

---

FIGURE 12.2 | **GROWTH OF B2B COMMERCE 2001–2006**

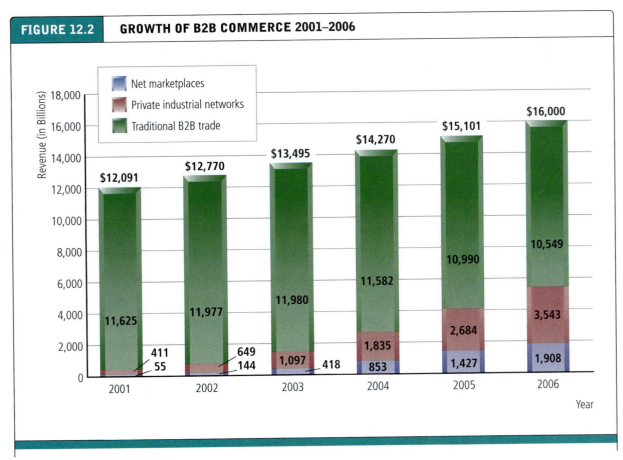

SOURCE: Jupiter Media Metrix, 2001c.

ketplaces are growing at a faster rate than private industrial networks, but in 2006, private industrial networks are still expected to be nearly twice the size of Net marketplaces — $3.5 trillion versus $1.9 trillion.

Several observations are important to note with respect to Figure 12.2. First, the common perception that electronic marketplaces will become the dominant form of B2B commerce is not supported. Second, private industrial networks will play a dominant role in B2B commerce both now and in the future. Third, B2B commerce is a tiny part of all inter-firm commerce today, suggesting the difficulties of adopting and successfully implementing B2B commerce. For instance, 25% of all U.S. consumers have purchased something on the Web, but this level of penetration is not true of corporate purchasing agents. A recent survey found that 50% of purchasing agents believed they will do less than 20% of their purchasing online by 2002 (Jupiter Media Metrix, 2001a).

Industry Forecasts

Not all industries will be similarly affected by B2B, and not all industries can similarly benefit from B2B. Figure 12.3 shows a projection of the percentage that Internet-based B2B will constitute of an industry's total inter-firm trade for various industries for 2001–2006.

Several factors influence the speed with which industries migrate to B2B and the volume of transactions. Those industries in which there is already significant utilization of EDI (indicating concentration of buyers and suppliers) and large investments in information technology and Internet infrastructure can be expected to move first and fastest to B2B utilization. The computer, automotive, aerospace and defense, and industrial equipment industries meet these criteria. Where the marketplace is highly concentrated on either the purchasing or selling side, or both, conditions are also ripe for rapid B2B growth, as in energy and chemicals.

POTENTIAL BENEFITS OF B2B E-COMMERCE

Regardless of the specific type of B2B commerce, as a whole, Internet-based B2B commerce promises many strategic benefits to participating firms — both buyers and sellers — and impressive gains for the economy as whole. B2B e-commerce can:

- Lower administrative costs,
- Lower search costs for buyers,
- Reduce inventory costs by increasing competition among suppliers (increasing price transparency) and reducing inventory to the bare minimum,
- Lower transaction costs by eliminating paperwork and automating parts of the procurement process,
- Increase production flexibility by ensuring delivery of parts "just in time,"

FIGURE 12.3	INDUSTRY FORECASTS FOR INTERNET-BASED B2B COMMERCE, 2001–2006

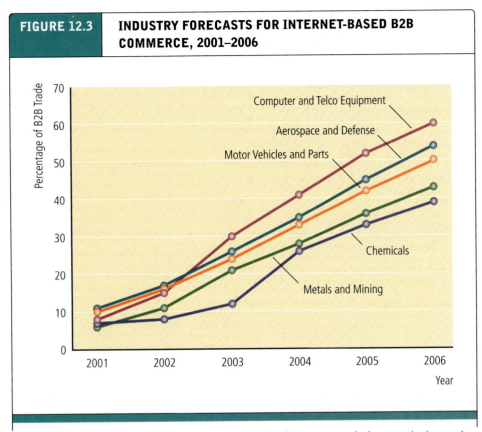

The greatest increase in B2B e-commerce is expected to occur in the computer and telecommunications equipment industries, aerospace and defense industries, and motor vehicle and other motor vehicle parts industries.

SOURCE: Jupiter Media Metrix, 2001c.

- Improve quality of products by increasing cooperation among buyers and sellers and reducing quality issues,
- Decrease product cycle time by sharing designs and production schedules with suppliers,
- Increase opportunities for collaborating with suppliers and distributors, and
- Create greater price transparency — the ability to see the actual buy and sell prices in a market.

B2B e-commerce offers potential first-mover strategic benefits for individual firms as well. Firms who move their procurement processes online first will experience impressive gains in productivity, cost reduction, and potentially much faster introduction of new, higher quality products. While these gains may be imitated by other competing firms, it is also clear from the brief history of B2B e-commerce that firms making sustained investments in information technology and Internet-based B2B commerce can adapt much faster to new technologies as they emerge, creating a string of first-mover advantages.

THE PROCUREMENT PROCESS AND THE SUPPLY CHAIN

procurement process
the way firms purchase the goods they need to produce goods for consumers

supply chain
firms that purchase goods, their suppliers, and their suppliers' suppliers. Includes not only the firms themselves, but also the relationships among them, and the processes that connect them.

The subject of B2B e-commerce can be complex because there are so many ways the Internet can be used to support the exchange of goods and payments among organizations. Ultimately, B2B e-commerce is about changing the **procurement process** (the way business firms purchase the goods they need to produce the goods they will ultimately sell to consumers) of thousands of firms across the United States and the world.

One way to enter this area of Internet-based B2B commerce is to examine the existing procurement process (see Figure 12.4). Firms purchase goods from a set of suppliers, and they in turn purchase their inputs from a set of suppliers. This set of firms is linked through a series of transactions referred to as the **supply chain**. The supply chain includes not just the firms themselves, but also the relationships among them and the processes that connect them.

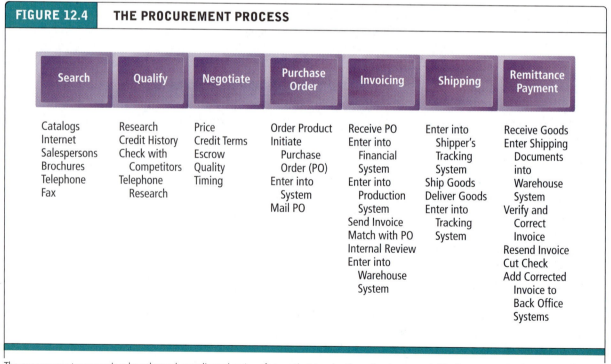

FIGURE 12.4   **THE PROCUREMENT PROCESS**

Search	Qualify	Negotiate	Purchase Order	Invoicing	Shipping	Remittance Payment
Catalogs	Research	Price	Order Product	Receive PO	Enter into	Receive Goods
Internet	Credit History	Credit Terms	Initiate	Enter into	Shipper's	Enter Shipping
Salespersons	Check with	Escrow	Purchase	Financial	Tracking	Documents
Brochures	Competitors	Quality	Order (PO)	System	System	into
Telephone	Telephone	Timing	Enter into	Enter into	Ship Goods	Warehouse
Fax	Research		System	Production	Deliver Goods	System
			Mail PO	System	Enter into	Verify and
				Send Invoice	Tracking	Correct
				Match with PO	System	Invoice
				Internal Review		Resend Invoice
				Enter into		Cut Check
				Warehouse		Add Corrected
				System		Invoice to
						Back Office
						Systems

The procurement process is a lengthy and complicated series of steps that involve the seller, buyer, and shipping companies in a series of connected transactions.

There are seven separate steps in the procurement process. The first three steps involve the decision of who to buy from and what to pay: searching for suppliers of specific products, qualifying both the seller and the products they sell, and negotiating prices, credit terms, escrow requirements, quality and scheduling of delivery. Once a supplier is identified, purchase orders are issued, the buyer is sent an invoice, the goods are shipped, and the buyer sends a payment. Each of these steps in the procurement process is composed of many separate sub-activities. Each of these activities must be recorded in the information systems of the seller, buyer, and shipper. Often, this data entry is not automatic and involves some manual labor.

Types of Procurement

Two distinctions are important for understanding how B2B can improve the procurement process. First, firms make purchases of two kinds of goods from suppliers: direct goods and indirect goods. **Direct goods** are goods integrally involved in the production process; for instance, when an automobile manufacturer purchases sheet steel for auto body production. **Indirect goods** are all other goods not directly involved in the production process, such as office supplies and maintenance products. Often these goods are called **MRO goods** — products for maintenance, repair, and operations.

Second, firms use two different methods for purchasing goods: contract purchasing and spot purchasing. **Contract purchasing** involves long-term written agreements to purchase specified products, with agreed upon terms and quality, for an extended period of time. Generally, firms purchase direct goods using long-term contracts. **Spot purchasing** involves the purchase of goods based on immediate needs in larger marketplaces that involve many suppliers. Generally, firms use spot purchases for indirect goods, although in some cases, firms use spot markets for direct goods.

According to several estimates, about 80% of inter-firm trade involves contract purchasing of direct goods, and 20% involves spot purchasing of indirect goods (Sodhi, 2001; Kaplan and Sawhney, 2000). This finding is significant for understanding B2B e-commerce as we see below.

Although the procurement process involves the purchasing of goods, it is extraordinarily information intense, involving the movement of information among many existing corporate systems. The procurement process today is also very labor intensive, involving directly about 5.6 million employees in the United States, not including truckers, shippers, bankers, insurers, and others involved in the administration of purchasing. Table 12.1 lists the occupational groups directly involved in the procurement process.

In the long term, the success or failure of B2B e-commerce depends on changing the day-to-day behavior of 5.6 million people. The key players in the procurement process are the purchasing managers. They ultimately decide who to buy from, what to buy, and on what terms. Purchasing managers ("procurement managers" in the

direct goods
goods directly involved in the production process

indirect goods
all other goods not directly involved in the production process

MRO goods
products for maintenance, repair, and operations

contract purchasing
involves long-term written agreements to purchase specified products, under agreed upon terms and quality, for an extended period of time

spot purchasing
involves the purchase of goods based on immediate needs in larger marketplaces that involve many suppliers

TABLE 12.1	DIRECT LABOR INVOLVEMENT IN THE PROCUREMENT PROCESS
TASK/OPERATION	**NUMBER**
Purchasing managers	114,000
Material recording, scheduling	1,930,000
Adjusters and investigators	1,701,000
Miscellaneous, administrative	3,576,000
Total	**7,321,000**

SOURCE: Table 512, Statistical Abstract of the United States, 2000.

business press) are also the key decision makers for the adoption of B2B e-commerce solutions.

Examining Table 12.1, one can see that the Internet could make an important contribution in simplifying the procurement process by bringing buyers and sellers together in a single marketplace and reducing search, research, and negotiating costs. This would appear to be very helpful for spot purchases of indirect goods. Later in the procurement process, the Internet could make an important contribution simply as a powerful communications medium, transferring information among the sellers, buyers, and shippers, and helping managers coordinate the procurement process. This would appear to be very helpful for contract purchases of direct goods. To a large extent, this is the promise of B2B e-commerce. But it is not the whole story.

Multi-tier Supply Chains

Although Figure 12.4 captures some of the complexity of the procurement process, it is important to realize that firms purchase thousands of goods from thousands of suppliers. The suppliers, in turn, must purchase their inputs from their suppliers. Large manufacturers such as Chrysler Corporation have over 20,000 suppliers of parts, packaging, and technology (IBM, 2001). The number of secondary and tertiary suppliers is at least as large. Together, this extended **multi-tier supply chain** (the chain of primary, secondary, and tertiary suppliers) constitutes a crucial aspect of the industrial infrastructure of the economy. Figure 12.5 depicts a firm's multi-tier supply chain.

The supply chain depicted in Figure 12.5 is a three-tier chain simplified for the sake of illustration. In fact, large Fortune 1000 firms have thousands of suppliers, who in turn have thousands of smaller suppliers. The complexity of the supply chain suggests a combinatorial explosion. Assuming a manufacturer has four primary suppliers and each one has three primary suppliers, and each of these has three primary sup-

multi-tier supply chain
the chain of primary, secondary, and tertiary suppliers

FIGURE 12.5	THE MULTI-TIER SUPPLY CHAIN

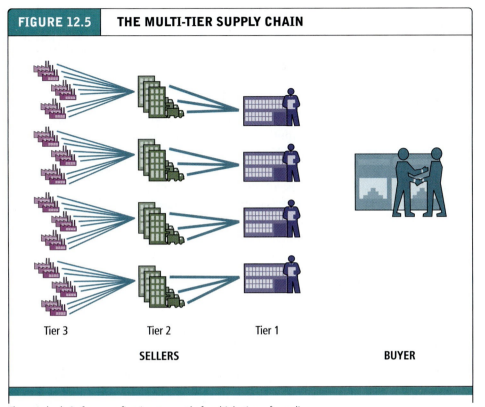

Tier 3   Tier 2   Tier 1

SELLERS   **BUYER**

The supply chain for every firm is composed of multiple tiers of suppliers.

pliers, then the total number of suppliers in the chain (including the buying firm) rises to 53. This figure does not include the shippers, insurers, and financiers involved in the transactions.

Immediately, one can see from Figure 12.5 that the procurement process involves a very large number of suppliers, each of whom must be coordinated with the production needs of the ultimate purchaser — the buying firm.

The Role of Existing Legacy Computer Systems

Complicating any efforts to coordinate the many firms in a supply chain is the fact that each firm generally has its own set of legacy computer systems, often home grown, that cannot easily pass information to other systems. **Legacy computer systems** generally are older mainframe and minicomputer systems used to manage key business processes within a firm in a variety of functional areas from manufacturing, logistics, financial, and human resources. Converting these older systems to new Internet and client/server-based systems is very expensive and takes many years.

legacy computer systems

generally are older mainframe and minicomputer systems used to manage key business processes within a firm in a variety of functional areas

materials requirements planning (MRP) system

legacy system that enables companies to predict, track, and manage all the constituent parts of complex manufactured goods

One typical legacy system is a **materials requirements planning (MRP) system** that enables companies to predict, track, and manage all the constituent parts of complex manufactured goods such as automobiles, machine tools, and industrial equipment. An MRP system stores and generates a bill of material or BOM that lists all the parts needed to manufacture a product. The MRP system also generates a production schedule that describes the order in which parts are used and the production time for each step in production. The BOM and production schedule are then used to generate purchase orders to suppliers. The MRP system can be run as often as needed, generating a dynamic production environment.

enterprise resource planning (ERP) system

a more sophisticated MRP system that includes human resource and financial components

Many larger firms have installed **enterprise resource planning (ERP) systems**, which are more sophisticated MRP systems that include human resource and financial components. With an ERP system in place, orders from customers are translated into BOMs, production schedules, and human resource and financial requirements, including notifying the finance department to issue invoices to customers and pay suppliers. However, ERP systems were not originally designed to coordinate the flow of information among a large set of supplier firms, and they require expensive modification before they can become part of an enterprise-wide B2B system.

TRENDS IN SUPPLY CHAIN MANAGEMENT AND COLLABORATIVE COMMERCE

It is impossible to understand the actual and potential contribution of Internet-based B2B commerce, or the successes and failures of B2B e-commerce vendors and markets without understanding ongoing efforts to improve the procurement process through a variety of supply chain management programs that long preceded the development of e-commerce.

supply chain management (SCM)

refers to a wide variety of activities that firms and industries use to coordinate the key players in their procurement process

Supply chain management (SCM) refers to a wide variety of activities that firms and industries use to coordinate the key players in their procurement process. For the most part, today's procurement managers work with telephones, fax machines, face-to-face conversations, and instinct, relying on trusted long-term suppliers for their strategic purchases of goods directly involved in the production process.

There have been four major developments in supply chain management over the two decades that preceded the development of the Internet and set the ground rules for understanding how B2B e-commerce works (or fails to work). These developments are supply chain simplification, electronic data interchange (EDI), supply chain management systems, and collaborative commerce.

Supply Chain Simplification

Many manufacturing firms have spent the past two decades reducing the size of their supply chains and working more closely with a smaller group of "strategic" supplier firms to reduce both product costs and administrative costs, while improving quality.

Following the lead of Japanese industry, for instance, the automobile industry has systematically reduced the number of its suppliers by over 50%. Instead of open bidding for orders, large manufacturers have chosen to work with strategic partner supply firms under long-term contracts that guarantee the supplier business, but also establish quality, cost, and timing goals. These strategic partnership programs are essential for just-in-time production models, and often involve joint product development and design, integration of computer systems, and tight coupling of the production processes of two or more companies. **Tight coupling** is a method for ensuring that suppliers precisely deliver the ordered parts, at a specific time and to a particular location, to ensure the production process is not interrupted for lack of parts.

tight coupling
a method for ensuring that suppliers precisely deliver the ordered parts, at a specific time and particular location, to ensure the production process is not interrupted for lack of parts

Electronic Data Interchange (EDI)

As noted in the previous section, B2B e-commerce did not originate with the Internet, but in fact has its roots in technologies such as EDI that were first developed in the mid-1970s and 1980s. EDI is a broadly defined communications protocol for exchanging documents among computers using technical standards developed by the American National Standards Institute (ANSI X12 standards) and international bodies such as the United Nations (EDIFACT standards).

EDI was developed to reduce the cost, delays, and errors inherent in the manual exchanges of documents such as purchase orders, shipping documents, price lists, payments, and customer data. EDI differs from an unstructured message because its messages are organized with distinct fields for each of the important pieces of information in a commercial transaction such as transaction date, product purchased, amount, sender's name, address, and recipient's name.

Each major industry in the United States and throughout much of the industrial world has EDI industry committees that define the structure and information fields of electronic documents for that industry. EDI communications at first relied on private point-to-point circuit-switched communication networks and private value-added networks that connected key participants in the supply chain (Laudon and Laudon, 2001). Today, EDI is directly involved in nearly half of the $11.5 trillion trade among firms, whereas the Internet accounts for only 3% of inter-firm trade (General Electric Information Services, 2001). In this sense, EDI is particularly important in the development of B2B e-commerce.

EDI has evolved significantly since the 1980s (see Figure 12.6). Initially, EDI focused on document automation (Stage 1). Procurement agents would create purchase orders electronically and send them to trading partners, who in turn would ship order fulfillment and shipping notices electronically back to the purchaser. Invoices, payments, and other documents would follow. These early implementations replaced the postal system for document transmission, and resulted in same-day shipping of orders (rather than a week's delay caused by the postal system), reduced errors, and lower costs.

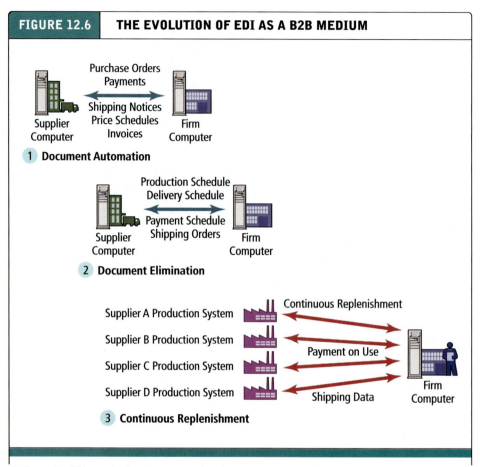

FIGURE 12.6	THE EVOLUTION OF EDI AS A B2B MEDIUM

Purchase Orders
Payments

Supplier Computer ←→ Firm Computer

Shipping Notices
Price Schedules
Invoices

1 Document Automation

Production Schedule
Delivery Schedule

Supplier Computer ←→ Firm Computer

Payment Schedule
Shipping Orders

2 Document Elimination

Supplier A Production System
Supplier B Production System
Supplier C Production System
Supplier D Production System

Continuous Replenishment
Payment on Use
Shipping Data

Firm Computer

3 Continuous Replenishment

EDI has evolved from a simple point-to-point digital communications media to a many-to-one enabling tool for continuous inventory replenishment.

The second stage of EDI development began in the early 1990s, driven largely by the automation of internal industrial processes and movement toward just-in-time production and continuous production. The new methods of production called for greater flexibility in scheduling, shipping, and financing of supplies. EDI evolved to become a system for document elimination. To support the new automated production processes used by manufacturers, EDI was used to eliminate purchase orders and other documents entirely, replacing them with production schedules and inventory balances. Supplier firms were sent monthly statements of production requirements and precise scheduled delivery times, and the orders would be fulfilled continuously, with inventory and payments being adjusted at the end of each month.

In the third stage of EDI, beginning in the mid-1990s, suppliers were given online access to selected parts of the purchasing firm's production and delivery schedules, and, under long-term contracts, were required to meet those schedules on their own without intervention by firm purchasing agents. Movement toward this continuous access model of EDI was spurred in the 1990s by large manufacturing and process firms (such as oil and chemical companies) that were implementing ERP systems. These systems required standardization of business processes and resulted in the automation of production, logistics, and many financial processes. These new production processes required much closer relationships with suppliers, who were required to be more precise in delivery scheduling and more flexible in inventory management. This level of supplier precision could never be achieved economically by human purchasing agents. This third stage of EDI introduced the era of continuous replenishment. For instance, Wal-Mart and ToysR-Us provide their suppliers with access to their store inventories, and the suppliers are expected to keep the stock of items on the shelf within prespecified targets. Similar developments occurred in the grocery industry.

Today, EDI must be viewed as a general enabling technology that provides for the exchange of critical business information between computer applications supporting a wide variety of business processes. EDI is an important industrial network technology, suited to support communications among a small set of strategic partners in direct, long-term trading relationships. The technical platform of EDI has changed from mainframes to personal computers, and the telecommunications environment is changing from private dedicated networks to the Internet. Most industry groups are moving toward XML as the language for expressing EDI commercial documents and communications.

The strength of EDI is its ability to support direct commercial transactions among strategically related firms in an industrial network, but this is its weakness as well. EDI is not well suited for the development of electronic marketplaces, where thousands of suppliers and purchasers meet in a digital arena to negotiate prices. EDI supports direct bilateral communications among a small set of firms and does not permit the multilateral, dynamic relationships of a true marketplace. EDI does not provide for price transparency among a large number of suppliers, does not scale easily to include new participants, and is not a real-time communications environment. It is instead a "batch processing" environment in which messages are exchanged in batches (although even this feature is changing as EDI moves toward XML and the Internet). EDI does not have a rich communications environment that can simultaneously support e-mail messaging, sharing of graphic documents, network meetings, or user friendly flexible database creation and management. For these features, new Internet-based software has emerged that is described below. EDI is also an expensive proposition, and a staff of dedicated programmers is required to implement it in large firms; in some cases, a considerable amount of time is also needed to reprogram existing enterprise systems to work with EDI protocols. Small firms are typically required to adopt EDI in order to supply large firms, and there are less expensive small-firm solutions for implementing EDI.

Supply Chain Management Systems

supply chain management (SCM) systems

continuously link the activities of buying, making, and moving products from suppliers to purchasing firms, as well as integrating the demand side of the business equation by including the order entry system in the process

Supply chain simplification, focusing on strategic partners in the production process, ERP systems, and continuous inventory replenishment are the foundation for contemporary supply chain management (SCM) systems. **Supply chain management (SCM) systems** continuously link the activities of buying, making, and moving products from suppliers to purchasing firms, as well as integrating the demand side of the business equation by including the order entry system in the process. With an SCM system and continuous replenishment, inventory is eliminated and production begins only when an order is received (see Figure 12.7). This is especially important in industries in which the product is perishable or experiences declining market value rapidly after production. Personal computers fit this description.

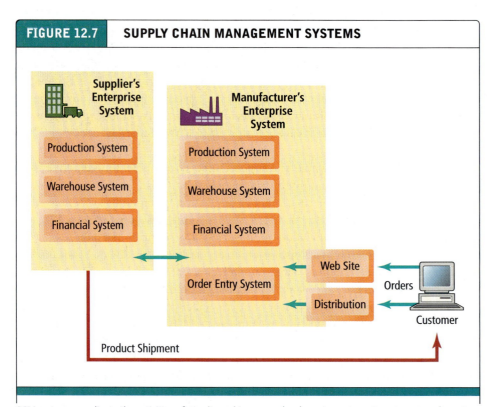

| FIGURE 12.7 | SUPPLY CHAIN MANAGEMENT SYSTEMS |

SCM systems coordinate the activities of suppliers, shippers, and order entry systems to automate order entry through production, payment, and shipping business processes.

Hewlett Packard has developed a Web-based order-driven supply chain management system that begins with either a customer placing an order online or the receipt of an order from a dealer. The order is forwarded from the order entry system to HP's production and delivery system. From there, the order is routed to one of several HP contractor supplier firms. One such firm is Synnex in Fremont, California. At Synnex, computers verify the order with HP and validate the ordered configuration to ensure the PC can be manufactured (e.g., will not have missing parts or fail a design specification set by HP). The order is then forwarded to a computer-based production control system that issues a bar-coded production ticket to factory assemblers. Simultaneously, a parts order is forwarded to Synnex's warehouse and inventory management system. A worker assembles the computer, the computer is boxed and tagged, and then shipped to the customer. The delivery is monitored and tracked by HP's supply chain management system that links directly to one of several overnight delivery systems operated by Airborne Express, Federal Express, and UPS. The elapsed time from order entry to shipping is 48 hours. With this system, Synnex and HP have eliminated inventory of perishable PCs, reduced cycle time from one week to 48 hours, and reduced errors (O'Connor, 2000).

Implementing an order-driven Web-based supply chain management system is not always easy however, as *Insight on Technology: Nike and i2 Just Can't Do It* illustrates.

Collaborative Commerce

Collaborative commerce is a direct extension of supply chain management systems, as well as supply chain simplification. **Collaborative commerce** is defined as the use of digital technologies to permit organizations to collaboratively design, develop, build, and manage products through their life cycles. This is a much broader mission than EDI or simply managing the flow of information among organizations. Collaborative commerce involves a definitive move from a *transaction focus* to a *relationship focus* among the supply chain participants. Rather than having an arm's-length adversarial relationship with suppliers, collaborative commerce fosters sharing of sensitive internal information with suppliers and purchasers. Managing collaborative commerce requires knowing exactly what information to share with whom. Collaborative commerce extends beyond supply chain management activities to include the collaborative development of new products and services by multiple cooperating firms.

A good example of a collaborative commerce system is provided by Group Dekko, a collection of 12 independently operated manufacturing companies headquartered in Kendallville, Indiana. Group Dekko produces a variety of components including wire harnesses, molded plastic parts, and metal stamping for automobiles, appliances, and office furniture. The group generates $300 million in annual revenues. In order to work with its large customers — automobile and appliance manufacturers — Group Dekko had to implement quality control procedures conforming with international standard ISO 9000. The Group Dekko Services Department implemented a common,

collaborative commerce
the use of digital technologies to permit organizations to collaboratively design, develop, build, and manage products through their life cycles

NIKE AND I2 JUST CAN'T DO IT

In the Fall of 2000, Nike, the world's largest maker of sport shoes, threw the switch on a $400 million 18-month project to revolutionize Nike's demand and supply chain management system. The new system, built using software from a leading supply chain management firm, i2 Technologies, sought to replace an older supply chain and demand-side management system built in the 1980s with a newer Web-enabled system. With the old system, built by a team of over 100 programmers and modified thousands of times over the years, retailers needed to place orders six months in advance of delivery. The new system promised to reduce the advance order period to a matter of weeks, making it possible for retailers to discover what shoes the market wanted, and then order and receive more shipments before a hot trend cooled off. Excess inventory would be nearly eliminated because no unwanted shoes would be produced. Nike was attempting to build a private industrial network that would closely coordinate the activities of its designers, Far Eastern fabricators, and large retailers such as The Foot Locker.

The new system failed almost from the start. In the span of six months, more than 5 million pairs of the wrong shoes were ordered from Nike's suppliers, creating shortages of popular shoes and excess inventory of less popular shoes. Once the shortages were discovered, Nike resorted to air shipment of fast-selling shoes to retailers at a cost of $5–$8 per pair, as opposed to boat shipment that cost 75 cents a pair. Nike then began discounting the overstocked shoes at half their list price. Nike managers estimate it will take nine months to get over the supply glitch and return to "normal."

Nike's stock dropped $2.61 billion in market value after the company announced the supply chain foul up. The mistake is expected to cost Nike over $100 million in revenue for the third quarter of 2001.

How could this happen? How could an experienced shoe manufacturer such as Nike, with two sophisticated supply chain management systems in place, nevertheless produce 5 million pairs of the wrong shoes?

The profile of the application at Nike was complex. There was a large SKU count, a large part number count, more than 136 separate manufacturing steps, a wide variety of information sources, and a global supply and distribution network with many Far Eastern contractors actually assembling the shoes. But this is exactly the situation that sophisticated supply chain management is supposed to handle easily. Even the Chairman of the U.S. Federal Reserve Bank, Alan Greenspan, was singing the promises of the new technology to save the U.S. economy from a history of business cycles caused by poor management of inventories and supply chains. Greenspan said, "New technologies for supply chain management can perceive imbalances in inventories at a very early stage — virtually in real time — and can cut production promptly in response to the developing signs of unintended inventory building."

Nike management decided not follow a standard implementation of i2 Technologies supply chain template that requires firms to adjust their business processes to those supported by the software. Instead, Nike chose to change the software to fit its own business processes, an entirely reasonable proposition on the face of it, given that Nike had a relatively unique manufacturing and distribution process that did not fit easily into i2's templates. However, this raised costs, slowed the project, and, during this longer implementation period, many senior managers involved in the project left—including the Chief Information Officer.

Instead of pilot testing the new system for a few months to work out the kinks, Nike management chose a "Big Bang" conversion in which the new system is turned on and run in parallel with the old system (in some cases of "Big Bang" implementations, the old system is turned off!). After this point, it is unclear exactly what happened, but management claims that unbeknownst to it, orders placed through both the old and new systems were counted as valid, resulting in overproduction of some slow-selling shoes, and underproduction of fast-selling shoes.

Over the past few years, a wide range of large companies have experienced similar expensive, nearly fatal supply chain management and enterprise system implementations, including Hershey Foods, Whirlpool, W.W. Gore and Associates, and others. Even Cisco Systems, the oft-described leader in supply chain management, took one of the largest write-offs of inventory in American industrial history when it wrote off $2.5 billion in parts inventory in its warehouses. The Cisco case differed somewhat from the other disasters because Cisco's supply chain management system actually worked, but its managers refused to listen to the system's predictions for inventory, instead relying on their own somewhat inflated "sense of the market."

The message to managers of large-scale supply chain management projects is clear: Move slowly and deliberately toward the goal and test before running live, remembering always that changing the behavior of thousands of employees, suppliers, and their employees is the most difficult task.

SOURCES: "Putting Out Supply Chain Fires," by Weld Royal, *IndustryWeek*.com, May 21, 2001; "The Swoosh Stumbles," by Eric Young and Mark Roberti, *Industry Standard*, March 12, 2001; "Nike: i2 Software Just Didn't Do it," by Tim Wilson, *InternetWeek*, March 1, 2001.

shared database of ISO documents using a software package called Lotus Domino to coordinate the efforts of the partner firms in Group Dekko. Lotus Domino is the Internet-based version of Lotus Notes, a collaborative document management and communications package. In this way, the separate Dekko companies could share standards, documents, graphics, and experiences in implementing the quality standards. This environment is being extended to share engineering drawings, bills of material, pricing, and routing information for new products. The goal is to involve Group Dekko companies, as well as their suppliers and customers, in the complete flow of design and product information (Manufacturing Systems Information, 2001).

Although collaborative commerce can involve customers as well as suppliers in the development of products, for the most part, collaborative commerce is concerned with the development of a rich communications environment to enable inter-firm sharing of designs, production plans, inventory levels, delivery schedules, and even the development of shared products (see Figure 12.8).

Efforts to develop closer collaboration among suppliers and purchasers originated in the late 1970s at Xerox Parc, Xerox Corporation's research center in Palo Alto. Development of the appropriate software to enable rich communications was furthered by research conducted by Lotus Development Corporation in the early 1990s. The development of the Internet as a rich communications media has displaced proprietary software tools, and today, collaborative commerce almost always involves the use of Internet technologies to support sharing of graphic designs, documents, messages, and network meetings.

Collaborative commerce is very different from EDI. EDI is a technology for structured communications among firms. Collaborative commerce is more like an interactive teleconference among members of the supply chain. EDI and collaborative

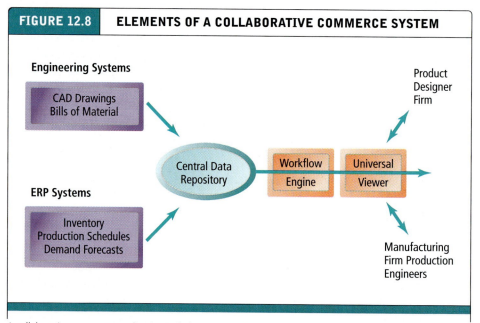

FIGURE 12.8   ELEMENTS OF A COLLABORATIVE COMMERCE SYSTEM

A collaborative commerce application includes a central data repository where employees at several different firms can store engineering drawings and other documents. A workflow engine determines who can see this data and what rules will apply for displaying the data on individual workstations. A viewer can be a browser operating on a workstation.

commerce share one characteristic: They are not open, competitive marketplaces, but instead are, technically, private industrial networks that connect strategic partners in a supply chain.

In Section 12.3, we discuss collaborative commerce in greater depth as an enabling industrial network technology.

MAIN TYPES OF INTERNET-BASED B2B COMMERCE

Based on the preceding discussion of supply chain management, there are two generic types of Internet-based B2B commerce systems: Net marketplaces and private industrial networks (see Figure 12.9). Within each of these general categories there are many different subtypes that we will discuss in following sections.

Net marketplaces (also referred to as *exchanges* or *hubs*) bring together potentially thousands of sellers and buyers into a single digital marketplace operated over the Internet. Net marketplaces are transaction-based, support many-to-many as well as one-to-many relationships, and bear some resemblance to financial markets such as the New York Stock Exchange. There are many different types of Net marketplaces, with different pricing mechanisms, biases, and value propositions that will be explored in Section 12.2 (Kerrigan, et al., 2001).

| FIGURE 12.9 | TWO MAIN TYPES OF INTERNET-BASED B2B COMMERCE |

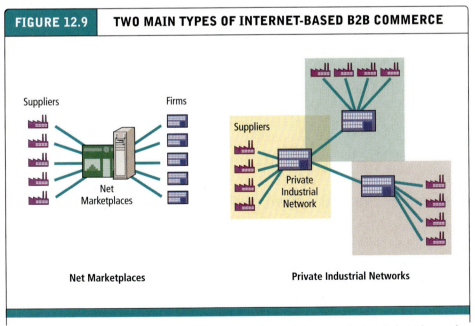

There are two main types of Internet-based B2B commerce: Net marketplaces and private industrial networks.

Private industrial networks bring together a small number of strategic business partner firms that collaborate to develop highly efficient supply chains and satisfy customer demand for products. Private industrial networks are relationship-based, support many-to-one or many-to-few relationships, and bear some resemblance to internal collaborative work environments. There are many different types of private industrial networks, as discussed in Section 12.3.

Private industrial networks are by far the largest form of B2B e-commerce. A recent survey by eMarketer found that only 7% of B2B e-commerce takes place using Net marketplaces, whereas 93% takes place through private industrial networks (Vanscoy, 2001). Forrester Research estimates that by 2004, Net marketplaces will account for 37% of all B2B e-commerce, but the largest share will be through private industrial networks (Deloitte Consulting, 2000) (see Figure 12.10). Jupiter Media Metrix estimates a 35% share for Net marketplaces in 2005 (Jupiter Media Metrix, 2000a).

12.2   NET MARKETPLACES

One of the most compelling visions of B2B e-commerce is that of an electronic marketplace on the Internet that would bring thousands of fragmented suppliers into contact with hundreds of major purchasers of industrial goods for the purpose of conducting "frictionless" commerce. The hope was that thousands of suppliers would compete with one another on price, transactions would be automated and low cost, and as a result, the price of industrial supplies would fall. By extracting fees from buyers and sellers on each transaction, third-party intermediary market makers could earn significant revenues. These Net marketplaces could scale easily as volume increased by simply adding more computers and communications equipment.

In pursuit of this vision, well over 1,000 Net marketplaces sprung up in E-commerce I. Unfortunately, nearly an equal number have disappeared in E-commerce II. Still, some survive, and they are joined by other Net marketplaces based on different assumptions that are quite successful.

THE VARIETY AND CHARACTERISTICS OF NET MARKETPLACES

There is a confusing variety of Net marketplaces today, and several different ways to classify them. For instance, some writers classify Net marketplaces on the basis of their pricing mechanisms — auction, bid/ask, negotiated price, and fixed prices — while others classify markets based on characteristics of the markets they serve (vertical versus horizontal, or sell-side versus buy-side), or ownership (industry-owned consortia versus independent third-party intermediaries). Table 12.2 describes some of the important characteristics of Net marketplaces.

FIGURE 12.10	THE PROJECTED RELATIVE SIZE OF NET MARKETPLACES AND PRIVATE INDUSTRIAL NETWORKS IN 2004

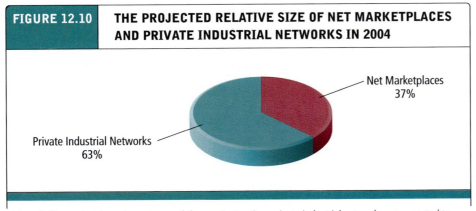

Net Marketplaces
37%

Private Industrial Networks
63%

Although Net marketplaces have attracted the most attention, private industrial networks are expected to capture 63% of all B2B e-commerce revenues by 2004.

SOURCE: Deloitte Consulting, 2000.

TABLE 12.2	OTHER CHARACTERISTICS OF NET MARKETPLACES: A B2B VOCABULARY

MARKET CHARACTERISTIC	MEANING
Bias	Sell side vs. buy side vs. neutral. Whose interests are advantaged: buyers, sellers, or no bias?
Ownership	Industry vs. third party. Who owns the marketplace?
Pricing mechanism	Fixed price catalogs, auctions, bid/ask, and RFPs/RFQs.
Scope/Focus	Horizontal vs. vertical markets.
Value creation	What benefits do they offer the customer?
Access to market	In public markets, any firm can enter, but in private markets, entry is by invitation only.

PURE TYPES OF NET MARKETPLACES

Although each of these distinctions helps describe the phenomenon of Net marketplaces, they do not focus on the central business functionality provided, and they are not capable by themselves of describing the variety of Net marketplaces.

In Figure 12.11, we present a classification of Net marketplaces that focuses on their business functionality; that is, what do these Net marketplaces provide for businesses seeking solutions? We use two dimensions of Net marketplaces to create a four-cell classification table. We distinguish Net marketplaces as providing either indirect goods (goods used to support production) or direct goods (goods used in production), and we distinguish markets as providing either contractual purchasing (where purchases take place over many years according to a contract between the firm and its vendor) or spot purchasing (where purchases are episodic and anonymous — vendors and buyers do not have an ongoing relationship and may not know one another). The intersection of these dimensions produces four "pure" types of Net marketplaces that are relatively straightforward: e-distributors, procurement networks, exchanges, and consortia. The term *pure* refers to the fact that in the real

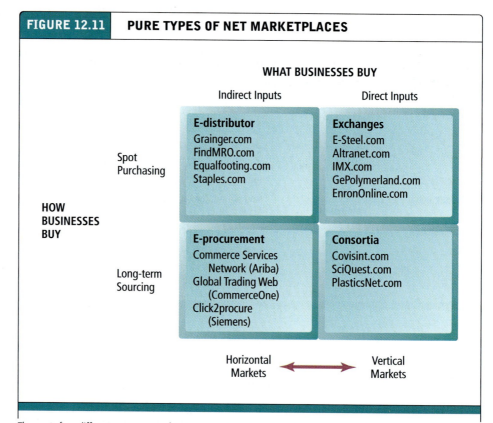

FIGURE 12.11	PURE TYPES OF NET MARKETPLACES

WHAT BUSINESSES BUY

	Indirect Inputs	Direct Inputs
Spot Purchasing	**E-distributor** Grainger.com FindMRO.com Equalfooting.com Staples.com	**Exchanges** E-Steel.com Altranet.com IMX.com GePolymerland.com EnronOnline.com

Long-term Sourcing	**E-procurement**
	Commerce Services
	   Network (Ariba)
	Global Trading Web
	   (CommerceOne)
	Click2procure
	   (Siemens)
		Consortia
		Covisint.com
		SciQuest.com
		PlasticsNet.com

HOW BUSINESSES BUY

Horizontal Markets ← → Vertical Markets

There are four different pure types of Net marketplaces based on the intersection of two dimensions: how businesses buy and what they buy. A third dimension — horizontal versus vertical markets — also distinguishes the different types of Net marketplaces.

world, some Net marketplaces can be found in multiple parts of this figure as business models change and opportunities appear and disappear. Nevertheless, the discussion of pure types of Net marketplaces is a useful starting point.

Each of these Net marketplaces seeks to provide value to customers in different ways. Below we discuss each type of Net marketplace in more detail.

E-DISTRIBUTORS

E-distributors are the most common and most easily understood type of Net market-place. **E-distributors** provide electronic catalogs that represent the products of thousands of direct manufacturers (see Figure 12.12). They are the equivalent of Amazon.com for industry. E-distributors are independently owned intermediaries that offer industrial customers a single source from which to order indirect goods (often referred to as MRO) on a spot, "as needed" basis. According to a recent report, about 40% of corporate purchases cannot be satisfied under a company's existing contracts, and must be purchased on a spot basis (Jupiter Media Metrix, 2001b; Devine et al., 2001). E-distributors make money by charging a markup on products they distribute.

Organizations and firms in all industries require MRO supplies. The MRO function maintains, repairs, and operates commercial buildings and maintains all the

e-distributors

provide electronic catalogs that represent the products of thousands of direct manufacturers

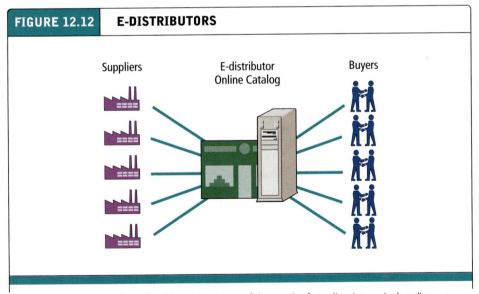

| FIGURE 12.12 | E-DISTRIBUTORS |

E-distributors are singular firms that bring the products of thousands of suppliers into a single online electronic catalog for sale to thousands of buyer firms. E-distributors are sometimes referred to as *one-to-many markets*, one seller serving many firms.

machinery of these buildings from heating, ventilating, and air conditioning systems to lighting fixtures.

E-distributors operate in horizontal markets because they serve many different industries with products from many different suppliers. E-distributors usually operate "public" markets in the sense that any firm can order from the catalog, as opposed to "private" markets, where membership is restricted to selected firms.

E-distributor prices are usually fixed, but large customers receive discounts and other incentives to purchase, such as credit, reporting on account activity, and limited forms of business purchasing rules (for instance, no purchases greater than $500 for a single item without a purchase order). The primary benefits offered to industrial customers are lower search costs, lower transaction costs, wide selection, rapid delivery, and low prices.

The most frequently cited example of a public e-distribution and procurement market is W.W. Grainger. Grainger is involved in both long-term systematic sourcing as well as spot sourcing, but its emphasis is on spot sourcing. Grainger's business model is to become the world's leading source of MRO suppliers, and its revenue model is that of a typical retailer: It owns the products, and takes a markup on the products it sells to customers.

Although the company is privately owned, most of its site is open to the public. Grainger is the largest distributor of MRO supplies in the United States, generating over $4 billion in revenue overall in a $350 billion MRO market, with nearly $200 million of that coming from its Web sites. At Grainger.com, users get an electronic online version of Grainger's famous seven-pound catalog, plus other parts not available in the catalog (adding up to over one million parts), and complete electronic ordering and payment. (Gardner, 2000).

E-PROCUREMENT

e-procurement companies
independently owned intermediaries connecting hundreds of online suppliers offering millions of maintenance and repair parts to business firms who pay fees to join the market

value chain management (VCM) services
include automation of a firm's entire procurement process on the buyer side and automation of the selling business processes on the seller side

E-procurement companies are independently owned intermediaries connecting hundreds of online suppliers offering millions of maintenance and repair parts to business firms who pay fees to join the market (see Figure 12.13). E-procurement Net marketplaces are typically used for long-term contractual purchasing of indirect goods (MRO); they create online horizontal markets, although they also provide for members' spot sourcing of MRO supplies. E-procurement companies make money by charging a percentage of each transaction, licensing consulting services and software, and assessing network use fees.

E-procurement companies expand on the business model of simpler e-distributors by including the online catalogs of hundreds of suppliers and offering value chain management services to both buyers and sellers. **Value chain management (VCM) services** provided by e-procurement companies include automation of a firm's entire procurement process on the buyer side and automation of the selling business

FIGURE 12.13 | **E-PROCUREMENT MARKETS**

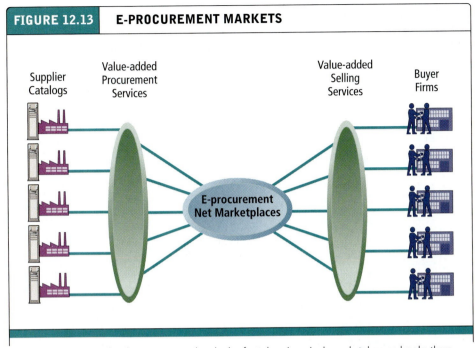

E-procurement Net marketplaces aggregate hundreds of catalogs in a single marketplace and make them available to firms, often on a custom basis that reflects only the suppliers desired by the participating firms.

processes on the seller side. For purchasers, e-procurement companies automate purchase orders, requisitions, sourcing, business rules enforcement, invoicing, and payment. For suppliers, e-procurement companies provide catalog creation and content management, order management, fulfillment, invoicing, shipment, and settlement.

E-procurement Net marketplaces are sometimes referred to as *many-to-many* markets. They are mediated by an independent third party that purports to represent both buyers and sellers, and hence claim to be neutral. On the other hand, because they may include the catalogs of both competing suppliers and competing e-distributors, they have a likely bias in favor of the buyers. Nevertheless, by aggregating huge buyer firms into their networks, they provide distinct marketing benefits for suppliers and reduce customer acquisition costs.

The two largest players in this market segment are Ariba and CommerceOne. Figure 12.14 illustrates Ariba's Commerce Services Network, which creates an e-procurement marketplace for firms who pay a fee to participate.

Federal Express, for instance, is using Ariba's e-distribution and procurement system to automate its $8 billion in purchases and 25,000 annual purchase requisitions. Over 180,000 FedEx employees now have access to Ariba's system and order from more than 32 suppliers and catalogs. The system automatically invokes FedEx's pur-

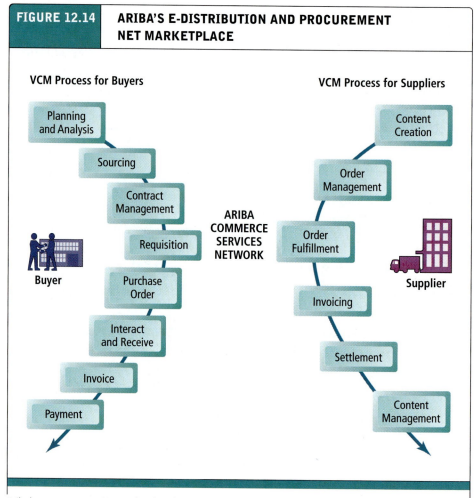

FIGURE 12.14 | **ARIBA'S E-DISTRIBUTION AND PROCUREMENT NET MARKETPLACE**

Ariba's e-procurement Net marketplace brings together buyers and suppliers in a single automated marketplace. It is much more than a simple transaction environment. It includes value chain management (VCM) services for both buyers and suppliers in which Ariba assists firms in streamlining the procurement process and order fulfillment process.

SOURCE: Ariba Inc, 2001b.

chasing business rules to route, review, and approve requisitions electronically. The result has been a 12% reduction in the prices paid for MRO supplies, a 75% reduction in the cost of processing purchases, and a reduction in parts-delivery time from an average of 7 days to 2 days (www.Ariba.com, 2001b). We discuss Ariba's Net marketplace in depth in the next section.

E-commerce in Action: Ariba

Ariba provides an excellent example of an a e-procurement Net marketplace. Ariba is a leading B2B software platform and service provider. The Menlo Park, California, company provides a suite of B2B procurement and market-maker software tools to corporate customers worldwide. Ariba also operates an e-procurement Net marketplace that offers a variety of software tools for rationalizing and automating the procurement process for both buyers and sellers. Established in 1996, the company sells its software and services in twenty-five countries and focuses on large Fortune 500 global firms.

The Ariba B2B e-commerce platform has four components. Ariba Buyer is the original application built by Ariba to automate the procurement business process within single firms. Ariba Marketplace and Ariba Dynamic Trade are software tools that permit users to establish B2B marketplaces internally on their corporate intranets, or externally on the public Internet. Ariba also offers customers access to Ariba Commerce Services Network, an Internet-based e-procurement Net marketplace that aggregates the catalogs of hundreds of suppliers and provides corporate buyers with a Web interface to Ariba procurement, payment, and shipping support services.

The Vision Ariba's vision is to become the leading Internet-based B2B commerce network platform. In the E-commerce I period (1996–1997), Ariba joined many other early B2B innovators such as CommerceOne and VerticalNet (now competitors for the B2B leadership position) in an effort to revolutionize the procurement and supply process in large corporations. Ariba wanted to replace the aging EDI platform used by large corporations to coordinate trade among a few firms at fixed prices and replace it with an Internet-based electronic marketplace where thousands of suppliers could be aggregated, open market prices could be seen by all, prices would be set dynamically based on supply and demand, and the resulting price transparency would ensure buyers the lowest cost for their goods. Ariba was aware that in 1997 — its first year of real sales — 95% of all corporate purchasing in the world was performed by hundreds of thousands of purchasing agents using paper and pencil documents, fax machines, and telephones. EDI was limited generally to contractual purchase of direct goods, which amounted to only 5% of all inter-firm trade, and ignored the MRO segment entirely, which accounts for 33% of all corporate purchasing. The average cost of these paper-based transactions was $75–$175. The traditional procurement process was slow to pay suppliers, and took several weeks to sometimes months to deliver supplies to corporate users. So-called "maverick purchasing" (off-contract purchasing by local units), the bane of all procurement officers, had grown to over 30% of the inter-firm procurement process in the United States, and resulted in premiums of 15% to 27%, according to AMR research (Ariba, Inc., 2000; 2001a).

Ariba promised to use the Internet to radically change the procurement process. Ariba Buyer enables organizations using their corporate intranets to automate the procurement cycle by linking in-house corporate purchasers with internal procurement approval officers and financial systems, thereby centralizing control over purchasing within the company. Ariba MarketPlace and Ariba Dynamic Trade allow organizations to establish fully functional electronic markets with integrated auction, reverse auction, exchange, and bid/ask exchanges. These marketplaces could be deployed on intranets or the public Internet. For firms that did not want to create their own Net marketplaces, Ariba offers Commerce Services Network, a global, Ariba-hosted B2B electronic marketplace. Client firms pay fees to join the network and take advantage of the network's large supplier base and procurement tools.

To a large extent, Ariba has developed the tools needed to bring about the revolution in procurement that it originally envisioned. However, Ariba did not count on the fact that implementation of its software by large companies is complex, time-consuming, and expensive. In most cases, customers must make significant changes in their business processes and expensive changes in existing systems. Because most customers have no experience with B2B e-commerce, Ariba must engage in a lengthy and expensive education program with customers. Inevitably, these considerations delay the sales cycle, which runs 6–9 months, and slow down implementation and payments. Ariba also did not count on the competitive response by Oracle, IBM, SAP, and other major technology players, each of which offers competing products (but who, in many cases, also partner with Ariba for specific customers). Finally, Ariba did not count on the difficulties it is facing in getting suppliers to join its Commerce Services Network. Suppliers have balked at the notion of joining such buyer-dominated networks, where their products and services would be put into direct competition with others. This reduces the liquidity of Net marketplaces and makes them less valuable for buyers, and also reduces the transaction fees paid to Ariba.

Business Model   Ariba's original business model was to charge licensing and maintenance fees for use of its software. For corporate buyers, Ariba offers the prospect of a reduction in procurement costs of 50% to 75%, a reduction in the cost of supplies, faster acquisition cycles, and reduced errors. Ariba offers suppliers similar reductions in selling costs, faster payment, and access to the aggregated purchasing power of hundreds of firms.

Ariba developed a related business model in 1999 by creating its own Net marketplace (Commerce Services Network) that charges fees based on transaction value among trading partners. By providing firms quick and easy access to its own network, Ariba believed it could attract purchasing agents and firms to a turnkey solution that did not require adopting firms to radically change their behavior, install software, or implement costly organizational change programs.

Financial Analysis Ariba has experienced extraordinary growth in revenues since 1998, growing from $8 million in 1998 to $279 million in 2000. However, revenue growth has slowed to a standstill in 2001 as the economy slowed. Table 12.3 presents Ariba's operating results and summary balance sheet data for 1998–2000.

Ariba receives most of its revenue from licensing fees. From 1999 to 2000, gross revenues increased from $45 million to $279 million, a stunning 643% growth. The increase resulted from a number of factors, including acquisitions, growth in new customers, and growth in strategic relationships with computer services giants such as IBM and Oracle, who offer Ariba-based solutions to their customers. Maintenance and service grew at over 400% from 1999–2000. However, the direct cost of generating these revenues also grew by over 500%, from $8.8 million to $47.5 million, causing overall gross margins to remain in the low 80% range.

Operating expenses mushroomed with gross revenues, primarily through large increases in the costs for marketing and sales that resulted from sales force compensation, advertising, and customer education programs. Both R&D (technology) costs and administrative costs grew rapidly as Ariba assimilated its acquisitions, assumed ongoing research projects of those businesses, and launched expensive human resource and financial management programs to control its own growth. The most striking operating expense increase is of course the amortization of goodwill, which was not present in previous years. Overall, the company paid $688 million more for acquired companies than they were worth in book values. Fortunately (for Ariba), it paid for these acquisitions mostly with stock and little of its own cash. Unfortunately, for those who received the stock, Ariba's stock values have plunged from their high of $183 to its current price of under $5!

The large increases in operating expenses offset the gains in revenue for 2000. The net loss for 2000 was $792 million, and a negative net margin of -342%. If one excluded the amortization of goodwill, the loss becomes only $104 million, still a hefty loss given revenues are only $279 million. Excluding the amortization, this would mean that for every dollar in net revenue made by Ariba in 2000, it lost 45 cents.

Revenue numbers for the first three quarters of 2001 offer little solace. Although in the first quarter, Ariba claimed an "operating profit," in later quarters it would take a billion dollar write-off of past investments. Licensing revenues were down by 8% as large global companies cut back expenditures on computer hardware and software, but licensing fees are up a bit. Management has initiated a restructuring of the company, a consolidation of physical office space, and a 30% reduction in staff for 2001.

A look at the balance sheet shows that the company had about $358 million in current assets at September 30, 2000, enough to see it through several years of losses at the current rate. Ariba has some breathing room to become a profitable company — if it makes the correct decisions in the near term future. Clearly, management is under pressure to do something different in the future to arrive at profitability.

TABLE 12.3	ARIBA'S CONSOLIDATED STATEMENTS OF OPERATIONS AND SUMMARY BALANCE SHEET DATA, 1998–2000

ARIBA, INC.
CONSOLIDATED STATEMENTS OF OPERATIONS
(in thousands)

For the fiscal year ended September 30	2000	1999	1998
Revenues			
License	$ 198,790	$ 26,768	$ 6,040
Maintenance and service	80,249	18,604	2,323
Gross revenues	279,039	45,372	8,363
Cost of revenues			
License	12,572	724	165
Maintenance and service	34,947	8,089	1,373
Total cost of revenues	47,519	8,813	1,538
Gross profit	231,520	36,559	6,825
Gross margin	83%	81%	82%
Operating expenses			
Sales and marketing	207,234	33,859	10,311
Research and development	39,017	11,620	4,499
General and administrative	29,172	7,917	2,580
Amortization of goodwill	688,588	—	—
In-process research and development	27,350	—	—
Business partner warrants	29,251	—	—
Amortization of stock-based compensation	18,051	14,584	956
Total operating expenses	1,038,663	67,980	18,346
Loss from operations	(807,143)	(31,421)	(11,521)
Other income, net	16,331	2,219	568
Net loss before taxes	(790,812)	(29,202)	(10,953)
Provision for income taxes	(1,963)	(98)	—
Net loss	(792,775)	(29,300)	(10,953)
Net margin	–342%	–80%	–160%

SUMMARY BALANCE SHEET
(in thousands)

At September 30	2000	1999	1998
Current Assets			
Cash, cash equivalents and investments (short and long term)	$ 364,691	$ 152,440	$ 13,932
Accounts receivable	61,892	5,157	2,129
Total current assets	358,064	106,045	14,292
Total assets	3,815,878	170,021	18,771
Total current liabilities	218,827	47,057	8,165
Long-term debt	402	781	647

SOURCE: Ariba, Inc. Form 10-K for the fiscal year ended September 30, 2000, filed with the Securities and Exchange Commission on December 29, 2000.

Strategic Analysis — Business Strategies Ariba has closely aligned its corporate strategy with every bend and twist in the B2B road. In the early years, it focused on procurement software that would supplement the large ERP systems being installed. Revenue was derived from licensing fees. As this market slowed because of direct competition from ERP firms and others such as Oracle and IBM, in 1999, Ariba began acquiring companies and expertise that would allow it to enter the market for Net marketplace software and operation of independent Net marketplaces. Ariba management believed that Net marketplaces would produce millions in revenue from transaction fees.

In 2000, Ariba made several acquisitions of companies that could extend the reach and power of its existing business model based on leasing software, and move the company more decisively toward the Net marketplace model that charges fees based on transactions. In January, Ariba purchased TradingDynamics for $465 million in stock. TradingDynamics provides B2B auction, request for quote, and bid-ask exchange operating software. In March, the company acquired Tradex Technologies Inc. for $2.3 billion in stock. Tradex produces software to operate exchanges. In August 2000, the company acquired SupplierMarket.com for $607 million in stock. Supplier-Market provides online collaborative sourcing software that permits buyers and sellers to locate trading partners, negotiate purchase prices, and collaborate over the Internet. None of these acquired companies had substantial book value — assets — and most of the purchase price involved "goodwill," an intangible asset equal to the purchase price minus any tangible assets.

From these acquisitions, we can conclude that management's initial strategy was to move toward the development of independent Net marketplaces while continuing to maintain licensing of its platform to companies that want to rebuild their own internal procurement processes. Independent Net marketplaces make it easier for large firms to make the transition to B2B e-commerce and away from the paper-and-pencil procurement process of the past as compared with building their own Net marketplaces using the Ariba platform. In an independent Net marketplace, all a buyer firm needs is a mouse and a PC with an Internet connection. All the software implementation and hosting is performed by Ariba. The challenge for independent Net marketplaces, however, is attracting a critical mass of large buyers and their suppliers into a single electronic marketplace in order to produce large transaction fees for Ariba. For this, Ariba will need partners with links to large multinational firms — IBM, for instance.

In addition, management emphasized other strategic directions, such as targeting large firms, creating a network effect for its Commerce Services Network, expanding globally, and expanding quickly through partnerships with key players such as IBM and through acquisitions. In 2000, Ariba entered into an alliance with IBM and i2 technologies called "b2bx3." IBM provides hardware and services, i2 provides software to coordinate purchase and delivery, and Ariba provides the software to automate online buying and selling.

By the end of 2000, however, it had become clear that Net marketplaces would not produce the pot of gold in transaction fees that so many Net marketplace firms had believed. Ariba management said in April 2001, as its stock took a sickening plunge to $4, that it no longer expected to receive "significant" revenue from exchanges. By this point, it was clear the entire industry of independent Net marketplaces was in trouble. Suppliers were balking, and very large firms were establishing their own markets or industrial networks rather than allow upstart independents to reap the benefits of B2B. As a result, Ariba's strategy changed again to move the company toward working with large firms rather than disrupting their supply chains.

In January 2001, Ariba announced its intention to purchase Agile Software Inc. for $2.4 billion in stock (when Ariba's shares were selling for about $40). Agile makes software that supports collaborative commerce among firms. However, in April 2001, the deal with Agile fell through as Ariba's shares plunged below $5. As a result of the drop in the value of its shares, Ariba has lost its most important currency — the ability to use highly valued stock to make acquisitions.

In the second quarter of 2001, Ariba also announced it would lay off 30% of its workforce. Although revenue had doubled to $90 million in the second quarter (when compared to a year earlier), it experienced an operating loss of $1.4 billion as it wrote off the earlier investment in Tradex and losses incurred in attempting to purchase Agile. Ariba was not alone. Its chief rival, CommerceOne, reported losses of $2 billion in this quarter, and sale of 20% of its equity to SAP AG, the German ERP software firm.

In September 2001, Ariba announced the resignation of Chief Executive Larry Mueller, one of the company's founders.

Strategic Analysis — Competition While Ariba pioneered the market for Internet-based B2B e-commerce software, it was quickly joined by powerful competitors such as IBM, Oracle, and GE Information Services, as well as entrepreneurial start-up companies such as CommerceOne, Captura Software, Clarus, Netscape Communications, and VerticalNet. In addition, the company faces significant competition from major enterprise software firms such as Oracle, SAP, and PeopleSoft, which have developed their own Internet-based procurement systems. The entry barriers to the market for B2B e-commerce software are low, and there are few technology-based differentiating features among the offerings. Increasingly, trust, longevity, and stability are becoming important factors for customers to be concerned about as they review competing products and firms.

Ariba has entered into strategic partnerships with some of its competitors, such as IBM and i2Technologies, to develop targeted solutions for specific customers.

Strategic Analysis — Technology Ariba is a B2B software applications company. All Ariba's software is built for the Internet using standard software tools such as HTML, Java, and XML. Perhaps its most differentiated software technology is found in its

Ariba Commerce Services Network. This network is an open-standards multi-protocol transaction network that routes and translates transactions between buyers and suppliers using most major electronic commerce standards such as XML, CXML (an Internet version of XML for commercial transactions), Internet EDI, VAN EDI, OBI (Open Buying Internet), HTML, e-mail, and fax. This enables buyers and sellers to conduct business with one another regardless of what protocol they are using. There is no need for a single B2B standard.

Strategic Analysis — Social and Legal Challenges At this time, there are no active legal challenges to Ariba. Nevertheless, a firm such as Ariba could face significant liabilities should its software fail to perform or its Commerce Services Network be unavailable for a period of time. As firms become more dependent on Ariba for procurement, any glitch in operation could be very expensive. In addition, given the volatility of its stock, it is fairly common for firms such as Ariba to become the target of investor lawsuits alleging misrepresentation of facts concerning the company's financial strength.

Future Prospects Ariba faces a number of daunting challenges. In the B2B software licensing business, it faces many established enterprise software firms who have similar offerings. In this business, entry costs are low, substitute products are plentiful, and customers themselves need significant selling on the product. In the Net marketplace business where it can receive transaction revenues, Ariba has found it challenging to attract sufficient suppliers or buyer organizations, and hence it has been difficult to collect substantial transaction fees. Instead, many of its potential customers have either built private industrial networks or established industry consortia, using software from other providers. Many competitors also offer Net marketplaces, and entry costs are low to this market also. In any event, the model of one big electronic marketplace is not attracting sufficient customers. Ariba's move toward private industrial networks and collaborative commerce has also failed as the deal with Agile Software collapsed.

It is apparent that none of Ariba's strategies have worked particularly well. With such a low stock price, Ariba has become an acquisition target for an established B2B software firm seeking to strengthen its offerings, or even for one of its large customers attempting to create its own Net marketplace from the vantage point of a firm that has an established reputation (see the Siemens case at the end of the chapter).

EXCHANGES

Exchanges are independently owned online marketplaces that connect hundreds of suppliers to potentially thousands of buyers in a dynamic, real-time environment (see Figure 12.15). Exchanges generally create vertical markets focusing on the spot-purchasing requirements of large firms in a single industry such as computers and telecommunications, electronics, food, and industrial equipment, although there are

exchanges
independently owned online marketplaces that connect hundreds of suppliers to potentially thousands of buyers in a dynamic, real-time environment

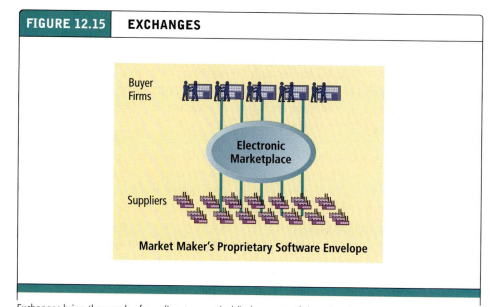

FIGURE 12.15   EXCHANGES

Buyer Firms

Electronic Marketplace

Suppliers

Market Maker's Proprietary Software Envelope

Exchanges bring thousands of suppliers to a vertical (industry-specific) marketplace to sell their goods to a much smaller number of buyer firms—usually the largest buyers in a market. Exchanges are sometimes referred to as *many-to-few* markets because they have many suppliers serving a smaller number of large buyer firms.

exceptions to this generalization as described below. Exchanges were the prototype Internet-based marketplace of E-commerce I; as noted above, several thousand were created in this period, but most have failed.

Exchanges make money by charging a commission on the transaction. The pricing model can be through an online negotiation, auction, RFQ (request for quote), or fixed buy-and-sell prices. The benefits offered to customers of exchanges include reduced search cost for parts and spare capacity. Other benefits include lower prices created by a global marketplace driven by competition among suppliers who would, presumably, sell goods at very low profit margins at one world-market price. The benefits offered suppliers are access to a global purchasing environment and the opportunity to unload production overruns (although at very competitive prices and low profit margins). Even though they are private intermediaries, exchanges are public in the sense of permitting any bona fide buyer or seller to participate.

Exchanges tend to be biased toward the buyer even though they are independently owned and presumably neutral. Suppliers are disadvantaged by the fact that exchanges put them in direct price competition with other similar suppliers around the globe, driving profit margins down. Exchanges have failed primarily because suppliers have refused to join them, and hence, the existing markets have very low liquidity, defeating the very purpose and benefits of an exchange. **Liquidity** is typically

liquidity

typically measured by the number of buyers and sellers in a market, the volume of transactions, and the size of transactions

measured by the number of buyers and sellers in a market, the volume of transactions, and the size of transactions. You know a market is liquid when you can buy or sell just about any size order at just about any time you want. On all of these measures, many exchanges failed, resulting in a very small number of participants, few trades, and small trade value per transaction. In a recent survey of procurement agents, the most common reason given for not using exchanges is the absence of their traditional, trusted suppliers (Jupiter Media Metrix, 2001c).

While most exchanges tend to be vertical marketplaces offering direct supplies, some exchanges offer indirect inputs as well, such as electricity and power, transportation services (usually to the transportation industry), and professional services. Table 12.4 describes a variety of exchanges extant at the time of this writing.

An example of an exchange is Altra Energy Technologies Inc. of Houston. Altra operates altranet.com, an online exchange where energy industry suppliers and buyers meet to trade natural gas, liquids, electricity and crude oil in a spot market for immediate delivery. In the Altra E-Gas market, about 7,500 trades per month occur. Trading partners can trade around the clock, preselect trading partners, confirm transactions, and obtain credit and insurance. The primary customers are small utilities and energy distributors.

CarrierPoint Inc. is an Atlanta-based spot market maker for trucking capacity. Ticona, Inc., the technical polymers business of the German-based Celanese Corporation, uses CarrierPoint's Dynamic Shipping MarketPlace to ship its products across the United States. Ticona posts trucking loads and schedules on a Web site, and truck-

TABLE 12.4	SOME EXCHANGES
EXCHANGE	**FOCUS**
E-Steel.com	Spot market for steel products.
Altranet.com (Altra Energy)	Real-time online network for trading gas, power, and liquids.
Smarterwork.com	Spare professional services from Web design to legal advice.
AskAD.com	Unsold advertising auctioned online.
Activeinternational.com	Trading in underutilized manufacturing capacity.
Foodtrader.com	One of the largest B2B spot trading sites for the food products industry.
E-greenbiz.com	Online spot market for nursery supplies.
Powerfarm.com	Online spot purchasing for the farm industry.
Textradeinternational.com	Global textile network for fiber and yarns trading.
Carrierpoint.com	Spot market for the trucking industry.

ing companies sign up for loads. In order to ensure that trusted long-term shippers did not feel they were competing in an auction, Ticona negotiates shipping rates with individual companies before permitting them on the site. Ticona is able to secure business for preferred shippers by restricting the loads viewable to Web site visitors. The objective of the Ticona application is to secure available shipping capacity and ensure that the best shippers deliver Ticona shipments. For trucking companies, the system helps them utilize spare trucking capacity by allowing them to sign up for future shipping jobs (Cottrill, 2001).

E-Commerce in Action: FreeMarkets Inc.

FreeMarkets Inc. is one of the leading B2B exchanges, generating revenues of $83 million in 2000. The Pittsburgh-based firm provides market-making services and a suite of software tools for Global 2000 firms purchasing direct goods from suppliers on a noncontractual basis. The company's market-making services enable industrial buyers of direct goods to find, screen, and qualify suppliers, and then to negotiate prices and terms through a dynamic, real-time, comprehensive bidding and auction process. The company offers proprietary technology, technical support facilities, market-making services, and access to a global database of suppliers, and call-center support to buyers and suppliers in over 30 languages. In a FreeMarkets online market created for large buyers, suppliers from around the world submit bids in real time. In addition to full-service market making, FreeMarkets also operates an online market for surplus assets and inventory.

Using its market-making software, FreeMarkets has conducted over 9,000 online auctions or what the company calls "markets" in 165 product categories such as ball bearings, corrugated packaging, die castings, printed circuit boards, fasteners, and molded rubbers for over 35 companies, generating transactions worth over $14 billion and saving customers an estimated $2.7 billion when compared to traditional sources.

The FreeMarkets offering has four components. The centerpiece is FreeMarkets Online, a hosted online market-making software application that is available over the Web and that does not require any installation or hosting by the customer. FullSource solution is a value-added service that helps the customer identify and screen suppliers, and prepare requests for quotation. QuickSource solution is a service for less complex sourcing situations, which enables customers to quickly run their own online markets without direct assistance from FreeMarkets. FreeMarkets Asset Exchange provides an ongoing marketplace where buyers and sellers of surplus suppliers can trade at any time.

FreeMarkets was an E-commerce I high-flyer. In an IPO on December 10, 1999, the stock went public at $48 a share, and soared on its first day to $282 (a 697% pop), with a market capitalization of over $8 billion on the first day! Bear Stearn's analysts put a $300 target price on the stock, with a "strong buy" recommendation. The stock lost value throughout 2000, however, and currently is selling for about $15.

The Vision The original vision of FreeMarkets was to create Internet-based efficient markets that would overcome inefficiencies in the goods market. Inefficiencies in the direct goods market arise from several factors. Custom-made direct goods have no standard prices and there are no catalog list prices, and therefore there is low price transparency for buyers. Quality is critical in direct goods, and buyers must do extensive time-consuming research to establish quality of goods and suppliers. Finally, supply markets for direct goods are fragmented and often localized. Buyers cannot "see" the whole market, given the hundreds of potential suppliers. These factors force buyers to pay high prices and to limit their sources to a few trusted suppliers under long-term contracts.

FreeMarkets' vision was to replace the existing localized and inefficient direct goods market with an easy-to-use market-making platform that would allow large Global 2000 firms to quickly prepare requests for quotation, search and qualify suppliers, and then conduct auctions involving a limited set of suppliers. In this sense, FreeMarkets was offering private marketplaces to corporations for their most basic and important goods.

FreeMarkets promised buyers substantial cost savings, a robust online dynamic bidding software application that required minimal installation, a customized approach for each company and product category, in-depth research and knowledge of suppliers, and a set of market rules that would discourage fraudulent bids and delivery failures. Settlement, payment, and shipping were negotiated directly by the parties involved in a transaction at a later time.

Benefits to suppliers were less clear. Suppliers would of course gain access to Global 2000 purchasing needs, but only if recognized and selected by the buyer. Suppliers also received detailed, clear specifications — more information. Yet suppliers who participated would be bidding against other global suppliers largely on price, and small suppliers not recognized by the Global 2000 firms because of their size generally could not participate at all.

Business Model FreeMarkets' business model is to charge transaction fees on the amount traded in each auction and service fees for value-added services. FreeMarkets is in essence an eBay for business, with substantial added-value services that assist customers. In its FullSource service, FreeMarkets identifies the potential savings, assists in the preparation of requests for quotation (RFQs), selects potential suppliers, conducts the online market for the customer, and helps the customer evaluate the results in terms of price, quality, terms, and delivery. For firms who do not require these services, FreeMarkets QuickSource service allows customers to conduct their markets without assistance for a transaction fee.

Financial Analysis FreeMarkets has experienced extraordinary revenue growth since beginning operations in 1998. In the first six months of 2001, its revenues were double the revenue generated in the comparable 2000 period. Hence FreeMarkets' revenue is continuing exceptional growth albeit at a slower pace than previous years. However, costs have mushroomed, and losses have progressively mounted at a faster rate than revenues. Table 12.5 shows the results of its operations and summary balance sheet data for 1998–2000.

FreeMarkets' revenue has grown explosively, from $7 million in 1998 to over $80 million in 2000. In the single year 1999–2000, revenues expanded over 400%. As noted above, revenue growth appears to be slowing in 2001, but still doubling year to year. The cost of revenues, however, has also been rising commensurately, and overall gross margins remain in the low 40% range.

Operating costs have kept pace with revenues, growing at 400% to 500% per year. The largest cost is for marketing, largely for the maintenance of an expensive sales force that can make sales to Global 2000 firms. Research and development for technology has also grown at explosive rates, along with general and administrative costs required to operate a rapidly expanding business. Total operating expenses 1999–2000 increased 576%, quite a bit faster than revenues. Even if goodwill amortization is excluded, costs are still rising at 367% in this period — nearly as fast as revenues are growing.

On balance, FreeMarkets does not appear to be scaling well or able to leverage its technology investment. Using standard accounting procedures for calculating margins that included amortization, net margins are worsening, from -250% to -454%. Removing the amortization charges for 2000, and recalculating a "net margin" (not an approved GAAP practice) shows net margins "improving" in 2000 to -191%. This translates to FreeMarkets paying out $1.91 for every dollar in net revenue it generates.

The outlook in 2001 offers little improvement. Revenues have doubled in the first half of 2001 when compared to the same period in 2000 (from $17 million to $34 million), but total operating costs for the six months — not including any goodwill write-downs — have also nearly doubled from $36 million in 2000 to $65 million in 2001. When FreeMarkets' failed investments of 2000 are included as a goodwill expense, the losses expand to an extraordinary $275 million loss in the first six months of 2001, compared to a $65 million loss in 2000. Acquisition investments gone sour have added to FreeMarkets' woes.

A look at the balance sheet summary shows how FreeMarkets can sustain these losses. At December 31, 2000, FreeMarkets had current assets of $154 million, enough to sustain it for a couple of years before running out of cash. It received some of this cash from private venture capital investments, but mostly from its sales of shares to the public. At this moment, it is unlikely that FreeMarkets can sell additional shares or receive additional funding from venture capitalists without selling the entire company. Clearly, management is under a great deal of pressure to reduce costs, leverage its past investments, and show at least so-called "operating profits."

TABLE 12.5	FREEMARKETS' CONSOLIDATED STATEMENTS OF OPERATIONS AND SUMMARY BALANCE SHEET DATA, 1998–2000

FREEMARKETS, INC.
CONSOLIDATED STATEMENTS OF OPERATIONS
(in thousands)

	2000	1999	1998
Revenues	$83,339	$20,880	$7,801
Cost of revenues	48,896	12,166	4,258
Gross profit	34,442	8,714	3,542
Gross margin	41%	42%	45%
Operating costs and expenses			
Research and development	19,121	4,913	842
Sales and marketing	41,506	11,939	656
General and administrative	34,081	9,316	2,025
Stock compensation	443	283	—
Stock compensation (sales/marketing)	5,965	4,669	—
Stock compensation (general & admin)	2	247	—
Goodwill amortization	90,749	—	—
Write-off of in-process R&D	7,397	—	—
Total operating costs and expenses	248,160	43,534	7,782
Operating (loss)/income	(164,821)	(22,654)	19
Interest and other income, net	8,409	833	215
Net (loss)/income	(156,412)	(21,821)	233
Net margin	−454%	−250%	7%

SUMMARY BALANCE SHEET DATA
(in thousands)

At December 31	2000	1999	1998
Current assets			
Cash and cash equivalents	52,991	177,204	1,656
Short-term investments	68,157	33,040	—
Accounts receivable	27,861	6,887	3,939
Total current assets	154,078	218,573	5,679
Total assets	462,546	231,654	6,870
Total current liabilities	45,204	9,722	1,864
Long-term debt	543	3,277	413

SOURCE: FreeMarkets, Inc. Form 10-K for the fiscal year ended December 31, 2000, filed with the Securities and Exchange Commission on May 10, 2001.

Strategic Analysis — Business Strategies FreeMarkets has changed its strategy frequently — like others in the B2B marketspace such as Ariba and CommerceOne — as its initial strategy of providing online exchanges failed to produce sufficient revenues. In 2000, FreeMarkets departed from its original strategy and attempted to build an online market for surplus. In 2001, FreeMarkets departed even more significantly from its original strategy by attempting to move into the collaborative commerce marketspace, helping small groups of very large firms work together closely. FreeMarkets has little experience in this market.

FreeMarkets made two acquisitions during 2000 as it attempted to build a global electronic market for surplus equipment. It acquired iMark in March 2000 for $334 million in stock. iMark is a B2B online marketplace for surplus equipment and inventory. In March 2000, the company also acquired Surplus Record and SR Auction (collectively "Surplus Record") for $18 million in cash. Surplus Record operated a directory and network of online dealers and buyers for surplus industrial equipment, machinery, and machine tools. Both of these acquisitions contributed toward the development of FreeMarkets' new online market for surplus industrial equipment called FreeMarkets Asset Recovery Marketplace.

In February 2001, as a part of its new strategic effort to break into the collaborative commerce arena, FreeMarkets entered into a merger with Adexa, Inc., a leading provider of software products for supply chain management and collaborative commerce within private industrial networks. FreeMarkets purchased all the shares of Adexa, worth at the time approximately $700 million. However, by June 2001, with the value of FreeMarkets shares plunging, the deal was called off. Also in June 2001, the company stopped using the iMark technology for surplus markets, and wrote off the entire investment, further damaging its earnings by taking a $204 million impairment of goodwill write-down.

Strategic Analysis — Competition In the marketspace for electronic online markets, there are low barriers to entry, many alternative substitute mechanisms, and great customer power, given that the customers tend to be Global 2000 established firms. In the exchange arena, FreeMarkets competes directly with PurchasePro, CommerceOne, and industry vertical markets such as E-Steel and GE Polymer. In January 2000, General Motors terminated its agreement with FreeMarkets and instead signed up with rival CommerceOne, which was chosen as a key participant in the industry consortium Covisint. In this instance, FreeMarkets lost out to the much larger CommerceOne because it lacked expertise in supply chain management and collaborative commerce.

In the E-commerce I period, thousands of start-up, venture-capital-backed firms offering exchanges appeared around the world. Many of these firms offered services before they had systems in place. The technology for creating exchanges is widely available and inexpensive, although the skilled programmers and systems engineers required to operate such exchanges are not inexpensive.

Large firms have many alternatives to the use of exchanges. Large firms can and often do build their own marketplaces (private industrial networks) or they can participate in industry consortia such as Covisint. Some firms are extending the capabilities of their EDI systems to Web-enabled EDI-based systems that fit seamlessly with backend legacy systems.

Yet FreeMarkets' advantage is also clear: It is totally hosted by FreeMarkets, and this reduces the costs of implementation for customers. Essentially, to take advantage of FreeMarkets' market-making technology requires only a mouse and a browser-enabled PC. No extensive business process changes are required, and no expensive implementation technology team is required.

Strategic Analysis — Technology FreeMarkets' technology consists primarily of its trading software called BidWare. BidWare was designed for high-value, online bidding in complex market situations where there are many variables. One of the challenges exchange designers face is building into the system some semblance of the complexity often found in face-to-face real-world purchasing decisions. For instance, a purchasing agent must consider multiple currencies, multiple country origins of shipments and financing, multiyear contracts, and differing quality standards. FreeMarkets' BidWare software has attempted to support these contingencies by enabling:

- *Transformation bidding* — Allows traders to make direct price comparisons of similar products with unique attributes (such as coal from different mines with different amounts of sulfur content).
- *Multicurrency bidding* — Allows customers and suppliers to conduct bidding in the currency of their choice, and to monitor bids in multiple currencies, all pegged to the real-time price of each currency.
- *Index bidding* — Allows customers to index their trading prices for volatile commodities against the price of known commodities (such as agricultural or oil futures).
- *Net present value bidding* — Allows customers to evaluate proposals that have varying prices over time.

These features of BidWare, while powerful, are also available from several competitors. On the other hand, other competitors such as CommerceOne do not offer a completely hosted product.

Strategic Analysis — Social and Legal Challenges FreeMarkets is currently facing several lawsuits alleging securities fraud. Some of these lawsuits result from a Securities and Exchange Commission order requiring the company to restate its 2000 earnings. Others allege improprieties in FreeMarkets' 1999 initial public offering. Specifically, the complaints allege that the underwriters in the IPO received excessive compensation and entered into unlawful agreements with their clients pursuant to which their clients agreed to purchase shares of the common stock in the after-market for the purpose of artificially inflating the price of the shares. The company and several of its officers are named in these complaints.

Future Prospects FreeMarkets faces a number of significant challenges to its survival as an independent company. It faces many competitors in the stagnant exchange space and must find ways in the near future to enter the more lucrative and faster growing areas of private industrial networks, where the focus is less on price and more on cooperating closely with a small group of suppliers. This is a significant mind-set and core competency change that FreeMarkets may find difficult to pursue. In this effort, the failed deal with Adexa resulting from declining stock market values of FreeMarkets does not bode well. Management needs to move quickly into those areas of B2B e-commerce that are expanding, but with a depressed stock price, it will not be able to acquire companies with those competencies.

INDUSTRY CONSORTIA

industry consortia
industry-owned vertical markets that enable buyers to purchase direct inputs (both goods and services) from a limited set of invited participants

Industry consortia are industry-owned vertical markets that enable buyers to purchase direct inputs (both goods and services) from a limited set of invited participants (see Figure 12.16). Industry consortia emphasize long-term contractual purchasing and the development of stable relationships (as opposed to merely an anonymous transaction emphasis). Industry consortia are more focused on optimizing supply chain relationships than exchanges, which tend to focus more on transaction cost. The ultimate objective of industry consortia is unification of supply chains within entire industries through a common network and computing platform. This objective is considerably broader than that of exchanges and constitutes the main thrust of B2B evolution for the foreseeable future. Ironically, but not unlike what we have observed in the B2C markets, this leading vision is being developed by established bricks-and-mortar Fortune 1000 firms and not visionary entrepreneurial start-ups that were involved in the development of exchanges.

Industry consortia sprang up in 1999 and 2000 in part as a reaction to the earlier development of independently owned exchanges, which were viewed by large industries (such as the automotive and chemical industries) as market interlopers who would not directly serve the interests of large buyers, but would instead line their own pockets. Rather than pay-to-play, large firms decided to pay-to-own their markets. Another concern of large firms was that Net marketplaces would work only if large suppliers and buyers participated, and only if there was liquidity. Independent exchanges were not attracting enough players to achieve liquidity. In addition,

---

FIGURE 12.16 | **INDUSTRY CONSORTIA**

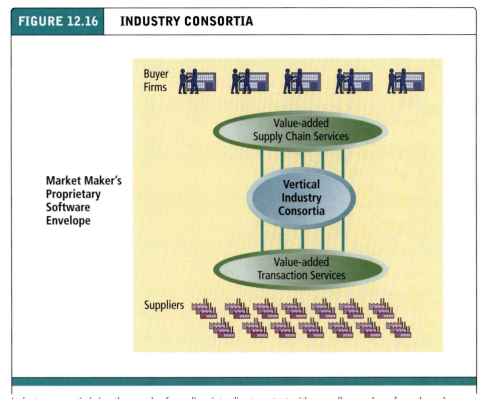

Industry consortia bring thousands of suppliers into direct contact with a smaller number of very large buyers. The market makers provide value-added software services for procurement, transaction management, shipping and payment for both buyers and suppliers. Industry consortia are sometimes referred to as *many-to-few* markets, where many suppliers (albeit selected by the buyers) serve a few very large buyers, mediated by a variety of value-added services.

---

exchanges often failed to provide additional value-added services that would transform the value chain for the entire industry, including linking the new marketplaces to firms' ERP systems.

More than 60 industry consortia now exist, with many industries having more than one (see Table 12.6). The industries with the most consortia are metals, chemicals, and retail, although these are not necessarily the largest consortia in terms of revenue. Many very large firms are equity funders of several industry consortia. For instance, Cargill — the world's largest private corporation — invested in six consortia that exist at various points in Cargill's and the food industry's tangled value chain.

Industry consortia make money in a number of ways. Industry members usually pay for the creation of the site and contribute initial operating capital. Then industry

TABLE 12.6	INDUSTRY CONSORTIA BY INDUSTRY (NOVEMBER 2000)
INDUSTRY	**NAME OF INDUSTRY CONSORTIA**
Aerospace	Aeroxchangewww.find; Cordiem.com; Exostar.com
Agriculture	Rooster.com
Automotive	Covisint.com; SupplyOn.com
Chemical	AllianceChem.com; Elemica.com; ChemConnect.com; RubberNetwork.com; ElastomerSolutions.com; Omnexus.com
Computers, Consumer Electronics, and Telecommunications	e2open.com; eHITEX.com
Construction	Mercadium.com
Consumer Products	RetailersMarketXchange (rmx.com); Transora.com; GlobalNetXchange (gnx.com); WorldWideRetailExchange.com; UCCnet.com
Energy and Utilities	Pantellos.com; Enporion.com
Engineering	ec4ec.com
Financial	MuniCenter.com
Food	CPGmarket.com; Dairy.com; Electronic Foodservice Network (eFSNetwork.com); FSXchange.com
Hospitality	Avendra.com
Legal	LawCommerce.com
Medical Services, Supplies	Global Healthcare Exchange (ghx.com); HealthNexis.com
Metals and Mining	WorldMetal.com; The Global Steel Exchange (gsx.com)
MRO	CorProcure.com
Manufacturing	ManufacturingCentral.com
Oils and Metals (Trading)	IntercontinentalExchange.com
Paper and Forest Products	ForestExpress.com
Petroleum	Trade-Ranger.com; Pepex.com
Real Estate	ConstellationRealTechnologies.com
Shipping	LevelSeas.com; OceanConnect.com
Textiles	TheSeam.com (Cotton Consortium)
Transportation	Transplace.com

SOURCE: Jupiter Media Metrix, 2000b; www.nmm.com,2001.

consortia charge the large buyer firms transaction and subscription fees. Industry members are expected to reap benefits far greater than their contributions through the rationalization of the procurement process, competition among vendors, and closer relationships with vendors.

Industry consortia offer many different pricing mechanisms, ranging from auctions to fixed prices to RFQs, depending on the products and the situation (see Figure 12.17). Prices can also be negotiated, and the environment, while competitive, is nevertheless restricted to a smaller number of buyer-selected, reliable, and long-term suppliers who are often viewed as "strategic industry" partners. The bias of industry consortia is clearly toward the large buyers who control access to this lucrative market channel and can benefit from competitive pricing offered by alternative suppliers. Benefits to suppliers come from access to large buyer firm procurement systems, long-term stable relationships, and large order sizes.

Industry consortia can and often do force suppliers to use the consortia's networks and proprietary software as a condition of selling to the industry's members. Although exchanges failed for a lack of suppliers and liquidity, the market power of consortia members ensures suppliers will participate and consortia can avoid the fate of voluntary exchanges. Clearly industry consortia are at an advantage when compared to exchanges because, unlike the venture-capital-backed exchanges, they have deep-pocket financial backing from the very start and guaranteed liquidity based on a steady flow of large firm orders. Yet industry consortia are a new phenomenon, and

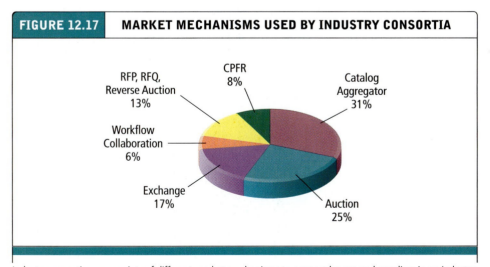

FIGURE 12.17 | **MARKET MECHANISMS USED BY INDUSTRY CONSORTIA**

Industry consortia use a variety of different market mechanisms to connect buyers and suppliers in an industry supply chain.

SOURCE: Jupiter Media Metrix, 2000b.

the long-term profitability of these consortia, especially when several consortia exist for a single industry, has yet to be demonstrated.

THE LONG-TERM DYNAMICS OF NET MARKETPLACES

Net marketplaces are changing rapidly because of the failures of early exchanges and a growing realization by key participants that real value will derive from B2B e-commerce only when it can change the entire procurement system, the supply chain, and the process of collaboration among firms.

Figure 12.18 depicts some of these changes. Pure Net marketplace exchanges are moving away from the simple "electronic marketplace" vision, and toward playing a more central role in changing the procurement process. Exchanges are ideal buy-out candidates for industry consortia because they have often developed the technology infrastructure. In any event, consortia and exchanges are beginning to work together in selected markets. Likewise, e-distributors are securing admission to large e-procurement systems and also seeking admission to industry consortia as suppliers of indirect goods.

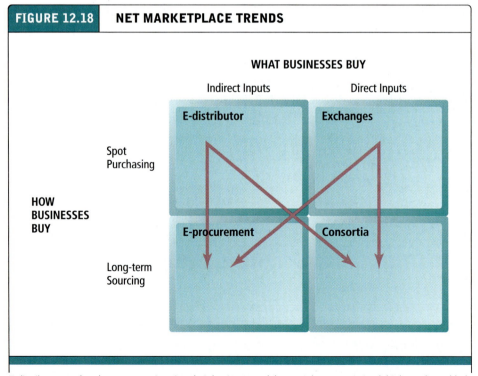

| FIGURE 12.18 | NET MARKETPLACE TRENDS |

E-distributors and exchanges are migrating their business models toward more sustained, higher value-added relationships with buyer firms by providing e-procurement services and participating in industry consortia.

Other notable trends include the movement from simple transactions involving spot purchasing to longer-term contractual relationships involving both indirect and direct goods (Wise and Morrison, 2000). The complexity and duration of transactions is increasing, and both buyers and suppliers are becoming accustomed to working in a digital environment, and making less use of the fax machine and telephone (Mott, 2001).

To date, Net marketplaces, as well as private industrial networks, have emerged in a political climate friendly to large-scale cooperation among very large firms. However, the possibility exists that Net marketplaces may provide some firms with an ideal platform to collude on pricing, market sharing, and market access, all of which would be anti-competitive and reduce the efficiency of the marketplace. *Insight on Society: Are Net Marketplaces Anti-Competitive?* considers the anti-competitive possibilities inherent in Net marketplaces.

12.3 PRIVATE INDUSTRIAL NETWORKS

Private industrial networks today form the largest part of B2B e-commerce, both on and off the Internet. AMR Research, a B2B research firm, estimates that as much as 75% of B2B expenditures by large firms in the next two years will be for the development of private industrial networks (Feuerstein, 2000).

WHAT ARE PRIVATE INDUSTRIAL NETWORKS?

As noted at the beginning of this chapter, private industrial networks are direct descendants of existing EDI networks, and they are closely tied to existing enterprise resource planning systems used by large firms. Private industrial networks (PINs) are Web-enabled networks for the coordination of trans-organizational business processes (sometimes also called *collaborative commerce*). A **trans-organizational business process** requires at least two independent firms to perform (Laudon and Laudon, 2002). For the most part, these networks originate in and closely involve the manufacturing and related support industries, and therefore we refer to them as "industrial" networks, although in the future they could just as easily apply to some services. These networks can be industry-wide, but often begin and sometimes focus on the voluntary coordination of a group of supplying firms centered about a single, very large firm. Private industrial networks can be viewed as "extended enterprises" in the sense that they often begin as enterprise resource planning systems in a single firm, and are then expanded to include (often using an extranet) the firm's major suppliers. Figure 12.19 illustrates a private industrial network originally built by Proctor & Gamble (P&G) in the United States to coordinate supply chains among its suppliers, distributors, truckers, and retailers.

trans-organizational business process
process that requires at least two independent firms to perform

ARE NET MARKETPLACES ANTICOMPETITIVE?

Although Net marketplaces and private industrial networks often lead to extraordinary gains in efficiency for both firms and industries as a whole, they also provide some equally powerful tools for reducing competition in the marketplace and driving up prices to consumers, and even reducing variety in the marketplace as well. There are two types of antitrust concerns: the market for goods and the market for B2B marketplaces themselves.

In the market for goods, the primary antitrust concerns are information sharing, monopsony, and exclusion. For instance, in a Net marketplace owned by large industry players (such as Covisint), owner-members could collude with one another on the prices they are willing to pay for inputs. Information sharing may also lead to market-sharing agreements in which manufacturers divide the market into segments and agree to produce only enough for their allocated segment. In a monopsony, buyers have so much power that they can control input prices by buying less of an input. Net marketplaces could be used to coordinate the reduction of purchases, forcing prices of suppliers below competitive levels. Net marketplaces owned by large industry players could be used to exclude rival competitive firms, forcing their rivals to pay higher prices for inputs.

In the market for Net marketplaces, a very large Net marketplace formed by buyers or sellers could prevent other entrepreneurial market-makers from starting up because of the high switching costs involved and the network effects of large markets. For instance, if Covisint succeeds, it may be the only Net marketplace for the automobile industry that large buyers use, and this by itself would become a monopoly. Such Net marketplaces may devise rules that specifically proscribe the members from purchasing in any other markets. Moreover, once a Net marketplace attracts, say, 90% of the buyers and sellers in a marketspace, it experiences powerful network effects and resulting high levels of liquidity; it becomes, in essence, the only marketplace with a sufficient number of buyers and sellers to support trading systematically.

Even though the technology of B2B markets is new, the antitrust issues and concepts are not. Information sharing among competitors, monopsony, and exclusion from necessary facilities are issues that have arisen in the context of airline reservation systems, railroad terminal facilities, and film distribution by the motion picture industry. There are Justice Department rules (Competitor Collaboration Guidelines) that describe permissible information sharing among competitors, and a large body of case law and scholarship that has developed principles for determining when collaboration among competing firms becomes illegal. In general, courts and scholars have sought to proscribe any behavior that would harm competition in the marketplace. A wide variety of behaviors are tolerated by courts up until the point where the consequences are harmful to competitors or to competition in general, and ultimately to the consumer or buyers who are forced to pay higher prices.

In a recent report on competition in B2B markets, the Federal Trade Commission concluded that no action was needed now to ensure B2B markets remained competitive. The FTC is, however, closely monitoring the behavior of large Net marketplaces, as well as the trading that occurs within them, for signs of collusion, monopsony power, and exclusionary behavior that might harm competition.

SOURCES: "Let It Be," *Wall Street Journal*, August 14, 2001; "Case Studies for Federal Trade Commission Public Workshop on Emerging Issues for Competition Policy in the World of E-Commerce," Federal Trade Commission, May 7, 2001; "Evaluating the Antitrust Risks of the Internet Entwined Business," by Shawn Potter, *West Virginia Journal of Law and Technology*, May 4, 2001; "Entering the 21st Century: Competition Policy in the World of B2B Marketplaces," Federal Trade Commission ,October 2000.

In Proctor & Gamble's private industrial network shown in Figure 12.19, customer sales are captured at the cash register, which then initiates a flow of information back to distributors, P&G, and its suppliers. This tells P&G and its suppliers the exact level of demand for thousands of products. This information is then used to initiate production, supply, and transportation to replenish products at the distributors and retailers. This process is called an *efficient customer response system* (a *demand-pull*

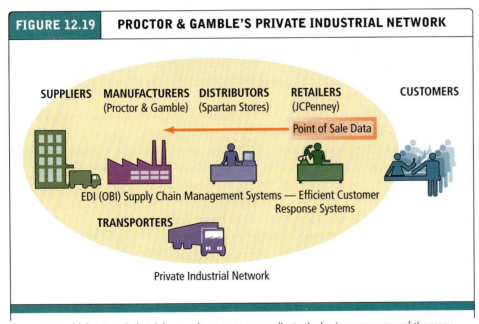

FIGURE 12.19   **PROCTOR & GAMBLE'S PRIVATE INDUSTRIAL NETWORK**

Proctor & Gamble's private industrial network attempts to coordinate the business processes of the many firms it deals with in the consumer products industry.

production model), and it relies on an equally efficient supply chain management system to coordinate the supply side.

CHARACTERISTICS OF PRIVATE INDUSTRIAL NETWORKS

The central focus of private industrial networks is to provide an industry-wide global solution to achieve the highest levels of efficiency. This effort extends far beyond the individual firm, even beyond an enterprise-sized Fortune 500 firm. The specific objectives of a private industrial network include:

- Developing efficient purchase and selling business processes industry-wide,
- Developing industry-wide resource planning to supplement enterprise-wide resource planning,
- Creating increasing supply chain visibility — knowing the inventory levels of buyers and suppliers,
- Achieving closer buyer–supplier relationships, including demand forecasting, communications, and conflict resolution,
- Operating on a global scale — globalization, and
- Reducing industry risk by preventing imbalances of supply and demand, including developing financial derivatives, insurance, and futures markets.

Private industrial networks serve different goals from the Net marketplaces described in the previous section. Net marketplaces are primarily transaction-oriented, whereas private industrial networks focus on continuous business process coordination between companies. This can include much more than simply supply chain management, such as product design, sourcing, demand forecasting, asset management, sales, and marketing. Private industrial networks do support transactions, but that is not their primary focus.

Private industrial networks usually focus on a single sponsoring company that "owns" the network, sets the rules, establishes governance (a structure of authority, rule enforcement, and control), and invites firms to participate at its sole discretion. Therefore, these networks are "private." This sets them apart from industry consortia, which are usually owned by major firms collectively through equity participation. Whereas Net marketplaces have a strong focus on indirect goods and services, private industrial networks focus on strategic, direct goods and services.

For instance, Ace Hardware, a cooperative of 5,100 retail hardware stores, uses a private industrial network to manage inventory levels and collaborate with suppliers by linking 14 Ace distribution centers and 9 key suppliers. In the past, a team of 30 Ace procurement managers would use faxes, phones, and an older EDI system to buy products for retail members. It took 7 to 10 days to process an order. Suppliers had no access to inventory levels in either retail stores or Ace distribution centers, forcing them to guess their likely production requirements. Manco, one large supplier of Ace, now uses the Internet-based private industrial network to accurately gauge demand for more than 200 products, from duct tape to shelf liners, that it supplies Ace. The more streamlined ordering process has allowed Manco to reduce distribution costs by 28% and freight costs by 18% (Harris, 2001).

Perhaps no single firm better illustrates the benefits of developing private industrial networks than Wal-Mart, described in *Insight on Business: Wal-Mart Transitions Toward a Private Industrial Network.*

PRIVATE INDUSTRIAL NETWORKS AND COLLABORATIVE COMMERCE

Private industrial networks can do much more than just serve a supply chain and efficient customer response system. They can also include other activities of a single large manufacturing firm, including design of products and engineering diagrams, as well as marketing plans and demand forecasting. Collaboration among businesses can take many forms and involve a wide range of activities — from simple supply chain management to coordinating market feedback to designers at supply firms (see Figure 12.20).

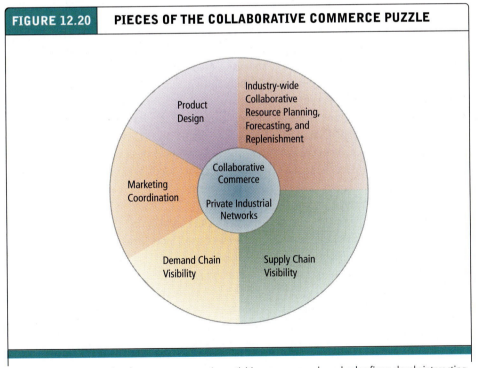

FIGURE 12.20   PIECES OF THE COLLABORATIVE COMMERCE PUZZLE

Collaborative commerce involves many cooperative activities among supply and sales firms closely interacting with a single large firm through a private industrial network.

INSIGHT ON BUSINESS

WAL-MART TRANSITIONS TOWARD A PRIVATE INDUSTRIAL NETWORK

Wal-Mart is a well-known leader in the application of network technology to the coordination of its supply chain. With sales of more than $191 billion in 2000 generated through its 4,189 locations worldwide, Wal-Mart has been able to use information technology to achieve a decisive cost advantage over competitors.

In the late 1980s, Wal-Mart developed the beginnings of collaborative commerce using an EDI-based supply chain management system that required its large suppliers to use Wal-Mart's proprietary EDI network to respond to orders from Wal-Mart purchasing managers. In 1991, Wal-Mart expanded the capabilities of its EDI-based network by introducing Retail Link. This system connected Wal-Mart's largest suppliers to Wal-Mart's own inventory management system, and it required large suppliers to track actual sales by stores and to replenish supplies as dictated by demand and following rules imposed by Wal-Mart. Wal-Mart also introduced financial payment systems that ensure that Wal-Mart does not own the goods until they arrive and are shelved.

In 1997, Wal-Mart moved Retail Link to an extranet that allowed suppliers to directly link over the Internet into Wal-Mart's inventory management system. In 2000, Wal-Mart hired an outside firm to upgrade Retail Link from being a supply chain management tool toward a more collaborative forecasting, planning, and replenishment system. Using demand aggregation software provided by Atlas Metaprise Software, Wal-Mart purchase agents can now aggregate demand from Wal-Mart's 4,189 separate stores into a single RFQ (request for quote) from suppliers. This gives Wal-Mart tremendous clout with even the largest suppliers. Wal-Mart and Atlas plan to first build a global sourcing network. Currently, Wal-Mart's 1,500 foreign location buyers rely on a mix of telephones, fax, and e-mail to communicate their spending forecasts. The new system will allow them to submit forecasts via the Internet. Wal-Mart headquarters in turn will issue worldwide RFQs for all stores. The Atlas software helps Wal-Mart purchasing agents select a winning bid and negotiate final contracts.

In addition, suppliers can now immediately access information on inventories, purchase orders, invoice status, and sales forecasts, based on 104 weeks of online, real-time, item-level data. The system now does not require smaller supplier firms to adopt expensive EDI software solutions. Instead, they can use standard browsers and PCs loaded with free software from Wal-Mart. Wal-Mart now has over 8,000 suppliers—small and large—participating in its network.

Wal-Mart's success has spurred its retail competitors to develop industry consortia—WorldWide Retail Exchange, GlobalNetXchange and Transora—in an effort to duplicate the success of Wal-Mart. For its part, Wal-Mart execu-

tives have said they would not join these consortia or an independent exchange because it would only help their competitors achieve what they have already accomplished with Retail Link.

SOURCES: "Atlas Shoulders The Private Exchange Load," by Norbert Turek, *Informationweek.com*, March 26, 2001; "Supplying Demand," by Mike Cleary, *Inter@ctive Week*, October 25, 2000; "Private E-Hubs vs. Public Exchanges: Wal-Mart Strengthens its e-Fortress," by Juhair Kashmeri, *eBizChronicle.com*, October 17, 2000; "Wal-Mart to Build Private Net Marketplace," by Adam Feuerstein *Upside Today*, October 16, 2000.

One form of collaboration — and perhaps the most profound — is industry-wide **collaborative resource planning, forecasting, and replenishment (CPFR)**, which involves working with network members to forecast demand, develop production plans, and coordinate shipping, warehousing, and stocking activities to ensure retail and wholesale shelf space is replenished with just the right amount of goods. If this goal is achieved, hundreds of millions of dollars of excess inventory and capacity could be wrung out of an industry. This activity alone is likely to produce the largest benefits and justify the cost of developing private industrial networks.

A second area of collaboration is *demand chain visibility*. In the past, it was impossible to know where excess capacity or supplies existed in the supply and distribution chains. For instance, retailers might have significantly overstocked shelves, but suppliers and manufacturers — not knowing this — might be building excess capacity or supplies for even more production. These excess inventories would raise costs for the entire industry and create extraordinary pressures to discount merchandise, reducing profits for everyone.

A third area of collaboration is *marketing coordination and product design*. Manufacturers that use or produce highly engineered parts use private industrial networks to coordinate both their internal design and marketing activities, as well as related activities of their supply and distribution chain partners. By involving their suppliers in product design and marketing initiatives, manufacturing firms can ensure that the parts produced actually fulfill the claims of marketers. On the reverse flow, feedback from customers can be used by marketers to speak directly to product designers at the firm and its suppliers. For the first time, "closed loop marketing" — customer feedback directly impacting design and production — described in Chapter 7 — can become a reality.

DaimlerChrysler, for instance, developed a collaborative commerce application called Chrysler Corporation Supply Partner Information Network (SPIN) for its 20,000 suppliers. SPIN is an intranet-based supply chain management and support system that permits 12,000 supplier employees at 3,500 locations around the world to access Chrysler's real-time procurement, inventory and demand forecasting systems, as well as longer-term strategy applications. Chrysler's Part Quality Supply System operating

collaborative resource planning, forecasting, and replenishment (CPFR)
involves working with network members to forecast demand, develop production plans, and to coordinate shipping, warehousing, and stocking activities to ensure retail and wholesale shelf space is replenished with just the right amount of goods

within SPIN tracks all production parts from supplier to shipper, factory installation, and after-market replacement. Chrysler estimates it has increased productivity of its entire "extended enterprise" family of suppliers by 20% (IBM, 2001).

IMPLEMENTATION BARRIERS

Although private industrial networks represent a large part of the future of B2B, there are many barriers to its complete implementation (Watson and Fenner, 2000). Participating firms are required to share sensitive data with their business partners, up and down the supply chain. What in the past was considered proprietary and secret must now be shared. In a digital environment, it can be difficult to control the limits of information sharing. Information a firm gives gladly to its largest customer may end up being shared with its closest competitor.

Integrating private industrial networks into existing ERP systems and EDI networks poses a significant investment of time and money. Most ERP systems were not designed initially to work as extranets, or even to be very Internet-friendly. Most ERP systems are based on models of business processes that are entirely internal to the firm.

Adopting private industrial networks also requires a change in mind-set and behavior for employees. Essentially, employees must shift their loyalties from the firm to the wider trans-organizational enterprise and recognize that their fate is intertwined with the fate of their suppliers and distributors. Suppliers in turn are required to change how they manage and allocate their resources because their own production is tightly coupled with the demands of their private industrial network partners. All participants in the supply and distribution chains, with the exception of the large network owner, lose some of their independence, and must initiate large behavioral change programs in order to participate (Laudon, 2000).

INDUSTRY-WIDE PRIVATE INDUSTRIAL NETWORKS

Single-firm networks can be so successful that they become adopted by the entire industry, and they can be used also to coordinate activities among firms in different industries altogether. For instance, the P&G system described above was so successful that P&G sold the software to IBM, which then re-sold the system to the entire consumer products industry in the United States. P&G believed that only by changing the entire industry of supply, procurement, and distribution could it achieve its goals of efficiency and effectiveness. Figure 12.21 illustrates an industry-wide private industrial network.

In the future, barring intervention by antitrust enforcers, we can expect many private industrial networks to expand into much larger industry-wide networks seeking to coordinate all the thousands of key players in vertical industries.

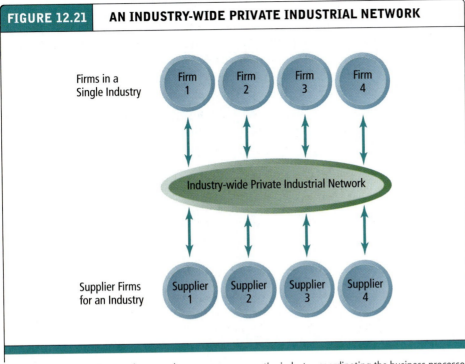

FIGURE 12.21 — **AN INDUSTRY-WIDE PRIVATE INDUSTRIAL NETWORK**

Firms in a Single Industry — Firm 1, Firm 2, Firm 3, Firm 4

Industry-wide Private Industrial Network

Supplier Firms for an Industry — Supplier 1, Supplier 2, Supplier 3, Supplier 4

Some private industrial networks expand to encompass an entire industry, coordinating the business processes for suppliers, transporters, production firms, and ultimately distributors and retailers.

THE LONG-TERM DYNAMICS OF PRIVATE INDUSTRIAL NETWORKS

It is apparent that as large firms become more accustomed to working closely with both their supply chain partners and their distributors on the demand side, they will seek to push the boundaries of their networks to extend across the industry as a whole, to other industries, and to elaborate new roles for themselves and others. For instance, the computer manufacturer Hewlett Packard discovered through its private industrial network that resin manufacturers were charging higher prices for resins they shipped to the molding manufacturers who make the plastic cases for HP computers. The molding manufacturers historically are very slow in paying their bills, and as a result their resin suppliers raised their prices. HP moved in as a market-maker and purchased resins from the suppliers at a market price, then re-sold at market to the molders. HP has more clout to collect from the molders than resin manufacturers (Turek and Gilbert, 2001). In the next five years, we may see that individual large firms will be able to intervene in global supply relationships in order to overcome bottlenecks that otherwise would be hidden from manufacturers.

In an effort to collaborate with firms in other industries, corporate giants such as Agilent, Coca-Cola, General Mills, Kellogg's, Land O'Lakes, and Monsanto have teamed up to form a new company called Nistevo, in Eden Prairie, Minnesota. This new company is intended to be a "trans-industry" system. Nistevo will coordinate the excess shipping capacity of community members in many different industries through a private industrial network. The system will attempt to bring underutilized shipping assets such as container trucks and railroad cars to nearly 100% utilization and cut out as much as 12% of logistics spending by the companies involved (Schwartz, 2001).

12.4   CASE STUDY

Siemens Clicks
with Click2procure

Siemens spent $871 million building its e-procurement system called click2procure, using technology provided by CommerceOne and SAP, the Austrian manufacturer of the widely adopted ERP system. Click2procure is poised to become one of the world's largest virtual buy-side private Net marketplaces.

Siemens is a German electrical engineering and electronics giant with 460,000 employees in 220 countries and revenues of $75 billion, making it the 21st biggest company in the world. This multinational conglomerate is a leading manufacturer of automation and control systems, communications, lighting, medical, semi-conductors, power, and transportation products and services.

Click2procure is used today by 3,000 professional buyers and 30,000 employees. Siemens purchases $29.3 billion a year in direct and indirect goods. Currently, click2procure has over 3,000 suppliers who pay a subscription fee of $2,500 a year for the opportunity to sell goods to Siemens. Siemens estimates that it has reduced the cost of a purchase transaction by 75% (from an average of $100 per purchase order, down to $25), and the cost of direct goods by 10% to 20%. Siemens hopes to be able to save nearly $1 billion per year by using click2procure.

Click2procure is a part of Siemens' efforts to put its entire business online by 2005. Powered by CommerceOne's MarketSite operating environment, click2procure provides a private, Web-based platform for standardizing and automating purchasing activities. The system also provides sourcing, procurement, and supply chain management services to outside firms through a separate business called Siemens Procurement and Logistics Services (SPLS) LLC, a separate business unit set up for the purpose of developing click2procure as a profit center. Siemens is leveraging the enormous cost of click2procure by selling the same capabilities to outside businesses.

Prior to SPLS and click2procure, each of Siemens' business units around the globe did its own purchasing and followed its own rules. This bloated the supply base to 5,000 separate suppliers for MRO goods alone — about $10 billion worth of products. The decentralized purchasing system meant that Siemens could not aggregate orders across all business units to obtain better prices, and a significant amount of maverick purchasing occurred. Generally, maverick purchasing results in higher costs. Under the old system, 50,000 indirect purchases per month cost about $100 each to process, and there was no central review of the prices paid for products.

Siemens wanted to centralize control over global purchasing into a single unit — SPLS. It wanted to build a solution with the following five characteristics:

- *Global reach* — supporting procurement in over 90 countries.

- *Effective catalog management* — providing the ability to aggregate and manage catalogs from hundreds of suppliers.

- *Web-based search engine* — providing the ability to compare prices from multiple suppliers.

- *Rules-based and approval tracking* — providing the ability to impose its own business rules on purchasing based on the type of product and the ability to track the approval process.

- *Integration with legacy systems* — providing a software solution that would easily integrate with a diverse range of legacy and ERP systems already in place.

Guided by these criteria, Siemens opted for CommerceOne's package Net Market Maker Solution. Net MarketMaker Solution leverages CommerceOne.net, a Web-based Net marketplace operated by CommerceOne. CommerceOne.net provides catalog management and transaction processing capabilities. In addition, CommerceOne.net provides access to catalog management, transaction processing, and business services such as auctions and electronic requests for quotes: e-RFQs (see Figure 12.22). Using CommerceOne's packaged solution allowed Siemens to develop its own "private" click2procure version in only four months! A system of this magnitude would have required three to five years if Siemens had chosen to build the system itself.

SPLS is the general contractor of the click2procure service. SPLS aggregates purchases from all Siemens buyers to negotiate better prices from suppliers. SPLS also works with buyer firms — both Siemens business units and other firms who use Siemens' system — to integrate click2procure with back-office legacy systems. This increases the switching costs for users who might want to use a different exchange.

FIGURE 12.22   SIEMENS' CLICK2PROCURE PRIVATE NET MARKETPLACE

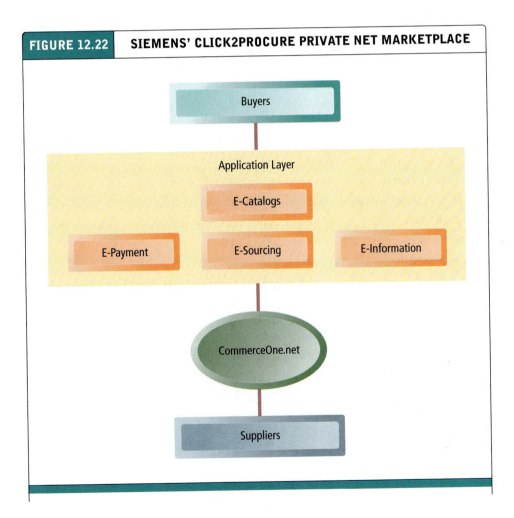

SPLS issues a single monthly invoice to business units, reflecting items purchased, tax, and freight charges. SPLS charges buyers either a flat fee per transaction, or takes a percentage of the discount it negotiates with suppliers.

For suppliers, click2procure automates the invoicing and payment process, ensuring that suppliers get paid rapidly. In the past, receiving payment for supplies could take months as invoices wended their way through a number of differing accounts payable systems at local and global levels. SPLS issues a single check to suppliers monthly for all orders processed through click2procure. In addition, suppliers gain access to click2procure's rapidly expanding network of buyers and potentially huge aggregated orders. For instance, whereas in the past, Siemens business units would buy PC computers from many different sources, by aggregating orders from all its business units, SPLC was able to purchase $30 million worth of PCs from a single vendor, Dell Computer, up from $2 million in previous years.

In the future, SPLS intends to market click2procure to other businesses as a "master distributor" for indirect and direct goods. Since it started in 2000, Siemens has recorded $1.5 billion in sales for businesses other than Siemens. In this future vision, SPLS will make its supplier base available to other firms directly, or through the Global Trading Web, a network of interoperable regional, vertical private Net marketplaces that run on CommerceOne's systems.

SPLS reports a number of significant benefits from click2procure for Siemens:

- 10% reduction in prices paid for goods,
- 75% reduction in administrative costs, bringing purchase order cost down to $25,
- 60% reduction in ordering lifecycles, from over eight days down to 48 hours,
- Significant reduction in accounts payable staff now that bills are paid on time,
- Enhanced inventory and asset utilization, and
- Improved demand planning and forecasting.

Despite these benefits, many business units at Siemens have resisted joining. In some cases, favorite local suppliers are not included in the marketplace. Local units have to give up their own purchasing process and forms, and completely change their procurement business procedures. Local units lose the ability to negotiate most favored terms, passing this activity on to central buyers who may not understand local requirements. For instance, local business units may want PCs with special monitors, processors, and disk drives, and they may not want to participate in a globally centralized order for the "standard" PC.

SOURCES: www.click2procure.com; "Siemens Launches E-Procurement at Full Throttle," by Ned Stafford, *CRM Daily*, August 31, 2001; "Siemens' Private Marketplace Turns Procurement in Profit Center," Aberdeen Group, 2001.

Case Study Questions

1. What would happen to Siemens if CommerceOne went out of business? What steps would you take as a manager to prepare for this possibility?

2. If you were the manager of a Siemens local business unit, what are some of the disadvantages for your local unit of moving toward the click2procure system?

3. If you were a manager of a manufacturing firm considering joining click2procure, what are some of the concerns you might have about tightly integrating click2procure with your back-end legacy ERP systems? What recommendations would you make to your senior management on how to address your concerns?

12.5 REVIEW

KEY CONCEPTS

■ Define B2B commerce and understand its scope and history.

Before the Internet, business-to-business transactions were referred to simply as *trade* or the *procurement process*. Today, we use the term *B2B commerce* to describe all types of computer-assisted inter-firm trade, and the term *Internet-based B2B commerce* or *B2B e-commerce* to describe specifically that portion of B2B commerce that uses the Internet to assist firms in buying and selling a variety of goods to each other. The process of conducting trade among businesses consumes many business resources, including the time spent by employees processing orders, making and approving purchasing decisions, searching for products, and arranging for their purchase, shipment, receipt, and payment. Across the economy, this amounts to trillions of dollars spent annually on procurement processes. If a significant portion of this inter-firm trade could be automated and parts of the procurement process assisted by the Internet, millions or even trillions of dollars could be freed up for other uses, resulting in increased productivity and increased national economic wealth.

In order to understand the history of B2B commerce, you must understand several key stages including:

- *Automated order entry systems*, developed in the 1970s, used the telephone to send digital orders to companies. Telephone modems were placed in the offices of the customers for a particular business. This enabled procurement managers to directly access the firm's inventory database to automatically reorder products.
- *EDI or electronic data interchange*, developed in the late 1970s, is a communications standard for sharing various procurement documents including invoices, purchase orders, shipping bills, product stocking numbers (SKUs) and settlement information for an industry. It was developed to reduce the costs, delays, and errors inherent in the manual exchange of documents.
- *Electronic storefronts* emerged in the 1990s along with the commercialization of the Internet. They are online catalogs containing the products that are made available to the general public by a single vendor.

- *Net marketplaces* emerged in the late 1990s as a natural extension and scaling up of the electronic storefront. The essential characteristic of all Net marketplaces is that they bring hundreds of suppliers, each with its own electronic catalog, together with potentially thousands of purchasing firms to form a single Internet-based marketplace.
- *Private industrial networks* also emerged in the late 1990s with the commercialization of the Internet as natural extensions of EDI systems and the existing close relationships that developed between large industrial firms and their suppliers.

Before you can understand each of the different types of Net marketplaces, you must be familiar with several other key concepts including:

- *Seller-side solutions* are owned by the suppliers of goods and are seller-biased markets that only display goods from a single seller. Customers benefit because these systems reduce the costs of inventory replenishment and are paid for by and large by the suppliers. Automated order entry systems are seller-side solutions.
- *Buyer-side solutions* are owned by the buyers of goods and are buyer-biased markets because they reduce procurement costs for the buyer. Sellers also benefit because the cost of serving a company's customers is reduced. EDI systems are buyer-side solutions.
- *Vertical markets* provide expertise and products targeted to a specific industry. EDI systems usually serve vertical markets.
- *Horizontal markets* serve a myriad of different industries. Electronic storefronts are an example of a horizontal market in that they tend to carry a wide variety of products that are useful to any number of different industries.

■ **Understand the procurement process, the supply chain, and collaborative commerce.**

- *The procurement process* refers to the way business firms purchase the goods they need in order to produce the goods they will ultimately sell to consumers. Firms purchase goods from a set of suppliers who in turn purchase their inputs from a set of suppliers. These firms are linked in a series of connected transactions.
- *The supply chain* is the series of transactions that links sets of firms that do business with each other. It includes not only the firms themselves but also the relationships between them and the processes that connect them.

There are seven steps in the procurement process.
- searching for suppliers for specific products;
- qualifying the sellers and the products they sell;
- negotiating prices, credit terms, escrow requirements, and quality requirements;
- scheduling delivery;
- issuing purchase orders;
- sending invoices; and

- shipping the product.

Each step is composed of separate sub-steps that must be recorded in the information systems of the buyer, seller, and shipper. There are two different types of procurements and two different methods of purchasing goods.

- *Purchases of direct goods* — goods that are directly involved in the production process.
- *Purchases of indirect goods* — goods needed to carry out the production process but that are not directly involved in creating the end product.
- *Contract purchases* — long-term agreements to buy a specified amount of a product. There are pre-specified quality requirements and pre-specified terms.
- *Spot purchases* — for goods that meet the immediate needs of a firm. Indirect purchases are most often made on a spot purchase basis in a large marketplace that includes many suppliers.

The term *multi-tier supply chain* is used to describe the complex series of transactions that exists between a single firm with multiple primary suppliers, the secondary suppliers who do business with those primary suppliers, and the tertiary suppliers who do business with the secondary suppliers.

Trends in supply chain management (the activities that firms and industries use to coordinate the key players in their procurement process) include:

- *Supply chain simplification*, which refers to the reduction of the size of a firm's supply chain. Firms today generally prefer to work closely with a strategic group of suppliers in order to reduce both product costs and administrative costs. Long-term contract purchases containing pre-specified product quality requirements and pre-specified timing goals have been shown to improve end product quality and ensure uninterrupted production.
- *Supply chain management systems*, which coordinate and link the activities of suppliers, shippers, and order entry systems to automate the order entry process from start to finish, including the purchase, production, and moving of a product from a supplier to a purchasing firm.
- *Collaborative commerce*, which is a direct extension of supply chain management systems as well as supply chain simplification. It is the use of digital technologies to permit the supplier and the purchaser to share sensitive company information in order to collaboratively design, develop, build, and manage products throughout their life cycles.

■ Identify the main types of B2B commerce: Net marketplaces and private industrial networks.

There are two generic types of B2B commerce and many different subtypes within those two main categories of Internet commerce.

- *Net marketplaces,* which are also referred to as *exchanges* or *hubs,* assemble thousands of sellers and buyers in a single digital marketplace on the Internet. They can be owned by either the buyer or the seller or they can operate as independent intermediaries between the buyer and seller.

- *Private industrial networks* bring together a small number of strategic business partners who collaborate with one another to develop highly efficient supply chains and to satisfy customer demand for product. They are by far the largest form of B2B commerce, presently comprising 93% of the total computer-assisted inter-firm trade.

■ Understand the four types of Net marketplaces.

There are four main types of "pure" Net marketplaces:
- *E-distributors* are independently owned intermediaries that offer industrial customers a single source from which to make spot purchases of indirect or MRO goods. E-distributors operate in a *horizontal* market that serves many different industries with products from many different suppliers.
- *E-procurement companies* are independently owned intermediaries connecting hundreds of online suppliers offering millions of MRO goods to business firms who pay a fee to join the market. E-procurement companies operate in a horizontal market in which long-term contractual purchasing agreements are used to buy indirect goods.
- *Exchanges* are independently owned online marketplaces that connect hundreds of suppliers to potentially thousands of buyers in a dynamic real-time environment. They are typically *vertical* markets in which spot purchases can be made for direct inputs (both goods and services). Exchanges make money by charging a commission on each transaction.
- *Industry consortia* are industry-owned vertical markets where long-term contractual purchases of direct inputs can be made from a limited set of invited participants. Consortia serve to reduce supply chain inefficiencies by unifying the supply chain for an industry through a common network and computing platform.

■ Identify the major trends in the development of Net marketplaces.

- In the E-commerce I period, independent exchanges were the prototype Internet-based marketplace and several thousand of them were created; however, most of them did not succeed. The main reason independent exchanges failed is that they did not attract enough players to achieve liquidity (measured by the number of buyers and sellers in the market, the transaction volume, and the size of the transactions.)
- Industry consortia sprang up in 1999 and 2000 partly in reaction to the earlier development of independently owned exchanges that were viewed by large industries as interlopers who would not directly serve their needs. Industry consortia are profitable because they charge the large buyer firms transaction and subscription fees, but the rationalization of the procurement process, the competition among the vendors, and the closer relationship with the vendors are benefits that more than offset the costs of membership to the firms. However, the long-term profitability of consortia has yet to be proven.

- The failure of the early exchanges is one reason Net marketplaces are changing so rapidly. Participants have come to realize that the real value of B2B commerce will only be realized when it succeeds in changing the entire procurement system, the supply chain, and the process of collaboration among firms.

■ **Identify the role of private industrial networks in transforming the supply chain.**

- *Private industrial networks,* which presently dominate B2B commerce, are Web-enabled networks for coordinating trans-organizational business processes (collaborative commerce). These networks range in scope from a single firm to an entire industry.
- Although the central purpose of a private industrial network is to provide industry-wide global solutions to achieve the highest levels of efficiency, they generally start with a single sponsoring company that "owns" the network. This differentiates private industrial networks from consortia that are usually owned collectively by major firms through equity participation.
- Private industrial networks are transforming the supply chain by focusing on continuous business process coordination between companies. This coordination includes much more than just transaction support and supply chain management. Product design, demand forecasting, asset management, and sales and marketing plans can all be coordinated among network members.

■ **Understand the role of private industrial networks in supporting collaborative commerce.**

Collaboration among businesses can take many forms and involve a wide range of activities. Some of the forms of collaboration used by private industrial networks include:

- *CPFR or industry-wide collaborative resource planning, forecasting, and replenishment* involves working with network members to forecast demand, develop production plans, and coordinate shipping, warehousing, and stocking activities. The goal is to ensure that retail and wholesale shelf space is precisely maintained.
- *Supply-chain and distribution chain visibility* refers to the fact that in the past it was impossible to know where excess capacity existed in a supply or distribution chain. Eliminating excess inventories by halting the production of overstocked goods can raise the profit margins for all network members because products will no longer need to be discounted in order to move them off the shelves.
- *Marketing and product design collaboration* can be used to involve a firm's suppliers in product design and marketing activities as well as in the related activities of their supply and distribution chain partners. This can ensure that the parts used to build a product live up to the claims of the marketers. Collaborative commerce applications used in a private industrial network can also make possible closed loop marketing in which customer feedback will directly impact product design.

QUESTIONS

1. Explain the differences among total inter-firm trade, B2B commerce, and B2B e-commerce.
2. What are the key attributes of an electronic storefront? What early technology are they descended from?
3. List at least five potential benefits of B2B e-commerce.
4. Name and define the two distinct types of procurements firms make. Explain the difference between the two.
5. Name and define the two methods of purchasing goods.
6. Define the term supply chain and explain what SCM systems attempt to do. What does supply chain simplification entail?
7. Explain the difference between a horizontal market and a vertical market.
8. How do the value chain management services provided by e-procurement companies benefit buyers? What services do they provide to suppliers?
9. What are the three dimensions that characterize an e-procurement market based on its business functionality? Name two other market characteristics of an e-procurement Net marketplace.
10. Identify and briefly explain the anti-competitive possibilities inherent in Net marketplaces.
11. List three of the objectives of a private industrial network.
12. What is the main reason why many of the independent exchanges developed in the E-commerce I period failed?
13. Explain the difference between an industry consortia and a private industrial network.
14. What is CPFR, and what benefits could it achieve for the members of a private industrial network?
15. What are the barriers to the complete implementation of private industrial networks?

PROJECTS

1. Go to www.netmarketmakers.com. Netmarketmakers.com (which also uses the URL NMM.com) is a Jupiter Media Metrix-affiliated market research firm that provides information, analysis, resources, and connections to the people who build and grow Net markets, as well as to the broader community of investors, technology service providers, and others who facilitate this growth. Its Web site contains a listing of over 4,000 Net marketplaces. Click the "Knowledgebase" link to find a list of market-makers organized by industry. Choose an industry and a B2B vertical market-maker that interests you. Investigate the site and prepare a report that describes the size of the industry served, the type of Net marketplace provided, the benefits promised by the site for both suppliers and purchasers, and the history of the company. You might also investigate the bias (buyer vs. seller), ownership (suppliers, buyers,

independents), pricing mechanism(s), scope and focus, and access (public vs. private) of the Net marketplace.

2. Examine the Web site of one of the e-distributors listed in Figure 12.11, and compare and contrast it to one of the Web sites listed for e-procurement Net marketplaces. If you were a business manager of a medium-sized firm, how would you decide where to purchase your indirect inputs — from an e-distributor or an e-procurement Net marketplace? Write a short report detailing your analysis.

3. Assume you are a procurement officer for an office furniture manufacturer of steel office equipment. You have a single factory located in the Midwest with 2,000 employees. You sell about 40% of your office furniture to retail-oriented catalog outlets such as Quill in response to specific customer orders, and the remainder of your output is sold to resellers under long-term contracts. You have a choice of purchasing raw steel inputs — mostly cold rolled sheet steel — from an exchange such as E-Steel and/or from an emerging industry consortium. Which alternative would you choose and why? Prepare a PowerPoint presentation for management supporting your position.

4. Find a Net marketplace that has failed (possible candidates include MetalSite.com; Aerospan.com; Chemdex.com; Petrocosm.com; Freightwise.com, or another of your choosing). Investigate the reasons behind its failure. Prepare a short report on your findings and your analysis of the lessons that can be learned from its demise.

WEB SITE RESOURCES www.LearnE-commerce.net

- News: Weekly updates on topics relevant to the material in this chapter
- Video Lecture: Professor Ken Laudon summarizes the key concepts of the chapter
- Research: Abstracts and links to articles referenced in the chapter, as well as other relevant research
- International Spotlight: More information about B2B e-commerce outside of the United States
- Additional Material: Business-to-Government (B2G) e-commerce; the use of intranets and extranets in e-commerce
- PowerPoint Slides: Illustrations from the chapter and more
- Additional projects and exercises

| CHAPTER 13 | AUCTIONS, PORTALS, AND COMMUNITIES |

and

| CHAPTER 14 | ONLINE CONTENT PROVIDERS: DIGITAL MEDIA |

appear on the E-commerce Web site:

www.LearnE-Commerce.Net

References

CHAPTER 1

Arthur, Brian. "Increasing Returns and the New World of Business." *Harvard Business Review* (July–August 1996).

Bailey, Joseph P. *Intermediation and Electronic Markets: Aggregation and Pricing in Internet Commerce*. Ph.D., Technology, Management and Policy, Massachusetts Institute of Technology (1998a).

Bailey, Joseph P. *Electronic Commerce: Prices and Consumer Issues for Three Products: Books, Compact Discs and Software*. Organisation for Economic Co-Operation and Development, OCDE/GD (1998b).

Bakos, Yannis. "The Emerging Landscape for Retail E-commerce." *Journal of Economic Perspectives* (January 2001).

Bakos, Yannis. "The Emerging Role of Electronic Marketplaces on the Internet." *Communications of the ACM* (August 1998).

Bakos, Yannis. "Reducing Buyer Search Costs: Implications for Electronic Marketplaces." *Management Science* (December 1997).

Brynjolfsson, Erik, and Michael Smith. "Frictionless Commerce? A Comparison of Internet and Conventional Retailers." *Management Science* (April 2001).

Clemons, Eric K.; Il-Horn Hann; and Lorin M. Hitt. "The Nature of Competition in Electronic Markets: An Empirical Investigation of Online Travel Agent Offerings." Working Paper, The Wharton School of the University of Pennsylvania (March 2000).

Computer Industry Almanac Inc. "U.S Has 33% Share of Internet Users Worldwide Year-end 2000 According to Computer Industry Almanac." (April 24, 2001). www.c-i-a.com/200103iu.htm

Cyveillance, Inc. "Internet Exceeds 2 Billion Pages." (July 10, 2000). www.cyveillance.com/us/newsroom/pressr/000710.asp

Dykema, E.B. "Online Retail's Ripple Effect." *Forrester Research Report*, Forrester Research Inc. (September 2000).

eBay.com. Report on Form 10-K for the fiscal year ended December 31, 2000, as filed with the Securities and Exchange Commission on March 28, 2001.

eTForecasts. "By 2005 55% of U.S. Internet Users Will Use Web Appliances." (June 12, 2000). www.etforecasts.com/pr/pr600.htm

Evans, Philip, and Thomas S. Wurster. *Blown to Bits: How the New Economics of Information Transforms Strategy*. Cambridge, MA: Harvard Business School Press (2000).

Evans, Philip, and Thomas S. Wurster. "Getting Real About Virtual Commerce." *Harvard Business Review* (November–December 1999).

Evans, Philip, and Thomas S. Wurster. "Strategy and the New Economics of Information." *Harvard Business Review* (September–October 1997).

Forrester Research, Inc. "Forrester Online Retail Index." (April 2001). www.forrester.com/NRF

Hallford, Joshua. "B-to-B Buying Picks Up Speed." *The Standard* (October 2, 2000).

International Council of Shopping Centers. *ICSC Econostats USA Economic Statistics for the Week Ending January 12, 2001*. Vol. 7 No. 2 (January 2001).

Inktomi, Inc. "Web Surpasses One Billion Documents." (January 18, 2000). www.inktomi.com/new/press/billion.html.

Internet Software Consortium Internet Domain Survey. (2001). www.isc.org/ds/WWW-200101/index.html

Jupiter Media Metrix (Jon Gibs, Lead Analyst). "B-to-B Spending in 2006." (September 24, 2001)

Kalakota, Ravi, and Marcia Robinson. *e-Business 2.0: A Roadmap to Success*. Reading MA: Addison-Wesley (2001).

Kambil, Ajit. "Doing Business in the Wired World." *IEEE Computer* (May 1997).

Laudon, Kenneth C., and Jane P. Laudon. *Management Information Systems: Managing the Digital Firm*. Upper Saddle River NJ: Prentice Hall (2002).

PriceWaterhouseCoopers. PriceWaterhouseCoopers MoneyTree Survey, Q1 2001, Aggregate National Data, National Internet-Related Investments, Internet Deals 1996–2000, Internet-Related Investments in Venture-Backed Companies. (2001). www.pwcmoneytree.com/aggregatemenu.asp

Rainie, Lee, and Dan Packel. "More Online, Doing More." *The Pew Internet and American Life Project* (February 18, 2001).

Rayport, Jeffrey, and Bernard Jaworski. *e-Commerce*. New York: McGraw-Hill (2000).

Sinha, Indajit. "Cost Transparency: The Net's Threat to Prices and Brands." *Harvard Business Review* (March–April 2000).

Shankar, Venkatesh; Arvind Rangaswamy; and Michael Pusater. "The Impact of Internet Marketing on Price Sensitivity and Price Competition." Presented at Marketing Science and the Internet, INFORM College on Marketing Mini-Conference (March 1998).

Shapiro, Carl, and Hal R. Varian. *Information Rules. A Strategic Guide to the Network Economy*. Boston MA: Harvard Business School Press (1999).

Smith, Michael; Joseph Bailey; and Erik Brynjolfsson. "Understanding Digital Markets: Review and Assessment." In Erik Brynjolfsson and Brian Kahin (eds.) *Understanding the Digital Economy*. Cambridge MA: MIT Press (2000).

Tagliabue, John. "Online Cohabitation: Internet and Minitel." *New York Times* (June 2, 2001).

Tehan, Rita. Congressional Research Service Issue Brief. "RL30435: Internet and E-Commerce Statistics: What They Mean and Where to Find Them on the Web." National Council for Science and the Environment (2000). www.cnie.org/nle/st-36.html.

Tversky, A., and D. Kahneman. "The Framing of Decisions and the Psychology of Choice." *Science* (January 1981).

Varian, Hal R. "5 Habits of Highly Effective Revolution." *Forbes ASAP* (February 21, 2000a).

Varian, Hal R. "When Commerce Moves On, Competition Can Work in Strange Ways." *New York Times* (August 24, 2000b).

CHAPTER 2

Amit, R., and C. Zott. "Value Drivers of E-commerce Business Models." INSEAD Working Papers Series, 2000/54/ENT/SM (2000).

Armstrong, Arthur, and John Hagel, III. "The Real Value of Online Communities." *Harvard Business Review* (May–June 1996).

Arthur, W. Brian. "Increasing Returns and the New World of Business." *Harvard Business Review* (July–August 1996).

Bakos, Yannis; Henry Lucas; Wonseok Oh; Sivakuman Viswanathan; Gary Simon; and Bruce Weber. "The Impact of Electronic Commerce in the Retail Brokerage Industry: Trading Costs of Internet Versus Full Service Firms." Center for Research on Information Systems, Stern School of Business, New York University (July 2000).

Bakos, Yannis. "The Emerging Role of Electronic Marketplaces on the Internet." *Communications of the ACM* (August 1998).

Bakos, Yannis. "The Emerging Landscape for Retail E-commerce." *Journal of Economic Perspectives* (January 2001).

Barney, J. B. "Firm Resources and Sustained Competitive Advantage." *Journal of Management* Vol. 17, No. 1 (1991).

"Behind the Numbers: The Mystery of B-to-B Forecasts Revealed." *Industry Standard.* (February 28, 2000).

Bellman, Steven; Gerland L. Lohse; and Eric J. Johnson. "Predictors of Online Buying Behavior." *Communications of the ACM* (December 1999).

Benjamin, Robert I., and Rolf T. Wigand. "Electronic Markets and Virtual Value Chains on the Information Superhighway." *Sloan Management Review* (Winter 1995).

Dykema, E. B. "Online Retail's Ripple Effect." *Forrester Research Report*, Forrester Research, Inc. (September 2000).

Fisher, William W. III. "The Growth of Intellectual Property: A History of the Ownership of Ideas in the United States." http://www.law.harvard.edu/Academic_Affairs/coursepages/tfisher/iphistory.html (1999).

GE Aircraft Engines Web site, www.geae.com

Gerace, Thomas. "Encyclopedia Britannica." Harvard Business School Case Study 396-051 (1999).

Ghosh, Shikhar. "Making Business Sense of the Internet." *Harvard Business Review* (March–April, 1998).

Glasner, Joanna. "EToys Epitaph: 'End of an Error'." *Wired News* (March 8, 2001).

Grainger Consulting Services. "The Economic Benefits of Utilizing Business to Business Electronic Commerce." Grainger Consulting Services, Inc. (September 1999).

Gulati, Ranjay, and Jason Garino. "Getting the Right Mix of Bricks and Clicks." *Harvard Business Review* (May–June 2000).

Hagel, J., III, and Jeffrey Rayport. "The Coming Battle for Customer Information" *Harvard Business Review* (January–February, 1997a).

Hagel, J., III, and Jeffrey Rayport. "The New Infomediaries." *McKinsey Quarterly* No. 4 (1997b).

Hallford, Joshua. "B-to-B Buying Picks Up Speed." *The Standard* (October 2, 2000).

International Council of Shopping Centers. *ICSC Econostats USA Economic Statistics for the Week Ending January 12, 2001*. Vol. 7, No. 2 (January 2001).

Jupiter Media Metrix (Jon Gibs, Lead Analyst). "B-to-B Spending in 2006." (September 24, 2001)

Kambil, Ajit. "Doing Business in the Wired World." *IEEE Computer* (May 1997).

Kambil, Ajit; Ari Ginsberg; and Michael Bloch. "Reinventing Value Propositions." Working Paper NYU Center for Research on Information Systems (1998).

Kanter, Elizabeth Ross. "The Ten Deadly Mistakes of Wanna-Dots." *Harvard Business Review* (January 2001).

Kaplan, Steven, and Mohanbir Sawhney. "E-Hubs: The New B2B Marketplaces." *Harvard Business Review* (May–June 2000).

Kim, W. Chan, and Renee Mauborgne. "Knowing a Winning Business Idea When You See One." *Harvard Business Review* (September–October 2000).

Knight, Leah. "Triggering the B2B Electronic Commerce Explosion." *GartnerTechWatch* (May 2001).

McAfee, Andrew. "The Napsterization of B2B." *Harvard Business Review* (November–December 2000).

Micrologic Research Inc. "Wireless 2001, A Study of the Worldwide Cellular Telephone Market." www.mosmicro.com/Wire99exec.html (2001).

Morneau, Jill. "E-Marketplaces Start to Take Off." *InternetWeek* (January 17, 2001).

Neilsen/Net Ratings Inc. "Hot Off the Net/April Internet Universe." www.neilsen-netratings.com (May 22, 2001).

Porter, Michael E. *Competitive Strategy*. New York: Free Press (1980).

Porter, Michael E. *Competitive Advantage: Creating and Sustaining Superior Performance*. New York: Free Press (1985).

Porter, Michael E. "Strategy and the Internet." *Harvard Business Review* (March 2001).

Porter, Michael E., and V. E. Millar. "How Information Gives You Competitive Advantage." *Harvard Business Review* (July–August 1985).

Rainie, Lee, and Dan Packel. "More Online, Doing More." The Pew Internet and American Life Project. Washington D.C. (www.pewinternet.org) (February 18, 2000).

Rigdon, Joan I. "The Second-Mover Advantage." *Red Herring* (September 1, 2000).

Searchenginewatch.com Web site, www.searchenginewatch.com

Timmers, Paul. "Business Models for Electronic Markets." *Electronic Markets* Vol. 8, No. 2 (1998).

Teece, David J. "Profiting from Technological Innovation: Implications for Integration, Collaboration, Licensing and Public Policy." *Research Policy* 15 (1986).

Werbach, Kevin. "Syndication: The Emerging Model for Business in the Internet Age." *Harvard Business Review* (May–June 2000).

Wise, Richard, and Morrison, David. "Beyond the Exchange: The Future of B2B." *Harvard Business Review* (November–December 2000).

CHAPTER 3

Berners-Lee, Tim; Robert Cailliau; Ari Luotonen; Henrik Frystyk Nielsen; and Arthur Secret. "The World Wide Web." *Communications of the ACM* (August 1994).

Boardwatch Magazine. Directory of Internet Service Providers. Golden, Colorado. Penton Media (1999). See http://boardwatch.internet.com/isp/summer 99/introduction.html.

Bush, Vannevar. "As We May Think." *The Atlantic Monthly* (July 1945).

Center for Media Education. "What the Market Will Bear: Cisco's Vision for Broadband Internet." Washington DC: Center for Media Education. (2000). www.cme.org/access/broadband

Computer Industry Almanac Inc. "U.S Has 33% Share of Internet Users Worldwide Year-end 2000 According to Computer Industry Almanac." (April 24, 2001). www.c-i-a.com/200103iu.htm

Computer Science and Telecommunications Board. National Research Council (NRC). "Realizing the Information Future." Washington DC: National Academy Press (1994).

Computer Science and Telecommunications Board. National Research Council (NRC). "Trust in Cyberspace." Washington DC: National Academy Press (1999).

Computer Science and Telecommunications Board. National Research Council (NRC). "Networking Health: Prescriptions for the Internet." Washington DC: National Academy Press (2000).

"Global Internet Statistics." *Global Reach* (2001). www.glreach.com/globstats

Kleinrock, Leonard. *1964 Communication Nets: Stochastic Message Flow and Delay.* New York, NY: McGraw-Hill (1964).

Leiner, Barry M.; Vinton G. Cerf; David D. Clark; Robert E. Kahn; Leonard Kleinrock; Daniel C. Lynch; Jon Postel; Larry G. Roberts; and Stephen Wolff. "All About the Internet: A Brief History of the Internet," Internet Society (ISOC) (August 2000). www.isoc.org/internet/history/brief.html

McGarr, Michael. "Tomorrow's Technologies Pushing E-Commerce to New Heights." *E-Commerce World Magazine* (July 1, 2000).

McGrane, Sally. "A Little E-Mail (or a lot of it) Eases the Workday." *New York Times* (March 8, 2001).

National Research Council. "The Internet's Coming of Age." Washington DC: National Academy Press (2000).

Sweeny, Terry. "Voice Over IP Builds Momentum." *Information Week* (November 20, 2000).

Ziff-Davis Publishing. "Ted Nelson: Hypertext Pioneer." (1998) http://www.techtv.com/screensavers_story/0,3656,2127396-2102293,00.html

CHAPTER 4

Albrecht, Allan J., and John E. Gaffney. "Software Function, Source Lines of Code, and Development Effort Prediction: A Software Science Validation." *IEEE Transactions on Software Engineering* Vol. SE-9, No. 6 (1983).

Banker, Rajiv D., and Chris F. Kemerer. "Scale Economies in New Software Development." *IEEE Transactions on Software Engineering*, Vol. 15, No. 10 (1989).

Glass, Robert L. "The Realities of Software Technology Payoffs," *Communications of the ACM*, Vol. 42., No. 2. (1999).

Hughes, Chris, and Gunther Birznieks. "Serving Up Web Server Basics." www.webcompare.internet.con/web-basics/webbasics_6.html (2001).

Jupiter Media Metrix (Joseph Lazlo, Lead Analyst). "Consumer Broadband: Differentiate Beyond Technology to Drive Consumer Adoption." (September 27, 2000).

Laudon, Kenneth C., and Jane P. Laudon. *Management Information Systems: Managing the Digital Firm.* Upper Saddle River NJ: Prentice Hall (2002).

Lientz, Bennet P., and E. Burton Swanson. *Software Maintenance Management.* Reading MA: Addison-Wesley (1980).

Loudcloud Inc. "Designing High-Performance Scalable Web Applications." White Paper, March 2001.

Microsoft Corporation. "Building High-Scalability Server Farms." Microsoft Site Server Commerce (1999). www.microsoft.com/technet/commerce/bldhsfrm.asp?a = printable

Microsoft Corporation. "Capacity Model for Internet Transactions." Microsoft Site Server Commerce. (1999). www.microsoft.com/mcis/reskit/rk_whatsnew.htm

Microsoft Corporation. "Windows 2000 > Server > Standard Performance Evaluation Corporation." (February 08, 2000). www.microsoft.com/windows2000/server/evaluation/performance/benchmarks/SPECbench.asp

Netcraft Web Server Survey. (May 2001). www.netcraft.com/survey.

Robinson, Tim; Ed Merenda; and Steve Curtis. "IBM RS/6000 Web Server Sizing Guide." In Capacity Planning & Performance Tuning for VisualInfoand Digital Library Servers, IBM Corp. (1999). publibz.boulder.ibm.com/cgi-bin/bookmgr_OS390/BOOKS/EZ30RU01/CCONTENTSC

Valdes, Ray. "The Perils of Platform Selection." *Webtechniques* (March 2000). www.webtechniques.com/archives/2000/03/platform.html

CHAPTER 5

Ackman, Dan. "Equifax, eHNC Join Forces To Fight Online Fraud." www.forbes.com (June 21, 2000)

ActivMedia Research. "Real Numbers Behind E-Transactions." *Fraud & Security.* (September 2000).

Atanasov, Maria. "The Truth about Internet Fraud." *Smart Business* (March 13, 2001).

Atkins, D.; P. Buis; C. Hare; R. Kelley; C. Nachenberg; A.B. Nelson; P. Phillips; T. Ritchey; T. Sheldon; and J. Snyder. *Internet Security Professional Reference Second Edition*, Indianapolis, IN: New Riders (1997).

Boncella, Robert J. "Web Security for E-Commerce." *Communications of the Association for Information Systems* Vol .4. (November 2000).

Bradsher, Keith. "With its E-Mail Infected, Ford Scrambled and Caught Up." *New York Times* (May 8, 2000).

Bridis, Ted. "Microsoft Takes Steps to Thwart Hacker Attacks." *Wall Street Journal* (January 29, 2001).

Catalano, Carla. "Proxy Servers." *Computerworld* (November 22, 1999).

Cheswick, W.R., and S.M. Bellovin. *Firewalls and Internet Security: Repelling the Wily Hacker.* Reading, MA: Addison-Wesley (1994).

Computer Security Institute, Inc. " 2001 CSI/FBI Computer Crime and Security Survey." *Computer Security Issues & Trends* (Spring, 2001).

Deming, Dorothy E., and William E. Bauugh. "Hiding

Crimes in Cyberspace." *Information, Communication, and Society* Vol. 2, No. 3 (Autumn 1999).

Denning, D., and P. J. Denning. *Internet Besieged Countering Cyberspace Scofflaws.* New York, NY: ACM Press (1998).

"E-Commerce Spotlight: Who's Cheating Whom." *The Industry Standard* (January 10–17, 2000).

Ellison, Carl, and Bruce Schneier. "Ten Risks of PKI: What You're Not Being Told About Public Key Infrastructure." *Computer Security Journal* Vol. XVI, No. 1 (Winter 2000).

Electronic Privacy Information Center (EPIC). "Cryptography and Liberty 2000. An International Survey of Encryption Policy." Washington D.C. (2000).

"Experts: Internet, Credit Card Scams Spanning the Globe." www.worldroom.com (January 16, 2001).

Finfacts. "Finfacts Internet Statistics: Online Credit Card Fraud." www.finfacts.ie/intcard.htm, (June 23, 2001).

Gaither, Chris. "Microsoft Sites Shut, This Time in Network Attack." *New York Times* (January 26, 2001).

Garfinkel, S., and G. Spafford. *Web Security & Commerce.* Cambridge, MA: O'Reilly and Associates (1997).

Gomes, Lee. "Internet Relay Chat is Suspected Launch Pad of Web Hackers." *Wall Street Journal* (February 14, 2000).

Greene, Thomas. "Win-NT/IIS Admins Made April Fools by Hackers." infowar.com Hacker Sitings and News. http://www.infowar.com/hacker/01/hack_040201a_j.shtml (April 2, 2001).

Gruman, Galen. "Point-to-Point Tunneling Protocol." *Computerworld* (August 2, 1999).

International Computer Security Association. *Study on Computer Crime* (2000).

Markoff, John. "Thief Reveals Credit Card Data when Web Extortion Plot Fails." *New York Times* (January 10, 2000).

Markoff, John, and Sara Robinson. "Chat Systems Yield Clues in Web Attacks by Hackers." *New York Times* (February 15, 2000).

McClure, S.; J. Scambry; and G. Kurtz. *Hacking Exposed: Network Security Secrets and Solutions.* Berkley, CA: Osborne/McGraw-Hill (1999).

McConnell, Mike. "Security and the Internet." *Wall Street Journal* (February 17, 2000).

McCormick, John. "Beware: E-Mail Wiretaps can Steal Sensitive Correspondence." *TechRepublic* (February 28, 2001).

Mullich, Joe. "Strategies for Firewall Protection." *Knowledge Management* (November, 2000).

National White Collar Crime Center and the Federal Bureau of Investigation. "Six Month Data Trends Report" (May–November 2000).

National Infrastructure Protection Center. "First Ever Federal Computer Hacking Trial in the Southern District of New York." Press Release. www.nipc.gov/pressroom/pressre/oquendo.htm (March 2001).

Radcliff, Deborah. "Authorization Management Tools Emerge." *Computerworld* (September 11, 2000).

Reuters News Service. "EU-Wide Credit Card Fraud Soars 50% in 2000." *The Industry Standard* (February 19, 2001)

Schwartz, John. "Fighting Crime Online: Who is in Harm's Way?" *New York Times* (February 8, 2001).

Sinrod, Eric J., and William P. Reilly. "Cybercrimes: A Practical Approach to the Application of Federal Computer Crime Laws." *Santa Clara University School of Law Review* (May 2000).

Smith, Richard. "Email Wiretapping." Privacy Foundation (February 5, 2001).

Smith, R.E. *Internet Cryptography.* Reading, MA: Addison-Wesley (1997).

Stein, Lincoln D. *Web Security: A Step-by-step Reference Guide.* Reading, MA: Addison-Wesley (1998).

Thibodeau, Patrick. "Feds' Math Is Fuzzy on Computer Crime." *Computerworld* (April 23, 2001).

Tran, Khanh. "Hackers Attack Major Internet Sites, Temporarily Shutting Buy.com, eBay." *Wall Street Journal* (February 9, 2000).

Tran, Khanh. "Yahoo! Portal is Shut Down by Web Attack." *Wall Street Journal* (February 8, 2000).

Wallerstein, Lisa. "Fraud in the New Economy." *Dbrief* Dun and Bradstreet (October 2000). http://dbrief.dnb.com.

Yankee Group Inc. "The Yankee Group Predicts over $1.2 Billion Impact as a Result of Recent Attacks Launched by Internet Hackers." *Yankee Group News Release* (February 10, 2000).

CHAPTER 6

"Payment Solutions," Internet.com, Product Reviews, 2001.

"What Is SET?" www.setco.com

Branscum, Deborah. "Smart and Smarter." *The Standard* (January 16, 2001).

Crockett, Roger. "No Plastic? No Problem." *Business Week* (October 23, 2000).

CyberCash, Inc. "Instabuy Consumer FAQs." www.instabuy.com (July 18, 2001).

Davies, Glyn. *A History of Money from Ancient Times to the Present Day.* Cardiff: University of Wales Press (1996).

Duffy, Daintry. "Cyber Checkout." *CIO* (November 15, 2000).

FIWG. "Institutional Payment Systems and the Internet." Financial Internet Working Group Issues Paper, Preliminary Draft, April 2001.

Financial Services Technology Consortium. Electronic Check Project (2001). www.fstc.org/projects/past.cfm

Gaskin, James. "Electronic Billing Revs Up." *InteractiveWeek* (April 3, 2000).

Hansell, Saul. "Credit Cards With Chips Have Little Use in U.S." *New York Times* (August 12, 2001).

Johnson, Amy Helen. "Looking for Big Profits in Small Purchases." *ComputerWorld* (May 15, 2000).

Jupiter Media Metrix. "Internet Payments." (2000).

King, Rachael. "E-Billing Still in the Ether." *The Net Economy* (March 19, 2001).

Lawrence, Stacy. "Study Peeks into Worldwide Wallets." *The Industry Standard* (April 11, 2000).

MacKie-Mason; K. Jeffrey; and Kimberly White. "Evaluating and Selecting Digital Payment Mechanisms." *Telecommunications Policy Research Conference* (October 5–7, 1996) Maryland.

Microsoft. "Microsoft Passport Technical White Paper." www.passport.com. (July 18, 2001).

Oreskovic, Alexei. "Short Changed." *The Standard* (July 3, 2000).

Patel, Jeetu. "B-to-B E-billing Heats Up." *InformationWeek.com* (October 23, 2000).

Paul, Lauren Gibbons. "E-billing: The Check Is in the Ether." EarthWeb.com (April 1, 1999).

Robinson, Teri. "Online Bill Payment: Ready to Break Through?" *Internetweek.com* (October 23, 2000).

Rosen, Cheryl. "E-Payments Get More Tempting." *InformationWeek.com* (December 18–25, 2000).

Sapsford, Jathon, and Paul Becket. "Credit-Card Firms Still Need A Strong Hand in Web Game." *Wall Street Journal* (April 2, 2001).

Schwartz, Karen. "Online Billing Slowly Gains Momentum." *Datamation* (September 26, 2000).

Trombly, Maria. "U.S. Brokerages and Banks Push to Close Wireless Cash Gap." *Computerworld* (January 15, 2001).

Weinberg, Ari. "Secret Shopper: Micropayments, Bigger Headaches." *The Standard* (July 3, 2000).

Winn, Jane Kaufman. "Clash of the Titans: Regulation the Competition between Established and Emerging Electronic Payment Systems." *Berkeley Technology Law Journal* (1999).

www.federalreserve.gov/pubs/shop

www.monthlyreview.org/500editr.htm

CHAPTER 7

Adomavicius, Gediminas, and Alexander Tuzhilin. "Expert-Driven Validation of Rule-Based User Models in Personalization Applications." *Data Mining and Knowledge Discovery* (January 2001).

Bailey, J., and Erik Brynjolfsson. "An Exploratory Study of the Emerging Role of Electronic Intermediaries." *International Journal of Electronic Commerce* (Spring, 1997).

Bakos, J.Y., and Erik Brynjolfsson. "Bundling Information Goods: Pricing, Profits and Efficiency." *Management Science* (December 1999).

Bakos, J.Y., and Erik Brynjolfsson. "Bundling and Competition on the Internet: Aggregation Strategies for Information Goods." *Marketing Science* (January 2000).

Bachelder, Beth. "Behind The Numbers: E-Business Communication Gets Personal." *InformationWeek* (August 7, 2000).

Bannan, Karen. "Chatting Up a Sale." *Wall Street Journal* (October 23, 2000).

Bellman, Steven; Gerald L. Lohse; and Eric J. Johnson. "Predictors of Online Buying Behavior." *Communications of the ACM* (December 1999).

Brynjolfsson, Erik, and M.D. Smith. "Frictionless Commerce? A Comparison of Internet and Conventional Retailer." *Management Science* (April 2000).

Carpenter, Phil. *eBrands: Building an Internet Business at Breakneck Speed*. Cambridge MA: Harvard Business School Press (2000).

Chan, P.K. "A Non-Invasive Learning Approach to Building Web User Profiles." In *Proceedings of ACM SIGKDD International Conference* (1999).

Clay, K.; K. Ramayya; and E. Wolff. "Retail Strategies on the Web: Price and Non-Price Competition in the On Line Book Industry." Working Paper, *MIT E-commerce Forum* (1999).

Compaq, Inc. Compaq White Paper, http://nonstop.compaq.com/view.asp?IOID=826, (November 1998).

Computer Industry Almanac Inc. "U.S. Has 33% Share of Internet Users Worldwide Year-end 2000 According to Computer Industry Almanac." (April 24, 2001) www.c-i-a.com/200103.iu.htm

Cross, Robert. "Launching the Revenue Rocket: How Revenue Management Can Work For Your Business." *Cornell Hotel and Restaurant Administration Quarterly* (April, 1997).

Ellison, Sarah. "Web-Brand Study Says Awareness Isn't Trust." *Wall Street Journal* (June 7, 2000).

Evans, P., and T. S. Wurster. "Getting Real About Virtual Commerce." *Harvard Business Review* (November-December 1999).

Fawcett, Tom, and Foster Provost. "Adaptive Fraud Detection." *Data Mining and Knowledge Discovery* (1997).

Fawcett, Tom, and Foster Provost, "Combining Data Mining and Machine Learning for Effective User Profiling." In *Proceedings of the Second International Conference on Knowledge Discovery and Data Mining* (1996).

Feldwick, Paul. "What Is Brand Equity Anyway, and How Do You Measure It?" *Journal of the Market Research Society* (April 1996).

Forrester Research, Inc. "Designing Transactive Content." (February, 1998).

Forrester Research, Inc. "Transactive Content." (October 1997).

Gilbert, Alorie, and Beth Bachelder. "The Big Squeeze." *InformationWeek* (March 27, 2000).

Golder, Peter. "What History Teaches Us About the Endurance of Brands." *Stern Business* (Fall 2000).

Golder, Peter, and Gerard Tellis. "Pioneer Advantage: Marketing Logic or Marketing Legend?" *Journal of Marketing Research*, Vol. 30, No. 2 (May 1993).

Godin, Seth. *Permission Marketing.* New York: Simon & Schuster (1999).

Grossnickle, Joshua, and Oliver Raskin. *Online Marketing Research.* New York: McGraw Hill (2001).

Gulati, Ranjay, and Jason Garino. "Getting the Right Mix of Bricks and Clicks." *Harvard Business Review* (May–June 2000).

Guthrie, Betty C. "Clicks & Mortar: Virtual Sales Combine with the Real Deal." *Smart Computing* (January 2000).

Hibbard, Justin. "Manufacturers Vie With Online Retailers." *InformationWeek* (April 12, 2000).

Interbrand, Inc. "World's Most Valuable Brands Ranked by Interbrand 2001" http://63.111.41.5/interbrand/test/html/events/ranking_methodology.pdf

Jupiter Media Metrix. "Online Activities." (July 2000a).

Jupiter Media Metrix. (Jean-Gabriel Henry, Lead Analyst). "Chat-Based Customer Service: Is It for Everyone?' (May 24, 2000b).

Jupiter Media Metrix. (Andrew Krucoff, Evan Cohen, Michael Saxon, Analysts). "Access, Activities and Transactions of the Online User: The Jupiter Online Consumer Survey Volume 6." (January 2001a).

Jupiter Media Metrix. (David Daniels, Lead Analyst). "Understanding Customer Loyalty: Technologies to Identify Truly High-Value Customers." (June 29, 2001b).

Jupiter Media Metrix. (David Daniels, Lead Analyst). "Jupiter Metrics: Customer Relationship Management, 2Q 2001." (August 27, 2001c).

Kenny, David, and John F. Marshall. "Contextual Marketing: The Real Business of the Internet." *Harvard Business Review* (November–December 2000).

King, Julia. "New Covenants Ease Online Channel War." *Computerworld* (May 17, 2000).

Kotler, Philip, and Gary Armstrong. *Principles of Marketing*, 9th Edition. Upper Saddle River, NJ: Prentice Hall (2001).

Kraemer, Kenneth L.; Jason Dedrick; and Sandra Yamashiro. "Refining and Extending the Business Model With Information Technology: Dell Computer Corporation." *The Information Society* (January–March 2000).

Lake, David. "CyberDialogue Files for IPO." *Industry Standard* (February 18, 2000).

Lohse, L.G.; G.Bellman; and E.J. Johnson. "Consumer Buying Behavior on the Internet: Findings from Panel Data." *Journal of Interactive Marketing* (Winter 2000).

Lorek, Laura. "Have It-Your-Way Web Sites Start to Catch On." *Interactive Week* (June 25, 2001).

McDowell, Edwin. "Cuts in Commission Sting Travel Agents." *New York Times* (October 12, 1999).

Neuborne, Ellen. "From One-way Marketing to Cyber Dialogue." *Business Week* (April 17, 2000).

Nielsen/Net Ratings, Inc. "Hot off the Net: June Internet Universe." http://www.nielsen-netratings.com/hot_of_the_net.htm (August 13, 2001).

Nie, Norman, and Lutz Erbring. "Internet and Society: A Preliminary Report." *Stanford Institute for the Quantitative Study of Society* (February 17, 2000).

Peppers, Don, and Martha Rogers. *Enterprise One to One.* New York: Doubleday (1997).

Rainie, Lee, and Dan Packel. "More Online, Doing More." *The Pew Internet and American Life Project* (February 18, 2001).

Rao, Sidhart. "Instant Surveys on the Internet." *The Economic Times* (December 2, 2000).

Rayport, J.F., and J.J. Sviokla. "Exploiting the Virtual Value Chain." *Harvard Business Review* (November–December 1995).

Reichheld, Frederick F., and Phil Schefter. "E-Loyalty: Your Secret Weapon on the Web." *Harvard Business Review* (July–August 2000).

Rozanski, Horacio D.; Gerry Bollman; and Martin Lipman. "Seize the Occasion: Usage Based Segmentation for Internet Marketers." *E Insights* Booz Allen & Hamilton (April 2001).

Shapiro, Carl, and Hal Varian. "Versioning: The Smart Way to Sell Information." *Harvard Business Review* (November–December 1998).

Shapiro, Carl, and Hal Varian. *Information Rules: A Strate-*

gic Guide to the Network Economy. Cambridge, MA: Harvard Business School Press (1999).

Sinha, Indrajit. "Cost Transparency: The Net's Real Threat to Prices and Brands." *Harvard Business Review* (March–April 2000).

Smith, M.D.; J. Bailey; and E. Brynjolfsson. "Understanding Digital Markets: Review and Assessment," in E. Brynjolfsson and B. Kahin (eds.), *Understanding the Digital Economy.* Cambridge, MA: MIT Press (1999).

Songini, Marc L. "NBA Shoots for Data Analysis." *Computerworld* (May 28, 2001).

Starbuck, William, and Paul C. Nystrom. "Why Many Firms Run Into Crises, and Why Some Survive." Working Paper. Stern School of Business, Management and Organizational Behavior (1997).

Sweat, Jeff, and Rick Whiting. "Instant Marketing." *InformationWeek* (August 2, 1999).

Tedeschi, Bob. "Conventional Retailers are Integrating Web Sites With Stores, Improving Service in Both Areas." *New York Times* (August 16, 1999).

Teece, David J. "Profiting from Technological Innovation: Implications for Integration, Collaboration, Licensing and Public Policy." *Research Policy,* 15 (1986).

Wagner, Mary. "Caring for Customers." *Internet World* (September 1, 1999).

Waltner, Charles. "CRM Makes Online Shopping Personal." www.informationweek.com (January 29, 2001).

Weber, Thomas. "Why Those Companies Are So Eager to Get Your E-mail Address." *Wall Street Journal* (February 12, 2001).

Wellner, Alison. "Every Day's A Holiday." *American Demographics* (December 2000).

Wigand, R.T., and R.I. Benjamin. "Electronic Commerce: Effects on Electronic Markets." *Journal of Computer Mediated Communication* (December 1995).

Wolfinbarger, Mary, and Mary Gilly. "Shopping Online for Freedom, Control and Fun." *California Management Review* (Winter 2001).

Zetlin, Minda. "Channel Conflicts." *Computerworld* (September 25, 2000).

CHAPTER 8

ActivMedia Research. "Real Numbers Behind Successful Web Site Promotion, 2000." (July 2000).

Briggs, Rex, and N. Hollis. "Advertising on the Web: Is There Response Before Click Through?" *Journal of Advertising Research* (1997).

Briggs, Rex. "How Internet Advertising Works." ESOMAR "Net Effects" Conference, London (February 22 1999).

Dahm, Tom. "Getting (and Keeping) a Top Search Engine Ranking." www.webdevelopersjournal.com (July 25, 2000).

Dellaert, B., and B.E. Khan. "How Tolerable is Delay? Consumers' Evaluations of Web Sites After Waiting." *Journal of Interactive Marketing* (Winter 1999).

Ernst and Young. "Global Online Retailing Report." (February 8, 2001).

Hansell, Saul. "Web Site Ads, Holding Sway, Start to Blare." *New York Times* (March 17, 2001a).

Hansell, Saul. "Marketers Find Internet Opens New Avenues to Customers." *New York Times* (March 26, 2001b).

Hansell, Saul. "Clicks for Sale." *New York Times* (June 4, 2001c).

Hansell, Saul. "Pop-Up Ads Pose a Measurement Puzzle." *New York Times* (July 23, 2001d).

Haubl, G., and V. Trifts. "Consumer Decisionmaking in Online Shopping Environments: The Effects of Interactive Decision Aids." *Marketing Science* (Winter 2000).

"How Dotcom Survivors Promote Their Web Sites." *Entrepreneur Magazine* (June 2001).

Internet Advertising Bureau and Millward Brown Interactive. "IAB Online Advertising Effectiveness Study." (1997).

Interactive Advertising Bureau. "Interactive Advertising Bureau (IAB), DoubleClick, MSN and CNET Networks Release Groundbreaking Online Brand Research Findings." Press Release (July 18, 2001).

Jupiter Media Metrix. (Marissa Gluck, Lead Analyst). "Online Advertising Through 2006: Prioritizing Opportunities in a Slowing Market." (August 8, 2001a).

Jupiter Media Metrix. (David Daniels, Jared Blank, Lead Analysts). "Analyzing Customer Drop-Off Rates: Understanding Why Customers Abandon Shopping Carts." (June 11, 2001b).

Jupiter Media Metrix. (Michele Slack, Lead Analyst). "E-mail Marketing: Closing the Loop from Acquisition to Retention." (April 17, 2000a).

Jupiter Media Metrix. (Lydia Loizides, Marissa Gluck, Lead Analysts). "Streaming Video Advertising: Despite Hype, Limited Opportunity." (December 7, 2000b).

Jupiter Media Metrix. "Media Planning and Buying: Navigating the Flood of Online Options." (November 29, 2000c).

Lohse, L.G.; G. Bellman; and E.J. Johnson. "Consumer Buying Behavior on the Internet: Findings from

Panel Data." *Journal of Interactive Marketing* (Winter 2000).

Miles, Stephanie. "People Like Us." *Wall Street Journal* (April 23, 2001).

Millward Brown Interactive. "Evaluating the Effectiveness of the Superstitial ™." (October 1999).

Mowrey, Mark. "Thank You, Please Come Again." *Industry Standard* (March 20, 2000).

Novak, T.P.; D.L. Hoffman; and Y.F.Yung. "Measuring the Customer Experience in Online Environments: A Structural Modeling Approach." *Marketing Science* (Winter, 2000).

Nua Internet Surveys. "CyberAtlas: Marketers Spend Little on Search Engines." (August 23, 2001).

Rewick, Jennifer. "Choices, Choices." *Wall Street Journal* (April 23, 2001).

Saunders, Christopher. "Industry Players Seek to Distance Themselves From Click-Throughs." *Internet News-Advertising Report* (July 9, 2001).

Tate, Ryan. "Executive Briefing: Search Engines Not in Good Favor with Nader." *UpsideToday* (July 18, 2001).

Weber, Thomas. "A "Sticky" Situation: How a Web Buzzword Spout Out of Control." *Wall Street Journal* (March 5, 2001).

www.searchenginewatch.com. "Tips About Search Engines." 2001.

CHAPTER 9

Apple Computer, Inc. v. *Microsoft Corp.*, 709 F. Supp. 925, 926 (N.D. Cal. 1989); 799 F. Supp. 1006, 1017 (N.D. Cal. 1992); 35 F.3d 1435 (9th Cir.); cert. denied, 63 U.S.L.W. 3518 (U.S. Feb. 21, 1995) (No.94-1121).

Bernina of America, Inc. v. *Fashion Fabrics Int'l, Inc.*, 2001 U.S. Dist. LEXIS 1211 (N.D. Ill. Feb. 8, 2001).

Brown Bag vs. *Symantec Corp.*, 960 F.2d 1465 (9th Cir. 1992).

Brown, Doug, and Julianna Gruenwald. "Taxing Questions." *Interactive Week* (June 25, 2001).

Bushkin, John. "The Web's Dirty Little Secret: What Porn Sites Lack in Respect They Make Up for in Profits." *Wall Street Journal* (April 17, 2000).

Chiappetta, Vincent. "Defining the Proper Scope of Internet Patents: If We Don't Know Where We Want to Go, We're Unlikely to Get There." *Michigan Telecommunications Technology Law Review* (May 2001).

Columbus Group and Ipsos-Reid. Privacy Policies Critical to Online Trust. Columbus Group (March 2001).

Congressional Research Service RS20035. "Internet Privacy––Protecting Personal Information: Overview and Pending Legislation." (January 16, 2001).

Diamond v. *Chakrabarty*, 447 US 303 (1980).

The Digital Millennium Copyright Act of 1998. www.loc.gov/copyright/legislation (December 1998).

Dueker, Kenneth Sutherlin. "Trademark Law Lost in Cyberspace: Trademark Protection for Internet Addresses." *Harvard Journal of Law and Technology* (Summer 1996).

E. & J. Gallo Winery v. *Spider Webs Ltd.*, 129 F.Supp. 2d 1033 (S.D. Tex. 2001).

Farah, Samar. "The War Over Patents on the Web: Who Owns an Idea?" *Christian Science Monitor* (July 27, 2000).

Federal Trade Commission. "Privacy Online: A Report to Congress." (June 1998).

Federal Trade Commission. "Privacy Online: Fair Information Practices in the Electronic Marketplace." (May 2000a).

Federal Trade Commission. "Online Profiling: A Report to Congress." (June 2000b).

Felten et al. v. *RIAA et al.*, Complaint for Declaratory Judgment and Injunctive Relief, U.S. District Court, New Jersey (June 6, 2001).

Fisher, William W. III. "The Growth of Intellectual Property: A History of the Ownership of Ideas in the United States." http://www.law.harvard.edu/Academic_Affairs/coursepages/tfisher/iphistory.html (1999)

Flynn, Laurie J. "New Economy; Whose Name Is It Anyway? Arbitration Panels Favoring Trademark Holders in Disputes over Web Names." *New York Times* (September 4, 2000).

Ford Motor Co. v. *Lapertosa*, 2001 U.S. Dist. LEXIS 253 (E.D. Mich. Jan. 3, 2001).

Gabber, Eran; Phillip B. Gibbons; David M. Kristol; Yossi Matias; and Alain Mayer. "Consistent, Yet Anonymous, Web Access with LPWA." *Communications of the ACM* (February 1999).

Goldschlag, David M.; Michael G. Reed; and Paul F. Syverson, "Onion Routing for Anonymous and Private Internet Connections." *Communications of the ACM* (February 1999).

Guernsey, Lisa. "Welcome to Web. Passport, Please?" *New York Times* (March 15, 2001).

Hansell, Saul. "So Far, Big Brother Isn't Big Business; At Web's Rear Window, Marketers in No Rush to Mine Private Data." *New York Times* (May 7, 2000).

Hansell, Saul. "After Complaints, Yahoo to Close Access to Pornographic Sites." *New York Times* (April 14, 2001).

Harvard Law School. "Business Methods Patents Online." Intellectual Property in Cyberspace 2000 http://eon.law.Harvard.edu/h2o/property/patents/main.html.

Howard, Philip E.N.; Lee Rainie; and Steve Jones. "Days and Nights on the Internet: The Impact of a Diffusion Technology." *American Behavioral Scientist* (Summer 2001).

Laudon, Kenneth. "Markets and Privacy." *Communications of the ACM* (September 1996).

Markoff, John. "Scientists Drop Plan to Present Music-Copying Study That Record Industry Opposed." *New York Times* (April 27, 2001).

Matthews, Anna Wilde. "Questions Dog the Granting of Broad Exclusivity Rights." *Wall Street Journal* (March 30, 2000).

Nash, David B. "Orderly Expansion of the International Top-Level Domains: Concurrent Trademark Users Need a Way Out of the Internet Trademark Quagmire." *The John Marshall Journal of Computer and Information Law*, Vol. 15, No. 3. (1997).

Nettis Environment Ltd. v. *IWI, Inc.*, 46 F. Supp. 2d 722 (N.D. Ohio 1999).

Nissan Motor Co., Ltd. v. *Nissan Computer Corp.*, 289 F. Supp. 2d 1154 (C.D. Cal.), aff'd, 2000 U.S. App. LEXIS 33937 (9th Cir. Dec. 26, 2000).

McGuire, David. "Far-reaching Net-Gambling Ban Gathers Steam in California." *BizReport.com* (June 1, 2001).

National Center for Missing and Exploited Children, Office of Juvenile Justice and Delinquency Prevention, United States Department of Justice (June 2000).

NetValue. "The NetValue Report on Minors Online." (December 19, 2000).

Nordland, Rod and Bartholet, Jeffrey. "The Web's Dark Secret." *Newsweek* (March 19, 2001).

PaineWebber Inc. v. *Fortuny, Civ.* A. No. 99-0456-A (E.D. Va. Apr. 9, 1999)

Perine, Keith. "The Privacy Police." *The Industry Standard* (February 21, 2000).

Playboy Enterprises, Inc. v. *Global Site Designs, Inc.*, 1999 WL 311707 (S.D. Fla. May 15, 1999).

Playboy Enterprises, Inc. v. *Netscape Communications, Inc.*, 55 F. Supp. 2d 1070 (C.D. Cal.), aff'd, 1999 U.S. App. LEXIS 30215 (9th Cir. 1999).

Rainie, Lee, and Dan Packel. "More Online, Doing More." The Pew Internet and American Life Project (February 18, 2001).

Rafter, Michelle V. "Trust or Bust?" *The Industry Standard* (March 13, 2000).

Richtel, Matt. "Survey Shows Few Trust Promises on Online Privacy." *New York Times* (April 17, 2000).

Richtel, Matt. "High Stakes in the Race to Invent a Bettor-Blocker." *New York Times* (June 28, 2001a).

Richtel, Matt. "Companies in US Profit From Surge in Internet Gambling." *New York Times* (July 6, 2001b).

Riordan, Teresa. "Patents: Historians Take a Longer View of Net Battles." *New York Times* (April 10, 2000).

Rosen , Cheryl, and Beth Bacheldor. "The Politics of Privacy Protection." *Information Week* (July 17, 2000).

State Street Bank & Trust Co. v. *Signature Financial Group*, 149 F. 3d 1368 (1998).

Stepanek, Marcia. "Weblining: Companies Are Using Your Personal Data to Limit Your Choices." *Business Week Online* (April 3, 2000).

Swisher, Kara. "E-tailers Faced Death; Now Can They Handle Taxes?" *New York Times* (April 9, 2001).

Takenaka, Toshiko. "International and Comparative Law Perspective on Internet Patents." *Michigan Telecommunications Technology Law Review* (May 15, 2001).

Thurm, Scott. "The Ultimate Weapon: It's the Patent." *Wall Street Journal* (April 17, 2000a).

Thurm, Scott. "Amazon.com Chief Executive Urges Shorter Duration for Internet Patents." *Wall Street Journal* (March 10, 2000b).

Ticketmaster v. *Tickets.com*, C.D. Cal. (August 2000).

Uiomonen, Terho, and Lawson, Stephen. "Beijing Cracks Down on Net." *Industry Standard* (October 3, 2000).

U.S. Department of Commerce. "Falling Through the Net: Toward Digital Inclusion," National Telecommunications and Information Administration (October 2000).

The Digital Millennium Copyright Act of 1998. www.loc.gov/copyright/legislation (December 1998).

U.S. Department of Health, Education and Welfare. *Records, Computers and the Rights of Citizens.* Cambridge, MA: MIT Press (1973).

United States Patent and Trademark Office. www.uspto.gov.

Varian, Hal, "Forget Taxing Internet Sales. In Fact, Just Forget Sales Taxes Altogether." *New York Times* (March 8, 2001).

Vijayan , Jaikumar, "Caught in the Middle." *Computerworld* (July 24, 2000).

The Washington Post, et al. v. *TotalNews, Inc., et al.*, S.D.N.Y, Civil Action Number 97-1190. (February 1997)

Winston, Brian. *Media Technology and Society: A History From the Telegraph to the Internet.* Routeledge (1998).

www.doubleclick.net

Yee, Chen May. "In Asia, It's Not a Wide-Open Web." *Wall Street Journal* (July 9, 2001).

CHAPTER 10

Amazon.com, Inc. Form 10-K for the fiscal year ended December 31, 2000 (March 23, 2001).

Ashford.com, Inc. Form 10-K for the fiscal year ended March 31, 2001 (June 29, 2001).

Ashford.com, Inc. Form 10-Q for the three-month period ended June 30, 2001 (August 14, 2001).

Bakos, Yannis. "The Emerging Landscape for Retail E-commerce." *Journal of Economic Perspectives* (January 2001).

Boston Consulting Group. "The State of Online Retailing 4.0." (May 2001).

Buy.com Inc. Form 10-K for the fiscal year ended December 31, 2000 (March 29, 2001).

Buy.com Inc. Press Release "Founder to Acquire Buy.com." (August 10, 2001).

Dell Computer Corporation. Form 10-K for the fiscal year ended February 2, 2001. (May 2, 2001).

Dykema, E.B. "Online Retail's Ripple Effect." *Forrester Research Report*, Forrester Research Inc. (September 2000).

Ernst and Young. *Global Online Retailing*. Special Report. (2001).

Evan, Philip, and Thomas S. Wurster, *Blown to Bits: How the New Economics of Information Transforms Strategy*. Cambridge, MA: Harvard Business School Press (2000).

Fashionmall.com, Inc. 10-K for the fiscal year ended December 31, 2000. (April 11, 2001).

Global Sports Inc. 10-Q for the three-month period ended June 30, 2001. (August 6, 2001).

Hansell, Saul. "Listen Up! It's Time for a Profit: A Front-Row Seat as Amazon Gets Serious." *New York Times* (May 20, 2001).

Hunt, J. Timothy. "Beyond Point and Click." *National Post* (May 1, 2001).

JC Penney Company, Inc. Form 10-K for the fiscal year ended January 2001 (April 24, 2001).

Koenig, David. "JCPenney.com Blooms into Surprise Success for Retailer." *Chicago Tribune* (April 8, 2001).

Lands' End Inc. Form 10-K for the fiscal year ended January 26, 2001. (April 23, 2001).

Mowry, Mark. "Pure-Play: A Losing Model." *Industry Standard* (June 26, 2000).

Nielsen/Net Ratings and Harris Interactive. "eCommercePulse." (March 2001).

Nielsen/NetRatings. "Nearly Half of All Americans Buy Online." (April 24, 2001).

Perman, Stacy. "Automate or Die." *eCompany Now* (July 2001).

Rigdon, Joan Indiana. "The Second Mover Advantage." *Red Herring* (September 2000).

Sandoval, Greg. "Global Sports Keeps Expansion Going." *CNET News.com* (September 14, 2001).

Tellis, Garard J., and Peter N. Golder. "First to Market, First to Fail? Real Causes of Enduring Market Leadership." *Sloan Management Review* (Winter 1996).

U.S. Census Bureau. Estimated Monthly Retail Sales, by Kinds of Business January 2000 to December 2000.

U.S. Census Bureau. *Statistical Abstract of the United States* (2000).

CHAPTER 11

Altman, Larry; Anju Simon; Ami Bhandari; and Zaki Hyatt-Shawi. "Run for the Money: The Battle for Online Aggregation Business," Booz Allen & Hamilton E-news (January 2001).

Armour, Stephanie. "Net Job Boards: More Hype than Help?" *USA Today* (August 8, 2001).

Baig, Edward, and Larry Armstrong. "Headhunting 2000: Upstarts, the Net, and Fussy Clients Are Altering the Rules." *Business Week* (May 17, 2000).

Bakos, Yannis; Henry C. Lucas; Wonseok Oh; Gary Simon; Siva Viswanathan; and Bruce Weber. "The Impact of Electronic Commerce on the Retail Brokerage Industry." Center For Information Systems Research, New York University, Stern School of Business (July 2000).

Bradford, Stacey. "SmartMoney.com: Click Here for a New Job." *Dow Jones News Service* (July 3, 2001).

Bray, Chad. "Online Small, But Increasing Sales Options for Insurers." *Dow Jones News Service* (May 10, 2001a).

Bray, Chad. "Insurance.com to Offer Binding Quotes, Expand Marketing." *Dow Jones News Service* (July 16, 2001b).

Brown, Jeffrey, and Austan Goolsbee. "Does the Internet Make Markets More Competitive? Evidence from the Life Insurance Industry." John F. Kennedy School of Government, Harvard University. Research Working Paper RWP00-007 (2000).

Brown, Ken, and Charles Gasparino. "Schwab, Like Many of Its Online Travelers, Hits New Lows." *Wall Street Journal* (August 14, 2001).

Caney, Derek. "USA Networks to Buy Stake in Expedia." *Reuters* (July16, 2001).

Dow Jones. "NASD Expected to Settle Its Advertising Dispute with E*Trade." *Dow Jones Business News* (June 27, 2001).

E-Trade Group, Inc. Form 10K for the fiscal year ended September 30, 2000, filed with the Securities and Exchange Commission (November 9, 2001).

E-Trade Group, Inc. Form 10-Q for the six-month period ended June 30, 2001, filed with the Securities and Exchange Commission (August 14, 2001).

Expedia.com, Inc. Form 10-K for the fiscal year ended

June, 30 2001, filed with the Securities and Exchange Commission (August 22, 2001).

Gill, Jennifer. "Now Hiring: Apply Online Only." *Business Week Online* (July 18, 2001).

Hallford, Joshua. "Europe Banking on the Net." *Industry Standard* (January 16, 2001).

Hodson, Mark. "E-flights Take Off." *Sunday Times-London* (June 24, 2001).

HotJobs.com, Inc. Form 10-K for the fiscal year ended December 31, 2000, filed with the Securities and Exchange Commission (March 30, 2001).

HotJobs.com, Inc. Form 10-Q for the six-month period ended June 30, 2001, filed with the Securities and Exchange Commission (August 14, 2001).

HotJobs.com, Inc. "HotJobs Announces Record $33.6 Million Revenue in First Quarter." Press Release, *Business Wire* (May 2, 2001).

Jupiter Media Metrix. (Robert Sterling, Lead Analyst) "Financial Services Projections: Complexity and Feature Bloat Drive Need for Moderated Experience." (October 2, 2000a).

Jupiter Media Metrix. (Steven Cutler, Lead Analyst). "The E*Trade Experience." (October, 2000b).

Jupiter Media Metrix. (Robert Sterling, Lead Analyst). "The Personal Finance Interface." (December 31, 2000c).

Jupiter Media Metrix. (Robert Sterling, Lead Analyst). "US 2000 Real Estate Projections." (November 3, 2000d).

Jupiter Media Metrix. "Online Growth of Multichannel Banks Forces a Re-thinking of Online-Only Strategy." (July 12, 2001a).

Jupiter Media Metrix. (Robert Rakowitz, Lead Analyst). "Online Bankers: Differences Between Multichannel Bankers and Internet-Only Bankers." (February 5, 2001b).

Jupiter Media Metrix. (Robert Sterling, Lead Analyst). "Real Estate: Jupiter Biannual Benchmarking Report." (July 19, 2001c).

Jupiter Media Metrix. (Fiona S. Swerdlow, Lead Analyst). "2001 US Travel Forecast Report." (July 9, 2001d).

Laudon, Kenneth C., and Jane P. Laudon. *Management Information Systems: Managing the Digital Firm*, 7th edition. Upper Saddle River, NJ: Prentice Hall (2002).

Luh, Shu Shin. "Monster.com Thrives As Rivals Struggle." *Asian Wall Street Journal* (June 11, 2001).

Massaro, Kerry. "Financial Institutions Embrace Account Aggregation." *Wall Street & Technology* (October 2000).

McGeehan, Patrick. "A Complete Financial Picture on One Site." *New York Times* (June 19, 2000).

McGeehan, Patrick. "Traditional Wall Street Firms Still Make the Investment Rules." *New York Times* (June 22, 2001).

Mantz, Beth M. "The Best Way to Find a Job." *Wall Street Journal* (November 27, 2000).

Marcial, Gene. "HotJobs May Start Lookin' Way Cool." *Business Week* (May 7, 2001).

Motoko, Rich. "Web Mortgage Broker Sidesteps Industry Fallout." *Wall Street Journal* (February 1, 2001).

Mowrey, Mark. "Net Traders Spooked." *Industry Standard* (January 16, 2001).

Mullaney, Tim. "Don't Expect Miracles. Online Financing Works Fine, But It's Not a Big Step Forward From the Old Ways." *Business Week* (April 16, 2001).

Reuters English News Service. "USA: Online Mortgage Sales Seen Up to 12% in 2005." *Reuters* (July 23, 2001).

Rich, Motoko. "Web Mortgage Broker Sidesteps Industry Fallout." *Wall Street Journal* (February 1, 2001).

Romano, Jay. "These Days, You Can Call It Real E-state." *New York Times* (March 12, 2000).

Sharkey, Joe. "Sales On Online Corporate Booking Systems Are Seen Growing Eightfold to $33 Billion by 2005." *New York Times* (February 7, 2001).

Tergesen, Anne. "An Insurance Hunter's Weapon of Choice: The Web." *Business Week* (June 11, 2001).

TMP WorldWide, Inc. Form 10-K for the fiscal year ended December 31, 2000, filed with the Securities and Exchange Commission (March 22, 2001).

U.S. Census Bureau. *Census of Service Industries* (2001). www.census.gov/econ/www/se0200.html.

U.S. Census Bureau. *Statistical Abstract of the United States* (2001).

U.S. Department of Labor. *Dictionary of Occupational Titles, 4th edition*. Revised 1991. www.oalj.dol.gov/public/dot/refrnc/dot03.htm.

Vaughan-Nichols, Steven J., and Rachel Schmutter. "Online Mortgages Gaining Ground." *Washington Post* (June 2, 2001).

Walker, Leslie. "Dog's New Search Trick." *Washington Post* (May 9, 2000).

Ybarra, Michael J. "The Brokerage Blues." *Upside* (July 16, 2001).

CHAPTER 12

Aberdeen Group. "Siemens' Private Marketplace Turns Procurement in to Profit Center." (2001).

Ariba, Inc. Form 10-K for the fiscal year ending September 30, 2000 filed with the Securities and Exchange Commission (December 29, 2000).

Ariba, Inc. Form 10-Q for the period ending June 30, 2001 filed with the Securities and Exchange Commission (August 14, 2001a).

Ariba, Inc. "Solutions Overview." (2001). www.ariba.com/solutions/solutions_overview.cfm

Brown, John Seely. Xerox Collaborative Design. (1985).

Cottril, Ken. "Timeout." *Traffic World* (May 21, 2001).

Deloitte Consulting. "B2B Exchanges." (November 2000).

Devine, Dennis A.; Christopher B. Dugan; Mikolaus D. Semaca; and Kevin J. Speicher. "Building Enduring Consortia." *McKinsey Quarterly* (2001).

Enos, Lori. "B2B Old-Timers Hitting Pay Dirt." *E-Commerce Times* (March 21, 2001).

Feuerstein, Adam. "Wal-Mart to Build Private Net Marketplace." *Upsidetoday.com* (October 16, 2000).

FreeMarkets, Inc. Form 10-K405A for the fiscal year ended December 30, 2000, filed with the Securities and Exchange Commission (May 10, 2001).

FreeMarkets, Inc. Form 10-Q for the six-month period ended June 30, 2001, filed with the Securities and Exchange Commission (August 18, 2001).

Gardner, Elizabeth. "A Supermiddleman––How Grainger.com Is changing Corporate Purchasing Habits." *Internet World* (January 15, 2000).

General Electric Information Services. Introduction to EDI. www.support.geis.com/edi. (2001).

Golden, Daniel. "IBM-led Trio Begins Campaign Touting its B2B Services." *Wall Street Journal* (August 17, 2000).

Gomes, Lee. "Vaunted Business-to-Business Sector is Blindside." *Wall Street Journal* (April 4, 2001).

Gomes, Lee. "Ariba, CommerceOne Report Big Losses Amid Tough Business-to-Business Market." *Wall Street Journal* (July 20, 2001).

Harris, Nicole. "Private Exchanges May Now Allow B-to-B Commerce to Thrive After All." *New York Times* (March 16, 2001).

International Business Machines. "Chrysler Boosts Efficiency by Catering to Suppliers." (2001) www.ibm.com/supplychainmanagement.

Jupiter Media Metrix. (Jean-Gabriel Henry and John Katsaros, Lead Analysts). "U.S. Business-to-Business Internet Trade Projections." (September 14, 2000a).

Jupiter Media Metrix. (Tim Clark, John Katsaros, and Jenna Pelaez, Lead Analysts). "Industry-Sponsored Marketplaces." (November 22, 2000b).

Jupiter Media Metrix, (Jean-Gabriel Henry, Lead Analyst). "Getting Procurement Agents to Buy Online." (February 22, 2001a).

Jupiter Media Metrix. (Jon Gibs, Lead Analyst). "B-to-B Supplier Strategies." (May 22, 2001b).

Jupiter Media Metrix. (Jon Gibs, Lead Analyst). "B-to-B Spending in 2006." (September 24, 2001c).

Kaplan, Steven, and Mohanbir Sawhney. "E-Hubs: The New B2B Marketplaces." *Harvard Business Review* (May–June 2000).

Kerrigan, Ryan; Eric Roegner; Dennis Swinford; and Craig Zawada. "B2B Basics." *McKinsey Quarterly* (2001).

Laudon, Kenneth C. "The Promise and Potential of Enterprise Systems and Industrial Networks." *The Concours Group* (2000).

Laudon, Kenneth C., and Jane P. Laudon. *Management Information Systems: Managing the Digital Firm.* 7th Edition. Upper Saddle River, NJ: Prentice Hall (2002).

Luening, Erich. "FreeMarkets Bullish on Sales Despite Woes." *CNET News.com* (September 6, 2001).

Manufacturing Systems Information. "c-Commerce: the Real Wave of the Future." *MSI Magazine* (2001).

Mott, Patrick. "Exchanges Grow Up." *Oracle Corporation* (2001). www.oracle.com.

O'Connor, Rory J. "Keeping Inventory Fresh." *Upside* (June 2000).

Saliba, Claire. "Netscape Marketplace Strikes Deal with Travelocity." *E-Commerce Times* (May 9, 2001).

Schwartz, Ephraim. "Old Economy Giants Team on Logistics." *InfoWorld.com* (February 16, 2001).

Sodhi, Manmohan S. "2001: A Cyberspace Odyssey." *OR.MS Today* (February 2001).

www.orms-today.com.

Turek, Norbert and Gilbert, Alorie, "Atlas Shoulders The Private Exchange Load." *InfoWeek* (March 26, 2001).

U.S. Census Bureau. *Statistical Abstract of the United States.* (2000).

Vanscoy, Kayte. "B2B. The Technology For Friction Free Commerce is Here. So How Come Nobody's Using It." *Smartbusiness Magazine* (March 2001).

Wang, Andy. "FreeMarkets Hit Hard After Losing GM Deal." *E-Commerce Times* (January 5, 2001).

Watson, James K., and Joe Fenner. "So Many Choices, So Little Integration." *Informationweek.com* (October 16, 2000).

Weinberg, Neil. "B2B Grows Up; Lessons from the B2B Roller Coaster." *Forbes Magazine* (September 10, 2001).

Wise, Richard, and Dave Morrison. "Beyond the Exchange: The Future of B2B." *Harvard Business Review* (November–December 2000).

Credits

CHAPTER 1

P. 3 screenshot from Amazon.com, p. 11 Figure 1.2: Reprinted by permission of Harvard Business Review, Sept-Oct. 1997, P. 16 Figure 1.3 from Internet Software Consortium (http://www.isc.org/). P. 17 Figure 1.4 from Cyveillance, Inc., July 10, 2000, www.cyveillance.com/us/newsroom/pressr/000710.asp. P. 25 Table 1.4 from Price Waterhouse Coopers MoneyTree Survey, 2001, www.pwcmoneytree.com/aggregatemenu.asp (adaptation). P. 33 Table 1.6 from Forrester Online Retail Index, www.cyberatlas.com/markets/retailing, May 15, 2001, adaptation. Pp. 34, 35 Tables 1.7, 1.8 from Nielsen/Net Ratings, Inc., www.cyberatlas.internet.com, adaptation, P. 46 screenshot from Napster.com.

CHAPTER 2

P. 55 screenshot from Kozmo.com, P. 60 screenshot from Yahoo.com, reproduced with permission of Yahoo! Inc. YAHOO! And the YAHOO! Logo are trademarks of Yahoo! Inc., P. 97 screenshot of Priceline.com, copyright 2001 Priceline.com. Used with permission. P. 59 screenshot from Amazon.com, P. 88 Figure 2.3 reprinted by permission of Harvard Business Review, Sept-Oct 1997, P. 76 screenshot from Google.com homepage.

CHAPTER 3

P. 105 screenshot from Akamai Technologies P. 122 Figure 3.10 screenshot from a VisualRoute message-tracing program, Visualware.com. P. 121 Figure 3.9 screenshot reproduced with permission of Azimuth Interactive, Inc., copyright 2000. P. 123 Figure 3.11 National Academy Press, P. 89, Figure 3.22 from Informationweek, November 20, 2000, P. 134, Figure 3.14 from Internet2.edu, P. 136 Figure 3.15 from 1999 Annual Report, Corning, Inc., P. 138 Figure 3.16 adapted from G. Forman and J. Zahorjan, "the Challenges of Mobile Computing," IEEE, March, 1994, P. 154 Figure 3.21 copyright 2001 SearchEngineWatch.com, P. 165 screenshot from Into Networks.com

CHAPTER 4

P. 193 four screenshots of WebTrends reports, copyright 2001 by WebTrends/NetlQ. Used by permission, P. 175 screenshot from Loudcloud.com, P. 204 Figure 4.10 from Robinson, Merenda, and Curtis, "IBM RS/600 Web Server Sizing Guide" in CAPACITY PLANNING, P. 184 Figure 4.5, from Laudon and Laudon, Management Information Systems: Managing the Digital Firm, Upper Saddle River, NJ: Prentice Hall, 2001, P. 190 Figure 4.7 from Netcraft Web Server Survey, May 2001, P. 201 Figure 4.8 from "Capacity Model for Internet Transactions, 1999", P. 202 Figure 4.9 from Microsoft, "Windows 2000 Server Standard Performance Evaluation Corporation, 2/8/2000, P. 205 Figure 4.11 from Robinson, Merenda, Curtis, "IBM RS/600 Web Server Sizing Guide" in CAPACITY PLANNING, P. 206 Figure 4.12 from Microsoft, 1999, p. 216 screenshot from REI.com

CHAPTER 5

P. 227 screenshot courtesy Merchant911.org, P. 271 screenshot from VeriSign, pp. 236, 237 Figures 5.3 and 5.4 from Communications of the Association for Information Systems, Vol 4, Article 11, November 2000

CHAPTER 6

P. 288 Figure 6.3 from Jupiter Media Metrix, P. 317 Figure 6.12 from Datamation, September 26, 2001, P. 279 screenshot from PayPal site, p. 322 screenshot of Checkfree.com homepage, P. 286 Table 6.1 from 1996 Telecommunications Policy Research Conference, 10/5-10/7, published by Lawrence Erlbaum Associates, Inc.

CHAPTER 7

P. 339, 353 Figures 7.1 and 7.10 adapted from Kotler and Armstrong, Principles of Marketing, 9e, 2001. Reprinted/electronically reproduced by permission of Pearson Education, Inc., Upper Saddle River, New Jersey, P. 360 Figure 7.12 from Azimuth-Interactive.com, P. 374 Figure 7.16 from http://non-stop.compaq.com/view.asp?/OID=826, November 1998, P. 342 Figure 7.2 from Lohse, Bellman, Johnson, "Consumer Buying on the Internet: Findings from Panel Data," Journal of Interactive Marketing, Winter 2000, © 2000 John Wiley & Sons, Inc. Reprinted by permission of John Wiley & Sons, Inc., P. 390 Figure 7.20 from "Bundling Information Goods: Pricing, Profits, and Efficiency," Management Science, December 1999, P. 399 AOL screenshot copyright 2001 America Online, Inc. Used with permission. P. 331 screenshot of MyPoints.com, P. 345 Table 7.4 from Booz, Allen, & Hamilton, E-Insights, April 2001, Pp. 334,336 Tables 7.1/7.3 from the Pew Internet and American Life Project, 2/18/2001, Pp.335, 351,347, 348, 349, 350 Tables 7.2, 7.5, and Figures 7.5, 7.6, 7.7, 7.8, 7.9 from Jupiter Media Metrix.

CHAPTER 8

Pp. 412, 413 Figures 8.1 and 8.2 from Jupiter Media Metrix, P. 415 Figure 8.3 copyright 2001 Interactive Advertising Bureau. Used with permission, P. 434 Figure 8.7 copyright 2001 by WebTrends/NetIQ. Used by permission. P. 423 screenshot from Beval.com, P. 418 screenshot from Overture, P. 409 screenshot of NextCard homepage, P. 442 screenshot of L90.com

CHAPTER 9

p. 453, screenshot from ElcomSoft.com

CHAPTER 10

P. 525, screenshot from Walmart.com

CHAPTER 11

P. 583, screenshot from NetBank.com; P. 604, screenshot from Yahoo.com; P. 608, screenshot from Quickenloans.com; P. 640, screenshot from Tesco.com; Pp. 590, 591,616, 618, 619, Figures 11.4, 11.5, 11.8; 11.9. 11.10 and Pp. 592, 596, Tables 11.2 , 11.4 from Jupiter Media Metrix.

CHAPTER 12

P. 651, screenshot from Covisint.com; P. 712, screenshot from click2procure.com; Pp. 657, 659, 699, Figures 12.2, 12.3 12.17 and P. 698, Table 12.6 from Jupiter Media Metrix.

Index

continued from inside front cover